T0338643

Machine Learning
A Journey to Deep Learning
with Exercises and Answers

Machine Learning
A Journey to Deep Learning
with Exercises and Answers

Andreas Wichert

Luis Sa-Couto

Instituto Superior Técnico - Universidade de Lisboa, Portugal
& INESC-ID, Portugal

 World Scientific

NEW JERSEY · LONDON · SINGAPORE · BEIJING · SHANGHAI · HONG KONG · TAIPEI · CHENNAI · TOKYO

Published by

World Scientific Publishing Co. Pte. Ltd.

5 Toh Tuck Link, Singapore 596224

USA office: 27 Warren Street, Suite 401-402, Hackensack, NJ 07601

UK office: 57 Shelton Street, Covent Garden, London WC2H 9HE

British Library Cataloguing-in-Publication Data
A catalogue record for this book is available from the British Library.

MACHINE LEARNING — A JOURNEY TO DEEP LEARNING
with Exercises and Answers

Copyright © 2021 by World Scientific Publishing Co. Pte. Ltd.

ISBN 978-981-123-405-7 (hardcover)
ISBN 978-981-123-406-4 (ebook for institutions)
ISBN 978-981-123-407-1 (ebook for individuals)

For any available supplementary material, please visit
https://www.worldscientific.com/worldscibooks/10.1142/12201#t=suppl

Printed in Singapore

Andreas:

To the memory of my father Andrzej Wichert

Luís:

In loving memory of Titi

Preface

Deep learning achieved tremendous results, and it is now common to identify artificial intelligence with deep learning and not with symbol manipulating systems. This results from the paradox of artificial intelligence, a discipline whose principal purpose is its own definition since the terms "intelligence" and "intelligent human behavior" are not very well defined and understood.

This book tells a story outgoing from a perceptron to deep learning highlighted with concrete examples. It discusses some core ideas for the development and implementation of machine learning from three different perspectives: the statistical perspective, the artificial neural network perspective and the deep learning methodology. The book represents a solid foundation in machine learning and should prepare the reader to apply and understand machine learning algorithms as well as to invent new machine learning methods.

The notes on which the book is based evolved in the course "Machine Learning" in the years $2018-2021$ at Department of Computer Science and Engineering, Instituto Superior Técnico, University of Lisbon. Our research benefited from discussions with Ana Paiva, Manuel Lopes, Eugénio Ribeiro, João Rico, Rui Henriques, Claudia Antunes, Diogo Ferrreira, Mikolas Janota and Luisa Coheur.

Most of the practical exercises were developed by Luís.

We would like to thank Senior Editor Steven Patt at World Scientific for his support.

Finally, we would like to thank our families, without their encouragement the book would never have been finished.

Andreas Wichert and Luís Sá-Couto

Contents

Chapter 1

Introduction

1.1   What is Machine Learning

It is difficult to define learning overall. There are some parallels between human learning and machine learning. During learning, humans attempt to gain some knowledge to adjust behavioral tendencies by experience.

Many of the techniques are derived from the efforts of psychologists and biologists to make sense of human learning through computational models [Anderson (1995)]. In this book, we cover statistical machine learning, such as linear regression, clustering, kernel machines and artificial neural networks. We will not cover symbolical machine learning, which was popular between 1970-1990. Symbolical machine learning includes inductive learning, knowledge learning and analogical learning [Winston (1992)].

To understand the difference between both approaches, we provide an example of symbolical machine learning in the next section, followed by examples of statistical machine learning. Both approaches differ mainly in the method with which the information is represented, either by symbols or vectors.

1.1.1   *Symbolical Learning*

Symbols are constructs of the human mind to simplify the process of problem solving. Symbols are used to denote or refer to something other than them, namely other things in the world (according to the pioneering work of Tarski [Tarski (1956)]). They are defined by their occurrence in a structure and by a formal language, which manipulates these structures [Simon (1991); Newell (1990)]. In this context, it is not possible to measure a meaningful similarity between symbols, only between the real world objects that they represent.

In symbolic concept acquisition, the system learns a symbolic representation by analyzing positive and negative examples of a concept. For example, the ARCH program learns concepts from examples represented by symbols in a structural domain of the block-world [Winston (1992)]. A scene is described by three blocks. In Figure 1.1, we see two examples of the concept arch. For each input, a symbolical representation is given through the symbolic graphs in Figure 1.2. Given these two positive examples of the concept, in Figure 1.3, we see how a symbolical learning procedure could use background knowledge to produce a unified graph representation of the concept.

Figure 1.4 shows two negative examples or near misses of the concept arch. Just like before, the input Figure 1.4 (a) is converted into the symbolical graph in Figure 1.5 (a). Afterward, the graph is used to update the unified graph that represents an arch such that it excludes the near miss example. Such update, would result in the graph in Figure 1.5 (b).

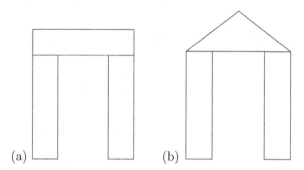

Fig. 1.1   (a) Arch with a brick on top and (b) arch with a pyramid on top.

1.1.2   *Statistical Machine Learning*

Another approach is to represent the objects directly. A way to this is to look into biology. In this approach, we represent a pattern that mirrors the way the biological sense organs describe the world. Since perception organs sense the world by receptors, we can create a vector where each dimension corresponds to a certain value in a receptor [Wichert (2009)].

Besides biology, we can justify the use of vectors with the idea of features. Let us imagine that we want to describe two species of fish, the sea bass and the salmon using their features (see Figure 1.6), [Duda *et al.* (2000)]. Each fish can be represented by a vector where each dimension corresponds to a feature and stores its value or presence.

Representing objects in this way, one can measure the dissimilarity between two objects by measuring the distance between the two D dimensional vectors that represent them. Concretely, one can measure this distance through the Euclidean distance function

$$d(\mathbf{x}, \mathbf{y}) = \|\mathbf{x} - \mathbf{y}\| = \sqrt{|x_1 - y_1|^2 + |x_2 - y_2|^2 + \cdots + |x_D - y_D|^2}.$$

The process of choosing the correct features to represent is called feature extraction. In our example, only two features are chosen, width and lightness. This allows us to plot each fish as point in a two-dimensional

(a)

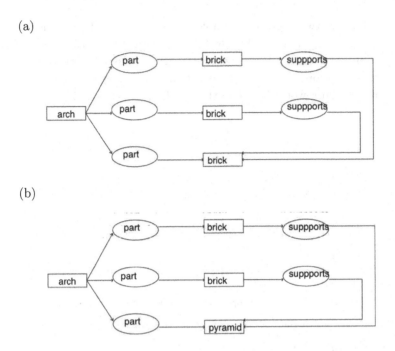

(b)

Fig. 1.2   (a) Graph description of an arch with a brick on top and (b) arch with a pyramid on top.

coordinate system. Figure 1.7 plots a sample of fish in feature space where each salmon is marked with a dot and each sea bass with a cross.

With this setting, the idea is to find the boundary that discriminates between the two types of fish. In a first approach, we attempt to separate the two classes using a straight line; we have some errors, but most examples are correctly separated. One of the most important machine learning algorithm, perceptron, attempts to determine (learn) this line from a given sample. Later, during classification, an unknown fish is described by a two-dimensional vector, and depending on which side of the separating line it falls, it is classified as either salmon or sea bass.

The two classes can be separated by a curve without errors; this is the best decision boundary for this specific sample (see Figure 1.8). However, if we attempt to correctly classify a fish outside the represented sample, we are not guaranteed to obtain a correct classification. We might misclassify this result due to the problem of overfitting.

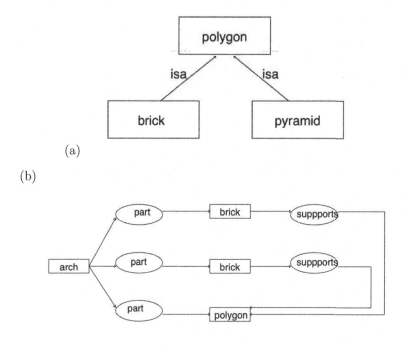

Fig. 1.3 (a) Graph representing background knowledge that bricks and pyramids are both types of polygon and (b) a generalized graph description that includes both, arch with a brick on top and arch with a pyramid on top.

Overfitting could be the result of some outliers; for example, some salmon can have some feature values that are related to sea basses distorting the boundary in such a way that all future sea basses around that point will be misclassified.

This phenomenon only occurs because a small training sample does not represent the population correctly. We can overcome this problem by increasing the size of the sample. However, this is often impossible. So, we have to reach a compromise in the sense that we do not want to divide the training sample perfectly; we allow a small error in the hope that the future fish will be classified mostly correctly. The compromise is described by the assumption that the curve has to be smooth (see Figure 1.9). The integration of such an assumption into the learning rule leads to regularization theory into which we will get later.

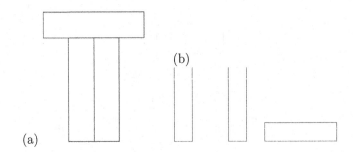

Fig. 1.4   (a) and (b) represent two examples of near misses of archs.

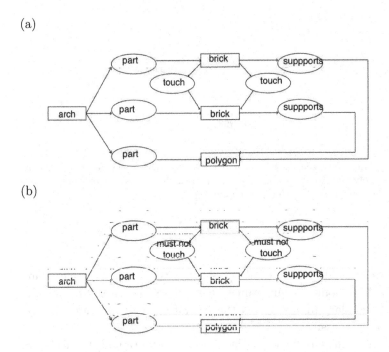

Fig. 1.5   (a) Graph description of near miss of Figure 1.4 (a) and (b) a specialized graph description that excludes the near miss.

1.1.3   *Supervised and Unsupervised Machine Learning*

In machine learning, we can distinguish between supervised learning, as described in the preceding example and unsupervised learning. In supervised learning, the algorithm is presented with examples of inputs and their

(a)

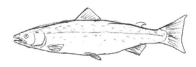

(b)

Fig. 1.6   (a) Sea bass and (b) salmon.

desired outputs. The goal is to learn a general rule that maps inputs to outputs. Supervised learning is frequently referred to as learning with a teacher because the desired outputs are indicated by a type of teacher. Consequently, unsupervised learning is referred to as learning without a teacher. In unsupervised learning, the algorithm groups information that is primarily represented by vectors into groups. The algorithm attempts to find the hidden structure of unlabeled data; clustering algorithms are an example of such kind of learning.

1.2   It all began with the Perceptron

The perceptron algorithm was invented in 1957 by Frank Rosenblatt [Rosenblatt (1962)], see Figure 1.10.

The algorithm was inspired by the neurons in the human brain. In Figure 1.11 (a), we present a drawing by Santiago Ramón y Cajal (1852-1934), the Spanish founder of modern neuroscience. Cajal deduced that nervous signals enter the neuron through dendrites and exit through its single slender axon. The dendrites receive signals from other neurons, the

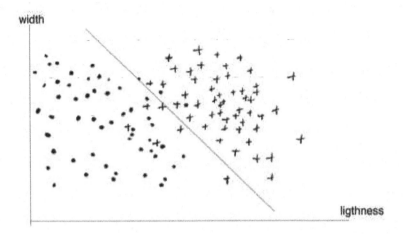

Fig. 1.7   In a sample, each salmon is represented by a dot and each sea bass by a cross. We separate the two classes using a straight line. Some errors are present, but most examples are correctly separated. Later, during classification, an unknown fish is described by a two-dimensional vector, and depending on which side of the separating line it falls, it is classified as either salmon or sea bass.

soma processes the information and the axon transmits the output. The synapses are the points of connection between neurons (see Figure 1.11 (b)).

In 1943, McCulloch, a neuroscientist, and Walter Pitts, a logician, developed the artificial neuron, a mathematical model that mimicks the functionality of a biological neuron. This model is called the McCulloch-Pitts model of a neuron.

1.2.1   *Artificial Neuron*

With two vectors of the same dimension D, the vector $\mathbf{x}$ represents an input pattern (signals incoming from other neurons) and the vector $\mathbf{w}$ represents a stored pattern (in the weights of each synapse). We can define a scalar product also called the dot product

$$\langle \mathbf{x} | \mathbf{w} \rangle = \sum_{j=1}^{D} w_j \cdot x_j = \cos \omega \cdot \|\mathbf{x}\| \cdot \|\mathbf{w}\|, \tag{1.1}$$

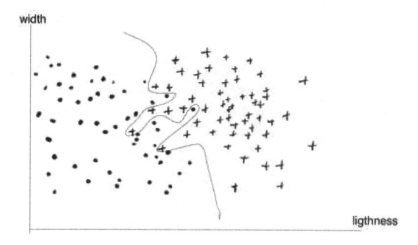

Fig. 1.8 The curve describes the best decision boundary for the sample. However, the decision boundary represents only the sample without any error. If we attempt to correctly classify a fish outside the represented sample, we are not guaranteed to obtain a correct classification. We might misclassify a new example due to the problem of overfitting. This problem, can be the result of some outliers; for example, some salmon can have some feature values that are most common in sea basses.

that measures the projection of one vector onto another. The dot product is a linear representation usually represented by the value *net*,

$$net = \sum_{j=1}^{D} w_j \cdot x_j.$$

The components w_j are called weights, they model the synapses representing the traces of memory. Non linearity of the linear representation can be achieved by a threshold operation in which the threshold T has a certain value with

$$o = \begin{cases} 1 & \text{if} \quad net \geq T \\ -1 & \text{if} \quad net < T \end{cases}, \tag{1.2}$$

being the output of the artificial neuron. This threshold operation can be described by a non liner transfer function like *sgn* for $T = 0$

$$o = sgn(net) = \begin{cases} 1 & \text{if} \quad net \geq 0 \\ -1 & \text{if} \quad net < 0 \end{cases}, \tag{1.3}$$

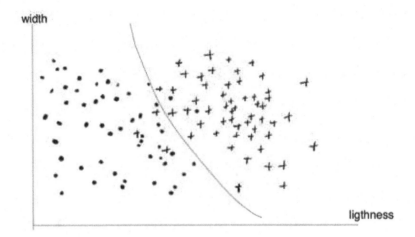

Fig. 1.9   Very often we are not able to increase the training sample and have to reach a compromise in the sense that we do not want to divide the training sample perfectly, we allow a small error in the hope that the future, unseen fish will be mostly classified correctly. The compromise can be described through assumptions like the requirement that the boundary has to be smooth.

The *sgn(net)* operation is related to the threshold operation of a real biological neuron with -1 meaning not firing and 1 firing, see Figure 1.12. Firing indicates that the neuron sends output information to other neurons to which it is connected. Not firing indicates that no information is sent. The transfer function is also called the activation function, with o being the output of the artificial neuron

$$o = sgn(net) = sgn(\langle \mathbf{x} | \mathbf{w} \rangle) = sgn \left(\sum_{j=1}^{D} w_j \cdot x_j \right). \qquad (1.4)$$

This model is also known as the linear threshold unit (LTU).

1.2.2   *Perceptron*

The perceptron is a model that uses a linear threshold unit to classify inputs into two classes [McCulloch and Pitts (1943)], [Rosenblatt (1962)].

Defining $x_0 = 1$[Hecht-Nielsen (1989); Hertz *et al.* (1991)], the percep-

Fig. 1.10 Frank Rosenblatt (1928-1971) was an American psychologist notable for the invention of the perceptron.

tron implements the mathematical function $sgn(net)$ with

$$net := \sum_{j=0}^{D} w_j \cdot x_j = \sum_{j=1}^{D} w_j \cdot x_j + w_0 = \langle \mathbf{x} | \mathbf{w} \rangle + w_0 \cdot x_0 \qquad (1.5)$$

The value w_0 is called the "bias", it is a constant value that does not depend on any input value and it can be seen as the symmetric of the threshold (see Figure 1.13).

The goal of the perceptron is to learn how to correctly classify patterns into one of two classes $C_1 = 1$ and $C_2 = -1$. To achieve this task, the model needs examples of correct associations between patterns and their respective classes.

$$Data = \{(\mathbf{x}_1, t_1), (\mathbf{x}_2, t_2), \cdots, , (\mathbf{x}_N, t_N)\}$$

with

$$t_k \in \{-1, 1\},$$

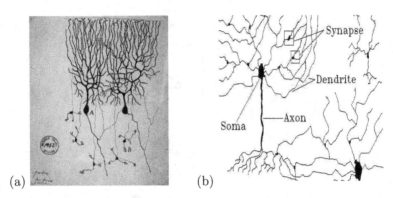

Fig. 1.11   (a) Drawing of neurons by Spanish neuroscientist Santiago Ramón y Cajal in 1899 (b) The dendrite receives signals from other neurons, the soma processes the information and the axon transmits the output of this neuron and the synapse is the point of connection to other neurons.

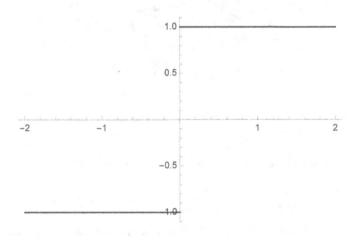

Fig. 1.12   Nonlinear *sgn* function gives −1 or 1 depending on whether *net* is negative, or positive with zero. The *sgn(net)* operation is related to the threshold operation of a real biological neuron with −1 not firing and 1 firing. It should be noted that *sgn* is non continuous

the output for class C_1 is $o = -1$ and for C_2 is $o = 1$ with

$$o = sgn\left(\sum_{j=0}^{D} w_j \cdot x_j\right) = sgn\left(\langle \mathbf{x} | \mathbf{w} \rangle + w_0 \cdot x_0\right) \tag{1.6}$$

and $x_0 = 1$.

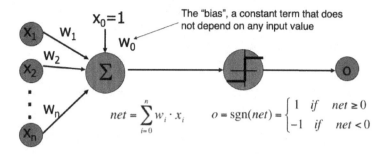

Fig. 1.13   The perceptron is based on a linear threshold unit (LTU) that models the McCulloch-Pitts model of a neuron (1943), [McCulloch and Pitts (1943)].

Simplified, the perceptron tries to learns the function $f(\mathbf{x})$

$$f(\mathbf{x}) = \begin{cases} 1 & \text{if} \quad \langle \mathbf{x}|\mathbf{w}\rangle + w_0 \geq 0 \\ -1 & \text{otherwise,} \end{cases} \tag{1.7}$$

This function applies the previously described idea of placing a straight line boundary in the feature space and, when given a new point, the model checks the side of the boundary where it falls. In a D dimensional space, this straight line becomes a hyperplane with equation

$$-w_0 = \langle \mathbf{x}|\mathbf{w}\rangle$$

or

$$0 = \langle \mathbf{x}|\mathbf{w}\rangle + w_0. \tag{1.8}$$

With this approach, the perceptron is only able to solve linearly separable problems (see Figure 1.14), that is, ones that can be separated by a line or hyperplane.

The hyperplane is described by the model weights $\mathbf{w}$ and w_0. The correct weights can be determined by a supervised learning algorithm.

Before learning, the weight values w_j are initialize to some small random values, so, the hyperplane is place randomly in the space. Then, the perceptron learning algorithm verifies whether, for a given input $\mathbf{x}_k$, the output value o_k belongs to the desired class represented by t_k. If the output matches the class, the algorithm does not touch the boundary, if it does not, then, the algorithm moves the boundary in a direction where the input $\mathbf{x}_k$ is closer to being correctly classified. This movement corresponds to the following update rule

$$\Delta w_j = \eta \cdot (t_k - o_k) \cdot x_j, \tag{1.9}$$

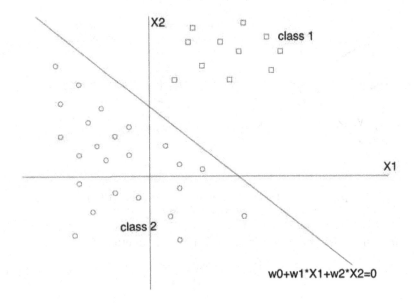

Fig. 1.14   The hyperplane is described by **w** and w_0, in two dimensions by a line $w_0 + w_1 \cdot x_1 + w_2 \cdot x_2 = 0$. The perceptron only solves linearly separable problems, in our example *class* 1 and *class* 2.

and

$$w_j^{new} = w_j^{old} + \Delta w_j, \tag{1.10}$$

where $\delta_k = (t_k - o_k)$ plays the role of the error signal with being either zero, 2 or -2

$$\delta_k = \begin{cases} 2 & \text{if } t_k = 1 \text{ and } o_k = -1 \\ -2 & \text{if } t_k = -1 \text{ and } o_k = 1 \\ 0 & \text{if } t_k = o_k \end{cases} \tag{1.11}$$

and η is called the learning rate that defines the size of the movement that is applied to the boundary with

$$0 < \eta \leq 1.$$

The algorithm converges to the correct classification if the training data are linearly separable, and η is sufficiently small. When assigning a value to η, we must consider two conflicting requirements: averaging of past inputs to provide stable weight estimates, which requires small η; however, fast adaptation with respect to real changes in the underlying distribution of the process responsible for generating the input vector $\mathbf{x}$, which requires a large η.

1.2.2.1 *Perceptron Algorithm*

The application of the previously described recipe to a whole sample of examples can be described in pseudocode:

(1) iterations=0;
(2) $\eta \in (0, 1]$;
(3) Initialise all the weights $w_0, w, \cdots, w_D$ to some random values;
(4) Choose a pattern $\mathbf{x}_k$ out of the training set;
(5) Compute $net_k = \sum_{i=1}^{D} w_j \cdot x_{k,j} + w_0 = \langle \mathbf{x}_k | \mathbf{w} \rangle + w_0 \cdot x_0$;
(6) Compute the output by the activation function $o_k = sgn(net_k)$;
(7) Compute $\Delta w_j = \eta \cdot (t_k - o_k) \cdot x_{k,j}$;
(8) Update the weights $w_j = w_j + \Delta w_j$;
(9) iterations++;
(10) If no change in weights for all training set or maximum number of iteration THEN STOP ELSE GOTO 4;

This simple algorithm is the basis for many supervised machine learning algorithms.

In general, an epoch corresponds to a full sweep through the training vectors (patterns) $\mathbf{x}_k$ with $k = 1, 2, \cdots, N$. So at any given iteration, we will be at $epoch = \lceil iterations/N \rceil$. Depending on the training set, the initialization and the size of the learning rate, we may need to run the algorithm across several epochs until a solution is reached.

If the training set is not linearly separable, then no solution exists. In this setting, after several epochs, the weights begin to oscillate. To get an approximate solution, the learning rate η has to decrease slowly to zero as the epochs go by.

1.2.2.2 *Example*

In this example a linearly separable training set is described by four vectors

$$\mathbf{x}_1 = \begin{pmatrix} 0 \\ 0 \end{pmatrix}, \mathbf{x}_2 = \begin{pmatrix} 0 \\ 2 \end{pmatrix}, \mathbf{x}_3 = \begin{pmatrix} 1 \\ 1 \end{pmatrix}, \mathbf{x}_4 = \begin{pmatrix} 1 \\ -1 \end{pmatrix},$$

and the corresponding targets

$$t_1 = -1, t_2 = 1, t_3 = 1, t_4 = -1.$$

The weights are initialized to 1 and the learning rate η for simplicity is set to 1 as well

$$w_0 = 1, w_1 = 1, w_2 = 1, \quad \eta = 1$$

Then we compute the change of the weights for one epoch

$$o_1 = sgn(1 \cdot 0 + 1 \cdot 0 + 1) = sgn(1) = 1; \quad \delta_1 = -2; \quad \mathbf{w} = \begin{pmatrix} -1 \\ 1 \\ 1 \end{pmatrix},$$

$$o_2 = sgn(1 \cdot 0 + 1 \cdot 2 - 1) = sgn(1) = 1; \quad \delta_2 = 0; \quad \mathbf{w} = \begin{pmatrix} -1 \\ 1 \\ 1 \end{pmatrix},$$

$$o_3 = sgn(1 \cdot 1 + 1 \cdot 1 - 1) = sgn(1) = 1; \quad \delta_3 = 0; \quad \mathbf{w} = \begin{pmatrix} -1 \\ 1 \\ 1 \end{pmatrix},$$

$$o_4 = sgn(1 \cdot 1 + 1 \cdot (-1) - 1) = sgn(-1) = -1; \quad \delta_4 = 0; \quad \mathbf{w} = \begin{pmatrix} -1 \\ 1 \\ 1 \end{pmatrix}.$$

For additional epochs, the weights do not change. The algorithm converged to a solution, as indicated in Figure 1.15. However if we change the

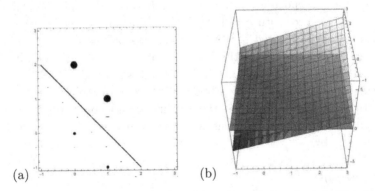

Fig. 1.15   (a) The two classes 1 (indicated by a big point) and -1 (indicated a small point) are separated by the line $-1 + x_1 + x_2 = 0$. (b) The hyperplane $-1 + x_1 + x_2 = y$ defines the line for $y = 0$.

initialization to

$$w_0 = 0, w_1 = 0, w_2 = 0, \quad \eta = 1$$

no solution is reached after one epoch; see Figure 1.16 (a). After an additional epoch, a solution is reached, and the weights do not change (see Figure 1.16 (b)). The solution is different from the solution in Figure 1.15 (a). For a given problem, there are infinitely many possible solutions that can be found using the perceptron algorithm depending on the weight initialization. The number of solutions can be reduced by increasing the size of the training set or by an alternative algorithm such as the support vector machine (which will be introduced later).

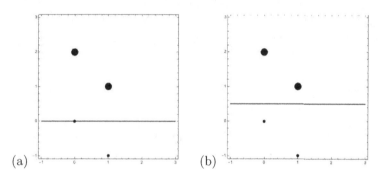

(a)   (b)

Fig. 1.16   (a) The two classes 1 (indicated by a big point) and -1 (indicated a small point) are not separated by the line $0 + 0 \cdot x_1 + 4 \cdot x_2 = 0$ after one training epoch. (b) The two classes 1 (indicated by a big point) and -1 (indicated a small point) are separated by the line $-2 + 0 \cdot x_1 + 4 \cdot x_2 = 0$ after the second epoch.

During its invention, the perceptron was intended to be a machine rather than a program due to the limited computing power. Even if the first implementation was in software for the IBM 704, it was then implemented in hardware as the "Mark 1 perceptron" for image recognition [Hecht-Nielsen (1989)]. Weights were encoded in resistors, and during learning, the weight updates were represented by adapting the resistors with the help of electric motors.

1.2.3   *XOR-Problem*

Perceptron describes an algorithm for supervised learning that considers only linearly separable problems in which groups can be separated by a line or hyperplane. In the 1960s, an active research program concerning machine learning with artificial neural networks was carried out by Rosenblatt.

After a press conference with Rosenblatt, the New York Times published an article in 1958 in which they claimed: "The Navy revealed the embryo of an electronic computer today that it expects will be able to walk, talk, see, write, reproduce itself and be conscious of its existence.... Later, perceptrons will be able to recognize people and call out their names and instantly translate speech in one language to speech and writing in another language".

In response, Rosenblatt's schoolmate at the Bronx High School of Science Marvin Minsky and his colleague, Seymour Aubrey Papert, published a book 1969 with the title "Perceptrons" [Minsky and Papert (1972)]. In the book, it was argued that perceptrons cannot model nonlinear functions such as the logical XOR operation (see Figure 1.17). Shortly after the book was published, Rosenblatt died in a boating accident. Some people assume it was suicide; he was definitely heartbroken.

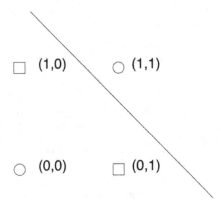

Fig. 1.17   "XOR" problem, there are two classes 0 and 1 as a result of the XOR operation. The class 0 results of the input $(0,0)$ and $(1,1)$ and the class 1 form the input $(0,1)$ and $(1,0)$. The classes cannot be separated by a straight line.

As a consequence of the published book, nearly no research was conducted in artificial neural networks for the next 10 years. Instead, symbolic artificial intelligence emerged. The term "artificial intelligence" was invented by the American computer scientist John McCarthy. It was used in the title of a conference that took place in 1956 at Dartmouth College in the USA. During this meeting, programs were presented that played chess and checkers, proved theorems and interpreted texts. The programs were thought to simulate human intelligent behavior. The use of symbols in algorithms that imitate human intelligent behavior led to the famous physical symbol system hypothesis by Newell and Simon (1976) [Newell and Simon

(1976)]: "The necessary and sufficient condition for a physical system to exhibit intelligence is that it be a physical symbol system." Machine learning was understood as symbolical learning, and statistical machine learning was seen as being outside the domain of computer science.

1.3 Road to Deep Learning

1.3.1 *Backpropagation*

The limitations of a simple perceptron do not apply to feedforward networks with nonlinear units, also called multilayer perceptrons. Such networks can be trained by the backpropagation learning algorithm. The algorithm itself was invented independently several times, [Bryson and Ho (1969)], [Werbos (1974)], [Parker (1985)], [McClelland and Rumelhart (1986b)]. However, it became popular with the books Parallel Distributed Processing (PDP) published by David Rumelhart and his colleagues (see Figure 1.18), [McClelland and Rumelhart (1986b)], [McClelland and Rumelhart (1986c)], [McClelland and Rumelhart (1986a)]. The books consist of three volumes, foundations, psychological and biological models and a handbook of models, programs, and exercises that included software on a diskette written in the programming language *C*. The authors returned to perceptrons and claimed to have overcome the problems presented by Minsky and Papert, the pessimism about learning in multilayer perceptrons was misplaced.

An example of a feedforward network with two hidden layers is shown in Figure 1.19. The hidden units are nonlinear; they are referred to as hidden units because we cannot see their outputs and cannot directly perform error correction [Hertz *et al.* (1991)].

The popularization of the backpropagation algorithm through the PDP books led to a connectionist movement that resulted in the "symbol wars" with the old symbolic artificial intelligence school. The symbol wars describe the emotional discussion of the two camps around the question as to whether the departure from the symbolic approach leads to something new and worthwhile.

1.4 Synopsis

This book discusses some core ideas for the development and implementation of machine learning from three different perspectives: the statistical

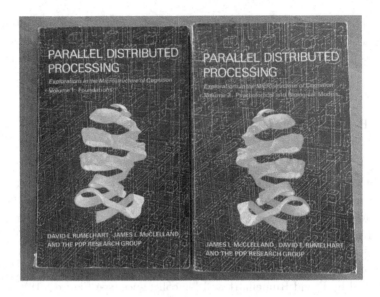

Fig. 1.18   Parallel Distributed Processing (PDP) Books, volume 1 foundations and volume 2 psychological and biological models.

perspective, the artificial neural network perspective and the deep learning methodology. The book represents a solid foundation in machine learning and should prepare the reader to apply and understand machine learning algorithms as well as to invent new machine learning methods.

It tells a story outgoing from a perceptron to deep learning highlighted with concrete examples.

The main parts of the book address linear and nonlinear regression, supervised learning, learning theory, feature extraction and unsupervised learning.

The statistical approach leads to the definition of regularization out of the example of regression. Building on regression, we develop the theory of perceptrons and logistic regression. We investigate the relation between bias and variance as a consequence of a finite training sample set that is used in machine learning. Out of backpropagation, we develop the theory of convolutional networks and deep learning. During the development we introduce the RBF networks and support vector machines that indicate us why neural networks with hidden nonlinear units can solve most problems.

Throughout the book we finish each chapter with lecture notes that contain the core ideas presented in the chapter and a lot of solved exercises

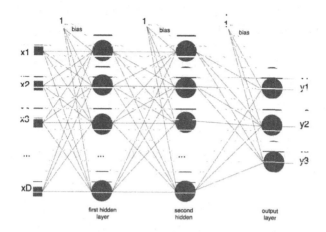

Fig. 1.19 The limitations of a simple perceptron do not apply to feedforward networks with hidden nonlinear units. An example of a feedforward network with two hidden layers.

so that the reader is able to learn through practice. By going through the procedures in a pen and paper manner, we believe that the reader will develop a comfort and familiarity with the techniques that will become indispensable in future usage. Furthermore, in many technical issues it is only in the lecture notes part of the chapter that we really cover and go into the details.

1.4.1 *Content*

Probability and Information - Chapter 2 Bayes' law and the law of total probability are introduced, followed by the normal distribution and the Laplace distribution. All play a central role in regularization theory. Then, we describe the essential tools of supervised machine learning, the Bernoulli distribution and information theory.

Linear Algebra and Optimization - Chapter 3 We describe some basic ideas of linear algebra. Examples of nonparametric models are the case-based reasoning and the k-nearest neighbor. We introduce the idea of the curse of dimensionality which has several consequences in many machine learning applications. It is followed by the central idea of supervised machine learning, the gradient descent method and Newton's method.

Linear and Nonlinear Regression - Chapter 4　The idea of linear regression is a central building block of a perceptron. Using linear and nonlinear regression, we introduce Bayesian regression. The normal distribution and Laplace distribution leads to ridge (l_2) or lasso (l_1) regularization.

Perceptron and Logistic Regression - Chapter 5　Expanding on linear regression, we introduce the perceptron and Adeline. The sigmoid function leads to logistic regression.

Multilayer Perceptrons - Chapter 6　The backpropagation algorithm is introduced based on the Euclidean squared error and the cross entropy error. Expressive capabilities of networks trained with this algorithm are analyzed.

Learning theory, Bias-Variance - Chapter 7　We discuss the learning theory through the finite sample size consideration that leads to the bias-variance dilemma. Then, we introduce the VC dimension for binary classifiers that allows us to estimate a desirable size for the training set.

Model Selection - Chapter 8　We introduce overfitting, the confusion matrix and cross-validation. Then, we describe the principle of model selection based on Occam's razor resulting in the minimum-description-length principle.

K-Means, EM-Clustering - Chapter 9　We describe two unsupervised learning algorithms that can be a basis for the later introduced radial basis function networks: K-means clustering and expectation maximization (EM) clustering.

Kernel Methods and RBF - Chapter 10　Cover's theorem is the basis of kernel methods. The interpolation problem and Micchelli's theorem lead to radial basis function networks. We then introduce kernel regression and indicate how to construct new kernels.

Support Vector Machines - Chapter 11　Two class problems define an optimal hyperplane that can be solved by quadratic optimization based on the dual problem. A support vector machine (SVM) can also be described as a kernel machine that is based on the kernel trick.

Deep Learning - Chapter 12　Deep learning introduces better generalization through the use of many hidden layers and a large training set. The vanishing gradient problem appears when many hidden layers are present. A solution is the ResNet approach and different activation functions, such as a rectified linear unit. To overcome the problem of local minima and saddle points, weight initialization and batch normalization are introduced. The problem of overfitting can be reduced by regularization methods. Through regularization, we can efficiently determine the correct complexity of a model. Transfer learning allows us to optimize a trained model for some related tasks without high computational costs.

Convolutional Neural Networks - Chapter 13 Expanding on the visual cortex, we introduce neocognitron and the map transformation cascade. Then, we describe the modern convolutional networks based on convolution and pooling that are trained by backpropagation, explain the principle of data augmentation and introduce AlexNet and GoogLeNet.

Recurrent Neural Networks - Chapter 14 Expanding the classic dynamic system, we introduce unfolding computational graphs that lead to recurrent neural networks (RNNs) trained by backpropagation through time.

Autoencoders - Chapter 15 The Karhunen-Loève transform is based on the covariance matrix and leads to the PCA algorithm which allows us to describe high dimensional vectors as lower dimensional ones. Autoencoders are neural networks that are trained with unsupervised learning to copy their input to the output through a hidden layer **h**. This hidden layer can be seen as a code that represents the input.

Epilogue - Chapter 16 Deep convolutional neural networks and deep learning artificial neural networks have many hidden layers usually trained by backpropagation. These models achieved tremendous results, and it is now common to identify artificial intelligence with deep learning and not with symbol manipulating systems. However there are still open questions.

1.5 Exercises and Answers

The perceptron can be seen as an extremely simplified model of a biological neuron that is trained to fire when presented with elements of a given class.

More specifically, for an input vector $\mathbf{x} = \begin{pmatrix} x_1 & x_2 & \cdots & x_d \end{pmatrix}^T$, the perceptron will, ideally, output $o = +1$ if $\mathbf{x}$ is an element of the learned class and $o = -1$ if it is not.

The knowledge that helps the perceptron decide if an element belongs to the class is stored in a vector of weights $\mathbf{w} = \begin{pmatrix} w_1 & w_2 & \cdots & w_d \end{pmatrix}^T$. For each feature x_i in the input vector, there is a weight w_i that decides the importance of that feature to recognize the class, more specifically:

- A very positive weight w_i indicates that if $\mathbf{x}$ has a large x_i than it is likely an instance of the class;
- A very negative weight w_i indicates that if $\mathbf{x}$ has a large x_i than it probably does not belong to the class;
- A w_i close to zero, indicates that x_i is not very relevant for the decision.

To implement this reasoning, the perceptron sums the input features weighted by their importance:

$$w_1 x_1 + w_2 x_2 + \cdots + w_d x_d$$

Now, if the sum is large, then $\mathbf{x}$ is probably a member of the class. But how large? We need a threshold! Let's start by calling it T. If the sum is above T, the perceptron outputs $+1$. Otherwise, it outputs -1. More specifically, we want the perceptron to fire if:

$$perceptron\,(\mathbf{x}) = \begin{cases} +1 & w_1 x_1 + w_2 x_2 + \cdots + w_d x_d \geq T \\ -1 & w_1 x_1 + w_2 x_2 + \cdots + w_d x_d < T \end{cases}$$

Which is the same as:

$$perceptron\,(\mathbf{x}) = \begin{cases} +1 & w_1 x_1 + w_2 x_2 + \cdots + w_d x_d - T \geq 0 \\ -1 & w_1 x_1 + w_2 x_2 + \cdots + w_d x_d - T < 0 \end{cases}$$

The well-known sign function $sgn\,(s) = \begin{cases} +1 & s \geq 0 \\ -1 & s < 0 \end{cases}$ can be used to write the perceptron computation in a more compact manner:

$$perceptron\,(\mathbf{x}) = sgn\,(w_1 x_1 + w_2 x_2 + \cdots + w_d x_d - T)$$

In the literature, the threshold is usually treated as just another parameter refered to as the bias $w_0 = -T$, which leads to:

$$perceptron\,(\mathbf{x}) = sgn\,(w_0 + w_1 x_1 + w_2 x_2 + \cdots + w_d x_d)$$

To write the model in an even more compact manner, we can add a dimension to $\mathbf{x}$ called x_0 that corresponds to the bias weight. Naturally, we must have $x_0 = 1$. Having said that, given the weight vector (augmented with the bias) $\mathbf{w} = \left(w_0 \; w_1 \; w_2 \; \cdots \; w_d \right)^T$, we expand all input vectors as follows:

$$\left(x_1 \; x_2 \; \cdots \; x_d \right)^T \rightarrow \left(x_0 \; x_1 \; x_2 \; \cdots \; x_d \right)^T \rightarrow \left(1 \; x_1 \; x_2 \; \cdots \; x_d \right)^T$$

So, we can write the perceptron output as the sign of a dot product between input features and weights:

$$perceptron\left(\mathbf{x} \right) = sgn \left(\sum_{i=0}^{d} w_i x_i \right) = sgn \left(\mathbf{w} \cdot \mathbf{x} \right)$$

Now that we have covered how the perceptron makes decisions, we need to know how to learn the correct weights from training examples. To achieve that we sweep the data using the following procedure:

(1) Initialize weights randomly
(2) Get training example $\mathbf{x} \in \mathbb{R}^d$ with target $t \in \{-1, +1\}$
(3) Compute the perceptron output: $o = perceptron\left(\mathbf{x} \right)$
(4) If it made a mistake: $o \neq t$, then for each feature x_i:

    (a) if output is positive $o = +1$ and it should be negative $t = -1$, subtract a fraction of x_i from w_i

    (b) if output is negative $o = -1$ and it should be positive $t = +1$, add a fraction of x_i to w_i

(5) If there are more examples, go back to 2.

More specifically, if we define the size of the step (fraction of x_i) as $0 < \eta \leq 1$, we can write the learning rule for each feature as follows.

$$w_i = w_i + \eta \left(t - o \right) x_i$$

1)

Consider the following linearly separable training set:

$$\left\{ \mathbf{x}^1 = \begin{pmatrix} 0 \\ 0 \end{pmatrix}, \mathbf{x}^2 = \begin{pmatrix} 0 \\ 2 \end{pmatrix}, \mathbf{x}^3 = \begin{pmatrix} 1 \\ 1 \end{pmatrix}, \mathbf{x}^4 = \begin{pmatrix} 1 \\ -1 \end{pmatrix} \right\}$$

$$\{ t_1 = -1, t_2 = +1, t_3 = +1, t_4 = -1 \}$$

a) Initialize all weights to one (including the bias). Use a learning rate of one for simplicity. Apply the perceptron learning algorithm until convergence.

Solution:

According to the question, we start with $\eta = 1$ and $\mathbf{w} = \begin{pmatrix} 1 & 1 & 1 \end{pmatrix}^T$.

Now, we take the first data point x^1 and augment it with a bias dedicated dimension:

$$\begin{pmatrix} x_0^1 & x_1^1 & x_2^1 \end{pmatrix}^T \rightarrow \begin{pmatrix} 1 & 0 & 0 \end{pmatrix}^T$$

and compute the perceptron output for it:

$$o^1 = sgn\,(\mathbf{w} \cdot \mathbf{x}) = sgn\,(1 \cdot 1 + 1 \cdot 0 + 1 \cdot 0) = +1$$

Since the perceptron made a mistake, we use the output to compute an update:

$$\mathbf{w} = \begin{pmatrix} 1 & 1 & 1 \end{pmatrix}^T + 1\,(-1 - 1) \begin{pmatrix} 1 & 0 & 0 \end{pmatrix}^T = \begin{pmatrix} -1 & 1 & 1 \end{pmatrix}^T$$

We can then repeat the same logic for the next data point:

$$o^2 = sgn\,(\mathbf{w} \cdot \mathbf{x}) = sgn\,(-1 \cdot 1 + 1 \cdot 0 + 1 \cdot 2) = +1$$

As no mistake was made, we move to the next point:

$$o^3 = sgn\,(\mathbf{w} \cdot \mathbf{x}) = sgn\,(-1 \cdot 1 + 1 \cdot 1 + 1 \cdot 1) = +1$$

Again, no mistake was made, so we can move to the next point:

$$o^4 = sgn\,(\mathbf{w} \cdot \mathbf{x}) = sgn\,(-1 \cdot 1 + 1 \cdot 1 + 1 \cdot -1) = -1$$

No mistake was done again, which concludes our first sweep through the data (i.e. the first epoch). If we do another epoch, we see that the weights don't change. Thus, we have convergence.

---

b) Draw the separation hyperplane.

Solution:

Since we are working in two dimensions the weights define a separation line between the two classes. We get the equation for this line by checking the critical point where the decision changes from +1 to -1:

$$w_0 x_0 + w_1 x_1 + w_2 x_2 = 0$$

$$w_0 x_0 + w_1 x_1 + w_2 x_2 = 0$$

$$(-1)1 + x_1 + x_2 = 0$$

$$x_2 = -x_1 + 1$$

Having the line's equation, we can draw it in a plot with our data points to see the separation:

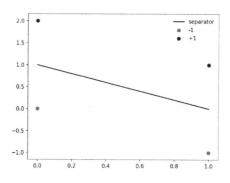

c) Does the perceptron converge on the first epoch if we change the weight initialization to zeros?

Solution:

According to the question, we start with $\eta = 1$ and $\mathbf{w} = \begin{pmatrix} 0 & 0 & 0 \end{pmatrix}^T$.

Now, we take the first data point $\mathbf{x}^1$ and augment it with a bias dedicated dimension:

$$\begin{pmatrix} x_0^1 & x_1^1 & x_2^1 \end{pmatrix}^T \rightarrow \begin{pmatrix} 1 & 0 & 0 \end{pmatrix}^T$$

and compute the perceptron output for it:

$$o^1 = sgn\left(\mathbf{w} \cdot \mathbf{x}\right) = sgn\left(0 \cdot 1 + 0 \cdot 0 + 0 \cdot 0\right) = +1$$

Since the perceptron made a mistake, we use the output to compute an update:

$$\mathbf{w} = \left(0\ 0\ 0\right)^T + 1\left(-1-1\right)\left(1\ 0\ 0\right)^T = \left(-2\ 0\ 0\right)^T$$

We can then repeat the same logic for the next data point:

$$o^2 = sgn\left(\mathbf{w} \cdot \mathbf{x}\right) = sgn\left(-2 \cdot 1 + 0 \cdot 0 + 0 \cdot 2\right) = -1$$

Since the perceptron made a mistake, we use the output to compute an update:

$$\mathbf{w} = \left(-2\ 0\ 0\right)^T + 1\left(1-(-1)\right)\left(1\ 0\ 2\right)^T = \left(0\ 0\ 4\right)^T$$

We can then repeat the same logic for the next data point:

$$o^3 = sgn\left(\mathbf{w} \cdot \mathbf{x}\right) = sgn\left(0 \cdot 1 + 0 \cdot 1 + 4 \cdot 1\right) = +1$$

No mistake was made, so we can move to the next point:

$$o^4 = sgn\left(\mathbf{w} \cdot \mathbf{x}\right) = sgn\left(0 \cdot 1 + 0 \cdot 1 + 4 \cdot -1\right) = +1$$

No mistake was made, so we finish the first epoch. We can plot the perceptron boundary and check that no convergence was achieved.

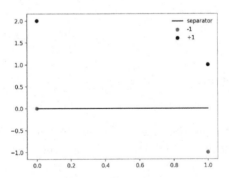

2)

Consider the following linearly separable training set:

$$\left\{ \mathbf{x}^1 = \begin{pmatrix} 0 \\ 0 \\ 0 \end{pmatrix}, \mathbf{x}^2 = \begin{pmatrix} 0 \\ 2 \\ 1 \end{pmatrix}, \mathbf{x}^3 = \begin{pmatrix} 1 \\ 1 \\ 1 \end{pmatrix}, \mathbf{x}^4 = \begin{pmatrix} 1 \\ -1 \\ 0 \end{pmatrix} \right\}$$

$$\{t_1 = -1, t_2 = +1, t_3 = +1, t_4 = -1\}$$

a) Initialize all weights to one (including the bias). Use a learning rate of one for simplicity. Apply the perception learning algorithm for one epoch.

Solution:

According to the question, we start with $\eta = 1$ and $\mathbf{w} = \begin{pmatrix} 1 & 1 & 1 & 1 \end{pmatrix}^T$.

Now, we take the first data point $\mathbf{x}^1$ and augment it with a bias dedicated dimension:

$$\begin{pmatrix} x_0^1 & x_1^1 & x_2^1 & x_3^1 \end{pmatrix}^T \to \begin{pmatrix} 1 & 0 & 0 & 0 \end{pmatrix}^T$$

and compute the perceptron output for it:

$$o^1 = sgn\,(\mathbf{w} \cdot \mathbf{x}) = sgn\,(1 \cdot 1 + 1 \cdot 0 + 1 \cdot 0 + 1 \cdot 0) = +1$$

Since the perceptron made a mistake, we use the output to compute an update:

$$\mathbf{w} = \begin{pmatrix} 1 & 1 & 1 & 1 \end{pmatrix}^T + 1\,(-1 - 1) \begin{pmatrix} 1 & 0 & 0 & 0 \end{pmatrix}^T = \begin{pmatrix} -1 & 1 & 1 & 1 \end{pmatrix}^T$$

We can then repeat the same logic for the next data point:

$$o^2 = sgn\,(\mathbf{w} \cdot \mathbf{x}) = sgn\,(-1 \cdot 1 + 1 \cdot 0 + 1 \cdot 2 + 1 \cdot 1) = +1$$

As no mistake was made, we move to the next point:

$$o^3 = sgn\,(\mathbf{w} \cdot \mathbf{x}) = sgn\,(-1 \cdot 1 + 1 \cdot 1 + 1 \cdot 1 + 1 \cdot 1) = +1$$

Again, no mistake was made, so we can move to the next point:

$$o^4 = sgn\,(\mathbf{w} \cdot \mathbf{x}) = sgn\,(-1 \cdot 1 + 1 \cdot 1 + 1 \cdot -1 + 1 \cdot 0) = -1$$

No mistake was done again, which concludes the epoch.

---

b) For an additional epoch, do the weights change?

Solution:

We take the weights at the end of the first epoch:

$$\mathbf{w} = \begin{pmatrix} -1 & 1 & 1 & 1 \end{pmatrix}^T$$

and compute the perceptron output for all points:

$$o^1 = sgn\left(\mathbf{w} \cdot \mathbf{x}\right) = sgn\left(-1 \cdot 1 + 1 \cdot 0 + 1 \cdot 0 + 1 \cdot 0\right) = -1$$

$$o^2 = sgn\left(\mathbf{w} \cdot \mathbf{x}\right) = sgn\left(-1 \cdot 1 + 1 \cdot 0 + 1 \cdot 2 + 1 \cdot 1\right) = +1$$

$$o^3 = sgn\left(\mathbf{w} \cdot \mathbf{x}\right) = sgn\left(-1 \cdot 1 + 1 \cdot 1 + 1 \cdot 1 + 1 \cdot 1\right) = +1$$

$$o^4 = sgn\left(\mathbf{w} \cdot \mathbf{x}\right) = sgn\left(-1 \cdot 1 + 1 \cdot 1 + 1 \cdot -1 + 1 \cdot 0\right) = -1$$

Since no mistakes occurred, we see that the perceptron converged.

c) What is the perceptron output for the query poin t $\begin{pmatrix} 0 & 0 & 1 \end{pmatrix}^T$?

Solution:

We start by augmenting the query with a bias dimension:

$$\begin{pmatrix} x_0 & x_1 & x_2 & x_3 \end{pmatrix}^T \rightarrow \begin{pmatrix} 1 & 0 & 0 & 1 \end{pmatrix}^T$$

We take the converged weights:

$$\mathbf{w} = \begin{pmatrix} -1 & 1 & 1 & 1 \end{pmatrix}^T$$

And compute the perceptron output for the point:

$$o = sgn\left(\mathbf{w} \cdot \mathbf{x}\right) = sgn\left(-1 \cdot 1 + 1 \cdot 0 + 1 \cdot 0 + 1 \cdot 1\right) = +1$$

We see that the point is on the boundary. So, because of the way we defined the sign function, the perceptron outputs +1, thus recognizing the point as a member of the learned class.

3)

What happens if we replace the sign function by the step function?

$$\Theta\left(x\right) = \begin{cases} 1 & x \geq 0 \\ 0 & x < 0 \end{cases}$$

Specifically, how would you change the learning rate to get the same results?

Solution:

Recall the lerning rule in question:

$$\mathbf{w} = \mathbf{w} + \eta\left(t - o\right)\mathbf{x}$$

The only term that depends on the perceptron output is the error $(y - o)$.

With the sign function, the error is:

$$\delta_{sgn} = t - o_{sgn} = t - sgn(\mathbf{w} \cdot \mathbf{x})$$

Which can be unfolded as:

$$\delta_{sgn} = \begin{cases} +2 & t = +1, \mathbf{w} \cdot \mathbf{x} < 0 \\ -2 & t = -1, \mathbf{w} \cdot \mathbf{x} \geq 0 \end{cases}$$

Whereas with the step function, the error is:

$$\delta_{step} = t - o_{step} = t - \Theta(\mathbf{w} \cdot \mathbf{x})$$

Which can be unfolded as:

$$\delta_{step} = \begin{cases} +1 & t = +1, \mathbf{w} \cdot \mathbf{x} < 0 \\ -1 & t = -1, \mathbf{w} \cdot \mathbf{x} \geq 0 \end{cases}$$

Having said that, we notice that there is a relation between the two error terms $\delta_{sgn} = 2\delta_{step}$.

So, since we had the update:

$$\mathbf{w} = \mathbf{w} + \eta_{sgn}\delta_{sgn}\mathbf{x}$$

If we replace the δ_{sgn} by the error for the step function we get:

$$\mathbf{w} = \mathbf{w} + 2\eta_{sgn}\delta_{step}\mathbf{x}$$

To get exactly the same update, we need to define a learning rate which is twice the one we used $\eta_{step} = 2\eta_{sgn}$ and get:

$$\mathbf{w} = \mathbf{w} + \eta_{step}\delta_{step}\mathbf{x}$$

---

4)

The perceptron can learn a relatively large number of functions. In this exercise, we focus on simple logical functions.

a) Show graphically that a perceptron can learn the logical *NOT* function. Give an example with specific weights.

Solution:

The *NOT* function receives as input a logical value $x \in \{-1, +1\}$ and outputs its logical negation $t \in \{-1, +1\}$. We can enumerate all possible inputs and their inputs:

- For $x = -1$ the output is $t = +1$
- For $x = +1$ the output is $t = -1$

To show that a perceptron can learn a given function we just need to show that all points that require a positive output $(+1)$ can be separated from all points that require a negative output by an hyperplane.

Since we are working with 1 dimensional inputs, an hyperplane is, in this case, a point.

So, is there a point that accurately separates the points? Yes, any point between -1 and $+1$ will achieve this.

An example comes from setting the perceptron weights to zero:

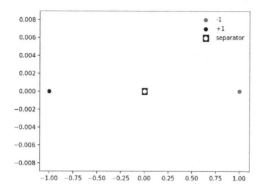

b) Show graphically that a perceptron can learn the logical AND function for two inputs. Give an example with specific weights.

Solution:

The AND function receives as input a pair of logical values $\mathbf{x} \in \mathbb{R}^2$ and outputs its logical conjunction $t \in \{-1, +1\}$. We can enumerate all possible inputs and their inputs:

- For $\mathbf{x} = \begin{pmatrix} -1 & -1 \end{pmatrix}^T$ the output is $t = -1$
- For $\mathbf{x} = \begin{pmatrix} -1 & +1 \end{pmatrix}^T$ the output is $t = -1$
- For $\mathbf{x} = \begin{pmatrix} +1 & -1 \end{pmatrix}^T$ the output is $t = -1$
- For $\mathbf{x} = \begin{pmatrix} +1 & +1 \end{pmatrix}^T$ the output is $t = +1$

To show that a perceptron can learn a given function we just need to show that all points that require a positive output $(+1)$ can be separated from all points that require a negative output by an hyperplane.

Since we are working with 2 dimensional inputs, an hyperplane is, in this case, a line.

So, is there a weight vector that defines a boundary line that accurately separates the points?

Yes, for instance $\mathbf{w} = \begin{pmatrix} -1 & 1 & 1 \end{pmatrix}^T$ achieves:

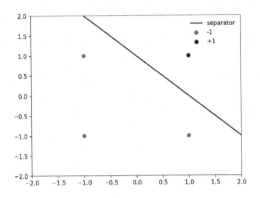

---

c) Show graphically that a perceptron can learn the logical OR function for two inputs. Give an example with specific weights.

Solution:

The OR function receives as input a pair of logical values $\mathbf{x} \in \mathbb{R}^2$ and outputs its logical disjunction $t \in \{-1, +1\}$. We can enumerate all possible inputs and their inputs:

- For $\mathbf{x} = \begin{pmatrix} -1 & -1 \end{pmatrix}^T$ the output is $t = -1$
- For $\mathbf{x} = \begin{pmatrix} -1 & +1 \end{pmatrix}^T$ the output is $t = +1$
- For $\mathbf{x} = \begin{pmatrix} +1 & -1 \end{pmatrix}^T$ the output is $t = +1$
- For $\mathbf{x} = \begin{pmatrix} +1 & +1 \end{pmatrix}^T$ the output is $t = +1$

To show that a perceptron can learn a given function we just need to show that all points that require a positive output ($+1$) can be separated from all points that require a negative output by an hyperplane.

Since we are working with 2 dimensional inputs, an hyperplane is, in this case, a line.

So, is there a weight vector that defines a boundary line that accurately separates the points?

Yes, for instance $\mathbf{w} = \begin{pmatrix} 1 & 1 & 1 \end{pmatrix}^T$ achieves:

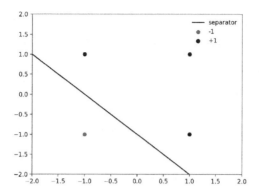

---

d) Show graphically that a perceptron can not learn the logical XOR function for two inputs.

Solution:

The XOR function receives as input a pair of logical values $\mathbf{x} \in \mathbb{R}^2$ and outputs the exclusive disjunction $t \in \{-1, +1\}$. We can enumerate all possible inputs and their inputs:

- For $\mathbf{x} = \begin{pmatrix} -1 & -1 \end{pmatrix}^T$ the output is $t = -1$
- For $\mathbf{x} = \begin{pmatrix} -1 & +1 \end{pmatrix}^T$ the output is $t = +1$
- For $\mathbf{x} = \begin{pmatrix} +1 & -1 \end{pmatrix}^T$ the output is $t = +1$
- For $\mathbf{x} = \begin{pmatrix} +1 & +1 \end{pmatrix}^T$ the output is $t = -1$

To show that a perceptron can learn a given function we need to show that all points that require a positive output (+1) can be separated from all points that require a negative output by an hyperplane.

Since we are working with 2 dimensional inputs, an hyperplane is, in this case, a line.

So, is there a weight vector that defines a boundary line that accurately separates the points?

No... If we plot the points we see right away that no line can separate the positive instances from the negative ones:

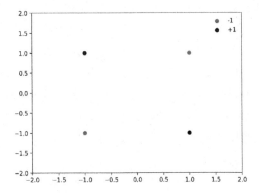

Thinking Questions

Could you implement a statistical machine learning application that classifies a number into two classes, primes and nonprimes? What is the main difference in the example of salmon and sea bass?

Chapter 2

Probability and Information

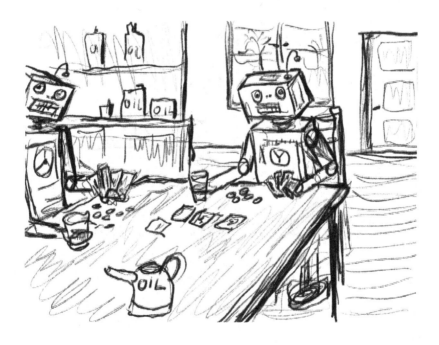

Fig. 2.1 The mathematical probability theory provides a consistent framework for the quantification and manipulation of uncertainty. It has its roots in attempts to analyze games of chance. Based on probability theory and statistics, information theory was developed. It measures the information of distributions of random variables. Random variables are variables whose values depend on outcomes of a stochastic phenomenon.

2.1   Probability Theory

A key concept in the field in machine learning is that of uncertainty. It arises both through noise on measurements, as well as through the finite size of data sets. Mathematical probability theory provides a consistent framework for the quantification and manipulation of uncertainty and forms one of the central foundations for pattern recognition. Probability theory is built around Kolmogorov's axioms [Kolmogorov (1933)], see Figure 2.2.

Fig. 2.2   A quotation attributed to Andrey Kolmogorov: "Every mathematician believes that he is ahead of the others. The reason none state this belief in public is because they are intelligent people."

All probabilities are between 0 and 1. For any proposition a,

$$0 \leq p(a) \leq 1$$

and

$$p(true) = 1, \quad p(false) = 0.$$

To each sentence, a numerical degree of belief between 0 and 1 is assigned, which provides a way of summarizing uncertainty. The last axiom expresses the probability of disjunction and is given by

$$p(a \vee b) = p(a) + p(b) - p(a \wedge b)$$

Where do these numerical degrees of belief come from?

- Humans can believe in a subjective viewpoint, which can be determined by some empirical psychological experiments. This approach is a very subjective way to determine the numerical degree of belief. This approach is called Bayesian.
- For a finite sample we can estimate a fraction by counting the relative frequency of an event in a sample. We do not know the true value because we cannot access the whole population. This approach is called frequentist.
- It appears that the true values can be determined from the true nature of the universe, for example, for a fair coin, the probability of heads is 0.5. This approach is related to the Platonic world of ideas. However, we can never verify whether a fair coin exists.

2.1.1 *Conditional probability*

The degree of belief $p(a)$ is attached to a sentence a before any evidence about the nature of the sentence is obtained; we call this probability the prior (before) probability. Arising from the frequentist approach, one can determine the probability of an event a by counting. If Ω is the set of all possible events, $p(\Omega) = 1$, then $a \in \Omega$. The cardinality determines the number of elements of a set, $card(\Omega)$ is the number of elements of the set Ω, $card(a)$ is the number of elements of the set a and

$$p(a) = \frac{card(a)}{card(\Omega)} \tag{2.1}$$

is the frequentist estimation for the probability of a.

Now we can define the posterior probability, the probability of a given that evidence b is obtained

$$p(a|b) = \frac{card(a \wedge b)}{card(b)}.$$

The posterior probability is also called the conditional probability. From

$$p(a \wedge b) = \frac{card(a \wedge b)}{card(\Omega)} \tag{2.2}$$

and

$$p(b) = \frac{card(b)}{card(\Omega)} \tag{2.3}$$

we get

$$p(a|b) = \frac{p(a \wedge b)}{p(b)} \tag{2.4}$$

and

$$p(b|a) = \frac{p(a \wedge b)}{p(a)}. \tag{2.5}$$

Bayes's rule follows from both equations

$$p(b|a) = \frac{p(a|b) \cdot p(b)}{p(a)}. \tag{2.6}$$

2.1.2 Law of Total Probability

For mutually exclusive events $b_1, ..., b_n$ with

$$\sum_{i=1}^{n} p(b_i) = 1 \tag{2.7}$$

the **law of total probability** is given by

$$p(a) = \sum_{i=1}^{n} p(a \wedge b_i) = \sum_{i=1}^{n} p(a, b_i) = \sum_{i=1}^{n} p(a|b_i) \cdot p(b_i). \tag{2.8}$$

The two key rules of probability are called:

- the sum rule

$$p(x) = \sum_{y} p(x, y)$$

- the product rule

$$p(x, y) = p(y|x) \cdot p(x) = p(x|y) \cdot p(y)$$

For binary events there are two states: true or false. In other words, for any event a there is an event $\neg a$ which corresponds to the event that a does not occur. Binary events are described by binary variables. For binary events,

$$p(x) + p(\neg x) = 1, \; p(y) + p(\neg y) = 1, \tag{2.9}$$

where the law of total probability is represented by

$$p(y) = p(y, x) + p(y, \neg x) \tag{2.10}$$

$$p(y) = p(y|x) \cdot p(x) + p(y|\neg x) \cdot p(\neg x).$$

and

$$p(\neg y) = p(\neg y, x) + p(\neg y, \neg x), \tag{2.11}$$

Fig. 2.3 Reverent Thomas Bayes (1702-1761). He set down his findings on probability in "Essay Towards Solving a Problem in the Doctrine of Chances" (1763), published posthumously in the Philosophical Transactions of the Royal Society of London. The drawing after a portrait of Bayes used in a 1936 book, it is not known if the portrait is actually representing him.

2.1.3 *Bayes's rule*

The Bayes's rule was discovered by Thomas Bayes, see Figure 2.3.

Bayes rule can be used to determine the total posterior probability $p(h_k|D)$ of hypothesis h_k given data D. For example, what is the probability that some illness is present?

- $p(D|h_k)$ is the probability that a hypothesis h_k generates the data D. $P(D|h_k)$ can be easily estimated. For example, what is the probability that some illness generates some symptoms?
- The probability that an illness is present given certain symptoms, can be then determined by the Bayes rule

$$p(h_k|D) = \frac{p(D|h_k) \cdot p(h_k)}{p(D)} = \frac{p(D, h_k)}{p(D)}. \tag{2.12}$$

The most probable hypothesis h_k out of a set of possible hypothesis $h_1, h_2, \cdots$ given some present data is according to the Bayes rule

$$p(h_k|D) = \frac{p(D|h_k) \cdot p(h_k)}{p(D)}. \tag{2.13}$$

We notice that $p(h_k|D)$ and $p(D, h_k)$ are related in a linear manner

$$p(h_k|D) \propto p(D|h_k) \cdot p(h_k). \tag{2.14}$$

So, to determine the maximum posteriori hypothesis h_{MAP} we maximize

$$h_{MAP} = \arg\max_{h_k} \frac{p(D|h_k) \cdot p(h_k)}{p(D)}. \tag{2.15}$$

As we can see, the maximization is independent of $p(D)$, it follows

$$h_{MAP} = \arg\max_{h_k} p(D|h_k) \cdot p(h_k). \tag{2.16}$$

If we assume $p(h_k) = p(h_\gamma)$ for all h_k and h_γ, then we can further simplify, and choose the maximum likelihood (ML) hypothesis

$$h_{ML} = \arg\max_{h_k} p(D|h_k). \tag{2.17}$$

2.1.3.1 *Bayesian Interpretation*

In the Bayesian (or epistemological) interpretation, probability measures a "degree of belief" and Bayes' rule links the degree of belief in a proposition before and after accounting for evidence [Bishop (2006)]. For example, for a given hypothesis h_k, with prior probability $p(h_k)$, $p(D|h_k)$ represents the likelihood of the data D if we assume h_k to be true. So, if we, in fact, observe D, we can update our belief about h_k through the rule

$$p(h_k|D) = \frac{p(D|h_k) \cdot p(h_k)}{p(D)}$$

2.1.3.2 *Example*

Cancer screening aims to detect cancer before symptoms appear [Mitchell (1997)]. This may involve for example a blood test. Suppose that a patient tests positive. The test is secure because in 99 percent of the cases the test returns a correct positive result ($= positive$) in which a rare form of cancer is actually present. Should the doctor tell the patient, that he has cancer?

The test has correct negative result ($= negative$) in 99 percent of the cases where the rare form of cancer is not present. It is also known that 0.001 of the entire population have the rare form of cancer ($h = cancer$).

$$p(cancer) = 0.001, \quad p(\neg cancer) = 0.999,$$

$$p(positive|cancer) = 0.99, \quad p(negative|cancer) = 0.01,$$

$$p(positive|\neg cancer) = 0.01, \quad p(negative|\neg cancer) = 0.99.$$

We determine h_{map} according to the linear relation

$$posterior \propto likelihood \times prior$$

$$p(cancer|positive) \propto p(positive|cancer) \cdot p(cancer) = 0.99 \cdot 0.001$$

$$p(\neg cancer|positive) \propto \cdot p(positive|\neg cancer) \cdot p(\neg cancer) \cdot 0.01 \cdot 0.999$$

it follows

$$h_{map} = \neg cancer$$

So, despite the positive result, we are still more confident that the patient is healthy than otherwise. The right thing to do would be to another test to try to accumulate more evidence in favor of the hypothesis that patient has the disease.

2.1.4 *Expectation*

The commonly used arithmetic mean

$$\mu = \bar{x} = \frac{1}{N}\sum_{k=1}^{N} x_k. \tag{2.18}$$

is defined as being equal to the sum of the numerical values of each and every observation divided by the total number of observations. For a random variable X with a finite number of outcomes $x_1, x_2, x_3, \cdots, x_N$ occurring with probabilities $p_1, p_2, p_3, \cdots, p_N$ with

$$1 = \sum_{k=1}^{N} p_k,$$

the expectation of X (usually a random variable is denoted with a capital letter) is defined as

$$\mathbb{E}(X) = \sum_{k=1}^{N} p_k \cdot x_k. \tag{2.19}$$

Another important operation involving probabilities is that of finding weighted averages of functions. The average value of some function $f(x)$ under a probability distribution $p(x)$ is called the expectation of $f(x)$

$$\mathbb{E}(f) = \int p(x)f(x)dx,$$

$$\mathbb{E}(f) = \sum_x p(x) f(x).$$ (2.20)

For a finite number N of points sampled according to their probabilities, the expectation can be approximated by a mean

$$\mathbb{E}(f) \simeq \frac{1}{N} \sum_{k=1}^{N} f(x_k).$$ (2.21)

A conditional expectation with respect to a conditional distribution is given by

$$\mathbb{E}(f|y) = \sum_x p(x|y) f(x).$$ (2.22)

The variance of $f(x)$ is defined by

$$var[f] = \mathbb{E}\left[(f(x) - \mathbb{E}[f(x)])^2 \right]$$ (2.23)

and provides a measure of how much variability there is in $f(x)$ around its mean value $\mathbb{E}[f(x)]$.

2.1.5 *Covariance*

When making inferences based on a sample, it may be useful to describe the relation between pairs of variables. This can be done through the sample covariance

$$cov(X, Y) = \frac{\sum_{k=1}^{N}(x_k - \overline{x}) \cdot (y_k - \overline{y})}{N - 1}$$ (2.24)

with $\overline{x}$ and $\overline{y}$ being the arithmetic mean of the two variables in the sample.

The arithmetic mean is the average value; the sum of all values in the sample divided by the number of values. If we have the whole population, the covariance is

$$cov(X, Y) = \frac{\sum_{k=1}^{N}(x_k - \overline{x}) \cdot (y_k - \overline{y})}{N}.$$ (2.25)

The sample covariance has $N - 1$ in the denominator rather than N due to Bessel's correction which allows us to avoid underestimating the real covariance.

In Machine Learning, we never have access to the whole population, so, in this book, we will use the sample covariance without further distinction; for example, when we introduce the covariance matrix, we will not distinguish between the sample covariance matrix and the population covariance matrix.

Covariance is a measure of how much two random variables change together in a linear way. In a linear relationship, either the high values of one variable are paired with the high values of another variable or the high values of one variable are paired with the low values of another variable. For example, for a two variable $((X, Y))$ dataset,

$$\{(2.1, 2), (2.3, 2), (2.9, 3), (4.1, 4), (5, 4.8), (2, 2.5), (2.2, 1.5),$$

$$(4, 5), (4, 2), (2.8, 4), (3, 3.4), (3.5, 3.8), (4.5, 4.7), (3.5, 3)\}$$

the sample covariance of the data set is 0.82456. Ordering the list by X, we notice that the ascending X values are matched by ascending Y values (see Figure 2.4).

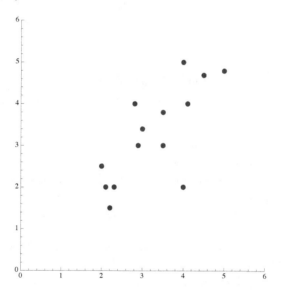

Fig. 2.4   The data points of the data set *Data*.

For data sets with more than two variables we may want to find out the relations between all pairs of variables. To that end, we use the covariance matrix. A position Σ_{ij} of this matrix measures the tendency of two features, x_i and x_j, to vary in the same direction. For n vectors, it is computed by

$$c_{ij} = \frac{\sum_{k=1}^{N}(x_{k,i} - \overline{x_i}) \cdot (x_{k,j} - \overline{x_j})}{N - 1} \tag{2.26}$$

with $\overline{x_i}$ and $\overline{x_j}$ being the arithmetic mean of the two variables of the sample.

Covariances are symmetric; $c_{ij} = c_{ji}$ and, so, the resulting covariance matrix Σ is symmetric and positive-definite,

$$\Sigma = \begin{pmatrix} c_{11} & c_{12} & \cdots & c_{1m} \\ c_{21} & c_{22} & \cdots & c_{2m} \\ \vdots & \vdots & \ddots & \vdots \\ c_{m1} & c_{m2} & \cdots & c_{mm} \end{pmatrix}. \tag{2.27}$$

For the aforementioned set of data, the covariance matrix Σ is given by

$$\Sigma = \begin{pmatrix} 0.912582 & 0.82456 \\ 0.82456 & 1.34247 \end{pmatrix}. \tag{2.28}$$

2.2   Distribution

A distribution is a mathematical function that provides a description of a random phenomenon in terms of the probabilities of events. We will present three common distributions that will be used:

- In Bayesian learning (e.g. Bayesian regression) to describe the prior assumption on the distribution of the data and model parameters by a Gaussian and a Laplace distribution. The prior assumption according to the Bayesian interpretation will lead to l_2 and l_1 regularization.
- To define an error function by a Bernoulli distribution which will lead to the cross entropy loss function.
- To describe a sample by a Gaussian distribution and a Gaussian mixture in EM clustering.
- To estimate the similarity between between vectors using a Gaussian Kernel in RBF networks.

2.2.1   *Gaussian Distribution*

A continuous random variable takes all values in a given interval of numbers describing a random phenomena. The probability distribution of a continuous random variable is shown by a probability density function (PDF). A PDF is a function whose value at any given sample (or point) in the sample space (the set of possible values taken by the random variable) is bigger if that point is more likely. Usually data or the model parameters are described by discrete values, however we assume that the distribution of the discrete random variables is approximately described by the probability density function.

The most important probability distribution for continuous variables is called the normal or Gaussian distribution and it was suggested by Johann Carl Friedrich Gauss, see Figure 2.5. For example, the normal distribution is seen in exams. Most students will score the average, while smaller numbers of students will score a bad or very good grade. An even smaller percentage of students score insufficient or excellent.

Fig. 2.5 Johann Carl Friedrich Gauss (30 April 1777 - 23 February 1855) was a German mathematician and physicist who made significant contributions to many fields in mathematics and sciences. He was the first to suggest the normal distribution law.

The Gaussian distribution or normal distribution is defined as PDF that reflects the relative probability

$$p(x|\mu, \sigma^2) = \mathcal{N}(x|\mu, \sigma^2) = \frac{1}{\sqrt{2 \cdot \pi \cdot \sigma}} \cdot \exp\left(-\frac{1}{2 \cdot \sigma^2} \cdot (x - \mu)^2\right) \quad (2.29)$$

where

- μ is the mean,
- σ is the standard deviation,
- σ^2 is the variance.

The notation $\mathcal{N}(x|\mu, \sigma^2)$ is often used to indicate the normal (Gaussian) distribution, in Figure 2.6 an example of a Normal distribution is shown.

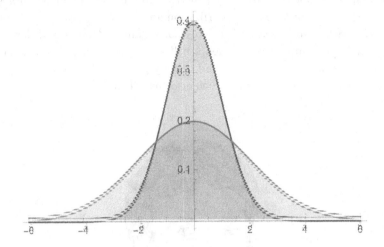

Fig. 2.6   Two Gaussian (normal) distribution with $\mu = 0$ $\sigma = 1$ and $\mu = 0$ $\sigma = 2$. μ describes the centre of the distribution and σ the width, the bigger σ the more flat the distribution. The PDF may give a value greater than one (small σ). It is the area under the curve that represents the probability. However, the PDF reflects the relative probability.

Instead of inverting σ one can use the precision (β) which is often used in Bayesian software

$$\beta = \frac{1}{\sigma^2}, \qquad \beta^{-1} = \sigma^2$$

$$p(x|\mu, \beta) = \mathcal{N}(x|\mu, \beta^{-1}) = \frac{\beta}{\sqrt{2 \cdot \pi}} \cdot \exp\left(-\frac{1}{2} \cdot \beta \cdot (x - \mu)^2\right)$$

The Gaussian distribution can be generalized to a D dimensional space defined as PDF that reflects the relative probability

$$p(\mathbf{x}|\boldsymbol{\mu}, \Sigma) = \mathcal{N}(\mathbf{x}|\boldsymbol{\mu}, \Sigma) = \frac{1}{(2 \cdot \pi)^{D/2}} \cdot \frac{1}{|\Sigma|^{1/2}} \cdot \exp\left(-\frac{1}{2} \cdot (\mathbf{x} - \boldsymbol{\mu})^T \Sigma^{-1} \cdot (\mathbf{x} - \boldsymbol{\mu})\right) \tag{2.30}$$

where

- $\boldsymbol{\mu}$ is the D dimensional mean vector
- Σ is a $D \times D$ covariance matrix
- $|\Sigma|$ is the determinant of Σ

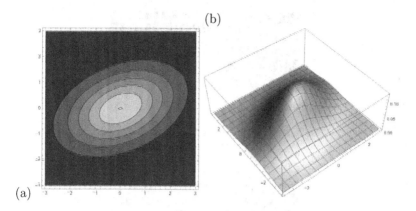

Fig. 2.7 (a) The Gaussian distribution over 2 dimensional space with $\boldsymbol{\mu} = (0,0)^T$ and the covariance matrix Σ (b). Three dimensional plot of the Gaussian. The PDF may give a value greater than one (small $|\Sigma|$). It is the volume under the PDF that represents the probability. However, the PDF reflects the relative probability.

In Figure 2.7 an example is shown with the covariance matrix

$$\Sigma = \begin{pmatrix} 2 & 0.5 \\ 0.5 & 1 \end{pmatrix}.$$

Again, instead of inverting Σ one can use the precision matrix $\boldsymbol{\beta}$

$$\boldsymbol{\beta} = \Sigma^{-1}$$

$$p(\mathbf{x}|\boldsymbol{\mu}, \boldsymbol{\beta}) = \mathcal{N}(\mathbf{x}|\boldsymbol{\mu}, \boldsymbol{\beta}^{-1}) = \sqrt{\frac{|\boldsymbol{\beta}|}{(2 \cdot \pi)^D}} \cdot \exp\left(-\frac{1}{2} \cdot (\mathbf{x} - \boldsymbol{\mu})^T \boldsymbol{\beta} \cdot (\mathbf{x} - \boldsymbol{\mu})\right)$$

2.2.1.1 *Central limit theorem*

The central limit theorem was formulated by Laplace, see Figure 2.8.

It states that the sum of N random variables $X_1, X_2, X_3, \cdots, X_N$ approaches a normal (Gaussian) distribution as N approaches infinity (under certain common conditions). For example, if we take 10000 samples from one random variable X_1 (i.e. $N = 1$) we can plot a 20 bin histogram of the samples in Figure 2.9 (a).

The height of a rectangle in a histogram represents the number of values in the corresponding bin. With the value $N = 1$ we have one histogram that represents a nearly uniform distribution. Now, if instead of using a single variable X_1, we repeat the same process for the normalized sum of two variables

$$\frac{X_1 + X_2}{2}$$

Fig. 2.8 Pierre-Simon Laplace (23 March 1749 - 5 March 1827) was a French mathematician and astronomer. The meaning of last words of Laplace according to Fourier: "What we know is little, and what we are ignorant of is immense."

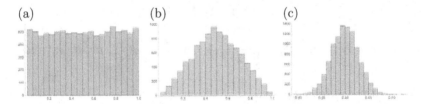

Fig. 2.9 (a) One random variable X_1, $N = 1$ with 10000 random values is represented by a histogram of 20 bins of equal size (b). Mean of two random variables with 10000 random values. (c) Mean of 100 random variables with 10000 random values, the distribution tends to a Gaussian. For a distribution the the sum of the height of the bins should be one.

(i.e. $N = 2$) we start to get the pyramid shape in Figure 2.9 (b).

If we go to larger numbers of variables, like $N = 100$

$$\frac{X_1 + X_2 + X_3 + X_4 + \cdots X_{100}}{100}$$

the distribution tends to a Gaussian, even with N being a finite number, see Figure 2.9 (c). In practice we can approximate the Gaussian distribution that is defined on continuous variables quite well with the discrete variables that are used in machine learning.

2.2.2 Laplace Distribution

The Laplace distribution is a continuous probability distribution named after Pierre-Simon Laplace, see Figure 2.8. It is the distribution of differences between two independent variates with identical exponential distributions, defined as PDF that reflects the relative probability

$$p(x|\mu, b) = Laplace(x|\mu, b) = \left(\frac{1}{2 \cdot b}\right) \exp\left(\frac{-|x - \mu|}{b}\right) \tag{2.31}$$

where $b > 0$ is a scale parameter referred to as the diversity. In Figure 2.10 an example of a Laplace distribution is shown.

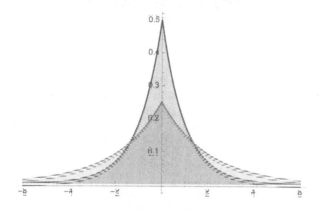

Fig. 2.10   Two Laplace distribution with $\mu = 0$, $b = 1$ and $\mu = 0$, $b = 2$. μ describes the centre of the distribution and b the width, the bigger diversity b the more flat the distribution.

2.2.3 Bernoulli Distribution

A discrete random variable is a variable whose value is obtained by counting occurrences of a random phenomenon, for example the number of heads when throwing two coins.

The Bernoulli distribution, named after Swiss mathematician Jacob Bernoulli (see Figure 2.11), is the discrete probability distribution of a binary random variable x which takes the value 1 with probability o and

Fig. 2.11   Jacob Bernoulli (1655 - 16 August 1705), Swiss mathematician.

0 with probability $1 - o$. It is the probability distribution of any single experiment that asks a yes-no question (for example tossing of a coin) of a binary variable y and it can be written as

$$Bern(y|o) = \begin{cases} o, & \text{if } y = 1 \\ 1 - o, & \text{if } y = 0, \end{cases} \qquad (2.32)$$

which can also be written compactly as

$$Bern(y|o) = o^y \cdot (1 - o)^{1-y}. \qquad (2.33)$$

For a data set $D = \{y^{(1)}, y^{(2)}, \cdots, y^{(N)}\}$ of N independent coin tosses, we can write the probability of the set of tosses as

$$p(D|o) = p(y^{(1)}, y^{(2)}, \cdots, y^{(N)}|o) = \prod_{n=1}^{N} p(y^{(n)}|o). \qquad (2.34)$$

Now, we can use the Bernoulli distribution to further write

$$p(D|o) = \prod_{n=1}^{N} Bern(y^{(n)}|o) = \prod_{n=1}^{N} o^{y^{(n)}} \cdot (1 - o)^{1-y^{(n)}}. \qquad (2.35)$$

Another interesting scenario is where the N independent coin tosses are done with N different coins with each having different heads and tails probabilities. If coin $n \in \{1, \cdots, N\}$ flips tails with probability $o^{(n)}$, then we can write the probability of observing the sequence D with $O = \{o^{(1)}, o^{(2)}, \cdots, o^{(N)}\}$ as

$$p(D|O) = p(y^{(1)}, y^{(2)}, \cdots, y^{(N)}|o^{(1)}, o^{(2)}, \cdots, o^{(N)}) = \prod_{n=1}^{N} p(y^{(n)}|o^{(n)}).$$
(2.36)

Again, we can use the Bernoulli to further write

$$p(D|O) = \prod_{n=1}^{N} Bern(y^{(n)}|o^{(n)}) = \prod_{n=1}^{N} (o^{(n)})^{y^{(n)}} \cdot (1 - (o^{(n)}))^{1-y^{(n)}}. \quad (2.37)$$

2.2.3.1 *Multinomial Variables*

A vector of binary variables can be used to describe one of K possible mutually exclusive states [Bishop (2006)]. In a K dimensional vector, one of the K dimensions is one and all others are zero. This is the typical representation to describe the outcome of a rolling of a K-sided die.

$$\mathbf{y} = \begin{pmatrix} y_1 \\ y_2 \\ \vdots \\ y_k \\ \vdots \\ y_K \end{pmatrix}$$

with one value $y_k = 1$ and all remaining values are zero, for example with $K = 6$ with $y_2 = 1$ we would have

$$\mathbf{y} = \begin{pmatrix} 0 \\ 1 \\ 0 \\ 0 \\ 0 \\ 0 \end{pmatrix}$$

So, for a general binary vector $\mathbf{y}$ with a 1-of-K representation we will have

$$y_k \in \{0, 1\}, \quad \sum_{k=1}^{K} y_k = 1.$$

Notice how this 1-of-K representation corresponds to the unary representation in which zero cannot be represented.

We can, thus, generalize the Bernoulli distribution for this case

$$p(\mathbf{y}|\mathbf{o}) = \prod_{k=1}^{K} o_k^{y_k} \tag{2.38}$$

with the vector $\mathbf{o}$ containing the probability of each outcome

$$\sum_{k=1}^{K} o_k = 1.$$

So, for a full data set of N independent vectors (where each represents something like a die toss).

$$D = \{\mathbf{y}^{(1)}, \mathbf{y}^{(2)}, \cdots, \mathbf{y}^{(N)}\}$$

the probability of the data is given by

$$p(D|\mathbf{o}) = \prod_{n=1}^{N} p(\mathbf{y}^{(n)}|\mathbf{o}) = \prod_{n=1}^{N} \prod_{k=1}^{K} o_k^{y_k^{(n)}}. \tag{2.39}$$

Again, it will be helpful in the future to think about the scenario where each toss n has its own outcomes probabilities. In that setting, for each $\mathbf{y}^{(n)}$ there is a corresponding probability vector $\mathbf{o}^{(n)}$. Like before, let us refer to the set of these vectors as $O = \{\mathbf{o}^{(1)}, \mathbf{o}^{(2)}, \cdots, \mathbf{o}^{(N)}\}$. Then we can similarly define a likelihood function for the data as

$$p(D|O) = p(\mathbf{y}^{(1)}, \mathbf{y}^{(2)}, \cdots, \mathbf{y}^{(N)}|\mathbf{o}^{(1)}, \mathbf{o}^{(2)}, \cdots, \mathbf{o}^{(N)}) = \prod_{n=1}^{N} p(\mathbf{y}^{(n)}|\mathbf{o}^{(n)}). \tag{2.40}$$

which simplifies to

$$p(D|O) = \prod_{n=1}^{N} \prod_{k=1}^{K} (o_k^{(n)})^{y_k^{(n)}}. \tag{2.41}$$

2.3   Information Theory

The concepts of information theory are widely used in Machine Learning. For example, Shannon's entropy is used with decision trees to chose the attributes during construction of a classification rule. Another example appears in the logistic regression and Deep Learning loss functions we will see in later chapters, most use cross entropy.

2.3.1 *Surprise and Information*

The larger the probability of an event, the lower the degree of surprised we get when it happens. For example the event "Dog bites man" is quite common, so we are not surprised if it occurs. However the event "Man bites dog" is more unusual and we are very surprised if read such news.

The surprise of an event x_k is defined as the inverse of its probability

$$s_k = \frac{1}{p(x_k)}. \tag{2.42}$$

The information of an event is defined as

$$I_i = \log_2 s_k = -\log_2 p(x_k), \tag{2.43}$$

and it is inversely related to probability.

Probabilities are multiplied and information is summed due to to the logarithm function. Usually in computer science one uses the logarithm base 2 so the information is represented in bits. A bit (binary digit) corresponds to the smallest information unit that could correspond to a yes or no answer of a most basic question.

Fig. 2.12 John Tukey an American mathematician best known for development of the Fast Fourier Transform (FFT) algorithm, Early in his career during a seminar 1943-44 he introduced the term "bit" (binary digi) for the smallest information unit.

2.3.2   *Entropy*

The theoretical minimum average number of bits that are required to represent information is known as the Shannon's entropy, see Figure 2.13.

Fig. 2.13   Claude Elwood Shannon (1916 - 2001) was an American mathematician, electrical engineer, and cryptographer known as "the father of information theory"

With N as the number of different events x_t and $p(x_t)$ as the probability of occurrence of the events, the theoretical minimum average number of bits is computed using Shannon's formula of entropy

$$H = -\sum_{t}^{K} p(x_t) \cdot \log_2 p(x_t) = -\sum_{x \in X} p(x) \cdot \log_2 p(x). \tag{2.44}$$

The relationship between $\log_2$ and any other base b requires a simple multiplication by a constant,

$$\log_2 x = \frac{log_b x}{log_b 2} = \frac{log_{10} x}{log_{10} 2}. \tag{2.45}$$

2.3.2.1   *Intuition of Entropy*

Let us imagine a simple experiment, for example, throwing a fair coin [Topsoe (1974)], [Wichert (2013)]. Before we perform the experiment, we do not know what will be the result; we are uncertain about the outcome. We measure the uncertainty by the entropy of the experiment. The experiment starts at time t_0 and ends at time t_1. At t_0, we have no information about the results of the experiment, and at t_1, we have all of the information, so that the entropy of the experiment is 0.

We can describe an experiment by probabilities. For the outcome of the flip of an honest coin, the probability for a head or tail is 0.5, $p = (0.5, 0.5)$. So, how can we define entropy? Imagine that person A knows the outcome of the experiment, but person B does not. Person B could ask A about the outcome of the experiment. If the question is of the most basic nature, then we could measure the minimum required number of optimal questions B must pose to A to know the result of the experiment.

A most basic question corresponds to the smallest information unit that could correspond to a yes or no answer. The smallest information unit is called a binary digit, or bit. For a fair coin, we pose just one question, for example, is it a tail? For a card game, to determine if a card is either red, clubs or spades, we have a different number of possible questions. If the card is red, then we need only one question. However, in the case in which the card is not red, we need another question to determine whether it is a spade or a club. So, with probability 0.5 we need one question (the case where the card is red) and with probability 0.5 we need two questions (the cases where the card is a spade or a club). So, on average we will need $1 \cdot 0.5 + 2 \cdot 0.25 + 2 \cdot 0.25$ questions, which would result in 1.5 questions.

Now consider a different example. In this scenario there are four cards and one of them is a joker. Upon extraction, the probability of getting the joker is 0.25 and of getting one of the other cards is $1 - 0.25 = 0.75$, $p = (0.25, 0.75)$. The goal is to find out if the extracted card was a joker or not. With probability 0.25 we need one question (is it a joker?) and with probability 0.75 we need one question again (is it a joker?). So, on expectation, we need $1 \cdot 0.25 + 1 \cdot 0.75 = 1$ question. Let us call the real entropy for this one experiment $H_0(F^1) = 1$.

Now consider the case where we perform the experiment twice (extract two cards from the aforementioned set of four with replacement). We want to compute the real entropy $H_0(F^2)$ to get the outcome of the experiments. The hierarchy of the probabilities for two experiments is shown in Table 2.1 and the binary search tree with the questions is represented in Figure 2.14. So, the real entropy for two experiments is $H_0(F^2)$:

$$H_0(F^2) = 1 \cdot 0.75 \cdot 0.75 + 2 \cdot 0.75 \cdot 0.25 + 3 \cdot 0.25 \cdot 0.75 + 3 \cdot 0.25 \cdot 0.25$$

For three experiments, we will have the probabilities shown in Table 2.2 and the binary search tree of questions represented in Figure 2.15. The real

Table 2.1   Hierarchy of the probabilities for two experiments.

results	probability
card, card	$0.75 \cdot 0.75$
joker, card	$0.25 \cdot 0.75$
card, joker	$0.75 \cdot 0.25$
joker, joker	$0.25 \cdot 0.25$

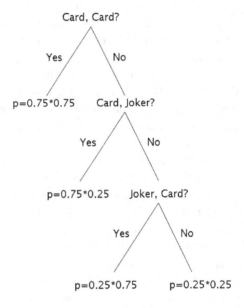

Fig. 2.14   The real entropy for two experiments as $H_0(F^2)$

entropy for this setting is:

$$H_0(F^3) = 1 \cdot 0.42188 + 3 \cdot 0.14062 + 3 \cdot 0.14062 + 3 \cdot 0.14062$$

$$+5 \cdot 0.046875 + 5 \cdot 0.046875 + 5 \cdot 0.046875 + 5 \cdot 0.015625$$

Now, if we define the mean number of questions per experiment for a sequence of k experiments as $h_k = 1/k \cdot H_0(F^k)$ we get, for the previously described scenarios:

- $H_0(F^1) = 1$, $h_1 = \frac{H_0(F^1)}{1} = 1.0$
- $H_0(F^2) = 1.6875$, $h_2 = \frac{H_0(F^2)}{2} = 0.84375$

Table 2.2 Hierarchy of the probabilities for three experiments.

results	probability
card, card, card	$0.75 \cdot 0.75 \cdot 0.75$
card, card, joker	$0.75 \cdot 0.75 \cdot 0.25$
card, joker, card	$0.75 \cdot 0.25 \cdot 0.75$
joker. card card	$0.25 \cdot 0.75 \cdot 0.75$
joker, joker, card	$0.25 \cdot 0.25 \cdot 0.75$
joker, card, joker	$0.25 \cdot 0.75 \cdot 0.25$
card, joker, joker	$0.75 \cdot 0.25 \cdot 0.25$
joker, joker, joker	$0.25 \cdot 0.25 \cdot 0.25$

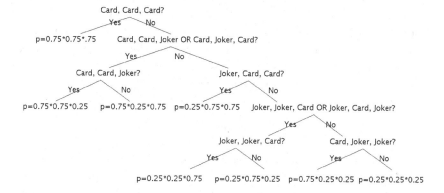

Fig. 2.15 The real entropy for three experiments as $H_0(F^3)$

- $H_0(F^3) = 2.4688, \quad h_3 = \frac{H_0(F^3)}{3} = 0.82292$

This setting begs the question: does the sequence $h_k := \frac{H_0(F^k)}{k}$, with the values $\{1, 0.84375, 0.82292, ...\}$ for $k = 1, 2, 3, ..$ have a limit for $\lim_{k \to \infty} h_k$? Can we use that limit as a better measure for the entropy?

2.3.2.2 *Ideal Entropy*

The limit for $\lim_{k \to \infty} h_k$ is defined as

$$H(F) := \lim_{k \to \infty} \frac{H_0(F^k)}{k} \tag{2.46}$$

which is called the ideal entropy and it converges to [Shannon (1948)]

$$H(F) = -\sum_t p(x_t) \cdot \log_2 p(x_t) = -\sum_{x \in X} p(x) \cdot \log_2 p(x). \tag{2.47}$$

For the four card case it is simply

$$H(F) = -0.25 \cdot \log_2 0.25 - 0.75 \cdot \log_2 0.75 = 0.81128.$$

The ideal entropy indicates the minimum number of optimal questions that B must pose to know the result of the experiment on A [Shannon (1948)], [Topsoe (1974)].

2.3.2.3   *Maximal Entropy*

Suppose that A repeated the experiment an infinite number of times. The ideal entropy is the essential information obtained by taking out the redundant information that corresponds to the ideal distribution to which the results converge. The flatter the distribution is, the higher the entropy, the sharper the distribution, the lower the entropy. The entropy is the highest for equal probabilities, for a distribution $p = (x_1, x_2, ..., x_K)$ with $p = (1/K, 1/K..., 1/K)$. The entropy is zero for for a distribution $p = (p_1, p_2, \cdots, p_K)$ with a one at a certain position $p = (0, 1, 0, \cdots, 0)$. For the case $p = (p_1, p_2, ..., p_K)$ the maximal ideal entropy is

$$H(F) = - \sum_t p(x_t) \cdot \log_2 p(x_t) = - \log_2 1/K = \log_2 K \qquad (2.48)$$

The equation $H(F) = \log_2 K$ is very similar to Boltzmann's equation, in which K *number of microstates* corresponds to a given macrostate, see Figure 2.16. Boltzmann's equation includes Boltzmann's constant, and it uses log instead of $\log_2$. Instead of measuring the information in bits (yes/no questions) it measures the information in   nepit (nat), which is based on Euler's number $e = 2.7182818...$ (sometimes also called Napier's constant). Euler's number is irrational and cannot be attributed to any questions.

2.3.2.4   *Coding*

The efficiency of a particular encoding scheme is frequently computed as a ratio of the entropy of the source to the average number of bits per codeword m_t required for the scheme

$$\sum_{t=1}^{K} N_t \cdot p(m_t). \qquad (2.49)$$

where N_t is the number of bits to message m_t. For example, for six letters (messages) A, B, C, D, E and F with $p(A) = p(B) = 0.25$ and $p(C) = p(D) = p(E) = p(F) = 0.125$, using the conversion of Table 2.3 the average

Fig. 2.16 Ludwig Eduard Boltzmann (1844 - 1906) was an Austrian physicist and philosopher. He developed the statistical concept of nature.

Table 2.3 Six letters and its representation in bits.

M	S
A	10
B	11
C	000
D	001
E	010
F	011

number of bits per codeword is

$$\sum_{t=1}^{6} N_t \cdot p(m_t) = \qquad (2.50)$$

$$2 \cdot 0.25 + 2 \cdot 0.25 + 4 \cdot 0.125 + 4 \cdot 0.125 + 4 \cdot 0.125 + 4 \cdot 0.125 = 2.5$$

and the entropy of the source is

$$H = -\sum_{t=1}^{6} p(m_t) \cdot \log_2 p(m_t) = \qquad (2.51)$$

$$-2 \cdot (0.25 \cdot log_2(0.25)) - 4 \cdot (0.125 \cdot log_2(0.125)) = 2.5 \; bits.$$

The ratio of the entropy of the source to the average number of bits per codeword in our example is one.

2.3.3   Conditional Entropy

Conditional entropy quantifies the amount of information needed to describe the outcome of a random variable Y given that the value of another random variable X is known.

$$H(Y|X) = - \sum_{x \in X, y \in Y} p(x,y) \log \left(\frac{p(x,y)}{p(x)} \right) \tag{2.52}$$

We assume that $0 \cdot \log 0 = 0$ and $0 \cdot \log c/0 = 0$ for $c > 0$. Notice what happens if both variables are independent, that is, if X provides no information about Y.

2.3.4   Relative Entropy

Kullback-Leibler divergence (also called relative entropy) is a measure of how one probability distribution is different from a second, reference probability distribution. For discrete probability distributions p and q defined on the same probability space, the Kullback-Leibler divergence is defined as

$$KL(p||q) = - \sum_{x \in X} p(x) \log q(x) - \left(- \sum_{x \in X} p(x) \log p(x) \right) \tag{2.53}$$

$$KL(p||q) = - \sum_{x \in X} p(x) \log \left(\frac{q(x)}{p(x)} \right) \tag{2.54}$$

For example, consider that random variable X follows an unknown distribution $p(x)$. Suppose that we have modeled X using an approximating distribution $q(x)$. If we use $q(x)$ to construct a coding scheme for the purpose of transmitting values of x to a receiver, then the average additional amount of information required to specify the values as a result of using $q(x)$ instead of the true distribution $p(x)$ is $KL(p||q)$.

2.3.5   Mutual Information

Mutual information measures the information that X and Y share, it tells us how much knowing one of these variables reduces uncertainty about the other.

$$I(X,Y) = -\sum_{y\in Y}\sum_{x\in X} p(x,y)\log\left(\frac{p(x)\cdot p(y)}{p(x,y)}\right) \tag{2.55}$$

$$I(X,Y) = \sum_{y\in Y}\sum_{x\in X} p(x,y)\log\left(\frac{p(x,y)}{p(x)\cdot p(y))}\right) \tag{2.56}$$

For example, if X and Y are independent, then $I(X,Y) = 0$. Then knowing X does not give any information about Y and their mutual information is zero. The Mutual information $I(X,Y)$ between X and Y is equal to the Kullback-Leibler divergence between the joint probability density function $p(x,y)$ and the product of the probability functions $p(x)$ and $p(y)$

$$KL(p_{x,y}\|p_x,p_y) = I(X,Y) = \sum_{y\in Y}\sum_{x\in X} p(x,y)\log\left(\frac{p(x,y)}{p(x)\cdot p(y))}\right) \tag{2.57}$$

$$KL(p_{x,y}\|p_x,p_y) = \sum_{y\in Y}\sum_{x\in X} p(x,y)\log p(x,y) - \sum_{y\in Y}\sum_{x\in X} p(x,y)\log(p(x)\cdot p(y)) \tag{2.58}$$

$$KL(p_{x,y}\|p_x,p_y) = -H(X,Y) - \sum_{y\in Y}\sum_{x\in X} p(x,y)\log(p(x)\cdot p(y)). \tag{2.59}$$

2.3.6 Relationship

In the following Figure 2.17 we indicate the relationship between

- $H(Y,X) = -\sum_{x\in X, y\in Y} p(x,y)\log p(x,y)$
- $H(X|Y)$
- $H(Y|X)$
- $H(X)$
- $H(Y)$

2.4 Cross Entropy

The cross entropy for discrete probability distributions p and q defined on the same probability space is a measure of difference between two probability distributions and can be written as

$$H(p,q) = -\sum_{x\in X} p(x)\log q(x), \tag{2.60}$$

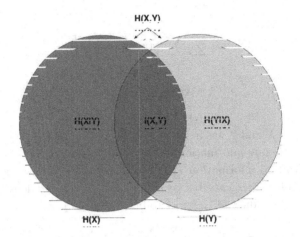

Fig. 2.17   The relationship between the several introduced entropies and mutual information.

or

$$H(p, q) = H(p) - KL(p||q) \qquad (2.61)$$

For $\log_2$, cross entropy measures the average number of bits needed to identify an event coded by a scheme optimized for the estimated distribution q instead of the true one p. We can also write it as an expectation

$$H(p, q) = \mathbb{E}_p(\log(q))$$

In supervised Machine learning it is often the case where we have target outputs $\mathbf{y}^{(n)}$ for a model and the current model outputs $\mathbf{o}^{(n)}$. This setting is equivalent to the scenarios we described for the Bernoulli and Multinomial distributions. As we will see, both these scenarios are extremely related to cross entropy.

As we have seen before, using the Bernoulli distribution for a data set of N independent binary events $D = \{y^{(1)}, y^{(2)}, \cdots, y^{(N)}\}$, where each event $y^{(n)}$ is true with a given probability $o^{(n)}$, we can write the probability of the observed data (i.e. the likelihood), with $O = \{o^{(1)}, o^{(2)}, \cdots, o^{(N)}\}$, as

$$p(D|O) = \prod_{n=1}^{N} (o^{(n)})^{y^{(n)}} \cdot (1 - (o^{(n)}))^{1-y^{(n)}} \qquad (2.62)$$

If we want to estimate the probabilities $o^{(n)}$, we can do so by finding the probabilities that maximize the likelihood of the observed data $p(D|O)$.

Equivalently, since log is a monotonic increasing function we can as well minimize the negative log likelihood

$$-\log p(D|O) = -\sum_{n=1}^{N} \log p(y^{(n)}|o^{(n)}) \tag{2.63}$$

which is the same as

$$-\log p(D|O) = -\sum_{n=1}^{N} \left(y^{(n)} \cdot \log o^{(n)} + (1 - y^{(n)}) \cdot \log(1 - o^{(n)}) \right). \tag{2.64}$$

Now, if we look at each each $y^{(n)}$ and $o^{(n)}$ as distributions with

$$\mathbf{y}^{(n)} = \begin{pmatrix} 1 - y^{(n)} \\ y^{(n)} \end{pmatrix}$$

$$\mathbf{o}^{(n)} = \begin{pmatrix} 1 - o^{(n)} \\ o^{(n)} \end{pmatrix}$$

We see that the negative log likelihood is just the sum of the N cross entropies between the distributions of each $y^{(n)}$ with each $o^{(n)}$

$$-\log p(D|O) = \sum_{n=1}^{N} H(\mathbf{y}^{(n)}, \mathbf{o}^{(n)}). \tag{2.65}$$

We have also seen before how to write the likelihood of observed data for a 1 out of K representation where for each $\mathbf{y}^{(n)}$ there is a corresponding probability vector $\mathbf{o}^{(n)}$. In fact, for data $D = \{\mathbf{y}^{(1)}, \mathbf{y}^{(2)}, \cdots, \mathbf{y}^{(N)}\}$ and probabilities $O = \{\mathbf{o}^{(1)}, \mathbf{o}^{(2)}, \cdots, \mathbf{o}^{(N)}\}$, we wrote

$$p(D|O) = \prod_{n=1}^{N} \prod_{k=1}^{K} (o_k^{(n)})^{y_k^{(n)}}. \tag{2.66}$$

Again, if we wanted to estimate the probability vectors, we could find the values that maximize the likelihood of observing the data. Which, again, is equivalent to minimizing the negative log likelihood

$$-\log p(D|O) = -\sum_{n=1}^{N} \sum_{k=1}^{K} y_k^{(n)} \cdot \log o_k^{(n)}. \tag{2.67}$$

With that in mind, we can see that just like in the previously described case, $-\log p(D|O)$ is nothing more than the sum of the N cross entropies between each $\mathbf{y}^{(n)}$ and $\mathbf{o}^{(n)}$

$$-\log p(D|O) = \sum_{n=1}^{N} H(\mathbf{y}^{(n)}, \mathbf{o}^{(n)}). \tag{2.68}$$

As we have seen, to learn the correct outputs, all we have to do is choose them such that they minimize the sum of the cross entropies. In Machine Learning, when we have to minimize a given function we call it the loss function. Alternatively, in other domains, we can also call it error function, cost function or energy function. With all that said, in this case, we can define the cross entropy loss

$$L(D, O) = \sum_{n=1}^{N} H(\mathbf{y}^{(n)}, \mathbf{o}^{(n)}). \tag{2.69}$$

Note that this loss is not a distance function since it is not symmetric and is only defined over probability distributions.

Another well-known loss function is the squared error or quadratic loss function

$$L_{sq}(D, O) = \sum_{n=1}^{N} \|\mathbf{y}^{(n)}, \mathbf{o}^{(n)}\|_2^2, \tag{2.70}$$

let us compare it with cross entropy using an example where the observed data is $D = \{y^{(1)}, y^{(2)}, y^{(3)}\} = \{1, 0, 1\}$. In a sense, both losses intend to tell us for some output probabilities $O = \{o^{(1)}, o^{(2)}, o^{(3)}\} = \{0.9, 0.1, 0.7\}$ how unlikely is the observed data.

Before moving on, let us convert the output probabilities and the data to distribution vectors. Using

$$\mathbf{y}^{(n)} = \begin{pmatrix} 1 - y^{(n)} \\ y^{(n)} \end{pmatrix}$$

$$\mathbf{o}^{(n)} = \begin{pmatrix} 1 - o^{(n)} \\ o^{(n)} \end{pmatrix}$$

we get

$$D = \left\{ \begin{pmatrix} 0 \\ 1 \end{pmatrix}, \begin{pmatrix} 1 \\ 0 \end{pmatrix}, \begin{pmatrix} 0 \\ 1 \end{pmatrix} \right\}$$

$$O = \left\{ \begin{pmatrix} 0.1 \\ 0.9 \end{pmatrix}, \begin{pmatrix} 0.4 \\ 0.6 \end{pmatrix}, \begin{pmatrix} 0.3 \\ 0.7 \end{pmatrix} \right\}$$

with which we can compute the values of the two losses.

First, let us compute the cross entropy loss:

$$L(D, O) = -\sum_{n=1}^{3} \sum_{k=1}^{2} \left(y_k^{(n)} \cdot \log o_k^{(n)} \right)$$

$$L(D,O) = -(0 \cdot \log 0.1 + 1 \cdot \log 0.9)$$
$$+ (1 \cdot \log 0.4 + 0 \cdot \log 0.6)$$
$$+ (0 \cdot \log 0.3 + 1 \cdot \log 0.7)$$
$$L(D,O) = -\log 0.9 - \log 0.4 - \log 0.7 = 1.378$$

Now, we compute the result for the quadratic loss

$$L_{sq}(D,O) = \sum_{n=1}^{3} \sum_{k=1}^{2} \left(y_k^{(n)} - o_k^{(n)} \right)^2$$
$$L_{sq}(D,O) = \left((0-0.1)^2 + (1-0.9)^2 \right)$$
$$+ \left((1-0.4)^2 + (0-0.6)^2 \right)$$
$$+ \left((0-0.3)^2 + (1-0.7)^2 \right)$$
$$L_{sq}(D,O) = 0.92$$

From this example, we can see that the squared loss is lower. This means that, in general, cross entropy is much steeper as it penalizes more the differences between observed data and the corresponding probabilities, see Figure 2.18. As it turns out this intuition will be very important later in the book. This will be the case because for the typical supervised Machine

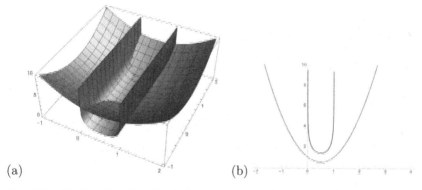

(a) (b)

Fig. 2.18   The loss function that is based on cross entropy is much steeper than the quadratic loss (a) Three dimensional plot, the distributions are only defined between 0 and 1. (b). One dimensional projection, since o and $\neg o$ represent one variable.

Learning problem where a continuously differentiable loss function in which for a given **y** we want to determine **o** that minimizes that function we will determine the minima of a solution numerically, by approximating the real zeros of the gradient of $\nabla_{\mathbf{o}} L(D,O)$ with gradient descent. We will see that a steeper loss will lead to a faster and clearer finding of this solution.

2.5   Exercises and Answers

A Probability and Distributions

1)

Consider the following registry where an experiment is repeated six times and four events (A, B, C and D) are detected. Considering frequentist estimates for probabilities, compute:

	D	C	B	A
1	0	0	1	1
2	0	1	1	1
3	1	0	0	0
4	1	0	0	0
5	0	0	0	0
6	0	0	0	0

- $p(A)$
- $p(A, B)$
- $p(B \mid A)$
- $p(A, B, C)$
- $p(A \mid B, C)$
- $p(A, B, C, D)$
- $p(D \mid A, B, C)$

Solution:

According to the question, what we want are frequentist estimates for probabilities. So, let us count occurrences of specific events and their combinations.

First and foremost let us define $\# \{X_1, \ldots, X_n\}$ as the number of experiment runs where events $X_1, \ldots, X_n$ appeared together. Given this definition, for example $\# \{D\} = 2$ since out of all experiment runs there are two where event D occurred. Out of the six runs, the frequencies of our measured events are:

$$\# \{D\} = 2 \; \# \{C\} = 1 \; \# \{B\} = 2 \; \# \{A\} = 2$$

So, we can get the marginal probabilities by normalizing by the total number of runs:

$$p(D) = \tfrac{2}{6} \; p(C) = \tfrac{1}{6} \; p(B) = \tfrac{2}{6} \; p(A) = \tfrac{2}{6}$$

We can repeat the same reasoning for pairs of events:

$$\# \{A, B\} = 2 \; \# \{A, D\} = 0 \; \# \{B, D\} = 0$$
$$\# \{A, C\} = 1 \; \# \{B, C\} = 1 \; \# \{C, D\} = 0$$

So, we can get the joint probabilities for the pairs by normalizing by the total number of runs:

$$p(A, B) = \tfrac{2}{6} \; p(A, D) = 0 \; p(B, D) = 0$$
$$p(A, C) = \tfrac{1}{6} \; p(B, C) = \tfrac{1}{6} \; p(C, D) = 0$$

Yet again, we repeat the process for triples:

$$\# \{A, B, C\} = 1 \; \# \{A, B, D\} = 0 \; \# \{A, C, D\} = 0 \; \# \{B, C, D\} = 0$$

$$p(A, B, C) = \tfrac{1}{6} \; p(A, B, D) = 0 \; p(A, C, D) = 0 \; p(B, C, D) = 0$$

Finally, for all events:

$$\# \{A, B, C, D\} = 0 \; p(A, B, C, D) = 0$$

Now, we can use the rules of probability to compute everything:

- $p(A) = \tfrac{2}{6}$
- $p(A, B) = \tfrac{2}{6}$
- $p(B \mid A) = \frac{p(A,B)}{p(A)} = \frac{\frac{2}{6}}{\frac{2}{6}} = 1$
- $p(A, B, C) = \tfrac{1}{6}$
- $p(A \mid B, C) = \frac{p(A,B,C)}{p(B,C)} = \frac{\frac{1}{6}}{\frac{1}{6}} = 1$
- $p(A, B, C, D) = 0$
- $p(D \mid A, B, C) = \frac{p(A,B,C,D)}{p(A,B,C)} = \frac{0}{\frac{1}{6}} = 0$

2)

Consider the following set of height measures in centimeters of a group of people:

$$X|180\ 160\ 200\ 171\ 159\ 150$$

What are the maximum likelihood parameters of a gaussian distribution for this set of points? Plot it approximately.

Solution:

The maximum likelihood gaussian is defined by the sample mean and standard deviation. Let us compute them:

$$\mu = \frac{180 + 160 + 200 + 171 + 159 + 150}{6} = 170$$

$$\sigma = \frac{1}{6-1}((180 - 170)^2 + (160 - 170)^2$$
$$+ (200 - 170)^2 + (171 - 170)^2 + (159 - 170)^2 + (150 - 170)^2)^{\frac{1}{2}} = 18.0111$$

Having the parameters, we can write the expression:

$$N\left(x \mid \mu, \sigma\right) = \frac{1}{18.0111\sqrt{2\pi}} \exp\left(-\frac{1}{2}\left(\frac{x - 170}{18.0111}\right)^2\right)$$

This gaussian can be plotted as a function of x as follows:

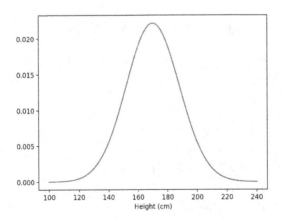

3)

Consider the following set of two dimensional measures:

$$\begin{array}{c|cccc} X_1 & -2 & -1 & 0 & -2 \\ X_2 & 2 & 3 & 1 & 1 \end{array}$$

What are the maximum likelihood parameters of a Gaussian distribution for this set of points? What is the shape of the Gaussian? Draw it approximately using a contour map.

Solution:

The maximum likelihood gaussian is defined by the sample mean vector and the covariance matrix. Let us compute them:

$$\mu = \frac{1}{4}\left(\begin{bmatrix} -2 \\ 2 \end{bmatrix} + \begin{bmatrix} -1 \\ 3 \end{bmatrix} + \begin{bmatrix} 0 \\ 1 \end{bmatrix} + \begin{bmatrix} -2 \\ 1 \end{bmatrix}\right) = \begin{bmatrix} -1.25 \\ 1.75 \end{bmatrix}$$

$$\Sigma_{00} = \frac{1}{4-1}[(-2+1.25)(-2+1.25) + (-1+1.25)(-1+1.25)$$
$$+ (0+1.25)(0+1.25) + (-2+1.25)(-2+1.25)] \approx 0.9167$$

$$\Sigma_{01} = \frac{1}{4-1}[(-2+1.25)(2-1.75) + (-1+1.25)(3-1.75)$$
$$+ (0+1.25)(1-1.75) + (-2+1.25)(1-1.75)] \approx -0.0833$$

$$\Sigma_{10} = \frac{1}{4-1}[(2-1.75)(-2+1.25) + (3-1.75)(-1+1.25)$$
$$+ (1-1.75)(0+1.25) + (1-1.75)(-2+1.25)] \approx -0.0833$$

$$\Sigma_{11} = \frac{1}{4-1}[(2-1.75)(2-1.75) + (3-1.75)(3-1.75)$$
$$+ (1-1.75)(1-1.75) + (1-1.75)(1-1.75)] \approx 0.9167$$

To compute the expression for the multivariate gaussian we need to compute the determinant of Σ and its inverse:

$$det\left(\Sigma\right) = det\begin{pmatrix} 0.9167 & -0.0833 \\ -0.0833 & 0.9167 \end{pmatrix}$$

$$det\left(\Sigma\right) = (0.9167 \cdot 0.9167) - (-0.0833 \cdot -0.0833) = 0.8333$$

$$\Sigma^{-1} = \frac{1}{0.8333}\begin{bmatrix} 0.9167 & 0.0833 \\ 0.0833 & 0.9167 \end{bmatrix} = \begin{bmatrix} 1.1 & 0.1 \\ 0.1 & 1.1 \end{bmatrix}$$

So, we can write the expression for a two dimensional input $\mathbf{x} = \begin{bmatrix} x_0 & x_1 \end{bmatrix}^T$ as follows.

$$N\left(\mathbf{x} \mid \mu, \Sigma\right) = \frac{1}{(2\pi)^{\frac{2}{2}}\sqrt{0.8333}}$$

$$\cdot \exp\left(-\frac{1}{2}\left(\begin{bmatrix} x_0 \\ x_1 \end{bmatrix} - \begin{bmatrix} -1.25 \\ 1.75 \end{bmatrix}\right)^T \begin{bmatrix} 1.1 & 0.1 \\ 0.1 & 1.1 \end{bmatrix}\left(\begin{bmatrix} x_0 \\ x_1 \end{bmatrix} - \begin{bmatrix} -1.25 \\ 1.75 \end{bmatrix}\right)\right)$$

Looking at the covariance matrix, we can see that the shape must be an ellipse, which can be plotted as follows.

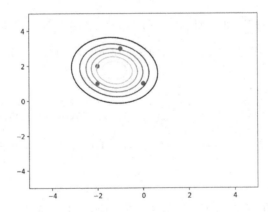

4)

Consider the following set of two dimensional measures:

$$\begin{array}{c|cccc} X_1 & 2 & 1 & 0 & 2 \\ X_2 & -2 & 3 & -1 & 1 \end{array}$$

What are the maximum likelihood parameters of a Gaussian distribution for this set of points? What is the shape of the Gaussian? Draw it approximately using a contour map.

Solution:

The maximum likelihood gaussian is defined by the sample mean vector and the covariance matrix. Let us compute them:

$$\mu = \frac{1}{4}\left(\begin{bmatrix} 2 \\ -2 \end{bmatrix} + \begin{bmatrix} 1 \\ 3 \end{bmatrix} + \begin{bmatrix} 0 \\ -1 \end{bmatrix} + \begin{bmatrix} 2 \\ 1 \end{bmatrix}\right) = \begin{bmatrix} 1.25 \\ 0.25 \end{bmatrix}$$

$$\Sigma_{00} = \frac{1}{4-1}[(2-1.25)(2-1.25) + (1-1.25)(1-1.25)$$
$$+ (0-1.25)(0-1.25) + (2-1.25)(2-1.25)] \approx 0.9167$$

$$\Sigma_{01} = \frac{1}{4-1}[(2-1.25)(-2-0.25) + (1-1.25)(3-0.25)$$
$$+ (0-1.25)(-1-0.25) + (2-1.25)(1-0.25)] \approx -0.0833$$

$$\Sigma_{10} = \frac{1}{4-1}[(-2-0.25)(2-1.25) + (3-0.25)(1-1.25)$$
$$+ (-1-0.25)(0-1.25) + (1-0.25)(2-1.25)] \approx -0.0833$$

$$\Sigma_{11} = \frac{1}{4-1}[(-2-0.25)(-2-0.25) + (3-0.25)(3-0.25)$$
$$+ (-1-0.25)(-1-0.25) + (1-0.25)(1-0.25)] \approx 4.9167$$

To compute the expression for the multivariate gaussian we need to compute the determinant of Σ and its inverse:

$$det(\Sigma) = det\begin{pmatrix} 0.9167 & -0.0833 \\ -0.0833 & 4.9167 \end{pmatrix}$$

$$det\left(\Sigma\right) = (0.9167 \cdot 4.9167) - (-0.0833 \cdot -0.0833) = 4.5$$

$$\Sigma^{-1} = \frac{1}{4.5} \begin{bmatrix} 4.9167 & 0.0833 \\ 0.0833 & 0.9167 \end{bmatrix} = \begin{bmatrix} 1.0926 & 0.0185 \\ 0.0185 & 0.2037 \end{bmatrix}$$

So, we can write the expression for a two dimensional input $\mathbf{x} = \begin{bmatrix} x_0 & x_1 \end{bmatrix}^T$ as follows.

$$N\left(\mathbf{x} \mid \mu, \Sigma\right) = \frac{1}{(2\pi)^{\frac{2}{2}} \sqrt{4.5}}$$

$$\cdot \exp\left(-\frac{1}{2}\left(\begin{bmatrix} x_0 \\ x_1 \end{bmatrix} - \begin{bmatrix} 1.25 \\ 0.25 \end{bmatrix}\right)^T \begin{bmatrix} 1.0926 & 0.0185 \\ 0.0185 & 0.2037 \end{bmatrix} \left(\begin{bmatrix} x_0 \\ x_1 \end{bmatrix} - \begin{bmatrix} 1.25 \\ 0.25 \end{bmatrix}\right)\right)$$

Looking at the covariance matrix, we can see that the shape must be an ellipse, which can be plotted as follows.

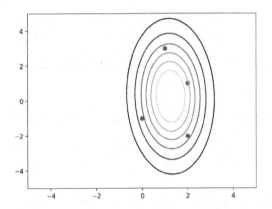

B Simple Bayesian Learning

Bayes rule tells us how we can compute the probability of a given hypothesis H given a set of observed data D:

$$p\left(H \mid D\right) = \frac{p\left(D \mid H\right) p\left(H\right)}{p\left(D\right)}$$

This formula is so widely used that all its terms have well established names:

- $p(H)$ is called the prior and denotes the a priori probability of a given hypothesis i.e. how likely a given explanation is before seeing any data;
- $p(D \mid H)$ is called the likelihood and measures how likely is the observed data if we assume that H is true;
- $p(D)$ is usually called the evidence and determines how likely the observed data is under all possible hypotheses;
- $p(H \mid D)$ is named the posterior to refer to the probability of the hypothesis after taking the observed data into account.

Classification with this rule amounts to choosing the most probable class given a specific set of features. For instance, if in our learning problem there are two features X_1 and X_2 to predict a class C, a Bayesian classifier outputs the class with the highest predictive posterior probability $p(C \mid X_1, X_2)$.

To compute posteriors using Bayes's rule, we need to compute likelihoods $p(X_1, X_2 \mid C)$. Often, these likelihoods are complex conditional joint distributions that are hard to estimate from limited data. In such cases, assumptions must be made. A well-known, rather useful one is the Naive Bayes assumption where features X_1 and X_2 are treated as conditionally independent given the class. Specifically, this allows us to factorize the conditional joint distributions into a product of simpler ones which are easier to estimate from limited data $p(X_1, X_2 \mid C) = p(X_1 \mid C) p(X_2 \mid C)$.

1)

Assuming that 1 means *True* and 0 means *False*, consider the following features and class:

- X_1: "Fast processing"
- X_2: "Decent Battery"
- X_3: "Good Camera"
- X_4: "Good Look and Feel"
- X_5: "Easiness of Use"
- *Class*: "iPhone"

You are given the following training set:

X_1	X_2	X_3	X_4	X_5	$Class$
1	1	0	1	0	1
1	1	1	0	0	0
0	1	1	1	0	0
0	0	0	1	1	0
1	0	1	1	1	1
0	0	1	0	0	1
0	0	0	0	1	1

And the query vector $\mathbf{x} = \begin{bmatrix} 1 & 1 & 1 & 1 & 1 \end{bmatrix}^T$.

a) Using Bayes' rule, without making any assumptions, compute the class for the query vector.

Solution:

In this exercise we will see that a small training sample will not be enough to make a decision. If we apply the same methodology of estimating probabilities by counting and normalizing, we will get lots of zeros in the likelihood distributions which will lead to posteriors that cannot be computed.

Let us apply the methodology and verify just that. So, to compute the class we must choose the one that yields the maximum posterior probability. To compute the posterior, we need the likelihoods and the priors:

$$p(C = 0) = \frac{3}{7}$$

$$p(C = 1) = \frac{4}{7}$$

Since we do not have the complete information, we assume

X_1	X_2	X_3	X_4	X_5	$p\left(X_1, X_2, X_3, X_4, X_5 \mid C=0\right)$	$p\left(X_1, X_2, X_3, X_4, X_5 \mid C=1\right)$
0	0	0	0	0	0	0
0	0	0	0	1	0	$\frac{1}{4}$
0	0	0	1	0	0	0
0	0	0	1	1	$\frac{1}{3}$	0
0	0	1	0	0	0	$\frac{1}{4}$
0	0	1	0	1	0	0
0	0	1	1	0	0	0
0	0	1	1	1	0	0
0	1	0	0	0	0	0
0	1	0	0	1	0	0
0	1	0	1	0	0	0
0	1	0	1	1	0	0
0	1	1	0	0	0	0
0	1	1	0	1	0	0
0	1	1	1	0	$\frac{1}{3}$	0
0	1	1	1	1	0	0
1	0	0	0	0	0	0
1	0	0	0	1	0	0
1	0	0	1	0	0	0
1	0	0	1	1	0	0
1	0	1	0	0	0	0
1	0	1	0	1	0	0
1	0	1	1	0	0	0
1	0	1	1	1	0	$\frac{1}{4}$
1	1	0	0	0	0	0
1	1	0	0	1	0	0
1	1	0	1	0	0	$\frac{1}{4}$
1	1	0	1	1	0	0
1	1	1	0	0	$\frac{1}{3}$	0
1	1	1	0	1	0	0
1	1	1	1	0	0	0
1	1	1	1	1	0	0

which can leas to some contradictions. Now, we would use Bayes's rule to get a posterior for each class:

$$p\left(C = 0 \mid X_1 = 1, X_2 = 1, X_3 = 1, X_4 = 1, X_5 = 1\right) =$$
$$\frac{p\left(C = 0\right)p\left(X_1 = 1, X_2 = 1, X_3 = 1, X_4 = 1, X_5 = 1 \mid C = 0\right)}{p\left(X_1 = 1, X_2 = 1, X_3 = 1, X_4 = 1, X_5 = 1\right)}$$

$$p\left(C = 1 \mid X_1 = 1, X_2 = 1, X_3 = 1, X_4 = 1, X_5 = 1\right) =$$
$$\frac{p\left(C = 1\right)p\left(X_1 = 1, X_2 = 1, X_3 = 1, X_4 = 1, X_5 = 1 \mid C = 1\right)}{p\left(X_1 = 1, X_2 = 1, X_3 = 1, X_4 = 1, X_5 = 1\right)}$$

However, according to our estimated likelihoods, the denominators are equal to zero:

$$p\left(X_1 = 1, X_2 = 1, X_3 = 1, X_4 = 1, X_5 = 1\right) =$$
$$p\left(X_1 = 1, X_2 = 1, X_3 = 1, X_4 = 1, X_5 = 1, C = 0\right) +$$
$$+p\left(X_1 = 1, X_2 = 1, X_3 = 1, X_4 = 1, X_5 = 1, C = 1\right) =$$
$$p\left(C = 0\right)p\left(X_1 = 1, X_2 = 1, X_3 = 1, X_4 = 1, X_5 = 1 \mid C = 0\right) +$$
$$p\left(C = 1\right)p\left(X_1 = 1, X_2 = 1, X_3 = 1, X_4 = 1, X_5 = 1 \mid C = 1\right) =$$
$$\frac{3}{7}0 + \frac{4}{7}0 =$$
$$0$$

So, both posteriors are not defined and, thus, we cannot classify the input.

---

b) What is the problem of working with this data set without assumptions?

Solution:
Nearly all entries are zero. There is not enough data to construct a meaningful joint distribution.

---

c) Compute the class for the same query vector under the Naive Bayes assumption.

Solution:

The Naive Bayes assumption of conditional independence posits that the conditional joint distribution that constitutes the likelihood can be written as a product of conditional distributions for each feature. So, for this exercise, instead of estimating a big table for all combinations of features, we need to estimate one table per feature.

X_1	$p(X_1 \mid C = 0)$	$p(X_1 \mid C = 1)$
0	$\frac{2}{3}$	$\frac{2}{4}$
1	$\frac{1}{3}$	$\frac{2}{4}$

X_2	$p(X_2 \mid C = 0)$	$p(X_2 \mid C = 1)$
0	$\frac{1}{3}$	$\frac{3}{4}$
1	$\frac{2}{3}$	$\frac{1}{4}$

X_3	$p(X_3 \mid C = 0)$	$p(X_3 \mid C = 1)$
0	$\frac{1}{3}$	$\frac{2}{4}$
1	$\frac{2}{3}$	$\frac{2}{4}$

X_4	$p(X_4 \mid C = 0)$	$p(X_4 \mid C = 1)$
0	$\frac{1}{3}$	$\frac{2}{4}$
1	$\frac{2}{3}$	$\frac{2}{4}$

X_5	$p(X_5 \mid C = 0)$	$p(X_5 \mid C = 1)$
0	$\frac{2}{3}$	$\frac{2}{4}$
1	$\frac{1}{3}$	$\frac{2}{4}$

Just like in the previous exercise we compute the posteriors:

$$p(C = 0 \mid X_1 = 1, X_2 = 1, X_3 = 1, X_4 = 1, X_5 = 1) =$$

$$\frac{p(C = 0)\, p(X_1 = 1, X_2 = 1, X_3 = 1, X_4 = 1, X_5 = 1 \mid C = 0)}{p(X_1 = 1, X_2 = 1, X_3 = 1, X_4 = 1, X_5 = 1)} =$$

$$\frac{p(C = 0)\, p(X_1 = 1 \mid C = 0)\, p(X_2 = 1 \mid C = 0)}{p(X_1 = 1, X_2 = 1, X_3 = 1, X_4 = 1, X_5 = 1)} \cdot$$

$$\frac{p(X_3 = 1 \mid C = 0)\, p(X_4 = 1 \mid C = 0)\, p(X_5 = 1 \mid C = 0)}{p(X_1 = 1, X_2 = 1, X_3 = 1, X_4 = 1, X_5 = 1)} =$$

$$\frac{\frac{3}{7}\,\frac{1}{3}\,\frac{2}{3}\,\frac{2}{3}\,\frac{2}{3}\,\frac{1}{3}}{p(X_1 = 1, X_2 = 1, X_3 = 1, X_4 = 1, X_5 = 1)}$$

Since the denominator is the same for both expressions, to classify, we just need to choose the larger numerator:

$$\frac{3}{7}\frac{1}{3}\frac{2}{3}\frac{2}{3}\frac{2}{3}\frac{1}{3} = 0.0141 > 0.0090 = \frac{4}{7}\frac{2}{4}\frac{1}{4}\frac{2}{4}\frac{2}{4}\frac{2}{4}$$

So the classifier outputs label $C = 0$ which means not an iPhone.

2)

From the following training set:

X_1	X_2	X_3	X_4	X_5	C
1	1	0	1	0	a
1	0	0	1	1	a
1	0	0	1	1	a
1	1	1	0	1	b
0	0	1	1	1	b
1	0	0	0	0	c

a) Compute the class for the pattern $\mathbf{x} = \begin{bmatrix} 1 & 0 & 1 & 0 & 1 \end{bmatrix}^T$ under the Naive Bayes assumption.

Solution:

Just like in the previous exercise, we have to estimate the priors and the likelihoods.

$$p(C = a) = \frac{3}{6}$$

$$p(C = b) = \frac{2}{6}$$

$$p(C = c) = \frac{1}{6}$$

X_1	$p(X_1 \mid C = a)$	$p(X_1 \mid C = b)$	$p(X_1 \mid C = c)$
0	$\frac{0}{3}$	$\frac{1}{2}$	$\frac{0}{1}$
1	$\frac{3}{3}$	$\frac{1}{2}$	$\frac{1}{1}$

X_2	$p(X_2 \mid C = a)$	$p(X_2 \mid C = b)$	$p(X_2 \mid C = c)$
0	$\frac{2}{3}$	$\frac{1}{2}$	$\frac{1}{1}$
1	$\frac{1}{3}$	$\frac{1}{2}$	$\frac{0}{1}$

X_3	$p(X_3 \mid C = a)$	$p(X_3 \mid C = b)$	$p(X_3 \mid C = c)$
0	$\frac{3}{3}$	$\frac{0}{2}$	$\frac{1}{1}$
1	$\frac{0}{3}$	$\frac{2}{2}$	$\frac{0}{1}$

X_4	$p(X_4 \mid C = a)$	$p(X_4 \mid C = b)$	$p(X_4 \mid C = c)$
0	$\frac{0}{3}$	$\frac{1}{2}$	$\frac{1}{1}$
1	$\frac{3}{3}$	$\frac{1}{2}$	$\frac{0}{1}$

X_5	$p(X_5 \mid C = a)$	$p(X_5 \mid C = b)$	$p(X_5 \mid C = c)$
0	$\frac{1}{3}$	$\frac{0}{2}$	$\frac{1}{1}$
1	$\frac{2}{3}$	$\frac{2}{2}$	$\frac{0}{1}$

Having estimated the required parameters, we can compute the posteriors:

$$p(C = a \mid X_1 = 1, X_2 = 0, X_3 = 1, X_4 = 0, X_5 = 1) =$$

$$\frac{p(C = a)\,p(X_1 = 1, X_2 = 0, X_3 = 1, X_4 = 0, X_5 = 1 \mid C = a)}{p(X_1 = 1, X_2 = 0, X_3 = 1, X_4 = 0, X_5 = 1)} =$$

$$\frac{p(C = a)\,p(X_1 = 1 \mid C = a)\,p(X_2 = 0 \mid C = a)}{p(X_1 = 1, X_2 = 0, X_3 = 1, X_4 = 0, X_5 = 1)}\cdot$$

$$\frac{p(X_3 = 1 \mid C = a)\,p(X_4 = 0 \mid C = a)\,p(X_5 = 1 \mid C = a)}{p(X_1 = 1, X_2 = 0, X_3 = 1, X_4 = 0, X_5 = 1)} =$$

$$\frac{\frac{3}{6}\frac{3}{3}\frac{2}{3}\frac{0}{3}\frac{0}{3}\frac{2}{3}}{p(X_1 = 1, X_2 = 0, X_3 = 1, X_4 = 0, X_5 = 1)} =$$

$$0$$

$$p(C = b \mid X_1 = 1, X_2 = 0, X_3 = 1, X_4 = 0, X_5 = 1) =$$

$$\frac{p(C = b)\,p(X_1 = 1, X_2 = 0, X_3 = 1, X_4 = 0, X_5 = 1 \mid C = b)}{p(X_1 = 1, X_2 = 0, X_3 = 1, X_4 = 0, X_5 = 1)} =$$

$$\frac{p(C = b)\,p(X_1 = 1 \mid C = b)\,p(X_2 = 0 \mid C = b)}{p(X_1 = 1, X_2 = 0, X_3 = 1, X_4 = 0, X_5 = 1)}\cdot$$

$$\frac{p(X_3 = 1 \mid C = b)\,p(X_4 = 0 \mid C = b)\,p(X_5 = 1 \mid C = b)}{p(X_1 = 1, X_2 = 0, X_3 = 1, X_4 = 0, X_5 = 1)} =$$

$$\frac{\frac{2}{6}\frac{1}{2}\frac{1}{2}\frac{2}{2}\frac{1}{2}\frac{2}{2}}{p(X_1 = 1, X_2 = 0, X_3 = 1, X_4 = 0, X_5 = 1)}$$

$$p\left(C = c \mid X_1 = 1, X_2 = 0, X_3 = 1, X_4 = 0, X_5 = 1\right) =$$

$$\frac{p\left(C = c\right)p\left(X_1 = 1, X_2 = 0, X_3 = 1, X_4 = 0, X_5 = 1 \mid C = c\right)}{p\left(X_1 = 1, X_2 = 0, X_3 = 1, X_4 = 0, X_5 = 1\right)} =$$

$$\frac{p\left(C = c\right)p\left(X_1 = 1 \mid C = c\right)p\left(X_2 = 0 \mid C = c\right)}{p\left(X_1 = 1, X_2 = 0, X_3 = 1, X_4 = 0, X_5 = 1\right)} \cdot$$

$$\frac{p\left(X_3 = 1 \mid C = c\right)p\left(X_4 = 0 \mid C = c\right)p\left(X_5 = 1 \mid C = c\right)}{p\left(X_1 = 1, X_2 = 0, X_3 = 1, X_4 = 0, X_5 = 1\right)} =$$

$$\frac{\frac{1}{6}\frac{1}{1}\frac{1}{1}\frac{0}{1}\frac{1}{1}\frac{0}{1}}{p\left(X_1 = 1, X_2 = 0, X_3 = 1, X_4 = 0, X_5 = 1\right)} =$$

$$0$$

The only non zero probability occurs for class $C = b$. So, that is the classifier's output.

---

b) What is the posterior probability $p\left(b \mid \mathbf{x}\right)$?

Solution:

To get the final values for all posterior elements, we need to get rid of the unknown quantity in the denominator $p(X_1 = 1, X_2 = 0, X_3 = 1, X_4 = 0, X_5 = 1)$:

$$\sum_{y \in \{a,b,c\}} p\left(C = y \mid X_1 = 1, X_2 = 0, X_3 = 1, X_4 = 0, X_5 = 1\right) = 1$$

$$\sum_{y \in \{a,b,c\}} p\left(C = y \mid X_1 = 1, X_2 = 0, X_3 = 1, X_4 = 0, X_5 = 1\right) = 1$$

$$\frac{\frac{2}{6}\frac{1}{2}\frac{1}{2}\frac{2}{2}\frac{1}{2}\frac{2}{2}}{p\left(X_1 = 1, X_2 = 0, X_3 = 1, X_4 = 0, X_5 = 1\right)} = 1$$

$$p\left(X_1 = 1, X_2 = 0, X_3 = 1, X_4 = 0, X_5 = 1\right) = \frac{2}{6}\frac{1}{2}\frac{1}{2}\frac{2}{2}\frac{1}{2}\frac{2}{2}$$

So, the required posterior is $p(C = b \mid X_1 = 1, X_2 = 0, X_3 = 1, X_4 = 0, X_5 = 1) = 1$.

---

c) What do you do if we have missing features? More specifically, under the Naive Bayes assumption, to what class does $\mathbf{x_{missing}} = \begin{bmatrix} 1 & ? & 1 & ? & 1 \end{bmatrix}^T$ belong to?

Solution:

We compute the posteriors for the features we have:

$$p(C = a \mid X_1 = 1, X_3 = 1, X_5 = 1) =$$
$$\frac{p(C = a) p(X_1 = 1, X_3 = 1, X_5 = 1 \mid C = a)}{p(X_1 = 1, X_3 = 1, X_5 = 1)} =$$
$$\frac{p(C = a) p(X_1 = 1 \mid C = a) p(X_3 = 1 \mid C = a) p(X_5 = 1 \mid C = a)}{p(X_1 = 1, X_3 = 1, X_5 = 1)} =$$
$$\frac{\frac{3}{6}\frac{3}{3}\frac{0}{3}\frac{2}{3}}{p(X_1 = 1, X_3 = 1, X_5 = 1)} =$$
$$0$$

$$p(C = b \mid X_1 = 1, X_3 = 1, X_5 = 1) =$$
$$\frac{p(C = b) p(X_1 = 1, X_3 = 1, X_5 = 1 \mid C = b)}{p(X_1 = 1, X_3 = 1, X_5 = 1)} =$$
$$\frac{p(C = b) p(X_1 = 1 \mid C = b) p(X_3 = 1 \mid C = b) p(X_5 = 1 \mid C = b)}{p(X_1 = 1, X_3 = 1, X_5 = 1)} =$$
$$\frac{\frac{2}{6}\frac{1}{2}\frac{2}{2}\frac{2}{2}}{p(X_1 = 1, X_3 = 1, X_5 = 1)}$$

$$p(C = c \mid X_1 = 1, X_3 = 1, X_5 = 1) =$$
$$\frac{p(C = c) p(X_1 = 1, X_3 = 1, X_5 = 1 \mid C = c)}{p(X_1 = 1, X_3 = 1, X_5 = 1)} =$$
$$\frac{p(C = c) p(X_1 = 1 \mid C = c) p(X_3 = 1 \mid C = c) p(X_5 = 1 \mid C = c)}{p(X_1 = 1, X_3 = 1, X_5 = 1)} =$$
$$\frac{\frac{1}{6}\frac{1}{1}\frac{0}{1}\frac{0}{1}}{p(X_1 = 1, X_2 = 0, X_3 = 1, X_4 = 0, X_5 = 1)} =$$
$$0$$

Again, class b is the only one with non zero probability.

---

3)

So far we have been dealing always with discrete feature domains. In this exercise, we will work with continuous values for features like Height and Weight. Assuming that 1means *True* and 0means *False*, consider the following features and class:

- X_1: "Weight (Kg)"
- X_2: "Height (Cm)"
- *Class*: "NBA Player"

You are given the following training set:

X_1	X_2	*Class*
170	160	0
80	220	1
90	200	1
60	160	0
50	150	0
70	190	1

And the query vector $\mathbf{x} = \begin{bmatrix} 100 & 225 \end{bmatrix}^T$.

a) Compute the most probable class for the query vector assuming that the likelihoods are 2-dimensional Gaussians.

Solution:

We start by estimating the priors:

$$p(C = 0) = \frac{1}{2}$$

$$p(C = 1) = \frac{1}{2}$$

Now, we will find the parameters of the two class conditional 2-d Gaussians that model the likelihoods:

$$
\begin{array}{ccc}
 & p(X_1, X_2 \mid C = 0) & p(X_1, X_2 \mid C = 1) \\
\mu & \begin{bmatrix} 93.3333 \\ 156.6667 \end{bmatrix} & \begin{bmatrix} 80 \\ 203.3333 \end{bmatrix} \\
\Sigma & \begin{bmatrix} 4433.3333 & 216.6667 \\ 216.6667 & 33.3333 \end{bmatrix} & \begin{bmatrix} 100 & 50 \\ 50 & 233.3333 \end{bmatrix}
\end{array}
$$

We can thus compute the posteriors:

$$p\left(C = 0 \mid X_1 = 100, X_2 = 225\right) =$$

$$\frac{p\left(C = 0\right) p\left(X_1 = 100, X_2 = 225 \mid C = 0\right)}{p\left(X_1 = 100, X_2 = 225\right)} =$$

$$\frac{\frac{1}{2} N\left(\begin{bmatrix} 100 \\ 225 \end{bmatrix} \mid \mu = \begin{bmatrix} 93.3333 \\ 156.6667 \end{bmatrix}, \Sigma = \begin{bmatrix} 4433.3333 & 216.6667 \\ 216.6667 & 33.3333 \end{bmatrix}\right)}{p\left(X_1 = 100, X_2 = 225\right)} =$$

$$\frac{3.4783 \times 10^{-48}}{p\left(X_1 = 100, X_2 = 225\right)}$$

$$p\left(C = 1 \mid X_1 = 100, X_2 = 225\right) =$$

$$\frac{p\left(C = 1\right) p\left(X_1 = 100, X_2 = 225 \mid C = 1\right)}{p\left(X_1 = 100, X_2 = 225\right)} =$$

$$\frac{\frac{1}{2} N\left(\begin{bmatrix} 100 \\ 225 \end{bmatrix} \mid \mu = \begin{bmatrix} 80 \\ 203.3333 \end{bmatrix}, \Sigma = \begin{bmatrix} 100 & 50 \\ 50 & 233.3333 \end{bmatrix}\right)}{p\left(X_1 = 100, X_2 = 225\right)} =$$

$$\frac{0.0001}{p\left(X_1 = 100, X_2 = 225\right)}$$

Comparing the numerators, we find that it is classified as an NBA player.

---

b) Compute the most probable class for the query vector, under the Naive Bayes assumption, using 1-dimensional Gaussians to model the likelihoods.

Solution:

We can estimate the priors in the same manner:

$$p\left(C = 0\right) = \frac{1}{2}$$

$$p\left(C = 1\right) = \frac{1}{2}$$

To estimate the likelihoods we will find the sample mean and standard deviation for each conditional distribution:

$$p(X_1 \mid C = 0) \; p(X_1 \mid C = 1)$$

	$p(X_1 \mid C = 0)$	$p(X_1 \mid C = 1)$
μ	93.3333	80
σ	66.5832	10

$$p(X_2 \mid C = 0) \; p(X_2 \mid C = 1)$$

	$p(X_2 \mid C = 0)$	$p(X_2 \mid C = 1)$
μ	156.6667	203.3333
σ	5.7735	15.2753

Now, for the query vector we have:

$$p(C = 0 \mid X_1 = 100, X_2 = 225) =$$
$$\frac{p(C = 0)\, p(X_1 = 100, X_2 = 225 \mid C = 0)}{p(X_1 = 100, X_2 = 225)} =$$
$$\frac{p(C = 0)\, p(X_1 = 100 \mid C = 0)\, p(X_2 = 225 \mid C = 0)}{p(X_1 = 100, X_2 = 225)} =$$
$$\frac{\frac{1}{2} N(100 \mid \mu = 93.3333, \sigma = 66.5832)\, N(225 \mid \mu = 156.6667, \sigma = 5.7735)}{p(X_1 = 100, X_2 = 225)} =$$
$$\frac{7.8542 \times 10^{-35}}{p(X_1 = 100, X_2 = 225)}$$

$$p(C = 1 \mid X_1 = 100, X_2 = 225) =$$
$$\frac{p(C = 1)\, p(X_1 = 100, X_2 = 225 \mid C = 1)}{p(X_1 = 100, X_2 = 225)} =$$
$$\frac{p(C = 1)\, p(X_1 = 100 \mid C = 1)\, p(X_2 = 225 \mid C = 1)}{p(X_1 = 100, X_2 = 225)} =$$
$$\frac{\frac{1}{2} N(100 \mid \mu = 80, \sigma = 10)\, N(225 \mid \mu = 203.3333, \sigma = 15.2753)}{p(X_1 = 100, X_2 = 225)} =$$
$$\frac{2.5783 \times 10^{-5}}{p(X_1 = 100, X_2 = 225)}$$

Comparing the numerators we determine that it is an NBA player.

C Decision Trees

A decision tree represents a data table where each data point has features and a class [Winston (1992)], [Mitchell (1997)], [Luger and Stubblefield

(1998)]. A node in the tree represents a test on a feature that partitions the original table in one table for each possible result of that test (see figure 2.19).

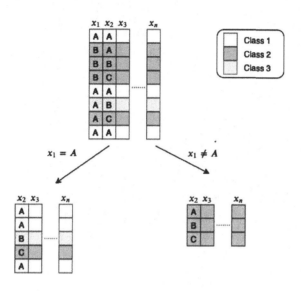

Fig. 2.19 A test node that creates two partitions.

The tree is built by inserting these test nodes until we reach all leafs. Leafs are nodes where the table partition has either all elements of the same class or no more tests can be applied, for instance the rightmost node in the aforementioned figure. Once the full tree is built, to perform classification of a given point, we traverse the tree by applying each node's test until a leaf is reached (see figure 2.20).

The size of the tree depends on the order we choose for the tests. Different orders will result in different decision trees, all of which can be correct. So, how do we decide which one we want? On the one hand, we want a tree that correctly captures the information present in the data table (i.e. classifies correctly its instances). On the other hand, we want a tree that classifies unseen examples correctly too. In that sense, a simple tree is preferrable because it is less likely to include unnecessary constraints that only appear true in this training set but are not true in general.

We could test all possible orders and choose the best tree but it grows extremely fast ($\Theta(n!)$). Since blind search won't do, we need a heuristic. A common procedure known as ID3 uses entropy as the heuristic.

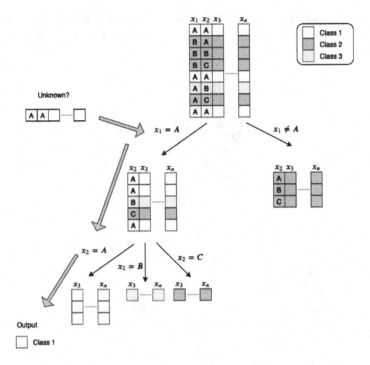

Fig. 2.20   Classifying a point with a decision tree.

Entropy is a function that receives a distribution and returns a value:

$$E(p_1, p_2, p_3, \ldots, p_n) = -\sum_{i=1}^{n} p_i \log_2 p_i$$

The higher the value the less deterministic the distribution is. More specifically, a high entropy tells us that the outcome of sampling that distribution is very hard to predict. Entropy of a given table is given by the entropy in the distribution of classes. How much entropy we need to get rid of to have perfect classification.

In ID3, a test node is a test on a specific feature, where one partition is created for each possible value. When building a tree, at a given moment, the entropy of that tree is the weighted average of the entropies of all partitions (see figure 2.21).

So, every time we want to choose the next attribute to test, we do:

• Compute the original entropy of the tree

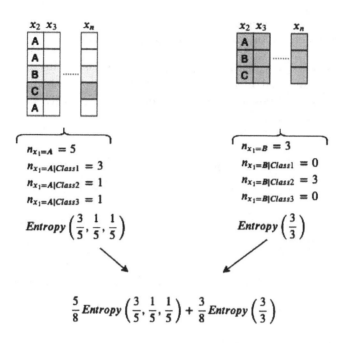

Fig. 2.21   Computing entropy from multiple partitions.

- For each possible feature test we can add to the tree
  - compute the partition tables that are created each possible feature assignment
  - compute the total entropy of each partition
  - compute the new entropy by taking the weighted average of entropies of all partitions
  - compute the test's information gain by computing the difference between the original entropy and the new entropy

- Choose the feature that provides the highest information gain and add it to the tree

An alternative method we will see is CART where all tests have binary outputs [Bishop (2006)]. Concretely, instead of testing a feature and creating a branch for all its possible values, we test a feature value assignment $x_i = a$ and create two branches:

- A branch for instances where $x_i == a$;
- A branch for all reamining instances.

The test to place on the tree is chosen in a mechanic which is very similar to the one we used in ID3 but instead of entropy we will use impurity. Impurity is measured with the *Gini* index that also receives a distribution and outputs a value:

$$Gini\,(p_1, p_2, \ldots, p_n) = 1 - \sum_{i=1}^{n} p_i^2$$

1)

Consider the following data table:

F_1	F_2	F_3	O
a	a	a	$+$
c	b	c	$+$
c	a	c	$+$
b	a	a	$-$
a	b	c	$-$
b	b	c	$-$

a) Determine the whole decision tree using ID3 (**information gain**), taking "O" as the target. Show all steps.

Solution:

Before anything, we need to compute the entropy we start with:

$$E_{start} = E\left(\frac{3}{3+3}, \frac{3}{3+3}\right) = 1bit$$

Let us test attribute F_1:

$$
\begin{array}{ccc}
F_1 = a & F_1 = b & F_1 = c \\
\downarrow & \downarrow & \downarrow \\
\#\{O = +\} = 1 & \#\{O = +\} = 0 & \#\{O = +\} = 2 \\
\#\{O = -\} = 1 & \#\{O = -\} = 2 & \#\{O = -\} = 0 \\
\downarrow & \downarrow & \downarrow \\
E\left(\frac{1}{1+1}, \frac{1}{1+1}\right) & E\left(\frac{2}{2+0}\right) & E\left(\frac{2}{2+0}\right)
\end{array}
$$

Total entropy after partitioning by F_1 is equal to the weighted average of each partition's entropy: $E_{F_1} = \frac{2}{6}E\left(\frac{1}{1+1}, \frac{1}{1+1}\right) + \frac{2}{6}E\left(\frac{2}{2+0}\right) + \frac{2}{6}E\left(\frac{2}{2+0}\right) \approx 0.33bit$.

So, the information gain is given by subtracting the entropy at begining from the remaining entropy after F_1: $G(F_1) = E_{start} - E_{F_1} \approx 0.66bit$.

Let us test the next attribute, namely F_2:

$$F_2 = a \qquad\qquad F_2 = b$$
$$\downarrow \qquad\qquad\qquad \downarrow$$
$$\#\{O = +\} = 2 \ \#\{O = +\} = 1$$
$$\#\{O = -\} = 1 \ \#\{O = -\} = 2$$
$$\downarrow \qquad\qquad\qquad \downarrow$$
$$E\left(\frac{2}{2+1}, \frac{1}{2+1}\right) \quad E\left(\frac{1}{1+2}, \frac{2}{1+2}\right)$$

Total entropy after partitioning by F_2 is equal to the weighted average of each partition's entropy: $E_{F_2} = \frac{3}{6}E\left(\frac{2}{2+1}, \frac{1}{2+1}\right) + \frac{3}{6}E\left(\frac{1}{1+2}, \frac{2}{1+2}\right) = 0.9183bit$.

So, the information gain is given by subtracting the entropy at begining from the remaining entropy after F_2: $G(F_2) = E_{start} - E_{F_2} = 0.0817bit$

For F_3:

$$F_3 = a \qquad\qquad F_3 = c$$
$$\downarrow \qquad\qquad\qquad \downarrow$$
$$\#\{O = +\} = 1 \ \#\{O = +\} = 2$$
$$\#\{O = -\} = 1 \ \#\{O = -\} = 2$$
$$\downarrow \qquad\qquad\qquad \downarrow$$
$$E\left(\frac{1}{1+1}, \frac{1}{1+1}\right) \quad E\left(\frac{2}{2+2}, \frac{2}{2+2}\right)$$

Total entropy after partitioning by F_3 is equal to the weighted average of each partition's entropy: $E_{F_3} = \frac{2}{6}E\left(\frac{1}{1+1}, \frac{1}{1+1}\right) + \frac{4}{6}E\left(\frac{2}{2+2}, \frac{2}{2+2}\right) = 1.0bit$.

So, the information gain is given by subtracting the entropy at begining from the remaining entropy after F_3: $G(F_3) = E_{start} - E_{F_3} = 0bit$

Since F_1 provides the highest gain, we use it as the first node in the tree and get this break down of the dataset:

$F_1 = a$			$F_1 = b$			$F_1 = c$		
F_2	F_3	O	F_2	F_3	O	F_2	F_3	O
a	a	$+$	a	a	$-$	b	c	$+$
b	c	$-$	b	c	$-$	a	c	$+$
				Done!			Done!	

The first partition ($F_1 = a$) still has uncertainty. For that reason, we will repeat the same process to decide the next attribute to test. Before anything, we need to compute the entropy we start with:

$$E_{start} = E\left(\frac{1}{1+1}, \frac{1}{1+1}\right) = 1bit$$

Let us test the next attribute, namely F_2:

$$F_2 = a \qquad\qquad F_2 = b$$
$$\downarrow \qquad\qquad\qquad \downarrow$$
$$\#\{O = +\} = 1 \;\#\{O = +\} = 0$$
$$\#\{O = -\} = 0 \;\#\{O = -\} = 1$$
$$\downarrow \qquad\qquad\qquad \downarrow$$
$$E\left(\frac{1}{1+0}\right) \qquad E\left(\frac{1}{0+1}\right)$$

Total entropy after partitioning by F_2 is equal to the weighted average of each partition's entropy: $E_{F_2} = \frac{1}{2}E\left(\frac{1}{1+0}\right) + \frac{1}{2}E\left(\frac{1}{0+1}\right) = 0bit$.

So, the information gain is given by subtracting the entropy at begining from the remaining entropy after F_2: $G(F_2) = E_{start} - E_{F_2} = 1bit$

For F_3:

$$F_3 = a \qquad\qquad F_3 = c$$
$$\downarrow \qquad\qquad\qquad \downarrow$$
$$\#\{O = +\} = 1 \;\#\{O = +\} = 0$$
$$\#\{O = -\} = 0 \;\#\{O = -\} = 1$$
$$\downarrow \qquad\qquad\qquad \downarrow$$
$$E\left(\frac{1}{1+0}\right) \qquad E\left(\frac{1}{0+1}\right)$$

Total entropy after partitioning by F_3 is equal to the weighted average of each partition's entropy: $E_{F_3} = \frac{1}{2}E\left(\frac{1}{1+0}\right) + \frac{1}{2}E\left(\frac{1}{0+1}\right) = 0.0bit$.

So, the information gain is given by subtracting the entropy at begining from the remaining entropy after F_3: $G(F_3) = E_{start} - E_{F_3} = 1bit$

Since both attributes have the same gain. we can choose either. Let us go with F_2 and get the following partioning:

$F_1 = a$		$F_1 = b$		$F_1 = c$	
$F_2 = a$		$F_2 = b$	F_2 F_3 O	F_2 F_3 O	
F_3	O	F_3	O	a a $-$	b c $+$
a	$+$	c	$-$	b c $-$	a c $+$
Done!		Done!		Done!		Done!

Since there is no more uncertainty, we needn't explore any further. Thus, we reach the final tree:

$$F_1$$
$$a \quad b \quad c$$
$$\swarrow \quad \downarrow \quad \searrow$$
$$F_2 \qquad - \qquad +$$
$$a \qquad b$$
$$\swarrow \qquad \searrow$$
$$+ \qquad\qquad -$$

b) Repeat the same exercise but this time use CART (**Gini**).

Solution:

Before anything, we need to compute the impurity we start with:

$$Gini_{start} = Gini\left(\frac{3}{3+3}, \frac{3}{3+3}\right) = 1 - \left(\frac{3}{6}\right)^2 - \left(\frac{3}{6}\right)^2 = 0.50$$

Let us start with all value splits for attribute F_1:

First, we evaluate the split $\{a\}\ vs\ \{b, c\}$ which yields the following partition:

$F_1 = \{a\}$	$F_1 = \{b, c\}$
$\downarrow$	$\downarrow$
$\#\{O = +\} = 1$	$\#\{O = +\} = 2$
$\#\{O = -\} = 1$	$\#\{O = -\} = 2$
$\downarrow$	$\downarrow$
$Gini\left(\frac{1}{1+1}, \frac{1}{1+1}\right)$	$Gini\left(\frac{2}{2+2}, \frac{2}{2+2}\right)$

Which gives the weighted impurity:

$$Gini_{\{a\}vs\{b,c\}}(F_1) = \frac{2}{2+4}Gini\left(\frac{1}{1+1}, \frac{1}{1+1}\right) + \frac{4}{2+4}Gini\left(\frac{2}{2+2}, \frac{2}{2+2}\right) = 0.5$$

Which yields an impurity reduction of:

$$\Delta Gini = Gini_{start} - Gini_{\{a\}vs\{b,c\}}(F_1) = 0.0$$

Second, we evaluate the split $\{b\}\ vs\ \{a, c\}$ which yields the following partition:

$F_1 = \{b\}$	$F_1 = \{a, c\}$
$\downarrow$	$\downarrow$

$$\# \{O = +\} = 0 \quad \# \{O = +\} = 3$$
$$\# \{O = -\} = 2 \quad \# \{O = -\} = 1$$

$$\downarrow \qquad\qquad \downarrow$$

$$Gini\left(\frac{2}{0+2}\right) \quad Gini\left(\frac{3}{3+1}, \frac{1}{3+1}\right)$$

Which gives the weighted impurity:

$$Gini_{\{b\}vs\{a,c\}}\left(F_1\right) = \frac{2}{2+4}Gini\left(\frac{2}{0+2}\right) + \frac{4}{2+4}Gini\left(\frac{3}{3+1}, \frac{1}{3+1}\right) = 0.25$$

Which yields an impurity reduction of:

$$\Delta Gini = Gini_{start} - Gini_{\{b\}vs\{a,c\}}\left(F_1\right) = 0.25$$

Finally, we evaluate the split $\{c\}$ *vs* $\{a, b\}$ which yields the following partition:

$F_1 = \{c\}$	$F_1 = \{a, b\}$
$\downarrow$	$\downarrow$

$$\# \{O = +\} = 2 \quad \# \{O = +\} = 1$$
$$\# \{O = -\} = 0 \quad \# \{O = -\} = 3$$

$$\downarrow \qquad\qquad \downarrow$$

$$Gini\left(\frac{2}{2+0}\right) \quad Gini\left(\frac{1}{1+3}, \frac{3}{1+3}\right)$$

Which gives the weighted impurity:

$$Gini_{\{c\}vs\{a,b\}}\left(F_1\right) = \frac{2}{2+4}Gini\left(\frac{2}{2+0}\right) + \frac{4}{2+4}Gini\left(\frac{1}{1+3}, \frac{3}{1+3}\right) = 0.25$$

Which yields an impurity reduction of:

$$\Delta Gini = Gini_{start} - Gini_{\{c\}vs\{a,b\}}\left(F_1\right) = 0.25$$

Now, we evaluate the next attribute:

$F_2 = \{a\}$	$F_2 = \{b\}$
$\downarrow$	$\downarrow$

$$\# \{O = +\} = 2 \quad \# \{O = +\} = 1$$
$$\# \{O = -\} = 1 \quad \# \{O = -\} = 2$$

$$\downarrow \qquad\qquad \downarrow$$

$$Gini\left(\frac{2}{2+1}, \frac{1}{2+1}\right) \quad Gini\left(\frac{1}{1+2}, \frac{2}{1+2}\right)$$

Which gives the weighted impurity:

$$Gini_{\{a\}vs\{b\}}\left(F_2\right) = \frac{3}{3+3}Gini\left(\frac{2}{2+1}, \frac{1}{2+1}\right) + \frac{3}{3+3}Gini\left(\frac{1}{1+2}, \frac{2}{1+2}\right) = 0.4444$$

Which yields an impurity reduction of:

$$\Delta Gini = Gini_{start} - Gini_{\{a\}vs\{b\}}\left(F_2\right) = 0.0006$$

Finally, let us evaluate F_3:

$F_3 = \{a\}$	$F_3 = \{c\}$
$\downarrow$	$\downarrow$
$\#\{O = +\} = 1$	$\#\{O = +\} = 2$
$\#\{O = -\} = 1$	$\#\{O = -\} = 2$
$\downarrow$	$\downarrow$
$Gini\left(\frac{1}{1+1}, \frac{1}{1+1}\right)$	$Gini\left(\frac{2}{2+2}, \frac{2}{2+2}\right)$

Which gives the weighted impurity:

$Gini_{\{a\}vs\{c\}}(F_3) = \frac{2}{2+4}Gini\left(\frac{1}{1+1}, \frac{1}{1+1}\right) + \frac{4}{2+4}Gini\left(\frac{2}{2+2}, \frac{2}{2+2}\right) = 0.5$

Which yields an impurity reduction of:

$\Delta Gini = Gini_{start} - Gini_{\{a\}vs\{c\}}(F_3) = 0$

According to the algorithm, we choose the split that yields the maximum reduction, so, in this case it could be either $F_1 - \{b\}\, vs\, \{a, c\}$ or $F_1 - \{a, b\}\, vs\, \{c\}$. Let us pick the former.

From the chosen split we get two tables:

	$F_1 = \{b\}$			$F_1 = \{a, c\}$	
F_2	F_3	O	F_2	F_3	O
a	a	$-$	a	a	$+$
b	c	$-$	b	c	$+$
			a	c	$+$
			b	c	$-$
	Done!				

The first one is done since it has no impurity: $Gini_{start} = Gini\left(\frac{2}{2}\right) = 1 - \left(\frac{2}{2}\right)^2 = 0$.

For the second one, we need to repeat the whole process since we still have impurity: $Gini_{start} = Gini\left(\frac{3}{3+1}, \frac{1}{3+1}\right) = 0.3750$.

Let us start with F_2:

$F_2 = \{a\}$	$F_2 = \{b\}$
$\downarrow$	$\downarrow$
$\#\{O = +\} = 2$	$\#\{O = +\} = 1$
$\#\{O = -\} = 0$	$\#\{O = -\} = 1$
$\downarrow$	$\downarrow$
$Gini\left(\frac{2}{2+2}\right)$	$Gini\left(\frac{1}{1+1}, \frac{1}{1+1}\right)$

Which gives the weighted impurity:

$Gini_{\{a\}vs\{b\}}(F_2) = \frac{2}{2+2}Gini\left(\frac{2}{2+2}\right) + \frac{2}{2+2}Gini\left(\frac{1}{1+1}, \frac{1}{1+1}\right) = 0.25$

Which yields an impurity reduction of:

$\Delta Gini = Gini_{start} - Gini_{\{a\}vs\{b\}}(F_2) = 0.1250$

Finally, let us evaluate F_3:

$F_3 = \{a\}$	$F_3 = \{c\}$
$\downarrow$	$\downarrow$
$\#\{O = +\} = 1$	$\#\{O = +\} = 2$
$\#\{O = -\} = 0$	$\#\{O = -\} = 1$
$\downarrow$	$\downarrow$
$Gini\left(\frac{1}{1}\right)$	$Gini\left(\frac{2}{2+1}, \frac{1}{2+1}\right)$

Which gives the weighted impurity:

$Gini_{\{a\}vs\{c\}}(F_3) = \frac{1}{1+3}Gini\left(\frac{1}{1}\right) + \frac{3}{1+3}Gini\left(\frac{2}{2+1}, \frac{1}{2+1}\right) = 0.3333$

Which yields an impurity reduction of:

$\Delta Gini = Gini_{start} - Gini_{\{a\}vs\{c\}}(F_3) = 0.042$

So, again we choose the split that maximizes the reduction of impurity, which, in this case, is $F_2 - \{a\}\ vs\ \{b\}$. This choice will split the table in two:

	$F_1 = \{b\}$			$F_1 = \{a,c\}$			
F_2	F_3	O	$F_2 = \{a\}$			$F_2 = \{a\}$	
a	a	$-$	F_3	O		F_3	O
b	c	$-$	a	$+$		c	$+$
			c	$+$		c	$-$
			Done!				
	Done!						

The first table we get shows no impurtiy, so that branch is done. Whereas the second table has no split that allows to reduce impurity any further. For that reason, the algorithm stops with uncertainty on that branch. More specifically, it returns the following tree:

$$F_1$$

a, c ↙   ↘ b

$$F_2$$ $$-$$

a ↙   ↘ b

$$+$$ $$+/-$$

2)

Consider the following data table:

F_1	F_2	F_3	O
d	a	b	m
c	a	b	n
c	a	a	y
d	a	a	y
c	b	a	f
c	b	b	f

a) Compute the first attribute to be tested using ID3.

Solution:

Before anything, we need to compute the entropy we start with:

$$E_{start} = E\left(\frac{\#\{O=m\}}{\sum_o \#\{O=o\}}, \frac{\#\{O=n\}}{\sum_o \#\{O=o\}}, \frac{\#\{O=y\}}{\sum_o \#\{O=o\}}, \frac{\#\{O=f\}}{\sum_o \#\{O=o\}}\right)$$

$$= E\left(\frac{1}{6}, \frac{1}{6}, \frac{1}{3}, \frac{1}{3}\right) = 1.9183bit$$

Let us test attribute F_1:

$$F_1 = d \qquad\qquad F_1 = c$$
$$\downarrow \qquad\qquad\qquad \downarrow$$
$$\#\{O=m\} = 1 \qquad \#\{O=m\} = 0$$
$$\#\{O=n\} = 0 \qquad \#\{O=n\} = 1$$
$$\#\{O=y\} = 1 \qquad \#\{O=y\} = 1$$
$$\#\{O=f\} = 0 \qquad \#\{O=f\} = 2$$
$$\downarrow \qquad\qquad\qquad \downarrow$$
$$E\left(\tfrac{1}{1+1}, \tfrac{1}{1+1}\right) \quad E\left(\tfrac{1}{1+1+2}, \tfrac{1}{1+1+2}, \tfrac{2}{1+1+2}\right)$$

Total entropy after partitioning by F_1 is equal to the weighted average of each partition's entropy: $E_{F_1} = \frac{2}{6}E\left(\tfrac{1}{1+1}, \tfrac{1}{1+1}\right) + \frac{4}{6}E\left(\tfrac{1}{1+1+2}, \tfrac{1}{1+1+2}, \tfrac{2}{1+1+2}\right) \approx 1.3333bit$.

So, the information gain is given by subtracting the entropy at begining from the remaining entropy after F_1: $G(F_1) = E_{start} - E_{F_1} \approx 0.5850bit$.

Let us test the next attribute, namely F_2:

$$F_2 = a \qquad\qquad F_2 = b$$
$$\downarrow \qquad\qquad\qquad \downarrow$$

$$\begin{array}{ll}
\#\{O = m\} = 1 & \#\{O = m\} = 0 \\
\#\{O = n\} = 1 & \#\{O = n\} = 0 \\
\#\{O = y\} = 2 & \#\{O = y\} = 0 \\
\#\{O = f\} = 0 & \#\{O = f\} = 2
\end{array}$$

$$\downarrow \qquad\qquad\qquad \downarrow$$

$$E\left(\frac{1}{1+1+2}, \frac{1}{1+1+2}, \frac{2}{1+1+2}\right) \qquad E\left(\frac{2}{2}\right)$$

Total entropy after partitioning by F_2 is equal to the weighted average of each partition's entropy: $E_{F_2} = \frac{4}{6}E\left(\frac{1}{1+1+2}, \frac{1}{1+1+2}, \frac{2}{1+1+2}\right) + \frac{2}{6}E\left(\frac{2}{2}\right) \approx 1.0bit$.

So, the information gain is given by subtracting the entropy at begining from the remaining entropy after F_2: $G(F_2) = E_{start} - E_{F_2} \approx 0.9183bit$

For F_3:

$$F_3 = b \qquad\qquad F_3 = a$$
$$\downarrow \qquad\qquad\qquad \downarrow$$

$$\begin{array}{ll}
\#\{O = m\} = 1 & \#\{O = m\} = 0 \\
\#\{O = n\} = 1 & \#\{O = n\} = 0 \\
\#\{O = y\} = 0 & \#\{O = y\} = 2 \\
\#\{O = f\} = 1 & \#\{O = f\} = 1
\end{array}$$

$$\downarrow \qquad\qquad\qquad \downarrow$$

$$E\left(\frac{1}{1+1+1}, \frac{1}{1+1+1}, \frac{1}{1+1+1}\right) \qquad E\left(\frac{2}{2+1}, \frac{1}{2+1}\right)$$

Total entropy after partitioning by F_3 is equal to the weighted average of each partition's entropy: $E_{F_3} = \frac{3}{6}E\left(\frac{1}{1+1+1}, \frac{1}{1+1+1}, \frac{1}{1+1+1}\right) + \frac{3}{6}E\left(\frac{2}{2+1}, \frac{1}{2+1}\right) \approx 1.2516bit$.

So, the information gain is given by subtracting the entropy at begining from the remaining entropy after F_3: $G(F_3) = E_{start} - E_{F_3} \approx 0.6667bit$

Since F_2 provides the highest gain, we would use it as the first node in the tree.

b) Complete the tree started in the previous question. There is no need to perform all computations. What do you need to take into account?

Solution:

From last question we got that the root node should be a test on F_2, this yields the following partition:

$F_2 = a$			$F_2 = b$		
F_1	F_3	O	F_1	F_3	O
d	b	m	c	a	f
c	b	n	c	b	f
c	a	y	*Done!*		
d	a	y			

Analyzing the second table, we see that no more uncertainty exists, so that branch is completed. The first table still provides uncertainty, so we would have to decide between testing F_1 or F_3. Testing F_1 would give no advantage since both branche would end up undecided. Whereas testing F_3 allows us to separate the y's from the rest. So, we would get the follwoing partition:

$F_2 = a$					$F_2 = b$		
$F_3 = b$		$F_3 = a$			F_1	F_3	O
F_1	O	F_1		O	c	a	f
d	m	c		f	c	b	f
c	n	d		f	*Done!*		
		Done!					

With this test, two branches appear. On the one hand, for $F_3 = a$, uncertainty disappears, so it is done. On the other hand, for $F_3 = a$, we require a final test on F_1 to get rid of the final bit of uncertainty. With that test, we get the final tree:

3)

Show if a decision tree can learn the following logical functions and if so plot the corresponding decision boundaries.

   a) *AND*

Solution:

   To show it is possible we only need to create a decision tree that solves the problem. The following does:

$$x_1$$

$$-1 \qquad +1$$

$$\swarrow \qquad \searrow$$

$$x_2 \qquad\qquad x_2$$

$$-1 \qquad +1 \qquad -1 \qquad +1$$

$$\swarrow \qquad \searrow \qquad \swarrow \qquad \searrow$$

$$-1 \qquad -1 \qquad -1 \qquad +1$$

The corresponding decision boundaries are shown below.

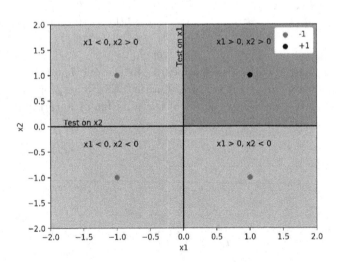

b) *OR*

Solution:

To show it is possible we only need to create a decision tree that solves the problem. The following does:

$$x_1$$

$$-1 \qquad +1$$

$$\swarrow \qquad \searrow$$

$$x_2 \qquad\qquad x_2$$

$$-1 \quad +1 \qquad -1 \quad +1$$

$$\swarrow \quad \searrow \quad \swarrow \quad \searrow$$

$$-1 \quad +1 \qquad +1 \quad +1$$

The corresponding decision boundaries are shown below.

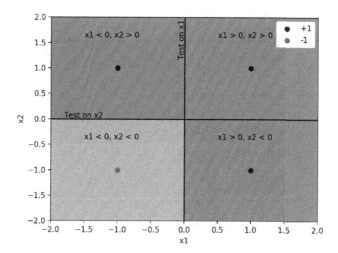

c) *XOR*

Solution:

To show it is possible we only need to create a decision tree that solves the problem. The following does:

$$x_1$$
$$-1 \qquad +1$$
$$\swarrow \qquad \searrow$$
$$x_2 \qquad\qquad x_2$$
$$-1 \quad +1 \qquad -1 \quad +1$$
$$\swarrow \quad \searrow \quad \swarrow \quad \searrow$$
$$-1 \quad +1 \qquad +1 \quad -1$$

The corresponding decision boundaries are shown below.

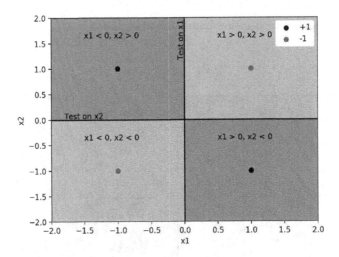

Thinking Questions

a) Assuming training examples with d boolean features, how many parameters do you have to estimate if you make no assumptions about how the data is distributed? What about if you make the Naive Bayes assumption?

b) Is Naive Bayes a linear classifier?

c) Taking into account the answers to the previous question reflect on how the decision tree can represent much more complex functions than the perceptron. Reflect also on how the size of the tree relates to the number of regions in which the space can be divided. Can you think why we want a good heuristic when building the tree? Why are usually smaller trees preferred?

Chapter 3

Linear Algebra and Optimization

Fig. 3.1 Descriptors of objects like patterns are mostly represented as feature vectors of a fixed dimension. Many machine learning algorithms are based on gradient based numerical optimization.

3.1   Vectors

A vector $\mathbf{x}$ of dimension D is represented as

$$\mathbf{x} = \begin{pmatrix} x_1 \\ x_2 \\ \vdots \\ x_D \end{pmatrix} = (x_1, x_2, \cdots, x_D)^T$$

One should be careful since $\mathbf{x}$ and the transpose $\mathbf{x}^T$ is not the same (as we will see later), this is sometimes confusing since some mathematical computer systems represent vectors incorrectly in lines due to the nature of the computer screen. We will see later, that physics found an efficient alternative notation.

3.1.1   *Norm*

A norm describes the length of a vector, it is a function given a vector space V that maps a vector into a real number with

$$\|\mathbf{x}\| \geq 0, \quad and \quad \|\mathbf{x}\| = 0 \quad for \quad \mathbf{x} = 0 \quad only,$$

with α scalar

$$\|\alpha \cdot \mathbf{x}\| = |\alpha| \cdot \|\mathbf{x}\|,$$

$$\|\mathbf{x} + \mathbf{y}\| \leq \|\mathbf{x}\| + |\mathbf{y}\|.$$

The l_p norm is defined as the following (for $p = 2$ it is the Euclidean norm):

$$\|\mathbf{x}\|_p = (|x_1|^p + |x_2|^p + \cdots + |x_D|^p)^{\frac{1}{p}} \tag{3.1}$$

l_p norms are equivalent and the following relation holds for $0 < q < p$

$$\|\mathbf{x}\|_p \leq \|\mathbf{x}\|_q \leq m^{\frac{1}{q} - \frac{1}{p}} \cdot \|\mathbf{x}\|_p \tag{3.2}$$

and

$$m^{\frac{1}{p} - \frac{1}{q}} \cdot \|\mathbf{x}\|_q \leq \|\mathbf{x}\|_p \leq \|\mathbf{x}\|_q. \tag{3.3}$$

The maximum l_∞ norm is defined as

$$\|\mathbf{x}\|_\infty = max\left(|x_1|, |x_2|, \cdots, |x_D|\right). \tag{3.4}$$

3.1.2 *Distance function*

A given metric d defines a distance between two vectors it is always positive or zero

$$d(\mathbf{x}, \mathbf{y}) \geq 0,$$

if it is symmetric

$$d(\mathbf{x}, \mathbf{y}) = d(\mathbf{y}, \mathbf{x})$$

and if the triangle inequality holds

$$d(\mathbf{x}, \mathbf{y}) \leq d(\mathbf{x}, \mathbf{z}) + d(\mathbf{z}, \mathbf{y}).$$

The l_p norms induce metrics that are distances between two points

$$d_p(\mathbf{x}, \mathbf{y}) = \|\mathbf{x} - \mathbf{y}\|_p = (|x_1 - y_1|^p + |x_2 - y_2|^p + \cdots + |x_D - y_D^p)^{\frac{1}{p}} \quad (3.5)$$

A very popular metric is based on the l_1 norm and it is called Taxicab or Manhattan metric d_1 with

$$d_1(\mathbf{x}, \mathbf{y}) = \|\mathbf{x} - \mathbf{y}\|_1 = |x_1 - y_1| + |x_2 - y_2| + \cdots + |x_D - y_D| \quad (3.6)$$

which can be written simply as

$$d_1(\mathbf{x}, \mathbf{y}) = \|\mathbf{x} - \mathbf{y}\|_1 = \sum_{j=1}^{D} |x_j - y_j|$$

The most used metric is based on the Euclidean distance (or l_2 norm)

$$d_2(\mathbf{x}, \mathbf{y}) = \|\mathbf{x} - \mathbf{y}\|_2 = \sqrt{|x_1 - y_1|^2 + |x_2 - y_2|^2 + \cdots + |x_D - y_D|^2}. \quad (3.7)$$

which can be written simply as

$$d_2(\mathbf{x}, \mathbf{y}) = \|\mathbf{x} - \mathbf{y}\| = \sqrt{\sum_{j=1}^{D} |x_j - y_j|^2}.$$

By normalizing the vector to length one the Euclidean distance function is constrained to a unit radius ball

$$0 \leq d\left(\frac{\mathbf{x}}{\|\mathbf{x}\|}, \frac{\mathbf{y}}{\|\mathbf{y}\|}\right) = \left\|\frac{\mathbf{x}}{\|\mathbf{x}\|} - \frac{\mathbf{y}}{\|\mathbf{y}\|}\right\| \leq \sqrt{2}. \quad (3.8)$$

(b)

(a)

Fig. 3.2   (a) David Hilbert, (1862 - 1943) one of the most famous German mathematicians, attended a banquet in 1934, and he was seated next to the new minister of education, Bernhard Rust [Reid (1996)]. Rust asked, "How is mathematics in Göttingen now that it has been freed of the Jewish influence?" Hilbert replied, "Mathematics in Göttingen? There is really none any more." (b) Stefan Banach (1892 -1945) a Polish mathematician who is generally considered one of the world's most important and influential 20th-century mathematicians.

3.1.3   *Scalar Product*

The Euclidean norm is induced by the inner product (scalar product)

$$\|\mathbf{x}\|_2 = \sqrt{\langle \mathbf{x}|\mathbf{x}\rangle} \tag{3.9}$$

and defines a Hilbert space, which extends the two or three dimensional Euclidean space to spaces with any finite or infinite number of dimensions, see Figure 3.2 (a). A scalar product exists in l_2 but not in l_1 space. A normed vector space (does not need to have a scalar product) is called a Banach space, see Figure Figure 3.2 (b). Without a scalar product there is no **orthogonality**. In Euclidean space, two vectors are orthogonal if and only if the scalar product is zero.

Two vectors are orthonormal if they are orthogonal and unit vectors. By normalizing the vector to the length one (unit vectors) the Euclidean distance function is constrained to the unit sphere and corresponds to the cosine of the angle ω between the vectors

$$\cos \omega = \frac{\langle \mathbf{x}|\mathbf{y}\rangle}{\|\mathbf{x}\| \cdot \|\mathbf{y}\|} \tag{3.10}$$

with a similarity function

$$-1 \le sim(\mathbf{x},\mathbf{y}) = \cos \omega \le 1 \tag{3.11}$$

called the cosine similarity. If we do not normalize the vectors, then we get the simple scalar product also called the dot product

$$\langle \mathbf{x} | \mathbf{w} \rangle = \cos \omega \cdot \|\mathbf{x}\| \cdot \|\mathbf{w}\|, \tag{3.12}$$

which is a measure of the projection of one vector onto another. The dot product of a vector with a unit vector is the projection of that vector in the direction given by the unit vector. The dot product is represented in a Perceptron by the value *net*,

$$net := \langle \mathbf{x} | \mathbf{w} \rangle = \sum_{i=1}^{D} w_j \cdot x_j,$$

The scalar product is commutative

$$\langle \mathbf{x} | \mathbf{w} \rangle = \mathbf{x}^T \cdot \mathbf{w} = \mathbf{w}^T \cdot \mathbf{x} = \langle \mathbf{w} | \mathbf{x} \rangle.$$

However, matrix multiplication between vectors is not, since

$$\mathbf{x}^T \cdot \mathbf{w} = \langle \mathbf{x} | \mathbf{w} \rangle = \begin{pmatrix} w_0 \ w_1 \end{pmatrix} \cdot \begin{pmatrix} x_0 \\ x_1 \end{pmatrix} = w_0 \cdot x_0 + w_1 \cdot x_1$$

is very different from

$$\mathbf{x} \cdot \mathbf{w}^T = | \mathbf{w} \rangle \langle \mathbf{x} | = \begin{pmatrix} w_0 \\ w_1 \end{pmatrix} \cdot \begin{pmatrix} x_0 \ x_1 \end{pmatrix} = \begin{pmatrix} w_0 \cdot x_0 \ w_0 \cdot x_1 \\ w_1 \cdot x_0 \ w_1 \cdot x_1 \end{pmatrix}.$$

In quantum physics a shorthand notation for a column vector and a vector is used that less confusing. Related to the scalar product $\langle \mathbf{x} | \mathbf{w} \rangle$ row vectors $\mathbf{x}^T$ are $\langle \mathbf{x} |$ "bra" and and column vectors $\mathbf{w}$ are $| \mathbf{w} \rangle$ "kets" from bra(c)kets. However this notation is usually not used outside the domain of quantum physics.

3.1.4 *Linear Independent Vectors*

A set of vectors is linearly dependent if at least one of the vectors in the set can be defined as a linear combination of the others, otherwise they are linearly independent.

D vectors of dimension D can be represented by a square matrix X with dimension $D \times D$

$$X = \begin{pmatrix} x_{11} \ x_{12} \ x_{13} \ \cdots \ x_{1D} \\ x_{21} \ x_{22} \ x_{23} \ \cdots \ x_{2D} \\ \vdots \ \vdots \ \ddots \ \vdots \\ x_{D1} \ x_{D2} \ x_{S3} \ \cdots \ x_{SD} \end{pmatrix}.$$

The vectors that represent the square matrix X are linearly dependent if the determinant of the matrix is zero $|X| = 0$, otherwise they are linearly independent. A square matrix that is not invertible is called singular or degenerate. A square matrix is singular if and only if it's determinant is 0.

3.1.5   *Matrix Operations*

Matrix multiplication is not commutative

$$A \cdot B \neq B \cdot A, \tag{3.13}$$

since

$$(A \cdot B)^T = B^T \cdot A^T \tag{3.14}$$

it is

$$A \cdot B = (B^T \cdot A^T)^T. \tag{3.15}$$

A symmetric matrix is

$$A^T = A. \tag{3.16}$$

An identity matrix of dimension D is defined as

$$I = \begin{pmatrix} 1 & 0 & 0 & \cdots & 0 \\ 0 & 1 & 0 & \cdots & 0 \\ \vdots & \vdots & & \ddots & \vdots \\ 0 & 0 & 0 & \cdots & 1 \end{pmatrix} \tag{3.17}$$

An orthogonal matrix is (its vectors are orthonormal)

$$A^T \cdot A = A \cdot A^T = I \tag{3.18}$$

it implies that

$$A^{-1} = A^T. \tag{3.19}$$

3.1.6   *Tensor Product*

The tensor product is defined for vector and matrices as

$$\begin{pmatrix} \omega_0 \\ \omega_1 \end{pmatrix} \otimes \begin{pmatrix} \omega_0 \\ \omega_1 \end{pmatrix} = \begin{pmatrix} \omega_0 \cdot \omega_0 \\ \omega_0 \cdot \omega_1 \\ \omega_1 \cdot \omega_0 \\ \omega_1 \cdot \omega_1 \end{pmatrix} \tag{3.20}$$

and

$$A \otimes B = \begin{pmatrix} a_{11} \cdot B & a_{12} \cdot B \\ a_{21} \cdot B & a_{22} \cdot B \end{pmatrix} = \begin{pmatrix} a_{11} \cdot b_{11} & a_{11} \cdot b_{12} & a_{12} \cdot b_{11} & a_{12} \cdot b_{12} \\ a_{11} \cdot b_{21} & a_{11} \cdot b_{22} & a_{12} \cdot b_{21} & a_{12} \cdot b_{22} \\ a_{21} \cdot b_{11} & a_{21} \cdot b_{12} & a_{22} \cdot b_{11} & a_{22} \cdot b_{12} \\ a_{21} \cdot b_{21} & a_{21} \cdot b_{22} & a_{22} \cdot b_{21} & a_{22} \cdot b_{22} \end{pmatrix}. \tag{3.21}$$

3.1.7 Hadamard product

The Hadamard product for matrices (also known as the Schur product) [Davis (1962)] is defined as

$$\begin{pmatrix} a_{11} & a_{12} \\ a_{21} & a_{22} \end{pmatrix} \circ \begin{pmatrix} b_{11} & b_{12} \\ b_{21} & b_{22} \end{pmatrix} = \begin{pmatrix} a_{11} \cdot b_{11} & a_{12} \cdot b_{12} \\ a_{21} \cdot b_{21} & a_{22} \cdot b_{22} \end{pmatrix} \tag{3.22}$$

and for vectors

$$\begin{pmatrix} a_{11} \\ a_{21} \end{pmatrix} \circ \begin{pmatrix} b_{11} \\ b_{21} \end{pmatrix} = \begin{pmatrix} a_{11} \\ a_{21} \end{pmatrix} \odot \begin{pmatrix} b_{11} \\ b_{21} \end{pmatrix} = \begin{pmatrix} a_{11} \cdot b_{11} \\ a_{21} \cdot b_{21} \end{pmatrix}. \tag{3.23}$$

where $\circ$ or sometimes $\odot$ represents the element-wise multiplication.

3.1.8 Element-wise division

Element-wise division is defined as

$$\begin{pmatrix} a_{11} & a_{12} \\ a_{21} & a_{22} \end{pmatrix} \oslash \begin{pmatrix} b_{11} & b_{12} \\ b_{21} & b_{22} \end{pmatrix} = \begin{pmatrix} \frac{a_{11}}{b_{11}} & \frac{a_{21}}{b_{21}} \\ \frac{a_{21}}{b_{21}} & \frac{a_{22}}{b_{22}} \end{pmatrix} \tag{3.24}$$

and for vectors

$$\begin{pmatrix} a_{11} \\ a_{21} \end{pmatrix} \oslash \begin{pmatrix} b_{11} \\ b_{21} \end{pmatrix} = \begin{pmatrix} \frac{a_{11}}{b_{11}} \\ \frac{a_{21}}{b_{21}} \end{pmatrix} \tag{3.25}$$

where $\oslash$ represents the element-wise division.

3.2 Matrix Calculus

3.2.1 Gradient

Consider a continuously differentiable function $f(\mathbf{x})$,

$$f : \mathbb{R}^D \to \mathbb{R} : f(\mathbf{x}) = y.$$

It maps the vector $\mathbf{x}$ into a real value. The gradient operator for $\mathbf{x}$ is

$$\nabla = \left[\frac{\partial}{\partial x_1}, \frac{\partial}{\partial x_2}, \cdots, \frac{\partial}{\partial x_D} \right]^T \tag{3.26}$$

or

$$\nabla f(\mathbf{x}) = \begin{pmatrix} \frac{\partial f}{\partial x_1} \\ \frac{\partial f}{\partial x_2} \\ \vdots \\ \frac{\partial f}{\partial x_D} \end{pmatrix}. \tag{3.27}$$

3.2.2   *Jacobian*

The Jacobian is the generalization of the gradient for vector-valued functions of several variables. Consider a continuously differentiable function $f(\mathbf{x})$, see Figure 3.3 (a).

$$\mathbf{f} : \mathbb{R}^D \rightarrow \mathbb{R}^K : f(\mathbf{x}) = \mathbf{y}$$

Then the Jacobian matrix J of $\mathbf{f}$ is a $K \times D$ matrix

$$J = \left(\frac{\partial \mathbf{f}}{\partial x_1}, \frac{\partial \mathbf{f}}{\partial x_2}, \cdots \frac{\partial \mathbf{f}}{\partial x_D} \right) \tag{3.28}$$

$$J = \begin{pmatrix} \frac{\partial f_1(\mathbf{x})}{\partial x_1} & \frac{\partial f_1(\mathbf{x})}{\partial x_2} & \cdots & \frac{\partial f_1(\mathbf{x})}{\partial x_D} \\ \frac{\partial f_2(\mathbf{x})}{\partial x_1} & \frac{\partial f(_2\mathbf{x})}{\partial x_2} & \cdots & \frac{\partial f_2(\mathbf{x})}{\partial x_D} \\ \vdots & \vdots & \ddots & \vdots \\ \frac{\partial f_K(\mathbf{x})}{\partial x_1} & \frac{\partial f_K(\mathbf{x})}{\partial x_2} & \cdots & \frac{\partial f_K(\mathbf{x})}{\partial x_D} \end{pmatrix}. \tag{3.29}$$

If $K = 1$ f is a scalar field and the Jacobian matrix is reduced to a row vector of partial derivatives of f. It is the **transpose** of the gradient of f, when denoted as a column vector.

3.2.2.1   *Important rules for gradient*

These are the three most important rules for gradients that we will use in the chapter about linear regression.

(1) Distributive properties

$$\nabla(a \cdot f(\mathbf{x}) + b \cdot g(\mathbf{x})) = a \cdot \nabla f(\mathbf{x}) + b \cdot \nabla g(\mathbf{x}), \quad a, b \in \mathbb{R}. \tag{3.30}$$

(2) For a bilinear form

$$\nabla \left(\mathbf{x}^T \cdot A \cdot \mathbf{x} \right) = \left(A + A^T \right) \cdot \mathbf{x}, \tag{3.31}$$

if A symmetric (symmetric bilinear form), then

$$\nabla \left(\mathbf{x}^T \cdot A \cdot \mathbf{x} \right) = 2 \cdot A \cdot \mathbf{x}. \tag{3.32}$$

(3) For a scalar product

$$\nabla_x \langle \mathbf{y} | \mathbf{x} \rangle = \nabla_x \left(\mathbf{y}^T \mathbf{x} \right) = \mathbf{y}. \tag{3.33}$$

3.2.3 Hessian Matrix

Consider a continuously twice differentiable function $f(\mathbf{x})$,

$$f : \mathbb{R}^D \to \mathbb{R} : f(\mathbf{x}) = y.$$

Then the Hessian matrix with respect to $\mathbf{x}$, written $\nabla^2 f(\mathbf{x})$ or simply as H is the $D \times D$ matrix of partial derivatives, see Figure 3.3 (b), it is the Jacobian of the gradient

$$\nabla^2 f(\mathbf{x}) = J \begin{pmatrix} \frac{\partial f}{\partial x_1} \\ \frac{\partial f}{\partial x_2} \\ \vdots \\ \frac{\partial f}{\partial x_D} \end{pmatrix}^T = \begin{pmatrix} \frac{\partial^2 f(\mathbf{x})}{\partial x_1^2} & \frac{\partial^2 f(\mathbf{x})}{\partial x_1 \partial x_2} & \cdots & \frac{\partial^2 f(\mathbf{x})}{\partial x_1 \partial x_D} \\ \frac{\partial^2 f(\mathbf{x})}{\partial x_2 \partial x_1} & \frac{\partial^2 f(\mathbf{x})}{\partial x_2 \partial x_2} & \cdots & \frac{\partial^2 f(\mathbf{x})}{\partial x_2 \partial x_D} \\ \vdots & \vdots & \ddots & \vdots \\ \frac{\partial^2 f(\mathbf{x})}{\partial x_D \partial x_1} & \frac{\partial^2 f(\mathbf{x})}{\partial x_D \partial x_2} & \cdots & \frac{\partial^2 f(\mathbf{x})}{\partial x_D^2} \end{pmatrix}. \tag{3.34}$$

Be careful, we cannot take the gradient of a vector but only the Jacobian of the gradient transpose, the relation is

$$H(f(\mathbf{x})) = J(\nabla(f(\mathbf{x}))^T. \tag{3.35}$$

(a)   (b)

Fig. 3.3 (a) Carl Gustav Jacob (1804 - 1851) was a German mathematician who made fundamental contributions to elliptic functions, dynamics, differential equations, determinants, and number theory. (b) Ludwig Otto Hesse (1811 - 1874) was a German mathematician. He worked mainly on algebraic invariants, and geometry.

3.3 Gradient based Numerical Optimization

3.3.1 Gradient descent

Consider a continuously differentiable function $y = f(x)$. The function has extreme points for $0 = f'(x)$. We can determine the solution numerically, by approximating the real zeros $f'(x) = 0$ by gradient descent. The gradient descent for one dimension is

$$x_{n+1} = x_n - \eta \cdot f'(x_n) \tag{3.36}$$

$$-\eta \cdot f'(x_n) = (x_{n+1} - x_n). \tag{3.37}$$

By first-order Taylor series expansion we have

$$f(x_{n+1}) \approx f(x_n) + f'(x_n) \cdot (x_{n+1} - x_n) = f(x_n) - \eta f'(x_n)^2 \tag{3.38}$$

and it follows

$$f(x_{n+1}) \leq f(x_n).$$

Using gradient descent we would like to arrive at the global minimum of a function that is not convex. A function is called convex if the line segment between any two points on the graph of the function lies above or on the graph, see Figure 3.4. For a non convex function the determined minima

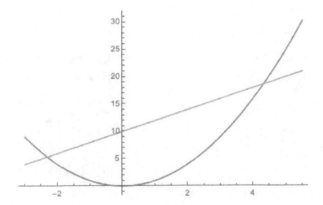

Fig. 3.4   A function is called convex if the line segment between any two points on the graph of the function lies above the graph between the two points.

depends on the initial value of x_1. We can arrive at a local minimum that is nearly as good as the global minimum or at another local minimum which value is quite different. When we stop the gradient descent, we do not know at which kind of minimum we arrived. An empirical method would be to start with different initial values of x_1, see Figure 3.5. Another problem arrives with a saddle points, whose derivative is zero but which is not a local extremum of the function, see Figure 3.6.

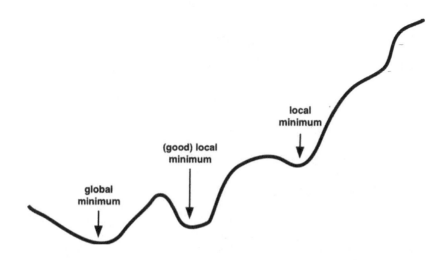

Fig. 3.5 Using gradient descent we would like to arrive at the global minimum of a function that is not convex. But this depend on the initial value of x_1. We can arrive at a local minimum that is nearly as good as the global minimum or at another local minimum which value is quite different. When we stop the gradient descent we do not know which kind of minimum we arrived at. An empirical method would be to start with different initial values of x_1.

Consider now a continuously differentiable function $f(\mathbf{x})$,

$$f : \mathbb{R}^D \to \mathbb{R} : f(\mathbf{x}) = y.$$

It maps the vector $\mathbf{x}$ into a real value. The gradient operator for $\mathbf{x}$ is

$$\nabla = \left[\frac{\partial}{\partial x_1}, \frac{\partial}{\partial x_2}, \cdots, \frac{\partial}{\partial x_D} \right]^T$$

and

$$\nabla f(\mathbf{x}) = \begin{pmatrix} \frac{\partial f}{\partial x_1} \\ \frac{\partial f}{\partial x_2} \\ \vdots \\ \frac{\partial f}{\partial x_D} \end{pmatrix}.$$

The gradient descent for D dimensions is

$$\mathbf{x}_{n+1} = \mathbf{x}_n - \eta \cdot \nabla f(\mathbf{x}_n) \tag{3.39}$$

$$-\eta \cdot \nabla f(\mathbf{x}_n) = (\mathbf{x}_{n+1} - \mathbf{x}_n) \tag{3.40}$$

By first-order Taylor series expansion we have

$$f(\mathbf{x}_{n+1}) \approx f(\mathbf{x}_n) + (\nabla f(\mathbf{x}_n))^T \cdot (\mathbf{x}_{n+1} - \mathbf{x}_n) \tag{3.41}$$

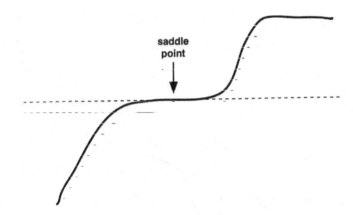

Fig. 3.6 Another problem arrives with a saddle points, whose derivative is zero but which is not a local extremum of the function.

$$f(\mathbf{x}_{n+1}) \approx f(\mathbf{x}_n) - \eta \left(\nabla f(\mathbf{x}_n)\right)^T \left(\nabla f(\mathbf{x}_n)\right) \qquad (3.42)$$

$$f(\mathbf{x}_{n+1}) \approx f(\mathbf{x}_n) - \eta \|\nabla f(\mathbf{x}_n)\|^2 \qquad (3.43)$$

and it follows

$$f(\mathbf{x}_{n+1}) \leq f(\mathbf{x}_n)$$

3.3.1.1   *Learning parameter η*

The learning-rate parameter η has a profound influence on the convergence behavior of the gradient descent method [Haykin (2008)], see Figure 3.7:

- When η is small, the transient response of the algorithm follows a smooth path but it may take a long time (slow)
- When η is large, the transient response of the algorithm follows a zigzagging (oscillatory) path
- When η exceeds a certain critical value, the algorithm becomes unstable (i.e., it diverges)

3.3.2   **Newton's Method**

Consider a continuously twice differentiable function $f(\mathbf{x})$.

$$f : \mathbb{R}^D \to \mathbb{R} : f(\mathbf{x}) = y$$

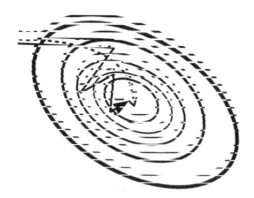

Fig. 3.7   When η is small, the transient response of the algorithm follows a smooth path (slow due too many steps), see the doted arrow. When η is large, the transient response of the algorithm follows a zigzagging (oscillatory) path, see continuous arrow.

It maps the vector $\mathbf{x}$ into a real value. Then the Hessian matrix with respect to $\mathbf{x}$, written $\nabla^2 f(\mathbf{x})$ or simply as H is the $D \times D$ matrix of partial derivatives,

$$\nabla^2 f(\mathbf{x}) = \begin{pmatrix} \frac{\partial^2 f(\mathbf{x})}{\partial x_1^2} & \frac{\partial^2 f(\mathbf{x})}{\partial x_1 \partial x_2} & \cdots & \frac{\partial^2 f(\mathbf{x})}{\partial x_1 \partial x_D} \\ \frac{\partial^2 f(\mathbf{x})}{\partial x_2 \partial x_1} & \frac{\partial^2 f(\mathbf{x})}{\partial x_2 \partial x_2} & \cdots & \frac{\partial^2 f(\mathbf{x})}{\partial x_2 \partial x_D} \\ \vdots & \vdots & \ddots & \vdots \\ \frac{\partial^2 f(\mathbf{x})}{\partial x_D \partial x_1} & \frac{\partial^2 f(\mathbf{x})}{\partial x_D \partial x_2} & \cdots & \frac{\partial^2 f(\mathbf{x})}{\partial x_D^2} \end{pmatrix}. \tag{3.44}$$

By second-order Taylor series expansion we have

$$f(\mathbf{x}_{n+1}) \approx f(\mathbf{x}_n) + (\nabla f(\mathbf{x}_n))^T \cdot (\mathbf{x}_{n+1} - \mathbf{x}_n) + \frac{(\mathbf{x}_{n+1} - \mathbf{x}_n)^T H_n (\mathbf{x}_{n+1} - \mathbf{x}_n)}{2} \tag{3.45}$$

We can reformulate to

$$f(\mathbf{x}_{n+1}) - f(\mathbf{x}_n) \approx (\nabla f(\mathbf{x}_n))^T \cdot (\mathbf{x}_{n+1} - \mathbf{x}_n) + \frac{(\mathbf{x}_{n+1} - \mathbf{x}_n)^T H_n (\mathbf{x}_{n+1} - \mathbf{x}_n)}{2} \tag{3.46}$$

We minimize the resulting change with

$$0 = (\nabla f(\mathbf{x}_n))^T \cdot (\mathbf{x}_{n+1} - \mathbf{x}_n) + \frac{(\mathbf{x}_{n+1} - \mathbf{x}_n)^T H_n (\mathbf{x}_{n+1} - \mathbf{x}_n)}{2} \tag{3.47}$$

$$0 = (\nabla f(\mathbf{x}_n))^T + \frac{(\mathbf{x}_{n+1} - \mathbf{x}_n)^T H_n}{2} \tag{3.48}$$

we minimize when

$$0 = \nabla f(\mathbf{x}_n) + H_n \left(\mathbf{x}_{n+1} - \mathbf{x}_n \right) \tag{3.49}$$

$$(\mathbf{x}_{n+1} - \mathbf{x}_n) = -H_n^{-1} \cdot \nabla f(\mathbf{x}_n) \tag{3.50}$$

and we get the update rule as

$$\mathbf{x}_{n+1} = \mathbf{x}_n - H_n^{-1} \cdot \nabla f(\mathbf{x}_n). \tag{3.51}$$

This method is named after Sir Isaac Newton, see Figure 3.8.

Fig. 3.8   Sir Isaac Newton (1642 -1726) was an English mathematician, physicist, astronomer, theologian, who is widely recognized as one of the most influential scientists of all time.

3.3.3   *Second and First Order Optimization*

Optimization algorithms that use only the gradient, such as gradient descent, are called first-order optimization algorithms like

$$\mathbf{x}_{n+1} = \mathbf{x}_n - \eta \cdot \nabla f(\mathbf{x}_n).$$

Optimization algorithms that also use the Hessian matrix, such as Newton's method,

$$\mathbf{x}_{n+1} = \mathbf{x}_n - H_n^{-1} \cdot \nabla f(\mathbf{x}_n)$$

are called second-order optimization algorithms [Haykin (2008)]. Newton's method converges quickly asymptotically and does not exhibit the zigzagging behavior that sometimes characterizes the method of steepest descent.

Iteratively updating the approximation and jumping to the minimum of the approximation can reach the critical point much faster than gradient descent. When f($\mathbf{x}$) is a positive definite quadratic function, Newton's method consists of one jump to the minimum of the function directly. However this useful property near a local minimum can be a harmful near a saddle point, a point of a function or surface which is a stationary point but not an extremum. An example of a one-dimensional function with a saddle point is $f(x) = x^3$ with a saddle point at $x_0 = 0$. Surfaces can also have saddle points, which the second derivative test can sometimes be used to identify, see Figure 3.9. Saddle points are common in high dimensional spaces, especially in deep learning. Another problem of the Newton's method is that

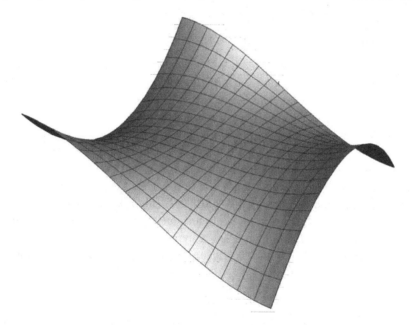

Fig. 3.9 A plot of the function $x^3 - 3 \cdot x \cdot y^2$ is shown, it is a saddle surface called the monkey saddle. The name derives from the observation that a saddle for a monkey would require three depressions, two for the legs and one for the tail.

the Hessian H_n has to be a positive definite matrix for all iteration steps n. A positive definite matrix means, that
$$\mathbf{x}^T \cdot H_n \cdot \mathbf{x} > 0$$
for every non zero vector $\mathbf{x}$. Unfortunately, in general, there is no guarantee that H_n is positive definite at every iteration of the algorithm [Haykin

(2008)]. Also the computational complexity is often a major limitation of Newton's method.

3.4   Dilemmas in Machine Learning

In this section we look into two known dilemmas. One is called the curse of high dimensionality that influences negatively most machine learning algorithms. Often, algorithms that work with low dimensional data will not work with high dimensional data. The other dilemma results from the rounding problem that can lead to wrong results or errors during computation.

3.4.1   *The Curse of Dimensionality*

The curse of dimensionality refers to various phenomena that arise when analyzing and organizing data in high-dimensional spaces. The volume of a hypercube exponentially increases; a hypercube graph in dimension D has 2^D vertices. For a hypercube with an edge of the size 2, the volume in dimension D is given by 2^D. If 100 points cover the one-dimensional unit interval $[0, 1]$ on a real line, considering the corresponding 10-dimensional unit hypercube, 100 points become isolated points in a vast empty space. The volume of a high-dimensional cube approaches its surface with an increase in dimension [Böhm *et al.* (2001)]. In high-dimensional spaces, a partition is only performed in a few dimensions, which touch the boundary of the data space in most dimensions. A hypercube corresponds to a sphere in l_∞ space; the volume v of a Euclidean ball of radius r in D-dimensional l_∞ space can be indicated by

$$v_D^\infty = (2 \cdot r)^D \tag{3.52}$$

Surprisingly the volume decreases for a sphere with fixed radius r in l_1 and l_2 space with the growing dimension. The volume v of a sphere with l_1 norm and with radius r in D-dimensional space is given by

$$v_D^1 = \frac{2^n}{n!} \cdot r^D, \tag{3.53}$$

suppose that r is fixed, then the volume v_D^1 approaches zero as D tends to infinity because

$$\lim_{D \to \infty} \frac{(2 \cdot r)^D}{D!} = 0. \tag{3.54}$$

On the other hand the radius r of a sphere with l_1 norm and with the volume v_n^1 in D-dimensional space is given by

$$r = \left(\frac{v_D^1 \cdot D!}{2^D} \right)^{1/D} = \frac{(v_D^1 \cdot D!)^{1/D}}{2}, \tag{3.55}$$

suppose that v_D^1 is fixed, then the radius r approaches infinity as D tends to infinity because

$$\lim_{D \to \infty} \frac{(v_D^1 \cdot D!)^{1/D}}{2} = \infty. \tag{3.56}$$

The same relation between the volume, the radius and the dimension are as well true for sphere with l_2 norm. Such a sphere with l_2 norm in dimension n is called a D ball, the volume can be indicated by explicit formulas

$$v_{2 \cdot D}^2 = \frac{\pi^D}{D!} \cdot r^{2 \cdot D}, \tag{3.57}$$

and

$$v_{2 \cdot D+1}^2 = \frac{2 \cdot D! \cdot (4 \cdot \pi)^D}{(2 \cdot D + 1)!} \cdot r^{2 \cdot D + 1}.. \tag{3.58}$$

This relation have serious consequences for the ϵ-similarity in popular l_1 and l_2 spaces, in high dimensions the value of ϵ that describes the radius of the sphere is mostly larger than the extension of the data space in most dimensions [Böhm *et al.* (2001)]. Let us consider a range query vector $\mathbf{y}$ from a collection of N vectors,

$$\mathbf{x}_1, \mathbf{x}_2, \mathbf{x}_3, \cdots, \mathbf{x}_N$$

all vectors $\mathbf{x}_i$ that are ϵ-similar according to the distance function d are searched

$$d(\mathbf{x}_i, \mathbf{y}) < \epsilon. \tag{3.59}$$

In high dimensional space the search is sensitive to the value of ϵ. With extreme minimal changes to the value of ϵ either *all* vectors $\mathbf{x}_i$ represent the solution or no vector at all. With the growing dimension of the space it becomes difficult to determine an adequate value for ϵ.

3.4.1.1 *Machine learning*

With the increase of the dimensionality the volume of the space increases exponentially. As a consequence in machine learning an exponential amount of training data with the dimensionality is required. With a fixed linear number of training data points with the dimensionality, the fixed points become isolated in a vast empty space. In the mostly empty space common data organization strategies cannot be implemented efficiently. Machine learning leads to overfitting, since in the vast space the population cannot be represented correctly. Usually we cannot overcome this problem by increasing the size of the sample because with the huge dimensionality the size becomes intractable.

We will discus later possible solutions when we introduce the principle component method for high dimensional data.

3.4.2 *Numerical Computation*

Machine learning algorithms require a high amount of numerical computation. Evaluating a mathematical function on a computer can be difficult when the function involves real numbers, which cannot be represented precisely. We need to represent real numbers with a finite number of bits. Rounding errors can cause algorithms that work in theory to fail in practice. There are two main problems:

- Numbers near zero are rounded to zero. This is called an **underflow**. As a consequence we cannot divide by zero and the algorithm breaks. Another possibility is that a small probability value becomes zero and influences the result.
- Huge numbers due to limited representation can become negative. This is called an **overflow**. As a consequence we cannot compute the negative logarithm and the algorithm breaks.

3.5 **Exercises and Answers**

Nearest Neighbour

The k Nearest Neighbors (kNN) classifier works under the assumption that examples that share similar features will likely have the same class [Mitchell (1997)]. With that, if we represent every example as a feature vector, we can, for instance, compute the euclidean distance between a new example and some known training data to find out what previously seen examples are similar to the new one. We can then use that information to perform classification.

To illustrate this idea let us describe a simple example task. Assuming that 1 means *True* and 0 means *False*, consider the following features and class:

- X_1: "Weight (Kg)"
- X_2: "Height (Cm)"
- *Class*: "NBA (National Basketball Association) Player"

Consider as well that you are given the following training set:

	$\mathbf{x}^{(1)}$	$\mathbf{x}^{(2)}$	$\mathbf{x}^{(3)}$	$\mathbf{x}^{(4)}$	$\mathbf{x}^{(5)}$	$\mathbf{x}^{(6)}$	$\mathbf{x}^{(7)}$	$\mathbf{x}^{(8)}$	$\mathbf{x}^{(9)}$	$\mathbf{x}^{(10)}$
X_1	170	80	90	60	50	70	90	100	110	80
X_2	160	220	200	160	150	190	170	180	178	210
Class	0	1	1	0	0	1	0	0	0	0

Because these data are two-dimensional, we can plot them in figure 3.10 to get a general sense.

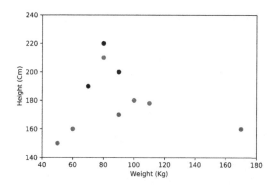

Fig. 3.10 The data collection of people represented in feature space where blue points are NBA players.

If we are given a new test example, represented in figure 3.5 by a dark cross, a nearest neighbor classifier starts by finding the k training examples that are most similar to this new point. In figure 3.11 we are assuming that $k = 1$, so figure 3.5 highlights the closest training example in euclidean distance. Having the set of closest neighbors, the classifier outputs the label of the majority within that set. In this case, the only element in the set is an NBA player, so the classifier outputs 1 as we see in figure 3.5.

The idea of choosing the majoritary label implies that we typically set k to be an odd number. Otherwise there would be ties to deal with.

To consolidate our undestanding of the process, let us focus on the example in figure 3.12. This time we set $k = 3$, so figure 3.5 highlights the

(a) (b)

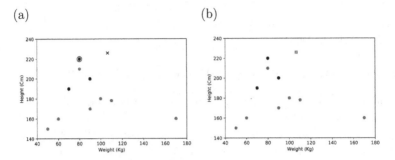

Fig. 3.11 An example of a one nearest neighbor classifier where in a) we find the closest training example and in b) we use the neighbor's label to classify the input.

three closest training examples. This three point set has two NBA players and one regular person. For that reason, the classifier would, yet again, output label 1 as is shown in figure 3.5.

(a) (b)

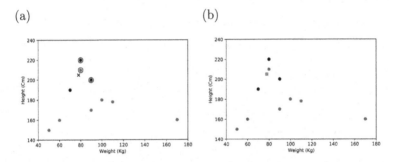

Fig. 3.12 An example of a three nearest neighbors classifier where in a) we find the set of closest training examples and in b) we use the set's majority label to classify the input.

In this case, increasing k did not produce an impact. However, this is not always the case. In fact, this is a key model parameter that needs to be chosen wisely. To see some of the key impacts let us focus on figure 3.13. In general, to build these plots, we have, for each scenario, classified every possible point in the feature space. This allows us to see which regions are labeled 1 and which are labeled 0 for four different scenarios for the parameter k. Let us analyze each one.

Figure 3.5 presents the regions for a one nearest neighbor. In this case, we see a manifestation of overfitting. An outlier example of a regular person in the middle of several NBA players leads the classifier to think that there is something particular about those heights and weights when there is not.

In figures 3.5 and 3.5, we increase k to three and five and we see that the overfitting problem seems to disappear. Both scenarios show a smoother decision boundary between classes and both look like reasonable classification rules. In fact, this pattern of reducing overfitting by increasing k usually appears. However, an increase of this parameter can also create problems.

The last scenario (figure 3.5), shows the classification regions for $k = 7$. In this case, we see that all points are classified as non-NBA players. This happens because there are not enough examples of this class.

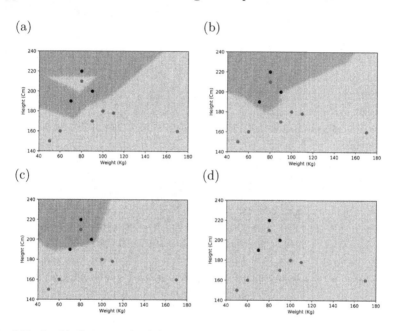

Fig. 3.13 In this figure we plot four scenarios with different values of k. In 3.5 we find a small classification region that appears due to overfitting. In 3.5 and 3.5 we see that increasing the number of neighbors yields a smoother, more general decision landscape. Finally, in 3.5 we see that a bigger increase of the number of neighbors creates problems and all new inputs will be classified as non-NBA players.

From the four described scenarios we can take away that the choice of k is bounded by trade-offs. As usual, to deal with this issue we need to conduct experiments with validation data to make an informed decision.

Unlike most classifiers we look at in this text, kNN does not use parameters and update rules to do learning. In fact one may wonder if there is any learning at all. This type of classifier is called non-parametric and because learning amounts to storing and using a collection of training instances, it is usually refered to as instance-based learning.

The fact that we need to store and use the whole collection of data can become a big drawback of this approach. However, for small data collections it can be very useful for three main reasons. First of all, it is extremely easy to implement and use. Second, learning is immediate. Finally, we can apply it to many kinds of data besides vectors. All we need is a similarity measure between examples to find out the most similar neighbors.

1)

a) Using the same data from the example above, use a k nearest neighbors classifier to classify vector $\mathbf{x} = \begin{bmatrix} 100 & 210 \end{bmatrix}^T$ with $k = 1$, $k = 3$ and $k = 5$.

Solution:

The first step is to measure the $l1$ distance from the input to all labeled data vectors.

	$\mathbf{x}^{(1)}$	$\mathbf{x}^{(2)}$	$\mathbf{x}^{(3)}$	$\mathbf{x}^{(4)}$	$\mathbf{x}^{(5)}$	$\mathbf{x}^{(6)}$	$\mathbf{x}^{(7)}$	$\mathbf{x}^{(8)}$	$\mathbf{x}^{(9)}$	$\mathbf{x}^{(10)}$
X_1	170	80	90	60	50	70	90	100	110	80
X_2	160	220	200	160	150	190	170	180	178	210
Class	0	1	1	0	0	1	0	0	0	0
$\left\|\mathbf{x} - \mathbf{x}^{(i)}\right\|_2$	86.0	22.4	14.1	64.0	78.1	36.1	41.2	30.0	33.5	20.0

For $k = 1$, the classifier outputs the label of the nearest neighbor. In this case, the closest example is $\mathbf{x}^{(3)}$ at a distance of 14.14, so the output class will be 1.

For $k = 3$, we need the three nearest neighbors. For this input the neighbors will be $\mathbf{x}^{(3)}$, $\mathbf{x}^{(10)}$ and $\mathbf{x}^{(2)}$ from nearest to farthest. Out of this group, a majority of two examples have class 1, so this would be the output.

Finally, for $k = 5$, the set of neighbors is $\mathbf{x}^{(3)}$, $\mathbf{x}^{(10)}$, $\mathbf{x}^{(2)}$, $\mathbf{x}^{(8)}$ and $\mathbf{x}^{(9)}$. In this case, we have a majority of three examples with label 0.

---

b) Redo the exercise computing the distance with the $l1$ norm $\|\mathbf{x}\|_1 = \sum_i |x_i|$.

Solution:

Since we are working in two dimensions, it would be easy to plot the point and check the region where it falls in the previously shown region plots. However, we want to use a more general approach. The first step is to measure the euclidean distance from the query vector to all labeled data vectors.

	$\mathbf{x}^{(1)}$	$\mathbf{x}^{(2)}$	$\mathbf{x}^{(3)}$	$\mathbf{x}^{(4)}$	$\mathbf{x}^{(5)}$	$\mathbf{x}^{(6)}$	$\mathbf{x}^{(7)}$	$\mathbf{x}^{(8)}$	$\mathbf{x}^{(9)}$	$\mathbf{x}^{(10)}$
X_1	170	80	90	60	50	70	90	100	110	80
X_2	160	220	200	160	150	190	170	180	178	210
$Class$	0	1	1	0	0	1	0	0	0	0
$\left\|\mathbf{x} - \mathbf{x}^{(i)}\right\|_1$	120	30	20	90	110	50	50	30	42	20

For $k = 1$, the classifier outputs the label of the nearest neighbor. In this case, we have a tie for the closest example between $\mathbf{x}^{(3)}$ and $\mathbf{x}^{(10)}$ at a distance of 20. In practice one can choose randomly and take the class from that example.

For $k = 3$, we need the three nearest neighbors. For this input the neighbors will be $\mathbf{x}^{(3)}$, $\mathbf{x}^{(10)}$ and $\mathbf{x}^{(2)}$ from nearest to farthest. Out of this group, a majority of two examples have class 1, so this would be the output. It was also possible to choose $\mathbf{x}^{(8)}$ instead of $\mathbf{x}^{(2)}$ and in that case the label would be 0.

Finally, for $k = 5$, the set of neighbors is $\mathbf{x}^{(3)}$, $\mathbf{x}^{(10)}$, $\mathbf{x}^{(2)}$, $\mathbf{x}^{(8)}$ and $\mathbf{x}^{(9)}$. In this case, we have a majority of three examples with label 0.

---

c) Again, repeat the exercise computing the distance with the infinity norm $\|\mathbf{x}\|_\infty = max_i |x_i|$.

Solution:

Since we are working in two dimensions, it would be easy to plot the point and check the region where it falls in the previously shown region plots. However, we want to use a more general approach. The first step is to measure the euclidean distance from the query vector to all labeled data vectors.

	$x^{(1)}$	$x^{(2)}$	$x^{(3)}$	$x^{(4)}$	$x^{(5)}$	$x^{(6)}$	$x^{(7)}$	$x^{(8)}$	$x^{(9)}$	$x^{(10)}$
X_1	170	80	90	60	50	70	90	100	110	80
X_2	160	220	200	160	150	190	170	180	178	210
Class	0	1	1	0	0	1	0	0	0	0
$\|x - x^{(i)}\|_\infty$	70	20	10	50	60	30	40	30	32	20

For $k = 1$, the classifier outputs the label of the nearest neighbor. In this case, the closest example is $x^{(3)}$ at a distance of 10, so the output class will be 1.

For $k = 3$, we need the three nearest neighbors. For this input the neighbors will be $x^{(3)}$, $x^{(10)}$ and $x^{(2)}$ from nearest to farthest. Out of this group, a majority of two examples have class 1, so this would be the output.

Finally, for $k = 5$, the set of neighbors is $x^{(3)}$, $x^{(10)}$, $x^{(2)}$, $x^{(6)}$ and $x^{(8)}$. In this case, we have a majority of three examples with label 1.

---

2)

Assuming that 1 means *True* and 0 means *False*, consider the following features and class:

- X_1: "Fast processing"
- X_2: "Decent Battery"
- X_3: "Good Camera"
- X_4: "Good Look and Feel"
- X_5: "Easiness of Use"
- *Class*: "iPhone"

You are given the following training set:

	$x^{(1)}$	$x^{(2)}$	$x^{(3)}$	$x^{(4)}$	$x^{(5)}$	$x^{(6)}$	$x^{(7)}$
X_1	1	1	0	0	1	0	0
X_2	1	1	1	0	0	0	0
X_3	0	1	1	0	1	1	0
X_4	1	0	1	1	1	0	0
X_5	0	0	0	1	1	0	1
Class	1	0	0	0	1	1	1

Use a k nearest neighbors classifier based on the Hamming distance to classify vector $\begin{bmatrix} 1 & 1 & 1 & 1 & 1 \end{bmatrix}^T$ with $k = 1$ and $k = 3$.

Solution:

When working with binary data it is common to use different, binary specific distance measures. In this example we will use the Hamming distance which counts the number of different bits between the two vectors. This is a good example to remind us that the nearest neighbor classifier is not tied to the euclidean distance measure.

Having chosen the Hamming distance, we need to compute it for all training examples.

	$\mathbf{x}^{(1)}$	$\mathbf{x}^{(2)}$	$\mathbf{x}^{(3)}$	$\mathbf{x}^{(4)}$	$\mathbf{x}^{(5)}$	$\mathbf{x}^{(6)}$	$\mathbf{x}^{(7)}$
X_1	1	1	0	0	1	0	0
X_2	1	1	1	0	0	0	0
X_3	0	1	1	0	1	1	0
X_4	1	0	1	1	1	0	0
X_5	0	0	0	1	1	0	1
$Class$	1	0	0	0	1	1	1
$Hamming\left(\mathbf{x}, \mathbf{x}^{(i)}\right)$	2	3	3	4	1	4	4

For $k = 1$, the classifier outputs the label of the nearest neighbor. In this case, the closest example is $\mathbf{x}^{(5)}$ at a distance of 1, so the output class will be 1.

For $k = 3$, we need the three nearest neighbors. For this input these neighbors will be $\mathbf{x}^{(5)}$, $\mathbf{x}^{(1)}$ and $\mathbf{x}^{(2)}$ (it could also be $\mathbf{x}^{(3)}$) from nearest to farthest. Out of this group, a majority of two examples have class 1, so this would be the output.

---

3)

Consider the following data where a few preprocessed restaurant reviews (without stopwords) are classified as positive (1) or negative (0).

	Sentence	*Class*
	{"*Great*", "*place*", "*go*", "*with*", "*friends*"}	1
	{"*Food*", "*amazing*"}	1
	{"*What*", "*terrible*", "*experience*", "*no*", "*words*"}	0
	{"*Waiting*", "*time*", "*too*", "*long*"}	0
	{"*Terrible*", "*place*", "*for*", "*family*", "*dinner*"}	0

Consider as well the Jaccard similarity between two sets:

$$Jaccard_{sim}(A, B) = \frac{|A \cap B|}{|A \cup B|}$$

Using the similarity measure, compute the k nearest neighbor output for input $\{"Terrible", "food", "overall", "lousy", "dinner"\}$ using $k = 1$ and $k = 3$.

Solution:

Much like before we start by computing the similarity between the input and the training data.

	Sentence	Class	Jaccard
$x^{(1)}$	$\{"Great", "place", "go", "with", "friends"\}$	1	$\frac{0}{10} = 0$
$x^{(2)}$	$\{"Food", "amazing"\}$	1	$\frac{1}{6}$
$x^{(3)}$	$\{"What", "terrible", "experience", "no", "words"\}$	0	$\frac{1}{9}$
$x^{(4)}$	$\{"Waiting", "time", "too", "long"\}$	0	$\frac{0}{9} = 0$
$x^{(5)}$	$\{"Terrible", "place", "for", "family", "dinner"\}$	0	$\frac{2}{8} = \frac{1}{4}$

For $k = 1$, we need to find the closest neighbor. Working with a similarity measure instead of a distance measure, the closest example will be the one with highest similarity. In this case $x^{(5)}$ is most similar, so the classifier outputs its label of 0.

For $k = 3$, we need the three nearest neighbors. For this query set these neighbors will be $x^{(5)}$, $x^{(2)}$ and $x^{(3)}$. Out of this group, a majority of two examples have class 0, so this would be the output.

Alternatively, we could have followed the same reasoning as in previous exercises by converting the similarity measure to a distance through:

$$Jaccard_{dist}(A, B) = 1 - Jaccard_{sim}(A, B)$$

Chapter 4

Linear and Nonlinear Regression

Fig. 4.1 The idea of linear regression is a central building block of a perceptron. Using linear and non linear regression we introduce the Bayesian regression. The normal distribution leads to ridge (l_2) regularization and the Laplace distribution to LASSO (l_1) regularization.

4.1   Linear Regression

4.1.1   *Regression of a Line*

The Conversion of a temperature from Celsius to Fahrenheit can be represented by a linear equation

$$Fahrenheit = 32 + 1.8 \cdot Celsius$$

with intercept $b = 32$ and slope $m = 1.8$. In regression of a line

$$y = w_0 + w_1 \cdot y = b + m \cdot x \qquad (4.1)$$

the parameters w_0 and w_1 are selected to find a best fit to a given data set, with w_0 being the intercept term and w_1 being the slope of the line (see Figure 4.2), x is the explanatory variable (or independent variable) and y the response. In case the line goes through the origin $w_0 = 0$.

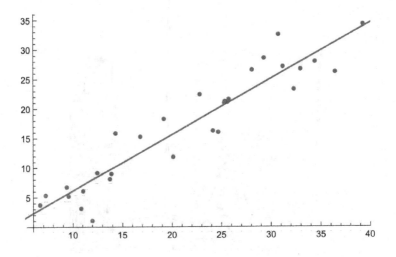

Fig. 4.2   A line $y = w_0 + w_1 \cdot x = b + m \cdot x$ is selected to find a best fit to a given data set, with w_0 being the intercept term and w_1 being the slope of the line.

4.1.2   *Multiple Linear Regression*

For more than one explanatory variable, the process is called multiple linear regression [Rao (1973)] and it can be written as a linear combination

$$y = y(\mathbf{x}, \mathbf{w}) = w_0 + \sum_{j=1}^{D} w_j \cdot x_j = w_0 + \langle \mathbf{w} | \mathbf{x} \rangle \qquad (4.2)$$

that represents an hyperplane (see Figure 4.3) parameterized by the w_j values.

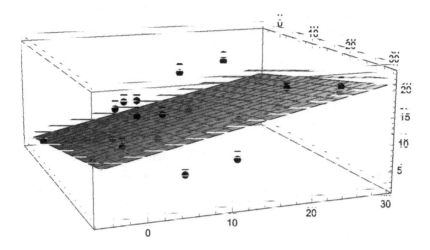

Fig. 4.3 A plane $y = y(\mathbf{x}, \mathbf{w}) = w_0 + \sum_{j=1}^{2} w_j \cdot x_j$ is selected to find a best fit to a given data set.

The intercept term w_0 is often called the bias parameter of the affine transformation because the output y is biased toward being w_0 in the absence of any input. This term is different from the idea of statistical bias to which we will look into later in another context.

In perceptron we had a similar linear combination. Yet, what we now are calling y was called *net*

$$net = bias + \sum_{j=1}^{D} w_j \cdot x_j = w_0 + \sum_{j=1}^{D} w_j \cdot x_j$$

and y was the activation of *net* ($y = sgn(net)$). So, we can look at a multiple regression as an artificial neuron without any activation function (or one where the activation function is the identity).

Finally, to simplify notation, just like in perceptron, we can assume a fixed value $x_0 = 1$ to write compactly

$$y = y(\mathbf{x}, \mathbf{w}) = \sum_{j=0}^{D} w_j \cdot x_j = \langle \mathbf{w} | \mathbf{x} \rangle = \mathbf{w}^T \cdot \mathbf{x}$$

4.1.3 *Design Matrix*

The data set to which one fits a regression is called the training set (or the sample). A set like this is composed by N observations with the corresponding target values. We can represent the sample with a matrix where each observation is placed on a row

$$X = (\mathbf{x}_1, \mathbf{x}_2, \cdots, \mathbf{x}_k, \cdots, \mathbf{x}_N)^T$$

and a vector where each target is placed on a row as well

$$\mathbf{t} = (t_1, t_2, \cdots, t_k, \cdots, t_N)^T.$$

If we take each row in the observations matrix and prepend a fixed $x_0 = 1$, we will get a matrix where where $x_{j,0} = 1$ for $j = 1, \cdots, N$. This augmented matrix is called the design matrix and it can be written as

$$X = \begin{pmatrix} \mathbf{x}_1^T \\ \vdots \\ \mathbf{x}_k^T \\ \vdots \\ \mathbf{x}_N^T \end{pmatrix} = \begin{pmatrix} x_{1,0} & x_{1,1} & x_{1,2} & \cdots & x_{1,D} \\ x_{2,0} & x_{2,1} & x_{2,2} & \cdots & x_{2,D} \\ \vdots & \vdots & \ddots & \vdots \\ x_{N,0} & x_{N,1} & x_{N,2} & \cdots & x_{N,D} \end{pmatrix}. \tag{4.3}$$

With this representation, it is simple to say that the multiple regression would have weights that map inputs to outputs in a linear way

$$\begin{pmatrix} y_1 \\ \vdots \\ y_k \\ \vdots \\ y_N \end{pmatrix} = \begin{pmatrix} 1 & x_{1,1} & x_{1,2} & \cdots & x_{1,D} \\ 1 & x_{2,1} & x_{2,2} & \cdots & x_{2,D} \\ \vdots & \vdots & \ddots & \vdots \\ 1 & x_{N,1} & x_{N,2} & \cdots & x_{N,D} \end{pmatrix} \cdot \begin{pmatrix} w_0 \\ w_1 \\ \vdots \\ w_j \\ \vdots \\ w_D \end{pmatrix}. \tag{4.4}$$

This problem can be compactly written in matrix notation

$$\mathbf{y} = X \cdot \mathbf{w} = \left(\mathbf{w}^T \cdot X^T\right)^T \tag{4.5}$$

4.1.4 *Squared-Error*

Although the weights are supposed to map inputs to outputs, often, a perfect linear mapping is not possible. So, we can measure how well a vector of weights makes our model perform by analyzing how the predicted values y_k differ from the sample's target values t_k. A typical way to do this is to compute the squared error (which is also called the squared loss)

$$E(\mathbf{w}) = \sum_{k=1}^{N} (y(\mathbf{x}_k, \mathbf{w}) - t_k)^2 = \|\mathbf{t} - \mathbf{y}\|^2 = \left\| \begin{pmatrix} t_1 \\ \vdots \\ t_k \\ \vdots \\ t_N \end{pmatrix} - \begin{pmatrix} y_1 \\ \vdots \\ y_k \\ \vdots \\ y_N \end{pmatrix} \right\|^2 . \quad (4.6)$$

Notice that given that the sample observations and targets are fixed, the error value depends on the choice of parameters w_j represented by the vector $\mathbf{w}$.

4.1.5 Closed-Form Solution

Much like in perceptron, the goal is to learn the correct model weights. In that case, we had a learning rule to find them. In this case, having defined an error measure, we can look for the weight vector that minimizes it. We can get a closed-form solution for $\mathbf{w}$ by looking for the gradient's zeros

$$\nabla E(\mathbf{w}) = 0 \quad (4.7)$$

where the gradient operator is

$$\nabla = \left[\frac{\partial}{\partial w_1}, \frac{\partial}{\partial w_2}, \cdots, \frac{\partial}{\partial w_D} \right]^T$$

$$\nabla E(\mathbf{w}) = \left[\frac{\partial E}{\partial w_1}, \frac{\partial E}{\partial w_2}, \cdots, \frac{\partial E}{\partial w_D} \right]^T .$$

With that in mind, we will write the problem in an easier way. The sum-of-squares error function over all N training points

$$E(\mathbf{w}) = \sum_{k=1}^{N} \left(t_k - \mathbf{w}^T \cdot \mathbf{x}_k \right)^2 = \sum_{k=1}^{N} \left(t_k - \mathbf{x}_k^T \cdot \mathbf{w} \right)^2 \quad (4.8)$$

can be represented in vector and matrix notation by

$$E(\mathbf{w}) = \|\mathbf{t} - X \cdot \mathbf{w}\|^2 = (\mathbf{t} - X \cdot \mathbf{w})^T (\mathbf{t} - X \cdot \mathbf{w}) . \quad (4.9)$$

Now, we can take its gradient and set it to zero

$$\nabla E(\mathbf{w}) = \nabla \left((\mathbf{t} - X \cdot \mathbf{w})^T \cdot (\mathbf{t} - X \cdot \mathbf{w}) \right) = 0 \quad (4.10)$$

and expand the equation to

$$\nabla \left(\mathbf{t}^T \cdot \mathbf{t} - 2 \cdot \mathbf{t}^T \cdot X \cdot \mathbf{w} + \mathbf{w}^T \cdot X^T \cdot X \cdot \mathbf{w} \right) = 0 \qquad (4.11)$$

using the gradient rule

$$\nabla(a \cdot f(\mathbf{w}) + b \cdot g(\mathbf{w})) = a \cdot \nabla f(\mathbf{w}) + b \cdot \nabla g(\mathbf{w}), \quad a, b \in \mathbb{R}$$

we expand

$$\nabla \left(\mathbf{t}^T \cdot \mathbf{t} \right) - 2 \cdot \nabla \left(\mathbf{t}^T \cdot X \cdot \mathbf{w} \right) + \nabla \left(\mathbf{w}^T \cdot X^T \cdot X \cdot \mathbf{w} \right) = 0. \qquad (4.12)$$

Using the gradient rules with $A = X^T \cdot X$ (A is symmetric)

$$\nabla \left((\mathbf{w}^T \cdot A \cdot \mathbf{w}) = 2 \cdot A \cdot \mathbf{w} \right.$$

and

$$\nabla_w \left(\mathbf{t}^T \mathbf{w} \right) = \mathbf{t}$$

we simplify to

$$-2 \cdot X^T \cdot \mathbf{t} + 2 \cdot X^T \cdot X \cdot \mathbf{w} = 0$$

$$X^T \cdot \mathbf{t} - X^T \cdot X \cdot \mathbf{w} = 0$$

$$X^T \cdot \mathbf{t} = X^T \cdot X \cdot \mathbf{w} \qquad (4.13)$$

and we get the closed-form solution for $\mathbf{w}$

$$\left(X^T \cdot X \right)^{-1} \cdot X^T \cdot \mathbf{t} = \mathbf{w}. \qquad (4.14)$$

4.1.6 *Example*

Let us go through an example where we employ our closed-form solution. In this example, we are given a training set that consists of 4 observations

$$\mathbf{x}_1 = \begin{pmatrix} 1 \\ 1 \end{pmatrix}, \mathbf{x}_2 = \begin{pmatrix} 2 \\ 1 \end{pmatrix}, \mathbf{x}_3 = \begin{pmatrix} 1 \\ 3 \end{pmatrix}, \mathbf{x}_4 = \begin{pmatrix} 3 \\ 3 \end{pmatrix},$$

with the corresponding targets

$$t_1 = 1.4, t_2 = 0.5, t_3 = 2, t_4 = 2.5.$$

We can represent our sample by a design matrix with $x_{j,0} = 1$ as

$$X = \begin{pmatrix} 1 & 1 & 1 \\ 1 & 2 & 1 \\ 1 & 1 & 3 \\ 1 & 3 & 3 \end{pmatrix}$$

and a target vector

$$\mathbf{t} = \begin{pmatrix} 1.4 \\ 0.5 \\ 2 \\ 2.5 \end{pmatrix}.$$

With that, we can employ our expression for the weights

$$\left(\begin{pmatrix} 1 & 1 & 1 & 1 \\ 1 & 2 & 1 & 3 \\ 1 & 1 & 3 & 3 \end{pmatrix} \cdot \begin{pmatrix} 1 & 1 & 1 \\ 1 & 2 & 1 \\ 1 & 1 & 3 \\ 1 & 3 & 3 \end{pmatrix} \right)^{-1} \cdot \begin{pmatrix} 1 & 1 & 1 & 1 \\ 1 & 2 & 1 & 3 \\ 1 & 1 & 3 & 3 \end{pmatrix} \cdot \begin{pmatrix} 1.4 \\ 0.5 \\ 2 \\ 2.5 \end{pmatrix} = \mathbf{w}$$

to get the final solution

$$\begin{pmatrix} 0.275 \\ 0.02 \\ 0.645 \end{pmatrix} = \mathbf{w},$$

see Figure 4.4.

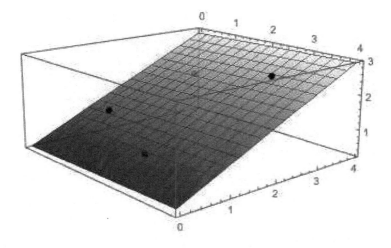

Fig. 4.4 A plane $y = y(\mathbf{w}) = 0.275 + 0.02 \cdot x_1 + 0.645 \cdot x_2$ is selected to find a best fit to a given data set.

Another example lets us confirm an intuition we developed at the beginning of the chapter. As we have seen, the kind of regression we are studying is nothing more than a perceptron without a nonlinear activation function.

For the perceptron example of the first chapter with the design matrix

$$X = \begin{pmatrix} 1 & 0 & 0 \\ 1 & 0 & 2 \\ 1 & 1 & 1 \\ 1 & 1 & -1 \end{pmatrix}$$

and the corresponding target of two classes

$$t_1 = -1, t_2 = 1, t_3 = 1, t_4 = -1.$$

the regression solution is

$$\mathbf{w} = \begin{pmatrix} -1 \\ 1 \\ 1 \end{pmatrix}.$$

With that, in mind look at Figure 4.5, where both the regression and the perceptron results are shown. It seems that the linear regression is the basic building block of a perceptron.

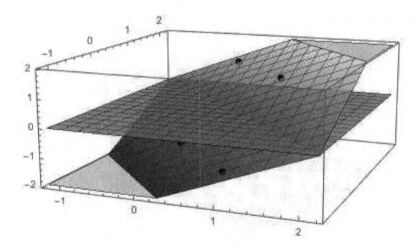

Fig. 4.5 A plane $y = y(\mathbf{w}) = -1 + x_1 + x_2$ is selected to find a best fit to a given data set of two classes 1 and -1. They are separated by the line $-1 + x_1 + x_2 = 0$.

4.1.7 *Moore-Penrose Matrix*

The matrix

$$X^\dagger = \left(X^T \cdot X \right)^{-1} \cdot X^T \tag{4.15}$$

(a)　　　　　　　　　　　(b)

Fig. 4.6　(a) Roger Penrose and (b) Eliakim Hastings Moore.

is known as the pseudo-inverse of X or as the Moore-Penrose matrix named after Roger Penrose and Eliakim Hastings Moore, see Figure 4.6.

With this new matrix defined, we can say that our closed-form solution is given by

$$X^\dagger \cdot \mathbf{t} = \mathbf{w}. \tag{4.16}$$

When some features are linear combinations of the others, or when the number of features D is larger than the number N of examples $N < D$, then the matrix $X^T \cdot X$ is not invertible, it is said to be singular or degenerate. So, our closed-form solution will not work.

Using a technique called SVD (more on that later) we can always find this Moore-Penrose pseudoinverse $X^\dagger$.

Let us go through an example. For the design matrix

$$X = \begin{pmatrix} 1 & 1 & 1 \\ 1 & 2 & 2 \\ 1 & 1 & 3 \\ 1 & 3 & 3 \end{pmatrix}$$

the matrix

$$X^T \cdot X = \begin{pmatrix} 4 & 10 & 10 \\ 10 & 30 & 30 \\ 10 & 30 & 30 \end{pmatrix}$$

is singular. However any matrix X can be factorized using SVD as

$$X = U \cdot S \cdot V^T \tag{4.17}$$

where U is an orthogonal matrix with orthonormal eigenvectors from the matrix $X \cdot X^T$ (more about eigenvectors in the chapter 15), V is an orthogonal matrix with orthonormal eigenvectors from $X^T \cdot X$ and S is a diagonal matrix with r elements equal to the root of the positive eigenvalues of $X \cdot X^T$ or $X^T \cdot X$. In our example,

$$U = \begin{pmatrix} 0.2019 & -0.8119 & 0.4082 & 0.3652 \\ 0.3748 & -0.3995 & -0.8165 & -0.1826 \\ 0.7204 & 0.4255 & 0. & 0.5477 \\ 0.5476 & 0.013 & 0.4082 & -0.7303 \end{pmatrix},$$

$$V = \begin{pmatrix} 0.2317 & -0.9728 & 0 \\ 0.6877 & 0.1639 & -0.7071 \\ 0.6879 & 0.1639 & 0.7071 \end{pmatrix},$$

$$S = \begin{pmatrix} 7.9605 & 0 & 0 \\ 0 & 0.7944 & 0 \\ 0 & 0 & 0 \\ 0 & 0 & 0 \end{pmatrix},$$

and the Pseudoinverse is defined as

$$X^\dagger = V \cdot S^\dagger U^T \tag{4.18}$$

where $S^\dagger$ is formed from S by taking the reciprocal of all the non-zero elements, leaving all the zeros alone and making the matrix the right shape: if S is an $m \times n$ matrix, then $S^\dagger$ must be an $n \times m$ matrix,

$$S^\dagger = \begin{pmatrix} 0.12562 & 0 & 0 & 0 \\ 0 & 1.2587 & 0 & 0 \\ 0 & 0 & 0 & 0 \end{pmatrix},$$

and we get

$$X^\dagger = \begin{pmatrix} 1 & 0.5 & -0.5 & 0 \\ -0.15 & -0.05 & 0.15 & 0.05 \\ -0.15 & -0.05 & 0.15 & 0.05 \end{pmatrix},$$

and

$$\mathbf{w} = X^\dagger \cdot \mathbf{t} = \begin{pmatrix} 0.65 \\ 0.19 \\ 0.19 \end{pmatrix}.$$

4.2 Linear Basis Function Models

The linear basis function model is the same as linear regression with nonlinear features [Seber and Wild (1989)]. Concretely, it is a linear combination of fixed nonlinear functions of the inputs $\phi_j(\mathbf{x})$

$$y(\mathbf{x}, \mathbf{w}) = w_0 + \sum_{j=1}^{M-1} w_j \cdot \phi_j(\mathbf{x}). \tag{4.19}$$

As before, to write things in a compact manner, we can define an extra function $\phi_0(x) = 1$ and, thus, write

$$y(\mathbf{x}, \mathbf{w}) = \sum_{j=0}^{M-1} w_j \cdot \phi_j(\mathbf{x}) = \langle \mathbf{w} | \Phi(\mathbf{x}) \rangle = \mathbf{w}^T \Phi(\mathbf{x}).$$

One should note that D and $M-1$ do not need to agree. For example, if we use as basis functions the first $M-1 = 9$ powers of a $D = 1$ dimensional x, writing

$$\phi_j(x) = x^j$$

we get

$$y(x, \mathbf{w}) = w_0 + \sum_{j=1}^{9} w_j \cdot x^j = \sum_{j=0}^{9} \phi_j(x)$$

and we have to determine $M = 10$ parameters. With the notation

$$\Phi_{k,j} = \phi_j(\mathbf{x}_k) \tag{4.20}$$

we get the design matrix Φ and the mapping

$$\begin{pmatrix} y_1 \\ \vdots \\ y_k \\ \vdots \\ y_N \end{pmatrix} = \begin{pmatrix} 1 & \phi_{1,1} & \phi_{1,2} & \cdots & \phi_{1,M-1} \\ 1 & \phi_{2,1} & \phi_{2,2} & \cdots & \phi_{2,M-1} \\ \vdots & \vdots & & \ddots & \vdots \\ 1 & \phi_{N,1} & \phi_{N,2} & \cdots & \phi_{N,M-1} \end{pmatrix} \cdot \begin{pmatrix} w_0 \\ w_1 \\ \vdots \\ w_j \\ \vdots \\ w_{M-1} \end{pmatrix} \tag{4.21}$$

in which M parameters have to be determined. The dimension $M - 1$ is dependent on the number of the basis functions and may be different from the dimension D of $\mathbf{x}$. The $\Phi^\dagger$ is Moore-Penrose or the pseudo-inverse matrix of Φ and is derived as before with

$$\Phi^\dagger = \left(\Phi^T \cdot \Phi \right)^{-1} \cdot \Phi^T. \tag{4.22}$$

4.2.1 *Example Logarithmic Curve*

Let us go through an example with a training set consisting of 5 observations with $D = 1$

$$\mathbf{x}_1 = \begin{pmatrix} 3 \end{pmatrix}, \mathbf{x}_2 = \begin{pmatrix} 4 \end{pmatrix}, \mathbf{x}_3 = \begin{pmatrix} 6 \end{pmatrix}, \mathbf{x}_4 = \begin{pmatrix} 10 \end{pmatrix}, \mathbf{x}_5 = \begin{pmatrix} 12 \end{pmatrix},$$

with targets

$$t_1 = 1.5, t_2 = 9.3, t_3 = 23.4, t_4 = 45.8, t_5 = 60.1.$$

Using as a basis function

$$\phi_1(x) = \log(x)$$

we will preform a logarithmic curve fitting

$$y(x, \mathbf{w}) = w_0 + w_1 \cdot \log(x).$$

To find the weights, we start by representing the design matrix Φ as

$$\Phi = \begin{pmatrix} 1 & 1.09861 \\ 1 & 1.38629 \\ 1 & 1.79176 \\ 1 & 2.30259 \\ 1 & 2.48491 \end{pmatrix}$$

with pseudo-inverse

$$\Phi^\dagger = \begin{pmatrix} 1.1355 & 0.758687 & 0.227601 & -0.441489 & -0.680298 \\ -0.516043 & -0.308185 & -0.0152252 & 0.35386 & 0.485593 \end{pmatrix}$$

and the closed-form solution is

$$\mathbf{w} = \Phi^\dagger \cdot \mathbf{t}$$

representing the logarithmic curve

$$y(x, \mathbf{w}) = -47.0212 + 41.3945 \cdot \log(x).$$

4.2.2 *Example Polynomial Regression*

To consolidate the understanding of the process, let us go through another example with a different basis function. In this case, the sample consists of 5 observations with $D = 1$

$$\mathbf{x}_1 = \begin{pmatrix} 0.8 \end{pmatrix}, \mathbf{x}_2 = \begin{pmatrix} 1 \end{pmatrix}, \mathbf{x}_3 = \begin{pmatrix} 1.2 \end{pmatrix}, \mathbf{x}_4 = \begin{pmatrix} 1.4 \end{pmatrix}, \mathbf{x}_5 = \begin{pmatrix} 1.6 \end{pmatrix},$$

with targets

$$t_1 = 24, t_2 = 20, t_3 = 10, t_4 = 13, t_5 = 12.$$

Using as basis functions the first $M = 4$ powers of x

$$\phi_j(x) = x^j$$

we get a polynomial regression

$$y(x, \mathbf{w}) = \sum_{j=0}^{3} w_j \cdot \phi_j(x) = w_0 + w_1 \cdot x + w_2 \cdot x^2 + w_3 \cdot x^3.$$

Again, to find the weights, we represent the sample by the design matrix

$$\Phi = \begin{pmatrix} 1 & 0.8 & 0.64 & 0.512 \\ 1 & 1 & 1 & 1 \\ 1 & 1.2 & 1.44 & 1.728 \\ 1 & 1.4 & 1.96 & 2.744 \\ 1 & 1.6 & 2.56 & 4.096 \end{pmatrix}$$

where the pseudo-inverse is given by

$$\Phi^\dagger = \begin{pmatrix} 22.5571 & -34.2286 & -4.65714 & 29.7714 & -12.4429 \\ -53.1548 & 90.9524 & 8.57143 & -82.381 & 36.0119 \\ 41.0714 & -76.7857 & -3.57143 & 73.2143 & -33.9286 \\ -10.4167 & 20.8333 & 0 & -20.8333 & 10.4167 \end{pmatrix}$$

and the closed-form solution is

$$\mathbf{w} = \Phi^\dagger \cdot \mathbf{t}$$

representing the polynomial regression

$$y(x, \mathbf{w}) = 47.9429 - 9.7619 \cdot x - 41.0714 \cdot x^2 + 20.8333 \cdot x^3,$$

see Figure 4.7.

4.3 Model selection

For two polynomials of different degrees, the polynomial of higher degree has greater expressive power as it can represent polynomials of a lower degree. Consider 11 points from the interval -5 to 5 in steps of one generated using the polynomial of degree 3, $1 + x + x^2 + x^3$ (with $D = 1$ and $M = 4$). These data points can be correctly fitted by a polynomial of degree 3, $M = 4$ and by a polynomial of degree 9, $M = 10$ (see Figure 4.8 (a)). With that in mind, it would be reasonable to assume that, if we do not know the generator polynomial and we want to fit a few points it would be

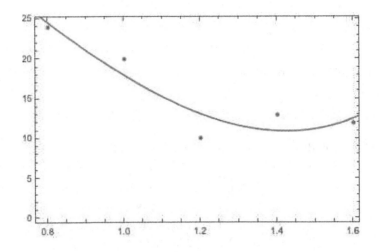

Fig. 4.7   The polynomial $y(x, \mathbf{w}) = 47.9429 - 9.7619 \cdot x - 41.0714 \cdot x^2 + 20.8333 \cdot x^3$ is selected to find a best fit to a given data set.

preferable to use a polynomial that has as much expressive power as possible. However, this apparently harmless assumption can bring tremendous problems if we add some noise to the generated points.

By adding random noise from the interval $[-0, 5, 0.5]$ to the points x_k and t_k, the information about the generating polynomial $1 + x + x^2 + x^3$ is blurred. The regression polynomial of degree 9, $M = 10$ correctly represents the interpolated point; however, the shape of the polynomial is different from the shape of the polynomial that truly generated the data (see Figure 4.8 (b)). So, if we would try to predict the outputs for other values in the domain with this model we would fail (sometimes terribly). This is an example of overfitting. The regression is very good at representing the sample, but not so good if we look at the whole population.

Using a simpler model of degree 3, $M = 4$, we can recover the shape information of the generator polynomial even if all points are not correctly interpolated (see Figure 4.8 (c)). So, we can see that choosing the right complexity for the polynomial is important to overcome overfitting.

Another solution to go around this problem is to use more data. By increasing the sample size of the noisy points to 1000, generated by adding Gaussian random noise having a standard deviation $\sigma = 20$, the regression polynomial of degree 9, $M = 10$ fits the shape of the generated polynomial (see Figure 4.8 (d)).

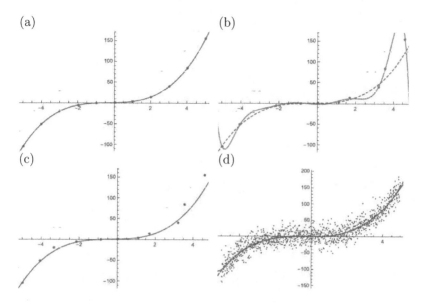

Fig. 4.8 (a) We generated 11 points from the interval -5 to 5 in a step of one using a polynomial of degree 3, $1 + x + x^2 + x^3$ (with $D = 1$ and $M = 4$). The data can be correctly fitted by the regression polynomial of degree 3, $M = 4$ and polynomial of degree 9, $M = 10$. (b) By adding random noise from the interval $[-0, 5, 0.5]$ to points x_k and t_k, the information about the generating polynomial $1 + x + x^2 + x^3$ is blurred. The regression polynomial of degree 9, $M = 10$, correctly represents the interpolated point; however, the shape of the polynomial is different from the shape of the generated polynomial. (c) Using a simpler regression model of degree 3, $M = 4$, we can recover the shape information of the generated polynomial even if not all points are correctly interpolated. (d) By increasing the sample size of the noisy points to 1000, generated by adding Gaussian random noise having standard deviation $\sigma = 20$, the regression polynomial of degree 9, $M = 10$ fits the shape of the generated polynomial.

We can reinforce the developed intuitions by looking at another example. This time, we generated 13 points from the interval -0.1 to 1.1 in steps of 0.1 using $\sin(2 \cdot \pi \cdot x)$. The data cannot be fitted by a polynomial of degree 3, $M = 4$, without errors since the model is too simple. However, the data can be fitted without an error by a polynomial of degree 9, $M = 10$ (see Figure 4.9 (a), (b)). By adding random noise from the interval $[-0, 5, 0.5]$ to points x_k and t_k the shape of the generated regression polynomial of degree 9, $M = 10$ overfits (see Figure 4.9 (c)). By increasing the sample of the noisy points to 2200, generated by Gaussian random noise having standard deviation $\sigma = 0.2$, the regression polynomial of degree 9, $M = 10$ fits the shape of the generated periodic function (see Figure 4.8 (d)).

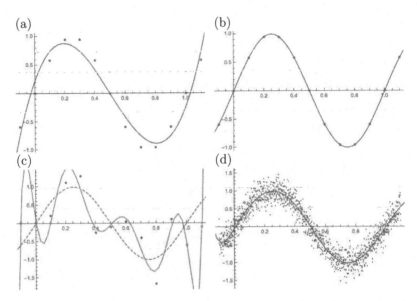

Fig. 4.9 (a) We generated 13 points from the interval -0.1 to 1.1 in steps of 0.1 using $\sin(2 \cdot \pi \cdot x)$. The data cannot be fitted by a polynomial of degree 3, $M = 4$, without errors since the model is too simple. (b) The data can be fitted without an error by a polynomial of degree 9, $M = 10$. (c) By adding random noise from the interval $[-0, 5, 0.5]$ to points x_k and t_k the shape of the generated regression polynomial of degree 9, $M = 10$ overfits. (d) By increasing the sample of the noisy points to 2200, generated by Gaussian random noise having standard deviation $\sigma = 0.2$, the regression polynomial of degree 9, $M = 10$ fits the shape of the generated periodic function.

With many features, the prediction function becomes very expressive, which can lead to overfitting if the sample is small. The best solution to this problem is to increase the size of the sample. If this is not possible, one can choose a simpler model. However, a model can be too simple and generate too many errors. An alternative idea is to constrain the expressive model that is trained on a small sample by some prior information about the population from which the sample is taken in relation to the model. This idea leads to Bayesian regression.

4.4 Bayesian Regression

In the Bayesian view, we think of the observed data D as fixed outputs of a regression model that is described by a weight vector $\mathbf{w}$. In this view, the data is fixed as it was indeed observed, and we have uncertainty about which weights parameterize the model that generated the data.

Before seeing any data, the uncertainty about which weights parameterize the model are described by the prior distribution over weights $p(\mathbf{w})$.

For every possible vector of weights, we can measure how likely the observed data is through the likelihood function $p(D|\mathbf{w})$ [Mitchell (1997)], [Bishop (2006)], [Robert (2007)].

After accounting for the observed data, the new uncertainty about the weights is expressed through the posterior distribution

$$p(\mathbf{w}|D) = \frac{p(D|\mathbf{w}) \cdot p(\mathbf{w})}{p(D)}. \qquad (4.23)$$

The prior information $p(\mathbf{w})$ constraints the model. It gives some information about the distribution of its parameters before seeing any data. $p(D)$ is a normalization constant which ensures that $p(\mathbf{w}|D)$ is a valid probability value. Given the likelihood we can state that *posterior* is related in a linear manner to *likelihood × prior*,

$$posterior \propto likelihood \times prior \qquad (4.24)$$

where all terms are viewed as a function of $\mathbf{w}$.

4.4.1 *Maximizing the Likelihood or the Posterior*

One way to estimate the best parameter vector is to choose $\mathbf{w}$ such that it maximizez the likelihood (ML). As we will see in a bit, this is basically what we did before to find a closed-form solution. So, in this setting we would choose

$$\mathbf{w}_{ML} = \arg\max_{\mathbf{w}} p(D|\mathbf{w}) \qquad (4.25)$$

and since log is monotonic increasing function this would be the same as choosing

$$\mathbf{w}_{ML} = \arg\max_{\mathbf{w}} \log(p(D|\mathbf{w})) \qquad (4.26)$$

Another approach is to choose the weights that maximize the posterior (MAP)

$$\mathbf{w}_{MAP} = \arg\max_{\mathbf{w}} \log(p(\mathbf{w}|D)), \qquad (4.27)$$

thus allowing prior information through $p(\mathbf{w})$ to constraint the result.

4.4.2   *Bayesian Learning*

For linear regression we have the linear combination

$$y = y(\mathbf{x}, \mathbf{w}) = \mathbf{w}^T \cdot \mathbf{x}$$

while for the linear basis function model we have

$$y(\mathbf{x}, \mathbf{w}) = \mathbf{w}^T \Phi(\mathbf{x}).$$

The nonlinear functions $\phi_j(\mathbf{x})$ determine the dimension of $\mathbf{w}$ (with the bias) which is M for linear basis function model and $D + 1$ for the linear regression. For both models the likelihood function is equal, it is

$$p(t_k|y_k) = p(t_k|y_k(\mathbf{x}_k, \mathbf{w})) \tag{4.28}$$

and describes the probability that the observed data point t_k is generated by $y_k(\mathbf{x}_k, \mathbf{w})$ given either by linear regression or by linear basis function model. So, without loss of generality we can focus on the simple linear regression case.

We know that the likelihood function is

$$p(t_k|\mathbf{w}, \mathbf{x}_k) \tag{4.29}$$

with $\mathbf{w}$ in relation with $\mathbf{x}_k$ generating the observed t_k. But we are interested in the posterior distribution

$$p(\mathbf{w}|t_k, \mathbf{x}_k). \tag{4.30}$$

So, we can use Bayes' rule to write the posterior for a given example

$$p(\mathbf{w}|t_k, \mathbf{x}_k) = \frac{p(t_k|\mathbf{w}, \mathbf{x}_k) \cdot p(\mathbf{w})}{p(t_k)}. \tag{4.31}$$

As we are only interested finding the MAP estimate for the weights, we can ignore all terms that do not depend on them and write

$$p(\mathbf{w}|t_k, \mathbf{x}_k) \propto p(t_k|\mathbf{w}, \mathbf{x}_k) \cdot p(\mathbf{w}). \tag{4.32}$$

Having this general view of the posterior, we need to get more concrete. In Bayesian regression, it is assumed that we are working in what is called a Gaussian environment.

4.4.2.1 *Assumptions about the Gaussian Environment*

The environment that characterizes this type of regression [Bishop (2006)], [Robert (2007)], [Haykin (2008)] is based on four key assumptions:

(1) The N training examples $\mathbf{x}_k$ are drown independently from the same distribution i.e. they are independent and identically distributed (iid).
(2) The process that generates target values is Gaussian distributed around points on the regression hyperplane. This just means that the noise in the linear regression model is described by a Gaussian distribution of zero mean and a common variance σ^2.
(3) The weight values are independent and Gaussian distributed around zero, with common variance σ_w^2
(4) The environment is stationary, that is, the parameter vector $\mathbf{w}$ is fixed but unknown.

All these assumptions have implications for likelihood and prior and, thus, posterior. We will go through each.

4.4.2.2 *Likelihood*

The second assumption tell us that the likelihood is a Gaussian around the predicted output with variance σ^2. So, we can use this information to detail the likelihood for a specific example

$$p(t_k|\mathbf{w}, \mathbf{x}_k, \sigma^2) = \frac{1}{\sqrt{2 \cdot \pi} \cdot \sigma} \cdot \exp\left(-\frac{1}{2 \cdot \sigma^2} \cdot (t_k - \mathbf{w}^T \cdot \mathbf{x}_k)^2\right) \qquad (4.33)$$

Having the likelihood for a specific example, we can write down the likelihood for the whole data set using the first assumption. Since, the samples are independent, we just need to multiply the individual likelihoods

$$p(\mathbf{t}|X, \mathbf{w}, \sigma^2) = \prod_{k=1}^{N} p(t_k|\mathbf{w}, \mathbf{x}_k, \sigma^2) \qquad (4.34)$$

4.4.2.3 *Prior*

The $D + 1$ elements of the vector $\mathbf{w}$ are independent and identically distributed and described by a Gaussian distribution of zero mean and a common variance σ_w^2 as a consequence of the third assumption. Then the prior is

$$p(\mathbf{w}|\sigma_w^2) = \prod_{j=0}^{D} p(w_j|\sigma_w^2) = \prod_{j=0}^{D} \mathcal{N}(\mathbf{w}|0, \sigma_w^2) \qquad (4.35)$$

$$p(\mathbf{w}|\sigma_w^2) = \frac{1}{\left(\sqrt{2\cdot\pi}\cdot\sigma_w\right)^{D+1}} \prod_{j=0}^{D}\left(\exp\left(-\frac{w_j^2}{2\cdot\sigma_w^2}\right)\right) \tag{4.36}$$

$$p(\mathbf{w}|\sigma_w^2) = \frac{1}{\left(\sqrt{2\cdot\pi}\cdot\sigma_w\right)^{D+1}} \exp\left(-\frac{1}{2\cdot\sigma_w^2}\sum_{j=0}^{D}w_j^2\right) \tag{4.37}$$

$$p(\mathbf{w}|\sigma_w^2) = \frac{1}{\left(\sqrt{2\cdot\pi}\cdot\sigma_w\right)^{D+1}} \exp\left(-\frac{1}{2\cdot\sigma_w^2}\mathbf{w}^T\cdot\mathbf{w}\right) \tag{4.38}$$

$$p(\mathbf{w}|\sigma_w^2) = \frac{1}{\left(\sqrt{2\cdot\pi}\cdot\sigma_w\right)^{D+1}} \exp\left(-\frac{1}{2\cdot\sigma_w^2}\|\mathbf{w}\|^2\right). \tag{4.39}$$

This prior will constrain our conclusions about the real parameters behind the model.

4.4.2.4   *Posterior*

The posterior is then

$$p(\mathbf{w}|X,\mathbf{t},\sigma^2) \propto p(\mathbf{t}|X,\mathbf{w},\sigma^2)\cdot p(\mathbf{w}|\sigma_w^2). \tag{4.40}$$

Simplifying, we get

$$p(\mathbf{w}|X,\mathbf{t},\sigma^2) \propto \exp\left(-\frac{1}{2\cdot\sigma^2}\cdot\sum_{k=1}^{N}(t_k-\mathbf{w}^T\cdot\mathbf{x}_k)^2 - \frac{1}{2\cdot\sigma_w^2}\|\mathbf{w}\|^2\right). \tag{4.41}$$

With

$$\lambda = \frac{\sigma^2}{\sigma_w^2}$$

Having the posterior, we can find the weight values that maximize it

$$\mathbf{w}_{MAP} = \arg\max_{\mathbf{w}}(p(\mathbf{w}|X,\mathbf{t},\lambda)).$$

As we have seen, this is the same as maximizing the log posterior

$$\mathbf{w}_{MAP} = \arg\max_{\mathbf{w}}\log(p(\mathbf{w}|X,\mathbf{t},\lambda)).$$

Which yields

$$\mathbf{w}_{MAP} = \arg\max_{\mathbf{w}}\left(-\frac{1}{2}\cdot\sum_{k=1}^{N}(t_k-\mathbf{w}^T\cdot\mathbf{x}_k)^2 - \frac{\lambda}{2}\|\mathbf{w}\|_2^2\right). \tag{4.42}$$

4.4.3 *Maximizing a posteriori*

Now we can define the MAP problem as a minimization of a quadratic loss function.

$$E(\mathbf{w}) = \frac{1}{2} \cdot \sum_{k=1}^{N} (t_k - \mathbf{w}^T \cdot \mathbf{x}_k)^2 + \frac{\lambda}{2} \|\mathbf{w}\|_2^2 \qquad (4.43)$$

with $\frac{\lambda}{2}\|\mathbf{w}\|^2$ being the regularization value that constraints our model resulting from the assumptions. Minimizing this function is equivalent to maximizing $\mathbf{w}_{MAP}$

4.4.3.1 *Closed-form Solution*

We set the gradient of $E(\mathbf{w})$ to zero with the gradient operator to compute a closed-form solution for $\mathbf{w}$ as before

$$\nabla E(\mathbf{w}) = \nabla \left(\frac{1}{2} \cdot (\mathbf{t} - X \cdot \mathbf{w})^T \cdot (\mathbf{t} - X \cdot \mathbf{w}) + \frac{\lambda}{2} \mathbf{w}^T \mathbf{w} \right) = 0 \qquad (4.44)$$

$$-2 \cdot X^T \cdot \mathbf{t} + 2 \cdot X^T \cdot X \cdot \mathbf{w} + 2 \cdot \lambda \cdot \mathbf{w} = 0$$

$$-X^T \cdot \mathbf{t} + X^T \cdot X \cdot \mathbf{w} + \lambda \cdot \mathbf{w} = 0$$

$$X^T \cdot \mathbf{t} = \left(X^T \cdot X + \lambda \cdot I \right) \cdot \mathbf{w}$$

$$\left(X^T \cdot X + \lambda \cdot I \right)^{-1} \cdot X^T \cdot \mathbf{t} = \mathbf{w}. \qquad (4.45)$$

4.4.4 *Relation between Regularized Least-Squares and MAP*

The ordinary least-squares estimator is the weight vector that minimizes the simple quadratic loss

$$E(\mathbf{w}) = \frac{1}{2} \sum_{k=1}^{N} \left(t_k - \mathbf{w}^T \cdot \mathbf{x}_k \right)^2$$

To overcome the problems of overfitting we can constraint the model freedom by adding a new term in l_2 norm (We usually simplify $\|\mathbf{w}\|_2 = \|\mathbf{w}\|$)

$$E(\mathbf{w}) = \frac{1}{2} \cdot \sum_{k=1}^{N} (t_k - \mathbf{w}^T \cdot \mathbf{x}_k)^2 + \frac{\lambda}{2} \|\mathbf{w}\|_2^2 \qquad (4.46)$$

which is identical to the MAP estimate.

Fig. 4.10   Andrey Nikolayevich Tikhonov a known Soviet and Russian mathematician and geophysicist.

This quadratic regularizer is also called ridge regression or Tikhonov regularization [Tikhonov and Arsenin (1977)], named after Andrey Nikolayevich Tikhonov, see Figure 4.10. In this formulation, one writes

$$E(\mathbf{w}) = \frac{1}{2} \cdot \sum_{k=1}^{N} (t_k - \mathbf{w}^T \cdot \mathbf{x}_k)^2 + \|\Gamma \cdot \mathbf{w}\|_2^2 \qquad (4.47)$$

where is the Γ Tikhonov matrix with

$$\Gamma = I \cdot \frac{\lambda}{\sqrt{2}}$$

4.4.4.1   *Example of Tikhonov Regularization*

In the following example, we generate 13 points from the interval -0.1 to 1.1 in steps of 0.1 using $\sin(2 \cdot \pi \cdot x)$. By adding random noise from the interval $[-0, 5, 0.5]$ to the points x_k and t_k, the shape of the generated regression polynomial of degree 9, $M = 10$ overfits (see Figure 4.9 (c)) The shape of the generated regression polynomial of degree 9, $M = 10$ with the Tikhonov regularization with $\log(\lambda/2) = -18$ does not overfit (see Figure 4.11 (a). For the Tikhonov regularization with $\log(\lambda/2) = 0$, the shape of the generated polynomial of degree 9, $M = 10$ is different from the shape of the generated function $\sin(2 \cdot \pi \cdot x)$; the regularization value is too large (see Figure 4.11 (b).

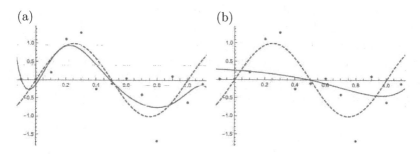

Fig. 4.11 (a) We generated 13 points from the interval -0.1 to 1.1 in steps of 0.1 using $\sin(2 \cdot \pi \cdot x)$. By adding random noise noise form the interval $[-0, 5, 0.5]$ to the points x_k and t_k the shape the generated regression polynomial of degree 9, $M = 10$ overfits. (a) The ridge regression or Tikhonov regularization with $\lambda/2 = 1.522997974471263 \cdot 10^{-8}$ or in a more compact notation $\log(\lambda/2) = -18$ with the generated regression polynomial of degree 9, $M = 10$ does not overfit. (b) The ridge regression or Tikhonov regularization with $\lambda/2 = 1$ or in a more compact notation $\log(\lambda/2) = 0$ with the generated regression polynomial of degree 9, $M = 10$ is different from the shape of the generated function $\sin(2 \cdot \pi \cdot x)$, the regularization value is too big.

4.4.5 LASSO Regularizer

A similar regularization reasoning using the l_1 norm gives us the LASSO (Least Absolute Shrinkage and Selection Operator) [Tibshirani (1996)]

$$E(\mathbf{w}) = \frac{1}{2} \cdot \sum_{k=1}^{N} (t_k - \mathbf{w}^T \cdot \mathbf{x}_k)^2 + \lambda \cdot \|\mathbf{w}\|_1 \qquad (4.48)$$

From a Bayesian interpretation LASSO results from a MAP estimate where the prior distribution is a Laplacian instead of a Gaussian. Specifically, the prior is

$$p(\mathbf{w}|b) = \left(\frac{1}{2 \cdot b}\right)^{D+1} \cdot \prod_{j=0}^{D} \left(\exp\left(\frac{-|w_j|}{b}\right)\right) \qquad (4.49)$$

$$p(\mathbf{w}|b) = \left(\frac{1}{2 \cdot b}\right)^{D+1} \cdot \exp\left(-\frac{1}{b} \cdot \|\mathbf{w}\|_1\right) \qquad (4.50)$$

where $b > 0$ is a scale parameter referred to as the diversity.

In general, unlike ridge, LASSO lacks a simple closed-form solution because $E(\mathbf{w})$ is not differentiable since for $\|\mathbf{w}\|_1$ there is no derivative at the zeros. However, a non closed-form solution can be achieved using gradient descent as is indicated in the next chapter.

When compared to a quadratic regularizer, LASSO tends to generate sparser solutions with lots of zeros in the weight vector (see Figure 4.12). This may be helpful since not only many applications benefit from sparse representations as it increases interpretability. Specifically, a feature that gets a weight of zero can be considered irrelevant for the problem.

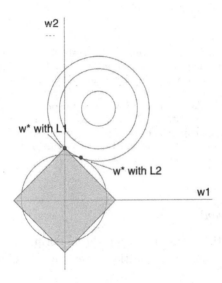

Fig. 4.12 The unregularized error function is represented by the upper three circles indicating the possible parameters w_1 and w_2. The optimal value for the parameter vector $\mathbf{w}^*$ for quadratic regularization with the l_2 norm indicated by $L2$ is represented by the lower circle corresponding to the l_2 norm. The optimal value for the parameter vector $\mathbf{w}^*$ for lasso regularization with the l_1 norm indicated by $L1$ is represented by the lower rectangle corresponding to the l_1 norm. Lasso tends to generate sparser solutions than a quadratic regularizer, in our example $w_1 = 0$.

4.4.5.1 *Example of LASSO Regularization*

In the following example we generated 13 points from the interval -0.1 to 1.1 in steps of 0.1 using $\sin(2 \cdot \pi \cdot x)$ with random noise noise form the interval $[-0, 5, 0.5]$. The LASSO regularization with $\log(\lambda) = -18$ is shown in Figure 4.13 (a) as a relatively good approximation of the real function. In Figure 4.13 (b), we see that LASSO regularization with $\log(\lambda) = 0$ is too restrictive as the shape of the regression polynomial of degree 9 ($M = 10$) is very different from the shape of the function $\sin(2 \cdot \pi \cdot x)$ that generated the data.

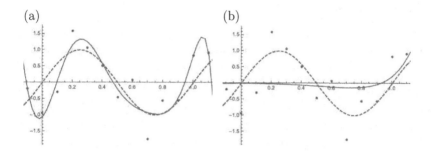

Fig. 4.13 We generated 13 a points from the interval -0.1 to 1.1 in steps of 0.1 using $\sin(2 \cdot \pi \cdot x)$ with random noise noise form the interval $[-0, 5, 0.5]$. (a) Good approximation using LASSO regularization with $\log(\lambda) = -18$. (b) LASSO regularization with $\log(\lambda) = 0$, too big regularization causes the shape of the regression polynomial of degree 9 ($M = 10$) to be very different from the shape of the function $\sin(2 \cdot \pi \cdot x)$ that generated the data.

4.5   Linear Regression for classification

We identified the multiple linear regression with an artificial neuron without any activation function

$$w_0 + \sum_{j=1}^{D} w_j \cdot x_j = \sum_{j=0}^{D} w_j \cdot x_j = \langle \mathbf{w} | \mathbf{x} \rangle = \mathbf{w}^T \cdot \mathbf{x}$$

Linear classification would imply an activation function f such as for example the *sgn* function as described before

$$f(net) = f\left(\sum_{j=0}^{D} w_j \cdot x_j \right).$$

We will investigation the relation between the activation function and the multiple linear regression in the following chapter. We will see that having an activation function, we cannot solve the optimization problem to find the weights in closed-form. However, we can solve it using iterative procedures that depend on learning rules.

4.6   Exercises and Answers

Linear Regression

In this section we will be focusing on the model of linear regression. Much like perceptron, this model works by learning a weight vector $\mathbf{w} = \left(w_0 \ w_1 \ \cdots \ w_d \right)^T$ that is used to compute a linear combination of the input features $\mathbf{x} = \left(x_1 \ \cdots \ x_d \right)^T$. However, this model focuses on regression instead of classification. So, for that reason, its output is not binary. It is, in fact, a real number $output\left(\mathbf{x}; \mathbf{w} \right) = o \in \mathbb{R}$. So, to achieve that, we get rid of the sign function and work directly with the linear combination (dot product).

We can think about the linear regression as providing a score for each point. Instead of making a binary decision for each point (i.e. belongs to the class or not) we give a score to each point where higher scores are more likely to belong to the class.

The following image shows a linearly separable problem with two input features:

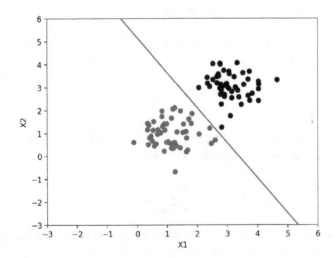

If we add a third dimension for the output, we can think of the perceptron as putting all points that don't belong to the class on the *Output* = 0 plane and all points that belong to the class on the *Output* = 1 plane:

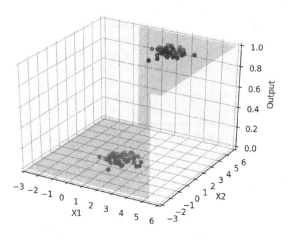

In linear regression, we have a similar picture but we don't make binary decisions, we provide an output score:

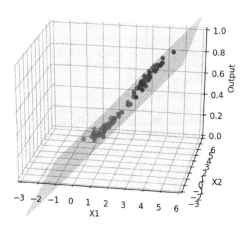

Looking at both plots we see that as the formulas suggest, the perceptron basically squashes the linear regression scores into a binary decision $perceptron(\mathbf{x}; \mathbf{w}) = \Theta(linear\_regression(\mathbf{x}; \mathbf{w}))$.

Closed form solution of squared error

So, let us assume we have training data

$$\left\{ \left(\mathbf{x}^{(1)}, t^{(1)}\right), \left(\mathbf{x}^{(2)}, t^{(2)}\right), \ldots, \left(\mathbf{x}^{(n)}, t^{(n)}\right) \right\}.$$

For a given weight vector $\mathbf{w}$, the linear regression outputs are:

$$output^{(1)}\left(\mathbf{x}^{(1)}; \mathbf{w}\right) = o^{(1)} = \mathbf{w}^T\mathbf{x}^{(1)}$$
$$output^{(2)}\left(\mathbf{x}^{(2)}; \mathbf{w}\right) = o^{(2)} = \mathbf{w}^T\mathbf{x}^{(2)}$$

$$\vdots$$

$$output^{(n)}\left(\mathbf{x}^{(n)}; \mathbf{w}\right) = o^{(n)} = \mathbf{w}^T\mathbf{x}^{(n)}$$

All computations we will need to do will be made easier by working in vector notation. So, we can write the whole system of equations as follows:

$$\begin{pmatrix} o^{(1)} \\ o^{(2)} \\ \vdots \\ o^{(n)} \end{pmatrix} = \begin{pmatrix} 1 & x_1^{(1)} & \cdots & x_d^{(1)} \\ 1 & x_1^{(2)} & \cdots & x_d^{(2)} \\ \vdots & \vdots & \ddots & \vdots \\ 1 & x_1^{(n)} & \cdots & x_d^{(n)} \end{pmatrix} \begin{pmatrix} w_0 \\ w_1 \\ \vdots \\ w_d \end{pmatrix}$$

$$\mathbf{O} = \mathbf{Xw}$$

Having stated how linear regression maps inputs to outputs, we can focus on the central problem of learning. We will look into the most common form of learning. That is, learning by optimization. More specifically, we want to find a weight vector such that our outputs closely approximate the targets $o^{(i)} \sim t^{(i)}$. To find that vector, it is common to define an error function that measures how wrong the outputs are. A well known error function is the sum of squared errors:

$$E\left(\mathbf{w}\right) = \sum_{i=1}^{n} \left(t^{(i)} - o^{(i)}\right)^2$$

Again, we can switch to vector notation as follows:

$$
\begin{aligned}
E\left(\mathbf{w}\right) &= \sum_{i=1}^{n} \left(t^{(i)} - o^{(i)}\right)^2 \\
&= \sum_{i=1}^{n} \left(t^{(i)} - \mathbf{w}^T \mathbf{x}^{(i)}\right)^2 \\
&= \left(\mathbf{T} - \mathbf{Xw}\right)^T \left(\mathbf{T} - \mathbf{Xw}\right)
\end{aligned}
$$

Having defined the error function, the learning problem can be solved by finding its minimum. For linear regression, we can compute a closed form solution for this problem. We do it by computing the derivative and finding its zero:

$$\frac{\partial E\left(\mathbf{w}\right)}{\partial \mathbf{w}} = 0$$

$$\frac{\partial \left(\mathbf{T} - \mathbf{Xw}\right)^T \left(\mathbf{T} - \mathbf{Xw}\right)}{\partial \mathbf{w}} = 0$$

$$\left(\frac{\partial}{\partial \mathbf{w}}\left(\mathbf{T} - \mathbf{Xw}\right)^T\right)\left(\mathbf{T} - \mathbf{Xw}\right) + \left(\mathbf{T} - \mathbf{Xw}\right)^T\left(\frac{\partial}{\partial \mathbf{w}}\left(\mathbf{T} - \mathbf{Xw}\right)\right) = 0$$

$$\left(-\mathbf{X}^T\right)\left(\mathbf{T} - \mathbf{Xw}\right) + \left(\mathbf{T} - \mathbf{Xw}\right)^T\left(-\mathbf{X}\right) = 0$$

$$\left(-\mathbf{X}^T\right)\left(\mathbf{T} - \mathbf{Xw}\right) + \left(-\mathbf{X}\right)^T\left(\mathbf{T} - \mathbf{Xw}\right) = 0$$

$$-2\mathbf{X}^T\left(\mathbf{T} - \mathbf{Xw}\right) = 0$$

$$\mathbf{X}^T\left(\mathbf{T} - \mathbf{Xw}\right) = 0$$

$$\mathbf{X}^T\mathbf{T} - \mathbf{X}^T\mathbf{Xw} = 0$$

$$\mathbf{X}^T\mathbf{Xw} = \mathbf{X}^T\mathbf{T}$$

$$\mathbf{w} = \left(\mathbf{X}^T\mathbf{X}\right)^{-1}\mathbf{X}^T\mathbf{T}$$

So, unlike perceptron where we had to take multiple iterative steps to learn the correct weights, in linear regression we can learn them directly.

Feature Transformations

Much like perceptron, the typical linear regression can only work well with linear problems. However, in many problems we can fix this by changing the feature space we are working in. For example, the following image shows points of two different classes that cannot be separated by a line:

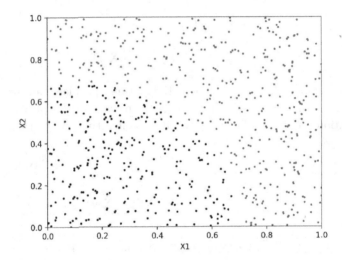

However, if we notice that the difference between classes is related to their distance from the origin (point $(0,0)$) we can work with the squares of the features x_1^2, x_2^2 instead of the features themselves. The following plot shows how this transformation turns the problem into a linear one. In this space, we could use a perceptron to solve the classification issue perfectly.

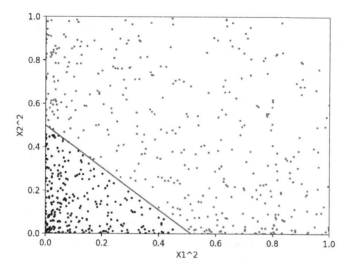

This idea of feature transformation can be used in general (both in classification and regression) to transform non-linear problems into linear ones. In practice, we take the input matrix:

$$\mathbf{X} = \begin{pmatrix} 1 & x_1^{(1)} & \cdots & x_d^{(1)} \\ 1 & x_1^{(2)} & \cdots & x_d^{(2)} \\ \vdots & \vdots & \ddots & \vdots \\ 1 & x_1^{(n)} & \cdots & x_d^{(n)} \end{pmatrix}$$

and we choose feature transforming functions (which in the previous example correspond to taking the squares of the features $\phi_k^{(i)}\left(x_1^{(i)}, \ldots, x_d^{(i)}\right) = x_k^{(i)2}$) to build the new input matrix:

$$\mathbf{\Phi} = \begin{pmatrix} 1 & \phi_1^{(1)}\left(x_1^{(1)}, \ldots, x_d^{(1)}\right) & \cdots & \phi_l^{(1)}\left(x_1^{(1)}, \ldots, x_d^{(1)}\right) \\ 1 & \phi_1^{(2)}\left(x_1^{(2)}, \ldots, x_d^{(2)}\right) & \cdots & \phi_l^{(2)}\left(x_1^{(2)}, \ldots, x_d^{(2)}\right) \\ \vdots & \vdots & \ddots & \vdots \\ 1 & \phi_1^{(n)}\left(x_1^{(n)}, \ldots, x_d^{(n)}\right) & \cdots & \phi_l^{(n)}\left(x_1^{(n)}, \ldots, x_d^{(n)}\right) \end{pmatrix}$$

the rest of the process stays exactly the same. We just have a different input!

1)

Consider the following training data:

$$\left\{ \mathbf{x}^{(1)} = \begin{pmatrix} 1 \\ 1 \end{pmatrix}, \mathbf{x}^{(2)} = \begin{pmatrix} 2 \\ 1 \end{pmatrix}, \mathbf{x}^{(3)} = \begin{pmatrix} 1 \\ 3 \end{pmatrix}, \mathbf{x}^{(4)} = \begin{pmatrix} 3 \\ 3 \end{pmatrix} \right\}$$

$$\left\{ t^{(1)} = 1.4, t^{(2)} = 0.5, t^{(3)} = 2, t^{(4)} = 2.5 \right\}$$

a) Find the closed form solution for a linear regression that minimizes the sum of squared errors on the training data.

Solution:

First, we need to build the $n \times (d + 1)$ design matrix to account for the bias parameter, where n is the number of examples and d is the original number of input features.

$$X = \begin{pmatrix} 1 & 1 & 1 \\ 1 & 2 & 1 \\ 1 & 1 & 3 \\ 1 & 3 & 3 \end{pmatrix}$$

Second, we construct a target vector:

$$Y = \begin{pmatrix} 1.4 \\ 0.5 \\ 2.0 \\ 2.5 \end{pmatrix}$$

Now, the goal is to find the weight vector $\mathbf{w} = \begin{pmatrix} w_0 & w_1 & w_2 \end{pmatrix}^T$ that minimizes the sum of squared errors. We can do it using the pseudo-inverse:

$$\mathbf{w} = \left(X^T X \right)^{-1} X^T Y$$

$$\mathbf{w} = \left(X^T X\right)^{-1} X^T Y$$

$$= \left[\begin{pmatrix} 1\ 1\ 1 \\ 1\ 2\ 1 \\ 1\ 1\ 3 \\ 1\ 3\ 3 \end{pmatrix}^T \begin{pmatrix} 1\ 1\ 1 \\ 1\ 2\ 1 \\ 1\ 1\ 3 \\ 1\ 3\ 3 \end{pmatrix}\right]^{-1} \begin{pmatrix} 1\ 1\ 1 \\ 1\ 2\ 1 \\ 1\ 1\ 3 \\ 1\ 3\ 3 \end{pmatrix}^T \begin{pmatrix} 1.4 \\ 0.5 \\ 2.0 \\ 2.5 \end{pmatrix}$$

$$= \left[\begin{pmatrix} 1\ 1\ 1\ 1 \\ 1\ 2\ 1\ 3 \\ 1\ 1\ 3\ 3 \end{pmatrix} \begin{pmatrix} 1\ 1\ 1 \\ 1\ 2\ 1 \\ 1\ 1\ 3 \\ 1\ 3\ 3 \end{pmatrix}\right]^{-1} \begin{pmatrix} 1\ 1\ 1\ 1 \\ 1\ 2\ 1\ 3 \\ 1\ 1\ 3\ 3 \end{pmatrix} \begin{pmatrix} 1.4 \\ 0.5 \\ 2.0 \\ 2.5 \end{pmatrix}$$

$$= \begin{pmatrix} 4\ 7\ 8 \\ 7\ 15\ 15 \\ 8\ 15\ 20 \end{pmatrix}^{-1} \begin{pmatrix} 1\ 1\ 1\ 1 \\ 1\ 2\ 1\ 3 \\ 1\ 1\ 3\ 3 \end{pmatrix} \begin{pmatrix} 1.4 \\ 0.5 \\ 2.0 \\ 2.5 \end{pmatrix}$$

$$= \begin{pmatrix} 1.875 & -0.5 & -0.375 \\ -0.5 & 0.4 & -0.1 \\ -0.375 & -0.1 & 0.275 \end{pmatrix} \begin{pmatrix} 1\ 1\ 1\ 1 \\ 1\ 2\ 1\ 3 \\ 1\ 1\ 3\ 3 \end{pmatrix} \begin{pmatrix} 1.4 \\ 0.5 \\ 2.0 \\ 2.5 \end{pmatrix}$$

$$= \begin{pmatrix} 1.0 & 0.5 & 0.25 & -0.75 \\ -0.2 & 0.2 & -0.4 & 0.4 \\ -0.2 & -0.3 & 0.35 & 0.15 \end{pmatrix} \begin{pmatrix} 1.4 \\ 0.5 \\ 2.0 \\ 2.5 \end{pmatrix}$$

$$= \begin{pmatrix} 0.275 \\ 0.02 \\ 0.645 \end{pmatrix}$$

b) Predict the target value for $x_{query} = \begin{pmatrix} 2\ 3 \end{pmatrix}^T$.

Solution:

From the previous question, we have our weights:

$$\mathbf{w} = \begin{pmatrix} 0.275 \\ 0.02 \\ 0.645 \end{pmatrix}$$

So, to compute the predicted value, we just need to augment the query vector with a bias dimension and apply the linear regression:

$$output\,(\mathbf{x}) = \mathbf{w} \cdot \mathbf{x} = \begin{pmatrix} 0.275 \\ 0.02 \\ 0.645 \end{pmatrix} \cdot \begin{pmatrix} 1 \\ 2 \\ 3 \end{pmatrix} = 2.25$$

c) Sketch the predicted hyperplane along which the linear regression predicts points will fall.

Solution:

We can get the hyperplane's equation by taking the linear regression output for a general input $\begin{pmatrix} 1 & x_1 & x_2 \end{pmatrix}^T$ and equating it to zero:

$$output\,(\mathbf{x}) = \mathbf{w} \cdot \mathbf{x} \qquad\qquad = 0$$

$$= \begin{pmatrix} 0.275 \\ 0.02 \\ 0.645 \end{pmatrix} \cdot \begin{pmatrix} 1 \\ x_1 \\ x_2 \end{pmatrix} \qquad = 0$$

$$= 0.02 x_1 + 0.645 x_1 + 0.275 \quad = 0$$

From the equation, we get the following plot:

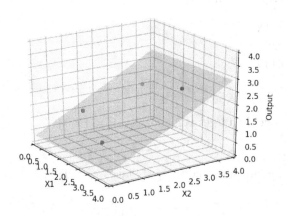

d) Compute the mean squared error produced by the the linear regression.

Solution:

For each point in the training data, we must compute the linear regression prediction and then compute its squared error:

$$\left(t^{(1)} - output\left(\mathbf{x}^{(1)}\right)\right)^2 = \left(t^{(1)} - \mathbf{w} \cdot \mathbf{x}^{(1)}\right)^2$$

$$= \left(1.4 - \begin{pmatrix} 0.275 \\ 0.02 \\ 0.645 \end{pmatrix} \cdot \begin{pmatrix} 1 \\ 1 \\ 1 \end{pmatrix}\right)^2 = (1.4 - 0.94)^2 = 0.2116$$

$$\left(t^{(2)} - output\left(\mathbf{x}^{(2)}\right)\right)^2 = \left(t^{(2)} - \mathbf{w} \cdot \mathbf{x}^{(2)}\right)^2$$

$$= \left(0.5 - \begin{pmatrix} 0.275 \\ 0.02 \\ 0.645 \end{pmatrix} \cdot \begin{pmatrix} 1 \\ 2 \\ 1 \end{pmatrix}\right)^2 = (0.5 - 0.96)^2 = 0.2116$$

$$\left(t^{(3)} - output\left(\mathbf{x}^{(3)}\right)\right)^2 = \left(t^{(3)} - \mathbf{w} \cdot \mathbf{x}^{(3)}\right)^2$$

$$= \left(2.0 - \begin{pmatrix} 0.275 \\ 0.02 \\ 0.645 \end{pmatrix} \cdot \begin{pmatrix} 1 \\ 1 \\ 3 \end{pmatrix}\right)^2 = (2.0 - 2.23)^2 = 0.0529$$

$$\left(t^{(4)} - output\left(\mathbf{x}^{(4)}\right)\right)^2 = \left(t^{(4)} - \mathbf{w} \cdot \mathbf{x}^{(4)}\right)^2$$

$$= \left(2.5 - \begin{pmatrix} 0.275 \\ 0.02 \\ 0.645 \end{pmatrix} \cdot \begin{pmatrix} 1 \\ 3 \\ 3 \end{pmatrix}\right)^2 = (2.5 - 2.27)^2 = 0.0529$$

So, the mean error is:

$$\frac{0.2116 + 0.2116 + 0.0529 + 0.0529}{4} = 0.13225$$

2)

Consider the following training data:

$$\left\{ \mathbf{x}^{(1)} = (-2.0), \mathbf{x}^{(2)} = (-1.0), \mathbf{x}^{(3)} = (0.0), \mathbf{x}^{(4)} = (2.0) \right\}$$

$$\left\{ t^{(1)} = 2.0, t^{(2)} = 3.0, t^{(3)} = 1.0, t^{(4)} = -1.0 \right\}$$

a) Find the closed form solution for a linear regression that minimizes the sum of squared errors on the training data.

Solution:

First, we need to build the $n \times (d+1)$ design matrix to account for the bias parameter, where n is the number of examples and d is the original number of input features.

$$X = \begin{pmatrix} 1 & -2.0 \\ 1 & -1.0 \\ 1 & 0.0 \\ 1 & 2.0 \end{pmatrix}$$

Second, we construct a target vector:

$$Y = \begin{pmatrix} 2.0 \\ 3.0 \\ 1.0 \\ -1.0 \end{pmatrix}$$

Now, the goal is to find the weight vector $\mathbf{w} = \begin{pmatrix} w_0 & w_1 \end{pmatrix}^T$ that minimizes the sum of squared errors. We can do it using the pseudo-inverse:

$$\mathbf{w} = \left(X^T X \right)^{-1} X^T Y$$

$$\mathbf{w} = (X^T X)^{-1} X^T Y$$

$$= \left[\begin{pmatrix} 1 & -2.0 \\ 1 & -1.0 \\ 1 & 0.0 \\ 1 & 2.0 \end{pmatrix}^T \begin{pmatrix} 1 & -2.0 \\ 1 & -1.0 \\ 1 & 0.0 \\ 1 & 2.0 \end{pmatrix} \right]^{-1} \begin{pmatrix} 1 & -2.0 \\ 1 & -1.0 \\ 1 & 0.0 \\ 1 & 2.0 \end{pmatrix}^T \begin{pmatrix} 2.0 \\ 3.0 \\ 1.0 \\ -1.0 \end{pmatrix}$$

$$= \left[\begin{pmatrix} 1 & 1 & 1 & 1 \\ -2.0 & -1.0 & 0.0 & 2.0 \end{pmatrix} \begin{pmatrix} 1 & -2.0 \\ 1 & -1.0 \\ 1 & 0.0 \\ 1 & 2.0 \end{pmatrix} \right]^{-1} \begin{pmatrix} 1 & 1 & 1 & 1 \\ -2.0 & -1.0 & 0.0 & 2.0 \end{pmatrix} \begin{pmatrix} 2.0 \\ 3.0 \\ 1.0 \\ -1.0 \end{pmatrix}$$

$$= \begin{pmatrix} 4.0 & -1.0 \\ -1.0 & 9.0 \end{pmatrix}^{-1} \begin{pmatrix} 1 & 1 & 1 & 1 \\ -2.0 & -1.0 & 0.0 & 2.0 \end{pmatrix} \begin{pmatrix} 2.0 \\ 3.0 \\ 1.0 \\ -1.0 \end{pmatrix}$$

$$= \begin{pmatrix} 0.2571 & 0.0286 \\ 0.0286 & 0.1143 \end{pmatrix} \begin{pmatrix} 1 & 1 & 1 & 1 \\ -2.0 & -1.0 & 0.0 & 2.0 \end{pmatrix} \begin{pmatrix} 2.0 \\ 3.0 \\ 1.0 \\ -1.0 \end{pmatrix}$$

$$= \begin{pmatrix} 0.2 & 0.2286 & 0.2571 & 0.3143 \\ -0.2 & -0.0857 & 0.0286 & 0.2571 \end{pmatrix} \begin{pmatrix} 2.0 \\ 3.0 \\ 1.0 \\ -1.0 \end{pmatrix}$$

$$= \begin{pmatrix} 1.0286 \\ -0.8857 \end{pmatrix}$$

---

b) Predict the target value for $x_{query} = (1)^T$.

Solution:
From the previous question, we have our weights:

$$\mathbf{w} = \begin{pmatrix} 1.0286 \\ -0.8857 \end{pmatrix}$$

So, to compute the predicted value, we just need to augment the query vector with a bias dimension and apply the linear regression:

$$output\left(\mathbf{x}\right) = \mathbf{w} \cdot \mathbf{x} = \begin{pmatrix} 1.0286 \\ -0.8857 \end{pmatrix} \cdot \begin{pmatrix} 1 \\ 1 \end{pmatrix} = 0.1429$$

c) Sketch the predicted hyperplane along which the linear regression predicts points will fall.

Solution:

We can get the hyperplane's equation by taking the linear regression output for a general input $\left(1 \; x_1\right)^T$ and equating it to zero:

$$output\left(\mathbf{x}\right) = \mathbf{w} \cdot \mathbf{x} \qquad\qquad = 0$$
$$= \begin{pmatrix} 1.0286 \\ -0.8857 \end{pmatrix} \cdot \begin{pmatrix} 1 \\ x_1 \end{pmatrix} \quad = 0$$
$$= -0.8857x_1 + 1.0286 \quad = 0$$

From the equation, we get the following plot:

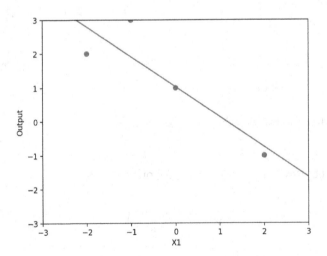

d) Compute the mean squared error produced by the the linear regression.

Solution:

For each point in the training data, we must compute the linear regression prediction and then compute its squared error:

$$\left(t^{(1)} - \mathbf{w} \cdot \mathbf{x}^{(1)}\right)^2 = \left(2.0 - \left(\begin{array}{c} 1.0286 \\ -0.8857 \end{array}\right) \cdot \left(\begin{array}{c} 1 \\ -2.0 \end{array}\right)\right)^2$$

$$= (2.0 - 2.800)^2 = 0.64$$

$$\left(t^{(2)} - \mathbf{w} \cdot \mathbf{x}^{(2)}\right)^2 = \left(3.0 - \left(\begin{array}{c} 1.0286 \\ -0.8857 \end{array}\right) \cdot \left(\begin{array}{c} 1 \\ -1.0 \end{array}\right)\right)^2$$

$$= (3.0 - 1.9143)^2 = 1.1788$$

$$\left(t^{(3)} - \mathbf{w} \cdot \mathbf{x}^{(3)}\right)^2 = \left(1.0 - \left(\begin{array}{c} 1.0286 \\ -0.8857 \end{array}\right) \cdot \left(\begin{array}{c} 1 \\ 0.0 \end{array}\right)\right)^2$$

$$= (1.0 - 1.0286)^2 = 0.0008$$

$$\left(t^{(4)} - \mathbf{w} \cdot \mathbf{x}^{(4)}\right)^2 = \left(-1.0 - \left(\begin{array}{c} 1.0286 \\ -0.8857 \end{array}\right) \cdot \left(\begin{array}{c} 1 \\ 2.0 \end{array}\right)\right)^2$$

$$= (-1.0 - (-0.7429))^2 = 0.0661$$

So, the mean error is:

$$\frac{0.64 + 1.1788 + 0.0008 + 0.0661}{4} = 0.4714$$

3)

Consider the following training data:

$$\left\{ \mathbf{x}^{(1)} = \begin{pmatrix} 1 \\ 1 \end{pmatrix}, \mathbf{x}^{(2)} = \begin{pmatrix} 2 \\ 1 \end{pmatrix}, \mathbf{x}^{(3)} = \begin{pmatrix} 1 \\ 3 \end{pmatrix}, \mathbf{x}^{(4)} = \begin{pmatrix} 3 \\ 3 \end{pmatrix} \right\}$$

$$\left\{ t^{(1)} = 1, t^{(2)} = 1, t^{(3)} = 0, t^{(4)} = 0 \right\}$$

a) Find the closed form solution for a linear regression that minimizes the sum of squared errors on the training data.

Solution:

First, we need to build the $n \times (d + 1)$ design matrix to account for the bias parameter, where n is the number of examples and d is the original number of input features.

$$X = \begin{pmatrix} 1 & 1 & 1 \\ 1 & 2 & 1 \\ 1 & 1 & 3 \\ 1 & 3 & 3 \end{pmatrix}$$

Second, we construct a target vector:

$$Y = \begin{pmatrix} 1 \\ 1 \\ 0 \\ 0 \end{pmatrix}$$

Now, the goal is to find the weight vector $\mathbf{w} = \begin{pmatrix} w_0 & w_1 & w_2 \end{pmatrix}^T$ that minimizes the sum of squared errors. We can do it using the pseudo-inverse:

$$\mathbf{w} = \left(X^T X \right)^{-1} X^T Y$$

$$\mathbf{w} = \left(X^T X \right)^{-1} X^T Y$$

$$= \left[\begin{pmatrix} 1\,1\,1 \\ 1\,2\,1 \\ 1\,1\,3 \\ 1\,3\,3 \end{pmatrix}^T \begin{pmatrix} 1\,1\,1 \\ 1\,2\,1 \\ 1\,1\,3 \\ 1\,3\,3 \end{pmatrix} \right]^{-1} \begin{pmatrix} 1\,1\,1 \\ 1\,2\,1 \\ 1\,1\,3 \\ 1\,3\,3 \end{pmatrix}^T \begin{pmatrix} 1 \\ 1 \\ 0 \\ 0 \end{pmatrix}$$

$$= \left[\begin{pmatrix} 1\,1\,1\,1 \\ 1\,2\,1\,3 \\ 1\,1\,3\,3 \end{pmatrix} \begin{pmatrix} 1\,1\,1 \\ 1\,2\,1 \\ 1\,1\,3 \\ 1\,3\,3 \end{pmatrix} \right]^{-1} \begin{pmatrix} 1\,1\,1\,1 \\ 1\,2\,1\,3 \\ 1\,1\,3\,3 \end{pmatrix} \begin{pmatrix} 1 \\ 1 \\ 0 \\ 0 \end{pmatrix}$$

$$= \begin{pmatrix} 4 & 7 & 8 \\ 7 & 15 & 15 \\ 8 & 15 & 20 \end{pmatrix}^{-1} \begin{pmatrix} 1\,1\,1\,1 \\ 1\,2\,1\,3 \\ 1\,1\,3\,3 \end{pmatrix} \begin{pmatrix} 1 \\ 1 \\ 0 \\ 0 \end{pmatrix}$$

$$= \begin{pmatrix} 1.875 & -0.5 & -0.375 \\ -0.5 & 0.4 & -0.1 \\ -0.375 & -0.1 & 0.275 \end{pmatrix} \begin{pmatrix} 1\,1\,1\,1 \\ 1\,2\,1\,3 \\ 1\,1\,3\,3 \end{pmatrix} \begin{pmatrix} 1 \\ 1 \\ 0 \\ 0 \end{pmatrix}$$

$$= \begin{pmatrix} 1.0 & 0.5 & 0.25 & -0.75 \\ -0.2 & 0.2 & -0.4 & 0.4 \\ -0.2 & -0.3 & 0.35 & 0.15 \end{pmatrix} \begin{pmatrix} 1 \\ 1 \\ 0 \\ 0 \end{pmatrix}$$

$$= \begin{pmatrix} 1.5 \\ 0.0 \\ -0.5 \end{pmatrix}$$

b) Use your linear regression to classify $x_{query} = \begin{pmatrix} 2 & 2.5 \end{pmatrix}^T$, assuming a threshold similarity of 0.5.

Solution:

From the previous question, we have our weights:

$$\mathbf{w} = \begin{pmatrix} 1.5 \\ 0.0 \\ -0.5 \end{pmatrix}$$

So, to compute the predicted value, we just need to augment the query vector with a bias dimension and apply the linear regression:

$$\text{output}\,(\mathbf{x}_{\text{query}}) = \mathbf{w} \cdot x_{\text{query}} = \begin{pmatrix} 1.5 \\ 0.0 \\ -0.5 \end{pmatrix} \cdot \begin{pmatrix} 1 \\ 2 \\ 2.5 \end{pmatrix} = 0.25$$

The input is classified as not belonging to the class.

---

4)

Consider the following training data:

$$\left\{ \mathbf{x}^{(1)} = (-2.0)\,, \mathbf{x}^{(2)} = (-1.0)\,, \mathbf{x}^{(3)} = (0.0)\,, \mathbf{x}^{(4)} = (2.0) \right\}$$

$$\left\{ t^{(1)} = 1, t^{(2)} = 0, t^{(3)} = 0, t^{(4)} = 0 \right\}$$

a) Find the closed form solution for a linear regression that minimizes the sum of squared errors on the training data.

Solution:

First, we need to build the $n \times (d + 1)$ design matrix to account for the bias parameter, where n is the number of examples and d is the original number of input features.

$$X = \begin{pmatrix} 1 & -2.0 \\ 1 & -1.0 \\ 1 & 0.0 \\ 1 & 2.0 \end{pmatrix}$$

Second, we construct a target vector:

$$Y = \begin{pmatrix} 1 \\ 0 \\ 0 \\ 0 \end{pmatrix}$$

Now, the goal is to find the weight vector $\mathbf{w} = \begin{pmatrix} w_0 & w_1 \end{pmatrix}^T$ that minimizes the sum of squared errors. We can do it using the pseudo-inverse:

$$\mathbf{w} = \left(X^T X \right)^{-1} X^T Y$$

$$\mathbf{w} = \left(X^T X\right)^{-1} X^T Y$$

$$= \left[\begin{pmatrix} 1 & -2.0 \\ 1 & -1.0 \\ 1 & 0.0 \\ 1 & 2.0 \end{pmatrix}^T \begin{pmatrix} 1 & -2.0 \\ 1 & -1.0 \\ 1 & 0.0 \\ 1 & 2.0 \end{pmatrix} \right]^{-1} \begin{pmatrix} 1 & -2.0 \\ 1 & -1.0 \\ 1 & 0.0 \\ 1 & 2.0 \end{pmatrix}^T \begin{pmatrix} 1 \\ 0 \\ 0 \\ 0 \end{pmatrix}$$

$$= \left[\begin{pmatrix} 1 & 1 & 1 & 1 \\ -2.0 & -1.0 & 0.0 & 2.0 \end{pmatrix} \begin{pmatrix} 1 & -2.0 \\ 1 & -1.0 \\ 1 & 0.0 \\ 1 & 2.0 \end{pmatrix} \right]^{-1} \begin{pmatrix} 1 & 1 & 1 & 1 \\ -2.0 & -1.0 & 0.0 & 2.0 \end{pmatrix} \begin{pmatrix} 1 \\ 0 \\ 0 \\ 0 \end{pmatrix}$$

$$= \begin{pmatrix} 4.0 & -1.0 \\ -1.0 & 9.0 \end{pmatrix}^{-1} \begin{pmatrix} 1 & 1 & 1 & 1 \\ -2.0 & -1.0 & 0.0 & 2.0 \end{pmatrix} \begin{pmatrix} 1 \\ 0 \\ 0 \\ 0 \end{pmatrix}$$

$$= \begin{pmatrix} 0.2571 & 0.0286 \\ 0.0286 & 0.1143 \end{pmatrix} \begin{pmatrix} 1 & 1 & 1 & 1 \\ -2.0 & -1.0 & 0.0 & 2.0 \end{pmatrix} \begin{pmatrix} 1 \\ 0 \\ 0 \\ 0 \end{pmatrix}$$

$$= \begin{pmatrix} 0.2 & 0.2286 & 0.2571 & 0.3143 \\ -0.2 & -0.0857 & 0.0286 & 0.2571 \end{pmatrix} \begin{pmatrix} 1 \\ 0 \\ 0 \\ 0 \end{pmatrix}$$

$$= \begin{pmatrix} 0.2 \\ -0.2 \end{pmatrix}$$

b) Use your linear regression to classify $x_{query} = (-0.3)^T$, assuming a threshold similarity of 0.15.

Solution:

From the previous question, we have our weights:

$$\mathbf{w} = \begin{pmatrix} 0.2 \\ -0.2 \end{pmatrix}$$

So, to compute the predicted value, we just need to augment the query vector with a bias dimension and apply the linear regression:

$$output\,(\mathbf{x}_{\text{query}}) = \mathbf{w} \cdot \mathbf{x}_{\text{query}} = \begin{pmatrix} 0.2 \\ -0.2 \end{pmatrix} \cdot \begin{pmatrix} 1 \\ -0.3 \end{pmatrix} = 0.26$$

The input is classified as belonging to the class.

---

5)

Consider the following training data:

$$\mathbf{x}^{(1)} = \begin{pmatrix} -0.95 \\ 0.62 \end{pmatrix}, \mathbf{x}^{(2)} = \begin{pmatrix} 0.63 \\ 0.31 \end{pmatrix}, \mathbf{x}^{(3)} = \begin{pmatrix} -0.12 \\ -0.21 \end{pmatrix}, \mathbf{x}^{(4)} = \begin{pmatrix} -0.24 \\ -0.5 \end{pmatrix},$$

$$\mathbf{x}^{(5)} = \begin{pmatrix} 0.07 \\ -0.42 \end{pmatrix}, \mathbf{x}^{(6)} = \begin{pmatrix} 0.03 \\ 0.91 \end{pmatrix}, \mathbf{x}^{(7)} = \begin{pmatrix} 0.05 \\ 0.09 \end{pmatrix}, \mathbf{x}^{(8)} = \begin{pmatrix} -0.83 \\ 0.22 \end{pmatrix}$$

$$\left\{ t^{(1)} = 0, t^{(2)} = 0, t^{(3)} = 1, t^{(4)} = 0, t^{(5)} = 1, t^{(6)} = 0, t^{(7)} = 1, t^{(8)} = 0 \right\}$$

a) Plot the data points and try to choose a non-linear transformation to apply.

Solution:

Plotting the data points we see that the labels seem to change with the distance from the origin. A way to capture is this is to perform a quadratic feature transform:

$$\phi\left(x_1, x_2\right) = \left(x_1^2, x_2^2\right)$$

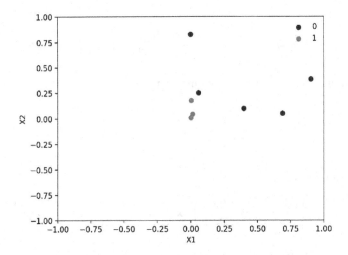

b) Adopt the non-linear transform you chose in a) and find the closed form solution.

Solution:

First, we need to build the $n \times (d+1)$ design matrix to account for the bias parameter, where n is the number of examples and d is the original number of input features. However, unlike previous exercises where we used the features themselves directly ($\phi(x) = x$), in this case, we have a non-linear transformation. So, we apply it:

$$\Phi = \begin{pmatrix} 1 & (-0.95)^2 & (0.62)^2 \\ 1 & (0.63)^2 & (0.31)^2 \\ 1 & (-0.12)^2 & (-0.21)^2 \\ 1 & (-0.24)^2 & (-0.5)^2 \\ 1 & (0.07)^2 & (-0.42)^2 \\ 1 & (0.03)^2 & (0.91)^2 \\ 1 & (0.05)^2 & (0.09)^2 \\ 1 & (-0.83)^2 & (0.22)^2 \end{pmatrix} = \begin{pmatrix} 1 & 0.9025 & 0.3844 \\ 1 & 0.3969 & 0.0961 \\ 1 & 0.0144 & 0.0441 \\ 1 & 0.0576 & 0.2500 \\ 1 & 0.0049 & 0.1764 \\ 1 & 0.0009 & 0.8281 \\ 1 & 0.0025 & 0.0081 \\ 1 & 0.6889 & 0.0484 \end{pmatrix}$$

Second, we construct a target vector:

$$Y = \begin{pmatrix} 0 \\ 0 \\ 1 \\ 0 \\ 1 \\ 0 \\ 1 \\ 0 \end{pmatrix}$$

Now, the goal is to find the weight vector $\mathbf{w} = \begin{pmatrix} w_0 & w_1 & w_2 \end{pmatrix}^T$ that minimizes the sum of squared errors. We can do it using the pseudo-inverse:

$$\mathbf{w} = \left(X^T X \right)^{-1} X^T Y$$

$$\mathbf{w} = \left(X^T X\right)^{-1} X^T Y$$

$$= \left[\begin{pmatrix} 1\ 0.9025\ 0.3844 \\ 1\ 0.3969\ 0.0961 \\ 1\ 0.0144\ 0.0441 \\ 1\ 0.0576\ 0.2500 \\ 1\ 0.0049\ 0.1764 \\ 1\ 0.0009\ 0.8281 \\ 1\ 0.0025\ 0.0081 \\ 1\ 0.6889\ 0.0484 \end{pmatrix}^{T} \begin{pmatrix} 1\ 0.9025\ 0.3844 \\ 1\ 0.3969\ 0.0961 \\ 1\ 0.0144\ 0.0441 \\ 1\ 0.0576\ 0.2500 \\ 1\ 0.0049\ 0.1764 \\ 1\ 0.0009\ 0.8281 \\ 1\ 0.0025\ 0.0081 \\ 1\ 0.6889\ 0.0484 \end{pmatrix} \right]^{-1} \begin{pmatrix} 1\ 0.9025\ 0.3844 \\ 1\ 0.3969\ 0.0961 \\ 1\ 0.0144\ 0.0441 \\ 1\ 0.0576\ 0.2500 \\ 1\ 0.0049\ 0.1764 \\ 1\ 0.0009\ 0.8281 \\ 1\ 0.0025\ 0.0081 \\ 1\ 0.6889\ 0.0484 \end{pmatrix}^{T}$$

$$\cdot \begin{pmatrix} 0 \\ 0 \\ 1 \\ 0 \\ 1 \\ 0 \\ 1 \\ 0 \end{pmatrix} =$$

$$= \begin{pmatrix} 8.0000\ 2.0686\ 1.8356 \\ 2.0686\ 1.4502\ 0.4351 \\ 1.8356\ 0.4351\ 0.9407 \end{pmatrix}^{-1} \begin{pmatrix} 1\ 0.9025\ 0.3844 \\ 1\ 0.3969\ 0.0961 \\ 1\ 0.0144\ 0.0441 \\ 1\ 0.0576\ 0.2500 \\ 1\ 0.0049\ 0.1764 \\ 1\ 0.0009\ 0.8281 \\ 1\ 0.0025\ 0.0081 \\ 1\ 0.6889\ 0.0484 \end{pmatrix}^{T} \begin{pmatrix} 0 \\ 0 \\ 1 \\ 0 \\ 1 \\ 0 \\ 1 \\ 0 \end{pmatrix}$$

$$= \begin{pmatrix} 0.3099\ -0.3026\ -0.4647 \\ -0.3026\ 1.0962\ 0.0835 \\ -0.4647\ 0.0835\ 1.9311 \end{pmatrix} \begin{pmatrix} 1\ 0.9025\ 0.3844 \\ 1\ 0.3969\ 0.0961 \\ 1\ 0.0144\ 0.0441 \\ 1\ 0.0576\ 0.2500 \\ 1\ 0.0049\ 0.1764 \\ 1\ 0.0009\ 0.8281 \\ 1\ 0.0025\ 0.0081 \\ 1\ 0.6889\ 0.0484 \end{pmatrix}^{T} \begin{pmatrix} 0 \\ 0 \\ 1 \\ 0 \\ 1 \\ 0 \\ 1 \\ 0 \end{pmatrix}$$

$$= \begin{pmatrix} -0.1419 & 0.1451 & 0.2850 & 0.1763 & 0.2264 & -0.0752 & 0.3053 & 0.0789 \\ 0.7188 & 0.1405 & -0.2831 & -0.2186 & -0.2825 & -0.2325 & -0.2992 & 0.4566 \\ 0.3529 & -0.2459 & -0.3783 & 0.0229 & -0.1236 & 1.1346 & -0.4488 & -0.3137 \end{pmatrix}$$

$$\cdot \begin{pmatrix} 0 \\ 0 \\ 1 \\ 0 \\ 1 \\ 0 \\ 1 \\ 0 \end{pmatrix} = \begin{pmatrix} 0.8168 \\ -0.8648 \\ -0.9508 \end{pmatrix}$$

c) Sketch the predicted surface along which the predictions will fall.

Solution:

$$output\,(\mathbf{x}) = \mathbf{w} \cdot \phi\,(\mathbf{x}) \qquad\qquad = 0$$

$$= \begin{pmatrix} 0.8168 \\ -0.8648 \\ -0.9508 \end{pmatrix} \cdot \begin{pmatrix} 1 \\ x_1^2 \\ x_2^2 \end{pmatrix} \qquad = 0$$

$$= -0.8648x_1^2 - 0.9508x_2^2 + 0.8168 \quad = 0$$

From the equation, we get the following plot:

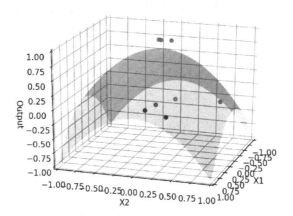

6)

Consider the following training data:

$$\left\{ \mathbf{x}^{(1)} = (3), \mathbf{x}^{(2)} = (4), \mathbf{x}^{(3)} = (6), \mathbf{x}^{(4)} = (10), \mathbf{x}^{(5)} = (12) \right\}$$

$$\left\{ t^{(1)} = 1.5, t^{(2)} = 9.3, t^{(3)} = 23.4, t^{(4)} = 45.8, t^{(5)} = 60.1 \right\}$$

a) Adopt a logarithmic feature transformation $\phi(x_1) = \log(x_1)$ and find the closed form solution for this non-linear regression that minimizes the sum of squared errors on the training data.

Solution:
First, we need to build the $n \times (d+1)$ design matrix to account for the bias parameter, where n is the number of examples and d is the original number of input features. However, unlike previous exercises where we used the features themselves directly ($\phi(x) = x$), in this case, we have a non-linear transformation. So, we apply it:

$$\Phi = \begin{pmatrix} 1 & \log(3) \\ 1 & \log(4) \\ 1 & \log(6) \\ 1 & \log(10) \\ 1 & \log(12) \end{pmatrix} = \begin{pmatrix} 1 & 1.0986 \\ 1 & 1.3863 \\ 1 & 1.7918 \\ 1 & 2.3026 \\ 1 & 2.4849 \end{pmatrix}$$

Second, we construct a target vector:

$$Y = \begin{pmatrix} 1.5 \\ 9.3 \\ 23.4 \\ 45.8 \\ 60.1 \end{pmatrix}$$

Now, the goal is to find the weight vector $\mathbf{w} = \begin{pmatrix} w_0 & w_1 \end{pmatrix}^T$ that minimizes the sum of squared errors. We can do it using the pseudo-inverse:

$$\mathbf{w} = \left(X^T X \right)^{-1} X^T Y$$

$$\mathbf{w} = \left(X^T X\right)^{-1} X^T Y$$

$$= \left[\begin{pmatrix} 1 \ 1.0986 \\ 1 \ 1.3863 \\ 1 \ 1.7918 \\ 1 \ 2.3026 \\ 1 \ 2.4849 \end{pmatrix}^T \begin{pmatrix} 1 \ 1.0986 \\ 1 \ 1.3863 \\ 1 \ 1.7918 \\ 1 \ 2.3026 \\ 1 \ 2.4849 \end{pmatrix} \right]^{-1} \begin{pmatrix} 1 \ 1.0986 \\ 1 \ 1.3863 \\ 1 \ 1.7918 \\ 1 \ 2.3026 \\ 1 \ 2.4849 \end{pmatrix}^T \begin{pmatrix} 1.5 \\ 9.3 \\ 23.4 \\ 45.8 \\ 60.1 \end{pmatrix}$$

$$= \left[\begin{pmatrix} 1 & 1 & 1 & 1 & 1 \\ 1.0986 & 1.3863 & 1.7918 & 2.3026 & 2.4849 \end{pmatrix} \begin{pmatrix} 1 \ 1.0986 \\ 1 \ 1.3863 \\ 1 \ 1.7918 \\ 1 \ 2.3026 \\ 1 \ 2.4849 \end{pmatrix} \right]^{-1}$$

$$\cdot \begin{pmatrix} 1 \ 1.0986 \\ 1 \ 1.3863 \\ 1 \ 1.7918 \\ 1 \ 2.3026 \\ 1 \ 2.4849 \end{pmatrix}^T \begin{pmatrix} 1.5 \\ 9.3 \\ 23.4 \\ 45.8 \\ 60.1 \end{pmatrix}$$

$$= \begin{pmatrix} 5.0 & 9.0642 \\ 9.0642 & 17.8158 \end{pmatrix}^{-1} \begin{pmatrix} 1 \ 1.0986 \\ 1 \ 1.3863 \\ 1 \ 1.7918 \\ 1 \ 2.3026 \\ 1 \ 2.4849 \end{pmatrix}^T \begin{pmatrix} 1.5 \\ 9.3 \\ 23.4 \\ 45.8 \\ 60.1 \end{pmatrix}$$

$$= \begin{pmatrix} 2.5745 & -1.3098 \\ -1.3098 & 0.7225 \end{pmatrix} \begin{pmatrix} 1 \ 1.0986 \\ 1 \ 1.3863 \\ 1 \ 1.7918 \\ 1 \ 2.3026 \\ 1 \ 2.4849 \end{pmatrix}^T \begin{pmatrix} 1.5 \\ 9.3 \\ 23.4 \\ 45.8 \\ 60.1 \end{pmatrix}$$

$$= \begin{pmatrix} 1.1355 & 0.7587 & 0.2276 & -0.4415 & -0.6803 \\ -0.5160 & -0.3082 & -0.0152 & 0.3539 & 0.4856 \end{pmatrix} \begin{pmatrix} 1.5 \\ 9.3 \\ 23.4 \\ 45.8 \\ 60.1 \end{pmatrix}$$

$$= \begin{pmatrix} -47.0212 \\ 41.3945 \end{pmatrix}$$

b) Repeat the exercise above for a quadratic feature transformation $\phi(x_1) = x_1^2$.

Solution:

First, we need to build the $n \times (d+1)$ design matrix to account for the bias parameter, where n is the number of examples and d is the original number of input features. However, unlike previous exercises where we used the features themselves directly ($\phi(x) = x$), in this case, we have a non-linear transformation. So, we apply it:

$$
\Phi = \begin{pmatrix} 1 & 3^2 \\ 1 & 4^2 \\ 1 & 6^2 \\ 1 & 10^2 \\ 1 & 12^2 \end{pmatrix} = \begin{pmatrix} 1 & 9 \\ 1 & 16 \\ 1 & 36 \\ 1 & 100 \\ 1 & 144 \end{pmatrix}
$$

Second, we construct a target vector:

$$
Y = \begin{pmatrix} 1.5 \\ 9.3 \\ 23.4 \\ 45.8 \\ 60.1 \end{pmatrix}
$$

Now, the goal is to find the weight vector $\mathbf{w} = \begin{pmatrix} w_0 & w_1 \end{pmatrix}^T$ that minimizes the sum of squared errors. We can do it using the pseudo-inverse:

$$
\mathbf{w} = \left(X^T X \right)^{-1} X^T Y
$$

$$\mathbf{w} = \left(X^T X\right)^{-1} X^T Y$$

$$= \left[\begin{pmatrix} 1 & 9 \\ 1 & 16 \\ 1 & 36 \\ 1 & 100 \\ 1 & 144 \end{pmatrix}^T \begin{pmatrix} 1 & 9 \\ 1 & 16 \\ 1 & 36 \\ 1 & 100 \\ 1 & 144 \end{pmatrix} \right]^{-1} \begin{pmatrix} 1 & 9 \\ 1 & 16 \\ 1 & 36 \\ 1 & 100 \\ 1 & 144 \end{pmatrix}^T \begin{pmatrix} 1.5 \\ 9.3 \\ 23.4 \\ 45.8 \\ 60.1 \end{pmatrix}$$

$$= \left[\begin{pmatrix} 1 & 1 & 1 & 1 & 1 \\ 9 & 16 & 36 & 100 & 144 \end{pmatrix} \begin{pmatrix} 1 & 9 \\ 1 & 16 \\ 1 & 36 \\ 1 & 100 \\ 1 & 144 \end{pmatrix} \right]^{-1} \begin{pmatrix} 1 & 1 & 1 & 1 & 1 \\ 9 & 16 & 36 & 100 & 144 \end{pmatrix} \begin{pmatrix} 1.5 \\ 9.3 \\ 23.4 \\ 45.8 \\ 60.1 \end{pmatrix}$$

$$= \begin{pmatrix} 5.0 & 305.0 \\ 305.0 & 32369.0 \end{pmatrix}^{-1} \begin{pmatrix} 1 & 1 & 1 & 1 & 1 \\ 9 & 16 & 36 & 100 & 144 \end{pmatrix} \begin{pmatrix} 1.5 \\ 9.3 \\ 23.4 \\ 45.8 \\ 60.1 \end{pmatrix}$$

$$= \begin{pmatrix} 0.4703 & -0.0044 \\ -0.0044 & 0.00007 \end{pmatrix} \begin{pmatrix} 1 & 1 & 1 & 1 & 1 \\ 9 & 16 & 36 & 100 & 144 \end{pmatrix} \begin{pmatrix} 1.5 \\ 9.3 \\ 23.4 \\ 45.8 \\ 60.1 \end{pmatrix}$$

$$= \begin{pmatrix} 0.4305 & 0.3994 & 0.3108 & 0.0272 & -0.1678 \\ -0.0038 & -0.0033 & -0.0018 & 0.0028 & 0.0060 \end{pmatrix} \begin{pmatrix} 1.5 \\ 9.3 \\ 23.4 \\ 45.8 \\ 60.1 \end{pmatrix}$$

$$= \begin{pmatrix} 2.7895 \\ 0.4136 \end{pmatrix}$$

c) Plot both regressions.

Solution:

For the logarithmic, we get:

$$output\,(\mathbf{x}) = w \cdot \phi\,(\mathbf{x}) = -47.0212 + 41.395\log\,(x_1)$$

For the quadratic, we get:

$$output\,(\mathbf{x}) = w \cdot \phi\,(\mathbf{x}) = 2.7895 + 0.4136x_1^2$$

With the equations, we can build the plots:

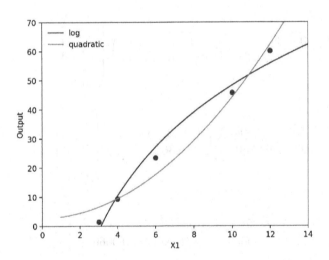

d) Which is a better fit a) or b)?

Solution:

Recall the equations for both regressions:

$$output_{log}\,(\mathbf{x}) = w \cdot \phi\,(\mathbf{x}) = -47.0212 + 41.395\log\,(x_1)$$

$$output_{quadratic}\,(\mathbf{x}) = w \cdot \phi\,(\mathbf{x}) = 2.7895 + 0.4136x_1^2$$

To measure which fit is better we will measure the mean squared errors. For the logarithmic transform, we have:

$$(\mathbf{\Phi w}_{\log} - \mathbf{Y})^2 = \left(\left(\begin{pmatrix} 1 & 1.0986 \\ 1 & 1.3863 \\ 1 & 1.7918 \\ 1 & 2.3026 \\ 1 & 2.4849 \end{pmatrix}\begin{pmatrix} -47.0212 \\ 41.3945 \end{pmatrix} - \begin{pmatrix} 1.5 \\ 9.3 \\ 23.4 \\ 45.8 \\ 60.1 \end{pmatrix}\right)\right)^2 = \begin{pmatrix} 9.2704 \\ 1.1315 \\ 14.0455 \\ 6.2155 \\ 18.1460 \end{pmatrix}$$

Which yields a mean squared error of:

$$\frac{9.2704 + 1.1315 + 14.0455 + 6.2155 + 18.1460}{5} = 9.7618$$

For the quadratic transform, we have:

$$(\mathbf{\Phi w}_{\text{quadratic}} - \mathbf{Y})^2 = \left(\left(\begin{pmatrix} 1 & 9 \\ 1 & 16 \\ 1 & 36 \\ 1 & 100 \\ 1 & 144 \end{pmatrix}\begin{pmatrix} 2.7895 \\ 0.4136 \end{pmatrix} - \begin{pmatrix} 1.5 \\ 9.3 \\ 23.4 \\ 45.8 \\ 60.1 \end{pmatrix}\right)\right)^2 = \begin{pmatrix} 25.1202 \\ 0.0152 \\ 32.7228 \\ 2.7192 \\ 5.0628 \end{pmatrix}$$

Which yields a mean squared error of:

$$\frac{25.1202 + 0.0152 + 32.7228 + 2.7192 + 5.0628}{5} = 13.1273$$

So, given the availabe data, the logarithmic transform appears to fit the data better.

Thinking Questions

When using the linear regression for classification, think about how the threshold changes the sensitivity of the model. Is it more or less likely that the model will fail to recognize a class member as the threshold increases?

Chapter 5

Perceptron

Fig. 5.1 Outgoing from linear regression we introduce perceptron and Adaline. The sigmoid function leads to the logistic regression.

5.1   Linear Regression and Linear Artificial Neuron

The multiple linear regression

$$y = y(\mathbf{x}, \mathbf{w}) = w_0 + \sum_{j=1}^{D} w_j \cdot x_j = w_0 + \langle \mathbf{w} | \mathbf{x} \rangle$$

corresponds to an artificial neuron without any activation function (or the activation function is the identity). For input $\mathbf{x}_k$ the neuron's output is given by

$$o_k = net_k = bias + \sum_{j=1}^{D} w_j \cdot x_{k,j} = w_0 + \sum_{j=1}^{D} w_j \cdot x_{k,j}$$

The training error for a training data set of N elements with inputs $\mathbf{x}_1, \cdots, \mathbf{x}_k, \cdots, \mathbf{x}_N$ and targets $t_1, \cdots, t_k, \cdots, t_N$ is given by

$$E(\mathbf{w}) = \frac{1}{2} \cdot \sum_{k=1}^{N} (t_k - o_k)^2 = \frac{1}{2} \cdot \sum_{k=1}^{N} \left(t_k - \sum_{j=0}^{D} w_j \cdot x_{k,j} \right)^2 \qquad (5.1)$$

with an additional scaling value $\frac{1}{2}$ and with $x_{k,0} = 1$. This kind of error is also called squared error (or sum-of-squared errors). We have seen that a closed-form solution that minimizes $E(\mathbf{w})$ for $\mathbf{w}$ exists with

$$\nabla E(\mathbf{w}) = 0$$

with the gradient operator

$$\nabla = \left[\frac{\partial}{\partial w_1}, \frac{\partial}{\partial w_2}, \cdots, \frac{\partial}{\partial w_D} \right]^T .$$

We can also get a non closed-form solution using gradient descent. To illustrate how one can do it, consider an example with $D = 1$. In such case, the training error is a function of $\mathbf{w}$, with $\mathbf{w} = (w_0, w_1)$. With that, we can represent all possible error values as a two dimensional function, see Figure 5.2. This function corresponds to an error surface with one global minimum. The task of the algorithm is to determine the corresponding minimum.

Plotting and looking for the minimum may work for this simple two dimensional case. However, in general, with more dimensions it is not possible to measure the error at all possible weight values. So, we need a procedure that allows us to find the solution without the need to determine all possible $\mathbf{w}$ value combinations. Such optimization procedure exists and is typically achieved through gradient descent [Mitchell (1997)].

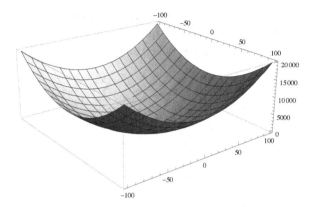

Fig. 5.2 The training error is a function of $\mathbf{w}$, with $\mathbf{w} = (w_0, w_1)$. We can plot all possible error values as a two dimensional function. The x-axis represents w_0, the y-axis represents w_1 and the z-axis the value $E(\mathbf{w}) = E((w_0, w_1))$. The function corresponds to the error surface with a minimum. The task of the learning algorithm is to determine the corresponding minimum. The error surface as defined by $E(\mathbf{w})$ contains only one global minimum since it is convex.

To find a minimum of a function $E(\mathbf{w})$ using gradient descent, we take steps proportional to the negative of the gradient

$$-\nabla E(\mathbf{w}) = -\left(\frac{\partial E}{\partial w_0}, \frac{\partial E}{\partial w_1}, \cdots, \frac{\partial E}{\partial w_n} \right)^T \tag{5.2}$$

of the function at the current point. Specifically, we start the process at some randomly chosen point $\mathbf{w}^{initial}$ and at each iteration the weights are updated according to the learning rule

$$w_j^{new} = w_j^{old} + \Delta w_j \tag{5.3}$$

with

$$\Delta w_j = -\eta \cdot \frac{\partial E}{\partial w_j}. \tag{5.4}$$

Which is the same as saying that we update the weight vector using

$$\mathbf{w}^{new} = \mathbf{w}^{old} + \Delta \mathbf{w} \tag{5.5}$$

where

$$\Delta \mathbf{w} = \eta \cdot (-\nabla E(\mathbf{w})). \tag{5.6}$$

The weight vector is moved by η in the direction that decreases $E(\mathbf{w})$, where η is called the learning rate. For a sufficiently small η, the algorithm will converge to a solution, because the error surface defined by $E(\mathbf{w})$ contains only one global minimum. For too large η the search could overstep the minimum in the error surface. The value

$$\frac{\partial E}{\partial w_j} = \frac{\partial}{\partial w_j} \frac{1}{2} \cdot \sum_{k=1}^{N} (t_k - o_k)^2 = \frac{1}{2} \cdot \sum_{k=1}^{N} \frac{\partial}{\partial w_j} (t_k - o_k)^2 \qquad (5.7)$$

is given by

$$\frac{\partial E}{\partial w_j} = \frac{1}{2} \cdot \sum_{k=1}^{N} 2 \cdot (t_k - o_k) \cdot \frac{\partial}{\partial w_j} (t_k - o_k) \qquad (5.8)$$

$$\frac{\partial E}{\partial w_j} = \sum_{k=1}^{N} (t_k - o_k) \cdot \frac{\partial}{\partial w_j} \left(t_k - \sum_{j=0}^{D} w_j \cdot x_{k,j} \right) \qquad (5.9)$$

$$\frac{\partial E}{\partial w_j} = \sum_{k=1}^{N} (t_k - o_k) \cdot (-x_{k,j}) \qquad (5.10)$$

$$\frac{\partial E}{\partial w_j} = - \sum_{k=1}^{N} (t_k - o_k) \cdot x_{k,j}. \qquad (5.11)$$

So, the update rule for gradient decent is given by

$$\Delta w_j = \eta \cdot \sum_{k=1}^{N} (t_k - o_k) \cdot x_{k,j} \qquad (5.12)$$

with

$$w_j^{new} = w_j^{old} + \Delta w_j$$

also called gradient learning rule.

Since the error surface contains one global minimum the gradient descent converge to a weight vector with a global minimum error for a sufficiently small learning rate η, even if the training examples are not linearly separable.

5.1.1 *Regularization*

The non closed-form solution for Tikhonov regularization or l_2 regularization (ridge regression) is given by

$$\frac{\partial E}{\partial w_j} = -\sum_{k=1}^{N}(t_k - o_k) \cdot x_{k,j} + \frac{\lambda}{2} \cdot w_j. \tag{5.13}$$

The update rule for gradient decent is given by

$$\Delta w_j = \eta \cdot \sum_{k=1}^{N}(t_k - o_k) \cdot x_{k,j} - \frac{\lambda}{2} \cdot w_j. \tag{5.14}$$

Often, for simplicity, the factor $\frac{1}{2}$ is not taken into account resulting in

$$\Delta w_j = \eta \cdot \sum_{k=1}^{N}(t_k - o_k) \cdot x_{k,j} - \lambda \cdot w_j. \tag{5.15}$$

As stated before the LASSO (l_1 regularization) lacks closed form solution because $E(\mathbf{w})$ is not differentiable since for $\|\mathbf{w}\|_1$ there is no derivative at the zeros. Instead of using the derivative for $|w_j|$ a subderivative with *sign* function is used

$$sign(w_j) = \begin{cases} -1 \ if \ w_j < 0 \\ 0 \ \ if \ w_j = 0 \\ 1 \ \ if \ w_j > 0 \end{cases} \tag{5.16}$$

which results in the gradient

$$\frac{\partial E}{\partial w_j} = -\sum_{k=1}^{N}(t_k - o_k) \cdot x_{k,j} + \lambda \cdot sign(w_j) \tag{5.17}$$

that yields the gradient descent update rule

$$\Delta w_j = \eta \cdot \sum_{k=1}^{N}(t_k - o_k) \cdot x_{k,j} - \eta \cdot \lambda \cdot sign(w_j). \tag{5.18}$$

5.1.2 *Stochastic gradient descent*

The gradient decent training rule uses the gradient of an error function that is computed for the whole set of N training examples. Stochastic gradient descent (SGD) approximates gradient decent by updating weights incrementally with the gradient of the error for each example according to the update rule

$$\Delta w_j = \eta \cdot (t_k - o_k) \cdot x_{k,j}. \tag{5.19}$$

This rule is known as delta-rule or LMS (least mean-squares) weight update. This rule is used in Adaline (Adaptive Linear Element) for adaptive filters and was developed by Widroff and Hoff [Widrow and Hoff (1960)], [Widrow and Hoff (1962)], see Figure 5.3. When the learning rate η decreases with an appropriate rate, stochastic gradient descent converges to a global minimum.

(a)　　　　　　　　　　　　　　　　　　(b)

Fig. 5.3　(a) Adaline (Adaptive Linear Element) as used in the sixties and (b) Widroff and Hoff, the inventor.

5.2　Continuous Differentiable Activation Functions

Most of these gradient descent solutions were simple alternatives for the closed-form solutions we had described for multiple linear regression. Remember that linear regression was like an artificial neuron without an activation function. Adding an activation function to neuron makes it impossible to get a closed-form solution. So, in this section we use the gradient descent idea to find solutions that optimize neurons with continuous differentiable activation functions $\phi()$. Such neurons will output

$$o_k = \phi \left(\sum_{j=0}^{D} w_j \cdot x_{k,j} \right) . \tag{5.20}$$

Following the same reasoning as before, we can define the update rule for gradient decent using the partial derivatives

$$\frac{\partial E}{\partial w_j} = \sum_{k=1}^{N} (t_k - o_k) \cdot \frac{\partial}{\partial w_j} \left(t_k - \phi \left(\sum_{j=0}^{D} w_j \cdot x_{k,j} \right) \right) \tag{5.21}$$

$$\frac{\partial E}{\partial w_j} = \sum_{k=1}^{N} (t_k - o_k) \cdot \left(-\phi' \left(\sum_{j=0}^{D} w_j \cdot x_{k,j} \right) \cdot x_{k,j} \right) \qquad (5.22)$$

$$\frac{\partial E}{\partial w_j} = -\sum_{k=1}^{N} (t_k - o_k) \cdot \phi' \left(\sum_{j=0}^{D} w_j \cdot x_{k,j} \right) \cdot x_{k,j}. \qquad (5.23)$$

5.2.1 Sigmoid Activation Functions

The $sgn(net)$ operation is related to the threshold operation of a real biological neuron with -1 not firing and 1 firing. Because of that an artificial neuron is a mathematical function $\phi(net)$ conceived as a model of biological neuron. The sgn activation function can be scaled to the two values 0 or 1 for not firing and firing,

$$\phi(net) := sgn_0(net) = \begin{cases} 1 \text{ if } net \geq 0 \\ 0 \text{ if } net < 0. \end{cases} \qquad (5.24)$$

Both non linear functions $sgn(net)$ and $sgn_0(net)$ are non continuous and, thus, non-differentiable. So, they are not suitable for the gradient descent procedure. However, the activation function $sgn_0(net)$ can be approximated by the non linear continuous function $\sigma(net)$

$$\phi(net) := \sigma(net) = \frac{1}{1 + e^{(-\alpha \cdot net)}} \in [0, 1] \qquad (5.25)$$

in which the value α determines its steepness, see Figure 5.4. As a consequence the class represented by the target value t_k can be chosen from the interval

$$t_k \in [0, 1].$$

This function is called sigmoid because it is S-shaped (it reassembles a big S). For the non linear continuous activation function $\sigma()$, the neuron's output is given by

$$o_k = \sigma \left(\sum_{j=0}^{D} w_j \cdot x_{k,j} \right).$$

Now, the derivative of this sigmoid function is given by

$$\sigma(x)' = \alpha \cdot \sigma(x) \cdot (1 - \sigma(x)) \qquad (5.26)$$

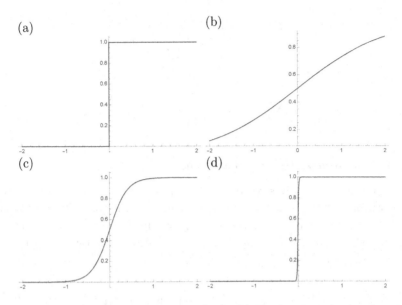

Fig. 5.4   (a) The activation function $sgn_0(net)$. (b) The function $\sigma(net)$ with $\alpha = 1$. (c) The function $\sigma(net)$ with $\alpha = 5$. (d) The function $\sigma(net)$ with $\alpha = 10$ is very similar to $sgn_0(net)$, bigger α make it even more similar. The sigmoid function has its name, since the shape of the function resembles a letter S.

so, we get the partial derivatives

$$\frac{\partial E}{\partial w_j} = -\alpha \cdot \sum_{k=1}^{N}(t_k - o_k) \cdot \sigma\left(net_k\right) \cdot (1 - \sigma\left(net_k,\right)) \cdot x_{k,j} \qquad (5.27)$$

resulting in the update rule for gradient decent

$$\Delta w_j = \eta \cdot \alpha \sum_{k=1}^{N}(t_k - o_k) \cdot x_{k,j} \cdot o_k \cdot (1 - o_k) \qquad (5.28)$$

$$w_j^{new} = w_j^{old} + \Delta w_j.$$

.

5.2.2   *Perceptron with sgn$_0$*

Working with the sigmoid function caused a small change to the typical setting we had with the original perceptron. Namely, we went from targets -1 and 1 to targets 0 and 1. For coherence, in this subsection we take a small detour to show how we can frame the original Rosenblatt's perceptron using sgn_0 instead of sgn.

So, we want to introduce a slight modification in Rosenblatt's (see Figure 5.5) perceptron [Rosenblatt (1962)] by using the activation function

Fig. 5.5   Frank Rosenblatt the father of machine learning, one cannot stress enough the importance of his model.

$$sgn_0(net) = \begin{cases} 1 \text{ if } net \geq 0 \\ 0 \text{ if } net < 0 \end{cases}$$

which yields output

$$o(net) = sgn_0\left(\sum_{j=0}^{D} w_j \cdot x_j\right) = sgn_0\left(\sum_{j=1}^{D} w_j \cdot x_j + w_0\right).$$

Assuming the training data is divided in two classes 0 an 1, the $\delta_k = (t_k - o_k)$ that plays the role of the error signal changes from the original 0, -2 or 2 to 0, 1 or -1

$$\delta_k = \begin{cases} 1 & \text{if } t_k = 1 \text{ and } x_k = 0 \\ -1 & \text{if } t_k = 0 \text{ and } x_k = 1 \end{cases}, \tag{5.29}$$

so, in practice, it is scaled by $\frac{1}{2}$. Otherwise, the learning rule is basically the same

$$\Delta w_j = \eta \cdot (t_k - o_k) \cdot x_j.$$

Now, notice how this rule is very similar to the stochastic gradient descent rule that was derived from squared error (sum-of-squared errors)

$$\Delta w_j = \eta^*(t_k - o_k) \cdot x_{k,j} \cdot o_k \cdot (1 - o_k), \quad \eta^* = \eta \cdot \alpha.$$

Taking into account that the function $\sigma(net)$ with high value α is very similar to $sgn_0(net)$, the rule differs by the positive scalar value $o_k \cdot (1 - o_k)$ that determines the size of the gradient. This positive scalar value is related to the fact that, in the SGD version, the target values t_k are from the interval $t_k \in [0, 1]$. If we constraint the target values to the two possible values 0 or 1 we can constraint our error function and simplify the solution.

5.2.3 Cross Entropy Loss Function

The sigmoid output unit uses the linear input net and the sigmoid activation function to convert net into a probability value [Bishop (2006)].

$$\sigma(net) = \frac{1}{1 + e^{(-net)}} \in [0, 1]$$

Because of that, assuming two opposite classes C_1 and C_2, we can interpret the neuron's output for a given input as the probability of class C_1 given the input

$$p(C_1|\mathbf{x}) = \sigma\left(\sum_{j=0}^{N} w_j \cdot x_j\right) = \sigma\left(\mathbf{w}^T \cdot \mathbf{x}\right) \tag{5.30}$$

and

$$p(C_2|\mathbf{x}) = 1 - p(C_1|\mathbf{x}). \tag{5.31}$$

From this probabilistic perspective, we can think about learning the weights in a different manner. Assume we are given a training set

$$D = \{(\mathbf{x}_1, t_1), (\mathbf{x}_2, t_2), \cdots, , (\mathbf{x}_N, t_N)\}, \quad t_k \in \{0, 1\}$$

that was generated by a given neuron and we want to find its weights. Now, since the targets are either fire 1 or not fire 0, let us assume that the neuron fires with probability $p(C_1|\mathbf{x}_k)$ and does not with probability $p(C_1|\mathbf{x}_k)$. This is the same as saying that the neuron follows a Bernoulli distribution.

For a given example, we can measure the likelihood that the neuron, with a given set of weights has generated a given output for a given input

$$p(t_k|\mathbf{w}, \mathbf{x}_k) = Bernoulli\left(p(C_1|\mathbf{x}_k)\right) \tag{5.32}$$

$$p(t_k|\mathbf{w}, \mathbf{x}_k) = p(C_1|\mathbf{x}_k)^{t_k} \cdot (1 - p(C_1|\mathbf{x}_k))^{1-t_k} \tag{5.33}$$

Given that we know how to write the likelihood of one example, if we assume that the data are independent, we can write the likelihood for the whole data set by simply multiplying the individual likelihoods

$$p(\mathbf{t}|\mathbf{x}_1, \cdots, \mathbf{x}_N, \mathbf{w}) = \prod_{k=1}^{N} p(C_1|\mathbf{x}_k)^{t_k} \cdot (1 - p(C_1|\mathbf{x}_k))^{1-t_k} \qquad (5.34)$$

with

$$o_k = p(C_1|\mathbf{x}_k) = \sigma\left(\mathbf{w}^T \cdot \mathbf{x}_k\right) = \sigma(net_k), \qquad (5.35)$$

we can simply write

$$p(\mathbf{t}|\mathbf{x}_1, \cdots, \mathbf{x}_N, \mathbf{w}) = \prod_{k=1}^{N} o_k^{t_k} \cdot (1 - o_k)^{1-t_k}. \qquad (5.36)$$

Now, as we have done before in other circumstances, having the likelihood, we can estimate the weights such that the likelihood is maximized. This is equivalent to minimizing the negative log likelihood, yielding the loss function

$$E(\mathbf{w}) = -\log(p(\mathbf{t}|\mathbf{w})) = -\sum_{k=1}^{N} (t_k \log o_k + (1 - t_k) \log(1 - o_k)). \qquad (5.37)$$

Notice that all of this reasoning and, as a consequence, the resulting loss function is the same as we have seen in the information theory chapter. In fact, the loss function is exactly the cross entropy between targets and output.

$$H(t, p) = -\sum_{k=1}^{N} (t_k \cdot \log(p(C_1|\mathbf{x}_k)) + \neg t_k \cdot \log(p(C_2|\mathbf{x}_k)))$$

Now, to find the weights that minimize the loss function we will use our typical gradient descent strategy. The error (loss) function's partial derivatives are given by

$$\frac{\partial E}{\partial w_j} = \frac{\partial}{\partial w_j} \left(-\sum_{k=1}^{N} (t_k \log o_k + (1 - t_k) \log(1 - o_k))\right) \qquad (5.38)$$

with

$$\frac{\partial E}{\partial w_j} = -\sum_{k=1}^{N} \left(\frac{t_k}{o_k} + -\frac{(1 - t_k)}{(1 - o_k)}\right) \cdot \frac{\partial}{\partial w_j}(o_k) \qquad (5.39)$$

$$\frac{\partial E}{\partial w_j} = \sum_{k=1}^{N} \left(\frac{(1 - t_k)}{(1 - o_k)} - \frac{t_k}{o_k}\right) \cdot \frac{\partial}{\partial w_j}(o_k) \qquad (5.40)$$

$$\frac{\partial E}{\partial w_j} = \sum_{k=1}^{N} \left(\frac{(1 - t_k)}{(1 - o_k)} - \frac{t_k}{o_k} \right) \cdot (o_k \cdot (1 - o_k)) \cdot \frac{\partial}{\partial w_j} \left(\sum_{j=0}^{D} w_j \cdot x_{k,j} \right) \quad (5.41)$$

$$\frac{\partial E}{\partial w_j} = \sum_{k=1}^{N} ((1 - t_k) \cdot (o_k)) - (t_k) \cdot (1 - o_k)) \cdot \frac{\partial}{\partial w_j} \left(\sum_{j=0}^{D} w_j \cdot x_{k,j} \right) \quad (5.42)$$

$$\frac{\partial E}{\partial w_j} = \sum_{k=1}^{N} (o_k - t_k) \cdot \frac{\partial}{\partial w_j} \left(\sum_{j=0}^{D} w_j \cdot x_{k,j} \right) \quad (5.43)$$

$$\frac{\partial E}{\partial w_j} = \sum_{k=1}^{N} (o_k - t_k) \cdot x_{k,j} \quad (5.44)$$

$$\frac{\partial E}{\partial w_j} = -\sum_{k=1}^{N} (t_k - o_k) \cdot x_{k,j}. \quad (5.45)$$

So, the update rule for gradient decent is given by

$$\Delta w_j = \eta \cdot \sum_{k=1}^{N} (t_k - o_k) \cdot x_{k,j}. \quad (5.46)$$

5.2.3.1   *Stochastic Gradient Decent of Cross Entropy Loss Function*

Converting the learning rule to its stochastic gradient decent version we get

$$\Delta w_j = \eta \cdot (t_k - o_k) \cdot x_j.$$

With a general sigmoid function

$$\sigma(net) = \frac{1}{1 + e^{(-\alpha \cdot net)}},$$

the learning rule becomes

$$\Delta w_j = \eta \cdot \alpha \cdot (t_k - o_k) \cdot x_j = \eta^* \cdot (t_k - o_k) \cdot x_j, \quad \eta^* = \eta \cdot \alpha.$$

Notice how this rule is similar to the perceptron learning rule since the function $\sigma(net)$ with high value α is similar to $sgn_0(net)$. Also, this rule converges faster than the stochastic gradient descent rule that was derived from the squared error loss (sum-of-square errors)

$$\Delta w_j = \eta^* (t_k - o_k) \cdot x_{k,j} \cdot o_k \cdot (1 - o_k), \quad \eta^* = \eta \cdot \alpha$$

since the positive scalar value $o_k \cdot (1 - o_k)$ that determines the size of the gradient is not present. However the target values for the stochastic gradient descent rule that was derived from the squared error are more expressive since they are from the interval

$$t_k \in [0, 1]$$

whereas the target values for cross entropy are only binary values

$$t_k \in \{0, 1\}.$$

5.2.4 *Linear Unit versus Sigmoid Unit*

A unit with sigmoid activation function gives a better decision boundary than a linear unit. Unlike in a linear function, for the sigmoid function, points that are far away from the decision boundary have a bounded impact since their values cannot exceed one or get below zero as indicated in the Figure 5.6. However the target values for linear unit are more expressive, since

$$t_k \in \mathbb{R}.$$

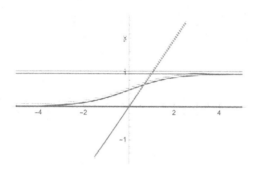

Fig. 5.6   For sigmoid function distant points from the decision boundary have the same impact, they are constrained by 1 one the right side and zero on the left side of the axis. This is not the case for a linear function as indicated, where more distant point have a bigger impact.

5.2.5 *Logistic Regression*

In statistics the artificial neuron with sigmoid activation function is called logistic regression and the sigmoid function called the logistic function. For an artificial neuron, the sigmoid activation function indicates the output of the neuron, in logistic regression the output of the neuron would be either 1 (neuron fires) or 0 (neuron does not fire) and the output would indicate the probability that the artificial neuron fires. Suppose we want to predict whether someone is female C_1 or male C_2 using height in centimeters. If linear regression is used,

$$net = y(\mathbf{w}, x) = \mathbf{w}^T \cdot \mathbf{x}$$

the predicted values will become greater than one and less than zero. Such values are inadmissible, however with

$$p(C_1|\mathbf{x}) = \frac{e^{(net)}}{1 + e^{(net)}} = \frac{1}{1 + e^{(-net)}} \in [0, 1] \qquad (5.47)$$

$$p(C_2|\mathbf{x}) = 1 - p(C_1|\mathbf{x}) = \frac{1}{1 + e^{(net)}} \in [0, 1] \qquad (5.48)$$

with odds being

$$odds = \frac{p(C_1|\mathbf{x})}{p(C_2|\mathbf{x})} = \frac{p(C_1|\mathbf{x})}{1 - p(C_1|\mathbf{x})} = e^{(net)}. \qquad (5.49)$$

we can overcome this problem.

The *logit* function that is the inverse of logistic (sigmoid σ) function with

$$\log(odds) = logit(\mathbf{w}^T \cdot \mathbf{x}) = \log\left(\frac{p(C_1|\mathbf{x})}{1 - p(C_1|\mathbf{x})}\right) = \mathbf{w}^T \cdot \mathbf{x} = net \qquad (5.50)$$

corresponds to the linear regression. It is common in machine learning community to call a sigmoid unit with cross entropy loss function a logistic regression.

5.3   Multiclass Linear Discriminant

For K artificial neurons with a continuous activation function ϕ an index t is used to identify the corresponding artificial linear neuron with

$$t \in \{1, 2, \cdots, K\}$$

to identify the weight vector $\mathbf{w}_t$ and the t the output o_t from the neuron, see Figure 5.7.

$$o_t = \phi\left(\sum_{j=1}^{D} w_{t,j} \cdot x_j\right)$$

Assuming that the training set consists of N observations

$$X = (\mathbf{x}_1, \mathbf{x}_2, \cdots, \mathbf{x}_k, \cdots, \mathbf{x}_N)^T$$

and respective target values represented as vectors of dimension K (since t is used as an index, we will use y_{kt} to indicate the specific target)

$$Y = (\mathbf{y}_1, \mathbf{y}_2, \cdots, \mathbf{y}_k, \cdots, \mathbf{y}_N)^T.$$

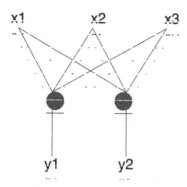

Fig. 5.7 2 artificial neurons correspond to two perceptrons with the same input **x** and two target values represented by the vector $\mathbf{y} = (y_1, y_2)$, the actual output computed by the network is $\mathbf{o} = (o_1, o_2)$.

During training, each neuron is trained individually with its target value y_{kt}

$$y_{kt} \in \{0, 1\}, \quad \sum_{t=1}^{K} y_{kt} = 1$$

After training, the prediction for an input pattern **x** is done using (see Figure 5.8).

$$\arg\max_t \left(\phi \left(\mathbf{w}_t^T \cdot \mathbf{x} \right) \right). \tag{5.51}$$

For the perceptron we cannot apply the $\arg\max_t$ operation since the output of each neuron is either 1 or 0 and building a $K - 1$ classifiers each of which solves a two class problem creates ambiguous regions (see Figure 5.9).

For K artificial neurons with the sigmoid activation the results cannot be interpreted as probabilities any more

$$o_t = \sigma \left(\sum_{j=1}^{D} w_{t,j} \cdot x_j \right) = \sigma(net_t)$$

since

$$\sum_{t=1}^{K} o_t \neq 1.$$

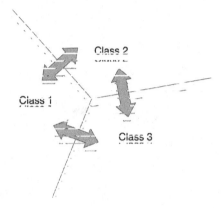

Fig. 5.8 Multiclass linear discrimination, in our example there are three classes that are determined by $\arg\max_t \left(\phi \left(\mathbf{w}_t^T \cdot \mathbf{x} \right) \right)$.

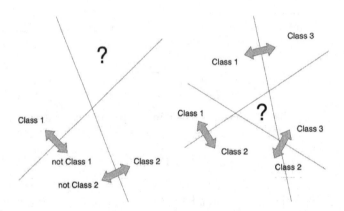

Fig. 5.9 It is not possible to construct K classes discriminant from two set without ambiguous regions. On the left we use two discriminants that distinguish C_1, not C_1 and C_2, not C_2 that leads to an ambiguous region represented by "?". On the right three discriminants are used to distinguish between classes C_1, C_2 and C_3 that lead to an ambiguous region represented by "?".

To be able to interpret them again as such, we can simply normalize the values with

$$o_s = \frac{\sigma(net_s)}{\sum_{t=1}^{K} \sigma(net_t)}. \tag{5.52}$$

Since each neuron can be viewed as a single classifier as well with odds being

$$odds_s = \frac{p(C_{s,1}|\mathbf{x})}{p(C_{s,2}|\mathbf{x})} = \frac{p(C_{s,1}|\mathbf{x})}{1 - p(C_{1,s}|\mathbf{x})} = e^{(net_s)} \qquad (5.53)$$

we could use the normalized odds to make the distinction more discriminative with

$$o_s = \frac{odd_s}{\sum_{t=1}^{K} odd_t} = \frac{\exp(net_s)}{\sum_{t=1}^{K} \exp(net_t)} \qquad (5.54)$$

and we arrive at the softmax function.

For two classes we can now use two alternative coding schemas: representation using a bit (one unit)) or 1-of-2 representation (2 units). The 1-of-K representation results in

$$p(C_s|\mathbf{x}) = \sigma(\mathbf{net})_s = \frac{\exp(net_s)}{\sum_{t=1}^{K} \exp(net_t)} \qquad (5.55)$$

which is called the normalized exponential or softmax function with many interesting properties. It is the generalization of the logistic sigmoid with the activation net_s

$$net_s = \mathbf{w}_s^T \cdot \mathbf{x}.$$

The softmax function is used in various multi class classification methods [Bishop (2006)], such as multinomial logistic regression (also known as softmax regression) with the prediction

$$\arg\max_s (\sigma(\mathbf{net})_s) = \arg\max_s \left(\mathbf{w}_s^T \cdot \mathbf{x} \right).$$

5.3.1 *Cross Entropy Loss Function for softmax*

Taking the error of the gradient function with respect to the vector $\mathbf{w}_j$ we obtain

$$\nabla_{\mathbf{w}_s} E(\mathbf{w}_1, \cdots, \mathbf{w}_K) = \sum_{k=1}^{N} (o_{ks} - y_{ks}) \cdot \mathbf{x}_k = -\sum_{k=1}^{N} (y_{ks} - o_{ks}) \cdot \mathbf{x}_k \qquad (5.56)$$

again, it is the same as making the gradient descent procedure for the sum-of-squares error function for several artificial neurons.

Let us see how to get there. The output of a unit is given by

$$o_{ks} = \sigma(net_{ks}) = \frac{\exp(net_{ks})}{\sum_{t=1}^{K} \exp(net_{kt})}$$

which is called the normalized exponential or softmax function. For simplification of the derivative function we drop the index k that indicates the k-th training pattern and we get

$$\frac{\partial \sigma(net_s)}{\partial net_t} = \sigma(net_s) \cdot (I_{st} - \sigma(net_t)) = o_s \cdot (I_{st} - o_t)$$

with the Kronecker Function

$$I_{st} = \delta_{st} = \begin{cases} 1, & \text{if } s = t \\ 0, & \text{otherwise.} \end{cases} \tag{5.57}$$

This just means that if $t = s$, we have

$$\frac{\partial \sigma(net_s)}{\partial net_t} = \sigma(net_s) \cdot (1 - \sigma(net_s)) = o_s \cdot (1 - o_s)$$

and if $t \neq s$ we have

$$\frac{\partial \sigma(net_s)}{\partial net_t} = -\sigma(net_t) \cdot \sigma(net_s)) = -o_t \cdot o_s.$$

For the cross entropy error function

$$E(\mathbf{w}) = -\sum_{k=1}^{N} \sum_{t=1}^{K} y_{kt} \cdot \log o_{kt}, \tag{5.58}$$

we can take the gradient with respect to net_s over all training patterns using the chain rule

$$\frac{\partial E(\mathbf{w})}{\partial net_s} = \frac{\partial E}{\partial o_{kt}} \frac{\partial o_{kt}}{\partial net_s}$$

$$\frac{\partial E}{\partial o_{kt}} = -\sum_{k=1}^{N} \sum_{t=1}^{K} \frac{y_{kt}}{o_{kt}}, \qquad \frac{\partial o_{kt}}{\partial net_s} = o_{kt} \cdot (I_{ts} - o_{ks}),$$

$$\frac{\partial E}{\partial net_s} = -\sum_{k=1}^{N} \sum_{t=1}^{K} \frac{y_{kt}}{o_{kt}} \cdot o_{kt} \cdot (I_{ts} - o_{ks}) \tag{5.59}$$

$$\frac{\partial E}{\partial net_s} = -\sum_{k=1}^{N} \sum_{t=1}^{K} y_{kt} \cdot (I_{ts} - o_{ks}). \tag{5.60}$$

Using the fact that

$$\sum_{t=1}^{K} y_{kt} = 1,$$

we can further simplify to

$$\frac{\partial E}{\partial net_s} = -\sum_{k=1}^{N}(y_{ks} - o_{ks}) \tag{5.61}$$

Using the same chain-rule reasoning, we can write the derivative of the error with respect to the weights

$$\frac{\partial E(\mathbf{w})}{\partial w_{js}} = \frac{\partial E(\mathbf{w})}{\partial net_s}\frac{\partial net_s}{\partial w_{js}}.$$

Since

$$net_s = \sum_{j=1}^{D} w_{js}x_j$$

we have that

$$\frac{\partial net_s}{\partial w_{js}} = x_j.$$

So, for all N training patterns

$$\frac{\partial E}{\partial w_{js}} = -\sum_{k=1}^{N}(y_{ks} - o_{ks}) \cdot x_{kj} \tag{5.62}$$

with the learning rule

$$\Delta w_{js} = \eta \cdot \sum_{k=1}^{N}(y_{ks} - o_{ks}) \cdot x_{kj} \tag{5.63}$$

$$w_{js}^{new} = w_{js}^{old} + \Delta w_{js}.$$

This learning rule applied iteratively results in the logistic regression algorithm.

5.3.2 *Logistic Regression Algorithm*

Given a training set (sample)

$$Data = \{(\mathbf{x}_1, \mathbf{y}_1), (\mathbf{x}_2, \mathbf{y}_2), \cdots, (\mathbf{x}_k, \mathbf{y}_k), \cdots, (\mathbf{x}_N, \mathbf{y}_N)\}$$

with $\mathbf{y}_k$ represented as vectors of dimension K. During the training each neuron is trained individually withs its target value y_{kt}

$$y_{kt} \in \{0, 1\}, \quad \sum_{t=1}^{K} y_{kt} = 1$$

the goal of the algorithm is to correctly classify the test set (population) into K classes $C_1 = 100 \cdots, C_2 = 010 \cdots, C_3 = 001 \cdots, \cdots$

Algorithm

(1) iterations=0;

(2) $\eta \in (0, 1]$;

(3) FOR t=1 TO K
{
    Initialise all the weights $w_{0t}, w_{1t}, \cdots, w_{Dt}$ to some random values;
}

(4) Choose a pattern $\mathbf{x}_k$ out of the training set;

(5) FOR t=1 TO K
{
    Compute $net_{kt} = \sum_{i=1}^{D} w_{jt} \cdot x_{kj} + w_{0t} = \langle \mathbf{x}_k | \mathbf{w}_t \rangle + w_{0t} \cdot x_0$;
    Compute $odds_{kt} = \exp(net_{kt})$;
}

(6) FOR t=1 TO K
{
    Compute $o_{kt} = \frac{odds_{kt}}{\sum_t odds_{kt}}$;
    Compute $\Delta w_{jt} = \eta \cdot (y_{kt} - o_{kt}) \cdot x_{k,j}$;
    Update the weights $w_{jt} = w_{jt} + \Delta w_{jt}$;
}

(7) iterations++;

(8) If no change in weights for all training set or maximum number of iteration THEN STOP ELSE GOTO 4;

An epoch corresponds to adapting all trainings vectors (patterns) $\mathbf{x}_k$ with $k = 1, 2, \cdots, N$, with $epoch = iterations/N$. Depending on the training set, the initialization and the size of the learning rate, the epochs have to be repeated several times untill a solution is reached.

5.4   Multilayer Perceptron

In the next chapter we will see that the linear limitations of a perceptron or logistic regression do not apply to feed-forward networks with multiple nonlinear units called multilayer perceptrons. Such models are also trained by gradient descent. However, to compute gradients for the multiple units we will need to use a lot of the chain rule. The efficient way to do it results in a new algorithm called backpropagation. We will see later that this algorithm plays a core role in deep learning and deep convolutional neural networks.

5.5 Exercises and Answers

We have already seen that the perceptron can work with other activation functions besides the sign. From that knowledge it is helpful to define what is called a generalized linear unit that receives an input vector $x = \left(x_0 \cdots x_d \right)^T$, takes the dot product with its weight vector $\mathbf{w} = \left(w_0 \cdots w_d \right)^T$ and passes it to a general activation function g. We can write the output of this generalized unit as follows:

$$unit\left(\mathbf{x}; \mathbf{w}\right) = g\left(\mathbf{w}^T \mathbf{x}\right)$$

In the original perceptron, g was the sign function. Afterwards, we worked with the sgn_0 function. In fact, we can use, in principle, any function as we will se in the exercises below.

To perform learning in a generalized linear unit we also define an error function and try to minimize it. However, the process of minimization is not so easy as with linear regression. The activation function makes it impossible to get the same kind of closed form solution. So, we will have to use an iterative procedure, gradient descent!

We want to find the weight vector that minimizes an error function. However, we do not know a priori the error for all possible weight vectors. All we can do is: given an error function (like the sum of squared errors in the previous section) and training data, compute the error for a specific weight vector on that training data.

Illustrated in the figure below is the idea of gradient descent. Specifically, we start with a given weight vector $\mathbf{w}_0$ and compute the error function gradient for that vector $\frac{\partial E(\mathbf{w})}{\partial \mathbf{w}}\left(\mathbf{w}_0\right)$. This gradient will point away from the closest minimum value of error. So, we update our weight vector by taking a step into the reverse direction of the gradient $\mathbf{w}^{(1)} = \mathbf{w}^{(0)} - \eta \frac{\partial E(\mathbf{w})}{\partial \mathbf{w}}\left(\mathbf{w}^{(0)}\right)$.

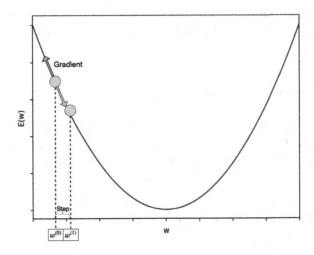

So, in general, for a differentiable error function, we have the general learning rule:

$$\mathbf{w}^{(t+1)} = \mathbf{w}^{(t)} - \eta \frac{\partial E\left(\mathbf{w}\right)}{\partial \mathbf{w}}\left(\mathbf{w}^{(t)}\right)$$

The error function gradient is computed on some training data. Sometimes, this process can take too long (if we have many examples) so we use stochastic gradient descent where the gradient of the error is computed for a single training example. So, instead of using all examples to take one update step we do one step per example. This makes learning faster. However, approximating the gradient with only one example can be very noisy so we can take very wrong steps sometimes.

Before moving to the exercises, let us make a quick note. When the error function is the cross-entropy loss and the unit's activation function is the sigmoid logistic function we call the model a logistic regression.

1)

Consider the following training data:

$$\left\{ \mathbf{x}^{(1)} = \begin{pmatrix} 1 \\ 1 \end{pmatrix}, \mathbf{x}^{(2)} = \begin{pmatrix} 2 \\ 1 \end{pmatrix}, \mathbf{x}^{(3)} = \begin{pmatrix} 1 \\ 3 \end{pmatrix}, \mathbf{x}^{(4)} = \begin{pmatrix} 3 \\ 3 \end{pmatrix} \right\}$$

$$\left\{ t^{(1)} = 1, t^{(2)} = 1, t^{(3)} = 0, t^{(4)} = 0 \right\}$$

In this exercise, we will work with a unit that computes the following function:

$$output\,(\mathbf{x}; \mathbf{w}) = \frac{1}{1 + \exp\,(-2\mathbf{w} \cdot \mathbf{x})}$$

And we will use the half sum of squared errors as our error (loss) function:

$$E\,(\mathbf{w}) = \frac{1}{2} \sum_{k=1}^{N} \left(t^{(k)} - output\,\left(\mathbf{x}^{(k)}; \mathbf{w} \right) \right)^2$$

a) Determine the gradient descent learning rule for this unit.

Solution:

To apply gradient descent, we want an update rule that moves a step of size η towards the opposite direction from the gradient of the error function with respect to the weights:

$$\mathbf{w} = \mathbf{w} - \eta \frac{\partial E\,(\mathbf{w})}{\partial \mathbf{w}}$$

To find the learning rule, we must compute the gradient. Before doing so, we should notice that the model is computing a sigmoid function, so:

$$output\,(\mathbf{x}; \mathbf{w}) = \frac{1}{1 + \exp\,(-2\mathbf{w} \cdot \mathbf{x})} = \sigma\,(2\mathbf{w} \cdot \mathbf{x})$$

Which has a well-known derivative that we will use later:

$$\frac{\partial \sigma\left(x\right)}{\partial x} = \frac{\partial \frac{1}{1+\exp(-x)}}{\partial x}$$

$$= \frac{\partial \frac{1}{1+\exp(-x)}}{\partial\left(1 + \exp\left(-x\right)\right)} \frac{\partial\left(1 + \exp\left(-x\right)\right)}{\partial\left(\exp\left(-x\right)\right)} \frac{\partial\left(\exp\left(-x\right)\right)}{\partial\left(-x\right)} \frac{\partial\left(-x\right)}{\partial x}$$

$$= -\frac{1}{\left(1 + \exp\left(-x\right)\right)^2} \exp\left(-x\right)\left(-1\right)$$

$$= \frac{1}{\left(1 + \exp\left(-x\right)\right)^2} \exp\left(-x\right)$$

$$= \frac{1}{1 + \exp\left(-x\right)} \frac{\exp\left(-x\right)}{1 + \exp\left(-x\right)}$$

$$= \frac{1}{1 + \exp\left(-x\right)} \frac{\exp\left(-x\right) + 1 - 1}{1 + \exp\left(-x\right)}$$

$$= \frac{1}{1 + \exp\left(-x\right)} \left(\frac{\exp\left(-x\right) + 1}{1 + \exp\left(-x\right)} - \frac{1}{1 + \exp\left(-x\right)}\right)$$

$$= \frac{1}{1 + \exp\left(-x\right)} \left(1 - \frac{1}{1 + \exp\left(-x\right)}\right)$$

$$= \sigma\left(x\right)\left(1 - \sigma\left(x\right)\right)$$

Having made this auxiliary computation, it is now easier to compute the derivative of the error function with respect to the parameter vector.

$$\frac{\partial E\left(\mathbf{w}\right)}{\partial \mathbf{w}} = \frac{\partial\left(-\sum_{k=1}^{N}\left(t^{(k)}\log output^{(k)}\left(\mathbf{x}^{(k)};\mathbf{w}\right) + \left(1-t^{(k)}\right)\log\left(1-output^{(k)}\left(\mathbf{x}^{(k)};\mathbf{w}\right)\right)\right)\right)}{\partial \mathbf{w}}$$

$$= -\sum_{k=1}^{N}\frac{\partial\left(t^{(k)}\log output^{(k)}\left(\mathbf{x}^{(k)};\mathbf{w}\right) + \left(1-t^{(k)}\right)\log\left(1-output^{(k)}\left(\mathbf{x}^{(k)};\mathbf{w}\right)\right)\right)}{\partial \mathbf{w}}$$

$$= -\sum_{k=1}^{N}\frac{\partial\left(t^{(k)}\log \sigma\left(\mathbf{w}\cdot\mathbf{x}^{(k)}\right) + \left(1-t^{(k)}\right)\log\left(1-\sigma\left(\mathbf{w}\cdot\mathbf{x}^{(k)}\right)\right)\right)}{\partial \mathbf{w}}$$

$$= -\sum_{k=1}^{N}\left(\frac{\partial\left(t^{(k)}\log \sigma\left(\mathbf{w}\cdot\mathbf{x}^{(k)}\right)\right)}{\partial \mathbf{w}} + \frac{\partial\left(\left(1-t^{(k)}\right)\log\left(1-\sigma\left(\mathbf{w}\cdot\mathbf{x}^{(k)}\right)\right)\right)}{\partial \mathbf{w}}\right)$$

$$= -\sum_{k=1}^{N}\left(t^{(k)}\frac{\partial\left(\log \sigma\left(\mathbf{w}\cdot\mathbf{x}^{(k)}\right)\right)}{\partial \mathbf{w}} + \left(1-t^{(k)}\right)\frac{\partial\left(\log\left(1-\sigma\left(\mathbf{w}\cdot\mathbf{x}^{(k)}\right)\right)\right)}{\partial \mathbf{w}}\right)$$

$$= -\sum_{k=1}^{N}(t^{(k)}\frac{\partial\left(\log \sigma\left(\mathbf{w}\cdot\mathbf{x}^{(k)}\right)\right)}{\partial \sigma\left(\mathbf{w}\cdot\mathbf{x}^{(k)}\right)}\frac{\partial \sigma\left(\mathbf{w}\cdot\mathbf{x}^{(k)}\right)}{\partial\left(\mathbf{w}\cdot\mathbf{x}^{(k)}\right)}\frac{\partial \mathbf{w}\cdot\mathbf{x}^{(k)}}{\partial \mathbf{w}}$$

$$+ \left(1-t^{(k)}\right)\frac{\partial\left(\log\left(1-\sigma\left(\mathbf{w}\cdot\mathbf{x}^{(k)}\right)\right)\right)}{\partial\left(1-\sigma\left(\mathbf{w}\cdot\mathbf{x}^{(k)}\right)\right)}\frac{\partial\left(1-\sigma\left(\mathbf{w}\cdot\mathbf{x}^{(k)}\right)\right)}{\partial \sigma\left(\mathbf{w}\cdot\mathbf{x}^{(k)}\right)}\frac{\partial \sigma\left(\mathbf{w}\cdot\mathbf{x}^{(k)}\right)}{\partial\left(\mathbf{w}\cdot\mathbf{x}^{(k)}\right)}\frac{\partial\left(\mathbf{w}\cdot\mathbf{x}^{(k)}\right)}{\partial \mathbf{w}}$$

$$= -\sum_{k=1}^{N}(t^{(k)}\frac{1}{\sigma\left(\mathbf{w}\cdot\mathbf{x}^{(k)}\right)}\sigma\left(\mathbf{w}\cdot\mathbf{x}^{(k)}\right)\left(1-\sigma\left(\mathbf{w}\cdot\mathbf{x}^{(k)}\right)\right)\mathbf{x}^{(k)}$$

$$+ \left(1-t^{(k)}\right)\frac{1}{1-\sigma\left(\mathbf{w}\cdot\mathbf{x}^{(k)}\right)}\left(-1\right)\sigma\left(\mathbf{w}\cdot\mathbf{x}^{(k)}\right)\left(1-\sigma\left(\mathbf{w}\cdot\mathbf{x}^{(k)}\right)\right)\mathbf{x}^{(k)}$$

$$= -\sum_{k=1}^{N}\left(t^{(k)}\left(1-\sigma\left(\mathbf{w}\cdot\mathbf{x}^{(k)}\right)\right)\mathbf{x}^{(k)} + \left(1-t^{(k)}\right)\left(-1\right)\sigma\left(\mathbf{w}\cdot\mathbf{x}^{(k)}\right)\mathbf{x}^{(k)}\right)$$

$$= -\sum_{k=1}^{N}\left(t^{(k)}\left(1-\sigma\left(\mathbf{w}\cdot\mathbf{x}^{(k)}\right)\right)\mathbf{x}^{(k)} - \left(1-t^{(k)}\right)\sigma\left(\mathbf{w}\cdot\mathbf{x}^{(k)}\right)\mathbf{x}^{(k)}\right)$$

$$= -\sum_{k=1}^{N}\mathbf{x}^{(k)}\left(t^{(k)}\left(1-\sigma\left(\mathbf{w}\cdot\mathbf{x}^{(k)}\right)\right) - \left(1-t^{(k)}\right)\sigma\left(\mathbf{w}\cdot\mathbf{x}^{(k)}\right)\right)$$

$$= -\sum_{k=1}^{N}\mathbf{x}^{(k)}\left(t^{(k)} - t^{(k)}\sigma\left(\mathbf{w}\cdot\mathbf{x}^{(k)}\right) - \left(\sigma\left(\mathbf{w}\cdot\mathbf{x}^{(k)}\right) - t^{(k)}\sigma\left(\mathbf{w}\cdot\mathbf{x}^{(k)}\right)\right)\right)$$

$$= -\sum_{k=1}^{N}\mathbf{x}^{(k)}\left(t^{(k)} - t^{(k)}\sigma\left(\mathbf{w}\cdot\mathbf{x}^{(k)}\right) - \sigma\left(\mathbf{w}\cdot\mathbf{x}^{(k)}\right) + t^{(k)}\sigma\left(\mathbf{w}\cdot\mathbf{x}^{(k)}\right)\right)$$

$$= -\sum_{k=1}^{N}\mathbf{x}^{(k)}\left(t^{(k)} - \sigma\left(\mathbf{w}\cdot\mathbf{x}^{(k)}\right)\right)$$

So, we can write our update rule as follows.

$$\mathbf{w} = \mathbf{w} - \eta \frac{\partial E(\mathbf{w})}{\partial \mathbf{w}}$$

$$= \mathbf{w} - \eta \left(-2 \sum_{k=1}^{N} \left(\left(t^{(k)} - \sigma \left(2\mathbf{w} \cdot \mathbf{x}^{(k)} \right) \right) \left(\sigma \left(2\mathbf{w} \cdot \mathbf{x}^{(k)} \right) \left(1 - \sigma \left(2\mathbf{w} \cdot \mathbf{x}^{(k)} \right) \right) \right) \mathbf{x}^{(k)} \right) \right)$$

$$= \mathbf{w} + 2\eta \sum_{k=1}^{N} \left(\left(t^{(k)} - \sigma \left(2\mathbf{w} \cdot \mathbf{x}^{(k)} \right) \right) \left(\sigma \left(2\mathbf{w} \cdot \mathbf{x}^{(k)} \right) \left(1 - \sigma \left(2\mathbf{w} \cdot \mathbf{x}^{(k)} \right) \right) \right) \mathbf{x}^{(k)} \right)$$

---

b) Compute the first gradient descent update assuming an initialization of all ones.

Solution:

The original gradient descent does one update per epoch because its learning rule requires contributions from all data points to do one step. Let us compute it.

According to the problem statement, we start with weights $\mathbf{w} = \begin{pmatrix} 1 \\ 1 \\ 1 \end{pmatrix}$ and learning rate $\eta = 1.0$.

$$\mathbf{w} = \mathbf{w} + 2\eta \sum_{k=1}^{4} \left(\left(t^{(k)} - \sigma \left(2\mathbf{w} \cdot \mathbf{x}^{(k)} \right) \right) \left(\sigma \left(2\mathbf{w} \cdot \mathbf{x}^{(k)} \right) \left(1 - \sigma \left(2\mathbf{w} \cdot \mathbf{x}^{(k)} \right) \right) \right) \mathbf{x}^{(k)} \right)$$

$$= \mathbf{w} + \sum_{k=1}^{4} 2\eta \left(\left(t^{(k)} - \sigma \left(2\mathbf{w} \cdot \mathbf{x}^{(k)} \right) \right) \left(\sigma \left(2\mathbf{w} \cdot \mathbf{x}^{(k)} \right) \left(1 - \sigma \left(2\mathbf{w} \cdot \mathbf{x}^{(k)} \right) \right) \right) \mathbf{x}^{(k)} \right)$$

$$= \mathbf{w} + 2\eta \left(\left(t^{(1)} - \sigma \left(2\mathbf{w} \cdot \mathbf{x}^{(1)} \right) \right) \left(\sigma \left(2\mathbf{w} \cdot \mathbf{x}^{(1)} \right) \left(1 - \sigma \left(2\mathbf{w} \cdot \mathbf{x}^{(1)} \right) \right) \right) \mathbf{x}^{(1)} \right)$$
$$+ 2\eta \left(\left(t^{(2)} - \sigma \left(2\mathbf{w} \cdot \mathbf{x}^{(2)} \right) \right) \left(\sigma \left(2\mathbf{w} \cdot \mathbf{x}^{(2)} \right) \left(1 - \sigma \left(2\mathbf{w} \cdot \mathbf{x}^{(2)} \right) \right) \right) \mathbf{x}^{(2)} \right)$$
$$+ 2\eta \left(\left(t^{(3)} - \sigma \left(2\mathbf{w} \cdot \mathbf{x}^{(3)} \right) \right) \left(\sigma \left(2\mathbf{w} \cdot \mathbf{x}^{(3)} \right) \left(1 - \sigma \left(2\mathbf{w} \cdot \mathbf{x}^{(3)} \right) \right) \right) \mathbf{x}^{(3)} \right)$$
$$+ 2\eta \left(\left(t^{(4)} - \sigma \left(2\mathbf{w} \cdot \mathbf{x}^{(4)} \right) \right) \left(\sigma \left(2\mathbf{w} \cdot \mathbf{x}^{(4)} \right) \left(1 - \sigma \left(2\mathbf{w} \cdot \mathbf{x}^{(4)} \right) \right) \right) \mathbf{x}^{(4)} \right)$$

$$= \begin{pmatrix} 1 \\ 1 \\ 1 \end{pmatrix}$$

$$+ 2 \left(1 - \sigma \left(2 \begin{pmatrix} 1 \\ 1 \\ 1 \end{pmatrix} \cdot \begin{pmatrix} 1 \\ 1 \\ 1 \end{pmatrix} \right) \right) \sigma \left(2 \begin{pmatrix} 1 \\ 1 \\ 1 \end{pmatrix} \cdot \begin{pmatrix} 1 \\ 1 \\ 1 \end{pmatrix} \right) \left(1 - \sigma \left(2 \begin{pmatrix} 1 \\ 1 \\ 1 \end{pmatrix} \cdot \begin{pmatrix} 1 \\ 1 \\ 1 \end{pmatrix} \right) \right) \begin{pmatrix} 1 \\ 1 \\ 1 \end{pmatrix}$$

$$+ 2 \left(1 - \sigma \left(2 \begin{pmatrix} 1 \\ 1 \\ 1 \end{pmatrix} \cdot \begin{pmatrix} 1 \\ 2 \\ 1 \end{pmatrix} \right) \right) \sigma \left(2 \begin{pmatrix} 1 \\ 1 \\ 1 \end{pmatrix} \cdot \begin{pmatrix} 1 \\ 2 \\ 1 \end{pmatrix} \right) \left(1 - \sigma \left(2 \begin{pmatrix} 1 \\ 1 \\ 1 \end{pmatrix} \cdot \begin{pmatrix} 1 \\ 2 \\ 1 \end{pmatrix} \right) \right) \begin{pmatrix} 1 \\ 2 \\ 1 \end{pmatrix}$$

$$+ 2 \left(0 - \sigma \left(2 \begin{pmatrix} 1 \\ 1 \\ 1 \end{pmatrix} \cdot \begin{pmatrix} 1 \\ 1 \\ 3 \end{pmatrix} \right) \right) \sigma \left(2 \begin{pmatrix} 1 \\ 1 \\ 1 \end{pmatrix} \cdot \begin{pmatrix} 1 \\ 1 \\ 3 \end{pmatrix} \right) \left(1 - \sigma \left(2 \begin{pmatrix} 1 \\ 1 \\ 1 \end{pmatrix} \cdot \begin{pmatrix} 1 \\ 1 \\ 3 \end{pmatrix} \right) \right) \begin{pmatrix} 1 \\ 1 \\ 3 \end{pmatrix}$$

$$+ 2 \left(0 - \sigma \left(2 \begin{pmatrix} 1 \\ 1 \\ 1 \end{pmatrix} \cdot \begin{pmatrix} 1 \\ 3 \\ 3 \end{pmatrix} \right) \right) \sigma \left(2 \begin{pmatrix} 1 \\ 1 \\ 1 \end{pmatrix} \cdot \begin{pmatrix} 1 \\ 3 \\ 3 \end{pmatrix} \right) \left(1 - \sigma \left(2 \begin{pmatrix} 1 \\ 1 \\ 1 \end{pmatrix} \cdot \begin{pmatrix} 1 \\ 3 \\ 3 \end{pmatrix} \right) \right) \begin{pmatrix} 1 \\ 3 \\ 3 \end{pmatrix}$$

$$= \begin{pmatrix} 1 \\ 1 \\ 1 \end{pmatrix} + 2 \left(1 - \sigma \left(6 \right) \right) \left(\sigma \left(6 \right) \left(1 - \sigma \left(6 \right) \right) \right) \begin{pmatrix} 1 \\ 1 \\ 1 \end{pmatrix} + 2 \left(1 - \sigma \left(8 \right) \right) \left(\sigma \left(8 \right) \left(1 - \sigma \left(8 \right) \right) \right) \begin{pmatrix} 1 \\ 2 \\ 1 \end{pmatrix}$$
$$+ 2 \left(0 - \sigma \left(10 \right) \right) \left(\sigma \left(10 \right) \left(1 - \sigma \left(10 \right) \right) \right) \begin{pmatrix} 1 \\ 1 \\ 3 \end{pmatrix} + 2 \left(0 - \sigma \left(14 \right) \right) \left(\sigma \left(14 \right) \left(1 - \sigma \left(14 \right) \right) \right) \begin{pmatrix} 1 \\ 3 \\ 3 \end{pmatrix}$$

$$= \begin{pmatrix} 1 \\ 1 \\ 1 \end{pmatrix} + \begin{pmatrix} 1.2197 \times 10^{-5} \\ 1.2197 \times 10^{-5} \\ 1.2197 \times 10^{-5} \end{pmatrix} + \begin{pmatrix} 2.2484 \times 10^{-7} \\ 4.4969 \times 10^{-7} \\ 2.2484 \times 10^{-7} \end{pmatrix}$$

$$+ \begin{pmatrix} -9.0787 \times 10^{-5} \\ -9.0787 \times 10^{-5} \\ -2.7236 \times 10^{-4} \end{pmatrix} + \begin{pmatrix} -1.6631 \times 10^{-6} \\ -4.9892 \times 10^{-6} \\ -4.9892 \times 10^{-6} \end{pmatrix}$$

$$= \begin{pmatrix} 0.99991997 \\ 0.99991687 \\ 0.99973507 \end{pmatrix}$$

c) Compute the first stochastic gradient descent update assuming an initialization of all ones.

Solution:

In stochastic gradient descent we make one update for each training example. So, instead of summing across all data points we adapt the learning rule for one example only:

$$\mathbf{w} = \mathbf{w} + 2\eta\left((t - \sigma(2\mathbf{w} \cdot \mathbf{x}))\left(\sigma(2\mathbf{w} \cdot \mathbf{x})(1 - \sigma(2\mathbf{w} \cdot \mathbf{x}))\right)\mathbf{x}\right)$$

We can now do the updates. Let us start with the first example:

$$\mathbf{w} = \mathbf{w} + 2\eta\left((t - \sigma(2\mathbf{w} \cdot \mathbf{x}))\left(\sigma(2\mathbf{w} \cdot \mathbf{x})(1 - \sigma(2\mathbf{w} \cdot \mathbf{x}))\right)\mathbf{x}\right)$$

$$= \begin{pmatrix} 1 \\ 1 \\ 1 \end{pmatrix} + 2\left(1 - \sigma\left(2\begin{pmatrix} 1 \\ 1 \\ 1 \end{pmatrix} \cdot \begin{pmatrix} 1 \\ 1 \\ 1 \end{pmatrix}\right)\right)\sigma\left(2\begin{pmatrix} 1 \\ 1 \\ 1 \end{pmatrix} \cdot \begin{pmatrix} 1 \\ 1 \\ 1 \end{pmatrix}\right)$$

$$\cdot\left(1 - \sigma\left(2\begin{pmatrix} 1 \\ 1 \\ 1 \end{pmatrix} \cdot \begin{pmatrix} 1 \\ 1 \\ 1 \end{pmatrix}\right)\right)\begin{pmatrix} 1 \\ 1 \\ 1 \end{pmatrix}$$

$$= \begin{pmatrix} 1 \\ 1 \\ 1 \end{pmatrix} + 2(1 - \sigma(6))(\sigma(6)(1 - \sigma(6)))\begin{pmatrix} 1 \\ 1 \\ 1 \end{pmatrix}$$

$$= \begin{pmatrix} 1 \\ 1 \\ 1 \end{pmatrix} + \begin{pmatrix} 1.2197 \times 10^{-5} \\ 1.2197 \times 10^{-5} \\ 1.2197 \times 10^{-5} \end{pmatrix}$$

$$= \begin{pmatrix} 1.0000122 \\ 1.0000122 \\ 1.0000122 \end{pmatrix}$$

---

2)

Consider the following training data:

$$\left\{\mathbf{x}^{(1)} = \begin{pmatrix} 1 \\ 1 \end{pmatrix}, \mathbf{x}^{(2)} = \begin{pmatrix} 2 \\ 1 \end{pmatrix}, \mathbf{x}^{(3)} = \begin{pmatrix} 1 \\ 3 \end{pmatrix}, \mathbf{x}^{(4)} = \begin{pmatrix} 3 \\ 3 \end{pmatrix}\right\}$$

$$\left\{t^{(1)} = 1, t^{(2)} = 1, t^{(3)} = 0, t^{(4)} = 0\right\}$$

In this exercise, we will work with a unit that computes the following function:

$$output\left(\mathbf{x}; \mathbf{w}\right) = \frac{1}{1 + \exp\left(-\mathbf{w} \cdot \mathbf{x}\right)}$$

And we will use the cross-entropy loss function:

$$E\left(\mathbf{w}\right) = -\log\left(p\left(\mathbf{t} \mid \mathbf{w}\right)\right) =$$

$$-\sum_{k=1}^{N} \left(t^{(k)} \log output^{(k)}\left(\mathbf{x}^{(k)}; \mathbf{w}\right) + \left(1 - t^{(k)}\right) \log\left(1 - output^{(k)}\left(\mathbf{x}^{(k)}; \mathbf{w}\right)\right)\right)$$

a) Determine the gradient descent learning rule for this unit.

Solution:

To apply gradient descent, we want an update rule that moves a step of size η towards the opposite direction from the gradient of the error function with respect to the weights:

$$\mathbf{w} = \mathbf{w} - \eta \frac{\partial E\left(\mathbf{w}\right)}{\partial \mathbf{w}}$$

To find the learning rule, we must compute the gradient. Before doing so, we should notice that the model is computing a sigmoid function, so:

$$output\left(\mathbf{x}; \mathbf{w}\right) = \frac{1}{1 + \exp\left(-\mathbf{w} \cdot \mathbf{x}\right)} = \sigma\left(\mathbf{w} \cdot \mathbf{x}\right)$$

Which has a well-known derivative that we computed earlier:

$$\frac{\partial \sigma\left(x\right)}{\partial x} = \sigma\left(x\right)\left(1 - \sigma\left(x\right)\right)$$

Having made this auxiliary computation, it is now easier to compute the derivative of the error function with respect to the parameter vector.

$$\frac{\partial E\left(\mathbf{w}\right)}{\partial \mathbf{w}} = \frac{\partial \left(-\sum_{k=1}^{N}\left(t^{(k)}\log output^{(k)}\left(\mathbf{x}^{(k)};\mathbf{w}\right) + \left(1 - t^{(k)}\right)\log\left(1 - output^{(k)}\left(\mathbf{x}^{(k)};\mathbf{w}\right)\right)\right)\right)}{\partial \mathbf{w}}$$

$$= -\sum_{k=1}^{N}\frac{\partial \left(t^{(k)}\log output^{(k)}\left(\mathbf{x}^{(k)};\mathbf{w}\right) + \left(1 - t^{(k)}\right)\log\left(1 - output^{(k)}\left(\mathbf{x}^{(k)};\mathbf{w}\right)\right)\right)}{\partial \mathbf{w}}$$

$$= -\sum_{k=1}^{N}\frac{\partial \left(t^{(k)}\log \sigma\left(\mathbf{w}\cdot\mathbf{x}^{(k)}\right) + \left(1 - t^{(k)}\right)\log\left(1 - \sigma\left(\mathbf{w}\cdot\mathbf{x}^{(k)}\right)\right)\right)}{\partial \mathbf{w}}$$

$$= -\sum_{k=1}^{N}\left(\frac{\partial \left(t^{(k)}\log \sigma\left(\mathbf{w}\cdot\mathbf{x}^{(k)}\right)\right)}{\partial \mathbf{w}} + \frac{\partial \left(\left(1 - t^{(k)}\right)\log\left(1 - \sigma\left(\mathbf{w}\cdot\mathbf{x}^{(k)}\right)\right)\right)}{\partial \mathbf{w}}\right)$$

$$= -\sum_{k=1}^{N}\left(t^{(k)}\frac{\partial \left(\log \sigma\left(\mathbf{w}\cdot\mathbf{x}^{(k)}\right)\right)}{\partial \mathbf{w}} + \left(1 - t^{(k)}\right)\frac{\partial \left(\log\left(1 - \sigma\left(\mathbf{w}\cdot\mathbf{x}^{(k)}\right)\right)\right)}{\partial \mathbf{w}}\right)$$

$$= -\sum_{k=1}^{N}(t^{(k)}\frac{\partial \left(\log \sigma\left(\mathbf{w}\cdot\mathbf{x}^{(k)}\right)\right)}{\partial \sigma\left(\mathbf{w}\cdot\mathbf{x}^{(k)}\right)}\frac{\partial \sigma\left(\mathbf{w}\cdot\mathbf{x}^{(k)}\right)}{\partial \left(\mathbf{w}\cdot\mathbf{x}^{(k)}\right)}\frac{\partial \mathbf{w}\cdot\mathbf{x}^{(k)}}{\partial \mathbf{w}}$$

$$+ \left(1 - t^{(k)}\right)\frac{\partial \left(\log\left(1 - \sigma\left(\mathbf{w}\cdot\mathbf{x}^{(k)}\right)\right)\right)}{\partial \left(1 - \sigma\left(\mathbf{w}\cdot\mathbf{x}^{(k)}\right)\right)}\frac{\partial \left(1 - \sigma\left(\mathbf{w}\cdot\mathbf{x}^{(k)}\right)\right)}{\partial \sigma\left(\mathbf{w}\cdot\mathbf{x}^{(k)}\right)}\frac{\partial \sigma\left(\mathbf{w}\cdot\mathbf{x}^{(k)}\right)}{\partial \left(\mathbf{w}\cdot\mathbf{x}^{(k)}\right)}\frac{\partial \left(\mathbf{w}\cdot\mathbf{x}^{(k)}\right)}{\partial \mathbf{w}}$$

$$= -\sum_{k=1}^{N}(t^{(k)}\frac{1}{\sigma\left(\mathbf{w}\cdot\mathbf{x}^{(k)}\right)}\sigma\left(\mathbf{w}\cdot\mathbf{x}^{(k)}\right)\left(1 - \sigma\left(\mathbf{w}\cdot\mathbf{x}^{(k)}\right)\right)\mathbf{x}^{(k)}$$

$$+ \left(1 - t^{(k)}\right)\frac{1}{1 - \sigma\left(\mathbf{w}\cdot\mathbf{x}^{(k)}\right)}(-1)\sigma\left(\mathbf{w}\cdot\mathbf{x}^{(k)}\right)\left(1 - \sigma\left(\mathbf{w}\cdot\mathbf{x}^{(k)}\right)\right)\mathbf{x}^{(k)})$$

$$= -\sum_{k=1}^{N}\left(t^{(k)}\left(1 - \sigma\left(\mathbf{w}\cdot\mathbf{x}^{(k)}\right)\right)\mathbf{x}^{(k)} + \left(1 - t^{(k)}\right)(-1)\sigma\left(\mathbf{w}\cdot\mathbf{x}^{(k)}\right)\mathbf{x}^{(k)}\right)$$

$$= -\sum_{k=1}^{N}\left(t^{(k)}\left(1 - \sigma\left(\mathbf{w}\cdot\mathbf{x}^{(k)}\right)\right)\mathbf{x}^{(k)} - \left(1 - t^{(k)}\right)\sigma\left(\mathbf{w}\cdot\mathbf{x}^{(k)}\right)\mathbf{x}^{(k)}\right)$$

$$= -\sum_{k=1}^{N}\mathbf{x}^{(k)}\left(t^{(k)}\left(1 - \sigma\left(\mathbf{w}\cdot\mathbf{x}^{(k)}\right)\right) - \left(1 - t^{(k)}\right)\sigma\left(\mathbf{w}\cdot\mathbf{x}^{(k)}\right)\right)$$

$$= -\sum_{k=1}^{N}\mathbf{x}^{(k)}\left(t^{(k)} - t^{(k)}\sigma\left(\mathbf{w}\cdot\mathbf{x}^{(k)}\right) - \left(\sigma\left(\mathbf{w}\cdot\mathbf{x}^{(k)}\right) - t^{(k)}\sigma\left(\mathbf{w}\cdot\mathbf{x}^{(k)}\right)\right)\right)$$

$$= -\sum_{k=1}^{N}\mathbf{x}^{(k)}\left(t^{(k)} - t^{(k)}\sigma\left(\mathbf{w}\cdot\mathbf{x}^{(k)}\right) - \sigma\left(\mathbf{w}\cdot\mathbf{x}^{(k)}\right) + t^{(k)}\sigma\left(\mathbf{w}\cdot\mathbf{x}^{(k)}\right)\right)$$

$$= -\sum_{k=1}^{N}\mathbf{x}^{(k)}\left(t^{(k)} - \sigma\left(\mathbf{w}\cdot\mathbf{x}^{(k)}\right)\right)$$

So, we can write our update rule as follows.

$$\mathbf{w} = \mathbf{w} - \eta \frac{\partial E(\mathbf{w})}{\partial \mathbf{w}}$$

$$= \mathbf{w} - \eta \left(-\sum_{k=1}^{N} \mathbf{x}^{(k)} \left(t^{(k)} - \sigma \left(\mathbf{w} \cdot \mathbf{x}^{(k)} \right) \right) \right)$$

$$= \mathbf{w} + \eta \sum_{k=1}^{N} \mathbf{x}^{(k)} \left(t^{(k)} - \sigma \left(\mathbf{w} \cdot \mathbf{x}^{(k)} \right) \right)$$

---

b) Compute the first gradient descent update assuming an initialization of all ones.

Solution:

The original gradient descent does one update per epoch because its learning rule requires contributions from all data points to do one step. Let us compute it.

According to the problem statement, we start with weights $\mathbf{w} = \begin{pmatrix} 1 \\ 1 \\ 1 \end{pmatrix}$ and learning rate $\eta = 1.0$.

$$\mathbf{w} = \mathbf{w} + \eta \sum_{k=1}^{N} \mathbf{x}^{(k)} \left(t^{(k)} - \sigma \left(\mathbf{w} \cdot \mathbf{x}^{(k)} \right) \right)$$

$$= \mathbf{w} + \eta \sum_{k=1}^{4} \mathbf{x}^{(k)} \left(t^{(k)} - \sigma \left(\mathbf{w} \cdot \mathbf{x}^{(k)} \right) \right)$$

$$= \mathbf{w} + \eta \mathbf{x}^{(1)} \left(t^{(1)} - \sigma \left(\mathbf{w} \cdot \mathbf{x}^{(1)} \right) \right) + \eta \mathbf{x}^{(2)} \left(t^{(2)} - \sigma \left(\mathbf{w} \cdot \mathbf{x}^{(2)} \right) \right)$$
$$+ \eta \mathbf{x}^{(3)} \left(t^{(3)} - \sigma \left(\mathbf{w} \cdot \mathbf{x}^{(3)} \right) \right) + \eta \mathbf{x}^{(4)} \left(t^{(4)} - \sigma \left(\mathbf{w} \cdot \mathbf{x}^{(4)} \right) \right)$$

$$= \begin{pmatrix} 1 \\ 1 \\ 1 \end{pmatrix} + \begin{pmatrix} 1 \\ 1 \\ 1 \end{pmatrix} \left(1 - \sigma \left(\begin{pmatrix} 1 \\ 1 \\ 1 \end{pmatrix} \cdot \begin{pmatrix} 1 \\ 1 \\ 1 \end{pmatrix} \right) \right) + \begin{pmatrix} 1 \\ 2 \\ 1 \end{pmatrix} \left(1 - \sigma \left(\begin{pmatrix} 1 \\ 1 \\ 1 \end{pmatrix} \cdot \begin{pmatrix} 1 \\ 2 \\ 1 \end{pmatrix} \right) \right)$$

$$+ \begin{pmatrix} 1 \\ 1 \\ 3 \end{pmatrix} \left(0 - \sigma \left(\begin{pmatrix} 1 \\ 1 \\ 1 \end{pmatrix} \cdot \begin{pmatrix} 1 \\ 1 \\ 3 \end{pmatrix} \right) \right) + \begin{pmatrix} 1 \\ 3 \\ 3 \end{pmatrix} \left(0 - \sigma \left(\begin{pmatrix} 1 \\ 1 \\ 1 \end{pmatrix} \cdot \begin{pmatrix} 1 \\ 3 \\ 3 \end{pmatrix} \right) \right)$$

$$= \begin{pmatrix} 1 \\ 1 \\ 1 \end{pmatrix} + \begin{pmatrix} 1 \\ 1 \\ 1 \end{pmatrix} (1 - \sigma(3)) + \begin{pmatrix} 1 \\ 2 \\ 1 \end{pmatrix} (1 - \sigma(4)) + \begin{pmatrix} 1 \\ 1 \\ 3 \end{pmatrix} (0 - \sigma(5)) + \begin{pmatrix} 1 \\ 3 \\ 3 \end{pmatrix} (0 - \sigma(7))$$

$$= \begin{pmatrix} 1 \\ 1 \\ 1 \end{pmatrix} + \begin{pmatrix} 0.0474 \\ 0.0474 \\ 0.0474 \end{pmatrix} + \begin{pmatrix} 0.0179 \\ 0.0359 \\ 0.0179 \end{pmatrix} + \begin{pmatrix} -0.9933 \\ -0.9933 \\ -2.9799 \end{pmatrix} + \begin{pmatrix} -0.9991 \\ -2.9973 \\ -2.9973 \end{pmatrix}$$

$$= \begin{pmatrix} -0.9269 \\ -2.9072 \\ -4.9118 \end{pmatrix}$$

c) Compute the first stochastic gradient descent update assuming an initialization of all ones.

Solution:

In stochastic gradient descent we make one update for each training example. So, instead of summing accross all data points we adapt the learning rule for one example only:

$$\mathbf{w} = \mathbf{w} + \eta \mathbf{x} \left(t - \sigma \left(\mathbf{w} \cdot \mathbf{x} \right) \right)$$

We can now do the updates. Let us start with the first example:

$$\mathbf{w} = \mathbf{w} + \eta \mathbf{x} \left(t - \sigma \left(\mathbf{w} \cdot \mathbf{x} \right) \right)$$

$$= \begin{pmatrix} 1 \\ 1 \\ 1 \end{pmatrix} + 1 \begin{pmatrix} 1 \\ 1 \\ 1 \end{pmatrix} \left(1 - \sigma \left(\begin{pmatrix} 1 \\ 1 \\ 1 \end{pmatrix} \cdot \begin{pmatrix} 1 \\ 1 \\ 1 \end{pmatrix} \right) \right)$$

$$= \begin{pmatrix} 1 \\ 1 \\ 1 \end{pmatrix} + \begin{pmatrix} 1 \\ 1 \\ 1 \end{pmatrix} \left(1 - \sigma \left(3 \right) \right)$$

$$= \begin{pmatrix} 1 \\ 1 \\ 1 \end{pmatrix} + \begin{pmatrix} 0.0474 \\ 0.0474 \\ 0.0474 \end{pmatrix}$$

$$= \begin{pmatrix} 1.0474 \\ 1.0474 \\ 1.0474 \end{pmatrix}$$

---

3)

Consider the following training data:

$$\left\{ \mathbf{x}^{(1)} = \begin{pmatrix} 1 \\ 1 \end{pmatrix}, \mathbf{x}^{(2)} = \begin{pmatrix} 2 \\ 1 \end{pmatrix}, \mathbf{x}^{(3)} = \begin{pmatrix} 1 \\ 3 \end{pmatrix}, \mathbf{x}^{(4)} = \begin{pmatrix} 3 \\ 3 \end{pmatrix} \right\}$$

$$\left\{ t^{(1)} = 1, t^{(2)} = 1, t^{(3)} = 0, t^{(4)} = 0 \right\}$$

In this exercise, we will work with a unit that computes the following function:

$$output\,(\mathbf{x};\mathbf{w}) = \exp\left(\left(\mathbf{w}\cdot\mathbf{x}\right)^2\right)$$

And we will use the half sum of squared errors as our error (loss) function:

$$E\,(\mathbf{w}) = \frac{1}{2}\sum_{k=1}^{N}\left(t^{(k)} - output\left(\mathbf{x}^{(k)};\mathbf{w}\right)\right)$$

a) Determine the gradient descent learning rule for this unit.

Solution:

To apply gradient descent, we want an update rule that moves a step of size η towards the opposite direction from the gradient of the error function with respect to the weights:

$$\mathbf{w} = \mathbf{w} - \eta\frac{\partial E\,(\mathbf{w})}{\partial \mathbf{w}}$$

To find the learning rule, we must compute the gradient of the error function with respect to the parameter vector.

$$
\begin{aligned}
\frac{\partial E\,(\mathbf{w})}{\partial \mathbf{w}} &= \frac{\partial \frac{1}{2}\sum_{k=1}^{N}\left(t^{(k)} - output\left(\mathbf{x}^{(k)};\mathbf{w}\right)\right)^2}{\partial \mathbf{w}} \\[2mm]
&= \frac{\partial \frac{1}{2}\sum_{k=1}^{N}\left(t^{(k)} - \exp\left(\left(\mathbf{w}\cdot\mathbf{x}^{(k)}\right)^2\right)\right)^2}{\partial \mathbf{w}} \\[2mm]
&= \frac{1}{2}\frac{\partial \sum_{k=1}^{N}\left(t^{(k)} - \exp\left(\left(\mathbf{w}\cdot\mathbf{x}^{(k)}\right)^2\right)\right)^2}{\partial \mathbf{w}} \\[2mm]
&= \frac{1}{2}\sum_{k=1}^{N}\frac{\partial \left(t^{(k)} - \exp\left(\left(\mathbf{w}\cdot\mathbf{x}^{(k)}\right)^2\right)\right)^2}{\partial \mathbf{w}} \\[2mm]
&= \frac{1}{2}\sum_{k=1}^{N}\frac{\partial \left(t^{(k)} - \exp\left(\left(\mathbf{w}\cdot\mathbf{x}^{(k)}\right)^2\right)\right)^2}{\partial \left(t^{(k)} - \exp\left(\left(\mathbf{w}\cdot\mathbf{x}^{(k)}\right)^2\right)\right)}\frac{\partial \left(t^{(k)} - \exp\left(\left(\mathbf{w}\cdot\mathbf{x}^{(k)}\right)^2\right)\right)}{\partial \exp\left(\left(\mathbf{w}\cdot\mathbf{x}^{(k)}\right)^2\right)} \\[2mm]
&\quad \frac{\partial \exp\left(\left(\mathbf{w}\cdot\mathbf{x}^{(k)}\right)^2\right)}{\partial \left(\left(\mathbf{w}\cdot\mathbf{x}^{(k)}\right)^2\right)}\frac{\partial \left(\left(\mathbf{w}\cdot\mathbf{x}^{(k)}\right)^2\right)}{\partial \left(\mathbf{w}\cdot\mathbf{x}^{(k)}\right)}\frac{\partial \left(\mathbf{w}\cdot\mathbf{x}^{(k)}\right)}{\partial \mathbf{w}} \\[2mm]
&= \frac{1}{2}\sum_{k=1}^{N}\left(2\left(t^{(k)} - \exp\left(\left(\mathbf{w}\cdot\mathbf{x}^{(k)}\right)^2\right)\right)\right)(-1)\exp\left(\left(\mathbf{w}\cdot\mathbf{x}^{(k)}\right)^2\right)2\left(\mathbf{w}\cdot\mathbf{x}^{(k)}\right)\mathbf{x}^{(k)} \\[2mm]
&= -2\sum_{k=1}^{N}\left(\left(t^{(k)} - \exp\left(\left(\mathbf{w}\cdot\mathbf{x}^{(k)}\right)^2\right)\right)\right)\exp\left(\left(\mathbf{w}\cdot\mathbf{x}^{(k)}\right)^2\right)\left(\mathbf{w}\cdot\mathbf{x}^{(k)}\right)\mathbf{x}^{(k)}
\end{aligned}
$$

So, we can write our update rule as follows.

$$\mathbf{w} = \mathbf{w} - \eta \frac{\partial E\left(\mathbf{w}\right)}{\partial \mathbf{w}}$$

$$= \mathbf{w} - \eta \left(-2 \sum_{k=1}^{N} \left(\left(t^{(k)} - \exp\left(\left(\mathbf{w} \cdot \mathbf{x}^{(k)} \right)^2 \right) \right) \exp\left(\left(\mathbf{w} \cdot \mathbf{x}^{(k)} \right)^2 \right) \left(\mathbf{w} \cdot \mathbf{x}^{(k)} \right) \mathbf{x}^{(k)} \right) \right)$$

$$= \mathbf{w} + 2\eta \sum_{k=1}^{N} \left(\left(t^{(k)} - \exp\left(\left(\mathbf{w} \cdot \mathbf{x}^{(k)} \right)^2 \right) \right) \exp\left(\left(\mathbf{w} \cdot \mathbf{x}^{(k)} \right)^2 \right) \left(\mathbf{w} \cdot \mathbf{x}^{(k)} \right) \mathbf{x}^{(k)} \right)$$

b) Compute the stochastic gradient descent update for input $\mathbf{x} = \begin{pmatrix} 1 \\ 1 \end{pmatrix}$,

$t = 0$ initialized with $\mathbf{w} = \begin{pmatrix} 0 \\ 1 \\ 0 \end{pmatrix}$ and learning rate $\eta = 2$.

Solution:

In stochastic gradient descent we make one update for each training example. So, instead of summing accross all data points we adapt the learning rule for one example only:

$$\mathbf{w} = \mathbf{w} + 2\eta \left(\left(t - \exp\left(\left(\mathbf{w} \cdot \mathbf{x} \right)^2 \right) \right) \exp\left(\left(\mathbf{w} \cdot \mathbf{x} \right)^2 \right) \left(\mathbf{w} \cdot \mathbf{x} \right) \mathbf{x} \right)$$

We can now do the updates. Let us start with the first example:

$$\mathbf{w} = \mathbf{w} + 2\eta \left(\left(t - \exp\left(\left(\mathbf{w} \cdot \mathbf{x} \right)^2 \right) \right) \exp\left(\left(\mathbf{w} \cdot \mathbf{x} \right)^2 \right) \left(\mathbf{w} \cdot \mathbf{x} \right) \mathbf{x} \right)$$

$$= \begin{pmatrix} 0 \\ 1 \\ 0 \end{pmatrix} + 2\left(2\right) \left(0 - \exp\left(\left(\begin{pmatrix} 0 \\ 1 \\ 0 \end{pmatrix} \cdot \begin{pmatrix} 1 \\ 1 \\ 1 \end{pmatrix} \right)^2 \right) \right)$$

$$\exp\left(\left(\begin{pmatrix} 0 \\ 1 \\ 0 \end{pmatrix} \cdot \begin{pmatrix} 1 \\ 1 \\ 1 \end{pmatrix} \right)^2 \right) \left(\begin{pmatrix} 0 \\ 1 \\ 0 \end{pmatrix} \cdot \begin{pmatrix} 1 \\ 1 \\ 1 \end{pmatrix} \right) \begin{pmatrix} 1 \\ 1 \\ 1 \end{pmatrix}$$

$$= \begin{pmatrix} 0 \\ 1 \\ 0 \end{pmatrix} + 4 \left(\left(0 - \exp\left(1\right) \right) \exp\left(1\right) \left(1\right) \begin{pmatrix} 1 \\ 1 \\ 1 \end{pmatrix} \right)$$

$$= \begin{pmatrix} 0 \\ 1 \\ 0 \end{pmatrix} - 4 \begin{pmatrix} e^2 \\ e^2 \\ e^2 \end{pmatrix}$$

$$= \begin{pmatrix} -4e^2 \\ 1 - 4e^2 \\ -4e^2 \end{pmatrix}$$

Thinking Questions

a) Until now we could only solve classification tasks where the two classes were separated by simple lines. Now we have seen that we can apply any feature transformations we want. Think about which kinds of problems we can solve now? Is it all a matter of finding the right transformation? Is it easy to choose the right transformation?

b) Think about the error functions we have seen. Do you think that one is clearly better than the other? What changes when one changes the error function?

Chapter 6

Multilayer Perceptron

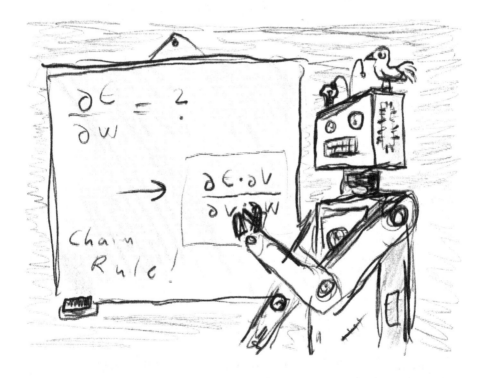

Fig. 6.1 The linear limitations of a perceptron or logistic regression do not apply to feed-forward networks with nonlinear units also called multilayer perceptrons. Such models are trained by gradient descent that is based on differentiable activation functions and the chain rule.

6.1 Motivations

The limitations of a simple perceptron do not apply to feed-forward networks with intermediate or "hidden" nonlinear units, for example a network with just one hidden unit can represent any Boolean function, see Figure 6.2. The great power of multi-layer networks was realized long ago, but it was only in the eighties that it was shown how to make them learn. Multiple layers of cascade linear units still produce only linear functions. For networks to be capable of representing nonlinear functions, units must use nonlinear activation functions.

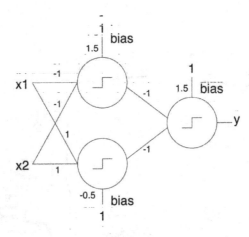

Fig. 6.2 An example of a network with one hidden layer and with the nonlinear *sgn* activation function that solves the *XOR* problem. The *sgn* is not differentiable, the values of the weights were determined manually.

6.2 Networks with Hidden Nonlinear Layers

An example of a feed-forward network with one hidden layer is shown in Figure 6.3. The input pattern is represented by the five-dimensional vector x; nonlinear hidden units compute their outputs V_1, V_2, V_3 and two output units compute their outputs o_1 and o_2. The units V_1, V_2, V_3 are referred to as hidden units because we cannot see their outputs and cannot directly perform error correction [Hertz *et al.* (1991)].

Feed-forward networks with hidden nonlinear units are universal ap-

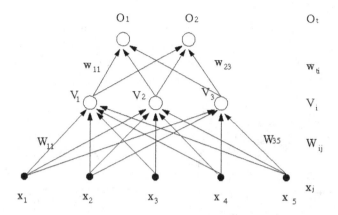

Fig. 6.3   The input pattern is represented by the five-dimensional vector **x**; nonlinear hidden units compute the output V_1, V_2, V_3 and two output units compute the output o_1 and o_2. The units V_1, V_2, V_3 are referred to as hidden units because we cannot see their outputs and cannot directly perform error correction.

proximators; they can approximate every bounded continuous function with an arbitrarily small error. Each Boolean function can be represented by a network with a single hidden layer. However, the representation may require an exponential number of hidden units. The hidden units should be nonlinear because multiple layers of linear units can only produce linear functions.

The output layer of a feed-forward network can be trained using the same strategies we used for single perceptrons. For simplification, we employ the notation in Figure 6.3. For continuous activation function $\phi()$

$$o_{k,t} = \phi\left(\sum_{i=0}^{3} w_{ti} \cdot V_{k,i}\right).$$

the squared error is given by

$$E(\mathbf{w}) = \frac{1}{2} \cdot \sum_{t=1}^{2}\sum_{k=1}^{N}(y_{kt} - o_{kt})^2 = \frac{1}{2} \cdot \sum_{t=1}^{2}\sum_{k=1}^{N}\left(y_{kt} - \phi\left(\sum_{i=0}^{3} w_{ti} \cdot V_{k,i}\right)\right)^2.$$

Since the error surface is not convex, $E(\mathbf{w})$ can have many local minima beside the global minimum.

6.2.1   *Backpropagation*

The backpropagation algorithm became popular with the books Parallel Distributed Processing (PDP) published by David Rumelhart and Mc-Clelland [McClelland and Rumelhart (1986b)], [McClelland and Rumelhart (1986c)], [McClelland and Rumelhart (1986a)], see Figure 6.4.

(a)   (b)

Fig. 6.4   (a) David Everett Rumelhart, Professor of Psychology and (b) Professor in the Social Sciences James L. (Jay) McClelland, Director, Center for Mind, Brain and Computation, Department of Psychology Stanford University.

To find a minimum of the function $E(\mathbf{w})$ using gradient descent, one takes steps proportional to the negative of the gradient. To compute the gradient we will make a distinction between the output units and the hidden units. For the output units we get

$$\frac{\partial E}{\partial w_{ti}} = -\sum_{k=1}^{N}(y_{kt} - o_{kt}) \cdot \phi'\left(\sum_{i=0}^{n} w_{ti} \cdot V_{k,i}\right) \cdot V_{k,i}. \qquad (6.1)$$

For the nonlinear continuous differentiable function $\sigma()$

$$\frac{\partial E}{\partial w_{ti}} = -\alpha \cdot \sum_{k=1}^{N}(y_{kt} - o_{kt}) \cdot \sigma(net_{k,t}) \cdot (1 - \sigma(net_{k,t})) \cdot V_{k,i} \qquad (6.2)$$

and

$$\Delta w_{ti} = \eta \cdot \alpha \cdot \sum_{k=1}^{N}(y_{kt} - o_{kt}) \cdot \sigma(net_{k,t}) \cdot (1 - \sigma(net_{k,t})) \cdot V_{k,i}. \qquad (6.3)$$

So, we basically used the same approach we did for single perceptron to determine Δw_{ti} for the output units. But what can we do about the hidden units? After all, we have no targets for them. So, how can we determine ΔW_{ij} for the hidden units? If the hidden units use a continuous differentiable non linear activation function $\phi()$

$$V_{k,i} = \phi\left(\sum_{j=0}^{5} W_{ij} \cdot x_{k,j}\right).$$

With that, we can define the training error for a training data set D_t of N elements as

$$E(\mathbf{w}, \mathbf{W}) =: E(\mathbf{w}) = \frac{1}{2} \cdot \sum_{k=1}^{N} \sum_{t=1}^{2} (y_{kt} - o_{kt})^2 \tag{6.4}$$

$$E(\mathbf{w}, \mathbf{W}) = \frac{1}{2} \cdot \sum_{k=1}^{N} \sum_{t=1}^{2} \left(y_{kt} - \phi\left(\sum_{i=0}^{3} w_{ti} \cdot V_{k,i}\right)\right)^2 \tag{6.5}$$

$$E(\mathbf{w}, \mathbf{W}) = \frac{1}{2} \cdot \sum_{k=1}^{N} \sum_{t=1}^{2} \left(y_{kt} - \phi\left(\sum_{i=0}^{3} w_{ti} \cdot \phi\left(\sum_{j=0}^{5} W_{ij} \cdot x_{k,j}\right)\right)\right)^2. \tag{6.6}$$

We already know

$$\frac{\partial E}{\partial w_{ti}} = -\sum_{k=1}^{N} (y_{kt} - o_{kt}) \cdot \phi'(net_{k,t}) \cdot V_{k,i}. \tag{6.7}$$

For $\frac{\partial E}{\partial W_{ij}}$ we can use the chain rule and we obtain

$$\frac{\partial E}{\partial W_{ij}} = \sum_{k=1}^{N} \frac{\partial E}{\partial V_{ki}} \cdot \frac{\partial V_{ki}}{\partial W_{ij}}, \tag{6.8}$$

with

$$\frac{\partial E}{\partial V_{ki}} = -\sum_{k=1}^{N} \sum_{t=1}^{2} (y_{kt} - o_{kt}) \cdot \phi'(net_{k,t}) \cdot w_{t,i}, \tag{6.9}$$

and

$$\frac{\partial V_{ki}}{\partial W_{ij}} = \phi'(net_{k,i}) \cdot x_{k,j} \tag{6.10}$$

it follows

$$\frac{\partial E}{\partial W_{ij}} = -\sum_{k=1}^{N} \sum_{t=1}^{2} (y_{kt} - o_{kt}) \cdot \phi'(net_{k,t}) \cdot w_{t,i} \cdot \phi'(net_{k,i}) \cdot x_{k,j}. \tag{6.11}$$

The algorithm is called backpropagation because we can reuse part of the computation that was used to determine Δw_{ti},

$$\Delta w_{ti} = \eta \cdot \sum_{k=1}^{N} (y_{kt} - o_{kt}) \cdot \phi'(net_{k,t}) \cdot V_{k,i}. \tag{6.12}$$

Namely, we take what are called the delta s

$$\delta_{kt} = (y_{kt} - o_{kt}) \cdot \phi'(net_{k,t}) \tag{6.13}$$

and we can use them for the output units

$$\Delta w_{ti} = \eta \cdot \sum_{k=1}^{N} \delta_{kt} \cdot V_{k,i}. \tag{6.14}$$

and

$$\Delta W_{ij} = \eta \sum_{k=1}^{N} \sum_{t=1}^{2} (y_{kt} - o_{kt}) \cdot \phi'(net_{k,t}) \cdot w_{t,i} \cdot \phi'(net_{k,i}) \cdot x_{k,j} \tag{6.15}$$

we reuse them for the hidden units

$$\Delta W_{ij} = \eta \sum_{k=1}^{N} \sum_{t=1}^{2} \delta_{kt} \cdot w_{t,i} \cdot \phi'(net_{k,i}) \cdot x_{k,j}. \tag{6.16}$$

The hidden layer has its own deltas

$$\delta_{ki} = \phi'(net_{k,i}) \cdot \sum_{t=1}^{2} \delta_{kt} \cdot w_{t,i} \tag{6.17}$$

which allows us to write

$$\Delta W_{ij} = \eta \sum_{k=1}^{N} \delta_{ki} \cdot x_{k,j}. \tag{6.18}$$

and these deltas would also be reused if there were more previous hidden layers.

6.2.2   *Example*

In this example we preform one training step of the stochastic gradient descent rule resulting from quadratic error on the network of Figure 6.3. For simplicity we assume that all units use the sigmoid activation function

$$\sigma(net) = \frac{1}{1 + e^{(-net)}} \in [0, 1]$$

with the derivative

$$\sigma(net)' = \sigma(net) \cdot (1 - \sigma(net)).$$

The initial weighs from input pattern to hidden units are

$$W_{10} = 0, W_{11} = 0.1, W_{12} = 0.1, W_{13} = 0.1, W_{14} = 0.1, W_{15} = 0.1$$

$$W_{20} = 0, W_{21} = 0.1, W_{22} = 0.1, W_{23} = 0.1, W_{24} = 0.1, W_{25} = 0.1$$

$$W_{30} = 0, W_{31} = 0.1, W_{32} = 0.1, W_{33} = 0.1, W_{34} = 0.1, W_{35} = 0.1$$

The initial weighs from hidden units to output units are

$$w_{10} = 0, w_{11} = 0.1, w_{12} = 0.1, w_{13} = 0.1$$

$$w_{20} = 0, w_{21} = 0.1, w_{22} = 0.1, w_{23} = 0.1$$

For simplicity we the corresponding weights for bias are set to zero. The training pattern is

$$\mathbf{x} = (1, 1, 0, 0, 0, 0)^T, \quad x_1 = 1, x_2 = 1, x_3 = 0, x_4 = 0, x_5 = 0$$

and the target pattern is

$$\mathbf{y} = (1, 0)^T, \quad y_1 = 1, y_2 = 0$$

First step In the first step the inputs are propagated forward and we compute the values V_1, V_2, V_3

$$V_i = \sigma \left(\sum_{j=0}^{5} W_{ij} \cdot x_j \right)$$

since it is a stochastic gradient we do not use the index k that indicates the input pattern index.

$$V_1 = \sigma(0 \cdot 1 + 0.1 \cdot 1 + 0.1 \cdot 1 + 0.1 \cdot 0 + 0.1 \cdot 0 + 0.1 \cdot 0) = \frac{1}{1 + e^{-0.2}} = 0.54983$$

and

$$V_1 = V_2 = V_3$$

Using the values V_1, V_2, V_3 as input we compute the output values o_1, o_2

$$o_t = \sigma \left(\sum_{i=0}^{3} w_{ti} \cdot V_i \right)$$

$$o_1 = \sigma(0 \cdot 1 + 0.1 \cdot 0.54983 + 0.1 \cdot 0.54983 + 0.1 \cdot 0.54983) = \frac{1}{1 + e^{-0.16495}} = 0.54114$$

and

$$o_1 = o_2$$

Second step   In the second step the errors represented by δ are propagated backward from the output units

$$\delta_t = (y_t - o_t) \cdot \sigma'(net_t)$$

with

$$\sigma'(net_t) = \sigma(net_t) \cdot (1 - \sigma(net_t)) = o_t \cdot (1 - o_t).$$

Since $y_1 = 1, y_2 = 0$ we get two δ^{output} for the two output units

$$\delta_1^{output} = (1 - 0.54114) \cdot 0.54114 \cdot (1 - 0.54114) = 0.113938$$

$$\delta_2^{output} = (0 - 0.54114) \cdot 0.54114 \cdot (1 - 0.54114) = -0.134369.$$

Using δ^{output} we compute the three δ for the three hidden units

$$\delta_i = \sigma'(net_i) \cdot \sum_{t=1}^{2} \delta_t \cdot w_{t,i}$$

with

$$\sigma'(net_i) = \sigma(net_i) \cdot (1 - \sigma(net_i)) = V_i \cdot (1 - V_i).$$

$$\delta_1^{hidden} = 0.54983 \cdot (1 - 0.54983) \cdot (0.113938 \cdot 0.1 + (-0.134369) \cdot 0.1)$$

$$\delta_1^{hidden} = -0.000505702$$

and

$$\delta_1^{hidden} = \delta_2^{hidden} = \delta_3^{hidden}$$

Third step   In the third step we update the weights

$$\Delta w_{ti} = \eta \cdot \delta_t^{output} \cdot V_i.$$

with

$$\delta_1^{output} = 0.113938, \quad \delta_2^{output} = -0.134369.$$

Taking into account bias we get with $\eta = 1$

$$\Delta w_{10} = \eta \cdot \delta_1^{output} \cdot 1 = 0.113938 \cdot 1 = 0.113938$$

$$\Delta w_{11} = \eta \cdot \delta_1^{output} \cdot 0.54983 = 0.113938 \cdot 0.54983 = 0.0626465$$

$$\Delta w_{12} = \eta \cdot \delta_1^{output} \cdot 0.54983 = 0.113938 \cdot 0.54983 = 0.0626465$$

$$\Delta w_{13} = \eta \cdot \delta_1^{output} \cdot 0.54983 = 0.113938 \cdot 0.54983 = 0.0626465$$

and

$$\Delta w_{20} = \eta \cdot \delta_2^{output} \cdot 1 = (-0.134369) \cdot 1 = -0.134369$$
$$\Delta w_{21} = \eta \cdot \delta_2^{output} \cdot 0.54983 = (-0.134369) \cdot 0.54983 = -0.0738801$$
$$\Delta w_{22} = \eta \cdot \delta_2^{output} \cdot 0.54983 = (-0.134369) \cdot 0.54983 = -0.0738801$$
$$\Delta w_{23} = \eta \cdot \delta_2^{output} \cdot 0.54983 = (-0.134369) \cdot 0.54983 = -0.0738801$$

and we update the weigths

$$w_{ti}^{new} = w_{ti}^{old} + \Delta w_{ti}$$

$$w_{10} = 0.113938, w_{11} = 0.162645, w_{12} = 0.1626465, w_{13} = 0.1626465$$
$$w_{20} = -0.134369, w_{21} = 0.02612, w_{22} = 0.02612, w_{23} = 0.02612$$

$$\Delta W_{ij} = \eta \cdot \delta_i^{hidden} \cdot x_j.$$

with

$$\delta_1^{hidden} = \delta_2^{hidden} = \delta_2^{hidden} = -0.000505702$$

Taking into account bias we get with $\eta = 1$

$$\Delta W_{10} = \eta \cdot \delta_1^{hidden} \cdot 1 = -0.000505702 \cdot 1 = -0.000505702$$
$$\Delta W_{11} = \eta \cdot \delta_1^{hidden} \cdot 1 = -0.000505702 \cdot 1 = -0.000505702$$
$$\Delta W_{12} = \eta \cdot \delta_1^{hidden} \cdot 1 = -0.000505702 \cdot 1 = -0.000505702$$
$$\Delta W_{13} = \eta \cdot \delta_1^{hidden} \cdot 0 = -0.000505702 \cdot 0 = 0$$
$$\Delta W_{14} = \eta \cdot \delta_1^{hidden} \cdot 0 = -0.000505702 \cdot 0 = 0$$
$$\Delta W_{15} = \eta \cdot \delta_1^{hidden} \cdot 0 = -0.000505702 \cdot 0 = 0$$
$$W_{ij}^{new} = W_{ij}^{old} + \Delta W_{ij}$$

and we update the weigths

$$W_{10} = 0.000505702, W_{11} = 0.099494, W_{12} = 0.999494,$$
$$W_{13} = 0.1, W_{14} = 0.1, W_{15} = 0.1$$
$$W_{20} = -0.000505702, W_{21} = 0.0999494, W_{22} = 0.099494,$$
$$W_{23} = 0.1, W_{24} = 0.1, W_{25} = 0.1$$
$$W_{30} = -0.000505702, W_{31} = 0.0999494, W_{32} = 0.999494,$$
$$W_{33} = 0.1, W_{34} = 0.1, W_{35} = 0.1$$

The most difficult part is the fact that one gets lost in indices, especially when an additional index is used to indicate the layer number. Since we have only one hidden layer, we simplified our notation by indicating the weights of different layers by different letters, w, W. In the Deep Learning chapter we will present the algorithm in a different manner that will allows us to work with more layers easily. However, this two-layered example is very important at this point to gain some practice with mechanics behind the process.

6.2.3   Activation Function

We have to use a nonlinear differentiable activation function in hidden units, like for example the sigmoid function

$$\sigma(net) = \frac{1}{1 + e^{(-\alpha \cdot net)}} \in [0, 1]$$

with the derivative

$$\sigma(net)' = \alpha \cdot \sigma(net) \cdot (1 - \sigma(net))$$

or the tanh function

$$f(net) = \tanh(\alpha \cdot net) = \frac{e^{\alpha \cdot net} - e^{-\alpha \cdot net}}{e^{\alpha \cdot net} + e^{-\alpha \cdot net}} \in [-1, 1] \qquad (6.19)$$

with the derivative

$$f'(net) = \alpha \cdot (1 - f(net)^2), \qquad (6.20)$$

see Figure 6.5. There is a relation between $\sigma(net)$ and $f(net)$, for simplifi-

(a)   (b)

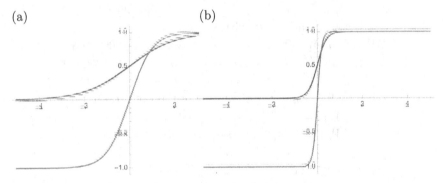

Fig. 6.5   (a) The sigmoid and the tanh activation function with $\alpha = 1$. (b) The sigmoid and the tanh activation function with $\alpha = 5$.

cation we assume $\alpha = 1$,

$$f(net) = \tanh(net) = \frac{e^{net} - e^{-net}}{e^{net} + e^{-net}} = \frac{e^{net}}{e^{net}} \cdot \frac{1 - e^{-2 \cdot net}}{1 + e^{-net}} \qquad (6.21)$$

$$f(net) = \frac{1}{1 + e^{-2 \cdot net}} - \frac{e^{-2 \cdot net}}{1 + e^{-net}} = \sigma(2 \cdot net) - \frac{e^{-2 \cdot net}}{1 + e^{-net}}$$

$$f(net) = \sigma(2 \cdot net) + \frac{1}{1 + e^{-2 \cdot net}} - \frac{e^{-2 \cdot net}}{1 + e^{-net}} - \frac{1}{1 + e^{-2 \cdot net}}$$

$$f(net) = \sigma(2 \cdot net) + \sigma(2 \cdot net) - \frac{e^{-2 \cdot net} + 1}{1 + e^{-net}}$$

$$f(net) = 2 \cdot \sigma(2 \cdot net) - 1 \qquad (6.22)$$

Hidden Units Hidden units preform feature extraction through nonlinear activation functions. They do not require bias, however it is commonly used and the universal approximation theorem uses hidden units with bias. Multiple layers of cascade linear units still produce only linear functions, for example consider in Figure 6.3 linear output units

$$o_{k,t} = \sum_{i=0}^{3} w_{ti} \cdot V_{k,i} = \mathbf{w}_t^T \cdot \mathbf{V}_k$$

and hidden linear units

$$V_{k,i} = \sum_{j=0}^{5} W_{ij} \cdot x_{k,j} = \mathbf{W}_j^T \cdot \mathbf{x}_k$$

Since W is a matrix

$$\mathbf{V}_k = W \cdot \mathbf{x}_k$$

we can write

$$o_{k,t} = \mathbf{w}_t^T \cdot W \cdot \mathbf{x}_k$$

with

$$(\mathbf{w}_t^*)^T = \mathbf{w}_t^T \cdot W$$

we get the same discrimination power (linear separable) as a simple perceptron

$$o_{k,t} = (\mathbf{w}_t^*)^T \cdot \mathbf{x}_k.$$

With nonlinear activation function,

$$\mathbf{V}_k = \phi(W \cdot \mathbf{x}_k)$$

we cannot do the matrix multiplication

$$o_{k,t} = \mathbf{w}_t^T \cdot \phi(W \cdot \mathbf{x}_k).$$

This process is related to what we have seen about linear basis function models. We can think about the output layer as the linear model and see the hidden layers as the basis functions. Remember that, to solve nonlinearly separable problems we needed good nonlinear basis functions (or features). So, in a network of neurons, we need to put activations functions on the hidden units (to make features nonlinear) and hope that the learning procedure will tune the hidden units in such a way that they represent good basis functions.

Output Units Output units require bias. They preform a linear separation, so, this means that the input to them had to be somehow linearized by the hidden units. They do not require a non linear activation function. However, many activation function can be useful depending on the output. If the output is $y_{kt} \in \mathbb{R}$, the output units should use a linear activation function. For outputs in the interval $y_{kt} \in [-1, 1]$, the output units should use the activation function $f(net) = \tanh(\alpha \cdot net)$. We should use sigmoid function or softmax to represent probabilities. Furthermore, when working with probabilities, if we assume the target values $y_{kt} \in \{0, 1\}$ with $\sum_t y_{kt} = 1$ we can use cross entropy that leads to faster convergence.

6.3 Cross Entropy Error Function

If we use cross entropy, learning consists of minimizing the error (loss) function [Bishop (2006)],

$$E(\mathbf{w}) = -\sum_{k=1}^{N} y_k \log o_k$$

in which $y_{kt} \in \{0, 1\}$ and o_k correspond to probabilities ($\sum_t y_{kt} = 1$). The resulting error surface is steeper than the error surface defined by squared error

$$E(\mathbf{w}) = \frac{1}{2} \cdot \sum_{k=1}^{N} \sum_{t=1}^{2} (y_{kt} - o_{kt})^2$$

and, thus, the gradient converges faster. The cross entropy error function can be alternatively written as a loss (cost) function with $\theta = \mathbf{w}$

$$L(\mathbf{x}, \mathbf{y}, \theta) = -\sum_{k=1}^{N} (y_k \log p(c_k|\mathbf{x}))$$

or as the loss function

$$J(\theta) = -\sum_{k=1}^{N} (y_k \log p(c_k|\mathbf{x})) = -\mathbb{E}_{x,y \sim p_{data}} \log p(c_k|\mathbf{x})$$

in which θ indicates the adaptive parameters of the model and $\mathbb{E}$ indicates the expectation. This notation is usually common in statistics.

6.3.1 *Backpropagation*

Working with the cross entropy loss, we need the network's outputs to represent probabilities. So, for output layer, we use the softmax function with

$$\phi(net) = \frac{\exp(net_k)}{\sum_{j=1}^{K} \exp(net_j)}.$$

For the hidden units, we could use any nonlinear function, but for familiarity reasons, let us use the sigmoid function

$$\phi(net) = \sigma(net) = \frac{1}{1 + e^{(-net))}}.$$

Using the sigmoid function we can reuse the results we developed when we introduced the logistic regression. With the output unit

$$o_{k,t} = \phi\left(\sum_{i=0}^{3} w_{ti} \cdot V_{k,i}\right).$$

and

$$E(\mathbf{w}) = -\sum_{k=1}^{N}\sum_{t=1}^{2} y_{kt} \log o_{kt} = -\sum_{k=1}^{N}\sum_{t=1}^{2} y_{kt} \log \phi\left(\sum_{i=0}^{3} w_{ti} \cdot V_{k,i}\right) \quad (6.23)$$

we get the logistic regression given the target values $y_{kt} \in \{0,1\}$ and

$$\sum_{t=1}^{K} y_{kt} = 1$$

$$\frac{\partial E}{\partial w_{ti}} = -\sum_{k=1}^{N}(y_{kt} - o_{kt}) \cdot V_{k,i}. \quad (6.24)$$

If the hidden units use a continuous differentiable non linear activation function $\phi()$

$$V_{k,i} = \phi\left(\sum_{j=0}^{5} W_{ij} \cdot x_{k,j}\right).$$

we can define the training error for a training data set D_t of N elements with

$$E(\mathbf{w}, \mathbf{W}) =: E(\mathbf{w}) = -\sum_{k=1}^{N}\sum_{t=1}^{2}(y_{kt} \cdot \log o_{kt}) \quad (6.25)$$

As before we will apply the chain rule and make the distinction between the hidden and output units,

$$E(\mathbf{w}, \mathbf{W}) = -\sum_{k=1}^{N}\sum_{t=1}^{2}\left(y_{kt} \cdot \log\phi\left(\sum_{i=0}^{3} w_{ti} \cdot V_{k,i}\right)\right)$$

$$E(\mathbf{w}, \mathbf{W}) = -\sum_{k=1}^{N}\sum_{t=1}^{2}\left(y_{kt} \cdot \log\phi\left(\sum_{i=0}^{3} w_{ti} \cdot \phi\left(\sum_{j=0}^{5} W_{ij} \cdot x_{k,j}\right)\right)\right)$$

We know that

$$\frac{\partial E}{\partial w_{ti}} = -\sum_{k=1}^{N}(y_{kt} - o_{kt}) \cdot V_{k,i}. \tag{6.26}$$

For $\frac{\partial E}{\partial W_{ij}}$ we can use the chain rule and we obtain

$$\frac{\partial E}{\partial W_{ij}} = \sum_{k=1}^{N} \frac{\partial E}{\partial V_{ki}} \cdot \frac{\partial V_{ki}}{\partial W_{ij}}.$$

with

$$\frac{\partial E}{\partial V_{ki}} = -\sum_{k=1}^{N}\sum_{t=1}^{2}(y_{kt} - o_{kt}) \cdot w_{t,i}, \qquad \frac{\partial V_{ki}}{\partial W_{ij}} = \phi'(net_{k,i}) \cdot x_{k,j}$$

it follows

$$\frac{\partial E}{\partial W_{ij}} = -\sum_{k=1}^{N}\sum_{t=1}^{2}(y_{kt} - o_{kt}) \cdot w_{t,i} \cdot \phi'(net_{k,i}) \cdot x_{k,j}. \tag{6.27}$$

We can reuse the computation that was used to determine Δw_{ti} as before

$$\Delta w_{ti} = \eta \cdot \sum_{k=1}^{N}(y_{kt} - o_{kt}) \cdot V_{k,i}.$$

and with

$$\delta_{kt} = (y_{kt} - o_{kt}) \tag{6.28}$$

we can write

$$\Delta w_{ti} = \eta \cdot \sum_{k=1}^{N}\delta_{kt} \cdot V_{k,i}. \tag{6.29}$$

With

$$\Delta W_{ij} = \eta \sum_{k=1}^{N}\sum_{t=1}^{2}(y_{kt} - o_{kt}) \cdot w_{t,i} \cdot \phi'(net_{k,i}) \cdot x_{k,j}$$

we can simplify (reuse the computation) to

$$\Delta W_{ij} = \eta \sum_{k=1}^{N} \sum_{t=1}^{2} \delta_{kt} \cdot w_{t,i} \cdot \phi'(net_{k,i}) \cdot x_{k,j}.$$

With

$$\delta_{ki} = \phi'(net_{k,i}) \cdot \sum_{t=1}^{2} \delta_{kt} \cdot w_{t,i} \qquad (6.30)$$

we can simplify to

$$\Delta W_{ij} = \eta \sum_{k=1}^{N} \delta_{ki} \cdot x_{k,j}. \qquad (6.31)$$

6.3.2 *Comparison*

Assuming hidden units with a sigmoid activation function. For the quadratic error the derivatives are

$$\frac{\partial E}{\partial w_{ti}} = -\sum_{k=1}^{N} (y_{kt} - o_{kt}) \cdot \phi'(net_{k,t}) \cdot V_{k,i}$$

and

$$\frac{\partial E}{\partial W_{ij}} = -\sum_{k=1}^{N} \sum_{t=1}^{2} (y_{kt} - o_{kt}) \cdot \phi'(net_{k,t}) \cdot w_{t,i} \cdot \phi'(net_{k,i}) \cdot x_{k,j}.$$

For cross entropy the derivatives are

$$\frac{\partial E}{\partial w_{ti}} = -\sum_{k=1}^{N} (y_{kt} - o_{kt}) \cdot V_{k,i},$$

and

$$\frac{\partial E}{\partial W_{ij}} = -\sum_{k=1}^{N} \sum_{t=1}^{2} (y_{kt} - o_{kt}) \cdot w_{t,i} \cdot \phi'(net_{k,i}) \cdot x_{k,j}.$$

The differences between the two setting reside in the small scalar factor $\phi'(net_{k,t})$. This factor shortens the gradient and, for that reason, the cross entropy gradient descent tends to converge faster.

δ notation   Using the δ notation for the squared error

$$\delta_{kt} = (y_{kt} - o_{kt}) \cdot \phi'(net_{k,t})$$

and for cross entropy

$$\delta_{kt} = (y_{kt} - o_{kt}).$$

The following expressions are the same for both errors

$$\Delta w_{ti} = \eta \cdot \sum_{k=1}^{N} \delta_{kt} \cdot V_{k,i}.$$

$$\delta_{ki} = \phi'(net_{k,i}) \cdot \sum_{t=1}^{2} \delta_{kt} \cdot w_{t,i}$$

$$\Delta W_{ij} = \eta \sum_{k=1}^{N} \delta_{ki} \cdot x_{k,j}.$$

6.3.3   *Computing Power*

Feed-forward networks with hidden nonlinear units are universal approximators; they can approximate every bounded continuous function with an arbitrarily small error. According to the universality theorem, a neural network with a single hidden layer is capable of approximating any bounded continuous function [Cybenko (1989)], [Hornik *et al.* (1989)]. However, attempting to build a network with only one layer to approximate complex functions often requires a very large number of nodes [Hornik (1991)], [White (1992)]. It was also shown that each Boolean function can be represented by a network with a single hidden layer (nonlinear units), however, the representation may require an exponential number of hidden units [Bebis and Georgiopoulos (1994)]. Because of these two theorems, from 1990 until the 2000s it was commonplace to use only one hidden layer.

6.3.4   *Generalization*

This approach can be extended to any numbers of layers [Hertz *et al.* (1991)], see Figure 6.6. The inputs are propagated forward, but the errors represented by δ are propagated backward. This why the algorithm is called backpropagation.

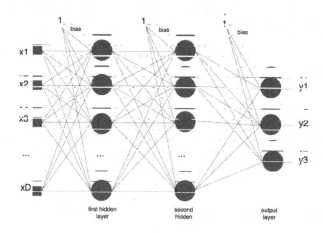

Fig. 6.6   A feed forward network with two hidden layers.

In general, with an arbitrary number of layers, the backpropagation update rule has always the form

$$\Delta w_{ti} = \eta \sum_{k=1}^{N} \delta_{output} \cdot V_{input}. \qquad (6.32)$$

Where output and input refers to the connections concerned, V stands for the appropriate input (hidden unit or real input) and δ depends on the layer concerned.

The backpropagation algorithm will find a local, not necessarily global error minimum. This is because the error surface defined by $E(\mathbf{w})$ can have many local minima besides the global minimum. The found minimum depends on the initial start of the gradient decent that is defined by random values of the initial weights. Stochastic gradient descent can some times overcome this problem. Additionally multiple nets can be trained with different initial weights preforming a blind search for the possible global minimum. The gradient descent can be very slow if η is too small, and can oscillate widely if η is too large. One can include weight momentum α with τ indicating the time step of the algorithm

$$\Delta w_{ti}(\tau + 1) = -\eta \frac{\partial E}{\partial w_{ti}} + \alpha \cdot \Delta w_{ti}(\tau), \qquad (6.33)$$

it prohibits fast changes of the direction of the gradient. The momentum parameter α is chosen between 0 and 1, usually 0.9 is a good value. Training can take thousands of iterations and is slow, however the classification after training is very fast.

6.4   Training

Using the backpropagation algorithm, categories can be learned through known labeled examples. Labels can include multiple things like faces vs. non-faces or man-made objects vs. non-man-made objects. In general, we try to learn a function $f : \mathbb{R}^n \to \mathbb{R}^m$,

$$\mathbf{y} = f(\mathbf{x})$$

that is described by a sample of training data D_t of the labeled data set D

$$D_t = \{(\mathbf{x}_1, \mathbf{y}_1), (\mathbf{x}_2, \mathbf{y}_2), \cdots , , (\mathbf{x}_N, \mathbf{y}_N)\} \tag{6.34}$$

called training data set.

After learning, the trained network can be seen as an hypothesis h that tries to represent the function f and it can be then used for mapping new examples.

The hypothesis h should represent the function f well on the training set. However, ideally, it should generalize from the training data set to unseen future data points.

To try to make sure this is the case, we can validate on an unseen validation data set D_v of the data set D

$$D_v = \{(\mathbf{x}_1', \mathbf{y}_1'), (\mathbf{x}_2', \mathbf{y}_2'), \cdots , , (\mathbf{x}_M', \mathbf{y}_M')\} \tag{6.35}$$

with

$$\emptyset = D_t \cap D_v, \quad D \supset D_t, \quad D \supset D_v.$$

The validation of our network is done by comparing the hypothesis h outputs

$$\mathbf{o}_k = h(\mathbf{x}_k') \tag{6.36}$$

with the correct values $\mathbf{y}_k'$ of the validation data set D_v by the mean squared error

$$MSE_{Dv}(h) = \frac{1}{N} \cdot \sum_{k=1}^{N} \|\mathbf{y}_k' - \mathbf{o}_k\|^2. \tag{6.37}$$

6.4.1   *Overfitting*

The training data contains information about the regularities in the mapping from input to output, but it also contains noise. For example the target values (labels) may be unreliable. There is sampling error and a flexible architecture can model the sampling error really well. We cannot tell which regularities are real and which are caused by sampling error.

The smaller the $MSE(D_v)$ the better the hypothesis h describing the function f. We can define the mean squared error for the training data set D_t

$$MSE_{Dt}(h) = \sum_{k=1}^{M} \frac{1}{M} \cdot \|\mathbf{y}_k - \mathbf{o}_k\|^2, \tag{6.38}$$

usually

$$MSE_{Dv}(h) > MSE_{Dt}(h).$$

If we have two hypothesis h_1 and h_2 with

$$MSE_{Dt}(h_1) < MSE_{Dt}(h_2), \quad MSE_{Dv}(h_1) > MSE_{Dv}(h_2). \tag{6.39}$$

then we say that the hypothesis h_1 overfits the training data set D_t, h_1 fits better the training examples than h_2, but performs more poorly over examples it didn't learn. It seems as if h_1 learned D_t by heart and not the topological structure that describes the function f, on the other hand h_2 learned the corresponding structure and can generalize [Mitchell (1997)].

To overcome overfitting we can increase the size of the labeled data set, this is the best possible approach. However due to the cost of generating labeled data, it is often not possible. Another approach is to use early stopping. In this strategy, tries to stop the learning before the network overfits.

6.4.2   *Early-Stopping Rule*

The model is trained on the training data set $= D_t$ and validated on the validation data set $= D_v$. Usually during training one determines validation-sample error for each epoch t

$$MSE_{Dv}(h(t)) = \sum_{k=1}^{M} \frac{1}{M} \cdot \|\mathbf{y}'_k - \mathbf{o(t)}_k\|^2. \tag{6.40}$$

and if

$$MSE_{Dv}(h(t+1)) > MSE_{Dv}(h(t)) \tag{6.41}$$

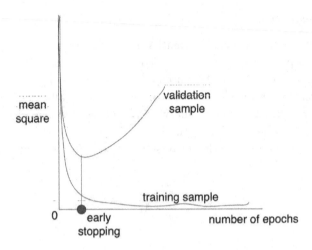

Fig. 6.7 Early stoping is used to prevent overfitting. If the mean squared error on the validation set becomes bigger, the training is stopped even if the mean squared error of the training goes down.

one stops the training, see Figure 6.7 [Haykin (2008)].

Since one usually preforms different experiments with different numbers of parameters (like number of hidden units, hidden layers), and validates the experiments on the validation set it may happen that the network structure is optimized for the validation set D_v. That is why it is a good practice to indicate the performance of the network on an additional independent test D_{test} with

$$\emptyset = D_t \cap D_v, \quad \emptyset = D_t \cap D_{test}, \quad \emptyset = D_v \cap D_{test}$$

and

$$D \supset D_t, \quad D \supset D_v, \quad D \supset D_{test}.$$

The test data is used to get a final, unbiased estimate of how well the network works. We expect this estimate to be worse than on the validation data. If the labeled data set D is too small, breaking it into three parts can be a problem. We will see how to solve this problem and go into more detail about all of these topics in the the chapter about model selection.

6.4.3 *Regularization*

To overcome overfitting one can use a model that has just the right capacity. That is, enough to model the true regularities and not enough to also model the spurious regularities. It is possible to increase the network's capacity by changing the number of neurons in each layer or by changing the number of layers. However, this choice may result in a very difficult task. Another approach is to use a relatively large network and then constraint its capacity through regularization on the weights. This makes it more difficult for the network to adapt to patterns in the training set. Hopefully, this difficulty will cause the network to learn only the really relevant ones. The typical way to achieve this is to penalize large weights through constraints on their squared values (l_2 regularization) or absolute values (l_1 regularization).

6.4.3.1 l_2 Regularization

$$\tilde{E}(\mathbf{w}) = \frac{1}{2} \cdot \sum_{k=1}^{N} (y_k - o_k)^2 + \frac{\lambda}{2} \|\mathbf{w}\|_2^2, \ \ or \ \ \tilde{E}(\mathbf{w}) = -\sum_{k=1}^{N} y_k \log o_k + \frac{\lambda}{2} \|\mathbf{w}\|_2^2$$

$$\tilde{E}(\mathbf{w}) = E(\mathbf{w}) + \frac{\lambda}{2} \|\mathbf{w}\|_2^2 \tag{6.42}$$

$$\frac{\partial \tilde{E}}{\partial w_j} = \frac{\partial E}{\partial w_j} + \lambda \cdot w_j.$$

$$\Delta w_j = -\eta \left(\frac{\partial E}{\partial w_j} + \lambda \cdot w_j \right) = -\eta \left(\frac{\partial E}{\partial w_j} \right) - \eta \lambda \cdot w_j = -\eta \left(\frac{\partial E}{\partial w_j} \right) - \alpha \cdot w_j$$

6.4.3.2 l_1 Regularization

$$\tilde{E}(\mathbf{w}) = \frac{1}{2} \cdot \sum_{k=1}^{N} (y_k - o_k)^2 + \lambda \cdot \|\mathbf{w}\|_1, \ \ or \ \ \tilde{E}(\mathbf{w}) = -\sum_{k=1}^{N} y_k \log o_k + \lambda \cdot \|\mathbf{w}\|_1$$

$$\tilde{E}(\mathbf{w}) = E(\mathbf{w}) + \lambda \|\mathbf{w}\|_1 \tag{6.43}$$

$$\frac{\partial \tilde{E}}{\partial w_j} = \frac{\partial E}{\partial w_j} + \lambda \cdot sign(w_j).$$

$$\Delta w_j = -\eta \left(\frac{\partial E}{\partial w_j} + \lambda \cdot sign(w_j) \right) = -\eta \left(\frac{\partial E}{\partial w_j} \right) - \eta \lambda \cdot sign(w_j)$$

$$\Delta w_j = -\eta \left(\frac{\partial E}{\partial w_j} \right) - \alpha \cdot sign(w_j)$$

6.4.3.3 l_p Regularization

Additionally we can define the l_p regularization as

$$\tilde{E}(\mathbf{w}) = \frac{1}{2} \cdot \sum_{k=1}^{N} (y_k - o_k)^2 + \frac{\lambda}{2} \|\mathbf{w}\|_p^p, \quad or \quad \tilde{E}(\mathbf{w}) = -\sum_{k=1}^{N} y_k \log o_k + \frac{\lambda}{2} \|\mathbf{w}\|_p^p$$

$$\tilde{E}(\mathbf{w}) = E(\mathbf{w}) + \frac{\lambda}{2} \|\mathbf{w}\|_p^p \tag{6.44}$$

$$\frac{\partial \tilde{E}}{\partial w_j} = \frac{\partial E}{\partial w_j} + \lambda \cdot p \cdot \cdot w_j^{p-1}.$$

$$\Delta w_j = -\eta \left(\frac{\partial E}{\partial w_j} + \lambda \cdot w_j^{p-1} \right) = -\eta \left(\frac{\partial E}{\partial w_j} \right) - \eta \cdot p\lambda \cdot w_j^{p-1} = -\eta \left(\frac{\partial E}{\partial w_j} \right) - \alpha \cdot w_j^{p-1}$$

6.5 Deep Learning and Backpropagation

According to the universality theorem, a neural network with a single hidden layer is capable of approximating any continuous function. Attempting to build a network with only one layer to approximate complex functions often requires a very large number of nodes. The immediate solution to this is to build networks with more hidden layers. In deep learning many hidden layers are used that reduce the training error on the validation set, see Figure 6.8. Empirical experiments indicate that "deep" neural networks

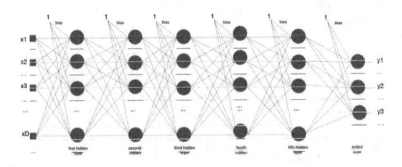

Fig. 6.8 A feed forward network with many hidden layers is called a deep network, in our example the network has five hidden layers.

give better results then "fat" neural networks. It seems that networks with many hidden layers have a different error landscape that is less prone to local minima. Before describing deep learning and indicating how to generalize the backpropagation algorithm to many hidden layers using the vector notation we describe learning theory and indicate why the model works through radial basis function networks and support vector machines.

6.6 Exercises and Answers

1)

Preform one training step of the stochastic gradient descent rule resulting from quadratic error on the network of Figure 6.3. For simplicity we assume that all units use the activation function

$$\sigma(net) = \frac{1}{1 + e^{-4 \cdot net}}$$

The initial weighs from input pattern to hidden units are

$$W_{10} = 0, W_{11} = 1, W_{12} = 1, W_{13} = 1, W_{14} = 1, W_{15} = 1$$

$$W_{20} = 0, W_{21} = 1, W_{22} = 1, W_{23} = 1, W_{24} = 1, W_{25} = 1$$

$$W_{30} = 0, W_{31} = 1, W_{32} = 1, W_{33} = 1, W_{34} = 1, W_{35} = 1$$

The initial weighs from hidden units to output units are

$$w_{10} = 0, w_{11} = 0, w_{12} = 0, w_{13} = 0$$

$$w_{20} = 0, w_{21} = 0, w_{22} = 0, w_{23} = 0$$

For simplicity the corresponding weights for bias are set to zero and the learning rate is $\eta = 1$. The training pattern is

$$\mathbf{x} = (0, 0, 0, 0, 0)^T, \quad x_1 = 0, x_2 = 0, x_3 = 0, x_4 = 0, x_5 = 0$$

and the target pattern is

$$\mathbf{y} = (2, 2)^T, \quad y_2 = 1, y_2 = 2.$$

Then show if the squared error reduced after one adaptation step as computed before.

Solution:

First step

$$V_1 = V_2 = V_3 = \frac{1}{1 + e^0} = 0.5$$

$$o_1 = o_2 = \frac{1}{1 + e^0} = 0.5$$

Second step   In the second step the errors represented by δ are propagated backward from the output units

$$\delta_t = (y_t - o_t) \cdot \sigma'(net_t)$$

$$\delta_1^{output} = \delta_2^{output} = (2 - 0.5) \cdot 4 \cdot \frac{1}{1 + e^0} \cdot (1 - \frac{1}{1 + e^0}) = 1.5$$

$$\delta_1^{input} = \delta_2^{input} = \delta_3^{input} = 1.5 \cdot 0 \cdot 1 + 1.5 \cdot 0 \cdot 1 = 0$$

Third step   In the third step we update the weights

$$\Delta w_{ti} = \eta \cdot \delta_t^{output} \cdot V_i.$$

Taking into account the symmetry with $\eta = 1$ we get

$$\Delta w_{tj} = \eta \cdot \delta_t^{output} \cdot 0.5 = 1.5 \cdot 0.5 = 0.75$$

and we update the weights

$$w_{ti}^{new} = w_{ti}^{old} + \Delta w_{ti} = 0.75$$

and

$$\Delta W_{ij} = \eta \cdot \delta_i^{input} \cdot 0 = 0 \cdot 0 = 0$$

$$W_{ij}^{new} = W_{ij}^{old} + \Delta W_{ij} = 1 + 0 = 1$$

Reduced error   After the training we have

$$V_1 = V_2 = V_3 = \frac{1}{1 + e^0} = 0.5$$

$$o_1 = o_2 = \frac{1}{1 + e^{-4 \cdot 1.5}} = 0.997527$$

Before the training the squared error is:

$$\frac{1}{2} \cdot (2 - 0.5)^2 = 2.25$$

After training the squared error is:

$$\frac{1}{2} \cdot (2 - 0.997527)^2 = 1.00495$$

The squared error reduced.

2)

Preform one training step of the stochastic gradient descent rule resulting from quadratic error on the network.

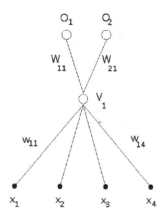

For simplicity we assume that all units use the activation function

$$\sigma(net) = \frac{1}{1 + e^{-2 \cdot net}}$$

The initial weighs from input pattern to hidden units are

$$w_{10} = 0, w_{11} = 1, w_{12} = 1, w_{13} = 0, w_{14} = 0$$

The initial weighs from hidden units to output units are

$$W_{10} = 0, W_{11} = 0, W_{21} = 1$$

For simplicity the corresponding weights for bias are set to zero and the learning rate is $\eta = 2$.

The training pattern is

$$\mathbf{x} = (4, 4, 1, 0)^T, \quad x_1 = 4, x_2 = 4, x_3 = 1, x_4 = 0,$$

and the target pattern is

$$\mathbf{y} = (0, 1)^T, \quad y_2 = 0, y_2 = 1.$$

Solution:

First step

$$V_1 = \frac{1}{1 + e^{-2 \cdot 8}} \approx 1$$

$$o_1 = o_2 = \frac{1}{1 + e^{-2 \cdot 0}} = 0.5$$

$$o_1 = o_2 = \frac{1}{1 + e^{-2 \cdot 1}} = 0.880797$$

Second step In the second step the errors represented by δ are propagated backward from the output units

$$\delta_t = (y_t - o_t) \cdot \sigma'(net_t)$$

$$\delta_1^{output} = \delta_2^{output} = (0 - 0.5) \cdot 2 \cdot 0.5 \cdot (1 - 0.5) = -0.25$$

$$\delta_2^{output} = \delta_2^{output} = (2 - 0.880797) \cdot 2 \cdot 0.880797 \cdot (1 - 0.880797) = 0.0250311$$

$$\delta_1^{input} = 2 \cdot 1 \cdot (1 - 1) \cdot (0 \cdot (-0.25) + 1 \cdot 0.880797) = 0$$

Third step In the third step we update the weights with $\eta = 2$ we get

$$\Delta W_{11} = \eta \cdot \delta_1^{output} \cdot 1 = -2 \cdot 0.25 = -0.5$$

$$\Delta W_{21} = \eta \cdot \delta_1^{output} \cdot 1 = 2 \cdot 0.0250311 = 0.0500622$$

and we update the weights

$$W_{11}^{new} = 0 - 0.5 = -0.5$$

$$W_{11}^{new} = 1 + 0.0500622 = 1.500622.$$

For the input weights there is no change since $\delta_1^{input} = 0$,

$$\Delta w_{ij} = 0$$

and we update the weights (no change)

$$w_{10}^{new} = 0, w_{11}^{new} = 1, w_{12}^{new} = 1, w_{13}^{new} = 0, w_{14}^{new} = 0$$

Thinking Questions

a) What are the main differences between using squared error and cross-entropy?

b) How do you think the MLP decision boundary will look like in two-dimensional problems?

c) Can we use MLP for a regression problem?

d) Try to apply an MLP to exercises from previous lectures. Notice that it can solve non-linearly separable problems.

Chapter 7

Learning Theory

Fig. 7.1 Learning theory tries to answer the following questions, under what conditions is successful learning possible? Under what conditions is a particular learning algorithm assured of learning successfully?

7.1   Supervised Classification Problem

In a learning problem there is an input space $\mathcal{X}$ (or population) and an unknown, correct classification function $f : \mathcal{X} \to \{0, 1\}$. From the population and sample, we are given a set of data (or a sample) that provides information about the correct function f on a few examples:

$$D = \{(x_1, f(x_1)), \cdots, (x_N, f(x_N))\}. \tag{7.1}$$

A learning algorithm has a set of possible hypotheses $\mathcal{H} = \{h_1, h_2, \cdots, h_M\}$, where each hypothesis $h \in \mathcal{H}$ is, just like f, a function that maps inputs to a classification $h : \mathcal{X} \to \{0, 1\}$. The goal of such an algorithm is to choose the hypothesis $h \in \mathcal{H}$ that best approximates f on the whole population $\mathcal{X}$.

A more accurate definition comes from defining the error of an hypothesis on the population

$$E_{population}(h) = \mathbb{E}_X \left[h(X) \neq f(X) \right], \tag{7.2}$$

and saying that the algorithm wants to choose the hypothesis from $\mathcal{H}$ that minimizes it

$$h^* = \arg \min_{h \in \mathcal{H}} E_{population}(h). \tag{7.3}$$

The big problem is that we do not know f, so we cannot compute $E_{population}$. All we are given is a sample D. For that reason, all we can do for an hypothesis is compute its error in the sample

$$E_{sample}(h) = \frac{1}{N} \sum_{n=1}^{N} \mathbb{I}\left[h(x_n) \neq f(x_n) \right]. \tag{7.4}$$

As an example, think about Rosenblatt's perceptron in a two-dimensional problem with two classes. The hypotheses set is the set of all possible straight lines and the goal of the procedure is to choose the line that best separates the two classes for all future examples and, yet, the algorithm chooses that line based on how it performs in the sample.

With that, we would like to be able to trust the performance of all hypotheses in the sample. If we know that their performance in the sample is representative of their performance in the population, then all the algorithm has to do is choose the hypothesis that best performs in the sample because it will, most likely, be the one that best performs in the population. So, the key question is: can we trust the sample? Or, more concretely, can we trust that $E_{sample}(h)$ is a good proxy for $E_{population}(h)$?

7.2 Probability of a bad sample

In answering the previous question, our intuition tells us that we can trust the proxy unless we are unlucky and get a non-representative sample. So, can we measure the probability that this will happen and guarantee that it is small?

Before going into the details of the answer, let us go through a small detour. Assume that the fraction of black marbles in a bin is μ. Looking at the marbles in the bin as a population, imagine we perform N extractions with replacement and, thus, get a sample of its contents. If we count the fraction ν of black marbles in the sample, what can we conclude about the population fraction μ? Figure 7.2 illustrates the described experiment.

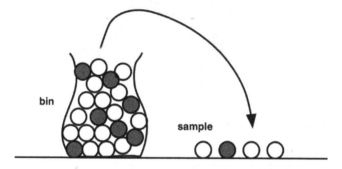

Fig. 7.2 We pick a random sample of N independent marbles (with replacement) from this bin, and observe the fraction ν of black marbles.

According to Hoeffding's Inequality [Hoeffding (1963)], see Figure 7.3, as the sample size N grows, it becomes exponentially unlikely that ν and μ differ by more than a certain error ϵ

$$P(|\nu - \mu| > \epsilon) \leq \frac{2}{e^{2 \cdot \epsilon^2 \cdot N}}. \tag{7.5}$$

If we define a bad sample as one where $|\nu - \mu| > \epsilon$, then this inequality is basically giving us the probability of getting a bad sample. Now, assume we want to know how big the sample must be for us to be guaranteed that the probability of getting a bad sample is smaller than a small value δ. Since

$$P(|\nu - \mu| > \epsilon) \leq \frac{2}{e^{2 \cdot \epsilon^2 \cdot N}}, \tag{7.6}$$

and we want that

$$P(|\nu - \mu| > \epsilon) \leq \delta. \tag{7.7}$$

Fig. 7.3   Wassily Hoeffding (June 12, 1914 - February 28, 1991) was a Finnish statistician and probabilist.

All we need to do is guarantee that

$$\frac{2}{e^{2 \cdot \epsilon^2 \cdot N}} \leq \delta. \tag{7.8}$$

Writing the inequality in terms of the sample size, we get

$$N \geq \frac{\ln\left(\frac{2}{\delta}\right)}{2\epsilon^2}. \tag{7.9}$$

Now, we can check our intuitions by checking what happens in the limits. If we want the error between sample and population to be null, we need an infinitely big sample

$$\lim_{\epsilon \to 0} \frac{\ln\left(\frac{2}{\delta}\right)}{2\epsilon^2} = \infty. \tag{7.10}$$

The same happens if we want the probability of getting a bad sample to be zero

$$\lim_{\delta \to 0} \frac{\ln\left(\frac{2}{\delta}\right)}{2\epsilon^2} = \infty. \tag{7.11}$$

After this detour, we are ready to tackle the initial problem. We can generalize the bins reasoning to Machine Learning [Abu-Mostafa *et al.* (2012)].

We can think about ν as the in sample error of a given hypothesis h and about μ as its population error. With that, we can write Hoeffding's inequality for the errors of an hypothesis h

$$P(|E_{sample}(h) - E_{population}(h)| > \epsilon) \leq \frac{2}{e^{2 \cdot \epsilon^2 \cdot N}}. \qquad (7.12)$$

Now, we want to be able to trust the in sample results for all our hypotheses. If we can, then the algorithm may choose based on that. With that, a bad sample would be one where at least one of the hypothesis is misleading. Let us denote the event where hypothesis h is misleading in the sample by $Misleading(h) = |E_{sample}(h) - E_{population}(h)| > \epsilon$. For the learning algorithm, the sample is bad if any hypothesis is misleading i.e. if $Misleading(h_1)$, or $Misleading(h_2)$, or $Misleading(h_3)$, and so on. We can write that event as $\cup_{h \in \mathcal{H}} Misleading(h)$. Let us try to bound the probability of a bad sample $P(\cup_{h \in \mathcal{H}} Misleading(h))$. For our finite hypotheses set with M hypotheses, we can write

$$P(\cup_{h \in \mathcal{H}} Misleading(h)) = P(\cup_{m=1}^{M} Misleading(h_m)) \qquad (7.13)$$

Using the union bound, we can write

$$P(\cup_{m=1}^{M} Misleading(h_m)) \leq \sum_{m=1}^{M} P(Misleading(h_m)). \qquad (7.14)$$

Since

$$P(Misleading(h)) = P(|E_{in}(h) - E_{out}(h)| > \epsilon) \leq \frac{2}{e^{2 \cdot \epsilon^2 \cdot N}}, \qquad (7.15)$$

we can write that

$$\sum_{m=1}^{M} P(Misleading(h_m)) \leq \sum_{m=1}^{M} \frac{2}{e^{2 \cdot \epsilon^2 \cdot N}}, \qquad (7.16)$$

which implies

$$P(\cup_{m=1}^{M} Misleading(h_m)) \leq \sum_{m=1}^{M} \frac{2}{e^{2 \cdot \epsilon^2 \cdot N}}. \qquad (7.17)$$

From there, we can develop the right-hand side into

$$P(\cup_{m=1}^{M} Misleading(h_m)) \leq \frac{2M}{e^{2 \cdot \epsilon^2 \cdot N}}. \qquad (7.18)$$

So, we have our bound on the probability of a bad sample

$$P(\text{``}BadSample\text{''}) \leq \frac{2M}{e^{2 \cdot \epsilon^2 \cdot N}}. \qquad (7.19)$$

Assuming we want the bad sample probability to be below a small value δ, we can write

$$\delta = \frac{2M}{e^{2 \cdot \epsilon^2 \cdot N}}. \tag{7.20}$$

As the sample grows, for a finite hypotheses set, we get closer and closer to be sure that it is not a bad one

$$\lim_{N \to \infty} \delta = \lim_{N \to \infty} \frac{2M}{e^{2 \cdot \epsilon^2 \cdot N}} = 0. \tag{7.21}$$

Another interesting thing is to look at the generalization error

$$\epsilon^2 = \frac{\ln \frac{2M}{\delta}}{2N}, \tag{7.22}$$

and see that it also goes to zero as the sample size grows

$$\lim_{N \to \infty} \epsilon^2 = \lim_{N \to \infty} \frac{\ln \frac{2M}{\delta}}{2N} = 0. \tag{7.23}$$

With that, we have shown that for a large enough sample size, we can guarantee that, with a large probability $1 - \delta$, we will get a training set on which all hypotheses in $\mathcal{H}$ will perform similarly to how they would perform in the whole population. This means that the learning algorithm can trust the conclusion it takes from the sample. Having that guarantee, all the algorithm needs to do is to find a hypothesis that performs well on the sample i.e. one where $E_{sample}(h)$ is small. So, to learn successfully we need two key ingredients:

(1) Large enough sample such that we can trust that it will not mislead us;
(2) A finite hypotheses set that contains at least one hypothesis that performs well on the sample.

Having these ingredients we can say that learning is possible.

7.3   Infinite hypotheses set

All this is well and good. Yet, we usually have a finite sample. And even worse, all learning algorithms we have seen have infinite hypotheses sets (think about the perceptron). In a case like that, using our derivation, the probability of a bad sample is unbounded

$$\lim_{M \to \infty} \delta = \lim_{M \to \infty} \frac{2M}{e^{2 \cdot \epsilon^2 \cdot N}} = \infty. \tag{7.24}$$

So, we are missing the first key ingredient. Now one may ask why to use an infinite hypotheses set in the first place. Well, to get the second ingredient this may be indispensable and some times not even enough (!). Think about how the perceptron is incapable of separating non-linearly separable classes.

It seems like, unless we are able to get a better bound on the probability of a bad sample, learning may be hopeless in practice after all. Fortunately it is not and we will try to get an intuition for why.

Looking at our bound, we see that the problem comes from the factor M that represents the size of the hypotheses set. However, we may have been too pessimistic. For example, for a given training set, a perceptron has an infinite amount of hypotheses (boundary lines) that result in the same classification, see Figure 7.4.

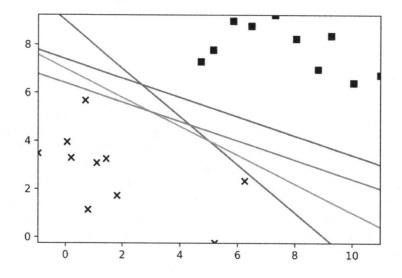

Fig. 7.4 All plotted boundaries classify all the points in the same way.

It seems that we could get a closer bound if instead of using the number of hypothesis in the hypotheses set, we use the "effective" number of hypotheses. Concretely, how many hypotheses in $\mathcal{H}$ generate different classifications for a given training set. To the set of different classifications that a hypotheses set can generate for some training data set of size N we call the dichotomies $DIC(N, \mathcal{H})$. If we define this set as

$$DIC(N, \mathcal{H}) = \{(h(\mathbf{x}_1), \cdots, h(\mathbf{x}_N)) \, | \, h \in \mathcal{H}\}, \qquad (7.25)$$

then the "effective" number of hypotheses is given by the size of the dichotomies set $|DIC(N, \mathcal{H})|$.

By now, the next step seems logically clear. We want to take the bound we had and substitute the number of hypothesis M by the number of dichotomies that our hypotheses set generates. Although this step is not completely mathematically correct, we will do it to get the intuition and by the end we will set the record straight. Having stated that, we get

$$P\left(\text{“}BadSample\text{”}\right) \leq \frac{2 \, |DIC(N, \mathcal{H})|}{e^{2 \cdot \epsilon^2 \cdot N}}. \qquad (7.26)$$

It is clear that the maximum possible number of dichotomies for N points is 2^N. Thus, we can write

$$\frac{2 \, |DIC(N, \mathcal{H})|}{e^{2 \cdot \epsilon^2 \cdot N}} \leq \frac{2 \cdot 2^N}{e^{2 \cdot \epsilon^2 \cdot N}} = \frac{2^{N+1}}{e^{2 \cdot \epsilon^2 \cdot N}}. \qquad (7.27)$$

This entails that

$$P\left(\text{“}BadSample\text{”}\right) \leq \frac{2^{N+1}}{e^{2 \cdot \epsilon^2 \cdot N}}. \qquad (7.28)$$

Unfortunately, for this bound, we are not guaranteed that as the sample size grows, the probability of getting a bad sample goes to zero. From that we can conclude that learning is not feasible if we are working with a hypotheses set that can generate all possible classifications for an infinitely large training set i.e. one where $\forall_{N>0} |DIC(N, \mathcal{H})| = 2^N$. However, most learning algorithms, like the perceptron, are not in this category. In a formal manner, most learning algorithms work with hypotheses sets where, for a large enough N, the number of dichotomies is strictly smaller than the maximum $|DIC(N, \mathcal{H})| < 2^N$. We need a better way to characterize the complexity of an hypotheses set to get a better bound.

7.4   The VC Dimension

In the theory of learning, if, for a given $\mathcal{H}$ there exists a set of N points such that $|DIC(N, \mathcal{H})| = 2^N$, it is said that $\mathcal{H}$ shatters N points. From the definition, we can restate our finding from the end of the previous section to state that learning is infeasible for hypotheses sets that shatter any number of points.

From the concept of shattering follows a key concept for us. The VC dimension of a set of hypotheses $\mathcal{H}$, written as $d_{VC}(\mathcal{H})$, is equal to the maximum number of points that it can shatter. We will see some examples and more details on how to compute the VC dimension of some sets of hypotheses, but, for now, the key thing is to state a very important result for our quest. It can be shown [Abu-Mostafa *et al.* (2012)] that

$$|DIC(N, \mathcal{H})| \leq N^{d_{VC}(\mathcal{H})} + 1. \tag{7.29}$$

Substituting this result into our bound, we get

$$P(\text{``BadSample''}) \leq \frac{2\,|DIC(N, \mathcal{H})|}{e^{2 \cdot \epsilon^2 \cdot N}} \leq \frac{2\left(N^{d_{VC}(\mathcal{H})} + 1\right)}{e^{2 \cdot \epsilon^2 \cdot N}}. \tag{7.30}$$

From which we see that, if we are working with an hypotheses set with finite VC dimension, call it k, learning is feasible since the probability of getting a bad sample goes to zero as the sample size grows

$$\lim_{N \to \infty} P(\text{``BadSample''}) \leq \lim_{N \to \infty} \frac{2\left(N^k + 1\right)}{e^{2 \cdot \epsilon^2 \cdot N}} = 0. \tag{7.31}$$

It seems like this intuitive path brought us to a point where learning seems to be feasible for a finite VC dimension, even if the hypotheses set itself is infinite. These are great news but does the mathematically rigorous path lead to the same place? Fortunately it does. When we substituted M by the number of dichotomies we said that it was not a mathematically rigorous step. To set the record straight, we should have got the bound

$$P(\text{``BadSample''}) \leq \frac{4\,|DIC(2N, \mathcal{H})|}{e^{\frac{1}{8} \cdot \epsilon^2 \cdot N}}. \tag{7.32}$$

Which leads to

$$P(\text{``BadSample''}) \leq \frac{4\,|DIC(2N, \mathcal{H})|}{e^{\frac{1}{8} \cdot \epsilon^2 \cdot N}} \leq \frac{4\left((2N)^{d_{VC}(\mathcal{H})} + 1\right)}{e^{\frac{1}{8} \cdot \epsilon^2 \cdot N}}. \tag{7.33}$$

Which, in turn, leads to exactly the same conclusion that learning is not hopeless if the VC dimension is finite.

7.5 A Fundamental Trade-off

All the steps we took led us to conclude that, for a finite VC dimension hypotheses set, if we have a large enough training sample, we can assume that the performance in the sample is a good proxy for the performance in the population. So, does this mean that learning is easy in such scenario?

Not at all. First of all, the bound only guarantees that we will not be mislead by the sample, for a large enough sample. This "large enough" can be too large for the data we have for a given task. Furthermore, remember the two key ingredients of learning feasibility. We not only need to guarantee a trustworthy sample, but we also need to be able to find a hypothesis that performs well in the sample. To get such hypothesis we may need to work with a more complex hypotheses space. But a more complex hypotheses space, will have a larger VC dimension and, thus, may require a prohibitively large sample size. There seems to be a trade-off between the two ingredients. This trade-off is fundamental and will haunt us throughout the book. Figure 7.5 puts a helpful image on the trade-off.

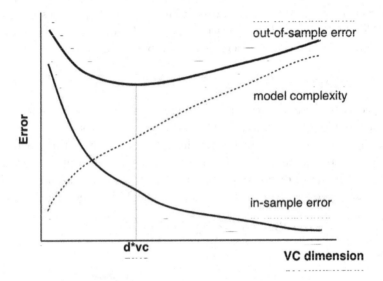

Fig. 7.5 When we use a more complex learning model, one that has higher VC dimension d_{vc}, we are likely to fit the training data better resulting in a lower in sample error, but we pay a higher penalty for model complexity. A combination of the two, which estimates the out of sample error, thus attains a minimum at some intermediate d_{vc}^*.

A good way to see what the knowledge of the trade-off can bring to the table is through regularization theory. Looking back at the bound, assume we want to guarantee that the probability of a bad sample is smaller than a small quantity δ. We can write

$$\delta = \frac{4\left((2N)^{d_{VC}(\mathcal{H})} + 1\right)}{e^{\frac{1}{8}\cdot\epsilon^2\cdot N}}. \tag{7.34}$$

From here, we may get an expression for the absolute difference between the sample and population errors

$$\epsilon = \sqrt{\frac{8}{N} \ln \left(\frac{4 \left((2N)^{d_{VC}(\mathcal{H})} + 1 \right)}{\delta} \right)}. \tag{7.35}$$

With a high probability $1 - \delta$, we will get a good sample, and, thus we will have that, for all hypotheses h,

$$|E_{sample}(h) - E_{population}(h)| \leq \epsilon. \tag{7.36}$$

From there it follows that

$$E_{population}(h) \leq E_{sample}(h) + \epsilon. \tag{7.37}$$

Which is the same as writting

$$E_{population}(h) \leq E_{sample}(h) + \sqrt{\frac{8}{N} \ln \left(\frac{4 \left((2N)^{d_{VC}(\mathcal{H})} + 1 \right)}{\delta} \right)}. \tag{7.38}$$

From this inequality, we can see that the error in the population can be seen as a combinations of two key terms. The leftmost term is the error in the sample and it can, most likely, be further reduced by an algorithm that works with a more complex hypotheses set. The rightmost term is a generalization error and is smaller for less complex hypotheses sets. This simple sum of terms aptly shows the aforementioned trade-off where complex sets are good on the one hand, but bad on the other hand.

In general terms, when we manage to get a very low sample error but a high generalization error, we are in the presence of overfitting. Most likely, our hypotheses set is too complex. The opposite scenario is referred to as underfitting and it occurs when the generalization error is very low, but the sample error is high.

It goes without saying that the ideal scenario would be one where the complexity of the hypotheses set is just right. However, we often have no idea about what "just right" means. For that reason, many algorithms try to choose the hypothesis that minimizes the sum of the in sample error and a regularization heuristic that measures the complexity of the hypothesis. Penalizing the complexity of the hypothesis restricts the hypotheses space in the sense that encourages the algorithm to choose from a subset of the space (the subset o simple hypotheses). However, it does not force it to choose form this subset. If the improvement in sample error pays off, then the algorithm has the freedom to go into the more complex subset of hypotheses.

Throughout the book we will see many examples of this type of reasoning driving the learning algorithms.

7.6   Computing VC Dimension

As we have seen before, the VC dimension plays a key role in learning theory for classification. VC stands for Vapnik-Chervonenkis, the surnames of its creators [Vapnik and Chervonenkis (1971)], see Figure 7.6.

Fig. 7.6   Alexey Chervonenkis and Vladimir Vapnik.

Although we have seen the key role that this dimension plays, we have not gone through the process of computing it for specific hypotheses sets. Remember that a dichotomy is a partition of a training set into two classes. The name comes from the ancient Greeks and it means equally divided, cut in half. Remember also that a training set is shattered by an hypotheses space $\mathcal{H}$ if and only if for EVERY dichotomy of the training set there exists SOME hypothesis in $\mathcal{H}$ consistent with this dichotomy [Mitchell (1997)]. For example for 3 points on a plane there are 2^3 possible dichotomies, see Figure 7.7. As long as the points are not collinear, we will be able to find 2^3 linear surfaces that shatter them. However, on a plane four points cannot be shattered by these simple lines, see Figure 7.8. Another example comes for simple boundaries on the real line. This hypotheses set of boundaries can shatter two points, however it cannot shatter three, see Figure 7.9.

Remember that the VC dimension of a hypothesis space $\mathcal{H}$ is the cardinality of the largest set that can be shattered by $\mathcal{H}$. Knowing that, to prove that the VC dimension of a given $\mathcal{H}$ is equal to k we would have to

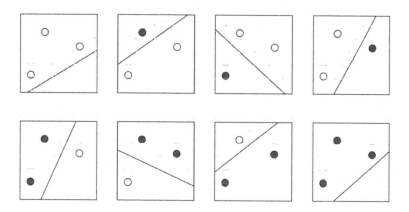

Fig. 7.7   Shattering of three points.

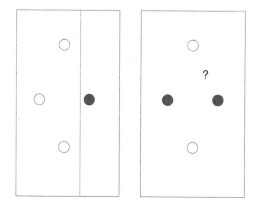

Fig. 7.8   On a plane four points cannot be shattered.

take a two-step argument:

(1) Find ONE set of k points that can be shattered by $\mathcal{H}$ concluding that $d_{VC}(\mathcal{H}) \geq k$;
(2) Prove that it is NOT POSSIBLE to find any set of $k+1$ points that can be shattered by $\mathcal{H}$ concluding that $d_{VC}(\mathcal{H}) < k+1$.

While the first step may be relatively easy, the second one is often quite difficult. The chapter's exercises provide several examples of this argument for simple scenarios. For now, let us show how unpractical this is with the

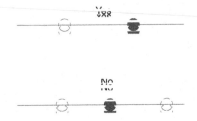

Fig. 7.9   Shattering of points on a line.

perceptron.

7.6.1   *The VC Dimension of a Perceptron*

In a d dimensional problem, the perceptron has $d + 1$ free learnable parameters: a weight for each input and a bias term

$$\mathbf{w} = (w_0, w_1, \cdots, w_d)^T. \tag{7.39}$$

We want to show that the VC dimension of such a perceptron with d inputs is $d + 1$,

$$d_{VC}(\mathcal{H}^{perceptron}) = d + 1. \tag{7.40}$$

First Step: In the aforementioned two-step argument, the first step is to find one set of $d + 1$ points in $\mathbb{R}^d$ that is shattered by a perceptron. With that, we would prove that

$$d_{VC} \leq d + 1. \tag{7.41}$$

Let us choose $d + 1$ linearly independent points and represent them as a matrix

$$X = \begin{pmatrix} \mathbf{x}_1^T \\ \mathbf{x}_2^T \\ \vdots \\ \mathbf{x}_{d+1}^T \end{pmatrix} = \begin{pmatrix} x_{1,0} & x_{1,1} & x_{1,2} & \cdots & x_{1,d+1} \\ x_{2,0} & x_{2,1} & x_{2,2} & \cdots & x_{2,d+1} \\ \vdots & \vdots & \ddots & \vdots \\ x_{d+1,0} & x_{d+1,1} & x_{d+1,2} & \cdots & x_{d+1,d+1} \end{pmatrix} \tag{7.42}$$

We can freely choose their position in the space

$$X = \begin{pmatrix} \mathbf{x}_1^T \\ \mathbf{x}_2^T \\ \mathbf{x}_3^T \\ \vdots \\ \mathbf{x}_d^T \\ \mathbf{x}_{d+1}^T \end{pmatrix} = \begin{pmatrix} 1 & 0 & 0 & \cdots & 0 & 0 \\ 1 & 1 & 0 & \cdots & 0 & 0 \\ 1 & 0 & 1 & \cdots & 0 & 0 \\ \vdots & \vdots & \ddots & \vdots \\ 1 & 0 & 0 & \cdots & 1 & 0 \\ 1 & 0 & 0 & \cdots & 0 & 1 \end{pmatrix}. \tag{7.43}$$

So, we did it in such a way, that the matrix X is invertible. Now, for every possible dichotomy of 2^{d+1} points

$$\mathbf{y} = \begin{pmatrix} 1 \\ 1 \\ \vdots \\ 1 \end{pmatrix}, \ \mathbf{y} = \begin{pmatrix} -1 \\ 1 \\ \vdots \\ 1 \end{pmatrix}, \ \mathbf{y} = \begin{pmatrix} 1 \\ -1 \\ \vdots \\ 1 \end{pmatrix}, \ \cdots, \ \mathbf{y} = \begin{pmatrix} -1 \\ -1 \\ \vdots \\ -1 \end{pmatrix}, \quad (7.44)$$

that is, for any

$$\mathbf{y} = \begin{pmatrix} y_1 \\ y_2 \\ \vdots \\ y_{d+1} \end{pmatrix} = \begin{pmatrix} \pm 1 \\ \pm 1 \\ \vdots \\ \pm 1 \end{pmatrix}, \quad (7.45)$$

we can find a weight vector $\mathbf{w}$ with

$$sgn(X \cdot \mathbf{w}) = \mathbf{y}. \quad (7.46)$$

As X contains only binary values, we can simplify to

$$X \cdot \mathbf{w} = \mathbf{y}, \quad (7.47)$$

and we get

$$\mathbf{w} = X^{-1} \cdot \mathbf{y}. \quad (7.48)$$

Since X is invertible, $\mathbf{w}$ exists and thus, a set of $d + 1$ points that a perceptron can shatter does exist.

Second Step: For the second step we need to universally prove that no set of $d + 2$ points can be shattered by a perceptron. By doing so, we will show that

$$d_{VC} \geq d + 1 \quad (7.49)$$

and thus conclude our proof. To achieve this, we will use the fact that for $d + 2$ points in a perceptron in d dimensions, some vectors (at least two) will be linearly dependent.

We have $d + 1$ dimensions and $d + 2$ points, since we have more points than dimensions, at least one point needs to be a linear combination of the other points

$$\mathbf{x}_k = \sum_{i \neq k} \alpha_i \cdot \mathbf{x}_i. \quad (7.50)$$

We can consider an example of a dichotomy that will lead to a contradiction since it cannot be generated by the perceptron. With $\mathbf{x}_i$ and non zero α_i we get

$$y_i = sgn(\alpha_i) \tag{7.51}$$

and

$$\mathbf{x}_k, \quad y_k = -1. \tag{7.52}$$

This is a contradiction, because

$$\mathbf{x}_k = \sum_{i \neq k} \alpha_i \cdot \mathbf{x}_i \tag{7.53}$$

$$\mathbf{w}^T \cdot \mathbf{x}_k = \sum_{i \neq k} \alpha_i \cdot \mathbf{w}^T \cdot \mathbf{x}_i. \tag{7.54}$$

If

$$y_i = sgn(\alpha_i) = sgn(\mathbf{w}^T \cdot \mathbf{x}_i) \tag{7.55}$$

then the multiplication must be positive

$$sgn(\alpha_i) \cdot sgn(\mathbf{w}^T \cdot \mathbf{x}_i) > 0, \tag{7.56}$$

$$\alpha_i \cdot \mathbf{w}^T \cdot \mathbf{x}_i > 0 \tag{7.57}$$

and since

$$\mathbf{w}^T \cdot \mathbf{x}_k = \sum_{i \neq k} \alpha_i \cdot \mathbf{w}^T \cdot \mathbf{x}_i > 0 \tag{7.58}$$

it follows that y_k cannot be negative,

$$y_k = sgn(\mathbf{w}^T \cdot \mathbf{x}_k) = 1. \tag{7.59}$$

Final Step:

$$\{d_{VC} \leq d+1, d_{VC} \geq d+1\} \rightarrow d_{VC} = d+1. \tag{7.60}$$

For a perceptron

$$d_{VC}(\mathcal{H}^{perceptron}) = d+1 \tag{7.61}$$

where d is the number of inputs.

7.6.2 *A Heuristic way to measure hypotheses space complexity*

A lot more important than knowing how to compute the VC dimension of a perceptron is to notice how tough it is to compute it. Knowing that, one can imagine how tougher it must be to compute it for more complex models [Blumer *et al.* (1989)]. From that, we can conclude that it would be very helpful to have a simple heuristic way to estimate the complexity of an hypotheses set.

Looking at the perceptron result, one notices that the VC dimension equals the number of free learnable parameters of the model. For other models, this is not always the case since many models have non-free or even redundant parameters. However, the intuition leads in the correct way. For a hypotheses set that is described by parameters that are learned by the learning algorithm, the number of such parameters is often a good approximation of how complex our model is. In practice, one estimates this number of parameters to make decisions about diagnosing and treating overfitting and underfitting.

7.7 The Regression Problem

All the theory we have seen was applied to classification. However, most lessons learned are applicable to regression. To see that let us look into the regression problem.

The main difference between classification and regression is in the targets. While the unknown target classification function mapped inputs to labels $f : \mathcal{X} \to \{0, 1\}$, in regression, inputs are mapped to real valued targets $f : \mathcal{X} \to \mathbb{R}$.

The rest can be seen as the same. There is an hypotheses space $\mathcal{H}$ from which the learning algorithm must choose the hypothesis that best approximates f on the population and, like in classification, all the algorithm is given is a sample

$$D = \{(\mathbf{x}_1, f(\mathbf{x}_1)), \cdots, (\mathbf{x}_N, f(\mathbf{x}_N))\}. \tag{7.62}$$

With real valued targets, when an hypothesis predicts a value, we need to measure its error in a different way. Specifically, an output that is close to the target is less wrong than an output that is far away from it. To that end, we will use the squared error between the hypothesis outputs and the sample targets [Haykin (2008)]. So, the sample error for a specific hypothesis is given by

$$E_{sample}(h) = \frac{1}{N} \sum_{n=1}^{N} (h(\mathbf{x}_n) - f(\mathbf{x}_n))^2 \qquad (7.63)$$

and the population error for that hypothesis is given by the expected squared loss across all possible inputs

$$E_{population}(h) = \mathbb{E}_{\mathbf{x}} \left[(h(\mathbf{x}) - f(\mathbf{x}))^2 \right]. \qquad (7.64)$$

Now, assume that, when given sample D, a learning algorithm chooses the hypothesis $h_D \in \mathcal{H}$. Then, the expected population error for a learning model can be written as the average population error of the chosen hypothesis for all possible training sets

$$\mathbb{E}_D \left[E_{population}(h_D) \right] \qquad (7.65)$$

which can be expanded into

$$\mathbb{E}_D \left[\mathbb{E}_{\mathbf{x}} \left[(h_D(\mathbf{x}) - f(\mathbf{x}))^2 \right] \right]. \qquad (7.66)$$

From the definition of expected value we can safely reverse the order of the expectations

$$\mathbb{E}_{\mathbf{x}} \left[\mathbb{E}_D \left[(h_D(\mathbf{x}) - f(\mathbf{x}))^2 \right] \right]. \qquad (7.67)$$

Now, a term $\mathbb{E}_D [h_D(\mathbf{x})]$ is a constant for a given $\mathbf{x}$. For that reason, we can add and subtract it safely as follows

$$\mathbb{E}_{\mathbf{x}} \left[\mathbb{E}_D \left[(h_D(\mathbf{x}) - \mathbb{E}_D [h_D(\mathbf{x})] + \mathbb{E}_D [h_D(\mathbf{x})] - f(\mathbf{x}))^2 \right] \right]. \qquad (7.68)$$

If we look at the expression inside the expectations we can identify the square of the sum of two terms. Now, we can expand it to get

$$\mathbb{E}_{\mathbf{x}}[\mathbb{E}_D[(h_D(\mathbf{x}) - \mathbb{E}_D [h_D(\mathbf{x})])^2$$
$$+ (\mathbb{E}_D [h_D(\mathbf{x})] - f(\mathbf{x}))^2$$
$$+ 2 (h_D(\mathbf{x}) - \mathbb{E}_D [h_D(\mathbf{x})]) (\mathbb{E}_D [h_D(\mathbf{x})] - f(\mathbf{x}))]].$$

Due to the linearity of expectation, we can break the inside expected value into a sum of three expectations

$$\mathbb{E}_{\mathbf{x}}[\mathbb{E}_D \left[(h_D(\mathbf{x}) - \mathbb{E}_D [h_D(\mathbf{x})])^2 \right]$$
$$+ \mathbb{E}_D \left[(\mathbb{E}_D [h_D(\mathbf{x})] - f(\mathbf{x}))^2 \right]$$
$$+ \mathbb{E}_D [2 (h_D(\mathbf{x}) - \mathbb{E}_D [h_D(\mathbf{x})]) (\mathbb{E}_D [h_D(\mathbf{x})] - f(\mathbf{x}))]].$$

Again due to the linearity of expectation, we can take the values that do not depend on D out of the last expectation

$$\mathbb{E}_{\mathbf{x}}[\mathbb{E}_D\left[(h_D(\mathbf{x}) - \mathbb{E}_D[h_D(\mathbf{x})])^2\right]$$
$$+ \mathbb{E}_D\left[(\mathbb{E}_D[h_D(\mathbf{x})] - f(\mathbf{x}))^2\right]$$
$$+ 2(\mathbb{E}_D[h_D(\mathbf{x})] - f(\mathbf{x}))\mathbb{E}_D[(h_D(\mathbf{x}) - \mathbb{E}_D[h_D(\mathbf{x})])]].$$

The rightmost factor of the last term is the expected value of a sum, which is the same as the sum of the expected values

$$\mathbb{E}_{\mathbf{x}}[\mathbb{E}_D\left[(h_D(\mathbf{x}) - \mathbb{E}_D[h_D(\mathbf{x})])^2\right]$$
$$+ \mathbb{E}_D\left[(\mathbb{E}_D[h_D(\mathbf{x})] - f(\mathbf{x}))^2\right]$$
$$+ 2(\mathbb{E}_D[h_D(\mathbf{x})] - f(\mathbf{x}))(\mathbb{E}_D[h_D(\mathbf{x})] - \mathbb{E}_D[h_D(\mathbf{x})])].$$

With that, we see that the rightmost term is zero and we get

$$\mathbb{E}_{\mathbf{x}}\left[\mathbb{E}_D\left[(h_D(\mathbf{x}) - \mathbb{E}_D[h_D(\mathbf{x})])^2\right] + \mathbb{E}_D\left[(\mathbb{E}_D[h_D(\mathbf{x})] - f(\mathbf{x}))^2\right]\right]. \quad (7.69)$$

The term on the right does not depend on the sample, so we can get rid of the expectation

$$\mathbb{E}_{\mathbf{x}}\left[\mathbb{E}_D\left[(h_D(\mathbf{x}) - \mathbb{E}_D[h_D(\mathbf{x})])^2\right] + (\mathbb{E}_D[h_D(\mathbf{x})] - f(\mathbf{x}))^2\right]. \quad (7.70)$$

All of this derivation showed us that the expected population error for a learning model depends on the sum of two terms:

- the variance $VAR(\mathbf{x}) = \mathbb{E}_D\left[(h_D(\mathbf{x}) - \mathbb{E}_D[h_D(\mathbf{x})])^2\right]$;
- and the squared bias $Bias^2(\mathbf{x}) = (\mathbb{E}_D[h_D(\mathbf{x})] - f(\mathbf{x}))^2$.

Looking at the first expression, we see that the variance measures how different are the outputs, for the same input, if the model learned with different data sets. This is a measure of how low the sample error can get with the hypotheses set in question. A very complex learning model can adapt to the details in the training sample and, so h_D will be very different for different samples. This will lead to very different outputs for the same input $\mathbf{x}$ which implies a high variance.

The squared bias measures how different the average hypothesis chosen by the model differs from the target function. This is a measure of the complexity of the hypotheses space. If the hypotheses space is too simple, even the best sample will lead to the choice of an unsuitable hypothesis.

So, again, the population error for a learning model is defined by our fundamental trade-off between the two key learning ingredients that in this case appear under the form of bias and variance

$$\mathbb{E}_D\left[E_{population}(h_D)\right] = \mathbb{E}_{\mathbf{x}}\left[VAR(\mathbf{x}) + Bias^2(\mathbf{x})\right]. \qquad (7.71)$$

It is only when the size of the training sample becomes infinitely large that we can hope to eliminate both bias and variance at the same time. In practice, in a model that learns by example and does so with a training sample of limited size, the price for achieving a small bias is a large variance. Very flexible models have a low bias and a high variance, see Figure 7.10. Whereas rigid models have high bias and low variance. The model with the optimal predictive capability is the one that leads to the best balance between bias and variance.

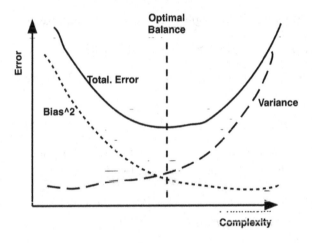

Fig. 7.10   The model with the optimal predictive capability is the one that leads to the best balance between bias and variance

7.7.1   *Example*

To see the trade-off in action we constructed a few examples. Specifically, we generated four datasets of 11 points from the interval -1 to 1 with increments of 0.1 using the function $\cos(1.5 \cdot \pi \cdot x) + noise$, where *noise* is a random value from the interval $[-0.2, 0.2]$.

High Bias For the case of high bias, we use the most simple model, a polynomial of degree 1

$$h(x, \mathbf{w}) = w_0 + w_1 \cdot x, \tag{7.72}$$

that we fit to the four generated data sets. In each of the four examples we see a very low variability between the generated curves, the variance is low. Yet, the model is not sufficient to fit the four training samples. This is an example of underfitting, see Figure 7.11.

High Variance For the case of high variance, we have a complex model, a polynomial of degree 15

$$h(x, \mathbf{w}) = w_0 + \sum_{j=1}^{15} w_j \cdot x^j, \tag{7.73}$$

that we fit to the four generated data sets (a), (b), (c) and (d). In each of the four examples we see a high variability between the generated curves, the variance is high. The model overfits the training data learning the present noise, see Figure 7.12.

Good Balance For the case of a good balance between variance and bias, we have a perfect model for this case, a polynomial of degree 4

$$h(x, \mathbf{w}) = w_0 + \sum_{j=1}^{4} w_j \cdot x^j, \tag{7.74}$$

that we fit to the four generated data sets (a), (b), (c) and (d). In each of the four examples we see a low variability between the generated curves, the variance is low. Furthermore, the polynomial of degree 4 approximates the true function almost perfectly achieving the optimal balance, see Figure 7.13

Good Balance trough Regularization Without knowing the right complexity to use, a possible approach is to try to find the optimal balance using a complex model with l_2 regularization. We minimize the regularized error function to give a prediction function

$$E(\mathbf{w}) = \frac{1}{2} \cdot \sum_{k=1}^{1} 1(t_k - \mathbf{w}^T \cdot \phi(\mathbf{x}_k))^2 + \frac{\lambda}{2} \|\mathbf{w}\|_2^2 \tag{7.75}$$

based on a polynomial of degree 15

$$h(x, \mathbf{w}) = w_0 + \sum_{j=1}^{15} w_j \cdot x^j. \tag{7.76}$$

We use $\frac{\lambda}{2} = 0.01$ and we fit it to the four generated data sets (a), (b), (c) and (d). In each of the four examples we see a low variability between the generated curves, the variance is low, see Figure 7.14. The model has a good balance. Instead of searching through models of different complexity, we chose one complex model and constrained it through the regularization value. This kind of search for a good balance between variance and bias is easier to implement, since it depends only on the value of λ.

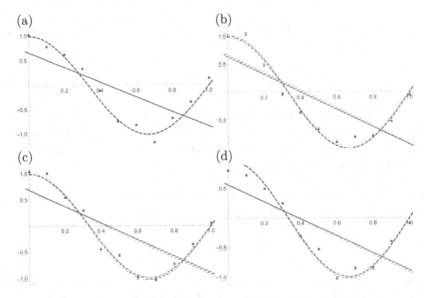

Fig. 7.11   We generated 11 points from the interval -1 to 1 with a step of 0.1 using the function $\cos(1.5 \cdot \pi \cdot x) + noise$, where *noise* is a random value from the interval $[-0, 2, 0.2]$. For the case of high bias, we have a very simple model, the most simple polynomial of degree 1, $w_0 + w_1 \cdot x$ that we fit to the four generated data sets (a), (b), (c) and (d). In each of the four examples we see a very low variability between the generated curves, the variance is low. However, the model is not sufficient to fit the four training samples. This is called underfitting.

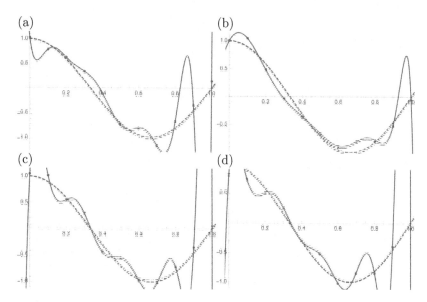

Fig. 7.12   We generated 11 points from the interval -1 to 1 in step of 0.1 using the function $\cos(1.5 \cdot \pi \cdot x) + noise$, where *noise* is a random value from the interval $[-0, 2, 0.2]$. For the case of high variance, we have a complex model. We use a polynomial of degree 15, $w_0 + \sum_{j=1}^{15} w_j \cdot x^j$ that we fit to the four generated data sets (a), (b), (c) and (d). In each of the four examples we see a high variability between the generated curves, the variance is high. The model overfits the training data by learning the noise in the training data.

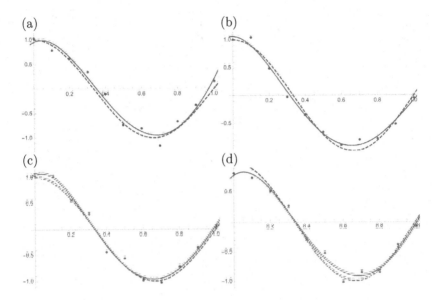

Fig. 7.13   We generated 11 points from the interval -1 to 1 with step of 0.1 using the function $\cos(1.5 \cdot \pi \cdot x) + noise$, where $noise$ is a random value from the interval $[-0.2, 0.2]$. For the case of good balance between variance and bias, we have a perfect model. We use a polynomial of degree 4, $w_0 + \sum_{j=1}^{4} w_j \cdot x^j$ that we fit to the four generated data sets (a), (b), (c) and (d). In each of the four examples we see a low variability between the generated curves, the variance is low. Furthermore, the polynomial of degree 4 approximates the true function almost perfectly, so it has the optimal balance.

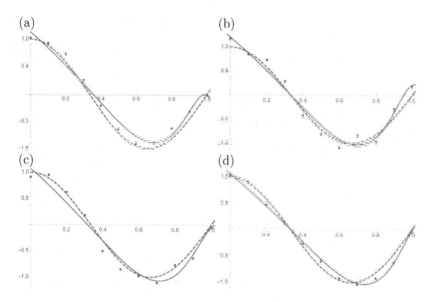

Fig. 7.14 We generated 11 points from the interval -1 to 1 with a step of 0.1 using the function $\cos(1.5 \cdot \pi \cdot x) + noise$, where *noise* is a random value from the interval $[-0.2, 0.2]$. We try to find the optimal balance using a complex model with l_2 regularization. We preform the l_2 regularization of a polynomial of degree 15 with $\frac{\lambda}{2} = 0.01$ and fit the model to the four generated data sets (a), (b), (c) and (d). In each of the four examples we see a low variability between the generated curves and nice approximation of the true generating function. The model has a good balance.

7.8 Exercises and Answers

The VC dimension is a way to measure the degrees of freedom of a classifier family. To make clear how to compute it, we will use as an example the set of 1 dimensional interval binary classifiers:

$$h(x; a, b) = \begin{cases} 1 & a \geq x \geq b \\ 0 & otherwise \end{cases} \tag{7.77}$$

Before going any further we need to recall the concept of a classifier family shattering n points.

Think about a game between you and an adversarial nature. In this game, you "play" first and take n points and place them anywhere you like. Afterwards, nature places targets (binary $+1$ or -1) on each point, this choice is called a dichotomy. Finally, you have the last move. If you can choose a classifier from the family in question that is able to correctly classify every point you win.

Having understood the rules of the game, the concept of shattering is simple. A classifier family can shatter n points if you can win at this game. More specifically, if you can find n points such that, regardless of the way nature chooses the targets, you can always choose a classifier from the family that solves the problem.

Let us look at our example. We would like to check if our family of classifiers can shatter one point. In the figure below, we can see that we are able to choose a point that is correctly classified for all possible targets that nature can give it.

But what is the relation between shattering and the VC dimension? Well, if a classifier family h shatters n points then we say that $d_{VC}(h) \geq n$. So, from our example follows that $d_{VC}(h) \geq 1$.

However, this game only allows us to compute lower bounds for the VC dimension. So, how can we get a final value for it?

We start by finding the tightest lower bound possible. In our example, this means increasing n until it is not obvious we can win. Let do it for $n = 2$:

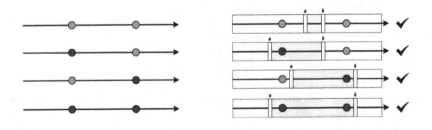

We see that we can win regardless of the targets, so $d_{VC}(h) \geq 2$. However, by increasing n again we see that it is not so easy:

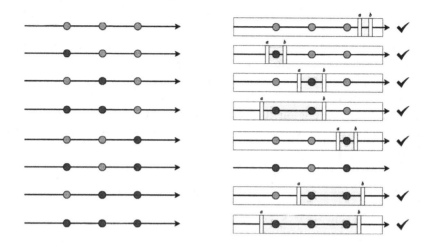

So, we need to prove that it is not possible to win the game when $n = 3$.

Given any three points $x_1 < x_2 < x_3$, the problematic dichotomy is such that $t_1 = +1, t_2 = -1, t_3 = +1$ since all others can be easily solved like in the figure above. If we try to place the interval, we either:

- Classify correctly x_1 and x_2 but miss x_3 using an interval around x_1: $a < x_1 < b < x_2 < x_3$
- Classify correctly x_3 and x_2 but miss x_1 using an interval around x_3: $x_1 < x_2 < a < x_3 < b$
- Classify correctly x_1 and x_3 but miss x_2 using an interval around the three points: $a < x_1 < x_2 < x_3 < b$

So, there is no way to correctly classify this dichotomy which means we cannot shatter three points and so we say that $d_{VC}(h) < 3$. Putting our lower bound together with the upper bound we conclude that $d_{VC}(h) = 2$.

With the example it becomes simple to see that the VC dimension of a classifier family equals the maximum number of points that it can shatter.

A simple way to get an approximation for the VC dimension is to count the number of free parameters in a classifier family. This number will sometimes not yield the correct value for the VC dimension since it can be the case that not all parameters correspond to degrees of freedom. However, it is generally a good heuristic to think about.

From knowing the VC dimension, several key insights can follow. On the one hand, a large VC dimension will mean a lot of capacity to accomodate to small changes in the data which can lead to overfitting. This relates to a high variance in the bias-variance view. In such scenario we will need more data to get a good parameter estimation and most likely regularization will be useful. On the other hand, a low VC dimension will restrict the freedom of the classifier to adjust to the data imposing a bias. However, the restricted freedom allows us to work with less data and possibly even do not require regularization. In reality, what high and low VC dimension means highly depends on the problem itself. In fact, it is only through exeprimental practice with a given classifier family that one can judge if its VC dimension is too low, too big or just right for the problem at hand.

1)

Show graphically what is the VC dimension of 1 dimensional threshold binary classifiers:

$$h\left(x; a\right) = \begin{cases} 1 & x \geq a \\ 0 & x < a \end{cases} \tag{7.78}$$

Solution:

To find the VC dimension of a classifier we need two key steps:

1) To prove that $d_{VC} \geq N$ we need to find a set of N points that can be shatter by the classifier.

2) To prove that $d_{VC} \leq N$ we need to show that it is not possible to find a set of $N + 1$ points that can be shatter by the classifier.

Having stated that, we want to find a lower bound on the VC dimension. To do that, we apply step 1 for $N = 1$ and then repeat it for increasing values of N.

So, for $N = 1$ we can find an example that can be shattered by h:

Thus, we can conclude $d_{VC} \geq 1$.

Now, for $N = 2$ it is not so easy. Specifically, one dichotomy is problematic.

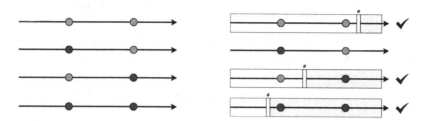

We cannot easily complete step 1. So, we try to get an upper-bound from step 2. Given any two points, there are three places where we can place a:

(1) On the left of the two points
(2) In the middle of the two points
(3) On the right of the two points

Now, for the dichotomy where the target of the leftmost point is $+1$ and the other is -1 it is not possible to correctly separate the two classes:

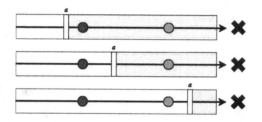

With that, we conclude that $d_{VC} \leq 1$.
   Putting all together, we get $d_{VC} = 1$.

---

2)

Show graphically what is the VC dimension of 2 dimensional axis-aligned rectangle binary classifiers:

$$h(x_1, x_2; a_1, a_2, h, w) = \begin{cases} 1 & a_1 + w \geq x_1 \geq a_1, a_2 + h \geq x_2 \geq a_2 \\ 0 & otherwise \end{cases} \quad (7.79)$$

Solution:
   To find the VC dimension of a classifier we need two key steps:

1) To prove that $d_{VC} \geq N$ we need to find a set of N points that can be shatter by the classifier.

2) To prove that $d_{VC} \leq N$ we need to show that it is not possible to find a set of $N + 1$ points that can be shatter by the classifier.

Having stated that, we want to find a lower bound on the VC dimension. To do that, we apply step 1 for $N = 1$ and then repeat it for increasing values of N.

So, for $N = 1$ we can find an example that can be shattered by h:

Thus, we can conclude $d_{VC} \geq 1$.

For $N = 2$ we can find an example that can be shattered by h:

Thus, we can conclude $d_{VC} \geq 2$.

For $N = 3$ we can find an example that can be shattered by h:

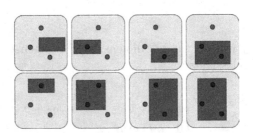

Thus, we can conclude $d_{VC} \geq 3$.

For $N = 4$ we can find an example that can be shattered by h:

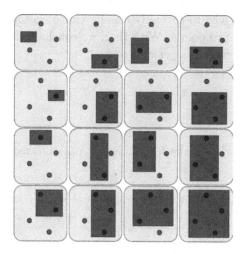

Thus, we can conclude $d_{VC} \geq 4$.

Now, for $N = 5$ it is not so easy. We cannot easily complete step 1. So, we try to get an upper-bound from step 2.

For any five points there are two possibilities:

(1) There are three or more collinear points
(2) The five points form one quadrilateral with a point in the middle

We cannot shatter scenario 1 for the same reasons presented in the previous exercise.

For scenario 2, consider the dichotomy where all four points that form the quadrilateral have $t_i = +1$ and the point in the middle has $t = 1$ like in the figure below.

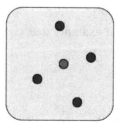

There is no way to classify all quadrilateral points correctly without miss-classifying the middle point.

So, there is no way to correctly classify this dichotomy. Which means we cannot shatter five points. With that, we conclude that $d_{VC} \leq 4$.

Putting all together, we get $d_{VC} = 4$.

---

3)

Show graphically what is the VC dimension of 2 dimensional perceptrons:

$$h(x_1, x_2; w_0, w_1, w_2) = sgn(w_0 + w_1 x_1 + w_2 x_2) \qquad (7.80)$$

Solution:

To find the VC dimension of a classifier we need two key steps:

1) To prove that $d_{VC} \geq N$ we need to find a set of N points that can be shatter by the classifier.

2) To prove that $d_{VC} \leq N$ we need to show that it is not possible to find a set of $N + 1$ points that can be shatter by the classifier.

Having stated that, we want to find a lower bound on the VC dimension. To do that, we apply step 1 for $N = 1$ and then repeat it for increasing values of N.

So, for $N = 1$ we can find an example that can be shattered by h:

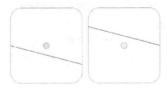

Thus, we can conclude $d_{VC} \geq 1$.

For $N = 2$ we can find an example that can be shattered by h:

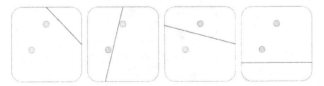

Thus, we can conclude $d_{VC} \geq 2$.

For $N = 3$ we can find an example that can be shattered by h:

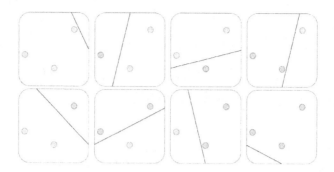

Thus, we can conclude $d_{VC} \geq 3$.

Now, for $N = 4$ it is not so easy. We cannot easily complete step 1. So, we try to get an upper-bound from step 2.

For any four points there are two possibilities:

(1) There are collinear points
(2) The four points form a quadrilateral

We cannot shatter scenario 1 for the same reasons presented in the first exercise.

For scenario 2, consider a dichotomy that resembles the XOR problem like in the figure below.

There is no way to classify all points correctly. Which means we cannot shatter four points. With that, we conclude that $d_{VC} \leq 3$.

Putting all together, we get $d_{VC} = 3$.

---

4)

Show analytically that the VC dimension of a d dimensional perceptron:

$$h(\mathbf{x}; \mathbf{w}) = sgn\left(\mathbf{w}^T \mathbf{x}\right) \tag{7.81}$$

where $\mathbf{x} = \left(1 \; x_1 \; \ldots \; x_d\right)^T$ and $\mathbf{w} = \left(w_0 \; w_1 \; \ldots \; w_d\right)^T$ is $d_{VC} = d + 1$.

Solution:

Step 1: Prove that there exists a set of $d+1$ points that the perceptron can shatter.

For a dataset with the data points $\mathbf{x}_i = \begin{pmatrix} x_1 & x_2 & \dots & x_d \end{pmatrix}^T$ placed on the rows (adding a bias dimension) of a matrix:

$$\mathbf{X} = \begin{pmatrix} 1 & -\mathbf{x}_1^T- \\ 1 & -\mathbf{x}_2^T- \\ 1 & -\mathbf{x}_3^T- \\ 1 & \vdots \\ 1 & -\mathbf{x}_{d+1}^T- \end{pmatrix} \tag{7.82}$$

With targets $t_i \in \{-1, 1\}$ placed on a column vector:

$$\mathbf{t} = \begin{pmatrix} t_1 \\ t_2 \\ t_3 \\ \vdots \\ t_{d+1} \end{pmatrix} \tag{7.83}$$

We need to prove that the perceptron can shatter this problem. To achieve that, all we need to do is to find a weight vector $\mathbf{w}^*$ such that the perceptron correctly classifies all possible targets (all dichotomies). This means that:

$$sgn\left(\mathbf{X}\mathbf{w}^*\right) = \mathbf{t} \tag{7.84}$$

A possible solution is $\mathbf{w}^* = \mathbf{X}^{-1}\mathbf{t}$, because:

$$sgn\left(\mathbf{X}\mathbf{w}^*\right) = sgn\left(\mathbf{X}\mathbf{X}^{-1}\mathbf{t}\right) = sgn\left(\mathbf{I}\mathbf{t}\right) = sgn\left(\mathbf{t}\right) = \mathbf{t} \tag{7.85}$$

Having showed this, all we need to do is to find a data matrix $\mathbf{X}$ that is invertible. An example that works is:

$$X = \begin{pmatrix} 1 & 0 & 0 & \cdots & 0 & 0 \\ 1 & 1 & 0 & \cdots & 0 & 0 \\ 1 & 0 & 1 & \cdots & 0 & 0 \\ \vdots & \vdots & \vdots & \ddots & \vdots & \vdots \\ 1 & 0 & 0 & 0 & 1 & 0 \\ 1 & 0 & 0 & 0 & 0 & 1 \end{pmatrix} \tag{7.86}$$

One check this by noticing that the columns form a base for R^{d+1} space. Which means that no column can be written as linear combination of the others.

So, since we have one example that works we conclude our proof and thus $d_{VC} \geq d + 1$.

Step 2: Prove that perceptron cannot shatter ANY $d + 2$ points.

Consider any $d + 2$ points: $\mathbf{x}_1, \mathbf{x}_2, \ldots, \mathbf{x}_d, \mathbf{x}_{d+1}, \mathbf{x}_{d+2}$.

We have more points than dimensions, so we must have:

$$\mathbf{x}_j = \sum_{i \neq j} a_i \mathbf{x}_i \tag{7.87}$$

where at least some $a_i \neq 0$.

Which can be rewritten as follows to make the net inputs appear:

$$\mathbf{x}_j = \sum_{i \neq j} a_i \mathbf{x}_i$$

$$\mathbf{w}^T \mathbf{x}_j = \mathbf{w}^T \sum_{i \neq j} a_i \mathbf{x}_i$$

$$\mathbf{w}^T \mathbf{x}_j = \sum_{i \neq j} a_i \mathbf{w}^T \mathbf{x}_i$$

To prove that the perceptron cannot shatter any $d + 2$ points we need to find a dichotomy it cannot learn. So, let us consider the following dichotomy:

(1) All $\mathbf{x}_i$ with $a_i \neq 0$ get $t_i = sgn\,(a_i)$
(2) $\mathbf{x}_j$ gets $t_j = -1$

For the perceptron to be correct, we need that its output equals the target:

$$t_i = sgn\,(a_i) = sgn\,\left(\mathbf{w}^T \mathbf{x}_i\right) \tag{7.88}$$

So, if a_i and $\mathbf{w}^T \mathbf{x}_i$ have the same sign, the product between the two will be positive:

$$a_i \mathbf{w}^T \mathbf{x}_i > 0 \tag{7.89}$$

Which means that the sum for all points except j is also positive:

$$\sum_{i \neq j} a_i \mathbf{w}^T \mathbf{x}_i > 0 \tag{7.90}$$

Which means that:

$$\mathbf{w}^T\mathbf{x}_j = \sum_{i \neq j} a_i \mathbf{w}^T \mathbf{x}_i > 0 \tag{7.91}$$

Thus, the target of j needs to be positive:

$$t_j = sgn\left(\mathbf{w}^T\mathbf{x}_j\right) = +1 \tag{7.92}$$

Which is an error! So, no perceptron can classify this dichotomy. Which means that the perceptron cannot shatter any set of $d + 2$ points. So, $d_{VC} \leq d + 1$.

Step 3: Combining the two steps

Combining both steps, we get:

$$d_{VC} \geq d + 1 \wedge d_{VC} \leq d + 1 \tag{7.93}$$

$$d + 1 \leq d_{VC} \leq d + 1 \Rightarrow d_{VC} = d + 1 \tag{7.94}$$

---

5)

Show analytically that the VC dimension of a Decision tree on inputs with d boolean features is 2^d.

Solution:

The first thing we need to do is to notice that 2^d is the maximum number of different points that can exist in this scenario. For that reason, we immediately know that $d_{VC} \leq 2^d$ for any classifier with this kind of input.

Noticing that, all we need to do is to create a decision tree that can shatter a data set with all possible points.

Using simple binary splits on all features, we can create a decision tree with height $d + 1$ that has one leaf for each point. Each leaf will have the label of that point. So, all points will be classified correctly regardless of the dichotomy chosen.

This proves that $d_{VC} \geq 2^d$.

Again, we can combine both facts and get:

$$d_{VC} \geq 2^d \wedge d_{VC} \leq 2^d \tag{7.95}$$

$$2^d \leq d_{VC} \leq 2^d \Rightarrow d_{VC} = 2^d \tag{7.96}$$

---

6)

For the following scenarios which would you **approximately** say has smallest VC dimension?

a) Three dimensional real inputs classified by:

(1) MLP with one hidden layer with the following units per layer $(3\ 2\ 2)$.
(2) Simple Bayesian classifier with multivariate gaussian likelihood function.

Solution:

We know that the VC dimension is a measure of the degrees of freedom of a classifier. A good proxy for the number of degrees of freedom is the number of parameters. So, let us estimate the number of parameters for each scenarion.

1.

Between the input layer and the hidden layer we will have:

- A 2×3 weight matrix $\mathbf{W}^{[1]}$, so 6 parameters
- A 3×1 bias vector $\mathbf{b}^{[1]}$, so 3 parameters

Between the hidden layer and the output layer we will have:

- A 2×2 weight matrix $\mathbf{W}^{[2]}$, so 4 parameters
- A 2×1 bias vector $\mathbf{b}^{[2]}$, so 2 parameters

There are no more parameters, so the total amounts to $6 + 3 + 4 + 2 = 15$.

2.

For the simple Bayesian classifier, we need to estimate prior and likelihood.

The prior is a distribution table with two entries (one for each class):

$$\frac{P\,(t=0)\,\big|\,P\,(t=1)}{p \quad \big| \quad 1-p} \qquad (7.97)$$

So, we have one parameter for the prior.

The likelihood $p\,(\mathbf{x}\mid t=0)$, being a multivariate gaussian, will require a mean vector and a covariance matrix:

- For three dimensions the mean vector is a 3×1 vector, so 3 parameters.
- For three dimensions, the covariance is a 3×3 matrix $\Sigma =$
$\begin{pmatrix} \Sigma_{11} & \Sigma_{12} & \Sigma_{13} \\ \Sigma_{21} & \Sigma_{22} & \Sigma_{23} \\ \Sigma_{31} & \Sigma_{32} & \Sigma_{33} \end{pmatrix}$, however the matrix is symmetric so, we only need
to count the diagonal and upper diagonal part of the matrix. So, 6 parameters.

The likelihood $p\,(\mathbf{x}\mid t=1)$, being a multivariate gaussian, requires the same number of parameters.

There are no more parameters to estimate, so the total is $2\times(3+6)+1=19$.

Finally, we can produce our guess on the VC dimensions of both classifiers. We would approximately say that the MLP classifier has a smaller VC dimension $d_{VC}\,(MLP) < d_{VC}\,(Bayesian)$.

---

b) Four dimensional boolean inputs classified by:

(1) Decision Tree.
(2) Naive Bayes.

Solution:

We know that the VC dimension is a measure of the degrees of freedom of a classifier. A good proxy for the number of degrees of freedom is the number of parameters. So, let us estimate the number of parameters for each scenarion.

   1.

We know from exercise 6 that $d_{VC}\,(DecisionTree) = 2^d$. So, in this case, we have that $d_{VC}\,(DecisionTree) = 2^4 = 16$

   2.

For the Naive Bayesian classifier, we need to estimate prior and likelihoods.

The prior is a distribution table with two entries (one for each class):

$$\begin{array}{c|c} P(t=0) & P(t=1) \\ \hline p & 1-p \end{array} \tag{7.98}$$

So, we have one parameter for the prior.

The likelihoods, like the prior are distributions over binary variables so for each class c and for each feature i we have a distribution $p(x_i \mid t = c)$ that requires one parameter.

Since there are 2 classes and 4features, we have $2 \times 4 \times 1 = 8$ parameters for the likelihoods.

There are no more parameters to estimate, so the total is $1 + 8 = 9$.

Finally, we can produce our guess on the VC dimensions of both classifiers. We would approximately say that the Naive Bayes classifier has a smaller VC dimension $d_{VC}(NB) < d_{VC}(DT)$.

---

c) N-dimensional real inputs classified by:

(1) Naive Bayes with Gaussian likelihoods.
(2) MLP with two hidden layers with the following units per layer $\left(N \ \frac{N}{2} \ \frac{N}{2} \ 2 \right)$.
(3) Simple Bayesian classifier with multivariate gaussian likelihood function.
(4) Perceptron.

Solution:

We know that the VC dimension is a measure of the degrees of freedom of a classifier. A good proxy for the number of degrees of freedom is the number of parameters. So, let us estimate the number of parameters for each scenarion.

1.

For the Naive Bayesian classifier, we need to estimate prior and likelihoods.

The prior is a distribution table with two entries (one for each class):

$$\begin{array}{c|c} P(t=0) & P(t=1) \\ \hline p & 1-p \end{array} \tag{7.99}$$

So, we have one parameter for the prior.

The likelihoods are one dimensional gaussians. Each one dimensional gaussian requires two parameters: mean and standard deviation. So for each class c and for each feature i we have a distribution $p(x_i \mid t = c)$ that requires two parameters.

Since there are 2 classes and N features, we have $2 \times N \times 2 = 4N$ parameters for the likelihoods.

There are no more parameters to estimate, so the total is $1 + 4N$.

2.

Between the input layer and the first hidden layer we will have:

- A $\frac{N}{2} \times N$ weight matrix $\mathbf{W}^{[1]}$, so $\frac{N^2}{2}$ parameters
- A $\frac{N}{2} \times 1$ bias vector $\mathbf{b}^{[1]}$, so $\frac{N}{2}$ parameters

Between the first hidden layer and the second one we will have:

- A $\frac{N}{2} \times \frac{N}{2}$ weight matrix $\mathbf{W}^{[2]}$, so $\frac{N^2}{4}$ parameters
- A $\frac{N}{2} \times 1$ bias vector $\mathbf{b}^{[2]}$, so $\frac{N}{2}$ parameters

Between the second hidden layer and the output layer we will have:

- A $2 \times \frac{N}{2}$ weight matrix $\mathbf{W}^{[3]}$, so N parameters
- A 2×1 bias vector $\mathbf{b}^{[3]}$, so 2 parameters

There are no more parameters, so the total amounts to $\frac{N^2}{2} + \frac{N}{2} + \frac{N^2}{4} + \frac{N}{2} + N + 2 = \frac{2N^2 + 2N + N^2 + 2N + 4N + 8}{4} = \frac{3N^2 + 8N + 8}{4}$.

3.

For the simple Bayesian classifier, we need to estimate prior and likelihood.

The prior is a distribution table with two entries (one for each class):

$$\begin{array}{c|c} P(t=0) & P(t=1) \\ \hline p & 1-p \end{array} \tag{7.100}$$

So, we have one parameter for the prior.

The likelihood $p(\mathbf{x} \mid t = 0)$, being a multivariate gaussian, will require a mean vector and a covariance matrix:

- For N dimensions the mean vector is an $N \times 1$ vector, so N parameters.
- For three dimensions, the covariance is an $N \times N$ matrix, however the matrix is symmetric so, we only need to count the diagonal and upper diagonal part of the matrix. So, $N + \frac{N^2 - N}{2}$ parameters.

The likelihood $p(\mathbf{x} \mid t = 1)$, being a multivariate gaussian, requires the same number of parameters.

There are no more parameters to estimate, so the total is $1 + 2 \times \left(N + N + \frac{N^2 - N}{2}\right) = 1 + \left(2N + 2N + N^2 - N\right) = 1 + 3N + N^2$.

4.

The perceptron has a weight vector $\mathbf{w} = \begin{pmatrix} w_1 & w_2 & \cdots & w_N \end{pmatrix}^T$ and a bias w_0. So, it has $N + 1$ parameters.

Finally, we can plot our guesses on the VC dimensions of the four scenarios:

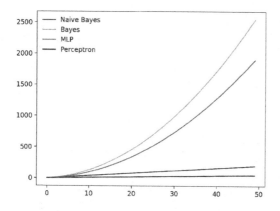

We would approximately order the VC dimensions as follows $d_{VC}(Perceptron) < d_{VC}(NB) < d_{VC}(MLP) < d_{VC}(Bayes)$.

---

7)

a) Choose between **increase, decrease, maintain** for each of the following factors:

- Training data
- Regularization
- VC dimension

For each of the following four scenarios:

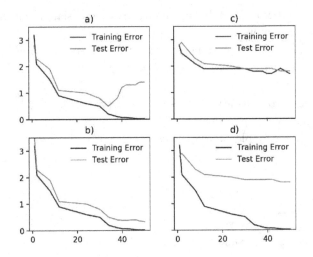

Justify every decision.

Solution:

    a) Increase, increase, maintain/decrease
    b) Increase, maintain, maintain
    c) Increase, decrease, increase
    d) Increase, increase, maintain/decrease

Thinking Questions

a) Try to show the VC dimension of a perceptron without bias.

b) Think about how learning theory can help you in practice. Namely, think about how one can use it to choose a classifier and to make decisions on regularization parameters.

c) Think about the relation between the Bias-Variance decomposition and the VC dimension.

Chapter 8

Model Selection

Fig. 8.1 With several possible models that can fit our data well, we often need to choose one. This is known as the problem of model selection and to solve it, we may need to estimate several interesting properties of each model like the number of degrees of freedom or even the models general structure.

8.1 The confusion matrix

So far we looked at the performance of classification models in terms of accuracy. Specifically, we measured error based on the fraction of mistakes. However, in some tasks, there are some types of mistakes that are worse than others. As an example consider a scenario where we are choosing between two models that diagnose a given infectious disease. Suppose that both models have the same accuracy. Now, if model A's mistakes are all false positives, that is, cases where the patient is not sick but the model predicted disease it will probably preferable to a model B where all mistakes are false negatives and contagious people are told they are healthy.

A helpful tool to perform this type of analysis is the confusion matrix (or error matrix). Each row of the matrix represents the instances in an actual class while each column represents the instances in a predicted class (or vice versa). Another good feature of this tool is for multiclass problems, it makes it easy to see if the system is confusing two classes (i.e. commonly mislabeling one as another).

If a classification system has been trained to distinguish between two classes (boolean classification), a confusion matrix will summarize the results. For two classes C_1 and *not* C_1 in which a binary classifier (for example a perceptron) preformed a classification out of 14 examples 8 were classified correctly and 6 wrong, we can represent the classification by a matrix like the one in represented in Table 8.1.

Table 8.1 Confusion matrix for two classes C_1 and *not* C_1. Out of 14 examples $8 = 7 + 1$ were classified correctly and $6 = 4 + 2$ wrong.

	predicted C_1	predicted *not* C_1
actual C_1	7	2
actual *not* C_1	4	1

8.1.1 *Precision and Recall*

Using a confusion matrix for a binary classifier we can define precision and recall with the renaming of the two classes as C_1=positive and *not* C_1=negative using Table 8.2, we define

$$Precision = \frac{true\ positive}{true\ positive + false\ positive} \tag{8.1}$$

and

$$Recall = \frac{true\ positive}{true\ positive + false\ negative}. \tag{8.2}$$

Table 8.2   Confusion matrix for for classes positive and negative.

	predicted positive	predicted negative
actual positive	true positive	false negative
actual negative	false positive	true negative

A high recall value without a high precision does not give us any confidence about the quality of the binary classifier. We can obtain a high recall value by classifying all patterns as positive (the recall value will be one); however, the precision value will be very low. Conversely, by classifying only one pattern correctly as positive, we obtain the maximal precision value of one but a low recall value. Both values have to be simultaneously interpreted. To that end, we can combine both values with the harmonic mean,

$$F = 2 \cdot \frac{Precision \cdot Recall}{Precision + Recall} \tag{8.3}$$

in which both values are evenly weighted. This measure is also called the balanced measure.

8.1.2   *Several Classes*

The MNIST database (Modified National Institute of Standards and Technology database) contains 60, 000 training images and 10, 000 testing images of 0 to 9 handwritten digits, see Figure 8.2. These images are represent by 28×28 pixel matrices with gray levels. Looking at each image as a vector yields 784 dimensional inputs.

We classified the test data set with a logistic regression where ten sigmoid units, with 785 parameters each, trained with the cross entropy loss function result in a fraction of correctly classified examples (or accuracy) of 0.8966. The resulting confusion matrix is represented in Figure 8.3.

8.2   Validation Set and Test Set

Using a supervised machine learning algorithm, categories can be learned through know labeled examples. The training data contains information

$0 \to 0,\ 3 \to 3,\ 9 \to 9,\ 0 \to 0,\ 2 \to 2,\ 1 \to 1,\ 1 \to 1,\ 3 \to 3,\ 9 \to 9$

$4 \to 4,\ 1 \to 1,\ 2 \to 2,\ 2 \to 2,\ 1 \to 1,\ 4 \to 4,\ 8 \to 8,\ 0 \to 0,\ 4 \to 4$

$4 \to 4,\ 7 \to 7,\ 7 \to 7,\ 2 \to 2,\ 9 \to 9,\ 6 \to 6,\ 5 \to 5,\ 5 \to 5,\ 4 \to 4$

$p \to 8,\ 2 \to 2,\ 5 \to 5,\ 9 \to 9,\ 5 \to 5,\ 4 \to 4,\ 1 \to 1,\ 3 \to 3,\ 7 \to 7$

$8 \to 8,\ 0 \to 0,\ 7 \to 7,\ 4 \to 4,\ 4 \to 4,\ 7 \to 7,\ 4 \to 4,\ 7 \to 7,\ 9 \to 9$

$8 \to 8,\ 9 \to 9,\ 9 \to 9,\ 2 \to 2,\ 2 \to 2,\ 0 \to 0,\ 1 \to 1,\ 6 \to 6,\ 5 \to 5$

$4 \to 4,\ 4 \to 4,\ 3 \to 3,\ 9 \to 9,\ 9 \to 9,\ 1 \to 1,\ 1 \to 1,\ 5 \to 5,\ 9 \to 9$

$2 \to 2,\ 7 \to 7,\ 0 \to 0,\ 3 \to 3,\ 4 \to 4,\ 7 \to 7,\ 5 \to 5,\ 8 \to 8,\ 7 \to 7$

$9 \to 9,\ 0 \to 0,\ 2 \to 2,\ 8 \to 8,\ 1 \to 1,\ 2 \to 2,\ 2 \to 2,\ 7 \to 7,\ 3 \to 3$

Fig. 8.2 Example of MNIST digits represented by gray images of size 28 × 28.

about the regularities in the mapping from input to output, but it also contains noise. For example the target values (labels) may be unreliable. There is sampling error and a flexible architecture can model the sampling error really well. Let h_1 and h_2 be two architectures fitted to a training set D_t. Consider also an independent validation set D_v. If we have the following mean squared errors

$$MSE_{Dt}(h_1) < MSE_{Dt}(h_2), \quad MSE_{Dv}(h_1) > MSE_{Dv}(h_2), \quad (8.4)$$

it suggests that hypothesis h_1 overfits the training data D_t as h_1 achieves a better fit with training examples when compared to h_2 but performs poorly with examples that it did not learn. So, using an independent validation set may be a good way to detect overfitting and to help us choose the best model.

Besides this simple strategy, we can use the idea of a validation set to implement other strategies. For instance, we can use it to implement an early-stopping rule where we can measure performance over this independent set and stop the learning procedure once the performance worsens. Another approach we have seen is regularization through weight penalties. In this case, we can use the validation set to determine the right regularization coefficient. Finally, another key factor to fight overfitting is to use a suitable model complexity. We can choose these architectural parameters using the validation set. However, when applying this kind of strategy we may run into a big problem. By choosing everything based on the validation set we may get an indirect overfitting to it. Because of that, to get a

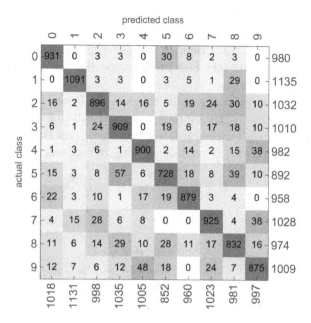

Fig. 8.3 Example of a confusion matrix of ten classes.

final estimate of the chosen model quality we need a third independent set, usually called the test set.

With all of that, under this paradigm, we would need to divide the labeled data set into three groups

$$D = D_t \cup D_v \cup D_{test}$$

with

$$\emptyset = D_t \cap D_v, \quad \emptyset = D_t \cap D_{test}, \quad \emptyset = D_v \cap D_{test}.$$

This can be also written as

$$D = D_t \,\dot\cup\, D_v \,\dot\cup\, D_{test}.$$

The partition of the data set D into a training data set D_t, a validation data set D_v and a test data set the D_{test} can lead us to have insufficient data in all of the three subgroups.

8.3 Cross-Validation

If the labeled data set D is too small to be partitioned one can use a technique called cross validation. Cross-validation enables us to estimate the accuracy of a hypothesis induced by a supervised learning algorithm. It enables us to predict the accuracy of a hypothesis over future unseen instances and to select the optimal hypothesis from a given set of alternative hypotheses. It evaluates the best architecture, like the number of hidden units and hidden layers.

The k-fold cross-validation splits the data set D into k mutually exclusive subsets $D_1, D_2, \cdots, D_k$ we then train and validate an architecture k times; each time, it is trained on $D - D_i$ and tested on D_i. For example, if we have $k = 4$, we divide the dataset D into four subsets

$$D = D_1 \dot\cup D_2 \dot\cup D_3 \dot\cup D_4 \qquad (8.5)$$

and the architecture is

- trained on $D_2 \cup D_3 \cup D_4$ and validated on D_1,
- trained on $D_1 \cup D_3 \cup D_4$ and validated on D_2,
- trained on $D_1 \cup D_2 \cup D_4$ and validated on D_3,
- trained on $D_1 \cup D_2 \cup D_3$ and validated on D_4.

Thus, cross-validation uses all the data for training and validating avoiding the problem of small partitions.

There are different types of cross-validation

- Complete k-fold cross-validation splits the dataset of size m in all (m over m/k) possible ways (choosing m/k instances out of m).
- Leave n-out cross-validation sets n instances aside for validating and uses the remaining ones for training (leave one-out is equivalent to n-fold cross-validation).
- In stratified cross-validation, the folds are stratified so that they contain approximately the same proportion of labels as the original data set.

One major drawback of cross-validation is that the number of training runs that must be performed is increased by a factor of k.

8.4 Minimum-Description-Length

Besides using independent data to choose between hypotheses, we can use a more general, yet heuristic approach. In this section we will focus on the principle of parsimony which can be expressed through Occam's razor.

8.4.1 *Occam's razor*

Occam's razor was first articulated by the medieval logician William of Occam in 1324: "It is vain do with more what can be done with less", see Figure 8.4. Occam's razor states that in life in general, all other things being equal, the simplest model is the best. In Machine Learning terms this means that we should choose the simplest model that correctly fits our data.

Fig. 8.4 William of Occam after stained glass window at a church in Surrey. Occam was born in the village of Ockham in Surrey (England) about 1285, believed that he died in a convent in Munich in 1349, a victim of the Black Death.

8.4.2 *Kolmogorov complexity theory*

Inspiration for the development of the Minimum-Description-Length (MDL) principle is traced back to Kolmogorov complexity theory [Kolmogorov (1998)], see Figure 8.5.

The basic idea is to try to find the shortest program that produces some data. The algorithmic (descriptive) complexity of a data sequence

Fig. 8.5 Andrey Nikolaevich Kolmogorov in Paris 1958.

is the length of the shortest binary computer program that prints out the sequence and then halts. This definition of complexity uses the computer that is the most general form of data compressor, rather than being based on the notion of probability distribution. When there are regularities in the data sequence it can be produced by a simpler program.

8.4.3 *Learning as Data Compression*

Since regularities in a sequence allow for a simpler compression, one can view learning as a form of data compression. This was the key insight used by Rissanen in formulating the Minimum-Description-Length (MDL) principle [Rissanen (1978)], [Rissanen (1998)], see Figure 8.6.

Why does the shorter encoding make sense as the product of learning?

- Shorter encoding implies regularities in the data.
- Regularities in the data imply patterns.
- Patterns are interesting.

Let us look at an example of regularity. The binary string

00001000010000100001000010000100001000010001000010000100001

can be very shortly described using its regularities. Namely, one can say just repeat 12 times 00001. The opposite case can be seen with the binary

Fig. 8.6   Jorma J. Rissanen is an information theorist, known for inventing the minimum description length principle and practical approaches to arithmetic coding for lossless data compression. His work inspired the development of the theory of stochastic chains with memory of variable length.

string

0100111001010011011010100001110101111011011010101110010011100.

This string is basically a random sequence and since no patterns can be found no compression can be achieved.

8.4.4   *Two-part code MDL principle*

Thinking about learning as data compression, given a set of hypotheses $\mathcal{H}$ and a data sequence d, we should try to find the particular hypothesis in H, that compresses the data sequence d the most.

The two-part code MDL principle then tells us [Haykin (2008)] to look for the hypothesis $h \in \mathcal{H}$ that minimizes the description length of h, which we denote by $L_1(p)$, and the description length of the data sequence d when it is encoded with the help of h, which is $L_2(d|h)$. So, with

$$L_{1,2} = L_1(h) + L_2(d|h) \tag{8.6}$$

we should chose the hypothesis $h \in M$ that minimizes $L_{1,2}$.

In finding the hypothesis that compresses the data sequence d the most, we must encode (describe or compress) the data in such a way that a decoder can retrieve the data even without knowing the hypothesis in advance. It is crucial as well that p itself is encoded.

Let us look at an example with polynomial regression. Consider a set of possible hypotheses described by parameter vectors $\mathbf{w}^{(m)}$ with $m = 1, 2, 3, \cdots$ of increasing dimensionality that correspond to polynomials of increasing order

$$y(x, \mathbf{w}^1) = w_0, \ y(x, \mathbf{w}^2) = w_0 + w_1 \cdot x, \ y(x, \mathbf{w}^3) = w_0 + w_1 \cdot x + w_2 \cdot x^2,$$

$$\cdots, \ y(x, \mathbf{w}^M) = w_0 + \sum_{j=1}^{M-1} w_j \cdot x^j.$$

The model selection problem tries to identify the model that best explains the generation of the training sample $d = (\mathbf{x}_k, t_k)$ for $k \in (1, 2, \cdots, N)$. The two-part code MDL principle that defines length $L_{12}(\mathbf{w}^m, d) =$ tells us to pick the model that minimizes

$$\min_m \left\{ L(\mathbf{w}^m) + E(\mathbf{w}^{(m)}) \right\}. \tag{8.7}$$

The leftmost term $L(\mathbf{w}^m)$ is the hypothesis complexity term, denoted by $\frac{2}{m}(N) + O(m)$, which relates to the model alone. In practice, the $O(m)$ term is often ignored to simplify matter. In the case of polynomials we can approximate the complexity by the number of bits needed to represent all numbers in the weight vector

$$L(\mathbf{w}^m) = m \cdot B \ bits \tag{8.8}$$

where B is the number of bits needed to represent each number. The rightmost term $E(\mathbf{w}^{(m)})$ is the error between the given data and the predicted values, which relates to the models ability to produce the data. Generally, for these polynomials, we use the squared error

$$E(\mathbf{w}^{(m)}) = \sum_{k=1}^{N} \left(y(\mathbf{x}_k, \mathbf{w}^{(m)}) - t_k \right)^2 = \|\mathbf{t} - \mathbf{y}\|^2 \tag{8.9}$$

The MDL principle corresponds to Occam's razor in stating a preference for simple theories. When we have two models that fit a given data sequence equally well, the MDL principle will pick the one that is the simplest.

Socrates teaches that a man must know how to choose the mean and avoid the extremes on either side, as far as possible, see Figure 8.8 (b). In ancient Greek philosophy (see Figure 8.7), especially that of Aristotle, the golden mean or golden middle way is the desirable middle between two extremes, one of excess and the other of deficiency, see Figure 8.8

Fig. 8.7 A symbol of ancient Greece: A bireme is an ancient oared warship with two decks of oars, invented and used by Greeks even before the 6th century BC.

(a). This is a good description of the MDL Principle as demonstrated by the polynomial regression, see Figure 8.9. We do not want a too simple hypothesis, because it cannot describe the data. However, a very complex hypothesis may not be general enough. This whole reasoning is extremely related to the bias-variance dilemma.

8.5 Paradox of Deep Learning Complexity

As we have stated before and will see in the next chapters, in deep learning we increase the complexity of the model by using many hidden layers with thousands (or even millions) of parameters. Let us denote a hypothesis by the large vector $\mathbf{w}$ that contains all the parameters in a deep network. By doing so, we can expect that the resulting hypotheses will be able to describe the data really well and as a consequence, we will be able to decrease a lot the $L_2(d|\mathbf{w})$ term.

However, it would seem that by using so many parameters, we would

Fig. 8.8   (a) Socrates (470 - 399 BC), after a marble, after roman artwork (1st century), perhaps a copy of a lost bronze statue made by Lysippos. (b) Aristotle (384 - 322 B.C), after roman artwork after a statue made by Lysippos (Lysippos was a Greek sculptor of the 4th century BC).

be increasing a lot the model complexity because we need to code all of these parameter values. If that is the case we are in direct contradiction of the principle of Parsimony. However, regularization can change this a lot. Assuming that the size of the numbers contained in parameter w_j is correlated to the coding costs

$$w_j \approx w_j \; bits, \tag{8.10}$$

$w = 0$ would require zero bits and a small number would be coded with less bits than a big number. Then, the hypothesis complexity term corresponds to the l_1 regularization

$$L(\mathbf{w}) = |\mathbf{w}| \cdot B \; bits = \|\mathbf{w}\|_1 \cdot B \; bits. \tag{8.11}$$

Similarly, for l_2 regularization we assume

$$L(\mathbf{w})| = \|\mathbf{w}\|_2^2 \cdot B \; bits. \tag{8.12}$$

According to this reasoning, the relation between the hypothesis complexity before learning and after learning changes. The complexity of a deep learning model before learning is tremendous, yet, after learning it is reduced considerably due to the use of regularization. Depending on the type of regularization (l_2 or l_1) most weights will have small values or become zero.

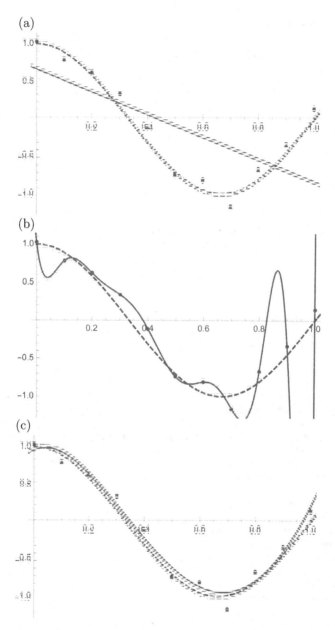

Fig. 8.9 Find the polynomial regression for describing the data, complexity of the model versus the goodness of fit. This approach is equivalent to the bias-variance dilemma. (a) Low model cost, high data cost, corresponds to high bias and low variance. (b) High model cost, low data cost, corresponds to low bias and high variance. (c) Low model cost and low data cost, corresponds to low bias and low variance.

8.6   Exercises and Answers

Get some information about scikit-learn at

$$https://scikit-learn.org/stable/$$

or Google it..

---

1) Confusion matrix and scikit-learn

You can use $scikit-learn$, for a simple experiment with logistic regression, iris dataset and confusion matrix

```
import from sklearn import datasets
import numpy as np

from sklearn.linear_model import LogisticRegression
from sklearn.model_selection import train_test_split
from sklearn.metrics import confusion_matrix

iris = datasets.load_iris()
X = iris.data
y = (iris["target"])
logreg = LogisticRegression()

# Split the data into a training set and a test set
X_train, X_test, y_train, y_test =
            train_test_split(X, y, test_size=0.25,random_state=0)
logreg.fit(X_train,y_train)

print("Size y train:",len(y_train))
print(y_train)
print("Size y test:",len(y_test))
print("Test:      ",  y_test)
y_pred=logreg.predict(X_test[:len(y_test), :])
print("Predict:",y_pred)
cm = confusion_matrix(y_test, y_pred)
print("Confusion matrix:")
print(cm)
```

Experiment with different $0 < test_size < 1$ values

---

2) *Cross-validation and scikit-learn*

You can use *scikit − learn*, for a simple experiment with logistic regression, iris dataset and fold count 5

```
from sklearn import datasets
import numpy as np

from sklearn.linear_model import LogisticRegression
from sklearn.model_selection import cross_val_score

iris = datasets.load_iris()
logreg = LogisticRegression()

scores = cross_val_score(logreg, iris.data, iris.target, cv=5)
print(*scores)
print("Mean: %0.4f,  Stdeviation:  %0.4f)"
                        % (scores.mean(), scores.std() ))
```

Experiment with different fold counts.

Thinking Questions

What do you think is the Kolmogorov complexity of π?

Chapter 9

Clustering

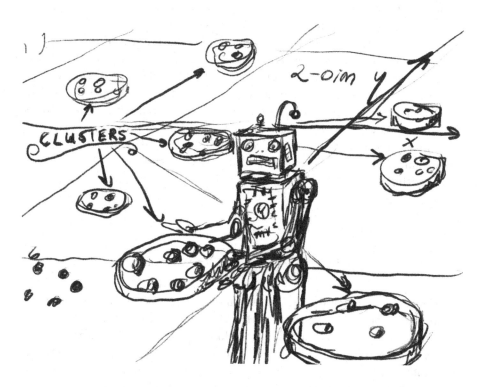

Fig. 9.1   A cluster is a collection of data objects that are similar to one another within the same cluster and dissimilar to the objects in other clusters.

9.1   Introduction

Clustering algorithms are an example of unsupervised learning. In this setting, we are given a training set with inputs but without targets. The main goal of the procedure is to find structure in the data by grouping points that are similar in the same group. The purpose of clustering in this book is to be a tool useful for developing supervised models. For that reason, we will not provide an extended review on all possible kinds of clustering methods. Instead, we will focus on two methods that are useful for data compression. Both methods generate cluster centers (also called centroids) that represent all points in that cluster. Taking into account the fact that the number of clusters K is much smaller than the number of data points, if we substitute the original data set by the set of centroids we get a compressed version of the same data. We will see why this is useful in the radial basis function networks chapter. The first algorithm we will look into is a non probabilistic technique called K-means [Lloyd (1982)], [Wichert (2015)]. After going through it, we introduce the latent variable view of mixture distributions. In this view, we can also characterize a cluster by its center, but we also have information about how the cluster is shaped. To get a clustering under this view we introduce a general technique for finding maximum likelihood estimators called the expectation-maximization (EM) algorithm.

9.2   *K*-means Clustering

In K-means, a training set consists of N observations without targets

$$X = (\mathbf{x}_1, \mathbf{x}_2, \cdots, \mathbf{x}_k, \cdots, \mathbf{x}_N). \tag{9.1}$$

The goal is to partition the data set into some number K of clusters, where we shall suppose for the moment that the value of K is given. This method uses a distance function to choose clusters such that distances between points in the same cluster are small when compared to the distances between points of different clusters. Specifically, the method maps N data points, represented by vectors of dimension D, into K centroids with

$$K \ll N$$

using the Euclidean distance function

$$d_2(\mathbf{x}, \mathbf{y}) = \|x - y\| = \sqrt{\sum_{j=1}^{D} (x_j - y_j)^2}.$$

After applying the method we end up with K vectors called centroids

$$\mathbf{c}_1, \mathbf{c}_2 \cdots, \mathbf{c}_K \tag{9.2}$$

and K sets called clusters

$$C_1, C_2 \cdots, C_K. \tag{9.3}$$

where cluster set C_k is defined as the set of points that are closer to centroid $\mathbf{c}_k$ than to all remaining centroids.

$$C_k = \{\mathbf{x} | d_2(\mathbf{x}, \mathbf{c}_k) = \min_{j=1,\cdots,K} d_2(\mathbf{x}, \mathbf{c}_j)\}. \tag{9.4}$$

A centroid $\mathbf{c}_k$ is the mean value of all points that belong to C_k

$$\mathbf{c}_k = \frac{1}{|C_k|} \cdot \sum_{\mathbf{x} \in C_k} \mathbf{x}. \tag{9.5}$$

Figure 9.2 shows an example of an output of K-means with $K = 2$.

To describe how the method works, we need to define some notation to describe the assignment of data points to clusters. For each data point $\mathbf{x}_n$, there is a corresponding set of binary indicator variables

$$r_{nk} \in \{0, 1\} \tag{9.6}$$

with

$$k = 1, ..., K$$

describing to which of the K clusters the data point $\mathbf{x}_n$ is assigned to. So if data point $\mathbf{x}_n$ is assigned to cluster k then $r_{nk} = 1$, and $r_{nj} = 0$ for $j \neq k$. This is known as the 1-of-K coding scheme and it can be written as

$$r_{nk} = \begin{cases} 1 \text{ if } k = \arg\min_j \|\mathbf{x}_n - \mathbf{c}_j\|^2 \\ 0 \text{ otherwise} \end{cases}. \tag{9.7}$$

With that notation, we can define an error function, sometimes called a distortion measure, given by

$$E = \sum_{n=1}^{N} \sum_{k=1}^{K} r_{nk} \cdot \|\mathbf{x}_n - \mathbf{c}_k\|^2 = \sum_{k=1}^{K} \sum_{x \in C_k} (d_2(\mathbf{x}, \mathbf{c}_k))^2. \tag{9.8}$$

Assuming we know the indicator variables that tell us to which clusters the points belong to, to minimize the error, all we need is to find the zeros of gradient with respect to the centroids

$$\frac{\partial E}{\partial \mathbf{c}_k} = -2 \cdot \sum_{n=1}^{N} r_{nk} \cdot (\mathbf{x} - \mathbf{c}_k) \tag{9.9}$$

(a)

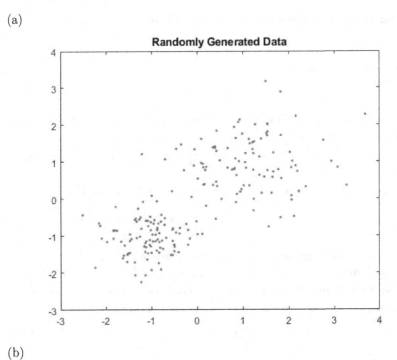

(b)

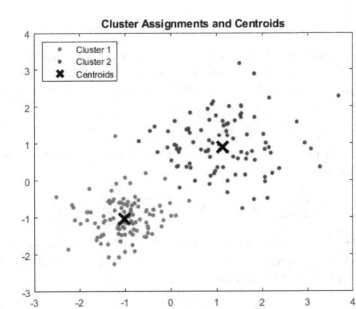

Fig. 9.2   (a) Two dimensional random points.   (b) Two clusters as determined by *K*-means.

$$\sum_{k=1}^{N} r_{kt} \cdot (\mathbf{x} - \mathbf{c}_t) = 0 \tag{9.10}$$

$$\sum_{k=1}^{N} r_{kt} \cdot \mathbf{x} - \sum_{k=1}^{N} r_{kt} \cdot \mathbf{c}_t = 0 \tag{9.11}$$

$$\mathbf{c}_t = \frac{\sum_{k=1}^{N} r_{kt} \cdot \mathbf{x}}{\sum_{k=1}^{N} r_{kt}} = \frac{1}{|C_t|} \cdot \sum_{x \in C_t} \mathbf{x} \tag{9.12}$$

From this, we see that the centroids that minimize the error are the means of the points inside each cluster.

So, can we just compute the means of each cluster of points? Well, not really. Remember that we assumed we knew the cluster for each point (the binary indicator variables). However, we do not.

We can solve this problem in an iterative manner. We start with random centroids and assign each point to the closest cluster. By doing so, we get values for our binary variables. This is sometimes called an expectation step (we will go into it later). Having the binary values, we can do a minimization step and compute the new centroids through our gradient derived expression, in this case the mean values. By this point, we have new updated centroids and we can go for the next iteration and do another expectation step and another minimization step after that. If we do this repeatedly, it can be shown that the procedure converges to a clustering.

9.2.1 *Standard K-means*

The aforementioned procedure can be written as an algorithm as follows

Random initialization of K centroids;
do
    {
        assign to each $\mathbf{x}_k$ in the dataset the nearest centroid $\mathbf{c}_t$ according to d_2;
        compute all new centroids $\mathbf{c}_t = \frac{1}{|C_t|} \cdot \sum_{x \in C_t} \mathbf{x}$;
    }
until ($|E_{new} - E_{old}| < \epsilon$ or number of iterations *max* iterations).

It is worth noting at this point, that the final clustering will depend on the initialization. Sometimes this small detail may have a big impact on the final result as we will see in the exercises section. Antoher key aspect of the described procedure is that we assumed we knew K beforehand. Usually, we do not know the correct K. For that reason, it is typical to run the method multiple times with different values to see which produces the best result.

Another approach to choose K is to provide a maximum radius r to start with. In a single sweep, one goes through the data and assigns the cluster seeds according to the chosen radius r. A data point becomes a new cluster seed if it is not covered by the spheres with the chosen radius of the other already assigned seeds [Wichert *et al.* (2002)]. By doing so, we not only get an estimate for K but also initialized centroids.

9.2.2 *Sequential K-means*

For large data sets, it is not useful to require a sweep through all points before doing an iteration. So, one can change the centroid update rule such that it computes a sequential mean

$$\mathbf{c}_t^{new} = \mathbf{c}_t^{old} + \eta_k \cdot (\mathbf{x}_k - \mathbf{c}_t^{old}) = \mathbf{c}_t^{old} + \frac{1}{|C_t^{old}| + 1} \cdot (\mathbf{x}_k - \mathbf{c}_t^{old}) \qquad (9.13)$$

where η_k is the learning rate parameter, which is typically made to decrease monotonically as more data points are considered and can be represented by $\frac{1}{|C_t^{old}|+1}$. With this rule, we can write another version of K-means that processes one point at a time.

Random initialisation of K centroids;
do
    {
        chose $\mathbf{x}_k$ from the dataset;
        determine the nearest centroid $\mathbf{c}_k$ according to d_2;
        compute the new centroid $\mathbf{c}_t^{new} = \mathbf{c}_t^{old} + \frac{1}{|C_t^{old}|+1} \cdot (\mathbf{x}_k - \mathbf{c}_t^{old})$;
    }
until ($|E_{new} - E_{old}| < \epsilon$ or number of iterations *max* iterations).

9.2.2.1 *Example: Color reduction*

K-means can be used for color reduction for RGB images. K would indicate the number of the reduced colors, and the dimension would be there for R, G, B. $x_i = R_i, G_i, B_i$ would correspond to the pixel at position i in a one dimensional array. Color segmentation represents a weak segmentation, in which the segmented parts (the same color) do not correspond necessarily to objects.

9.3 Mixture of Gaussians

Representing clusters by their centroid may be enough to capture the information present in the data. However, sometimes it can be useful to know the shape of that cluster. Using a mixture of gaussian, we can evolve the K-means procedure into something very similar but that captures this idea of shape.

First, let us recall that the Gaussian distribution or normal is defined over a D dimensional space as PDF that reflects the relative probability (can be bigger one for small $|\Sigma|$)

$$p(\mathbf{x}|\boldsymbol{\mu},\Sigma)=\mathcal{N}(\mathbf{x}|\boldsymbol{\mu},\Sigma)=\frac{1}{(2\cdot\pi)^{D/2}}\cdot\frac{1}{|\Sigma|^{1/2}}\cdot\exp\left(-\frac{1}{2}\cdot(\mathbf{x}-\boldsymbol{\mu})^T\Sigma^{-1}\cdot(\mathbf{x}-\boldsymbol{\mu})\right)$$

where

- $\boldsymbol{\mu}$ is the D dimensional mean vector,
- Σ is a $D \times D$ covariance matrix,
- $|\Sigma|$ is the determinant of Σ.

A Gaussian mixture distribution is a combination of multiple Gaussians where each has a certain weight

$$p(\mathbf{x}) = \sum_{k=1}^{K} \pi_k \cdot \mathcal{N}(\mathbf{x}|\boldsymbol{\mu}_k, \Sigma_k) \tag{9.14}$$

$$p(\mathbf{x}) = \sum_{k=1}^{K} \pi_k \cdot \frac{1}{(2\cdot\pi)^{D/2}} \cdot \frac{1}{|\Sigma_t|^{1/2}} \cdot \exp\left(-\frac{1}{2}\cdot(\mathbf{x}-\boldsymbol{\mu}_k)^T\Sigma_k^{-1}\cdot(\mathbf{x}-\boldsymbol{\mu}_k)\right) \tag{9.15}$$

with

$$0 \leq \pi_k \leq 1 \tag{9.16}$$

and

$$\sum_{k=1}^{K} \pi_k = 1 \tag{9.17}$$

Much like we did in K-means, let us introduce a K-dimensional binary random variable $\mathbf{c}$ having a 1-of-K representation in which a particular element c_k is equal to one and all other are equal to 0

$$c_k \in \{0,1\}, \qquad \sum_k c_k = 1 \tag{9.18}$$

with

$$p(\mathbf{x}, \mathbf{c}) = p(\mathbf{x}|\mathbf{c}) \cdot p(\mathbf{c}).$$

We can write

$$p(c_k = 1) = \pi_k \tag{9.19}$$

and

$$p(\mathbf{x}|c_k = 1) = \mathcal{N}(\mathbf{x}|\boldsymbol{\mu}_k, \Sigma_k) =$$
$$= \frac{1}{(2 \cdot \pi)^{D/2}} \cdot \frac{1}{|\Sigma_k|^{1/2}} \cdot \exp\left(-\frac{1}{2} \cdot (\mathbf{x} - \boldsymbol{\mu}_k)^T \Sigma_k^{-1} \cdot (\mathbf{x} - \boldsymbol{\mu}_k)\right)$$

Because $\mathbf{c}$ has a 1-of-K representation with $c_t \in \{0,1\}$ we can write its probability as

$$p(\mathbf{c}) = \prod_{k=1}^{K} \pi_k^{c_k} \tag{9.20}$$

and we can write

$$p(\mathbf{x}|\mathbf{c}) = \prod_{k=1}^{K} \mathcal{N}(\mathbf{x}|\boldsymbol{\mu}_k, \Sigma_k)^{c_k}. \tag{9.21}$$

Now, for each $\mathbf{x}$ there is a $\mathbf{c}$ and we are able to write the joint probability as $p(\mathbf{x}, \mathbf{c}) = p(\mathbf{c}) \cdot p(\mathbf{x}|\mathbf{c})$ to get

$$p(\mathbf{x}) = \sum_{\mathbf{c}} p(\mathbf{x}, \mathbf{c}) = \sum_{\mathbf{c}} p(\mathbf{c}) \cdot p(\mathbf{x}|\mathbf{c}) = \sum_{k=1}^{K} \pi_k \cdot \mathcal{N}(\mathbf{x}|\boldsymbol{\mu}_k, \Sigma_k). \tag{9.22}$$

With that, we can use Bayes' rule to write the probability of $\mathbf{c}$ given an $\mathbf{x}$

$$p(\mathbf{c}|\mathbf{x}) = \frac{p(\mathbf{x}|\mathbf{c}) \cdot p(\mathbf{c})}{p(\mathbf{x})}. \tag{9.23}$$

If we use $c_k = 1$ to denote cluster k we can write the probability that point $\mathbf{x}$ belongs to cluster k

$$p(c_k = 1|\mathbf{x}) = \frac{p(\mathbf{x}|c_k = 1) \cdot p(c_k = 1)}{p(\mathbf{x})} = \frac{\mathcal{N}(\mathbf{x}|\boldsymbol{\mu}_k, \Sigma_k) \cdot p(c_k = 1)}{\sum_{t=1}^{K} \mathcal{N}(\mathbf{x}|\boldsymbol{\mu}_t, \Sigma_t) \cdot p(c_t = 1)}. \tag{9.24}$$

For a given point $\mathbf{x}_n$, we define $\gamma(c_{nk})$ to be the probability that it belongs to cluster k i.e. $p(c_k = 1|\mathbf{x}_n)$. Specifically, we may write

$$\gamma(c_{kt}) \equiv p(c_k = 1|\mathbf{x}_n) = \frac{\pi_k \cdot \mathcal{N}(\mathbf{x}_n|\boldsymbol{\mu}_k, \Sigma_k)}{\sum_{t=1}^{K} \pi_t \cdot \mathcal{N}(\mathbf{x}_n|\boldsymbol{\mu}_t, \Sigma_t)}. \tag{9.25}$$

Now that we have the necessary notation, we need to find a way to get a clustering like we had in K-means.

9.3.1 *EM for Gaussian Mixtures*

Assume that the training set consists of N observations with no targets

$$X = (\mathbf{x}_1, \mathbf{x}_2, \cdots, \mathbf{x}_n, \cdots, \mathbf{x}_N)$$

We can represent the dataset as a design matrix X of dimensions $N \times D$ as before.

Now that we are working under a probabilistic perspective, we can use it to define our error measure. Given the mixture parameters, if we assume that the training examples are independent, the probability of the training set is given by the product of the individual likelihoods

$$p(X|\boldsymbol{\pi}, \boldsymbol{\mu}, \Sigma) = \prod_{n=1}^{N} \left(\sum_{k=1}^{K} \pi_k \cdot \mathcal{N}(\mathbf{x}_n|\boldsymbol{\mu}_k, \Sigma_k) \right). \tag{9.26}$$

As usual, it is easier to work with the log of the likelihood function

$$\log p(X|\boldsymbol{\pi}, \boldsymbol{\mu}, \Sigma) = \sum_{n=1}^{N} \log \left(\sum_{k=1}^{K} \pi_k \cdot \mathcal{N}(\mathbf{x}_n|\boldsymbol{\mu}_k, \Sigma_k) \right). \tag{9.27}$$

Now, much like in K-means, we can choose the clustering parameters such that they maximize our objective function (in this case the likelihood). To do so, we need to compute the gradient of $\log p(X|\boldsymbol{\pi}, \boldsymbol{\mu}, \Sigma)$ with respect to each parameter $\boldsymbol{\mu}_k$, then Σ_k and $\boldsymbol{\pi}_k$ and find where it goes to zero. Let us do it for the mean vectors of the Gaussian components

$$\frac{\partial \log p(X|\boldsymbol{\pi}, \boldsymbol{\mu}, \Sigma)}{\partial \boldsymbol{\mu}_k} = \sum_{n=1}^{N} \frac{\partial}{\partial \boldsymbol{\mu}_k} \log \left(\sum_{t=1}^{K} \pi_t \cdot \mathcal{N}(\mathbf{x}_n|\boldsymbol{\mu}_t, \Sigma_t) \right) \tag{9.28}$$

$$\frac{\partial \log p(X|\boldsymbol{\pi}, \boldsymbol{\mu}, \Sigma)}{\partial \boldsymbol{\mu}_k} = \sum_{n=1}^{N} \frac{1}{\sum_{t=1}^{K} \pi_t \cdot \mathcal{N}(\mathbf{x}_n|\boldsymbol{\mu}_t, \Sigma_t)} \cdot \frac{\partial}{\partial \boldsymbol{\mu}_k} \left(\sum_{t=1}^{K} \pi_t \cdot \mathcal{N}(\mathbf{x}_n|\boldsymbol{\mu}_t, \Sigma_t) \right) \tag{9.29}$$

$$\frac{\partial \log p(X|\boldsymbol{\pi}, \boldsymbol{\mu}, \Sigma)}{\partial \boldsymbol{\mu}_k} =$$

$$\sum_{n=1}^{N} \frac{\pi_k \cdot \mathcal{N}(\mathbf{x}_n|\boldsymbol{\mu}_k, \Sigma_k)}{\sum_{t=1}^{K} \pi_t \cdot \mathcal{N}(\mathbf{x}_n|\boldsymbol{\mu}_t, \Sigma_t)} \cdot \frac{1}{\partial \boldsymbol{\mu}_k} \left(-\frac{1}{2} \cdot (\mathbf{x}_n - \boldsymbol{\mu}_k)^T \Sigma_k^{-1} \cdot (\mathbf{x}_n - \boldsymbol{\mu}_k) \right) \tag{9.30}$$

and we get

$$\frac{\partial \log p(X|\boldsymbol{\pi}, \boldsymbol{\mu}, \Sigma)}{\partial \boldsymbol{\mu}_k} = \sum_{n=1}^{N} \frac{\pi_k \cdot \mathcal{N}(\mathbf{x}_n|\boldsymbol{\mu}_k, \Sigma_k)}{\sum_{t=1}^{K} \pi_t \cdot \mathcal{N}(\mathbf{x}_n|\boldsymbol{\mu}_t, \Sigma_t)} \cdot \Sigma_k^{-1} \cdot (\mathbf{x}_n - \boldsymbol{\mu}_k). \tag{9.31}$$

Now, let us see where it gets to zero

$$0 = \sum_{n=1}^{N} \frac{\pi_k \cdot \mathcal{N}(\mathbf{x}_n|\boldsymbol{\mu}_k, \Sigma_k)}{\sum_{t=1}^{K} \pi_t \cdot \mathcal{N}(\mathbf{x}_n|\boldsymbol{\mu}_t, \Sigma_t)} \cdot \Sigma_k^{-1} \cdot (\mathbf{x}_n - \boldsymbol{\mu}_k) \tag{9.32}$$

$$0 = \sum_{k=1}^{N} \gamma(c_{nk}) \cdot \Sigma_k^{-1} \cdot (\mathbf{x}_n - \boldsymbol{\mu}_k). \tag{9.33}$$

Multiplying by Σ_k we get

$$0 = \sum_{n=1}^{N} \gamma(c_{nk}) \cdot (\mathbf{x}_n - \boldsymbol{\mu}_k). \tag{9.34}$$

Solving for the mean vector yields

$$\boldsymbol{\mu}_k \cdot \left(\sum_{n=1}^{N} \gamma(c_{nk}) \right) = \sum_{n=1}^{N} \gamma(c_{nk}) \cdot \mathbf{x}_n \tag{9.35}$$

with

$$N_k = \sum_{n=1}^{N} \gamma(c_{nk}) \tag{9.36}$$

we get

$$\boldsymbol{\mu}_k = \frac{1}{N_k} \cdot \sum_{n=1}^{N} \gamma(c_{nk}) \cdot \mathbf{x}_n. \tag{9.37}$$

Now we maximize $\log p(X|\boldsymbol{\pi}, \boldsymbol{\mu}, \Sigma)$ with respect to Σ_k

$$\frac{\partial \log p(X|\boldsymbol{\pi}, \boldsymbol{\mu}, \Sigma)}{\partial \Sigma_k,} = \sum_{n=1}^{N} \frac{1}{\partial \Sigma_k} \log \left(\sum_{t=1}^{K} \pi_t \cdot \mathcal{N}(\mathbf{x}_n|\boldsymbol{\mu}_t, \Sigma_t) \right) = 0 \tag{9.38}$$

we get

$$\Sigma_k = \frac{1}{N_k} \cdot \sum_{n=1}^{N} \gamma(c_{nk}) \cdot (\mathbf{x}_n - \boldsymbol{\mu}_k) \cdot (\mathbf{x}_n - \boldsymbol{\mu}_k)^T \tag{9.39}$$

with

$$N_k = \sum_{n=1}^{N} \gamma(c_{nk}). \tag{9.40}$$

Finally, we maximize $\log p(X|\boldsymbol{\pi}, \boldsymbol{\mu}, \Sigma)$ with respect to π_k with the constraint

$$\sum_{t=1}^{K} \pi_t = 1. \tag{9.41}$$

This can be achieved using a Lagrange multiplier and maximizing the following quantity

$$\log p(X|\boldsymbol{\pi}, \boldsymbol{\mu}, \Sigma) + \lambda \left(\sum_{t=1}^{K} \pi_t - 1 \right) \tag{9.42}$$

$$\frac{\partial \log p(X|\boldsymbol{\pi}, \boldsymbol{\mu}, \Sigma) + \lambda \left(\sum_{t=1}^{K} \pi_t - 1 \right)}{\partial \pi_k} = 0 \tag{9.43}$$

which gives

$$0 = \sum_{n=1}^{N} \frac{\mathcal{N}(\mathbf{x}_n|\boldsymbol{\mu}_k, \Sigma_k)}{\sum_{t=1}^{K} \pi_t \mathcal{N}(\mathbf{x}_n|\boldsymbol{\mu}_t, \Sigma_t)} + \lambda \tag{9.44}$$

multiplying by π_k we get

$$0 = \sum_{n=1}^{N} \frac{\pi_k \cdot \mathcal{N}(\mathbf{x}_n|\boldsymbol{\mu}_k, \Sigma_k)}{\sum_{t=1}^{K} \pi_t \mathcal{N}(\mathbf{x}_n|\boldsymbol{\mu}_t, \Sigma_t)} + \pi_k \cdot \lambda \tag{9.45}$$

$$0 = \sum_{n=1}^{N} \gamma(c_{nk}) + \pi_k \cdot \lambda \tag{9.46}$$

$$0 = N_k + \pi_k \cdot \lambda \tag{9.47}$$

summing over K terms

$$0 = \sum_{t=1}^{K} (N_t + \pi_t \cdot \lambda) \tag{9.48}$$

$$-\sum_{t=1}^{K} N_t = \sum_{t=1}^{K} \pi_t \cdot \lambda \tag{9.49}$$

$$-N = \lambda \tag{9.50}$$

and we get

$$0 = N_k + \pi_k \cdot (-N) \tag{9.51}$$

$$\pi_k = \frac{N_k}{N}. \tag{9.52}$$

Now that we have expressions for how to choose all parameters, we can follow the same logic we did for K-means and build an algorithm.

Fig. 9.3 Two clusters with the distribution represented by the covariance matrices as determined by the EM clustering algorithm

9.3.2 *Algorithm: EM for Gaussian mixtures*

Given a Gaussian mixture model, the goal is to maximize the likelihood function with respect to the parameters (comprising the means and covariances of the components and the mixing coefficients), given a training set consisting of N observations

$$X = (\mathbf{x}_1, \mathbf{x}_2, \cdots, \mathbf{x}_k, \cdots, \mathbf{x}_N)$$

see Figure 9.3.

(1) Initialization:

Choose K, number of clusters. Then initialize:

- the means $\boldsymbol{\mu}_k$ (random data point or random value),

- Σ_k covariances (shape of clusters, usually we can start with identity matrix I),
- $\pi_k = p(c_k = 1)$ mixing coefficients (prior, importance of clusters, usually we can start with the value $\frac{1}{K}$, each cluster has the same importance.

(2) **E-Step** (Expectation):

Compute for each data point n and each cluster k

$$\gamma(c_{nk}) = p(c_k = 1 | \mathbf{x}_n) = \frac{\pi_k \cdot \mathcal{N}(\mathbf{x}_n | \boldsymbol{\mu}_k, \Sigma_k)}{\sum_{t=1}^{K} \pi_t \cdot \mathcal{N}(\mathbf{x}_n | \boldsymbol{\mu}_t, \Sigma_t)}. \tag{9.53}$$

Usually we can compute the likelihood

$$p(c_k = 1, \mathbf{x}_n) = \pi_k \cdot \mathcal{N}(\mathbf{x}_n | \boldsymbol{\mu}_k, \Sigma_k) \tag{9.54}$$

with

$$p(\mathbf{x}_n | c_k = 1) = \mathcal{N}(\mathbf{x}_n | \boldsymbol{\mu}_k, \Sigma_k) =$$

$$\frac{1}{(2 \cdot \pi)^{D/2}} \cdot \frac{1}{|\Sigma_k|^{1/2}} \cdot \exp\left(-\frac{1}{2} \cdot (\mathbf{x}_n - \boldsymbol{\mu}_k)^T \Sigma_k^{-1} \cdot (\mathbf{x}_n - \boldsymbol{\mu}_k)\right) \tag{9.55}$$

and after it

$$p(\mathbf{x}_n) = \sum_{k=1}^{K} p(c_k = 1, \mathbf{x}_n) = \sum_{k=1}^{K} \pi_k \cdot \mathcal{N}(\mathbf{x}_n | \boldsymbol{\mu}_k, \Sigma_k) \tag{9.56}$$

and normalize

$$\gamma(c_{nk}) = p(c_k = 1 | \mathbf{x}_n) = \frac{p(c_k = 1, \mathbf{x}_n)}{p(\mathbf{x}_n)}. \tag{9.57}$$

(3) **M-Step** (Maximization):

Update the parameters with the expressions we got from the gradients:

$$N_k = \sum_{n=1}^{N} \gamma(c_{nk}) \tag{9.58}$$

$$\boldsymbol{\mu}_k = \frac{1}{N_k} \cdot \sum_{n=1}^{N} \gamma(c_{nk}) \cdot \mathbf{x}_n \tag{9.59}$$

$$\Sigma_k = \frac{1}{N_k} \cdot \sum_{n=1}^{N} \gamma(c_{nk}) \cdot (\mathbf{x}_n - \boldsymbol{\mu}_k) \cdot (\mathbf{x}_n - \boldsymbol{\mu}_k)^T \tag{9.60}$$

$$\pi_k = p(c_k = 1) = \frac{N_k}{N} \tag{9.61}$$

(4) Evaluate the log likelihood

$$\log p(X | \boldsymbol{\pi}, \boldsymbol{\mu}, \Sigma) = \sum_{n=1}^{N} \log\left(\sum_{k=1}^{K} \pi_k \cdot \mathcal{N}(\mathbf{x}_n | \boldsymbol{\mu}_k, \Sigma_k)\right) \tag{9.62}$$

and check for convergence. Either the log likelihood or the number of iteration. If not satisfied go to step 2.

9.3.3 *Example*

Given the data

$$X = \left(\mathbf{x}_1 = \begin{pmatrix} 2 \\ 2 \end{pmatrix}, \ \mathbf{x}_2 = \begin{pmatrix} 0 \\ 2 \end{pmatrix}, \ \mathbf{x}_3 = \begin{pmatrix} 0 \\ 0 \end{pmatrix} \right)$$

with $K = 2$ and

$$\boldsymbol{\mu}_1 = \begin{pmatrix} 2 \\ 2 \end{pmatrix}, \ \boldsymbol{\mu}_2 = \begin{pmatrix} 0 \\ 2 \end{pmatrix},$$

and

$$\Sigma_1 = \begin{pmatrix} 1 & 0 \\ 0 & 1 \end{pmatrix}, \ \Sigma_2 = \begin{pmatrix} 1 & 0 \\ 0 & 1 \end{pmatrix},$$

$$\pi_1 = p(c_1 = 1) = 0.6, \quad \pi_2 = p(c_2 = 1) = 0.4,$$

we will perform a step of the EM clustering algorithm.

9.3.3.1 *E-Step (Expectation)*

Compute for each data point n and each cluster k

$$p(\mathbf{x}_n | c_k = 1) = \mathcal{N}(\mathbf{x}_n | \boldsymbol{\mu}_k, \Sigma_k) =$$

$$\frac{1}{(2 \cdot \pi)^{D/2}} \cdot \frac{1}{|\Sigma_k|^{1/2}} \cdot \exp\left(-\frac{1}{2} \cdot (\mathbf{x}_n - \boldsymbol{\mu}_k)^T \Sigma_k^{-1} \cdot (\mathbf{x}_n - \boldsymbol{\mu}_k) \right).$$

$$p(\mathbf{x}_1 | c_1 = 1) = \frac{1}{(2 \cdot \pi)^{2/2}} \cdot \frac{1}{1^{1/2}} \cdot \exp\left(-\frac{1}{2} \cdot (2-2, 2-2) \cdot \begin{pmatrix} 1 & 0 \\ 0 & 1 \end{pmatrix} \cdot \begin{pmatrix} 2-2 \\ 2-2 \end{pmatrix} \right),$$

$p(\mathbf{x}_1 | c_1 = 1) = 0.159155, \ p(\mathbf{x}_2 | c_1 = 1) = 0.0215393, \ p(\mathbf{x}_3 | c_1 = 1) = 0.00291502,$

$p(\mathbf{x}_1 | c_2 = 1) = 0.00291502, \ p(\mathbf{x}_2 | c_2 = 1) = 0.0215393, \ p(\mathbf{x}_3 | c_2 = 1) = 0.159155,$

Then

$$p(c_k = 1, \mathbf{x}_n) = \pi_k \cdot \mathcal{N}(\mathbf{x}_n | \boldsymbol{\mu}_k, \Sigma_k)$$

$p(\mathbf{x}_1, c_1 = 1) = 0.095493, \ p(\mathbf{x}_2, c_1 = 1) = 0.0129236, \ p(\mathbf{x}_3, c_1 = 1) = 0.00174901,$

$p(\mathbf{x}_1, c_2 = 1) = 0.00116601, \ p(\mathbf{x}_2, c_2 = 1) = 0.00861571, \ p(\mathbf{x}_3, c_2 = 1) = 0.063662,$

after it

$$p(\mathbf{x}_n) = \sum_{k=1}^{K} p(c_k = 1, \mathbf{x}_n) = \sum_{k=1}^{K} \pi_k \cdot \mathcal{N}(\mathbf{x}_n | \boldsymbol{\mu}_k, \Sigma_k)$$

$$p(\mathbf{x}_1) = 0.096659, \quad p(\mathbf{x}_2) = 0.0215393, \quad p(\mathbf{x}_3) = 0.065411,$$

using Bayes (normalizing)

$$\gamma(c_{nk}) = p(c_k = 1 | \mathbf{x}_n) = \frac{p(c_k = 1, \mathbf{x}_n)}{p(\mathbf{x}_n)}.$$

$$\gamma(c_{11}) = p(c_1 = 1 | \mathbf{x}_1) = 0.987937, \quad \gamma(c_{21}) = 0.6, \quad \gamma(c_{31}) = 0.0267388,$$

$$\gamma(c_{12}) = p(c_2 = 1 | \mathbf{x}_1) = 0.0120631, \quad \gamma(c_{22}) = 0.4, \quad \gamma(c_{32}) = 0.973261.$$

9.3.3.2 *M-Step* (*Maximization*)

We evaluate

$$N_k = \sum_{n=1}^{N} \gamma(c_{nk})$$

$$N_1 = 1.61468, \quad N_2 = 1.38532.$$

we determine the mean values

$$\boldsymbol{\mu}_k = \frac{1}{N_k} \cdot \sum_{n=1}^{N} \gamma(c_{nk}) \cdot \mathbf{x}_n$$

$$\boldsymbol{\mu}_1 = \frac{1}{1.61468} \cdot \left(0.987937 \cdot \begin{pmatrix} 2 \\ 2 \end{pmatrix} + 0.6 \cdot \begin{pmatrix} 0 \\ 2 \end{pmatrix} + 0.0267388 \cdot \begin{pmatrix} 0 \\ 0 \end{pmatrix} \right),$$

$$\boldsymbol{\mu}_1 = \begin{pmatrix} 1.2237 \\ 1.96688 \end{pmatrix}.$$

and

$$\boldsymbol{\mu}_2 = \frac{1}{1.38532} \cdot \left(0.0120631 \cdot \begin{pmatrix} 2 \\ 2 \end{pmatrix} + 0.4 \cdot \begin{pmatrix} 0 \\ 2 \end{pmatrix} + 0.973261 \cdot \begin{pmatrix} 0 \\ 0 \end{pmatrix} \right),$$

$$\boldsymbol{\mu}_2 = \begin{pmatrix} 0.0174156 \\ 0.594898 \end{pmatrix}.$$

and the new covariance matrix

$$\Sigma_k = \frac{1}{N_k} \cdot \sum_{n=1}^{N} \gamma(c_{nk}) \cdot (\mathbf{x}_n - \boldsymbol{\mu}_k) \cdot (\mathbf{x}_n - \boldsymbol{\mu}_k)^T$$

$$\Sigma_1 = \frac{1}{1.61468} \cdot \left(0.987937 \cdot \begin{pmatrix} 2 - 1.2237 \\ 2 - 1.96688 \end{pmatrix} \cdot (2 - 1.2237, 2 - 1.96688) + \right.$$

$$0.6 \cdot \begin{pmatrix} 0 - 1.2237 \\ 2 - 1.96688 \end{pmatrix} \cdot (0 - 1.2237, 2 - 1.96688) +$$

$$\left. 0.0267388 \cdot \begin{pmatrix} 0 - 1.2237 \\ 0 - 1.96688 \end{pmatrix} \cdot (0 - 1.2237, 0 - 1.96688) \right),$$

$$\Sigma_1 = \begin{pmatrix} 0.94996 & 0.0405286 \\ 0.0405286 & 0.0651426 \end{pmatrix},$$

and

$$\Sigma_2 = \begin{pmatrix} 0.0345279 & 0.0244707 \\ 0.0244707 & 0.835892 \end{pmatrix}.$$

and the new mixing parameter is

$$\pi_k = p(c_k = 1) = \frac{N_k}{N}$$

$$\pi_1 = p(c_1 = 1) = \frac{1.61468}{3} = 0.538227, \quad \pi_2 = p(c_2 = 1) = \frac{1.38532}{3} = 0.461775.$$

9.4   EM and *K*-means Clustering

Comparing K-means with the EM algorithm for Gaussian mixtures we see that there is a close similarity. For instance, both follow the same shape of learning procedure based on an alternation between expectation and optimization. However, there are differences. Whereas K-means performs a hard assignment of data points to clusters, in which each data point is associated uniquely with one cluster, the EM algorithm makes a soft assignment based on the posterior probabilities. Furthermore, while K-means yields the centroids of each cluster, the Gaussian Mixture clustering also yields a cluster shape and weight through the covariance and mixing coefficients respectively.

9.5   Exercises and Answers

K-means clustering

The k-means clustering algorithm finds structure in a set of unlabeled data points. More specifically, we choose a number of clusters k and the algorithm tries to group the data points by proximity. Let us go through an example. The following figure presents the data set.

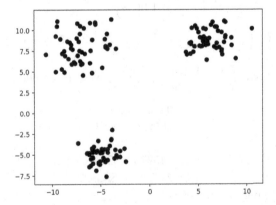

Analyzing it, we can see that there seem to be three distinct groups of points. For that reason, we will use $k = 3$. This is a key parameter. However, it is not always easy to make this choice. For one the problem can be a high dimensional one so we cannot plot the points and see. Furthermore, the points may be much closer so it is not obvious where a group starts and the other begins. Or even worse, there may be no groups at all.

After choosing the number of clusters, we can start the algorithm.

Step 0: Initialize the clusters

The algorithm starts by initializing each of the k clusters. There are many ways to do this each with its own advantages and disadvantages. A typical approach is to choose k random points from the data set or even to choose k random points from the whole space.

Initialization plays a key role in the procedure so we will procede our example with two different initializations.

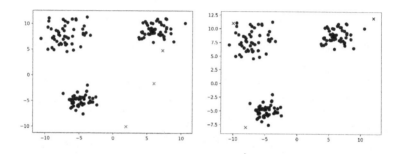

For each initialization, we have our initial centroids of each cluster μ^1, μ^2 and μ^3. We distinguish them by using different colors: red, green and blue.

Having initialized the procedure, we can now start to iterate towards a solution. The iterative procedure is made by three steps.

Step 1: Assign points to clusters

K-means is deterministic in the sense that each point belongs to one and only one cluster. However, it is helpful to use probabilities to describe the assignment of a point to a cluster. More specifically, we say that the probability that point $\mathbf{x}^{(n)}$ belongs to cluster c, $p\left(C = c \mid \mathbf{x}^{(n)}\right) = 1$ if point $\mathbf{x}^{(n)}$ is closer to centroid μ^c than to any other and $p\left(C = c \mid \mathbf{x}^{(n)}\right) = 0$ otherwise. This logic can be written with the indicator function as follows.

$$p\left(C = c \mid \mathbf{x}^{(n)}\right) = \mathbb{I}\left[c = \arg\min_{l \in \{1,2,\ldots,k\}} \left\|\mathbf{x}^{(n)} - \mu^l\right\|\right]$$

Applying this logic to our ongoing examples, we get:

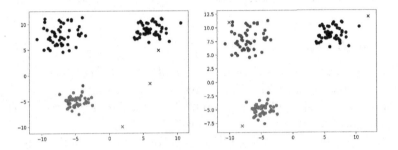

Having assigned all points to a cluster, we can move on to the next step.

Step 2: Adjust cluster centers

Each cluster centroid is updated to the mean of the points that belong to it:

$$\mu^c = \frac{\sum_{n=1}^{N} p\left(C = c \mid \mathbf{x}^{(n)}\right) \mathbf{x}^{(n)}}{\sum_{n=1}^{N} p\left(C = c \mid \mathbf{x}^{(n)}\right)}$$

As we can see below, the centroids move closer to the points that were assigned to them.

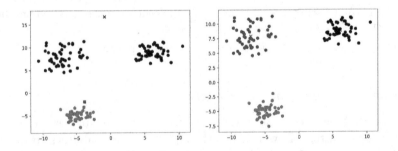

At this point, we can see the impact of initialization. Whereas the example on the right as already identified the three groups correctly, the left one is still far from it. In fact, it may never even find them.

Step 3: Check convergence

If no centroid changed position the algorithm terminates. Otherwise, we go back to step 1.

1)

Consider the following training data without labels:

$$\left\{ \mathbf{x}^{(1)} = \begin{pmatrix} 0 \\ 0 \end{pmatrix}, \mathbf{x}^{(2)} = \begin{pmatrix} 1 \\ 0 \end{pmatrix}, \mathbf{x}^{(3)} = \begin{pmatrix} 0 \\ 2 \end{pmatrix}, \mathbf{x}^{(4)} = \begin{pmatrix} 2 \\ 2 \end{pmatrix} \right\}$$

Also, consider the following initialization centroids for $k = 2$ clusters $\mu^1 = \begin{pmatrix} 2 \\ 0 \end{pmatrix}$ and $\mu^2 = \begin{pmatrix} 2 \\ 1 \end{pmatrix}$.

a) Apply the k-means clustering algorithm until convergence.

Solution:

Let us start the first iteration.

Step 1: Assign points to clusters

Let us start with $\mathbf{x}^{(1)}$:

$$\left\| \mathbf{x}^{(1)} - \mu^1 \right\|_2^2 = \left\| \begin{pmatrix} 0 \\ 0 \end{pmatrix} - \begin{pmatrix} 2 \\ 0 \end{pmatrix} \right\|_2^2 = \left\| \begin{pmatrix} -2 \\ 0 \end{pmatrix} \right\|_2^2 = 4$$

$$\left\| \mathbf{x}^{(1)} - \mu^2 \right\|_2^2 = \left\| \begin{pmatrix} 0 \\ 0 \end{pmatrix} - \begin{pmatrix} 2 \\ 1 \end{pmatrix} \right\|_2^2 = \left\| \begin{pmatrix} -2 \\ -1 \end{pmatrix} \right\|_2^2 = 5$$

$$\arg \min_{c \in \{1,2\}} \left\| \mathbf{x}^{(1)} - \mu^c \right\|_2^2 = \arg \min_{c \in \{1,2\}} \{4, 5\} = 1$$

Now $\mathbf{x}^{(2)}$:

$$\left\| \mathbf{x}^{(2)} - \mu^1 \right\|_2^2 = \left\| \begin{pmatrix} 1 \\ 0 \end{pmatrix} - \begin{pmatrix} 2 \\ 0 \end{pmatrix} \right\|_2^2 = \left\| \begin{pmatrix} -1 \\ 0 \end{pmatrix} \right\|_2^2 = 1$$

$$\left\| \mathbf{x}^{(2)} - \mu^2 \right\|_2^2 = \left\| \begin{pmatrix} 1 \\ 0 \end{pmatrix} - \begin{pmatrix} 2 \\ 1 \end{pmatrix} \right\|_2^2 = \left\| \begin{pmatrix} -1 \\ -1 \end{pmatrix} \right\|_2^2 = 2$$

$$\arg \min_{c \in \{1,2\}} \left\| \mathbf{x}^{(2)} - \mu^c \right\|_2^2 = \arg \min_{c \in \{1,2\}} \{1, 2\} = 1$$

Now $\mathbf{x}^{(3)}$:

$$\left\|\mathbf{x}^{(3)} - \mu^1\right\|_2^2 = \left\|\begin{pmatrix} 0 \\ 2 \end{pmatrix} - \begin{pmatrix} 2 \\ 0 \end{pmatrix}\right\|_2^2 = \left\|\begin{pmatrix} -2 \\ 2 \end{pmatrix}\right\|_2^2 = 8$$

$$\left\|\mathbf{x}^{(3)} - \mu^2\right\|_2^2 = \left\|\begin{pmatrix} 0 \\ 2 \end{pmatrix} - \begin{pmatrix} 2 \\ 1 \end{pmatrix}\right\|_2^2 = \left\|\begin{pmatrix} -2 \\ 1 \end{pmatrix}\right\|_2^2 = 5$$

$$\arg\min_{c \in \{1,2\}} \left\|\mathbf{x}^{(3)} - \mu^c\right\|_2^2 = \arg\min_{c \in \{1,2\}} \{8, 5\} = 2$$

Now $\mathbf{x}^{(4)}$:

$$\left\|\mathbf{x}^{(4)} - \mu^1\right\|_2^2 = \left\|\begin{pmatrix} 2 \\ 2 \end{pmatrix} - \begin{pmatrix} 2 \\ 0 \end{pmatrix}\right\|_2^2 = \left\|\begin{pmatrix} 0 \\ 2 \end{pmatrix}\right\|_2^2 = 4$$

$$\left\|\mathbf{x}^{(4)} - \mu^2\right\|_2^2 = \left\|\begin{pmatrix} 2 \\ 2 \end{pmatrix} - \begin{pmatrix} 2 \\ 1 \end{pmatrix}\right\|_2^2 = \left\|\begin{pmatrix} 0 \\ 1 \end{pmatrix}\right\|_2^2 = 1$$

$$\arg\min_{c \in \{1,2\}} \left\|\mathbf{x}^{(4)} - \mu^c\right\|_2^2 = \arg\min_{c \in \{1,2\}} \{4, 1\} = 2$$

Step 2: Compute new clusters

Cluster 1has two elements: $\mathbf{x}^{(1)}$ and $\mathbf{x}^{(2)}$. The new centroid can be computing by averaging the two cluster elements.

$$\mu^1 = \frac{\mathbf{x}^{(1)} + \mathbf{x}^{(2)}}{2} = \frac{1}{2}\left[\begin{pmatrix} 0 \\ 0 \end{pmatrix} + \begin{pmatrix} 1 \\ 0 \end{pmatrix}\right] = \frac{1}{2}\begin{pmatrix} 1 \\ 0 \end{pmatrix} = \begin{pmatrix} \frac{1}{2} \\ 0 \end{pmatrix}$$

Cluster 2 has two elements: $\mathbf{x}^{(3)}$ and $\mathbf{x}^{(4)}$. The new centroid can be computing by averaging the two cluster elements.

$$\mu^2 = \frac{\mathbf{x}^{(3)} + \mathbf{x}^{(4)}}{2} = \frac{1}{2}\left[\begin{pmatrix} 0 \\ 2 \end{pmatrix} + \begin{pmatrix} 2 \\ 2 \end{pmatrix}\right] = \frac{1}{2}\begin{pmatrix} 2 \\ 4 \end{pmatrix} = \begin{pmatrix} 1 \\ 2 \end{pmatrix}$$

Step 3: Verify convergence

Change in cluster 2:

$$\left\|\mu_{old}^1 - \mu^1\right\|_2^2 = \left\|\begin{pmatrix} 2 \\ 0 \end{pmatrix} - \begin{pmatrix} \frac{1}{2} \\ 0 \end{pmatrix}\right\|_2^2 = \left\|\begin{pmatrix} \frac{3}{2} \\ 0 \end{pmatrix}\right\|_2^2 = \frac{9}{4}$$

$$\left\|\mu_{old}^2 - \mu^2\right\|_2^2 = \left\|\begin{pmatrix} 2 \\ 1 \end{pmatrix} - \begin{pmatrix} 1 \\ 2 \end{pmatrix}\right\|_2^2 = \left\|\begin{pmatrix} 1 \\ -1 \end{pmatrix}\right\|_2^2 = 2$$

Centroids changed. We need to do another iteration.

Step 1: Assign points to clusters

Let us start with $\mathbf{x}^{(1)}$:

$$\left\|\mathbf{x}^{(1)} - \mu^1\right\|_2^2 = \left\|\begin{pmatrix} 0 \\ 0 \end{pmatrix} - \begin{pmatrix} \frac{1}{2} \\ 0 \end{pmatrix}\right\|_2^2 = \left\|\begin{pmatrix} -\frac{1}{2} \\ 0 \end{pmatrix}\right\|_2^2 = \frac{1}{4}$$

$$\left\|\mathbf{x}^{(1)} - \mu^2\right\|_2^2 = \left\|\begin{pmatrix} 0 \\ 0 \end{pmatrix} - \begin{pmatrix} 1 \\ 2 \end{pmatrix}\right\|_2^2 = \left\|\begin{pmatrix} -1 \\ -2 \end{pmatrix}\right\|_2^2 = 5$$

$$\arg\min_{c\in\{1,2\}} \left\|\mathbf{x}^{(1)} - \mu^c\right\|_2^2 = \arg\min_{c\in\{1,2\}} \left\{\frac{1}{4}, 5\right\} = 1$$

Now $\mathbf{x}^{(2)}$:

$$\left\|\mathbf{x}^{(2)} - \mu^1\right\|_2^2 = \left\|\begin{pmatrix} 1 \\ 0 \end{pmatrix} - \begin{pmatrix} \frac{1}{2} \\ 0 \end{pmatrix}\right\|_2^2 = \left\|\begin{pmatrix} \frac{1}{2} \\ 0 \end{pmatrix}\right\|_2^2 = \frac{1}{4}$$

$$\left\|\mathbf{x}^{(2)} - \mu^2\right\|_2^2 = \left\|\begin{pmatrix} 1 \\ 0 \end{pmatrix} - \begin{pmatrix} 1 \\ 2 \end{pmatrix}\right\|_2^2 = \left\|\begin{pmatrix} 0 \\ -2 \end{pmatrix}\right\|_2^2 = 4$$

$$\arg\min_{c\in\{1,2\}} \left\|\mathbf{x}^{(2)} - \mu^c\right\|_2^2 = \arg\min_{c\in\{1,2\}} \left\{\frac{1}{4}, 4\right\} = 1$$

Now $\mathbf{x}^{(3)}$:

$$\left\|\mathbf{x}^{(3)} - \mu^1\right\|_2^2 = \left\|\begin{pmatrix} 0 \\ 2 \end{pmatrix} - \begin{pmatrix} \frac{1}{2} \\ 0 \end{pmatrix}\right\|_2^2 = \left\|\begin{pmatrix} -\frac{1}{2} \\ 2 \end{pmatrix}\right\|_2^2 = \frac{9}{2}$$

$$\left\|\mathbf{x}^{(3)} - \mu^2\right\|_2^2 = \left\|\begin{pmatrix} 0 \\ 2 \end{pmatrix} - \begin{pmatrix} 1 \\ 2 \end{pmatrix}\right\|_2^2 = \left\|\begin{pmatrix} -1 \\ 0 \end{pmatrix}\right\|_2^2 = 1$$

$$\arg\min_{c\in\{1,2\}} \left\|\mathbf{x}^{(3)} - \mu^c\right\|_2^2 = \arg\min_{c\in\{1,2\}} \left\{\frac{9}{2}, 1\right\} = 2$$

Now $\mathbf{x}^{(4)}$:

$$\left\|\mathbf{x}^{(4)} - \mu^1\right\|_2^2 = \left\|\begin{pmatrix} 2 \\ 2 \end{pmatrix} - \begin{pmatrix} \frac{1}{2} \\ 0 \end{pmatrix}\right\|_2^2 = \left\|\begin{pmatrix} \frac{3}{2} \\ 2 \end{pmatrix}\right\|_2^2 = \frac{11}{2}$$

$$\left\|\mathbf{x}^{(4)} - \mu^2\right\|_2^2 = \left\|\begin{pmatrix} 2 \\ 2 \end{pmatrix} - \begin{pmatrix} 1 \\ 2 \end{pmatrix}\right\|_2^2 = \left\|\begin{pmatrix} 1 \\ 0 \end{pmatrix}\right\|_2^2 = 1$$

$$\arg \min_{c \in \{1,2\}} \left\|\mathbf{x}^{(4)} - \mu^c\right\|_2^2 = \arg \min_{c \in \{1,2\}} \left\{\frac{11}{2}, 1\right\} = 2$$

Step 2: Compute new clusters
Cluster 1has two elements: $\mathbf{x}^{(1)}$ and $\mathbf{x}^{(2)}$. The new centroid can be computing by averaging the two cluster elements.

$$\mu^1 = \frac{\mathbf{x}^{(1)} + \mathbf{x}^{(2)}}{2} = \frac{1}{2}\left[\begin{pmatrix} 0 \\ 0 \end{pmatrix} + \begin{pmatrix} 1 \\ 0 \end{pmatrix}\right] = \frac{1}{2}\begin{pmatrix} 1 \\ 0 \end{pmatrix} = \begin{pmatrix} \frac{1}{2} \\ 0 \end{pmatrix}$$

Cluster 2 has two elements: $\mathbf{x}^{(3)}$ and $\mathbf{x}^{(4)}$. The new centroid can be computing by averaging the two cluster elements.

$$\mu^2 = \frac{\mathbf{x}^{(3)} + \mathbf{x}^{(4)}}{2} = \frac{1}{2}\left[\begin{pmatrix} 0 \\ 2 \end{pmatrix} + \begin{pmatrix} 2 \\ 2 \end{pmatrix}\right] = \frac{1}{2}\begin{pmatrix} 2 \\ 4 \end{pmatrix} = \begin{pmatrix} 1 \\ 2 \end{pmatrix}$$

Step 3: Verify convergence
Change in cluster 2:

$$\left\|\mu_{old}^1 - \mu^1\right\|_2^2 = \left\|\begin{pmatrix} \frac{1}{2} \\ 0 \end{pmatrix} - \begin{pmatrix} \frac{1}{2} \\ 0 \end{pmatrix}\right\|_2^2 = \left\|\begin{pmatrix} 0 \\ 0 \end{pmatrix}\right\|_2^2 = 0$$

$$\left\|\mu_{old}^2 - \mu^2\right\|_2^2 = \left\|\begin{pmatrix} 1 \\ 2 \end{pmatrix} - \begin{pmatrix} 1 \\ 2 \end{pmatrix}\right\|_2^2 = \left\|\begin{pmatrix} 0 \\ 0 \end{pmatrix}\right\|_2^2 = 0$$

No centroid change, so the algorithm converged.

b) Plot the data points and draw the clusters.

Solution:

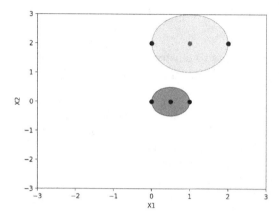

2)

Consider the following training data without labels:

$$\mathbf{x}^{(1)} = \begin{pmatrix} 1.0 \\ 0.0 \\ 0.0 \end{pmatrix}, \mathbf{x}^{(2)} = \begin{pmatrix} 8.0 \\ 8.0 \\ 4.0 \end{pmatrix}, \mathbf{x}^{(3)} = \begin{pmatrix} 3.0 \\ 3.0 \\ 0.0 \end{pmatrix}, \mathbf{x}^{(4)} = \begin{pmatrix} 0.0 \\ 0.0 \\ 1.0 \end{pmatrix},$$

$$\mathbf{x}^{(5)} = \begin{pmatrix} 0.0 \\ 1.0 \\ 0.0 \end{pmatrix}, \mathbf{x}^{(6)} = \begin{pmatrix} 3.0 \\ 2.0 \\ 1.0 \end{pmatrix}$$

Every time you need to initialize k clusters, do it by taking the first k points of the dataset and using them as centroids.

a) For $k = 2$ perform k-means clustering until convergence.

Solution:

Let us start the first iteration.

$$\mu^1 = \begin{pmatrix} 1.0 \\ 0.0 \\ 0.0 \end{pmatrix}$$

$$\mu^2 = \begin{pmatrix} 8.0 \\ 8.0 \\ 4.0 \end{pmatrix}$$

Step 1: Assign points to clusters.

Since there is only one cluster all points are assigned to it.

$$\left\| \mathbf{x}^{(1)} - \mu^1 \right\|_2^2 = \left\| \begin{pmatrix} 1.0 \\ 0.0 \\ 0.0 \end{pmatrix} - \begin{pmatrix} 1.0 \\ 0.0 \\ 0.0 \end{pmatrix} \right\|_2^2 = 0$$

$$\left\| \mathbf{x}^{(1)} - \mu^2 \right\|_2^2 = \left\| \begin{pmatrix} 1.0 \\ 0.0 \\ 0.0 \end{pmatrix} - \begin{pmatrix} 8.0 \\ 8.0 \\ 4.0 \end{pmatrix} \right\|_2^2 = 129$$

$$\arg \min_{c \in \{1,2\}} \left\| \mathbf{x}^{(1)} - \mu^c \right\|_2^2 = \arg \min_{c \in \{1,2\}} \{0, 129\} = 1$$

$$\left\| \mathbf{x}^{(2)} - \mu^1 \right\|_2^2 = \left\| \begin{pmatrix} 8.0 \\ 8.0 \\ 4.0 \end{pmatrix} - \begin{pmatrix} 1.0 \\ 0.0 \\ 0.0 \end{pmatrix} \right\|_2^2 = 129$$

$$\left\| \mathbf{x}^{(2)} - \mu^2 \right\|_2^2 = \left\| \begin{pmatrix} 8.0 \\ 8.0 \\ 4.0 \end{pmatrix} - \begin{pmatrix} 8.0 \\ 8.0 \\ 4.0 \end{pmatrix} \right\|_2^2 = 0$$

$$\arg \min_{c \in \{1,2\}} \left\| \mathbf{x}^{(2)} - \mu^c \right\|_2^2 = \arg \min_{c \in \{1,2\}} \{129, 0\} = 2$$

$$\left\| \mathbf{x}^{(3)} - \mu^1 \right\|_2^2 = \left\| \begin{pmatrix} 3.0 \\ 3.0 \\ 0.0 \end{pmatrix} - \begin{pmatrix} 1.0 \\ 0.0 \\ 0.0 \end{pmatrix} \right\|_2^2 = 13$$

$$\left\| \mathbf{x}^{(3)} - \mu^2 \right\|_2^2 = \left\| \begin{pmatrix} 3.0 \\ 3.0 \\ 0.0 \end{pmatrix} - \begin{pmatrix} 8.0 \\ 8.0 \\ 4.0 \end{pmatrix} \right\|_2^2 = 66$$

$$\arg\min_{c\in\{1,2\}}\left\|\mathbf{x}^{(3)}-\mu^c\right\|_2^2 = \arg\min_{c\in\{1,2\}}\{13,66\} = 1$$

$$\left\|\mathbf{x}^{(4)}-\mu^1\right\|_2^2 = \left\|\begin{pmatrix}0.0\\0.0\\1.0\end{pmatrix}-\begin{pmatrix}1.0\\0.0\\0.0\end{pmatrix}\right\|_2^2 = 2$$

$$\left\|\mathbf{x}^{(4)}-\mu^2\right\|_2^2 = \left\|\begin{pmatrix}0.0\\0.0\\1.0\end{pmatrix}-\begin{pmatrix}8.0\\8.0\\4.0\end{pmatrix}\right\|_2^2 = 137$$

$$\arg\min_{c\in\{1,2\}}\left\|\mathbf{x}^{(4)}-\mu^c\right\|_2^2 = \arg\min_{c\in\{1,2\}}\{2,137\} = 1$$

$$\left\|\mathbf{x}^{(5)}-\mu^1\right\|_2^2 = \left\|\begin{pmatrix}0.0\\1.0\\0.0\end{pmatrix}-\begin{pmatrix}1.0\\0.0\\0.0\end{pmatrix}\right\|_2^2 = 2$$

$$\left\|\mathbf{x}^{(5)}-\mu^2\right\|_2^2 = \left\|\begin{pmatrix}0.0\\1.0\\0.0\end{pmatrix}-\begin{pmatrix}8.0\\8.0\\4.0\end{pmatrix}\right\|_2^2 = 129$$

$$\arg\min_{c\in\{1,2\}}\left\|\mathbf{x}^{(5)}-\mu^c\right\|_2^2 = \arg\min_{c\in\{1,2\}}\{2,129\} = 1$$

$$\left\|\mathbf{x}^{(6)}-\mu^1\right\|_2^2 = \left\|\begin{pmatrix}3.0\\2.0\\1.0\end{pmatrix}-\begin{pmatrix}1.0\\0.0\\0.0\end{pmatrix}\right\|_2^2 = 9$$

$$\left\|\mathbf{x}^{(6)}-\mu^2\right\|_2^2 = \left\|\begin{pmatrix}3.0\\2.0\\1.0\end{pmatrix}-\begin{pmatrix}8.0\\8.0\\4.0\end{pmatrix}\right\|_2^2 = 70$$

$$\arg\min_{c\in\{1,2\}}\left\|\mathbf{x}^{(6)}-\mu^c\right\|_2^2 = \arg\min_{c\in\{1,2\}}\{9,70\} = 1$$

Step 2: Compute new centroids

The new centroids can be computing by averaging the cluster elements.

$$\mu^1 = \frac{\sum_{n=1}^{6} p\left(C = 1 \mid \mathbf{x}^{(n)}\right) \mathbf{x}^{(n)}}{\sum_{n=1}^{6} p\left(C = 1 \mid \mathbf{x}^{(n)}\right)}$$

$$\mu^1 = \frac{1}{5}\left[\begin{pmatrix} 1.0 \\ 0.0 \\ 0.0 \end{pmatrix} + \begin{pmatrix} 3.0 \\ 3.0 \\ 0.0 \end{pmatrix} + \begin{pmatrix} 0.0 \\ 0.0 \\ 1.0 \end{pmatrix} + \begin{pmatrix} 0.0 \\ 1.0 \\ 0.0 \end{pmatrix} + \begin{pmatrix} 3.0 \\ 2.0 \\ 1.0 \end{pmatrix}\right]$$

$$\mu^1 = \frac{1}{5}\begin{pmatrix} 7 \\ 6 \\ 2 \end{pmatrix} = \begin{pmatrix} \frac{7}{5} \\ \frac{6}{5} \\ \frac{2}{5} \end{pmatrix}$$

$$\mu^2 = \frac{\sum_{n=1}^{6} p\left(C = 2 \mid \mathbf{x}^{(n)}\right) \mathbf{x}^{(n)}}{\sum_{n=1}^{6} p\left(C = 2 \mid \mathbf{x}^{(n)}\right)} = \frac{1}{1}\left[\begin{pmatrix} 8.0 \\ 8.0 \\ 4.0 \end{pmatrix}\right] = \begin{pmatrix} 8.0 \\ 8.0 \\ 4.0 \end{pmatrix}$$

Step 3: Verify convergence
Change in cluster 2:

$$\left\|\mu_{old}^1 - \mu^1\right\|_2^2 = \left\|\begin{pmatrix} 1 \\ 0 \\ 0 \end{pmatrix} - \begin{pmatrix} \frac{7}{5} \\ \frac{6}{5} \\ \frac{2}{5} \end{pmatrix}\right\|_2^2 = 1.33$$

$$\left\|\mu_{old}^2 - \mu^2\right\|_2^2 = \left\|\begin{pmatrix} 8.0 \\ 8.0 \\ 4.0 \end{pmatrix} - \begin{pmatrix} 8.0 \\ 8.0 \\ 4.0 \end{pmatrix}\right\|_2^2 = 0.0$$

Centroids changed. We need to do another iteration.
Step 1: Assign points to clusters.
Since there is only one cluster all points are assigned to it.

$$\left\|\mathbf{x}^{(1)} - \mu^1\right\|_2^2 = \left\|\begin{pmatrix} 1.0 \\ 0.0 \\ 0.0 \end{pmatrix} - \begin{pmatrix} \frac{7}{5} \\ \frac{6}{5} \\ \frac{2}{5} \end{pmatrix}\right\|_2^2 = 1.76$$

$$\left\|\mathbf{x}^{(1)} - \mu^2\right\|_2^2 = \left\|\begin{pmatrix} 1.0 \\ 0.0 \\ 0.0 \end{pmatrix} - \begin{pmatrix} 8.0 \\ 8.0 \\ 4.0 \end{pmatrix}\right\|_2^2 = 129$$

$$\arg\min_{c \in \{1,2\}} \left\|\mathbf{x}^{(1)} - \mu^c\right\|_2^2 = \arg\min_{c \in \{1,2\}} \{1.76, 129\} = 1$$

$$\left\|\mathbf{x}^{(2)} - \mu^1\right\|_2^2 = \left\|\begin{pmatrix} 8.0 \\ 8.0 \\ 4.0 \end{pmatrix} - \begin{pmatrix} \frac{7}{5} \\ \frac{6}{5} \\ \frac{2}{5} \end{pmatrix}\right\|_2^2 = 102.76$$

$$\left\|\mathbf{x}^{(2)} - \mu^2\right\|_2^2 = \left\|\begin{pmatrix} 8.0 \\ 8.0 \\ 4.0 \end{pmatrix} - \begin{pmatrix} 8.0 \\ 8.0 \\ 4.0 \end{pmatrix}\right\|_2^2 = 0$$

$$\arg\min_{c\in\{1,2\}} \left\|\mathbf{x}^{(2)} - \mu^c\right\|_2^2 = \arg\min_{c\in\{1,2\}} \{102.76, 0\} = 2$$

$$\left\|\mathbf{x}^{(3)} - \mu^1\right\|_2^2 = \left\|\begin{pmatrix} 3.0 \\ 3.0 \\ 0.0 \end{pmatrix} - \begin{pmatrix} \frac{7}{5} \\ \frac{6}{5} \\ \frac{2}{5} \end{pmatrix}\right\|_2^2 = 5.96$$

$$\left\|\mathbf{x}^{(3)} - \mu^2\right\|_2^2 = \left\|\begin{pmatrix} 3.0 \\ 3.0 \\ 0.0 \end{pmatrix} - \begin{pmatrix} 8.0 \\ 8.0 \\ 4.0 \end{pmatrix}\right\|_2^2 = 66$$

$$\arg\min_{c\in\{1,2\}} \left\|\mathbf{x}^{(3)} - \mu^c\right\|_2^2 = \arg\min_{c\in\{1,2\}} \{5.96, 66\} = 1$$

$$\left\|\mathbf{x}^{(4)} - \mu^1\right\|_2^2 = \left\|\begin{pmatrix} 0.0 \\ 0.0 \\ 1.0 \end{pmatrix} - \begin{pmatrix} \frac{7}{5} \\ \frac{6}{5} \\ \frac{2}{5} \end{pmatrix}\right\|_2^2 = 3.76$$

$$\left\|\mathbf{x}^{(4)} - \mu^2\right\|_2^2 = \left\|\begin{pmatrix} 0.0 \\ 0.0 \\ 1.0 \end{pmatrix} - \begin{pmatrix} 8.0 \\ 8.0 \\ 4.0 \end{pmatrix}\right\|_2^2 = 137$$

$$\arg\min_{c\in\{1,2\}} \left\|\mathbf{x}^{(4)} - \mu^c\right\|_2^2 = \arg\min_{c\in\{1,2\}} \{3.76, 137\} = 1$$

$$\left\|\mathbf{x}^{(5)} - \mu^1\right\|_2^2 = \left\|\begin{pmatrix} 0.0 \\ 1.0 \\ 0.0 \end{pmatrix} - \begin{pmatrix} \frac{7}{5} \\ \frac{6}{5} \\ \frac{2}{5} \end{pmatrix}\right\|_2^2 = 2.16$$

$$\left\| \mathbf{x}^{(5)} - \mu^2 \right\|_2^2 = \left\| \begin{pmatrix} 0.0 \\ 1.0 \\ 0.0 \end{pmatrix} - \begin{pmatrix} 8.0 \\ 8.0 \\ 4.0 \end{pmatrix} \right\|_2^2 = 129$$

$$\arg\min_{c \in \{1,2\}} \left\| \mathbf{x}^{(5)} - \mu^c \right\|_2^2 = \arg\min_{c \in \{1,2\}} \{2.16, 129\} = 1$$

$$\left\| \mathbf{x}^{(6)} - \mu^1 \right\|_2^2 = \left\| \begin{pmatrix} 3.0 \\ 2.0 \\ 1.0 \end{pmatrix} - \begin{pmatrix} \frac{7}{5} \\ \frac{6}{5} \\ \frac{2}{5} \end{pmatrix} \right\|_2^2 = 3.56$$

$$\left\| \mathbf{x}^{(6)} - \mu^2 \right\|_2^2 = \left\| \begin{pmatrix} 3.0 \\ 2.0 \\ 1.0 \end{pmatrix} - \begin{pmatrix} 8.0 \\ 8.0 \\ 4.0 \end{pmatrix} \right\|_2^2 = 70$$

$$\arg\min_{c \in \{1,2\}} \left\| \mathbf{x}^{(6)} - \mu^c \right\|_2^2 = \arg\min_{c \in \{1,2\}} \{3.56, 70\} = 1$$

Step 2: Compute new centroids

The new centroids can be computing by averaging the cluster elements.

$$\mu^1 = \frac{\sum_{n=1}^{6} p\left(C = c \mid \mathbf{x}^{(n)}\right) \mathbf{x}^{(n)}}{\sum_{n=1}^{6} p\left(C = c \mid \mathbf{x}^{(n)}\right)} =$$

$$\mu^1 = \frac{1}{5}\left[\begin{pmatrix} 1.0 \\ 0.0 \\ 0.0 \end{pmatrix} + \begin{pmatrix} 3.0 \\ 3.0 \\ 0.0 \end{pmatrix} + \begin{pmatrix} 0.0 \\ 0.0 \\ 1.0 \end{pmatrix} + \begin{pmatrix} 0.0 \\ 1.0 \\ 0.0 \end{pmatrix} + \begin{pmatrix} 3.0 \\ 2.0 \\ 1.0 \end{pmatrix} \right]$$

$$\mu^1 = \frac{1}{5}\begin{pmatrix} 7 \\ 6 \\ 2 \end{pmatrix} = \begin{pmatrix} \frac{7}{5} \\ \frac{6}{5} \\ \frac{2}{5} \end{pmatrix}$$

$$\mu^2 = \frac{\sum_{n=1}^{6} p\left(C = 2 \mid \mathbf{x}^{(n)}\right) \mathbf{x}^{(n)}}{\sum_{n=1}^{6} p\left(C = 2 \mid \mathbf{x}^{(n)}\right)} = \frac{1}{1}\left[\begin{pmatrix} 8.0 \\ 8.0 \\ 4.0 \end{pmatrix} \right] = \begin{pmatrix} 8.0 \\ 8.0 \\ 4.0 \end{pmatrix}$$

Step 3: Verify convergence

Change in cluster 2:

$$\left\|\mu_{old}^1 - \mu^1\right\|_2^2 = \left\|\begin{pmatrix} \frac{7}{5} \\ \frac{6}{5} \\ \frac{2}{5} \end{pmatrix} - \begin{pmatrix} \frac{7}{5} \\ \frac{6}{5} \\ \frac{2}{5} \end{pmatrix}\right\|_2^2 = 0.0$$

$$\left\|\mu_{old}^2 - \mu^2\right\|_2^2 = \left\|\begin{pmatrix} 8.0 \\ 8.0 \\ 4.0 \end{pmatrix} - \begin{pmatrix} 8.0 \\ 8.0 \\ 4.0 \end{pmatrix}\right\|_2^2 = 0.0$$

No centroid change, so the algorithm converged.

b) For $k = 3$ perform k-means clustering until convergence.

Solution:

Let us start the first iteration.

$$\mu^1 = \begin{pmatrix} 1.0 \\ 0.0 \\ 0.0 \end{pmatrix}$$

$$\mu^2 = \begin{pmatrix} 8.0 \\ 8.0 \\ 4.0 \end{pmatrix}$$

$$\mu^3 = \begin{pmatrix} 3.0 \\ 3.0 \\ 0.0 \end{pmatrix}$$

Step 1: Assign points to clusters.

Since there is only one cluster all points are assigned to it.

$$\left\|\mathbf{x}^{(1)} - \mu^1\right\|_2^2 = \left\|\begin{pmatrix} 1.0 \\ 0.0 \\ 0.0 \end{pmatrix} - \begin{pmatrix} 1.0 \\ 0.0 \\ 0.0 \end{pmatrix}\right\|_2^2 = 0$$

$$\left\|\mathbf{x}^{(1)} - \mu^2\right\|_2^2 = \left\|\begin{pmatrix} 1.0 \\ 0.0 \\ 0.0 \end{pmatrix} - \begin{pmatrix} 8.0 \\ 8.0 \\ 4.0 \end{pmatrix}\right\|_2^2 = 129$$

$$\left\|\mathbf{x}^{(1)} - \mu^3\right\|_2^2 = \left\|\begin{pmatrix} 1.0 \\ 0.0 \\ 0.0 \end{pmatrix} - \begin{pmatrix} 3.0 \\ 3.0 \\ 0.0 \end{pmatrix}\right\|_2^2 = 13$$

$$\arg\min_{c \in \{1,2\}} \left\|\mathbf{x}^{(1)} - \mu^c\right\|_2^2 = \arg\min_{c \in \{1,2\}} \{0, 129, 13\} = 1$$

$$\left\|\mathbf{x}^{(2)} - \mu^1\right\|_2^2 = \left\|\begin{pmatrix} 8.0 \\ 8.0 \\ 4.0 \end{pmatrix} - \begin{pmatrix} 1.0 \\ 0.0 \\ 0.0 \end{pmatrix}\right\|_2^2 = 129$$

$$\left\|\mathbf{x}^{(2)} - \mu^2\right\|_2^2 = \left\|\begin{pmatrix} 8.0 \\ 8.0 \\ 4.0 \end{pmatrix} - \begin{pmatrix} 8.0 \\ 8.0 \\ 4.0 \end{pmatrix}\right\|_2^2 = 0$$

$$\left\|\mathbf{x}^{(2)} - \mu^3\right\|_2^2 = \left\|\begin{pmatrix} 8.0 \\ 8.0 \\ 4.0 \end{pmatrix} - \begin{pmatrix} 3.0 \\ 3.0 \\ 0.0 \end{pmatrix}\right\|_2^2 = 66$$

$$\arg\min_{c \in \{1,2\}} \left\|\mathbf{x}^{(2)} - \mu^c\right\|_2^2 = \arg\min_{c \in \{1,2\}} \{129, 0, 66\} = 2$$

$$\left\|\mathbf{x}^{(3)} - \mu^1\right\|_2^2 = \left\|\begin{pmatrix} 3.0 \\ 3.0 \\ 0.0 \end{pmatrix} - \begin{pmatrix} 1.0 \\ 0.0 \\ 0.0 \end{pmatrix}\right\|_2^2 = 13$$

$$\left\|\mathbf{x}^{(3)} - \mu^2\right\|_2^2 = \left\|\begin{pmatrix} 3.0 \\ 3.0 \\ 0.0 \end{pmatrix} - \begin{pmatrix} 8.0 \\ 8.0 \\ 4.0 \end{pmatrix}\right\|_2^2 = 66$$

$$\left\|\mathbf{x}^{(3)} - \mu^3\right\|_2^2 = \left\|\begin{pmatrix} 3.0 \\ 3.0 \\ 0.0 \end{pmatrix} - \begin{pmatrix} 3.0 \\ 3.0 \\ 0.0 \end{pmatrix}\right\|_2^2 = 0$$

$$\arg\min_{c \in \{1,2\}} \left\|\mathbf{x}^{(3)} - \mu^c\right\|_2^2 = \arg\min_{c \in \{1,2\}} \{13, 66, 0\} = 3$$

$$\left\| \mathbf{x}^{(4)} - \mu^1 \right\|_2^2 = \left\| \begin{pmatrix} 0.0 \\ 0.0 \\ 1.0 \end{pmatrix} - \begin{pmatrix} 1.0 \\ 0.0 \\ 0.0 \end{pmatrix} \right\|_2^2 = 2$$

$$\left\| \mathbf{x}^{(4)} - \mu^2 \right\|_2^2 = \left\| \begin{pmatrix} 0.0 \\ 0.0 \\ 1.0 \end{pmatrix} - \begin{pmatrix} 8.0 \\ 8.0 \\ 4.0 \end{pmatrix} \right\|_2^2 = 137$$

$$\left\| \mathbf{x}^{(4)} - \mu^3 \right\|_2^2 = \left\| \begin{pmatrix} 0.0 \\ 0.0 \\ 1.0 \end{pmatrix} - \begin{pmatrix} 3.0 \\ 3.0 \\ 0.0 \end{pmatrix} \right\|_2^2 = 19$$

$$\arg \min_{c \in \{1,2\}} \left\| \mathbf{x}^{(4)} - \mu^c \right\|_2^2 = \arg \min_{c \in \{1,2\}} \{2, 137, 19\} = 1$$

$$\left\| \mathbf{x}^{(5)} - \mu^1 \right\|_2^2 = \left\| \begin{pmatrix} 0.0 \\ 1.0 \\ 0.0 \end{pmatrix} - \begin{pmatrix} 1.0 \\ 0.0 \\ 0.0 \end{pmatrix} \right\|_2^2 = 2$$

$$\left\| \mathbf{x}^{(5)} - \mu^2 \right\|_2^2 = \left\| \begin{pmatrix} 0.0 \\ 1.0 \\ 0.0 \end{pmatrix} - \begin{pmatrix} 8.0 \\ 8.0 \\ 4.0 \end{pmatrix} \right\|_2^2 = 129$$

$$\left\| \mathbf{x}^{(5)} - \mu^3 \right\|_2^2 = \left\| \begin{pmatrix} 0.0 \\ 1.0 \\ 0.0 \end{pmatrix} - \begin{pmatrix} 3.0 \\ 3.0 \\ 0.0 \end{pmatrix} \right\|_2^2 = 13$$

$$\arg \min_{c \in \{1,2\}} \left\| \mathbf{x}^{(5)} - \mu^c \right\|_2^2 = \arg \min_{c \in \{1,2\}} \{2, 129, 13\} = 1$$

$$\left\| \mathbf{x}^{(6)} - \mu^1 \right\|_2^2 = \left\| \begin{pmatrix} 3.0 \\ 2.0 \\ 1.0 \end{pmatrix} - \begin{pmatrix} 1.0 \\ 0.0 \\ 0.0 \end{pmatrix} \right\|_2^2 = 9$$

$$\left\| \mathbf{x}^{(6)} - \mu^2 \right\|_2^2 = \left\| \begin{pmatrix} 3.0 \\ 2.0 \\ 1.0 \end{pmatrix} - \begin{pmatrix} 8.0 \\ 8.0 \\ 4.0 \end{pmatrix} \right\|_2^2 = 70$$

$$\left\| \mathbf{x}^{(6)} - \mu^3 \right\|_2^2 = \left\| \begin{pmatrix} 3.0 \\ 2.0 \\ 1.0 \end{pmatrix} - \begin{pmatrix} 3.0 \\ 3.0 \\ 0.0 \end{pmatrix} \right\|_2^2 = 2$$

$$\arg\min_{c \in \{1,2\}} \left\| \mathbf{x}^{(6)} - \mu^c \right\|_2^2 = \arg\min_{c \in \{1,2\}} \{9, 70, 2\} = 3$$

Step 2: Compute new centroids

The new centroids can be computing by averaging the cluster elements.

$$\mu^1 = \frac{\sum_{n=1}^6 p\left(C = 1 \mid \mathbf{x}^{(n)}\right) \mathbf{x}^{(n)}}{\sum_{n=1}^6 p\left(C = 1 \mid \mathbf{x}^{(n)}\right)}$$

$$\mu^1 = \frac{1}{3} \left[\begin{pmatrix} 1.0 \\ 0.0 \\ 0.0 \end{pmatrix} + \begin{pmatrix} 0.0 \\ 0.0 \\ 1.0 \end{pmatrix} + \begin{pmatrix} 0.0 \\ 1.0 \\ 0.0 \end{pmatrix} \right] = \frac{1}{3} \begin{pmatrix} 1 \\ 1 \\ 1 \end{pmatrix} = \begin{pmatrix} \frac{1}{3} \\ \frac{1}{3} \\ \frac{1}{3} \end{pmatrix}$$

$$\mu^2 = \frac{\sum_{n=1}^6 p\left(C = 2 \mid \mathbf{x}^{(n)}\right) \mathbf{x}^{(n)}}{\sum_{n=1}^6 p\left(C = 2 \mid \mathbf{x}^{(n)}\right)} = \frac{1}{1} \left[\begin{pmatrix} 8.0 \\ 8.0 \\ 4.0 \end{pmatrix} \right] = \begin{pmatrix} 8.0 \\ 8.0 \\ 4.0 \end{pmatrix}$$

$$\mu^3 = \frac{\sum_{n=1}^6 p\left(C = 3 \mid \mathbf{x}^{(n)}\right) \mathbf{x}^{(n)}}{\sum_{n=1}^6 p\left(C = 3 \mid \mathbf{x}^{(n)}\right)}$$

$$\mu^3 = \frac{1}{2} \left[\begin{pmatrix} 3.0 \\ 3.0 \\ 0.0 \end{pmatrix} + \begin{pmatrix} 3.0 \\ 2.0 \\ 1.0 \end{pmatrix} \right] = \frac{1}{2} \begin{pmatrix} 6 \\ 5 \\ 1 \end{pmatrix} = \begin{pmatrix} 3 \\ \frac{5}{2} \\ \frac{1}{2} \end{pmatrix}$$

Step 3: Verify convergence

Change in cluster 2:

$$\left\| \mu_{old}^1 - \mu^1 \right\|_2^2 = \left\| \begin{pmatrix} 1 \\ 0 \\ 0 \end{pmatrix} - \begin{pmatrix} \frac{1}{3} \\ \frac{1}{3} \\ \frac{1}{3} \end{pmatrix} \right\|_2^2 = 0.67$$

$$\left\| \mu_{old}^2 - \mu^2 \right\|_2^2 = \left\| \begin{pmatrix} 8.0 \\ 8.0 \\ 4.0 \end{pmatrix} - \begin{pmatrix} 8.0 \\ 8.0 \\ 4.0 \end{pmatrix} \right\|_2^2 = 0.0$$

$$\left\| \mu_{old}^3 - \mu^3 \right\|_2^2 = \left\| \begin{pmatrix} 3.0 \\ 3.0 \\ 0.0 \end{pmatrix} - \begin{pmatrix} 3 \\ \frac{5}{2} \\ \frac{1}{2} \end{pmatrix} \right\|_2^2 = 0.5$$

Centroids changed. We need to do another iteration.

Step 1: Assign points to clusters.

Since there is only one cluster all points are assigned to it.

$$\left\| \mathbf{x}^{(1)} - \mu^1 \right\|_2^2 = \left\| \begin{pmatrix} 1.0 \\ 0.0 \\ 0.0 \end{pmatrix} - \begin{pmatrix} \frac{1}{3} \\ \frac{1}{3} \\ \frac{1}{3} \end{pmatrix} \right\|_2^2 = 0.67$$

$$\left\| \mathbf{x}^{(1)} - \mu^2 \right\|_2^2 = \left\| \begin{pmatrix} 1.0 \\ 0.0 \\ 0.0 \end{pmatrix} - \begin{pmatrix} 8.0 \\ 8.0 \\ 4.0 \end{pmatrix} \right\|_2^2 = 129$$

$$\left\| \mathbf{x}^{(1)} - \mu^3 \right\|_2^2 = \left\| \begin{pmatrix} 1.0 \\ 0.0 \\ 0.0 \end{pmatrix} - \begin{pmatrix} 3 \\ \frac{5}{2} \\ \frac{1}{2} \end{pmatrix} \right\|_2^2 = 10.5$$

$$\arg \min_{c \in \{1,2\}} \left\| \mathbf{x}^{(1)} - \mu^c \right\|_2^2 = \arg \min_{c \in \{1,2\}} \{0.67, 129, 10.5\} = 1$$

$$\left\| \mathbf{x}^{(2)} - \mu^1 \right\|_2^2 = \left\| \begin{pmatrix} 8.0 \\ 8.0 \\ 4.0 \end{pmatrix} - \begin{pmatrix} \frac{1}{3} \\ \frac{1}{3} \\ \frac{1}{3} \end{pmatrix} \right\|_2^2 = 131$$

$$\left\| \mathbf{x}^{(2)} - \mu^2 \right\|_2^2 = \left\| \begin{pmatrix} 8.0 \\ 8.0 \\ 4.0 \end{pmatrix} - \begin{pmatrix} 8.0 \\ 8.0 \\ 4.0 \end{pmatrix} \right\|_2^2 = 0$$

$$\left\| \mathbf{x}^{(2)} - \mu^3 \right\|_2^2 = \left\| \begin{pmatrix} 8.0 \\ 8.0 \\ 4.0 \end{pmatrix} - \begin{pmatrix} 3 \\ \frac{5}{2} \\ \frac{1}{2} \end{pmatrix} \right\|_2^2 = 67.5$$

$$\arg \min_{c \in \{1,2\}} \left\| \mathbf{x}^{(2)} - \mu^c \right\|_2^2 = \arg \min_{c \in \{1,2\}} \{131, 0, 67.5\} = 2$$

$$\left\| \mathbf{x}^{(3)} - \mu^1 \right\|_2^2 = \left\| \begin{pmatrix} 3.0 \\ 3.0 \\ 0.0 \end{pmatrix} - \begin{pmatrix} \frac{1}{3} \\ \frac{1}{3} \\ \frac{1}{3} \end{pmatrix} \right\|_2^2 = 14.33$$

$$\left\| \mathbf{x}^{(3)} - \mu^2 \right\|_2^2 = \left\| \begin{pmatrix} 3.0 \\ 3.0 \\ 0.0 \end{pmatrix} - \begin{pmatrix} 8.0 \\ 8.0 \\ 4.0 \end{pmatrix} \right\|_2^2 = 66$$

$$\left\| \mathbf{x}^{(3)} - \mu^3 \right\|_2^2 = \left\| \begin{pmatrix} 3.0 \\ 3.0 \\ 0.0 \end{pmatrix} - \begin{pmatrix} 3 \\ \frac{5}{2} \\ \frac{1}{2} \end{pmatrix} \right\|_2^2 = 0.5$$

$$\arg \min_{c \in \{1,2\}} \left\| \mathbf{x}^{(3)} - \mu^c \right\|_2^2 = \arg \min_{c \in \{1,2\}} \{14.33, 66, 0.5\} = 3$$

$$\left\| \mathbf{x}^{(4)} - \mu^1 \right\|_2^2 = \left\| \begin{pmatrix} 0.0 \\ 0.0 \\ 1.0 \end{pmatrix} - \begin{pmatrix} \frac{1}{3} \\ \frac{1}{3} \\ \frac{1}{3} \end{pmatrix} \right\|_2^2 = 0.67$$

$$\left\| \mathbf{x}^{(4)} - \mu^2 \right\|_2^2 = \left\| \begin{pmatrix} 0.0 \\ 0.0 \\ 1.0 \end{pmatrix} - \begin{pmatrix} 8.0 \\ 8.0 \\ 4.0 \end{pmatrix} \right\|_2^2 = 137$$

$$\left\| \mathbf{x}^{(4)} - \mu^3 \right\|_2^2 = \left\| \begin{pmatrix} 0.0 \\ 0.0 \\ 1.0 \end{pmatrix} - \begin{pmatrix} 3 \\ \frac{5}{2} \\ \frac{1}{2} \end{pmatrix} \right\|_2^2 = 15.5$$

$$\arg \min_{c \in \{1,2\}} \left\| \mathbf{x}^{(4)} - \mu^c \right\|_2^2 = \arg \min_{c \in \{1,2\}} \{0.67, 137, 15.5\} = 1$$

$$\left\| \mathbf{x}^{(5)} - \mu^1 \right\|_2^2 = \left\| \begin{pmatrix} 0.0 \\ 1.0 \\ 0.0 \end{pmatrix} - \begin{pmatrix} \frac{1}{3} \\ \frac{1}{3} \\ \frac{1}{3} \end{pmatrix} \right\|_2^2 = 0.67$$

$$\left\| \mathbf{x}^{(5)} - \mu^2 \right\|_2^2 = \left\| \begin{pmatrix} 0.0 \\ 1.0 \\ 0.0 \end{pmatrix} - \begin{pmatrix} 8.0 \\ 8.0 \\ 4.0 \end{pmatrix} \right\|_2^2 = 129$$

$$\left\| \mathbf{x}^{(5)} - \mu^3 \right\|_2^2 = \left\| \begin{pmatrix} 0.0 \\ 1.0 \\ 0.0 \end{pmatrix} - \begin{pmatrix} 3 \\ \frac{5}{2} \\ \frac{1}{2} \end{pmatrix} \right\|_2^2 = 11.5$$

$$\arg\min_{c \in \{1,2\}} \left\| \mathbf{x}^{(5)} - \mu^c \right\|_2^2 = \arg\min_{c \in \{1,2\}} \{0.67, 129, 11.5\} = 1$$

$$\left\| \mathbf{x}^{(6)} - \mu^1 \right\|_2^2 = \left\| \begin{pmatrix} 3.0 \\ 2.0 \\ 1.0 \end{pmatrix} - \begin{pmatrix} \frac{1}{3} \\ \frac{1}{3} \\ \frac{1}{3} \end{pmatrix} \right\|_2^2 = 10.33$$

$$\left\| \mathbf{x}^{(6)} - \mu^2 \right\|_2^2 = \left\| \begin{pmatrix} 3.0 \\ 2.0 \\ 1.0 \end{pmatrix} - \begin{pmatrix} 8.0 \\ 8.0 \\ 4.0 \end{pmatrix} \right\|_2^2 = 70$$

$$\left\| \mathbf{x}^{(6)} - \mu^3 \right\|_2^2 = \left\| \begin{pmatrix} 3.0 \\ 2.0 \\ 1.0 \end{pmatrix} - \begin{pmatrix} 3 \\ \frac{5}{2} \\ \frac{1}{2} \end{pmatrix} \right\|_2^2 = 0.5$$

$$\arg\min_{c \in \{1,2\}} \left\| \mathbf{x}^{(6)} - \mu^c \right\|_2^2 = \arg\min_{c \in \{1,2\}} \{10.33, 70, 0.5\} = 3$$

Step 2: Compute new centroids

The new centroids can be computing by averaging the cluster elements.

$$\mu^1 = \frac{\sum_{n=1}^{6} p\left(C = 1 \mid \mathbf{x}^{(n)}\right) \mathbf{x}^{(n)}}{\sum_{n=1}^{6} p\left(C = 1 \mid \mathbf{x}^{(n)}\right)}$$

$$\mu^1 = \frac{1}{3} \left[\begin{pmatrix} 1.0 \\ 0.0 \\ 0.0 \end{pmatrix} + \begin{pmatrix} 0.0 \\ 0.0 \\ 1.0 \end{pmatrix} + \begin{pmatrix} 0.0 \\ 1.0 \\ 0.0 \end{pmatrix} \right] = \frac{1}{3} \begin{pmatrix} 1 \\ 1 \\ 1 \end{pmatrix} = \begin{pmatrix} \frac{1}{3} \\ \frac{1}{3} \\ \frac{1}{3} \end{pmatrix}$$

$$\mu^2 = \frac{\sum_{n=1}^{6} p\left(C = 2 \mid \mathbf{x}^{(n)}\right) \mathbf{x}^{(n)}}{\sum_{n=1}^{6} p\left(C = 2 \mid \mathbf{x}^{(n)}\right)} = \frac{1}{1} \left[\begin{pmatrix} 8.0 \\ 8.0 \\ 4.0 \end{pmatrix} \right] = \begin{pmatrix} 8.0 \\ 8.0 \\ 4.0 \end{pmatrix}$$

$$\mu^3 = \frac{\sum_{n=1}^{6} p\left(C = 3 \mid \mathbf{x}^{(n)}\right) \mathbf{x}^{(n)}}{\sum_{n=1}^{6} p\left(C = 3 \mid \mathbf{x}^{(n)}\right)}$$

$$\mu^3 = \frac{1}{2}\left[\begin{pmatrix} 3.0 \\ 3.0 \\ 0.0 \end{pmatrix} + \begin{pmatrix} 3.0 \\ 2.0 \\ 1.0 \end{pmatrix}\right] = \frac{1}{2}\begin{pmatrix} 6 \\ 5 \\ 1 \end{pmatrix} = \begin{pmatrix} 3 \\ \frac{5}{2} \\ \frac{1}{2} \end{pmatrix}$$

Step 3: Verify convergence

Change in cluster 2:

$$\left\|\mu_{old}^1 - \mu^1\right\|_2^2 = \left\|\begin{pmatrix} \frac{1}{3} \\ \frac{1}{3} \\ \frac{1}{3} \\ \frac{1}{3} \end{pmatrix} - \begin{pmatrix} \frac{1}{3} \\ \frac{1}{3} \\ \frac{1}{3} \\ \frac{1}{3} \end{pmatrix}\right\|_2^2 = 0.0$$

$$\left\|\mu_{old}^2 - \mu^2\right\|_2^2 = \left\|\begin{pmatrix} 8.0 \\ 8.0 \\ 4.0 \end{pmatrix} - \begin{pmatrix} 8.0 \\ 8.0 \\ 4.0 \end{pmatrix}\right\|_2^2 = 0.0$$

$$\left\|\mu_{old}^3 - \mu^3\right\|_2^2 = \left\|\begin{pmatrix} 3 \\ \frac{5}{2} \\ \frac{1}{2} \end{pmatrix} - \begin{pmatrix} 3 \\ \frac{5}{2} \\ \frac{1}{2} \end{pmatrix}\right\|_2^2 = 0.0$$

Centroids changed. We need to do another iteration.

No centroid change, so the alogorithm converged.

---

c) Which k provides a better clustering in terms of sum of intra-cluster euclidean distances.

Solution:

For $k = 2$:

$$D_{intra-cluster} = \sum_{n=1}^{6} \sum_{c=1}^{2} p\left(C = c \mid \mathbf{x}^{(n)}\right) \left\| \mathbf{x}^{(n)} - \mu^c \right\|_2^2$$

$$= \left\| \begin{pmatrix} 1.0 \\ 0.0 \\ 0.0 \end{pmatrix} - \begin{pmatrix} \frac{7}{5} \\ \frac{6}{5} \\ \frac{2}{5} \end{pmatrix} \right\|_2^2 + \left\| \begin{pmatrix} 8.0 \\ 8.0 \\ 4.0 \end{pmatrix} - \begin{pmatrix} 8.0 \\ 8.0 \\ 4.0 \end{pmatrix} \right\|_2^2$$

$$+ \left\| \begin{pmatrix} 3.0 \\ 3.0 \\ 0.0 \end{pmatrix} - \begin{pmatrix} 3 \\ \frac{5}{2} \\ \frac{1}{2} \end{pmatrix} \right\|_2^2 + \left\| \begin{pmatrix} 0.0 \\ 0.0 \\ 1.0 \end{pmatrix} - \begin{pmatrix} \frac{7}{5} \\ \frac{6}{5} \\ \frac{2}{5} \end{pmatrix} \right\|_2^2$$

$$+ \left\| \begin{pmatrix} 0.0 \\ 1.0 \\ 0.0 \end{pmatrix} - \begin{pmatrix} \frac{7}{5} \\ \frac{6}{5} \\ \frac{2}{5} \end{pmatrix} \right\|_2^2 + \left\| \begin{pmatrix} 3.0 \\ 2.0 \\ 1.0 \end{pmatrix} - \begin{pmatrix} 3 \\ \frac{5}{2} \\ \frac{1}{2} \end{pmatrix} \right\|_2^2$$

$$= 1.76 + 0 + 5.96 + 3.76 + 2.16 + 3.56$$

$$= 17.2$$

For $k = 3$:

$$E = \sum_{n=1}^{6} \sum_{c=1}^{2} p\left(C = c \mid \mathbf{x}^{(n)}\right) \left\| \mathbf{x}^{(n)} - \mu^c \right\|_2^2$$

$$= \left\| \begin{pmatrix} 1.0 \\ 0.0 \\ 0.0 \end{pmatrix} - \begin{pmatrix} \frac{1}{3} \\ \frac{1}{3} \\ \frac{1}{3} \end{pmatrix} \right\|_2^2 + \left\| \begin{pmatrix} 8.0 \\ 8.0 \\ 4.0 \end{pmatrix} - \begin{pmatrix} 8.0 \\ 8.0 \\ 4.0 \end{pmatrix} \right\|_2^2$$

$$+ \left\| \begin{pmatrix} 3.0 \\ 3.0 \\ 0.0 \end{pmatrix} - \begin{pmatrix} \frac{7}{5} \\ \frac{6}{5} \\ \frac{2}{5} \end{pmatrix} \right\|_2^2 + \left\| \begin{pmatrix} 0.0 \\ 0.0 \\ 1.0 \end{pmatrix} - \begin{pmatrix} \frac{1}{3} \\ \frac{1}{3} \\ \frac{1}{3} \end{pmatrix} \right\|_2^2$$

$$+ \left\| \begin{pmatrix} 0.0 \\ 1.0 \\ 0.0 \end{pmatrix} - \begin{pmatrix} \frac{1}{3} \\ \frac{1}{3} \\ \frac{1}{3} \end{pmatrix} \right\|_2^2 + \left\| \begin{pmatrix} 3.0 \\ 2.0 \\ 1.0 \end{pmatrix} - \begin{pmatrix} \frac{7}{5} \\ \frac{6}{5} \\ \frac{2}{5} \end{pmatrix} \right\|_2^2$$

$$= 0.67 + 0 + 0.5 + 0.67 + 0.67 + 0.5$$

$$= 3.0$$

So, $k = 3$ has more tightly packed clusters which is in general better.

d) Which k provides a better clustering in terms of mean inter-cluster centroid distance.

Solution:

The mean distance between centroids can be computed as follows.

$$D_{inter-cluster} = \sum_{i=1}^{k}\sum_{j=1}^{k} \left\| \mu^i - \mu^j \right\|_2^2$$

So, for $k = 2$:

$$D_{inter-cluster} = \frac{1}{k^2}\sum_{i=1}^{k}\sum_{j=1}^{k} \left\| \mu^i - \mu^j \right\|_2^2$$

$$= \frac{1}{4}\left(0 + 102.76 + 0 + 102.76\right)$$

$$= 51.39$$

For $k = 3$:

$$D_{inter-cluster} = \frac{1}{k^2}\sum_{i=1}^{k}\sum_{j=1}^{k} \left\| \mu^i - \mu^j \right\|_2^2$$

$$= \frac{1}{9}\left(0 + 131 + 11.83 + 131 + 0 + 67.5 + 11.83 + 67.5 + 0\right)$$

$$= 46.67$$

Looks like $k = 3$ has better separated clusters which is in general better.

2 Expectation-Maximization Clustering

Like k-means, EM-clustering finds structure in a set of unlabeled data points. However, it does so in a probabilistic manner. As in k-means the goal is to assign a probability $p\left(C = c \mid \mathbf{x}^{(n)}\right)$ that a point belongs to a cluster. Yet, unlike k-means, in EM we allow for non-deterministic distributions. This means that a point does not necessarily belong to one cluster. It is a member of every cluster but with different degrees of probability.

To estimate this posterior probability, we use Bayes rule to decompose it into a prior $p\left(C = c\right)$ and likelihood $p\left(\mathbf{x}^{(n)} \mid C = c\right)$. So, we will use this two probabilities for each cluster as we go along.

To make things more specific, let us go through an example. The following figure presents the data set.

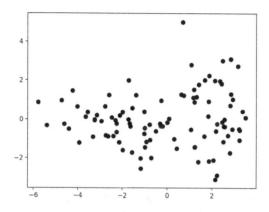

Analyzing it, we can see that there seem to be two distinct groups of points. For that reason, we will use $k = 2$ clusters. This is a key parameter. However, just like in k-means, it is not always easy to make this choice.

After choosing the number of clusters, we can start the algorithm.

Step 0: Initialize the clusters

The algorithm starts by initializing the likelihood and prior of each of the k clusters. In our example we will use two-dimensional Gaussians as likelihoods. However, the procedure can be generalized to other distributions. So, we start with uniform priors for each cluster ($p\left(C = 1\right) = p\left(C = 2\right) = 0.5$) and, for the likelihoods, we randomly choose the means and use identity matrix covariances. The following figure plots the likelihoods.

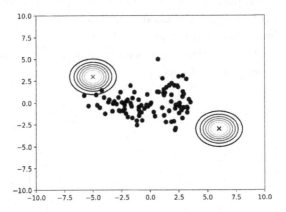

Having initialized the procedure, we can now start to iterate towards a solution. The iterative procedure is made by three steps.

Expectation Step: Assign points to clusters

With Bayes rule, we can write the posterior probability of each point belonging to each cluster as follows.

$$p\Big(C = c \mid \mathbf{x}^{(n)}\Big) = \frac{p\big(\mathbf{x}^{(n)} \mid C = c; \theta^c\big)p(C = c)}{p\big(\mathbf{x}^{(n)}\big)}$$

Applying this logic to our ongoing example, we get the figure below. Note that the strength of the color represents the probability that a point belongs to that cluster.

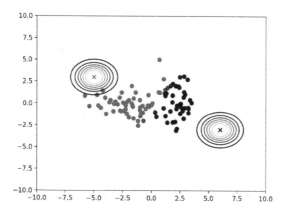

Having assigned probabilities to all points for all cluster, we can move on to the next step.

Maximization Step: Adjust cluster parameters

The posterior probability of a cluster for a given point represents how much that point contributes to estimate the distributions of that cluster. So, for instance, since we would estimate the prior of a cluster by counting the number of points in that cluster and dividing by the total number of points, we, instead sum and normalize the contributions of each point to that cluster as follows.

$$p\left(C = c\right) = \frac{\sum_{n=1}^{N} p\left(C = c \mid \mathbf{x}^{(n)}\right)}{\sum_{l=1}^{k} \sum_{n=1}^{N} p\left(C = l \mid \mathbf{x}^{(n)}\right)}$$

Specifically, if, for a given point, $p\left(C = 1 \mid \mathbf{x}^{(n)}\right) = 1$ then this point counts totally for cluster one and nothing to all other clusters. The same reasoning can be applied, in general, for the likelihoods. So, if the likelihood is defined by a parameter θ^c, then we estimated by averaging the contribution of each point to this parameter, weighted by the posterior probability that each point belongs to the cluster:

$$\theta^c = \frac{\sum_{n=1}^{N} p\left(C = c \mid \mathbf{x}^{(n)}\right) Contribution\left(\theta, \mathbf{x}^{(n)}\right)}{\sum_{n=1}^{N} p\left(C = c \mid \mathbf{x}^{(n)}\right)}$$

For example, for a multivariate gaussian, we have two parameters. For the mean, the contribution of each point is itself $x_i^{(n)}$. So, it can be estimated as:

$$\mu_i^c = \frac{\sum_{n=1}^{N} p\left(C = c \mid \mathbf{x}^{(n)}\right) Contribution\left(\mu_i, \mathbf{x}^{(n)}\right)}{\sum_{n=1}^{N} p\left(C = c \mid \mathbf{x}^{(n)}\right)}$$

$$\mu_i^c = \frac{\sum_{n=1}^{N} p\left(C = c \mid \mathbf{x}^{(n)}\right) \left[x_i^{(n)}\right]}{\sum_{n=1}^{N} p\left(C = c \mid \mathbf{x}^{(n)}\right)}$$

For position ij of the covariance matrix, the contribution of each point is the deviation from the dimensional means of its dimensions $\left(\mu_i^c - x_i^{(n)}\right)\left(\mu_j^c - x_j^{(n)}\right)$. So, it can be estimated as follows:

$$\Sigma_{ij}^c = \frac{\sum_{n=1}^{N} p\left(C = c \mid \mathbf{x}^{(n)}\right) Contribution\left(\Sigma_{ij}, \mathbf{x}^{(n)}\right)}{\sum_{n=1}^{N} p\left(C = c \mid \mathbf{x}^{(n)}\right)}$$

$$\Sigma_{ij}^c = \frac{\sum_{n=1}^{N} p\left(C = c \mid \mathbf{x}^{(n)}\right) \left[\left(\mu_i^c - x_i^{(n)}\right)\left(\mu_j^c - x_j^{(n)}\right)\right]}{\sum_{n=1}^{N} p\left(C = c \mid \mathbf{x}^{(n)}\right)}$$

As we can see below, the clusters are now more suited to the points that were assigned to them.

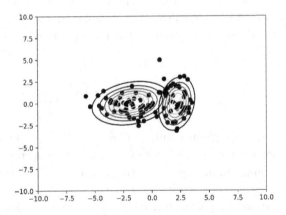

This terminates the M-step. Afterwards, the algorithm checks for convergence by seeing if any parameters changed. If they did not, then it terminates. If they did, then it goes back to the E-step. For curiosity, the next E-step would yield the follwoing probabilities.

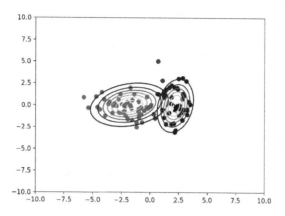

1)

Consider the following training data with boolean features:

$$\left\{ \mathbf{x}^{(1)} = \begin{pmatrix} 1 \\ 0 \\ 0 \\ 0 \end{pmatrix}, \mathbf{x}^{(2)} = \begin{pmatrix} 0 \\ 1 \\ 1 \\ 1 \end{pmatrix}, \mathbf{x}^{(3)} = \begin{pmatrix} 0 \\ 1 \\ 0 \\ 1 \end{pmatrix}, \mathbf{x}^{(4)} = \begin{pmatrix} 0 \\ 0 \\ 1 \\ 0 \end{pmatrix}, \mathbf{x}^{(5)} = \begin{pmatrix} 1 \\ 1 \\ 0 \\ 0 \end{pmatrix} \right\}$$

We want to model the data with three clusters. Initialize all priors uniformly and initialize using the following table:

	$p(x_1 = 1 \mid C = c)$	$p(x_2 = 1 \mid C = c)$	$p(x_3 = 1 \mid C = c)$	$p(x_4 = 1 \mid C = c)$
$c = 1$	0.8	0.5	0.1	0.1
$c = 2$	0.1	0.5	0.4	0.8
$c = 3$	0.1	0.1	0.9	0.2

Assume all features are conditionally independent given the cluster.

a) Perform one expectation maximization iteration.

Solution:

The question tells us that all features are conditionally independent given the cluster. So, we can write the likelihoods as follows:

$$p(\mathbf{x} \mid C = 1) = p(x_1 \mid C = 1)\, p(x_2 \mid C = 1)\, p(x_3 \mid C = 1)\, p(x_4 \mid C = 1)$$

Furthermore, the questions tells us that all distributions are initialized uniformly. So, we will have priors:

$$p\left(C=1\right)=\frac{1}{3}$$

$$p\left(C=2\right)=\frac{1}{3}$$

$$p\left(C=3\right)=\frac{1}{3}$$

And for the likelihoods:

	$p\left(x_1=1\mid C=c\right)$	$p\left(x_2=1\mid C=c\right)$	$p\left(x_3=1\mid C=c\right)$	$p\left(x_4=1\mid C=c\right)$
$c=1$	0.8	0.5	0.1	0.1
$c=2$	0.1	0.5	0.4	0.8
$c=3$	0.1	0.1	0.9	0.2

Which means:

	$p\left(x_1=0\mid C=c\right)$	$p\left(x_2=0\mid C=c\right)$	$p\left(x_3=0\mid C=c\right)$	$p\left(x_4=0\mid C=c\right)$
$c=1$	0.2	0.5	0.9	0.9
$c=2$	0.9	0.5	0.6	0.2
$c=3$	0.9	0.9	0.1	0.8

Each iteration has two steps. Let us do one:

E-Step: Assign each point to the cluster that yields higher posterior

- For $\mathbf{x}^{(1)}$:
  - For cluster $C=1$:
    * Prior: $p\left(C=1\right)=\frac{1}{3}$
    * Likelihood:
      $p\left(\mathbf{x}^{(1)}\mid C=1\right)=$
      $p\left(x_1^{(1)}=1\mid C=1\right)p\left(x_2^{(1)}=0\mid C=1\right)p\left(x_3^{(1)}=0\mid C=1\right)p\left(x_4^{(1)}=0\mid C=1\right)$ $=$
      $0.8\times0.5\times0.9\times0.9=0.324$
    * Joint Probability: $p\left(C=1\mid\mathbf{x}^{(1)}\right)=p(C=1)\,p\left(\mathbf{x}^{(1)}\mid C=1\right)=\frac{1}{3}\times0.324=0.108$
  - For cluster $C=2$:
    * Prior: $p\left(C=2\right)=\frac{1}{3}$
    * Likelihood:
      $p\left(\mathbf{x}^{(1)}\mid C=2\right)=$
      $p\left(x_1^{(1)}=1\mid C=2\right)p\left(x_2^{(1)}=0\mid C=2\right)p\left(x_3^{(1)}=0\mid C=2\right)p\left(x_4^{(1)}=0\mid C=2\right)$ $=$
      $0.1\times0.5\times0.6\times0.2=0.006$
    * Joint Probability: $p\left(C=2,\mathbf{x}^{(1)}\right)=p(C=2)\,p\left(\mathbf{x}^{(1)}\mid C=2\right)=\frac{1}{3}\times0.006=0.002$
  - For cluster $C=3$:
    * Prior: $p\left(C=3\right)=\frac{1}{3}$
    * Likelihood:
      $p\left(\mathbf{x}^{(1)}\mid C=3\right)=$
      $p\left(x_1^{(1)}=1\mid C=3\right)p\left(x_2^{(1)}=0\mid C=3\right)p\left(x_3^{(1)}=0\mid C=3\right)p\left(x_4^{(1)}=0\mid C=3\right)$ $=$
      $0.1\times0.9\times0.1\times0.8=0.0072$
    * Joint Probability: $p\left(C=3,\mathbf{x}^{(1)}\right)=p(C=3)\,p\left(\mathbf{x}^{(1)}\mid C=3\right)=\frac{1}{3}\times0.0072=0.0024$
  - So, we can compute the normalized posteriors for each cluster:

* $C = 1$: $p\left(C=1\mid \mathbf{x}^{(1)}\right) = \dfrac{p\left(C-1,\mathbf{x}^{(1)}\right)}{p\left(C=1,\mathbf{x}^{(1)}\right)+p\left(C=2,\mathbf{x}^{(1)}\right)+p\left(C=3,\mathbf{x}^{(1)}\right)} =$

$\dfrac{0.108}{0.108+0.002+0.0024} = 0.961$

* $C = 2$: $p\left(C=2\mid \mathbf{x}^{(1)}\right) = \dfrac{p\left(C=2,\mathbf{x}^{(1)}\right)}{p\left(C=1,\mathbf{x}^{(1)}\right)+p\left(C=2,\mathbf{x}^{(1)}\right)+p\left(C=3,\mathbf{x}^{(1)}\right)} =$

$\dfrac{0.002}{0.108+0.002+0.0024} = 0.018$

* $C = 3$: $p\left(C=3\mid \mathbf{x}^{(1)}\right) = \dfrac{p\left(C=3,\mathbf{x}^{(1)}\right)}{p\left(C=1,\mathbf{x}^{(1)}\right)+p\left(C=2,\mathbf{x}^{(1)}\right)+p\left(C=3,\mathbf{x}^{(1)}\right)} =$

$\dfrac{0.0024}{0.108+0.002+0.0024} = 0.021$

- For $\mathbf{x}^{(2)}$:
  - For cluster $C = 1$:
    * Prior: $p\left(C=1\right) = \frac{1}{3}$
    * Likelihood:
      $p\left(\mathbf{x}^{(2)} \mid C=1\right) =$
      $p\left(x_1^{(2)}=0\mid C=1\right)p\left(x_2^{(2)}=1\mid C=1\right)p\left(x_3^{(2)}=1\mid C=1\right)p\left(x_4^{(2)}=1\mid C=1\right) =$
      $0.2\times0.5\times0.1\times0.1 = 0.001$
    * Joint Probability: $p\left(C=1\mid \mathbf{x}^{(1)}\right) = p\left(C=1\right)p\left(\mathbf{x}^{(1)}\mid C=1\right) = \frac{1}{3}\times0.001 = 0.0003$
  - For cluster $C = 2$:
    * Prior: $p\left(C=2\right) = \frac{1}{3}$
    * Likelihood:
      $p\left(\mathbf{x}^{(2)} \mid C=2\right) =$
      $p\left(x_1^{(2)}=0\mid C=2\right)p\left(x_2^{(2)}=1\mid C=2\right)p\left(x_3^{(2)}=1\mid C=2\right)p\left(x_4^{(2)}=1\mid C=2\right) =$
      $0.9\times0.5\times0.4\times0.8 = 0.144$
    * Joint Probability: $p\left(C=2,\mathbf{x}^{(1)}\right) = p\left(C=2\right)p\left(\mathbf{x}^{(1)}\mid C=2\right) = \frac{1}{3}\times0.144 = 0.048$
  - For cluster $C = 3$:
    * Prior: $p\left(C=3\right) = \frac{1}{3}$
    * Likelihood:
      $p\left(\mathbf{x}^{(2)} \mid C=3\right) =$
      $p\left(x_1^{(2)}=0\mid C=3\right)p\left(x_2^{(2)}=1\mid C=3\right)p\left(x_3^{(2)}=1\mid C=3\right)p\left(x_4^{(2)}=1\mid C=3\right) =$
      $0.9\times0.1\times0.9\times0.2 = 0.0162$
    * Joint Probability: $p\left(C=3,\mathbf{x}^{(1)}\right) = p\left(C=3\right)p\left(\mathbf{x}^{(1)}\mid C=3\right) = \frac{1}{3}\times0.0162 = 0.0054$
  - So, we can compute the normalized posteriors for each cluster:

    * $C = 1$: $p\left(C=1\mid \mathbf{x}^{(2)}\right) = \dfrac{p\left(C=1,\mathbf{x}^{(2)}\right)}{p\left(C=1,\mathbf{x}^{(2)}\right)+p\left(C=2,\mathbf{x}^{(2)}\right)+p\left(C=3,\mathbf{x}^{(2)}\right)} =$

    $\dfrac{0.0003}{0.0003+0.048+0.0054} = 0.006$

    * $C = 2$: $p\left(C=2\mid \mathbf{x}^{(2)}\right) = \dfrac{p\left(C=2,\mathbf{x}^{(2)}\right)}{p\left(C=1,\mathbf{x}^{(2)}\right)+p\left(C=2,\mathbf{x}^{(2)}\right)+p\left(C=3,\mathbf{x}^{(2)}\right)} =$

    $\dfrac{0.048}{0.0003+0.048+0.0054} = 0.894$

    * $C = 3$: $p\left(C=3\mid \mathbf{x}^{(2)}\right) = \dfrac{p\left(C=3,\mathbf{x}^{(2)}\right)}{p\left(C=1,\mathbf{x}^{(2)}\right)+p\left(C=2,\mathbf{x}^{(2)}\right)+p\left(C=3,\mathbf{x}^{(2)}\right)} =$

    $\dfrac{0.0054}{0.0003+0.048+0.0054} = 0.100$

- For $\mathbf{x}^{(3)}$:
  - For cluster $C = 1$:
    * Prior: $p\left(C=1\right) = \frac{1}{3}$
    * Likelihood:
      $p\left(\mathbf{x}^{(3)} \mid C=1\right) =$
      $p\left(x_1^{(3)}=0\mid C=1\right)p\left(x_2^{(3)}=1\mid C=1\right)p\left(x_3^{(3)}=0\mid C=1\right)p\left(x_4^{(3)}=1\mid C=1\right) =$
      $0.2\times0.5\times0.9\times0.1 = 0.009$
    * Joint Probability: $p\left(C=1,\mathbf{x}^{(3)}\right) = p\left(C=1\right)p\left(\mathbf{x}^{(3)}\mid C=1\right) = \frac{1}{3}\times0.009 = 0.003$
  - For cluster $C = 2$:
    * Prior: $p\left(C=2\right) = \frac{1}{3}$
    * Likelihood:
      $p\left(\mathbf{x}^{(3)} \mid C=2\right) =$
      $p\left(x_1^{(3)}=0\mid C=2\right)p\left(x_2^{(3)}=1\mid C=2\right)p\left(x_3^{(3)}=0\mid C=2\right)p\left(x_4^{(3)}=1\mid C=2\right) =$
      $0.9\times0.5\times0.6\times0.8 = 0.216$

* Joint Probability: $p\left(C = 2, \mathbf{x}^{(3)}\right) = p\left(C = 2\right) p\left(\mathbf{x}^{(3)} \mid C = 2\right) = \frac{1}{3} \times 0.216 = 0.072$

– For cluster $C = 3$:

* Prior: $p\left(C = 3\right) = \frac{1}{3}$
* Likelihood:
  $p\left(\mathbf{x}^{(3)} \mid C = 3\right) =$
  $p\left(x_1^{(3)} = 0 \mid C = 3\right) p\left(x_2^{(3)} = 1 \mid C = 3\right) p\left(x_3^{(3)} = 0 \mid C = 3\right) p\left(x_4^{(3)} = 1 \mid C = 3\right) \quad =$
  $0.9 \times 0.1 \times 0.1 \times 0.2 = 0.0018$
* Joint Probability: $p\left(C = 3, \mathbf{x}^{(3)}\right) = p\left(C = 3\right) p\left(\mathbf{x}^{(3)} \mid C = 3\right) = \frac{1}{3} \times 0.0018 = 0.0006$

– So, we can compute the normalized posteriors for each cluster:

* $C \quad = \quad 1: \quad p\left(C = 1 \mid \mathbf{x}^{(3)}\right) \quad = \quad \dfrac{p\left(C=1, \mathbf{x}^{(3)}\right)}{p\left(C=1, \mathbf{x}^{(3)}\right) + p\left(C=2, \mathbf{x}^{(3)}\right) + p\left(C=3, \mathbf{x}^{(3)}\right)} \quad =$

  $\dfrac{0.003}{0.003 + 0.072 + 0.0006} = 0.0397$

* $C \quad = \quad 2: \quad p\left(C = 2 \mid \mathbf{x}^{(3)}\right) \quad = \quad \dfrac{p\left(C=2, \mathbf{x}^{(3)}\right)}{p\left(C=1, \mathbf{x}^{(3)}\right) + p\left(C=2, \mathbf{x}^{(3)}\right) + p\left(C=3, \mathbf{x}^{(3)}\right)} \quad =$

  $\dfrac{0.072}{0.003 + 0.072 + 0.0006} = 0.9524$

* $C \quad = \quad 3: \quad p\left(C = 3 \mid \mathbf{x}^{(3)}\right) \quad = \quad \dfrac{p\left(C=3, \mathbf{x}^{(3)}\right)}{p\left(C=1, \mathbf{x}^{(3)}\right) + p\left(C=2, \mathbf{x}^{(3)}\right) + p\left(C=3, \mathbf{x}^{(3)}\right)} \quad =$

  $\dfrac{0.0006}{0.003 + 0.072 + 0.0006} = 0.0079$

- For $\mathbf{x}^{(4)}$:

  – For cluster $C = 1$:

  * Prior: $p\left(C = 1\right) = \frac{1}{3}$
  * Likelihood:
    $p\left(\mathbf{x}^{(4)} \mid C = 1\right) =$
    $p\left(x_1^{(4)} = 0 \mid C = 1\right) p\left(x_2^{(4)} = 0 \mid C = 1\right) p\left(x_3^{(4)} = 1 \mid C = 1\right) p\left(x_4^{(4)} = 0 \mid C = 1\right) \quad =$
    $0.2 \times 0.5 \times 0.1 \times 0.9 = 0.009$
  * Joint Probability: $p\left(C = 1, \mathbf{x}^{(4)}\right) = p\left(C = 1\right) p\left(\mathbf{x}^{(4)} \mid C = 1\right) = \frac{1}{3} \times 0.009 = 0.003$

  – For cluster $C = 2$:

  * Prior: $p\left(C = 2\right) = \frac{1}{3}$
  * Likelihood:
    $p\left(\mathbf{x}^{(4)} \mid C = 2\right) =$
    $p\left(x_1^{(4)} = 0 \mid C = 2\right) p\left(x_2^{(4)} = 0 \mid C = 2\right) p\left(x_3^{(4)} = 1 \mid C = 2\right) p\left(x_4^{(4)} = 0 \mid C = 2\right) \quad =$
    $0.9 \times 0.5 \times 0.4 \times 0.2 = 0.036$
  * Joint Probability: $p\left(C = 2, \mathbf{x}^{(4)}\right) = p\left(C = 2\right) p\left(\mathbf{x}^{(4)} \mid C = 2\right) = \frac{1}{3} \times 0.036 = 0.012$

  – For cluster $C = 3$:

  * Prior: $p\left(C = 3\right) = \frac{1}{3}$
  * Likelihood:
    $p\left(\mathbf{x}^{(4)} \mid C = 3\right) =$
    $p\left(x_1^{(4)} = 0 \mid C = 3\right) p\left(x_2^{(4)} = 0 \mid C = 3\right) p\left(x_3^{(4)} = 1 \mid C = 3\right) p\left(x_4^{(4)} = 0 \mid C = 3\right) \quad =$
    $0.9 \times 0.9 \times 0.9 \times 0.8 = 0.5832$
  * Joint Probability: $p\left(C = 3, \mathbf{x}^{(4)}\right) = p\left(C = 3\right) p\left(\mathbf{x}^{(4)} \mid C = 3\right) = \frac{1}{3} \times 0.5832 = 0.1944$

  – So, we can compute the normalized posteriors for each cluster:

  * $C \quad = \quad 1: \quad p\left(C = 1 \mid \mathbf{x}^{(4)}\right) \quad = \quad \dfrac{p\left(C=1, \mathbf{x}^{(4)}\right)}{p\left(C=1, \mathbf{x}^{(4)}\right) + p\left(C=2, \mathbf{x}^{(4)}\right) + p\left(C=3, \mathbf{x}^{(4)}\right)} \quad =$

    $\dfrac{0.003}{0.003 + 0.012 + 0.1944} = 0.0143$

  * $C \quad = \quad 2: \quad p\left(C = 2 \mid \mathbf{x}^{(4)}\right) \quad = \quad \dfrac{p\left(C=2, \mathbf{x}^{(4)}\right)}{p\left(C=1, \mathbf{x}^{(4)}\right) + p\left(C=2, \mathbf{x}^{(4)}\right) + p\left(C=3, \mathbf{x}^{(4)}\right)} \quad =$

    $\dfrac{0.012}{0.003 + 0.012 + 0.1944} = 0.0573$

  * $C \quad = \quad 3: \quad p\left(C = 3 \mid \mathbf{x}^{(4)}\right) \quad = \quad \dfrac{p\left(C=3, \mathbf{x}^{(4)}\right)}{p\left(C=1, \mathbf{x}^{(4)}\right) + p\left(C=2, \mathbf{x}^{(4)}\right) + p\left(C=3, \mathbf{x}^{(4)}\right)} \quad =$

    $\dfrac{0.1944}{0.003 + 0.012 + 0.1944} = 0.9284$

- For $\mathbf{x}^{(5)}$:

  – For cluster $C = 1$:

  * Prior: $p\left(C = 1\right) = \frac{1}{3}$

* Likelihood:
  $p\left(\mathbf{x}^{(5)} \mid C = 1\right) =$

  $p\left(x_1^{(5)} = 1 \mid C = 1\right) p\left(x_2^{(5)} = 1 \mid C = 1\right) p\left(x_3^{(5)} = 0 \mid C = 1\right) p\left(x_4^{(5)} = 0 \mid C = 1\right)$ =
  $0.8 \times 0.5 \times 0.9 \times 0.9 = 0.324$
* Joint Probability: $p\left(C = 1, \mathbf{x}^{(5)}\right) = p\left(C = 1\right) p\left(\mathbf{x}^{(5)} \mid C = 1\right) = \frac{1}{3} \times 0.324 = 0.108$

− For cluster $C = 2$:

* Prior: $p\left(C = 2\right) = \frac{1}{3}$
* Likelihood:
  $p\left(\mathbf{x}^{(5)} \mid C = 2\right) =$

  $p\left(x_1^{(5)} = 1 \mid C = 2\right) p\left(x_2^{(5)} = 1 \mid C = 2\right) p\left(x_3^{(5)} = 0 \mid C = 2\right) p\left(x_4^{(5)} = 0 \mid C = 2\right)$ =
  $0.1 \times 0.5 \times 0.6 \times 0.2 = 0.006$
* Joint Probability: $p\left(C = 2, \mathbf{x}^{(5)}\right) = p\left(C = 2\right) p\left(\mathbf{x}^{(5)} \mid C = 2\right) = \frac{1}{3} \times 0.006 = 0.002$

− For cluster $C = 3$:

* Prior: $p\left(C = 3\right) = \frac{1}{3}$
* Likelihood:
  $p\left(\mathbf{x}^{(5)} \mid C = 3\right) =$

  $p\left(x_1^{(5)} = 1 \mid C = 3\right) p\left(x_2^{(5)} = 1 \mid C = 3\right) p\left(x_3^{(5)} = 0 \mid C = 3\right) p\left(x_4^{(5)} = 0 \mid C = 3\right)$ =
  $0.1 \times 0.1 \times 0.1 \times 0.8 = 0.0008$
* Joint Probability: $p\left(C = 3, \mathbf{x}^{(5)}\right) = p\left(C = 3\right) p\left(\mathbf{x}^{(5)} \mid C = 3\right) = \frac{1}{3} \times 0.0008 = 0.000267$

− So, we can compute the normalized posteriors for each cluster:

* $C = 1$: $p\left(C = 1 \mid \mathbf{x}^{(5)}\right) = \dfrac{p\left(C=1,\mathbf{x}^{(5)}\right)}{p\left(C=1,\mathbf{x}^{(5)}\right)+p\left(C=2,\mathbf{x}^{(5)}\right)+p\left(C=3,\mathbf{x}^{(5)}\right)}$ =
  $\dfrac{0.108}{0.108+0.002+0.000267} = 0.9795$

* $C = 2$: $p\left(C = 2 \mid \mathbf{x}^{(5)}\right) = \dfrac{p\left(C=2,\mathbf{x}^{(5)}\right)}{p\left(C=1,\mathbf{x}^{(5)}\right)+p\left(C=2,\mathbf{x}^{(5)}\right)+p\left(C=3,\mathbf{x}^{(5)}\right)}$ =
  $\dfrac{0.002}{0.108+0.002+0.000267} = 0.0181$

* $C = 3$: $p\left(C = 3 \mid \mathbf{x}^{(5)}\right) = \dfrac{p\left(C=3,\mathbf{x}^{(5)}\right)}{p\left(C=1,\mathbf{x}^{(5)}\right)+p\left(C=2,\mathbf{x}^{(5)}\right)+p\left(C=3,\mathbf{x}^{(5)}\right)}$ =
  $\dfrac{0.000267}{0.108+0.002+0.000267} = 0.0024$

M-Step: Re-estimate cluster parameters such that they fit their assigned elements

For each cluster we need to find the new prior and likelihood parameters. For each likelihood, we compute count and normalize occurrences for each cluster, weigthed by the corresponding posterior:

$$p\left(x_l = 1 \mid C = c\right) = \frac{\sum_{n=1}^{3} p\left(C = c \mid \mathbf{x}^{(n)}\right) \mathbb{I}\left[x_l^{(n)} = 1\right]}{\sum_{n=1}^{3} p\left(C = c \mid \mathbf{x}^{(n)}\right)}$$

For the priors we perform a weighted mean of the posteriors:

$$p\left(C = c\right) = \frac{\sum_{n=1}^{N} p\left(C = c \mid \mathbf{x}^{(n)}\right)}{\sum_{l=1}^{k} \sum_{n=1}^{N} p\left(C = l \mid \mathbf{x}^{(n)}\right)}$$

So, let us estimate the new parameters for each cluster.

• For $C = 1$:

  − For the likelihood:

* $p(x_1 = 1 \mid C = 1) =$
$\frac{0.961 \times 1 + 0.006 \times 0 + 0.0397 \times 0 + 0.0143 \times 0 + 0.9795 \times 1}{0.961 + 0.006 + 0.0397 + 0.0143 + 0.9795} = 0.97$

* $p(x_2 = 1 \mid C = 1) =$
$\frac{0.961 \times 0 + 0.006 \times 1 + 0.0397 \times 1 + 0.0143 \times 0 + 0.9795 \times 1}{0.961 + 0.006 + 0.0397 + 0.0143 + 0.9795} = 0.51$

* $p(x_3 = 1 \mid C = 1) =$
$\frac{0.961 \times 0 + 0.006 \times 1 + 0.0397 \times 0 + 0.0143 \times 1 + 0.9795 \times 0}{0.961 + 0.006 + 0.0397 + 0.0143 + 0.9795} = 0.01$

* $p(x_4 = 1 \mid C = 1) =$
$\frac{0.961 \times 0 + 0.006 \times 1 + 0.0397 \times 1 + 0.0143 \times 0 + 0.9795 \times 0}{0.961 + 0.006 + 0.0397 + 0.0143 + 0.9795} = 0.02$

– For the prior:

$$p(C = 1) = \frac{0.961 + 0.006 + 0.0397 + 0.0143 + 0.9795}{2.005 + 1.9397 + 1.0597} = 0.4$$

with

$$2.005 = 0.961 + 0.006 + 0.0397 + 0.0143 + 0.9795,$$

$$1.9397 = 0.018 + 0.894 + 0.9524 + 0.0573 + 0.0181,$$

$$1.0597 = 0.021 + 0.1 + 0.0079 + 0.9284 + 0.0024.$$

• For $C = 2$:

– For the likelihood:

* $p(x_1 = 1 \mid C = 2) =$
$\frac{0.018 \times 1 + 0.894 \times 0 + 0.9524 \times 0 + 0.0573 \times 0 + 0.0181 \times 1}{0.018 + 0.894 + 0.9524 + 0.0573 + 0.0181} = 0.0186$

* $p(x_2 = 1 \mid C = 2) =$
$\frac{0.018 \times 0 + 0.894 \times 1 + 0.9524 \times 1 + 0.0573 \times 0 + 0.0181 \times 1}{0.018 + 0.894 + 0.9524 + 0.0573 + 0.0181} = 0.9612$

* $p(x_3 = 1 \mid C = 2) =$
$\frac{0.018 \times 0 + 0.894 \times 1 + 0.9524 \times 0 + 0.0573 \times 1 + 0.0181 \times 0}{0.018 + 0.894 + 0.9524 + 0.0573 + 0.0181} = 0.4904$

* $p(x_4 = 1 \mid C = 2) =$
$\frac{0.018 \times 0 + 0.894 \times 1 + 0.9524 \times 1 + 0.0573 \times 0 + 0.0181 \times 0}{0.018 + 0.894 + 0.9524 + 0.0573 + 0.0181} = 0.9519$

– For the prior:

$$p(C = 2) = \frac{0.018 + 0.894 + 0.9524 + 0.0573 + 0.0181}{2.005 + 1.9397 + 1.0597} = 0.39$$

• For $C = 3$:

– For the likelihood:

* $p(x_1 = 1 \mid C = 3) = \frac{0.021 \times 1 + 0.1 \times 0 + 0.0079 \times 0 + 0.9284 \times 0 + 0.0024 \times 1}{0.021 + 0.1 + 0.0079 + 0.9284 + 0.0024} = 0.0221$

* $p(x_2 = 1 \mid C = 3) = \frac{0.021 \times 0 + 0.1 \times 1 + 0.0079 \times 1 + 0.9284 \times 0 + 0.0024 \times 1}{0.021 + 0.1 + 0.0079 + 0.9284 + 0.0024} = 0.1041$

* $p(x_3 = 1 \mid C = 3) = \frac{0.021 \times 0 + 0.1 \times 1 + 0.0079 \times 0 + 0.9284 \times 1 + 0.0024 \times 0}{0.021 + 0.1 + 0.0079 + 0.9284 + 0.0024} = 0.9705$

* $p(x_4 = 1 \mid C = 3) = \frac{0.021 \times 0 + 0.1 \times 1 + 0.0079 \times 1 + 0.9284 \times 0 + 0.0024 \times 0}{0.021 + 0.1 + 0.0079 + 0.9284 + 0.0024} = 0.1018$

- For the prior:

$$p(C = 3) = \frac{0.021 + 0.1 + 0.0079 + 0.9284 + 0.0024}{2.005 + 1.9397 + 1.0597} = 0.21$$

Having the new priors and likelihoods we could go for another iteration. However, the exercise only asks for one.

---

b) Verify that after one iteration the probability of the data increased.

Solution:

The probability of the observed data $p\left(\mathbf{x}^{(1)}, \mathbf{x}^{(2)}, \mathbf{x}^{(3)}, \mathbf{x}^{(4)}, \mathbf{x}^{(5)}\right)$ can be decomposed into the product of the probability of each point assuming indepent, identically distributed samples:

$$p\left(\mathbf{x}^{(1)}, \mathbf{x}^{(2)}, \mathbf{x}^{(3)}, \mathbf{x}^{(4)}, \mathbf{x}^{(5)}\right) = p\left(\mathbf{x}^{(1)}\right) p\left(\mathbf{x}^{(2)}\right) p\left(\mathbf{x}^{(3)}\right) p\left(\mathbf{x}^{(4)}\right) p\left(\mathbf{x}^{(5)}\right)$$

So, we need to compute the probability of each point before and after the EM update.

By the law of total probability we have that:

$$p\left(\mathbf{x}^{(n)}\right) = p\left(\mathbf{x}^{(n)}, C = 1\right) + p\left(\mathbf{x}^{(n)}, C = 2\right) + p\left(\mathbf{x}^{(n)}, C = 3\right)$$

Which can be rewritten as follows:

$$p\left(\mathbf{x}^{(n)}\right) = p(C = 1) p\left(\mathbf{x}^{(n)} \mid C = 1\right) + p(C = 2) p\left(\mathbf{x}^{(n)} \mid C = 2\right) +$$

$$+ p(C = 3) p\left(\mathbf{x}^{(n)} \mid C = 3\right)$$

With that in mind let us analyze each scenario. Before the iteration we had:

$$
\begin{array}{cc}
 & p(C = c) \\
c = 1 & \frac{1}{3} \\
c = 2 & \frac{1}{3} \\
c = 3 & \frac{1}{3}
\end{array}
$$

	$p(x_1=1 \mid C=c)$	$p(x_2=1 \mid C=c)$	$p(x_3=1 \mid C=c)$	$p(x_4=1 \mid C=c)$
$c=1$	0.8	0.5	0.1	0.1
$c=2$	0.1	0.5	0.4	0.8
$c=3$	0.1	0.1	0.9	0.2

- For $\mathbf{x}^{(1)}$:
  - Likelihood:
    $p\left(\mathbf{x}^{(1)} \mid C=1\right) =$
    $p\left(x_1^{(1)} = 1 \mid C = 1\right) p\left(x_2^{(1)} = 0 \mid C = 1\right) p\left(x_3^{(1)} = 0 \mid C = 1\right) p\left(x_4^{(1)} = 0 \mid C = 1\right) =$
    0.324
  - Likelihood:
    $p\left(\mathbf{x}^{(1)} \mid C=2\right) =$
    $p\left(x_1^{(1)} = 1 \mid C = 2\right) p\left(x_2^{(1)} = 0 \mid C = 2\right) p\left(x_3^{(1)} = 0 \mid C = 2\right) p\left(x_4^{(1)} = 0 \mid C = 2\right) =$
    0.006
  - Likelihood:
    $p\left(\mathbf{x}^{(1)} \mid C=3\right) =$
    $p\left(x_1^{(1)} = 1 \mid C = 3\right) p\left(x_2^{(1)} = 0 \mid C = 3\right) p\left(x_3^{(1)} = 0 \mid C = 3\right) p\left(x_4^{(1)} = 0 \mid C = 3\right) =$
    0.0072
  - Probability: $p\left(\mathbf{x}^{(1)}\right) = \frac{1}{3}0.324 + \frac{1}{3}0.006 + \frac{1}{3}0.0072 = 0.1124$

- For $\mathbf{x}^{(2)}$:
  - Likelihood:
    $p\left(\mathbf{x}^{(2)} \mid C=1\right) =$
    $p\left(x_1^{(2)} = 0 \mid C = 1\right) p\left(x_2^{(2)} = 1 \mid C = 1\right) p\left(x_3^{(2)} = 1 \mid C = 1\right) p\left(x_4^{(2)} = 1 \mid C = 1\right) =$
    0.001
  - Likelihood:
    $p\left(\mathbf{x}^{(2)} \mid C=2\right) =$
    $p\left(x_1^{(2)} = 0 \mid C = 2\right) p\left(x_2^{(2)} = 1 \mid C = 2\right) p\left(x_3^{(2)} = 1 \mid C = 2\right) p\left(x_4^{(2)} = 1 \mid C = 2\right) =$
    $0.9 \times 0.5 \times 0.4 \times 0.8 = 0.144$
  - Likelihood:
    $p\left(\mathbf{x}^{(2)} \mid C=3\right) =$
    $p\left(x_1^{(2)} = 0 \mid C = 3\right) p\left(x_2^{(2)} = 1 \mid C = 3\right) p\left(x_3^{(2)} = 1 \mid C = 3\right) p\left(x_4^{(2)} = 1 \mid C = 3\right) =$
    $0.9 \times 0.1 \times 0.9 \times 0.2 = 0.0162$
  - Probability: $p\left(\mathbf{x}^{(2)}\right) = \frac{1}{3}0.001 + \frac{1}{3}0.144 + \frac{1}{3}0.0162 = 0.0537$

- For $\mathbf{x}^{(3)}$:
  - Likelihood:
    $p\left(\mathbf{x}^{(3)} \mid C=1\right) =$
    $p\left(x_1^{(3)} = 0 \mid C = 1\right) p\left(x_2^{(3)} = 1 \mid C = 1\right) p\left(x_3^{(3)} = 0 \mid C = 1\right) p\left(x_4^{(3)} = 1 \mid C = 1\right) =$
    $0.2 \times 0.5 \times 0.9 \times 0.1 = 0.009$
  - Likelihood:
    $p\left(\mathbf{x}^{(3)} \mid C=2\right) =$
    $p\left(x_1^{(3)} = 0 \mid C = 2\right) p\left(x_2^{(3)} = 1 \mid C = 2\right) p\left(x_3^{(3)} = 0 \mid C = 2\right) p\left(x_4^{(3)} = 1 \mid C = 2\right) =$
    $0.9 \times 0.5 \times 0.6 \times 0.8 = 0.216$
  - Likelihood:
    $p\left(\mathbf{x}^{(3)} \mid C=3\right) =$
    $p\left(x_1^{(3)} = 0 \mid C = 3\right) p\left(x_2^{(3)} = 1 \mid C = 3\right) p\left(x_3^{(3)} = 0 \mid C = 3\right) p\left(x_4^{(3)} = 1 \mid C = 3\right) =$
    $0.9 \times 0.1 \times 0.1 \times 0.2 = 0.0018$

- Probability: $p\left(\mathbf{x}^{(1)}\right) = \frac{1}{3}0.009 + \frac{1}{3}0.216 + \frac{1}{3}0.0018 = 0.0756$

- For $\mathbf{x}^{(4)}$:
  - Likelihood:
    $p\left(\mathbf{x}^{(4)} \mid C = 1\right) =$
    $p\left(x_1^{(4)} = 0 \mid C = 1\right) p\left(x_2^{(4)} = 0 \mid C = 1\right) p\left(x_3^{(4)} = 1 \mid C = 1\right) p\left(x_4^{(4)} = 0 \mid C = 1\right) =$
    $0.2 \times 0.5 \times 0.1 \times 0.9 = 0.009$
  - Likelihood:
    $p\left(\mathbf{x}^{(4)} \mid C = 2\right) =$
    $p\left(x_1^{(4)} = 0 \mid C = 2\right) p\left(x_2^{(4)} = 0 \mid C = 2\right) p\left(x_3^{(4)} = 1 \mid C = 2\right) p\left(x_4^{(4)} = 0 \mid C = 2\right) =$
    $0.9 \times 0.5 \times 0.4 \times 0.2 = 0.036$
  - Likelihood:
    $p\left(\mathbf{x}^{(4)} \mid C = 3\right) =$
    $p\left(x_1^{(4)} = 0 \mid C = 3\right) p\left(x_2^{(4)} = 0 \mid C = 3\right) p\left(x_3^{(4)} = 1 \mid C = 3\right) p\left(x_4^{(4)} = 0 \mid C = 3\right) =$
    $0.9 \times 0.9 \times 0.9 \times 0.8 = 0.5832$
  - Probability: $p\left(\mathbf{x}^{(1)}\right) = \frac{1}{3}0.009 + \frac{1}{3}0.036 + \frac{1}{3}0.5832 = 0.2094$

- For $\mathbf{x}^{(5)}$:
  - Likelihood:
    $p\left(\mathbf{x}^{(5)} \mid C = 1\right) =$
    $p\left(x_1^{(5)} = 1 \mid C = 1\right) p\left(x_2^{(5)} = 1 \mid C = 1\right) p\left(x_3^{(5)} = 0 \mid C = 1\right) p\left(x_4^{(5)} = 0 \mid C = 1\right) =$
    $0.8 \times 0.5 \times 0.9 \times 0.9 = 0.324$
  - Likelihood:
    $p\left(\mathbf{x}^{(5)} \mid C = 2\right) =$
    $p\left(x_1^{(5)} = 1 \mid C = 2\right) p\left(x_2^{(5)} = 1 \mid C = 2\right) p\left(x_3^{(5)} = 0 \mid C = 2\right) p\left(x_4^{(5)} = 0 \mid C = 2\right) =$
    $0.1 \times 0.5 \times 0.6 \times 0.2 = 0.006$
  - Likelihood:
    $p\left(\mathbf{x}^{(5)} \mid C = 3\right) =$
    $p\left(x_1^{(5)} = 1 \mid C = 3\right) p\left(x_2^{(5)} = 1 \mid C = 3\right) p\left(x_3^{(5)} = 0 \mid C = 3\right) p\left(x_4^{(5)} = 0 \mid C = 3\right) =$
    $0.1 \times 0.1 \times 0.1 \times 0.8 = 0.0008$
  - Probability: $p\left(\mathbf{x}^{(1)}\right) = \frac{1}{3}0.324 + \frac{1}{3}0.006 + \frac{1}{3}0.0008 = 0.1103$

So, we have that:

$$p\left(\mathbf{x}^{(1)}, \mathbf{x}^{(2)}, \mathbf{x}^{(3)}, \mathbf{x}^{(4)}, \mathbf{x}^{(5)}\right) = p\left(\mathbf{x}^{(1)}\right) p\left(\mathbf{x}^{(2)}\right) p\left(\mathbf{x}^{(3)}\right) p\left(\mathbf{x}^{(4)}\right) p\left(\mathbf{x}^{(5)}\right),$$

$$p\left(\mathbf{x}^{(1)}, \mathbf{x}^{(2)}, \mathbf{x}^{(3)}, \mathbf{x}^{(4)}, \mathbf{x}^{(5)}\right) = 1.054 \times 10^{-5}$$

From a) we have that after one iteration the parameters are as follows.

$$p\left(C = c\right)$$

$c = 1$	0.40
$c = 2$	0.39
$c = 3$	0.21

	$p(x_1 = 1 \mid C = c)$	$p(x_2 = 1 \mid C = c)$	$p(x_3 = 1 \mid C = c)$	$p(x_4 = 1 \mid C = c)$
$c = 1$	0.97	0.51	0.01	0.02
$c = 2$	0.02	0.96	0.49	0.95
$c = 3$	0.02	0.10	0.97	0.10

- For $\mathbf{x}^{(1)}$:
  - Likelihood:
    $p\left(\mathbf{x}^{(1)} \mid C = 1\right) =$
    $p\left(x_1^{(1)} = 1 \mid C = 1\right) p\left(x_2^{(1)} = 0 \mid C = 1\right) p\left(x_3^{(1)} = 0 \mid C = 1\right) p\left(x_4^{(1)} = 0 \mid C = 1\right) =$
    0.46
  - Likelihood:
    $p\left(\mathbf{x}^{(1)} \mid C = 2\right) =$
    $p\left(x_1^{(1)} = 1 \mid C = 2\right) p\left(x_2^{(1)} = 0 \mid C = 2\right) p\left(x_3^{(1)} = 0 \mid C = 2\right) p\left(x_4^{(1)} = 0 \mid C = 2\right) =$
    0.0000204
  - Likelihood:
    $p\left(\mathbf{x}^{(1)} \mid C = 3\right) =$
    $p\left(x_1^{(1)} = 1 \mid C = 3\right) p\left(x_2^{(1)} = 0 \mid C = 3\right) p\left(x_3^{(1)} = 0 \mid C = 3\right) p\left(x_4^{(1)} = 0 \mid C = 3\right) =$
    0.000486
  - Probability: $p\left(\mathbf{x}^{(1)}\right) = 0.4 \times 0.46 + 0.39 \times 0.0000204 + 0.21 \times 0.000486 = 0.1846$

- For $\mathbf{x}^{(2)}$:
  - Likelihood:
    $p\left(\mathbf{x}^{(2)} \mid C = 1\right) =$
    $p\left(x_1^{(2)} = 0 \mid C = 1\right) p\left(x_2^{(2)} = 1 \mid C = 1\right) p\left(x_3^{(2)} = 1 \mid C = 1\right) p\left(x_4^{(2)} = 1 \mid C = 1\right) =$
    0.00000306
  - Likelihood:
    $p\left(\mathbf{x}^{(2)} \mid C = 2\right) =$
    $p\left(x_1^{(2)} = 0 \mid C = 2\right) p\left(x_2^{(2)} = 1 \mid C = 2\right) p\left(x_3^{(2)} = 1 \mid C = 2\right) p\left(x_4^{(2)} = 1 \mid C = 2\right) =$
    0.438
  - Likelihood:
    $p\left(\mathbf{x}^{(2)} \mid C = 3\right) =$
    $p\left(x_1^{(2)} = 0 \mid C = 3\right) p\left(x_2^{(2)} = 1 \mid C = 3\right) p\left(x_3^{(2)} = 1 \mid C = 3\right) p\left(x_4^{(2)} = 1 \mid C = 3\right) =$
    0.009506
  - Probability: $p\left(\mathbf{x}^{(2)}\right) = 0.4 \times 0.00000306 + 0.39 \times 0.438 + 0.21 \times 0.009506 = 0.1728$

- For $\mathbf{x}^{(3)}$:
  - Likelihood:
    $p\left(\mathbf{x}^{(3)} \mid C = 1\right) =$
    $p\left(x_1^{(3)} = 0 \mid C = 1\right) p\left(x_2^{(3)} = 1 \mid C = 1\right) p\left(x_3^{(3)} = 0 \mid C = 1\right) p\left(x_4^{(3)} = 1 \mid C = 1\right) =$
    0.000303
  - Likelihood:
    $p\left(\mathbf{x}^{(3)} \mid C = 2\right) =$
    $p\left(x_1^{(3)} = 0 \mid C = 2\right) p\left(x_2^{(3)} = 1 \mid C = 2\right) p\left(x_3^{(3)} = 0 \mid C = 2\right) p\left(x_4^{(3)} = 1 \mid C = 2\right) =$
    0.456
  - Likelihood:
    $p\left(\mathbf{x}^{(3)} \mid C = 3\right) =$
    $p\left(x_1^{(3)} = 0 \mid C = 3\right) p\left(x_2^{(3)} = 1 \mid C = 3\right) p\left(x_3^{(3)} = 0 \mid C = 3\right) p\left(x_4^{(3)} = 1 \mid C = 3\right) =$
    0.000294
  - Probability: $p\left(\mathbf{x}^{(3)}\right) = 0.4 \times 0.000303 + 0.39 \times 0.456 + 0.21 \times 0.000294 = 0.178$

- For $\mathbf{x}^{(4)}$:
  - Likelihood:
    $p\left(\mathbf{x}^{(4)} \mid C = 1\right) =$
    $p\left(x_1^{(4)} = 0 \mid C = 1\right) p\left(x_2^{(4)} = 0 \mid C = 1\right) p\left(x_3^{(4)} = 1 \mid C = 1\right) p\left(x_4^{(4)} = 0 \mid C = 1\right) =$
    0.0001441

- Likelihood:

$$p\left(\mathbf{x}^{(4)} \mid C = 2\right) =$$

$$p\left(x_1^{(4)} = 0 \mid C = 2\right) p\left(x_2^{(4)} = 0 \mid C = 2\right) p\left(x_3^{(4)} = 1 \mid C = 2\right) p\left(x_4^{(4)} = 0 \mid C = 2\right) =$$
0.00096

- Likelihood:

$$p\left(\mathbf{x}^{(4)} \mid C = 3\right) =$$

$$p\left(x_1^{(4)} = 0 \mid C = 3\right) p\left(x_2^{(4)} = 0 \mid C = 3\right) p\left(x_3^{(4)} = 1 \mid C = 3\right) p\left(x_4^{(4)} = 0 \mid C = 3\right) =$$
0.77

- Probability: $p\left(\mathbf{x}^{(4)}\right) = 0.4 \times 0.0001441 + 0.39 \times 0.00096 + 0.21 \times 0.77 = 0.1621$

- For $\mathbf{x}^{(5)}$:

- Likelihood:

$$p\left(\mathbf{x}^{(5)} \mid C = 1\right) =$$

$$p\left(x_1^{(5)} = 1 \mid C = 1\right) p\left(x_2^{(5)} = 1 \mid C = 1\right) p\left(x_3^{(5)} = 0 \mid C = 1\right) p\left(x_4^{(5)} = 0 \mid C = 1\right) =$$
0.48

- Likelihood:

$$p\left(\mathbf{x}^{(5)} \mid C = 2\right) =$$

$$p\left(x_1^{(5)} = 1 \mid C = 2\right) p\left(x_2^{(5)} = 1 \mid C = 2\right) p\left(x_3^{(5)} = 0 \mid C = 2\right) p\left(x_4^{(5)} = 0 \mid C = 2\right) =$$
0.0004896

- Likelihood:

$$p\left(\mathbf{x}^{(5)} \mid C = 3\right) =$$

$$p\left(x_1^{(5)} = 1 \mid C = 3\right) p\left(x_2^{(5)} = 1 \mid C = 3\right) p\left(x_3^{(5)} = 0 \mid C = 3\right) p\left(x_4^{(5)} = 0 \mid C = 3\right) =$$
0.000054

- Probability: $p\left(\mathbf{x}^{(5)}\right) = 0.4 \times 0.48 + 0.39 \times 0.0004896 + 0.21 \times 0.000054 = 0.1922$

So, we have that:

$$p\left(\mathbf{x}^{(1)}, \mathbf{x}^{(2)}, \mathbf{x}^{(3)}, \mathbf{x}^{(4)}, \mathbf{x}^{(5)}\right) = p\left(\mathbf{x}^{(1)}\right) p\left(\mathbf{x}^{(2)}\right) p\left(\mathbf{x}^{(3)}\right) p\left(\mathbf{x}^{(4)}\right) p\left(\mathbf{x}^{(5)}\right),$$

$$p\left(\mathbf{x}^{(1)}, \mathbf{x}^{(2)}, \mathbf{x}^{(3)}, \mathbf{x}^{(4)}, \mathbf{x}^{(5)}\right) = 0.00018$$

As we can see, after the iteration, the data is more probable which suggests that the model captures the data better.

2)

Consider the following training data without labels:

$$\left\{\mathbf{x}^{(1)} = \left(4\right), \mathbf{x}^{(2)} = \left(0\right), \mathbf{x}^{(3)} = \left(1\right)\right\}$$

We want to model the data with a mixture of two normal distributions. Initialize the likelihoods as follows:

$$p\left(\mathbf{x} \mid C = 1\right) = \mathcal{N}\left(\mu^1 = 0, \sigma^1 = 1\right)$$

$$p\left(\mathbf{x} \mid C = 2\right) = \mathcal{N}\left(\mu^2 = 1, \sigma^2 = 1\right)$$

Also, initialize the priors as follows:

$$p\left(C = 1\right) = 0.5$$

$$p\left(C = 2\right) = 0.5$$

a) Perform one expectation maximization iteration.

Solution:

Each iteration has two steps. Let us do one:

E-Step: Assign each point to the cluster that yields higher posterior

- For $\mathbf{x}^{(1)}$:
  - For cluster $C = 1$:
    * Prior: $p\left(C = 1\right) = 0.5$
    * Likelihood: $p\left(\mathbf{x}^{(1)} \mid C = 1\right) = \frac{1}{\sqrt{2\pi\sigma^2}} \exp\left(-\frac{1}{2} \frac{\left(\mathbf{x}^{(1)} - \mu^1\right)^2}{(\sigma^1)^2}\right) = $
      $\frac{1}{\sqrt{2\pi}} \exp\left(-\frac{1}{2} \frac{(4-0)^2}{1^2}\right) = \frac{1}{\sqrt{2\pi}} \exp\left(-8\right) = 0.000134$
    * Joint Probability:
      $p\left(C = 1, \mathbf{x}^{(1)}\right) = p\left(C = 1\right) p\left(\mathbf{x}^{(1)} \mid C = 1\right) = 0.5 \times 0.000134 = $
      0.000067
  - For cluster $C = 2$:
    * Prior: $p\left(C = 2\right) = 0.5$
    * Likelihood: $p\left(\mathbf{x}^{(1)} \mid C = 2\right) = \frac{1}{\sqrt{2\pi\sigma^2}} \exp\left(-\frac{1}{2} \frac{\left(\mathbf{x}^{(1)} - \mu^2\right)^2}{(\sigma^2)^2}\right) = $
      $\frac{1}{\sqrt{2\pi}} \exp\left(-\frac{1}{2} \frac{(4-1)^2}{1^2}\right) = \frac{1}{\sqrt{2\pi}} \exp\left(-4.5\right) = 0.0044$
    * Joint Probability:
      $p\left(C = 2, \mathbf{x}^{(1)}\right) = p\left(C = 2\right) p\left(\mathbf{x}^{(1)} \mid C = 2\right) = 0.5 \times 0.0044 = $
      0.0022

  - So, we can compute the normalized posteriors for each cluster:
    * $C = 1$: $\quad p\left(C = 1 \mid \mathbf{x}^{(1)}\right) = \frac{p\left(C=1, \mathbf{x}^{(1)}\right)}{p\left(C=1, \mathbf{x}^{(1)}\right) + p\left(C=2, \mathbf{x}^{(1)}\right)} = $
      $\frac{0.000067}{0.000067 + 0.0022} = 0.0293$
    * $C = 2$: $\quad p\left(C = 2 \mid \mathbf{x}^{(1)}\right) = \frac{p\left(C=2, \mathbf{x}^{(1)}\right)}{p\left(C=1, \mathbf{x}^{(1)}\right) + p\left(C=2, \mathbf{x}^{(1)}\right)} = $
      $\frac{0.0022}{0.000067 + 0.0022} = 0.9707$

- For $\mathbf{x}^{(2)}$:

  - For cluster $C = 1$:

    * Prior: $p\left(C = 1\right) = 0.5$
    * Likelihood: $p\left(\mathbf{x}^{(2)} \mid C = 1\right) = \frac{1}{\sqrt{2\pi\sigma^2}} \exp\left(-\frac{1}{2}\frac{\left(\mathbf{x}^{(2)} - \mu^1\right)^2}{\left(\sigma^1\right)^2}\right) = \frac{1}{\sqrt{2\pi}} \exp\left(-\frac{1}{2}\frac{(0-0)^2}{1^2}\right) = 0.399$
    * Joint Probability:
      $p\left(C = 1, \mathbf{x}^{(2)}\right) = p\left(C = 1\right)p\left(\mathbf{x}^{(2)} \mid C = 1\right) = 0.5 \times 0.3989 = 0.1995$

  - For cluster $C = 2$:

    * Prior: $p\left(C = 2\right) = 0.4$
    * Likelihood: $p\left(\mathbf{x}^{(2)} \mid C = 2\right) = \frac{1}{\sqrt{2\pi\sigma^2}} \exp\left(-\frac{1}{2}\frac{\left(\mathbf{x}^{(2)} - \mu^2\right)^2}{\left(\sigma^2\right)^2}\right) = \frac{1}{\sqrt{2\pi}} \exp\left(-\frac{1}{2}\frac{(0-1)^2}{1^2}\right) = 0.242$
    * Joint Probability:
      $p\left(C = 2, \mathbf{x}^{(2)}\right) = p\left(C = 2\right)p\left(\mathbf{x}^{(2)} \mid C = 2\right) = 0.5 \times 0.242 = 0.121$

  - So, we can compute the posteriors for each cluster:

    * $C = 1$: $p\left(C = 1 \mid \mathbf{x}^{(2)}\right) = \frac{p\left(C=1, \mathbf{x}^{(2)}\right)}{p\left(C=1, \mathbf{x}^{(2)}\right) + p\left(C=2, \mathbf{x}^{(2)}\right)} = \frac{0.1995}{0.1995 + 0.121} = 0.62$
    * $C = 2$: $p\left(C = 2 \mid \mathbf{x}^{(2)}\right) = \frac{p\left(C=2, \mathbf{x}^{(2)}\right)}{p\left(C=1, \mathbf{x}^{(2)}\right) + p\left(C=2, \mathbf{x}^{(2)}\right)} = \frac{0.121}{0.1995 + 0.121} = 0.38$

- For $\mathbf{x}^{(3)}$:

  - For cluster $C = 1$:

    * Prior: $p\left(C = 1\right) = 0.5$
    * Likelihood: $p\left(\mathbf{x}^{(3)} \mid C = 1\right) = \frac{1}{\sqrt{2\pi\left(\sigma^1\right)^2}} \exp\left(-\frac{1}{2}\frac{\left(\mathbf{x}^{(3)} - \mu^1\right)^2}{\left(\sigma^1\right)^2}\right) = \frac{1}{\sqrt{2\pi}} \exp\left(-\frac{1}{2}\frac{(1-0)^2}{1^2}\right) = 0.242$
    * Joint Probability:
      $p\left(C = 1, \mathbf{x}^{(3)}\right) = p\left(C = 1\right)p\left(\mathbf{x}^{(3)} \mid C = 1\right) = 0.5 \times 0.242 = 0.121$

- For cluster $C = 2$:

  * Prior: $p(C = 2) = 0.5$
  * Likelihood: $p\left(\mathbf{x}^{(3)} \mid C = 2\right) = \frac{1}{\sqrt{2\pi(\sigma^2)^2}} \exp\left(-\frac{1}{2} \frac{\left(\mathbf{x}^{(3)} - \mu^2\right)^2}{(\sigma^2)^2}\right) =$
    $\frac{1}{\sqrt{2\pi}} \exp\left(-\frac{1}{2} \frac{(1-1)^2}{1^2}\right) = 0.399$
  * Joint Probability:
    $p\left(C = 2, \mathbf{x}^{(3)}\right) = p(C = 2)\, p\left(\mathbf{x}^{(3)} \mid C = 2\right) = 0.5 \times 0.399 = 0.1995$

- So, we can compute the posteriors for each cluster:

  * $C = 1$: $p\left(C = 1 \mid \mathbf{x}^{(3)}\right) = \frac{p\left(C=1, \mathbf{x}^{(3)}\right)}{p\left(C=1, \mathbf{x}^{(3)}\right) + p\left(C=2, \mathbf{x}^{(3)}\right)} =$
    $\frac{0.121}{0.121 + 0.1995} = 0.38$
  * $C = 2$: $p\left(C = 2 \mid \mathbf{x}^{(3)}\right) = \frac{p\left(C=2, \mathbf{x}^{(3)}\right)}{p\left(C=1, \mathbf{x}^{(3)}\right) + p\left(C=2, \mathbf{x}^{(3)}\right)} =$
    $\frac{0.1995}{0.121 + 0.1995} = 0.62$

M-Step: Re-estimate cluster parameters such that they fit their assigned elements

For each cluster we need to find the new prior and likelihood parameters. For each likelihood, we compute the mean and standard deviation using all points weighted by their posteriors:

$$\mu^c = \frac{\sum_{n=1}^{3} p\left(C = c \mid \mathbf{x}^{(n)}\right) \mathbf{x}^{(n)}}{\sum_{n=1}^{3} p\left(C = c \mid \mathbf{x}^{(n)}\right)}$$

And the covariance matrix as follows.

$$\sigma^c = \sqrt{\frac{\sum_{n=1}^{3} p\left(C = c \mid \mathbf{x}^{(n)}\right) \left(\mathbf{x}^{(n)} - \mu^c\right)^2}{\sum_{n=1}^{3} p\left(C = c \mid \mathbf{x}^{(n)}\right)}}$$

For the priors we perform a weighted mean of the posteriors:

$$p(C = c) = \frac{\sum_{n=1}^{N} p\left(C = c \mid \mathbf{x}^{(n)}\right)}{\sum_{l=1}^{k} \sum_{n=1}^{N} p\left(C = l \mid \mathbf{x}^{(n)}\right)}$$

So, let us estimate the new parameters for each cluster.

- For $C = 1$:

  - For the likelihood:

    * $\mu^1 = \dfrac{0.0293\left(4\right)+0.62\left(0\right)+0.38\left(1\right)}{0.0293+0.62+0.38} = 0.495$

    * $\sigma^1 = \sqrt{\dfrac{0.0293(4-0.495)^2+0.62(0-0.495)^2+0.38(1-0.495)^2}{0.0293+0.62+0.38}} = 0.769$

    * So, the new likelihood is:

      $p\left(\mathbf{x} \mid C = 1\right) = \mathcal{N}\left(\mu^1 = 0.495, \sigma^1 = 0.769\right)$

  - For the prior: $p\left(C = 1\right) =$

    $\dfrac{p\left(C=1|\mathbf{x}^{(1)}\right)+p\left(C=1|\mathbf{x}^{(2)}\right)+p\left(C=1|\mathbf{x}^{(3)}\right)}{p\left(C=1|\mathbf{x}^{(1)}\right)+p\left(C=1|\mathbf{x}^{(2)}\right)+p\left(C=1|\mathbf{x}^{(3)}\right)+p\left(C=2|\mathbf{x}^{(1)}\right)+p\left(C=2|\mathbf{x}^{(2)}\right)+p\left(C=2|\mathbf{x}^{(3)}\right)}$

    $= \dfrac{0.0293+0.6225+0.3775}{(0.0293+0.6225+0.3775)+(0.9707+0.3775+0.6225)} = 0.3431$

- For $C = 2$:

  - For the likelihood:

    * $\mu^2 = \dfrac{0.9707\left(4\right)+0.3775\left(0\right)+0.6225\left(1\right)}{0.9707+0.3775+0.6225} = 4.5$

    * $\sigma^2 = \sqrt{\dfrac{0.9707(4-4.5)^2+0.3775(0-4.5)^2+0.6225(1-4.5)^2}{0.9707+0.3775+0.6225}} = 2.81$

    * So, the new likelihood is:

      $p\left(\mathbf{x} \mid C = 2\right) = \mathcal{N}\left(\mu^2 = 4.5, \sigma^2 = 2.81\right)$

  - For the prior:

    $p\left(C = 2\right) =$

    $\dfrac{p\left(C=2|\mathbf{x}^{(1)}\right)+p\left(C=2|\mathbf{x}^{(2)}\right)+p\left(C=2|\mathbf{x}^{(3)}\right)}{p\left(C=1|\mathbf{x}^{(1)}\right)+p\left(C=1|\mathbf{x}^{(2)}\right)+p\left(C=1|\mathbf{x}^{(3)}\right)+p\left(C=2|\mathbf{x}^{(1)}\right)+p\left(C=2|\mathbf{x}^{(2)}\right)+p\left(C=2|\mathbf{x}^{(3)}\right)}$

    $= \dfrac{0.9707+0.3775+0.6225}{(0.0293+0.6225+0.3775)+(0.9707+0.3775+0.6225)} = 0.6569$

Having the new priors and likelihoods we could go for another iteration. However, the exercise only asks for one.

b) Plot the points and sketch the clusters.

Solution:

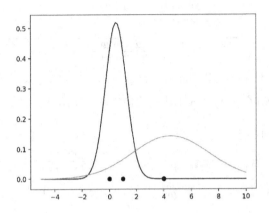

---

3)

Consider the following training data without labels:

$$\left\{ \mathbf{x}^{(1)} = \begin{pmatrix} 2 \\ 2 \end{pmatrix}, \mathbf{x}^{(2)} = \begin{pmatrix} 0 \\ 2 \end{pmatrix}, \mathbf{x}^{(3)} = \begin{pmatrix} 0 \\ 0 \end{pmatrix} \right\}$$

We want to model the data with a mixture of two multivariate normal distributions. Initialize the likelihoods as follows:

$$p\left(\mathbf{x} \mid C = 1\right) = \mathcal{N}\left(\mu^1 = \begin{pmatrix} 2 \\ 2 \end{pmatrix}, \Sigma^1 = \begin{pmatrix} 1 & 0 \\ 0 & 1 \end{pmatrix}\right)$$

$$p\left(\mathbf{x} \mid C = 2\right) = \mathcal{N}\left(\mu^2 = \begin{pmatrix} 0 \\ 0 \end{pmatrix}, \Sigma^2 = \begin{pmatrix} 1 & 0 \\ 0 & 1 \end{pmatrix}\right)$$

Also, initialize the priors as follows:

$$p\left(C = 1\right) = 0.6$$

$$p\left(C = 2\right) = 0.4$$

a) Perform one expectation maximization iteration.

Solution:

Each iteration has two steps. Let us do one:

E-Step: Assign each point to the cluster that yields higher posterior

- For $\mathbf{x}^{(1)}$:

  - For cluster $C = 1$:

    * Prior: $p(C = 1) = 0.6$
    * Likelihood: $p\left(\mathbf{x}^{(1)} \mid C = 1\right) =$

    $\frac{1}{2\pi} \frac{1}{det(\Sigma^1)} \exp\left(-\frac{1}{2}\left(\mathbf{x}^{(1)} - \mu^1\right)^T \left(\Sigma^1\right)^{-1}\left(\mathbf{x}^{(1)} - \mu^1\right)\right) =$

    $\frac{1}{2\pi} \frac{1}{1} \exp\left(-\frac{1}{2}\left(\begin{pmatrix} 2 \\ 2 \end{pmatrix} - \begin{pmatrix} 2 \\ 2 \end{pmatrix}\right)^T \begin{pmatrix} 1 & 0 \\ 0 & 1 \end{pmatrix}\left(\begin{pmatrix} 2 \\ 2 \end{pmatrix} - \begin{pmatrix} 2 \\ 2 \end{pmatrix}\right)\right) =$

    $\frac{1}{2\pi} \exp\left(-\frac{1}{2}\begin{pmatrix} 0 \\ 0 \end{pmatrix}^T \begin{pmatrix} 1 & 0 \\ 0 & 1 \end{pmatrix}\begin{pmatrix} 0 \\ 0 \end{pmatrix}\right) =$

    $\frac{1}{2\pi} \exp\left(-\frac{1}{2}\begin{pmatrix} 0 & 0 \end{pmatrix} \begin{pmatrix} 1 & 0 \\ 0 & 1 \end{pmatrix}\begin{pmatrix} 0 \\ 0 \end{pmatrix}\right) = \frac{1}{2\pi} \exp(0) = \frac{1}{2\pi}$

    * Joint Probability:
      $p\left(C = 1, \mathbf{x}^{(1)}\right) = p(C = 1)\, p\left(\mathbf{x}^{(1)} \mid C = 1\right) = 0.6 \times \frac{1}{2\pi} = 0.095$

  - For cluster $C = 2$:

    * Prior: $p(C = 2) = 0.4$
    * Likelihood: $p\left(\mathbf{x}^{(1)} \mid C = 2\right) =$

    $\frac{1}{2\pi} \frac{1}{det(\Sigma^2)} \exp\left(-\frac{1}{2}\left(\mathbf{x}^{(1)} - \mu^2\right)^T \left(\Sigma^2\right)^{-1}\left(\mathbf{x}^{(1)} - \mu^2\right)\right) =$

    $\frac{1}{2\pi} \frac{1}{1} \exp\left(-\frac{1}{2}\left(\begin{pmatrix} 2 \\ 2 \end{pmatrix} - \begin{pmatrix} 0 \\ 0 \end{pmatrix}\right)^T \begin{pmatrix} 1 & 0 \\ 0 & 1 \end{pmatrix}\left(\begin{pmatrix} 2 \\ 2 \end{pmatrix} - \begin{pmatrix} 0 \\ 0 \end{pmatrix}\right)\right) =$

    $\frac{1}{2\pi} \exp\left(-\frac{1}{2}\begin{pmatrix} 2 \\ 2 \end{pmatrix}^T \begin{pmatrix} 1 & 0 \\ 0 & 1 \end{pmatrix}\begin{pmatrix} 2 \\ 2 \end{pmatrix}\right) =$

    $\frac{1}{2\pi} \exp\left(-\frac{1}{2}\begin{pmatrix} 2 & 2 \end{pmatrix} \begin{pmatrix} 1 & 0 \\ 0 & 1 \end{pmatrix}\begin{pmatrix} 2 \\ 2 \end{pmatrix}\right) = \frac{1}{2\pi} \exp(-4) = 0.003$

    * Joint Probability:
      $p\left(C = 2, \mathbf{x}^{(1)}\right) = p(C = 2)\, p\left(\mathbf{x}^{(1)} \mid C = 2\right) = 0.4 \times 0.003 = 0.0012$

– So, we can compute the normalized posteriors for each cluster:

* $C = 1$: $p\left(C = 1 \mid \mathbf{x}^{(1)}\right) = \dfrac{p\left(C=1,\mathbf{x}^{(1)}\right)}{p\left(C=1,\mathbf{x}^{(1)}\right)+p\left(C=2,\mathbf{x}^{(1)}\right)} =$

  $\dfrac{0.095}{0.095+0.0012} = 0.9879$

* $C = 2$: $p\left(C = 2 \mid \mathbf{x}^{(1)}\right) = \dfrac{p\left(C=2,\mathbf{x}^{(1)}\right)}{p\left(C=1,\mathbf{x}^{(1)}\right)+p\left(C=2,\mathbf{x}^{(1)}\right)} =$

  $\dfrac{0.0012}{0.095+0.0012} = 0.0121$

- For $\mathbf{x}^{(2)}$:

  – For cluster $C = 1$:

  * Prior: $p\left(C = 1\right) = 0.6$
  * Likelihood: $p\left(\mathbf{x}^{(2)} \mid C = 1\right) =$

  $\dfrac{1}{2\pi}\dfrac{1}{det(\Sigma^{1})}\exp\left(-\frac{1}{2}\left(\mathbf{x}^{(2)} - \mu^{1}\right)^{T}\left(\Sigma^{1}\right)^{-1}\left(\mathbf{x}^{(2)} - \mu^{1}\right)\right) =$

  $\dfrac{1}{2\pi}\dfrac{1}{1}\exp\left(-\frac{1}{2}\left(\begin{pmatrix}0\\2\end{pmatrix} - \begin{pmatrix}2\\2\end{pmatrix}\right)^{T}\begin{pmatrix}1&0\\0&1\end{pmatrix}\left(\begin{pmatrix}0\\2\end{pmatrix} - \begin{pmatrix}2\\2\end{pmatrix}\right)\right) =$

  $\dfrac{1}{2\pi}\exp\left(-\frac{1}{2}\begin{pmatrix}-2\\0\end{pmatrix}^{T}\begin{pmatrix}1&0\\0&1\end{pmatrix}\begin{pmatrix}-2\\0\end{pmatrix}\right) =$

  $\dfrac{1}{2\pi}\exp\left(-\frac{1}{2}\begin{pmatrix}-2&0\end{pmatrix}\begin{pmatrix}1&0\\0&1\end{pmatrix}\begin{pmatrix}-2\\0\end{pmatrix}\right) = \dfrac{1}{2\pi}\exp\left(-2\right) = 0.0215$

  * Joint Probability:
  $p\left(C = 1, \mathbf{x}^{(2)}\right) = p\left(C = 1\right)p\left(\mathbf{x}^{(2)} \mid C = 1\right) = 0.6 \times 0.0215 = 0.0129$

  – For cluster $C = 2$:

  * Prior: $p\left(C = 2\right) = 0.4$
  * Likelihood: $p\left(\mathbf{x}^{(2)} \mid C = 2\right) =$

  $\dfrac{1}{2\pi}\dfrac{1}{det(\Sigma^{2})}\exp\left(-\frac{1}{2}\left(\mathbf{x}^{(2)} - \mu^{2}\right)^{T}\left(\Sigma^{2}\right)^{-1}\left(\mathbf{x}^{(2)} - \mu^{2}\right)\right) =$

  $\dfrac{1}{2\pi}\dfrac{1}{1}\exp\left(-\frac{1}{2}\left(\begin{pmatrix}0\\2\end{pmatrix} - \begin{pmatrix}0\\0\end{pmatrix}\right)^{T}\begin{pmatrix}1&0\\0&1\end{pmatrix}\left(\begin{pmatrix}0\\2\end{pmatrix} - \begin{pmatrix}0\\0\end{pmatrix}\right)\right) =$

  $\dfrac{1}{2\pi}\exp\left(-\frac{1}{2}\begin{pmatrix}0\\2\end{pmatrix}^{T}\begin{pmatrix}1&0\\0&1\end{pmatrix}\begin{pmatrix}0\\2\end{pmatrix}\right) =$

  $\dfrac{1}{2\pi}\exp\left(-\frac{1}{2}\begin{pmatrix}0&2\end{pmatrix}\begin{pmatrix}1&0\\0&1\end{pmatrix}\begin{pmatrix}0\\2\end{pmatrix}\right) = \dfrac{1}{2\pi}\exp\left(-2\right) = 0.0215$

  * Joint Probability:
  $p\left(C = 2, \mathbf{x}^{(2)}\right) = p\left(C = 2\right)p\left(\mathbf{x}^{(2)} \mid C = 2\right) = 0.4 \times 0.0215 = 0.0086$

– So, we can compute the posteriors for each cluster:

* $C = 1$: $p\left(C = 1 \mid \mathbf{x}^{(2)}\right) = \dfrac{p\left(C=1,\mathbf{x}^{(2)}\right)}{p\left(C=1,\mathbf{x}^{(2)}\right)+p\left(C=2,\mathbf{x}^{(2)}\right)} =$
$\dfrac{0.0129}{0.0129+0.0086} = 0.6$

* $C = 2$: $p\left(C = 2 \mid \mathbf{x}^{(2)}\right) = \dfrac{p\left(C=2,\mathbf{x}^{(2)}\right)}{p\left(C=1,\mathbf{x}^{(2)}\right)+p\left(C=2,\mathbf{x}^{(2)}\right)} =$
$\dfrac{0.0086}{0.0129+0.0086} = 0.4$

- For $\mathbf{x}^{(3)}$:

  – For cluster $C = 1$:

  * Prior: $p\left(C = 1\right) = 0.6$
  * Likelihood: $p\left(\mathbf{x}^{(3)} \mid C = 1\right) =$

  $\frac{1}{2\pi} \frac{1}{det(\Sigma^1)} \exp\left(-\frac{1}{2}\left(\mathbf{x}^{(3)} - \mu^1\right)^T \left(\Sigma^1\right)^{-1}\left(\mathbf{x}^{(3)} - \mu^1\right)\right) =$

  $\frac{1}{2\pi}\frac{1}{1} \exp\left(-\frac{1}{2}\left(\begin{pmatrix}0\\0\end{pmatrix} - \begin{pmatrix}2\\2\end{pmatrix}\right)^T \begin{pmatrix}1 & 0\\0 & 1\end{pmatrix}\left(\begin{pmatrix}0\\0\end{pmatrix} - \begin{pmatrix}2\\2\end{pmatrix}\right)\right) =$

  $\frac{1}{2\pi} \exp\left(-\frac{1}{2}\begin{pmatrix}-2\\-2\end{pmatrix}^T \begin{pmatrix}1 & 0\\0 & 1\end{pmatrix}\begin{pmatrix}-2\\-2\end{pmatrix}\right) =$

  $\frac{1}{2\pi} \exp\left(-\frac{1}{2}\left(-2\ -2\right)\begin{pmatrix}1 & 0\\0 & 1\end{pmatrix}\begin{pmatrix}-2\\-2\end{pmatrix}\right) = \frac{1}{2\pi}\exp\left(-4\right) = 0.003$

  * Joint Probability:
  $p\left(C = 1, \mathbf{x}^{(3)}\right) = p\left(C = 1\right)p\left(\mathbf{x}^{(3)} \mid C = 1\right) = 0.6 \times 0.003 = 0.0017$

  – For cluster $C = 2$:

  * Prior: $p\left(C = 2\right) = 0.4$
  * Likelihood: $p\left(\mathbf{x}^{(3)} \mid C = 2\right) =$

  $\frac{1}{2\pi} \frac{1}{det(\Sigma^2)} \exp\left(-\frac{1}{2}\left(\mathbf{x}^{(3)} - \mu^2\right)^T \left(\Sigma^2\right)^{-1}\left(\mathbf{x}^{(3)} - \mu^2\right)\right) =$

  $\frac{1}{2\pi}\frac{1}{1} \exp\left(-\frac{1}{2}\left(\begin{pmatrix}0\\0\end{pmatrix} - \begin{pmatrix}0\\0\end{pmatrix}\right)^T \begin{pmatrix}1 & 0\\0 & 1\end{pmatrix}\left(\begin{pmatrix}0\\0\end{pmatrix} - \begin{pmatrix}0\\0\end{pmatrix}\right)\right) =$

  $\frac{1}{2\pi} \exp\left(-\frac{1}{2}\begin{pmatrix}0\\0\end{pmatrix}^T \begin{pmatrix}1 & 0\\0 & 1\end{pmatrix}\begin{pmatrix}0\\0\end{pmatrix}\right) =$

  $\frac{1}{2\pi} \exp\left(-\frac{1}{2}\left(0\ 0\right)\begin{pmatrix}1 & 0\\0 & 1\end{pmatrix}\begin{pmatrix}0\\0\end{pmatrix}\right) = \frac{1}{2\pi}\exp\left(0\right) = \frac{1}{2\pi}$

  * Joint Probability:
  $p\left(C = 2, \mathbf{x}^{(3)}\right) = p\left(C = 2\right)p\left(\mathbf{x}^{(3)} \mid C = 2\right) = 0.4 \times \frac{1}{2\pi} = 0.0637$

- So, we can compute the posteriors for each cluster:

  * C = 1: $p\left(C = 1 \mid \mathbf{x}^{(3)}\right)$ = $\dfrac{p\left(C=1,\mathbf{x}^{(3)}\right)}{p\left(C=1,\mathbf{x}^{(3)}\right)+p\left(C=2,\mathbf{x}^{(3)}\right)}$ =

  $\dfrac{0.0017}{0.0017+0.0637} = 0.0267$

  * C = 2: $p\left(C = 2 \mid \mathbf{x}^{(3)}\right)$ = $\dfrac{p\left(C=2,\mathbf{x}^{(3)}\right)}{p\left(C=1,\mathbf{x}^{(3)}\right)+p\left(C=2,\mathbf{x}^{(3)}\right)}$ =

  $\dfrac{0.0637}{0.0017+0.0637} = 0.9733$

M-Step: Re-estimate cluster parameters such that they fit their assigned elements

For each cluster we need to find the new prior and likelihood parameters. For each likelihood, we compute the mean and covariances using all points weighted by their posteriors:

$$\mu^c = \frac{\sum_{n=1}^{3} p\left(C = c \mid \mathbf{x}^{(n)}\right) \mathbf{x}^{(n)}}{\sum_{n=1}^{3} p\left(C = c \mid \mathbf{x}^{(n)}\right)}$$

And the covariance matrix as follows.

$$\Sigma_{ij}^c = \frac{\sum_{n=1}^{3} p\left(C = c \mid \mathbf{x}^{(n)}\right) \left(\mathbf{x}_i^{(n)} - \mu_i^c\right)\left(\mathbf{x}_j^{(n)} - \mu_j^c\right)}{\sum_{n=1}^{3} p\left(C = c \mid \mathbf{x}^{(n)}\right)}$$

For the priors we perform a weighted mean of the posteriors:

$$p\left(C = c\right) = \frac{\sum_{n=1}^{N} p\left(C = c \mid \mathbf{x}^{(n)}\right)}{\sum_{l=1}^{k} \sum_{n=1}^{N} p\left(C = l \mid \mathbf{x}^{(n)}\right)}$$

So, let us estimate the new parameters for each cluster.

- For $C = 1$:

  - For the likelihood:

  $- \mu^1 = \dfrac{0.9879\begin{pmatrix} 2 \\ 2 \end{pmatrix} + 0.6\begin{pmatrix} 0 \\ 2 \end{pmatrix} + 0.0267\begin{pmatrix} 0 \\ 0 \end{pmatrix}}{0.9879+0.6+0.0267} = \dfrac{\begin{pmatrix} 1.9759 \\ 3.1759 \end{pmatrix}}{1.6147} = \begin{pmatrix} 1.2237 \\ 1.9669 \end{pmatrix}$

  $- \Sigma_{11}^1 = $
  $\dfrac{0.9879(2-1.2237)(2-1.2237)+0.6(0-1.2237)(0-1.2237)+0.0267(0-1.2237)(0-1.2237)}{0.9879+0.6+0.0267} =$

  0.94996

  $- \Sigma_{12}^1 = \Sigma_{21}^1 = $
  $\dfrac{0.9879(2-1.2237)(2-1.9669)+0.6(0-1.2237)(2-1.9669)+0.0267(0-1.2237)(0-1.9669)}{0.9879+0.6+0.0267} =$

  0.0405

- $\Sigma_{22}^1 =$
$\dfrac{0.9879(2-1.9669)(2-1.9669)+0.6(2-1.9669)(2-1.9669)+0.0267(0-1.9669)(0-1.9669)}{0.9879+0.6+0.0267} =$
0.0651

- $\Sigma^1 = \begin{pmatrix} 0.94996 & 0.0405 \\ 0.0405 & 0.0651 \end{pmatrix}$

- So, the new likelihood is:

$$p\left(\mathbf{x} \mid C = 1\right) = \mathcal{N}\left(\mu^1 = \begin{pmatrix} 1.2237 \\ 1.9669 \end{pmatrix}, \Sigma^1 = \begin{pmatrix} 0.94996 & 0.0405 \\ 0.0405 & 0.0651 \end{pmatrix}\right)$$

- For the prior:
$p\left(C = 1\right) =$

$$\dfrac{p\left(C=1|\mathbf{x}^{(1)}\right)+p\left(C=1|\mathbf{x}^{(2)}\right)+p\left(C=1|\mathbf{x}^{(3)}\right)}{p\left(C=1|\mathbf{x}^{(1)}\right)+p\left(C=1|\mathbf{x}^{(2)}\right)+p\left(C=1|\mathbf{x}^{(3)}\right)+p\left(C=2|\mathbf{x}^{(1)}\right)+p\left(C=2|\mathbf{x}^{(2)}\right)+p\left(C=2|\mathbf{x}^{(3)}\right)} =$$
$\dfrac{0.9879+0.6+0.0267}{(0.9879+0.6+0.0267)+(0.0121+0.4+0.9733)} = 0.5382$

- For $C = 2$:

  - For the likelihood:
  - $\mu^2 = \dfrac{0.0121\begin{pmatrix} 2 \\ 2 \end{pmatrix}+0.4\begin{pmatrix} 0 \\ 2 \end{pmatrix}+0.9733\begin{pmatrix} 0 \\ 0 \end{pmatrix}}{0.0121+0.4+0.9733} = \begin{pmatrix} 0.0174 \\ 0.5949 \end{pmatrix}$

  - $\Sigma_{11}^2 =$
  $\dfrac{0.0121(2-0.0174)(2-0.0174)+0.4(0-0.0174)(0-0.0174)+0.9733(0-0.0174)(0-0.0174)}{0.0121+0.4+0.9733} =$
  0.0345

  - $\Sigma_{12}^2 = \Sigma_{21}^2 =$
  $\dfrac{0.0121(2-0.0174)(2-0.5949)+0.4(0-0.0174)(2-0.5949)+0.9733(0-0.0174)(0-0.5949)}{0.0121+0.4+0.9733} =$
  0.0245

  - $\Sigma_{22}^1 =$
  $\dfrac{0.0121(2-0.5949)(2-0.5949)+0.4(2-0.5949)(2-0.5949)+0.9733(0-0.5949)(0-0.5949)}{0.0121+0.4+0.9733} =$
  0.8359

  - $\Sigma^2 = \begin{pmatrix} 0.0345 & 0.0245 \\ 0.0245 & 0.8359 \end{pmatrix}$

  - So, the new likelihood is:

  $$p\left(\mathbf{x} \mid C = 2\right) = \mathcal{N}\left(\mu^2 = \begin{pmatrix} 0.0174 \\ 0.5949 \end{pmatrix}, \Sigma^2 = \begin{pmatrix} 0.0345 & 0.0245 \\ 0.0245 & 0.8359 \end{pmatrix}\right)$$

- For the prior:
$p\left(C = 2\right) =$

$$\dfrac{p\left(C=2|\mathbf{x}^{(1)}\right)+p\left(C=2|\mathbf{x}^{(2)}\right)+p\left(C=2|\mathbf{x}^{(3)}\right)}{p\left(C=1|\mathbf{x}^{(1)}\right)+p\left(C=1|\mathbf{x}^{(2)}\right)+p\left(C=1|\mathbf{x}^{(3)}\right)+p\left(C=2|\mathbf{x}^{(1)}\right)+p\left(C=2|\mathbf{x}^{(2)}\right)+p\left(C=2|\mathbf{x}^{(3)}\right)} =$$
$\dfrac{0.0121+0.4+0.9733}{(0.9879+0.6+0.0267)+(0.0121+0.4+0.9733)} = 0.4618$

Having the new priors and likelihoods we could go for another iteration. However, the exercise only asks for one.

---

b) Plot the points and sketch the clusters.

Solution:

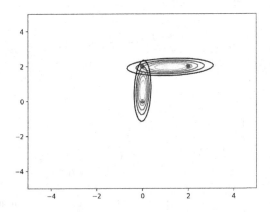

---

c) Verify that after one iteration the probability of the data increased.

Solution:
The probability of the observed data $p\left(\mathbf{x}^{(1)}, \mathbf{x}^{(2)}, \mathbf{x}^{(3)}\right)$ can be decomposed into the product of the probability of each point assuming independent, identically distributed samples:

$$p\left(\mathbf{x}^{(1)}, \mathbf{x}^{(2)}, \mathbf{x}^{(3)}\right) = p\left(\mathbf{x}^{(1)}\right) p\left(\mathbf{x}^{(2)}\right) p\left(\mathbf{x}^{(3)}\right)$$

So, we need to compute the probability of each point before and after the EM update.

By the law of total probability we have that:

$$p\left(\mathbf{x}^{(n)}\right) = p\left(\mathbf{x}^{(n)}, C = 1\right) + p\left(\mathbf{x}^{(n)}, C = 2\right)$$
$$= p(C = 1) p\left(\mathbf{x}^{(n)} \mid C = 1\right) + p(C = 2) p\left(\mathbf{x}^{(n)} \mid C = 2\right)$$

From a) we have that before the iteration:

- For $\mathbf{x}^{(1)}$:
  - $p\left(\mathbf{x}^{(1)}, C = 1\right) = 0.095$
  - $p\left(\mathbf{x}^{(1)}, C = 2\right) = 0.0012$
  - $p\left(\mathbf{x}^{(1)}\right) = 0.095 + 0.0012 = 0.0962$
- For $\mathbf{x}^{(2)}$:
  - $p\left(\mathbf{x}^{(2)}, C = 1\right) = 0.0129$
  - $p\left(\mathbf{x}^{(2)}, C = 2\right) = 0.0086$
  - $p\left(\mathbf{x}^{(2)}\right) = 0.0129 + 0.0086 = 0.0215$
- For $\mathbf{x}^{(3)}$:
  - $p\left(\mathbf{x}^{(3)}, C = 1\right) = 0.0017$
  - $p\left(\mathbf{x}^{(3)}, C = 2\right) = 0.0637$
  - $p\left(\mathbf{x}^{(3)}\right) = 0.0017 + 0.0637 = 0.0654$

$$p\left(\mathbf{x}^{(1)}, \mathbf{x}^{(2)}, \mathbf{x}^{(3)}\right) = p\left(\mathbf{x}^{(1)}\right) p\left(\mathbf{x}^{(2)}\right) p\left(\mathbf{x}^{(3)}\right) = 0.00014$$

For after the iteration:

- For $\mathbf{x}^{(1)}$:
  - $p\left(\mathbf{x}^{(1)}, C = 1\right) =$

    $0.5382 \mathcal{N}\left(\mathbf{x}^{(1)}; \mu^1 = \begin{pmatrix} 1.2237 \\ 1.9669 \end{pmatrix}, \mathbf{\Sigma}^1 = \begin{pmatrix} 0.94996 & 0.0405 \\ 0.0405 & 0.0651 \end{pmatrix}\right) \quad =$

    0.2542
  - $p\left(\mathbf{x}^{(1)}, C = 2\right) =$

    $0.4618 \mathcal{N}\left(\mathbf{x}^{(1)}; \mu^2 = \begin{pmatrix} 0.0174 \\ 0.5949 \end{pmatrix}, \mathbf{\Sigma}^2 = \begin{pmatrix} 0.0345 & 0.0245 \\ 0.0245 & 0.8359 \end{pmatrix}\right) \quad =$

    7.953×10^{-26}
  - $p\left(\mathbf{x}^{(1)}\right) = 0.2542 + 7.953 \times 10^{-26} = 0.2542$
- For $\mathbf{x}^{(2)}$:
  - $p\left(\mathbf{x}^{(2)}, C = 1\right) =$

    $0.5382 \mathcal{N}\left(\mathbf{x}^{(2)}; \mu^1 = \begin{pmatrix} 1.2237 \\ 1.9669 \end{pmatrix}, \mathbf{\Sigma}^1 = \begin{pmatrix} 0.94996 & 0.0405 \\ 0.0405 & 0.0651 \end{pmatrix}\right) \quad =$

    0.1499
  - $p\left(\mathbf{x}^{(2)}, C = 2\right) =$

    $0.4618 \mathcal{N}\left(\mathbf{x}^{(2)}; \mu^2 = \begin{pmatrix} 0.0174 \\ 0.5949 \end{pmatrix}, \mathbf{\Sigma}^2 = \begin{pmatrix} 0.0345 & 0.0245 \\ 0.0245 & 0.8359 \end{pmatrix}\right) = 0.128$
  - $p\left(\mathbf{x}^{(2)}\right) = 0.1499 + 0.128 = 0.2779$

- For $\mathbf{x}^{(3)}$:
  - $p\left(\mathbf{x}^{(3)}, C = 1\right) =$
    $0.5382\mathcal{N}\left(\mathbf{x}^{(3)}; \mu^1 = \begin{pmatrix} 1.2237 \\ 1.9669 \end{pmatrix}, \mathbf{\Sigma}^1 = \begin{pmatrix} 0.94996 & 0.0405 \\ 0.0405 & 0.0651 \end{pmatrix}\right)$ $=$
    4.351×10^{-14}
  - $p\left(\mathbf{x}^{(3)}, C = 2\right) =$
    $0.4618\mathcal{N}\left(\mathbf{x}^{(3)}; \mu^2 = \begin{pmatrix} 0.0174 \\ 0.5949 \end{pmatrix}, \mathbf{\Sigma}^2 = \begin{pmatrix} 0.0345 & 0.0245 \\ 0.0245 & 0.8359 \end{pmatrix}\right) = 0.354$
  - $p\left(\mathbf{x}^{(3)}\right) = 4.351 \times 10^{-14} + 0.354 = 0.354$

$$p\left(\mathbf{x}^{(1)}, \mathbf{x}^{(2)}, \mathbf{x}^{(3)}\right) = p\left(\mathbf{x}^{(1)}\right) p\left(\mathbf{x}^{(2)}\right) p\left(\mathbf{x}^{(3)}\right) = 0.025$$

As we can see, after the iteration, the data is more probable which suggests that the model captures the data better.

---

4)

Consider the following four scenarios of plotted data sets:

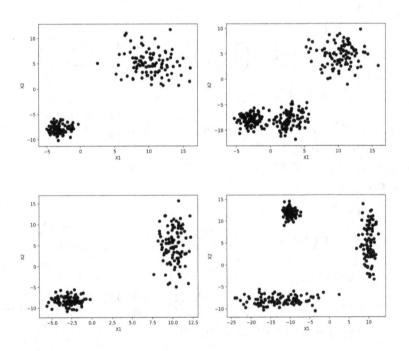

a) For each scenario justify wether or not k-means would be suitable.

Solution:

In k-means all clusters are assumed to have a circle like shape. So, we can analyze these scenarios and see if that property holds.

i) $k = 2$ would provide two circle like clusters.

ii) $k = 3$ would provide three circle like clusters. However, if $k = 2$ we would get a bad fit on the points with negative x_2 coordinate.

iii) The right most cluster of points is clearly and ellipsis so k-means would not be able to capture this shape.

iv) We have two sets of points where the shape is oval so k-means would be a relatively bad fit to this data.

---

b) Assuming you apply EM clustering to model all scenarios what would the means and covariances look like? For simplicity, assume all covariance matrices are diagonal.

Solution:

After EM clustering, the means stay at the cluster centroids and the covariances describe the shape of the cluster.

i)

For the leftmost cluster the mean would be around $\begin{pmatrix} -3 \\ -8 \end{pmatrix}$ and the covariance must capture a tightly packed circle so the identity matrix could do it.

For the right most cluster the mean would be around $\begin{pmatrix} 10 \\ 5 \end{pmatrix}$ and the covariance must capture a spread circle so we could use a multiple of the identity matrix like $\begin{pmatrix} f & 0 \\ 0 & f \end{pmatrix}$ with $f > 1$.

ii)

Assuming $k = 3$, we have three circles with increasing levels of spread. Following the same logic from i), the values could be:

$\mu^1 = \begin{pmatrix} -3 \\ -8 \end{pmatrix}$ and $\Sigma^1 = \begin{pmatrix} 1 & 0 \\ 0 & 1 \end{pmatrix}$

$\mu^2 = \begin{pmatrix} 3 \\ -8 \end{pmatrix}$ and $\Sigma^2 = \begin{pmatrix} f & 0 \\ 0 & f \end{pmatrix}$ with $f > 1$.

$$\mu^3 = \begin{pmatrix} 10 \\ 5 \end{pmatrix} \text{ and } \Sigma^3 = \begin{pmatrix} l & 0 \\ 0 & l \end{pmatrix} \text{ with } l > f.$$

iii)

Assuming $k = 2$ we have one tightly packed circle and a vertically spread ellipsis.

Like before, the circle could be $\mu^1 = \begin{pmatrix} -3 \\ -8 \end{pmatrix}$ and $\Sigma^1 = \begin{pmatrix} 1 & 0 \\ 0 & 1 \end{pmatrix}$.

The ellipsis is centered at around $\mu^2 = \begin{pmatrix} 10 \\ 5 \end{pmatrix}$ and dimension x_1 as a smaller variance then x_2, so the covariance matrix could be $\Sigma^2 = \begin{pmatrix} f & 0 \\ 0 & k \end{pmatrix}$ with $k > f$.

iv)

Assuming $k = 3$ we have a tightly packed circle and two ellipsis.

For the circle again we can use the identiy as covariance and the mean is $\begin{pmatrix} -10 \\ 12 \end{pmatrix}$.

For the horizontally spread ellipsis we have mean $\begin{pmatrix} -13 \\ -8 \end{pmatrix}$ and a covariance $\Sigma^2 = \begin{pmatrix} f & 0 \\ 0 & k \end{pmatrix}$ where $f > k$.

For the vertically spread ellipsis we have mean $\begin{pmatrix} 10 \\ 5 \end{pmatrix}$ and a covariance $\Sigma^2 = \begin{pmatrix} f & 0 \\ 0 & k \end{pmatrix}$ where $k > f$.

Thinking Questions

a) Think about what measures would be desirable in a clustering. Think about distance between centroids and intra-cluster distances.

b) Think about initialization mechanisms and how they affect the final clustering.

c) Why do we need the covariance in EM? What is the difference between k-means and EM in terms of cluster shapes we can capture.

d) Is k-means really a kind of EM clustering?

Chapter 10

Radial Basis Networks

Fig. 10.1 A complex pattern-classification problem, cast in a high-dimensional space nonlinearly, is more likely to be linearly separable than in a low-dimensional space, provided that the space is not densely populated.

10.1   Cover's theorem

A complex pattern-classification problem, cast in a high-dimensional space nonlinearly, is more likely to be linearly separable than in a low-dimensional space, provided that the space is not densely populated as stated by [Cover (1965)], see Figure 10.2. Once we have linearly separable patterns, the

Fig. 10.2   Thomas M. Cover (1938 - 2012) was an information theorist and professor jointly in the Departments of Electrical Engineering and Statistics at Stanford University.

classification problem can be easily solved.

Consider a training set that consists of N observations

$$(\mathbf{x}_1, \mathbf{x}_2, \cdots, \mathbf{x}_k, \cdots, \mathbf{x}_N)$$

where each of which is assigned to one of two classes C_1 and C_2. This dichotomy (binary partition) of the points is said to be separable with respect to a family of boundary surfaces if a surface exists in the family that separates the points in class C_1 from those in class C_2.

For each point $\mathbf{x}_k$ define a function Φ as

$$\Phi_k = \Phi(\mathbf{x}_k) = \begin{pmatrix} \phi_1(\mathbf{x}_k) \\ \phi_2(\mathbf{x}_k) \\ \vdots \\ \phi_M(\mathbf{x}_k) \end{pmatrix}. \qquad (10.1)$$

This function maps each point $\mathbf{x}_k$ in the D-dimensional input space into corresponding points Φ_k in a new space of dimension M with $D \leq M$. Φ is called a hidden function, because it plays a role similar to that of a hidden unit in a feedforward neural network. In this setting, a dichotomy C_1, C_2 of C is said to be separable if there exists an M-dimensional vector $\mathbf{w}$ such that we may write the following [Cover (1965)]:

$$\mathbf{w}^T \cdot \Phi(\mathbf{x}) > 0, \quad if \ \ \mathbf{x} \in C_1,$$

$$\mathbf{w}^T \cdot \Phi(\mathbf{x}) < 0, \quad if \ \ \mathbf{x} \in C_2.$$

Thus, the hyperplane is defined by the equation

$$\mathbf{w}^T \cdot \Phi(\mathbf{x}) = 0.$$

10.1.1 *Cover's theorem on the separability (1965)*

Given a set of training data that is not linearly separable, one can with high probability transform it into a training set that is linearly separable by projecting it into a higher-dimensional space via some non-linear transformation Φ. The proof is easy, we lift N samples onto the vertices of the simplex in the $N - 1$ dimensional real space. Every partition of the samples into two sets is separable by a linear separator, see VC-dimension of a perceptron [Cover (1965)].

10.2 Interpolation Problem

Given a set of N different points $\mathbf{x}_k \in \mathbb{R}^D$ and a set of real numbers $d_k \in \mathbb{R}^1$ with $k = 1, 2, \cdots, N$, find a function $F : \mathbb{R}^N \to \mathbb{R}^1$ that satisfies the interpolation condition:

$$F(\mathbf{x}_k) = d_k, \quad k = 1, 2, \cdots, N$$

The radial-basis-functions (RBF) technique consists of choosing a function F that has the form

$$d_k = F(\mathbf{x}) = \sum_{k=1}^{N} w_k \cdot \phi(\|\mathbf{x} - \mathbf{x}_k\|) \tag{10.2}$$

with $\phi(\|\mathbf{x} - \mathbf{x}_k\|)$ being a set of N arbitrary (generally nonlinear) functions called radial-basis functions [Powell (1988)]. The N known data points $\mathbf{x}_k \in \mathbb{R}^D$ are taken to be the centers of the radial-basis functions with

$$\phi_{ij} = \phi(\|\mathbf{x}_i - \mathbf{x}_j\|) \tag{10.3}$$

resulting in N linear equations

$$
\begin{pmatrix}
\phi_{11} & \phi_{12} & \phi_{13} & \cdots & \phi_{1N} \\
\phi_{21} & \phi_{22} & \phi_{23} & \cdots & \phi_{2N} \\
\vdots & \vdots & \ddots & & \vdots \\
\phi_{N1} & \phi_{N2} & \phi_{N3} & \cdots & \phi_{NN}
\end{pmatrix}
\cdot
\begin{pmatrix}
w_1 \\
w_2 \\
\vdots \\
w_N
\end{pmatrix}
=
\begin{pmatrix}
d_1 \\
d_2 \\
\vdots \\
d_N
\end{pmatrix} .
\tag{10.4}
$$

The interpolation matrix is given by

$$
\Phi = \{\phi_{ij}\}_{i,j}^N
$$

and with the vector notation

$$
\mathbf{w} =
\begin{pmatrix}
w_1 \\
w_2 \\
\vdots \\
w_N
\end{pmatrix} , \quad
\mathbf{d} =
\begin{pmatrix}
d_1 \\
d_2 \\
\vdots \\
d_N
\end{pmatrix}
$$

with

$$
\Phi \cdot \mathbf{w} = \mathbf{d}
\tag{10.5}
$$

assuming that Φ is nonsingular the solution is simply given by

$$
\mathbf{w} = \Phi^{-1} \cdot \mathbf{d} .
\tag{10.6}
$$

Fig. 10.3 Charles A. Micchelli recieved a doctor honoris causa from the university of Zaragoza (Spain) 1994.

10.2.1 *Micchelli's Theorem*

According to Micchelli's Theorem, we can be sure that the interpolation matrix Φ is nonsingular (see Figure 10.3) if Φ is one of the following functions with $r = \|\mathbf{x}_i - \mathbf{x}_j\|$:

(1) Multiquadratics:

$$\phi(r) = \sqrt{r^2 + c^2}, \quad c > 0; \tag{10.7}$$

(2) Inverse Multiquadratics:

$$\phi(r) = \frac{1}{\sqrt{r^2 + c^2}}, \quad c > 0; \tag{10.8}$$

(3) Gaussian functions:

$$\phi(r) = \exp\left(-\frac{r^2}{2 \cdot \sigma^2}\right), \quad \sigma > 0. \tag{10.9}$$

10.3 Radial Basis Function Networks

The radial basis function (RBF) network is composed of a hidden layer and an output layer. These networks were first formulated in a 1988 paper by Broomhead and Lowe, both researchers at the Royal Signals and Radar Establishment [Broomhead and Lowe (1988)].

(1) Input: Dimension D of the input vector $\mathbf{x}$
(2) Hidden Layer: Same number N of units as the size of the training sample

$$\phi_k = \phi(\|\mathbf{x} - \mathbf{x}_k\|), \quad k = 1, 2, \cdots, N$$

$\mathbf{x}_k$ defines the centre of the radial-basis function.
(3) Output Layer: Consists of a single unit. However there is no constraint on the size. The output layer corresponds to a perceptron or logistic regression. With several output layers we can use the *softmax* function. The hidden units preform a nonlinear transformation in such a way, that their output represents a linearly separable problem that can be learned by a perceptron or logistic regression. In this case, a bias parameter can be introduced into the linear sum of activations at the output

$$o = \sigma\left(\sum_{k=1}^{N} w_k \cdot \phi(\|\mathbf{x} - \mathbf{x}_k\|) + w_0\right) \tag{10.10}$$

Usually we use the radial basis function

$$\phi_k = \phi(\|\mathbf{x} - \mathbf{x}_k\|) = \exp\left(-\frac{\|\mathbf{x} - \mathbf{x}_k\|^2}{2 \cdot \sigma^2}\right), \quad k = 1, 2, \cdots, N \quad (10.11)$$

with σ^2 being the variance that is commonly equal for each hidden unit, see Figure 10.4. The problem with this approach is that the number of

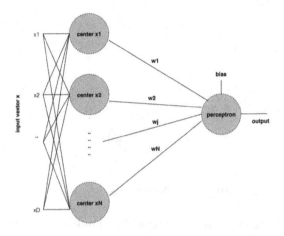

Fig. 10.4   A RBF network with N hidden units. The problem with this approach is that the number of hidden units grows with the size of training set N resulting in the curse of dimensionality.

hidden units grows with the size of training set resulting in the curse of dimensionality. However we can reduce this number considerably using an unsupervised clustering algorithm.

10.3.1   *Modifications of Radial Basis Function Networks*

The number if units in the hidden layer is the same number N of units as the size of the training sample [Wasserman (1993)]. Yet, we can reduce the number of hidden units to $K \ll N$ using K means clustering on

$$F(\mathbf{x}) = \sum_{k=1}^{K} w_k \cdot \phi(\|\mathbf{x} - \mathbf{c}_k\|) \quad (10.12)$$

or with bias

$$o = \sigma\left(\sum_{k=1}^{K} w_k \cdot \phi(\|\mathbf{x} - \mathbf{c}_k\|) + w_0\right). \quad (10.13)$$

Each cluster C_k contains the points that are closest to the centroid $\mathbf{c}_k$. The centroid $\mathbf{c}_k$ is represented by the mean value of all the points of C_k

$$\mathbf{c}_k = \frac{1}{|C_k|} \cdot \sum_{x \in C_k} \mathbf{x}. \tag{10.14}$$

and with the same width

$$\sigma = \frac{d_{max}}{\sqrt{2 \cdot K}} \tag{10.15}$$

where K is the number of clusters and d_{max} is the maximum distance between them [Wasserman (1993)]. Using this value we ensure that the individual Gaussian units are not too peaked or too flat.

Instead of K means we can use EM clustering of Gaussian mixtures with

$$\phi_k = \phi(\|\mathbf{x} - \boldsymbol{\mu}_k\|) = \exp\left(-\frac{1}{2} \cdot (\mathbf{x}_k - \boldsymbol{\mu}_k)^T \Sigma_k^{-1} \cdot (\mathbf{x}_k - \boldsymbol{\mu}_k)\right), \tag{10.16}$$

in which the covariance matrix Σ_k is determined by the algorithm resulting in

$$F(\mathbf{x}) = \sum_{k=1}^{K} w_k \cdot \phi(\|\mathbf{x} - \boldsymbol{\mu}_k\|)$$

or using bias

$$o = \sigma\left(\sum_{k=1}^{K} w_k \cdot \phi(\|\mathbf{x} - \boldsymbol{\mu}_k\|) + w_0\right).$$

So, to train an RBFN, we first use the inputs to learn the hidden functions. Then, we map the inputs through the hidden units to get a linearly separable problem. Finally, we use the mapped version to train the output layer perceptron. Usually the training process performed on the RBF network is significantly faster than that performed on the MLP.

10.3.2 *Interpretation of Hidden Units*

10.3.2.1 *Neurobiology*

In a neurobiological context, a receptive field is defined as that region of a sensory field from which an adequate sensory stimulus will elicit a response [Churchland and Sejnowski (1994)]. So, we can interpret each hidden unit as a receptive field positioned at $\mathbf{c}_k$ or $\boldsymbol{\mu}_k$ with a shape described by σ or Σ_k.

10.3.2.2   *Statistics*

The function

$$\phi(\mathbf{x}, \mathbf{x}_k) = \exp\left(-\frac{\|\mathbf{x} - \mathbf{x}_k\|^2}{2 \cdot \sigma^2}\right), \quad k = 1, 2, \cdots, K$$

is called a Gaussian function. In statistics a function is a kernel, denoted by $k(\mathbf{x})$, if it has similar properties to those associated with the probability density function of a random variable [Haykin (2008)]:

(1) The kernel $k(\mathbf{x})$ is a continuous, bounded, and real function of $\mathbf{x}$ and symmetric about the origin, where it attains its maximum value.

(2) The total volume under the surface of the kernel $k(\mathbf{x})$ is unity; that is, for an D-dimensional vector $\mathbf{x}$, we have

$$\int k(\mathbf{x})d\mathbf{x} = 1$$

Except for a scaling factor, the Gaussian function $\phi(\mathbf{x}, \mathbf{x}_k)$ satisfies both of these properties for the centre , $\mathbf{x}_k$ located at the origin. Because of the interpretation of the Gaussian function as a kernel the term kernel methods is used.

10.4   Exercises and Answers

1)

The training set is described by five vectors

$$\mathbf{x}_1 = \begin{pmatrix} 1 \\ 9 \end{pmatrix}, \mathbf{x}_2 = \begin{pmatrix} 0 \\ 8 \end{pmatrix}, \mathbf{x}_3 = \begin{pmatrix} 1 \\ 0 \end{pmatrix} \mathbf{x}_4 = \begin{pmatrix} 1 \\ 1 \end{pmatrix}, \mathbf{x}_5 = \begin{pmatrix} 0 \\ -10 \end{pmatrix}$$

and the corresponding target of the two classes is indicated as

$$t_1 = -1, t_2 = -1, t_3 = 1, t_4 = 1, t_5 = -1$$

Determine the parameters of the RBF network. Use an RBF with k-Means clustering with $k = 3$ and $\sigma = 5$ for the clusters and one output unit implemented as the original perceptron. The cluster centers are initialized with

$$\mathbf{c}_1 = \begin{pmatrix} 1 \\ 9 \end{pmatrix}, \mathbf{c}_2 = \begin{pmatrix} 1 \\ 0 \end{pmatrix}, \mathbf{c}_3 = \begin{pmatrix} 0 \\ -10 \end{pmatrix}$$

Initialize all weights of the perceptron to one (including the bias). Use a learning rate of one for simplicity. Apply the perceptron learning algorithm (the original from Rosenblatt) until convergence. Hint you can determine the cluster centers of k-Means by drawing the values in 2 dim coordinate system. It is enough to indicate what are the cluster centers after applying k-Means algorithm. No computation for k-Means algorithm are required!

Solution:

We can determine the cluster centers by drawing the values in 2 dim coordinate system without computation since the points are well separated. It follows

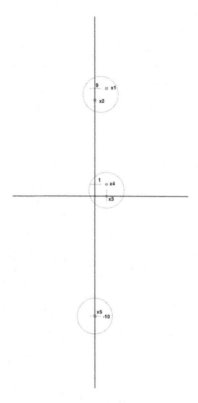

$$c_1 = \frac{x_1 + x_2}{2} = \begin{pmatrix} 0.5 \\ 8.5 \end{pmatrix}, \quad c_2 = \frac{x_3 + x_4}{2} = \begin{pmatrix} 1 \\ 0.5 \end{pmatrix}, \quad c_3 = \frac{x_5}{1} = \begin{pmatrix} 0 \\ -10 \end{pmatrix}$$

$$\phi_1 = \exp\left(-\frac{\|x - c_1\|^2}{2 \cdot 25}\right), \quad \phi_2 = \exp\left(-\frac{\|x - c_2\|^2}{2 \cdot 25}\right), \quad \phi_3 = \exp\left(-\frac{\|x - c_3\|^2}{2 \cdot 25}\right).$$

$$\Phi_k = \begin{pmatrix} \phi_1(\mathbf{x}_k) \\ \phi_2(\mathbf{x}_k) \\ \phi_3(\mathbf{x}_k) \end{pmatrix}.$$

Taking into account the bias we get

$$\Phi_1 = \begin{pmatrix} 1 \\ 0.99005 \\ 0.235746 \\ 0.00072 \end{pmatrix}, \quad \Phi_2 = \begin{pmatrix} 1 \\ 0.99005 \\ 0.318224 \\ 0.00153 \end{pmatrix}, \quad \Phi_3 = \begin{pmatrix} 1 \\ 0.23457 \\ 0.995012 \\ 0.132655 \end{pmatrix},$$

$$\Phi_4 = \begin{pmatrix} 1 \\ 0.323033 \\ 0.995012 \\ 0.087161 \end{pmatrix}, \quad \Phi_5 = \begin{pmatrix} 1 \\ 0.00106 \\ 00.10807 \\ 1 \end{pmatrix}.$$

Using original perceptron rule, delta is either -2, 2, or 0.

First epoch:

- $net_1 = 2.22651$, $o_1 = 1$, $\sigma_1 = -2$, $\mathbf{w} = \begin{pmatrix} -1 \\ -0.9801 \\ 0.52850 \\ 0.998565 \end{pmatrix}$,

- $net_2 = 1.80063$, $o_2 = -1$, $\sigma_2 = 0$, $\mathbf{w} = \begin{pmatrix} -1 \\ -0.9801 \\ 0.52850 \\ 0.998565 \end{pmatrix}$,

- $net_3 = 0.571565$, $o_3 = -1$, $\sigma_3 = -2$, $\mathbf{w} = \begin{pmatrix} 1 \\ -0.510959 \\ 2.51853 \\ 1.26388 \end{pmatrix}$,

- $net_4 = 3.4510$, $o_4 = 1$, $\sigma_4 = 0$, $\mathbf{w} = \begin{pmatrix} 1 \\ -0.510959 \\ 2.51853 \\ 1.26388 \end{pmatrix}$,

- $net_5 = 2.53551$, $o_5 = 1$, $\sigma_5 = -2$, $\mathbf{w} = \begin{pmatrix} -1 \\ -0.513078 \\ 2.3024 \\ -0.736124 \end{pmatrix}.$

Second epoch:

- $net_1 = -0.96572$, $o_1 = -1$, $\sigma_1 = 0$, $\mathbf{w} = \begin{pmatrix} -1 \\ -0.513078 \\ 2.3024 \\ -0.736124 \end{pmatrix}$,

- $net_2 = 0.776424$, $o_2 = -1$, $\sigma_2 = 0$, $\mathbf{w} = \begin{pmatrix} -1 \\ -0.513078 \\ 2.3024 \\ -0.736124 \end{pmatrix}$,

- $net_3 = 1.07291$, $o_3 = 1$, $\sigma_3 = 0$, $\mathbf{w} = \begin{pmatrix} -1 \\ -0.513078 \\ 2.3024 \\ -0.736124 \end{pmatrix}$,

- $net_4 = 1.06101$, $o_4 = 1$, $\sigma_4 = 0$, $\mathbf{w} = \begin{pmatrix} -1 \\ -0.513078 \\ 2.3024 \\ -0.736124 \end{pmatrix}$,

- $net_5 = -1.48785$, $o_5 = -1$, $\sigma_5 = 0$, $\mathbf{w} = \begin{pmatrix} -1 \\ -0.513078 \\ 2.3024 \\ -0.736124 \end{pmatrix}$.

The perceptron converged.

---

2)

The training set is described by four vectors

$$\mathbf{x}_1 = \begin{pmatrix} 0 \\ 0 \end{pmatrix}, \mathbf{x}_2 = \begin{pmatrix} 0 \\ -1 \end{pmatrix}, \mathbf{x}_3 = \begin{pmatrix} -1 \\ 0 \end{pmatrix}, \mathbf{x}_4 = \begin{pmatrix} -1 \\ -1 \end{pmatrix}$$

and the corresponding target of the two classes is indicated as

$$t_1 = 1, t_2 = 0, t_3 = 0, t_4 = 1$$

Determine the parameters of a RBF network. Use an RBF with k-Means clustering with $k = 2$ and $\sigma = 1$ for both clusters and one output unit implemented as a logistic regression. Initialize the first cluster center weights to zero $c_1 = (0,0)^T$ and the second cluster center weights to $c_2 = (-1,0)^T$.

Apply the k-Means clustering algorithm until convergence or for a maximum of two epochs (whichever happens first). Can the mapping be learned by the perceptron?

Solution:

First we preform k-Means clustering by computing the Euclidean distance of the data points to the cluster centers $c_1 = (0,0)^T$, $c_2 = (-1,0)^|T$.

$$d_2(\mathbf{x}_1, \mathbf{c}_1) = 0, d_2(\mathbf{x}_2, \mathbf{c}_1) = 1, d_2(\mathbf{x}_3, \mathbf{c}_1) = 1, d_2(\mathbf{x}_4, \mathbf{c}_1) = 1.41421$$

$$\mathbf{x}_1, \mathbf{x}_2 \in C_1$$

$$d_2(\mathbf{x}_1, \mathbf{c}_2) = 1, d_2(\mathbf{x}_2, \mathbf{c}_2) = 1.41421, d_2(\mathbf{x}_3, \mathbf{c}_2) = 0, d_2(\mathbf{x}_4, \mathbf{c}_2) = 1$$

$$\mathbf{x}_3, \mathbf{x}_4 \in C_2$$

$$\mathbf{c}_1 = \frac{\mathbf{x}_1 + \mathbf{x}_2}{2} = \begin{pmatrix} 0 \\ -0.5 \end{pmatrix}, \quad \mathbf{c}_2 = \frac{\mathbf{x}_3 + \mathbf{x}_4}{2} = \begin{pmatrix} -1 \\ -0.5 \end{pmatrix}$$

Second epoch:

$$d_2(\mathbf{x}_1, \mathbf{c}_1) = 0.5, d_2(\mathbf{x}_2, \mathbf{c}_1) = 0.5, d_2(\mathbf{x}_3, \mathbf{c}_1) = 1.11803, d_2(\mathbf{x}_4, \mathbf{c}_1) = 1.11803$$

$$\mathbf{x}_1, \mathbf{x}_2 \in C_1$$

$$d_2(\mathbf{x}_1, \mathbf{c}_2) = 1.11803, d_2(\mathbf{x}_2, \mathbf{c}_2) = 1.11803, d_2(\mathbf{x}_3, \mathbf{c}_2) = 0.5, d_2(\mathbf{x}_4, \mathbf{c}_2) = 0.5$$

$$\mathbf{x}_3, \mathbf{x}_4 \in C_2$$

$$\mathbf{c}_1 = \frac{\mathbf{x}_1 + \mathbf{x}_2}{2} = \begin{pmatrix} 0 \\ -0.5 \end{pmatrix}, \quad \mathbf{c}_2 = \frac{\mathbf{x}_3 + \mathbf{x}_4}{2} = \begin{pmatrix} -1 \\ -0.5 \end{pmatrix}$$

k-Means converged.

$$\phi_1 = \exp\left(-\frac{\|\mathbf{x} - \mathbf{c}_1\|^2}{2 \cdot 2}\right), \quad \phi_2 = \exp\left(-\frac{\|\mathbf{x} - \mathbf{c}_2\|^2}{2 \cdot 2}\right).$$

$$\Phi_k = \begin{pmatrix} \phi_1(\mathbf{x}_k) \\ \phi_2(\mathbf{x}_k) \end{pmatrix}.$$

Taking into account the bias we get

$$\Phi_1 = \begin{pmatrix} 1 \\ 0.882497 \\ 0.535261 \end{pmatrix}, \Phi_2 = \begin{pmatrix} 1 \\ 0.882497 \\ 0.535261 \end{pmatrix}, \Phi_3 = \begin{pmatrix} 1 \\ 0.535261 \\ 0.882497 \end{pmatrix}, \Phi_4 = \begin{pmatrix} 1 \\ 0.535261 \\ 0.882497 \end{pmatrix}$$

the target is $t_1 = 1$, $t_2 = 0$, $t_3 = 0$, $t_4 = 1$ which leads to a contradiction, the perceptron cannot learn the mapping.

---

3)

Solve the XOR problem The training set is described by four vectors

$$\mathbf{x}_1 = \begin{pmatrix} 0 \\ 0 \end{pmatrix}, \mathbf{x}_2 = \begin{pmatrix} 1 \\ 0 \end{pmatrix}, \mathbf{x}_3 = \begin{pmatrix} 0 \\ 1 \end{pmatrix}, \mathbf{x}_4 = \begin{pmatrix} 1 \\ 1 \end{pmatrix}$$

and the corresponding target of the two classes is indicated as

$$t_1 = -1, t_2 = 1, t_3 = 1, t_4 = -1$$

using an RBF network with 4 hidden units with $\sigma = 1$. Choose the four RBF units such that the problem is easily solvable by a perceptron (Hint: Interpolation Problem). Then, apply the perceptron (the original from Rosenblatt) and find the solution. To initialize your perceptron with bias $b = w_0 = 0$, you can choose one of the following weight vectors (see as well the definition of XOR problem). Note that a smart choice will save you a lot of work (only one iteration):

- $\mathbf{w} = (1, 1, -1, -1)^T$
- $\mathbf{w} = (-1, 1, 1, 1)^T$
- $\mathbf{w} = (-1, 1, 1, -1)^T$
- $\mathbf{w} = (1, -1, -1, 1)^T$

Solution:

We can center each RBF unit on our data points:

$$\phi_1 = \exp\left(-\frac{\left\| \mathbf{x} - \begin{pmatrix} 0 \\ 0 \end{pmatrix} \right\|^2}{2}\right), \quad \phi_2 = \exp\left(-\frac{\left\| \mathbf{x} - \begin{pmatrix} 1 \\ 0 \end{pmatrix} \right\|^2}{2}\right),$$

$$\phi_3 = \exp\left(-\frac{\left\| \mathbf{x} - \begin{pmatrix} 0 \\ 1 \end{pmatrix} \right\|^2}{2}\right), \quad \phi_4 = \exp\left(-\frac{\left\| \mathbf{x} - \begin{pmatrix} 1 \\ 1 \end{pmatrix} \right\|^2}{2}\right).$$

with

$$\phi_1 = (\exp(0), \exp(-0.5), \exp(-0.5), \exp(-1))^T$$

$$\phi_2 = (\exp(-0,5), \exp(0), \exp(-1), \exp(-0.5))^T$$

$$\phi_3 = (\exp(-0.5), \exp(-1), \exp(0), \exp(-0.5))^T$$

$$\phi_4 = (\exp(-1), \exp(-0.5), \exp(-0.5), \exp(0))^T$$

Looking at the new features, we see that the two middle features should push towards a positive output while the two outer features should pull for a negative output, since

$$(\exp(0) + \exp(-1)) > (\exp(-0.5) + \exp(-0.5))$$

So, let us choose to start with the weight vector (with bias $w_0 = 0$):

$$\mathbf{w} = (-1, 1, 1, -1)^T$$

Now, let us run the perceptron learning algorithm:

- $sgn(\mathbf{w}^T \cdot \mathbf{x}_1) = sgn(\exp(-0.5) + \exp(-0.5) - \exp(-1) - \exp(0)) = sgn(-0.154818) = -1$, no update since $t_1 = -1$
- $sgn(\mathbf{w}^T \cdot \mathbf{x}_2) = sgn(exp(0) + exp(-1) - exp(-0.5) - exp(-0.5)) = sgn(0.6166) = +1$, no update since $t_2 = 1$
- $sgn(\mathbf{w}^T \cdot \mathbf{x}_3) = sgn(exp(-1) + exp(0) - exp(-0.5) - exp(-0.5)) = sgn(0.158418) = +1$, no update since $t_3 = 1$
- $sgn(\mathbf{w}^T \cdot \mathbf{x}_4) = sgn(exp(-0.5) + exp(-0.5) - exp(-1) - exp(0)) = sgn(-0.154818) = -1$, no update since $t_4 = -1$

so, we get convergence.

Chapter 11

Support Vector Machines

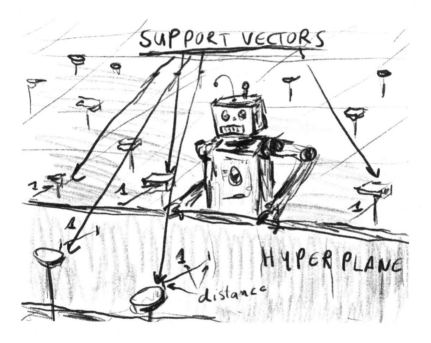

Fig. 11.1 In RBF networks we reduced the number of hidden units to $K \ll N$ using clustering. Can we reduce this number further? This question is related to the question of how to define a decision boundary. In a two class problem that is linearly separable there are many decision boundaries that can separate the two classes. But which one is the best?

11.1 Margin

In a two class problem that is linearly separable there are many decision boundaries that can separate the two classes, see Figure 11.2. Which bound-

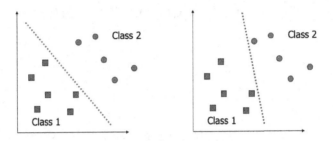

Fig. 11.2 In two class problem that is linear separable there are many decision boundaries can separate these two classes. Which one of these boundaries should we choose?

ary should we choose?

Like in the perceptron, a linear classifier decides based on a linear boundary. Such boundary can be described by two important parameters. First, we have the weight vector $\mathbf{w}$ which is orthogonal to the boundary and, thus, defines its slope. Second, we have a bias term w_0 that shifts the boundary from the origin. With that, we can write the equation for points on the boundary as described by

$$\mathbf{w}^T \cdot \mathbf{x} + w_0 = 0.$$

So, it is usual to say that a linear classifier defines the output class based on the sign of its discriminant function

$$y(\mathbf{x}) = \mathbf{w}^T \cdot \mathbf{x} + w_0.$$

In the perceptron all we wanted was some boundary that worked as a separator. However, as we have noticed, many such boundaries exist. In this chapter we want to find a way to choose the best possible boundary. To do so, we need a definition for what best means. Our intuitions tell us that such boundary would be one that perfectly separates both classes while being as far away from each class as possible. If we are able to find such separator, we have a margin on which future points of both classes may fall without being misclassified.

Let us try to quantify this margin for a given set of parameters. Any input vector $\mathbf{x}$ can be decomposed as a sum of two components: $\mathbf{x}_b$ a component vector orthogonal to $\mathbf{w}$ and, thus, parallel to the boundary; and $\mathbf{x}_w$ a component vector along the direction of the weight vector and, thus, orthogonal to the boundary. Take a quick look at Figure 11.3 to get a visual intuition for this decomposition.

So, we can start by writing $\mathbf{x} = \mathbf{x}_b + \mathbf{x}_w$. But, we can go further. Since we know that $\mathbf{x}_w$ is a component along the direction of the weight vector, we can write it in terms of a normalized weight vector $\mathbf{x}_w = r\frac{\mathbf{w}}{\|\mathbf{w}\|}$. With that, our general input vector becomes $\mathbf{x} = \mathbf{x}_b + r\frac{\mathbf{w}}{\|\mathbf{w}\|}$. For such vector, the discriminant output would be

$$y(\mathbf{x}) = y\left(\mathbf{x}_b + r\frac{\mathbf{w}}{\|\mathbf{w}\|}\right) = \mathbf{w}^T \cdot \left(\mathbf{x}_b + r\frac{\mathbf{w}}{\|\mathbf{w}\|}\right) + w_0.$$

If we further develop the expression we get

$$y(\mathbf{x}) = \mathbf{w}^T \cdot \mathbf{x}_b + \mathbf{w}^T \cdot \left(r\frac{\mathbf{w}}{\|\mathbf{w}\|}\right) + w_0.$$

Which can be rewritten into

$$y(\mathbf{x}) = \mathbf{w}^T \cdot \mathbf{x}_b + r\frac{\mathbf{w}^T \cdot \mathbf{w}}{\|\mathbf{w}\|} + w_0.$$

Using the fact that $\mathbf{w}^T \cdot \mathbf{w} = \|\mathbf{w}\|^2$

$$y(\mathbf{x}) = \mathbf{w}^T \cdot \mathbf{x}_b + r\frac{\|\mathbf{w}\|^2}{\|\mathbf{w}\|} + w_0.$$

Which is the same as

$$y(\mathbf{x}) = \mathbf{w}^T \cdot \mathbf{x}_b + r\|\mathbf{w}\| + w_0.$$

Now, since, by definition, $\mathbf{x}_b$ is orthogonal to the weight vector. Then, their inner product is equal to zero. So, the leftmost term vanishes

$$y(\mathbf{x}) = r\|\mathbf{w}\| + w_0.$$

If we solve for r

$$r = \frac{y(\mathbf{x}) - w_0}{\|\mathbf{w}\|} = \frac{y(\mathbf{x})}{\|\mathbf{w}\|} + \frac{-w_0}{\|\mathbf{w}\|}$$

we see that we can write it as a sum of two terms: the signed distance between the input point and the boundary $\frac{y(\mathbf{x})}{\|\mathbf{w}\|}$; and the signed distance between the origin and the boundary $\frac{-w_0}{\|\mathbf{w}\|}$. Again, Figure 11.3 provides a visual intuition for this reasoning.

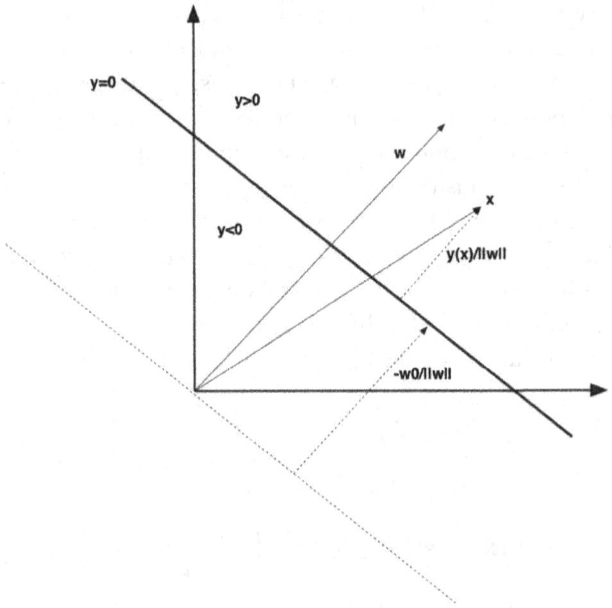

Fig. 11.3   The geometry of a linear discriminant function in two dimensions. The decision surface is orthogonal to $\mathbf{w}$ and its signed orthogonal distance from the origin is given by $-\frac{w_0}{\|\mathbf{w}\|}$. The signed orthogonal distance of a general point $\mathbf{x}$ from the decision surface is given by $\frac{y(\mathbf{x})}{\|\mathbf{w}\|}$.

11.2   Optimal Hyperplane for Linear Separable Patterns

Having an expression for the signed distance between a point $\mathbf{x}$ and the boundary, we can write the real distance by taking its absolute value

$$\rho = \left| \frac{y(\mathbf{x})}{\|\mathbf{w}\|} \right| = \frac{|y(\mathbf{x})|}{\|\mathbf{w}\|}.$$

Since $y(\mathbf{x}) \in \{-1, 1\}$, we have that $|y(\mathbf{x})| = 1$. So, we can write

$$\rho = \frac{|y(\mathbf{x})|}{\|\mathbf{w}\|} = \frac{1}{\|\mathbf{w}\|}.$$

To find the weight vector that yields the maximum possible margin, we need to choose the weight vector such that

$$\arg\max_{\mathbf{w}} \frac{1}{\|\mathbf{w}\|}.$$

Which is the same as minimizing the norm of the weight vector

$$\arg\min_{\mathbf{w}} \|\mathbf{w}\|.$$

So, can we just choose the weight vector with the smallest possible norm? Not really. We need also to guarantee that the weight vector corresponds to a boundary that correctly separates the two classes. For that reason, we will have to add constraints to our optimization. Given a training set $\{\mathbf{x}_i, t_i\}_{i=1}^{N}$, with $t_i \in \{-1, +1\}$ of linearly separable patterns we have

$$\mathbf{w}^T \cdot \mathbf{x}_i + w_0 \geq 0, \quad for \ \ t_i = +1$$

$$\mathbf{w}^T \cdot \mathbf{x}_i + w_0 < 0, \quad for \ \ t_i = -1$$

with a hyperplane

$$\mathbf{w}^T \cdot \mathbf{x} + w_0 = \mathbf{w}^T \cdot \mathbf{x} + b = 0$$

Since we want to have a margin between each class and the boundary, we want to find the parameters $\mathbf{w}_{opt}$ and b_{opt} such that

$$\mathbf{w}_{opt}^T \cdot \mathbf{x}_i + b_{opt} \geq 1, \quad for \ \ t_i = +1 \tag{11.1}$$

$$\mathbf{w}_{opt}^T \cdot \mathbf{x}_i + b_{opt} \leq 1, \quad for \ \ t_i = -1 \tag{11.2}$$

for the hyperplane

$$\mathbf{w}_{opt}^T \cdot \mathbf{x}_i + b_{opt} = 0. \tag{11.3}$$

The value of 1 is set for convenience because we can always rescale $\mathbf{w}_{opt}$ and b_{opt} correspondingly.

Now that we know what to optimize and what constraints to include we are ready to move on and try to solve the optimization task. But first, let us just take a small detour to talk about the name of this learning model.

11.3 Support Vectors

The data points that are closest to the boundary, that is, those points $\{\mathbf{x}_i, t_i\}$ for which

$$\mathbf{w}_{opt}^T \cdot \mathbf{x}_i + b_{opt} = \pm 1 \tag{11.4}$$

are called support vectors $\mathbf{x}^{(s)}$. That is why the algorithm is called a support vector machine. All the remaining examples in the training sample are really **irrelevant** to determine where to place the hyperplane, see Figure 11.4.

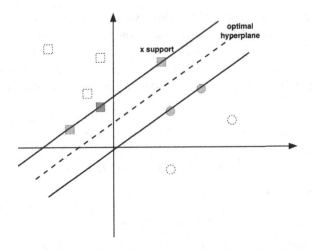

Fig. 11.4   The data points $\{\mathbf{x}_i, t_i\}$ for which $\mathbf{w}_{opt}^T \cdot \mathbf{x}_i + b_{opt} = \pm 1$ are called support vectors. All the remaining examples in the training sample are irrelevant for the determination of the hyperplane,

11.4   Quadratic Optimization for Finding the Optimal Hyperplane

Having finished the small detour, we may now look into solving the optimization task. Remember that we wanted to maximize the margin of a boundary that perfectly solves a linearly separable problem. We wrote this goal as an optimization problem subject to a few constraints. Specifically, we had the objective function

$$\Phi(\mathbf{w}) = \frac{1}{2} \cdot \mathbf{w}^T \mathbf{w} = \frac{1}{2} \cdot \|\mathbf{w}\|^2 \tag{11.5}$$

where a scaling factor $\frac{1}{2}$ was introduced for convenience. We also had the constraints that force the resulting boundary to solve the problem. Concretely, for a training set $\{\mathbf{x}_i, t_i\}_{i=1}^N$, with $t_i \in \{-1, +1\}$ of linearly separable patterns we must have that

$$\mathbf{w}^T \cdot \mathbf{x}_i + b \geq 1, \quad for \ \ t_i = +1$$

$$\mathbf{w}^T \cdot \mathbf{x}_i + b \leq 1, \quad for \ \ t_i = -1.$$

These constraints can be expressed in a single line as

$$t_i \cdot \left(\mathbf{w}^T \cdot \mathbf{x}_i + b\right) \geq 1, \quad for \ \ t_i = \pm 1. \tag{11.6}$$

Before moving forward, we must note that

- the cost function $\Phi(\mathbf{w})$ is a convex function of $\mathbf{w}$,
- the constraints are linear in $\mathbf{w}$.

For these reasons, we may solve the constrained optimization problem by using the method of Lagrange multipliers with

$$J(\mathbf{w}, b, \alpha) = \frac{1}{2} \cdot \mathbf{w}^T \mathbf{w} - \sum_{i=1}^{N} \alpha_i \cdot \left(t_i \cdot \left(\mathbf{w}^T \cdot \mathbf{x}_i + b \right) - 1 \right) \qquad (11.7)$$

where the α_i's are called Lagrange multipliers.

The solution to the constrained optimization problem is determined by the saddle point of the Lagrangian function $J(\mathbf{w}, b, \alpha)$. To find this point we have to minimize J with respect to $\mathbf{w}$ and b and maximize with respect to α. With that, we get two conditions

$$\frac{\partial J(\mathbf{w}, b, \alpha)}{\partial \mathbf{w}} = \mathbf{0}, \qquad \frac{\partial J(\mathbf{w}, b, \alpha)}{\partial b} = 0 \qquad (11.8)$$

leading to

$$\mathbf{w} = \sum_{i=1}^{N} \alpha_i \cdot t_i \cdot \mathbf{x}_i, \qquad \sum_{i=1}^{N} \alpha_i \cdot t_i = 0. \qquad (11.9)$$

This solution is unique by virtue of the convexity of the Lagrangian, but not with respect of the Lagrange multipliers α_i. For all constraints

$$t_i \cdot \left(\mathbf{w}^T \cdot \mathbf{x}_i + b \right) - 1 \neq 0$$

that are not satisfied as equalities, the corresponding multiplier α_i must be zero. The following Karush-Kuhn-Tucker conditions must be satisfied

$$\alpha_i \cdot \left(t_i \cdot \left(\mathbf{w}^T \cdot \mathbf{x}_i + b \right) - 1 \right) = 0. \qquad (11.10)$$

11.4.1 *Dual Problem*

It is possible to construct another problem called the dual problem that has the same optimal value as the primal problem. If the primal problem has an optimal solution, the dual problem also has an optimal solution, and the corresponding optimal values are equal.

In order for $\mathbf{w}_{opt}$ to be an optimal primal solution and α_{opt} to be an optimal dual solution, it is necessary and sufficient that $\mathbf{w}_{opt}$ is feasible for the primal problem, and that

$$\Phi(\mathbf{w}_{opt}) = J(\mathbf{w}_{opt}, b_{opt}, \alpha_{opt}) = \min_{\mathbf{w}} J(\mathbf{w}, b, \alpha). \qquad (11.11)$$

To convert the primal into the dual problem will be extremely helpful in the end of the chapter. So let us show how to do it.

We can expand the Lagrangian from

$$J(\mathbf{w}, b, \alpha) = \frac{1}{2} \cdot \mathbf{w}^T \mathbf{w} - \sum_{i=1}^{N} \alpha_i \cdot \left(t_i \cdot \left(\mathbf{w}^T \cdot \mathbf{x}_i + b \right) - 1 \right)$$

to

$$J(\mathbf{w}, b, \alpha) = \frac{1}{2} \cdot \mathbf{w}^T \mathbf{w} - \sum_{i=1}^{N} \alpha_i \cdot t_i \cdot \mathbf{w}^T \mathbf{x}_i - b \cdot \sum_{i=1}^{N} \alpha_i \cdot t_i + \sum_{i=1}^{N} \alpha_i. \quad (11.12)$$

Now, since

$$\mathbf{w} = \sum_{i=1}^{N} \alpha_i \cdot t_i \cdot \mathbf{x}_i,$$

we have that

$$\mathbf{w}^T \mathbf{w} = \sum_{i=1}^{N} \alpha_i \cdot t_i \cdot \mathbf{w}^T \mathbf{x}_i = \sum_{i=1}^{N} \sum_{j=1}^{N} \alpha_i \cdot \alpha_j \cdot t_i \cdot t_j \cdot \mathbf{x}_i^T \mathbf{x}_j,$$

which yields

$$J(\mathbf{w}, b, \alpha) = \frac{1}{2} \cdot \sum_{i=1}^{N} \alpha_i \cdot t_i \cdot \mathbf{w}^T \mathbf{x}_i - \sum_{i=1}^{N} \alpha_i \cdot t_i \cdot \mathbf{w}^T \mathbf{x}_i - b \cdot \sum_{i=1}^{N} \alpha_i \cdot t_i + \sum_{i=1}^{N} \alpha_i. \quad (11.13)$$

Simplifying we get

$$J(\mathbf{w}, b, \alpha) = -b \cdot \sum_{i=1}^{N} \alpha_i \cdot t_i + \sum_{i=1}^{N} \alpha_i - \frac{1}{2} \cdot \sum_{i=1}^{N} \alpha_i \cdot t_i \cdot \mathbf{w}^T \mathbf{x}_i \quad (11.14)$$

and substituting

$$\mathbf{w} = \sum_{i=1}^{N} \alpha_i \cdot t_i \cdot \mathbf{x}_i,$$

into the equation we get

$$J(\mathbf{w}, b, \alpha) = -b \cdot \sum_{i=1}^{N} \alpha_i \cdot t_i + \sum_{i=1}^{N} \alpha_i - \frac{1}{2} \cdot \sum_{i=1}^{N} \sum_{j=1}^{N} \alpha_i \cdot \alpha_j \cdot t_i \cdot t_j \cdot \mathbf{x}_i^T \mathbf{x}_j. \quad (11.15)$$

Since the Lagrangian condition is

$$\sum_{i=1}^{N} \alpha_i \cdot t_i = 0,$$

and setting

$$Q(\alpha) = J(\mathbf{w}, b, \alpha)$$

we get

$$Q(\alpha) = \sum_{i=1}^{N} \alpha_i - \frac{1}{2} \cdot \sum_{i=1}^{N} \sum_{j=1}^{N} \alpha_i \cdot \alpha_j \cdot t_i \cdot t_j \cdot \mathbf{x}_i^T \mathbf{x}_j \tag{11.16}$$

with α_i being non negative.

With that, we get a new optimization problem that depends entirely on the training data and the Lagrange multipliers. Given the training sample $\{\mathbf{x}_i, t_i\}_{i=1}^{N}$, with $t_i \in \{-1, +1\}$ of linearly separable patterns, we want to find the Lagrange multipliers $\{\alpha_i\}_{i=1}^{N}$ that maximize

$$Q(\alpha) = \sum_{i=1}^{N} \alpha_i - \frac{1}{2} \cdot \sum_{i=1}^{N} \sum_{j=1}^{N} \alpha_i \cdot \alpha_j \cdot t_i \cdot t_j \cdot \mathbf{x}_i^T \mathbf{x}_j$$

subject to the constraints

$$\sum_{i=1}^{N} \alpha_i \cdot t_i = 0, \quad \alpha_i \geq 0, \quad i = 1, 2, \cdots, N.$$

We said that the problem was cast in terms of the training data. However, we can say something further than that. The dual problem is cast entirely in terms of dot products between training inputs $\mathbf{x}_i^T \mathbf{x}_j$. This will be extremely important later on.

The dual problem $\alpha_i \geq 0$ is satisfied with the inequality sign for all the support vectors for which the α's are nonzero, and with the equality sign for all the other data points in the training sample, for which the α's are all zero. The support vectors constitute a subset of the training sample, which means that the solution vector is sparse.

Having determined the optimum Lagrange multipliers $\alpha_{opt,i}$ (not equal zero) we may recover

$$\mathbf{w}_{opt} = \sum_{i=1}^{N} \alpha_{opt,i} \cdot t_i \cdot \mathbf{x}_i, \tag{11.17}$$

$$\mathbf{w}_{opt}^T \cdot \mathbf{x}_i + b_{opt} = \pm 1 \tag{11.18}$$

and

$$b_{opt} = 1 - \mathbf{w}_{opt}^T \cdot \mathbf{x}^{(s)}, \quad for \ \ t^{(s)} = 1 \tag{11.19}$$

since

$$b_{opt} = 1 - \left(\sum_{i=1}^{N} \alpha_{opt,i} \cdot t_i \cdot \mathbf{x}_i^T \right) \cdot \mathbf{x}^{(s)}, \quad for \ \ t^{(s)} = 1.$$

Later we will see, how to determine the bias for a non optimal case.

This supervised learning algorithm is called support vector machines (SVM) and was developed by Corinna Cortes and Vladimir Vapnik [Cortes and Vapnik (1995)], see Figure 7.6 and 11.5.

Fig. 11.5   Corinna Cortes is a Danish computer scientist that developed together with Vladimir Vapnik the SVM learning algorithm.

11.5   Optimal Hyperplane for Non-separable Patterns

Although we have seen how to solve the problem for linearly separable cases, in most real data, such cleanliness does not occur. If the problem is almost linearly separable but there are some outliers that cross boundaries, we would like to able to find a good boundary nonetheless. We can use the exact same reasoning as before but allowing for a small "error" (or violation of the margin) $\xi_i > 0$ resulting in the new constraints

$$t_i \cdot \left(\mathbf{w}^T \cdot \mathbf{x}_i + b\right) \geq 1 - \xi_i, \quad for \ \ i = 1, 2, \cdots, N \qquad (11.20)$$

where ξ_i are called the slack variables.

In a sense, these variables measure the deviation of a data point from the ideal condition of pattern separability.

- For $0 < \xi_i \leq 1$ the data point falls inside the margin of separation, but on the correct side of the decision surface,

- For $\xi_i > 1$ falls on the wrong side of the separating hyperplane

11.5.1 *Dual Problem*

As before, we can reformulate our problem as a dual problem. Given the training sample $\{\mathbf{x}_i, t_i\}_{i=1}^N$, with $t_i \in \{-1, +1\}$, find the Lagrange multipliers $\{\alpha_i\}_{i=1}^N$ that maximize

$$Q(\alpha) = \sum_{i=1}^N \alpha_i - \frac{1}{2} \cdot \sum_{i=1}^N \sum_{j=1}^N \alpha_i \cdot \alpha_j \cdot t_i \cdot t_j \cdot \mathbf{x}_i^T \mathbf{x}_j \qquad (11.21)$$

subject to the usual constraints

$$\sum_{i=1}^N \alpha_i \cdot t_i = 0 \qquad (11.22)$$

and adding a new constraint

$$0 \le \alpha_i \le C, \quad i = 1, 2, \cdots, N \qquad (11.23)$$

where C is a user specified positive parameter. The one difference is that $0 \le \alpha_i$ constraint is bounded by the value C, $0 \le \alpha_i \le C$, This is a quadratic-programming (QP that can be solved by a QP solver). Later in the example XOR problem we show how to solve this problem by hand.

11.6 Support Vector Machine as a Kernel Machine

Much like in basis-function linear models, multilayer perceptrons and radial-basis function networks we will try to solve a nonlinear classification problem by preforming a nonlinear mapping of the input vectors into a high-dimensional feature space where an optimal hyperplane that separates the classes linear can be found [Shawe-Taylor and Cristianini (2004)].

Let $\mathbf{x}$ be a vector from the input space of dimension D and let $\{\phi_j(\mathbf{x})\}_{j=1}^\infty$ be a set of nonlinear functions, from D dimension to infinite dimension. In that feature space, the hyperplane would be defined as

$$\sum_{j=1}^\infty w_j \cdot \phi_j(\mathbf{x}) + b = 0 \qquad (11.24)$$

or, using vector notation

$$\mathbf{w}^T \cdot \Phi(\mathbf{x}) + b = 0 \qquad (11.25)$$

with $\Phi(\mathbf{x})$ being a feature vector with infinite dimension and $\mathbf{w}$ being the wight vector with infinite dimension.

But how can we deal with an infinite dimensional vector? It is here that the formulation in terms of the dual problems will come in handy.

First, with N_s being the number of support vectors, we can represent the weight vector as

$$\mathbf{w} = \sum_{i=1}^{N_s} \alpha_i \cdot t_i \cdot \Phi(\mathbf{x}_i). \tag{11.26}$$

However, this expression still uses a feature vector of infinite dimension

$$\Phi(\mathbf{x}_i) = \begin{pmatrix} \phi_1(\mathbf{x}_i) \\ \phi_2(\mathbf{x}_i) \\ \vdots \end{pmatrix}. \tag{11.27}$$

But we do not need the weight vector itself, all we need is the boundary or decision surface and we can represent it by

$$\sum_{i=1}^{N_s} \alpha_i \cdot t_i \cdot \Phi^T(\mathbf{x}_i)\Phi(\mathbf{x}) = 0. \tag{11.28}$$

In this expression for the boundary, all we need are inner products between support vectors $\langle \Phi(\mathbf{x}_i)|\Phi(\mathbf{x})\rangle$ (or $\Phi^T(\mathbf{x}_i)\Phi(\mathbf{x})$). We can look at these inner products as the result of a kernel function

$$k(\mathbf{x}, \mathbf{x}_i) = \Phi^T(\mathbf{x}_i)\Phi(\mathbf{x}) = \langle \Phi(\mathbf{x}_i)|\Phi(\mathbf{x})\rangle \tag{11.29}$$

$$k(\mathbf{x}, \mathbf{x}_i) = \langle \Phi(\mathbf{x}_i)|\Phi(\mathbf{x})\rangle = \sum_{j=1}^{\infty} \phi(\mathbf{x}_i) \cdot \phi(\mathbf{x}). \tag{11.30}$$

With that, all we need is to have a kernel function which we can evaluate, that receives two input vectors and outputs the result of their inner product in an infinite dimensional space. For a function to be a kernel function it must have two properties:

(1) The function $k(\mathbf{x}, \mathbf{x}_i)$ is symmetric about the center point $\mathbf{x}_i$ that is,

$$k(\mathbf{x}, \mathbf{x}_i) = k(\mathbf{x}_i, \mathbf{x})$$

and it attains its maximum value at the point $\mathbf{x} = \mathbf{x}_i$.

(2) The total volume under the surface of the function $k(\mathbf{x}, \mathbf{x}_i)$ is a constant.

11.6.1 *Kernel Trick*

So, we have seen that specifying the kernel $k(\mathbf{x}, \mathbf{x}_i)$ is sufficient, we need never explicitly compute the weight vector $\mathbf{w}_{opt}$. Having the kernel we can take full advantage of the fact that

$$\sum_{j=1}^{\infty} w_j \cdot \phi_j(\mathbf{x}) + b = \sum_{i=1}^{N_s} \alpha_i \cdot t_i \cdot k(\mathbf{x}, \mathbf{x}_i) + b = 0. \qquad (11.31)$$

For that reason, even though we assumed that the feature space could be of infinite dimensionality, defining the optimal hyperplane, consists of a finite number of terms that is equal to the number of training patterns used in the classifier. A support vector machine with a kernel is also referred to as a kernel machine.

A kernel $k(\mathbf{x}_i, \mathbf{x}_j)$ needs to satisfy the Mercer condition specified by Mercer's theorem [Mercer (1909)], see Figure 11.6. Mercer's theorem tells

Fig. 11.6 James Mercer (1883 - 1932) was a British mathematician. He proved Mercer's theorem, which states that positive-definite kernels can be expressed as a dot product in a high-dimensional space

us only whether a candidate kernel actually corresponds to an inner-product in some space and therefore if it is admissible for use in a support vector machine. If such kernel respects this condition it is called a Mercer kernel. To see wether the condition is met or not it is helpful to construct a kernel matrix where $k(\mathbf{x}_i, \mathbf{x}_j)$ is the ij-th element of the $N \times N$ matrix. Resulting in something like

$$K = \begin{pmatrix} k(\mathbf{x}_1, \mathbf{x}_1) & k(\mathbf{x}_1, \mathbf{x}_2) & k(\mathbf{x}_1, \mathbf{x}_3) & \cdots & k(\mathbf{x}_1, \mathbf{x}_N) \\ k(\mathbf{x}_2, \mathbf{x}_1) & k(\mathbf{x}_2, \mathbf{x}_2) & k(\mathbf{x}_2, \mathbf{x}_3) & \cdots & k(\mathbf{x}_2, \mathbf{x}_N) \\ \vdots & \vdots & \ddots & \vdots \\ k(\mathbf{x}_N, \mathbf{x}_1) & k(\mathbf{x}_N, \mathbf{x}_2) & k(\mathbf{x}_N, \mathbf{x}_3) & \cdots & k(\mathbf{x}_N, \mathbf{x}_N) \end{pmatrix} \tag{11.32}$$

Mercer kernels give rise to positive (or nonnegative definite) matrices [Saitoh (1988)] where a matrix K is nonnegative definite if

$$\mathbf{a}^T K \mathbf{a} \geq 0.$$

for any real valued vector $\mathbf{a}$.

11.6.2 *Dual Problem*

In the dual problem formulation we replace the scalar multiplication

$$\mathbf{x}_i^T \mathbf{x}_j = \langle \mathbf{x}_i | \mathbf{x}_j \rangle$$

by the kernel

$$k(\mathbf{x}_i, \mathbf{x}_j),$$

every thing else stays the same. So, given the training sample $\{\mathbf{x}_i, t_i\}_{i=1}^N$, with $t_i \in \{-1, +1\}$ we want to find the Lagrange multipliers $\{\alpha_i\}_{i=1}^N$ that maximize

$$Q(\alpha) = \sum_{i=1}^N \alpha_i - \frac{1}{2} \cdot \sum_{i=1}^N \sum_{j=1}^N \alpha_i \cdot \alpha_j \cdot t_i \cdot t_j \cdot k(\mathbf{x}_i, \mathbf{x}_j) \tag{11.33}$$

subject to constraints

$$\sum_{i=1}^N \alpha_i \cdot t_i = 0 \tag{11.34}$$

$$0 \leq \alpha_i \leq C, \quad i = 1, 2, \cdots, N \tag{11.35}$$

where C is a user specified positive parameter. A quadratic-programming (QP) solver can solve the maximization problem.

11.6.3 *Classification*

In order to classify data points, we evaluate the *sgn* that indicates us on which side of the decision boundary the query point is

$$o = sgn\left(\mathbf{w}^T \cdot \Phi(\mathbf{x}) + b\right)$$

$$o = sgn\left(\sum_{i=1}^{N_s} \alpha_i \cdot t_i \cdot \Phi(\mathbf{x}_i)^T \Phi(\mathbf{x}) + b\right) \tag{11.36}$$

using the kernel trick to avoid high or infinite dimension

$$o = sgn\left(\sum_{i=1}^{N} \alpha_i \cdot t_i \cdot k(\mathbf{x}, \mathbf{x}_i) + b\right) = sgn\left(\sum_{i=1}^{N_s} \alpha_i \cdot t_i \cdot k(\mathbf{x}, \mathbf{x}_i) + b\right)$$

with $N_s \ll N$ since for all non-support vectors $\alpha_i = 0$. The bias is given by

$$b = \frac{1}{N_s} \sum_{i=1}^{N_s} \left(t_i - \sum_{j=1}^{N_s} \alpha_j \cdot t_j \cdot k(\mathbf{x}_i, \mathbf{x}_j)\right). \tag{11.37}$$

To compute the output

(1) First we determine the bias

$$b = \frac{1}{N_s} \sum_{i=1}^{N_s} \left(t_i - \sum_{j=1}^{N_s} \alpha_j \cdot t_j \cdot k(\mathbf{x}_i, \mathbf{x}_j)\right), \tag{11.38}$$

(2) then the output

$$o = sgn\left(\sum_{i=1}^{N_s} \alpha_i \cdot t_i \cdot k(\mathbf{x}, \mathbf{x}_i) + b\right). \tag{11.39}$$

11.6.3.1 *Example: XOR Problem*

The XOR Problem is described by four vectors [Haykin (2008)], instead of 0 we will use (-1)

$$\mathbf{x}_1 = \begin{pmatrix} -1 \\ -1 \end{pmatrix}, \mathbf{x}_2 = \begin{pmatrix} 1 \\ 1 \end{pmatrix}, \mathbf{x}_3 = \begin{pmatrix} 1 \\ -1 \end{pmatrix}, \mathbf{x}_4 = \begin{pmatrix} 1 \\ 1 \end{pmatrix},$$

and the corresponding target of the two classes is indicated as

$$t_1 = -1, t_2 = 1, t_3 = 1, t_4 = -1.$$

We will use a polynomial kernel

$$k(\mathbf{x}_i, \mathbf{x}_j) = \left(1 + \mathbf{x}_i^T \mathbf{x}_j\right)^2$$

with

$$k(\mathbf{x}_i, \mathbf{x}_j) = 1 + x_{i1}^2 \cdot x_{j1}^2 + 2 \cdot x_{i1} \cdot x_{i2} \cdot x_{j1} \cdot x_{j2} + x_{i2}^2 \cdot x_{j2}^2 + 2 \cdot x_{i1} \cdot x_{j1} + 2 \cdot x_{i2} \cdot x_{j2}$$

with the feature vectors (not required, indeed for certain kernels the vector can have an infinite dimension)

$$\Phi(\mathbf{x}_i) = \begin{pmatrix} 1 \\ x_{i1}^2 \\ \sqrt{2} \cdot x_{i1} \cdot x_{i2} \\ x_{i2}^2 \\ \sqrt{2} \cdot x_{i1} \\ \sqrt{2} \cdot x_{i2} \end{pmatrix}, \quad \Phi(\mathbf{x}_j) = \begin{pmatrix} 1 \\ x_{j1}^2 \\ \sqrt{2} \cdot x_{j1} \cdot x_{j2} \\ x_{j2}^2 \\ \sqrt{2} \cdot x_{j1} \\ \sqrt{2} \cdot x_{j2} \end{pmatrix}$$

We obtain the Gram

$$K = \begin{pmatrix} k(\mathbf{x}_1, \mathbf{x}_1) & k(\mathbf{x}_1, \mathbf{x}_2) & k(\mathbf{x}_1, \mathbf{x}_3) & k(\mathbf{x}_1, \mathbf{x}_4) \\ k(\mathbf{x}_2, \mathbf{x}_1) & k(\mathbf{x}_2, \mathbf{x}_2) & k(\mathbf{x}_2, \mathbf{x}_3) & k(\mathbf{x}_2, \mathbf{x}_4) \\ k(\mathbf{x}_3, \mathbf{x}_1) & k(\mathbf{x}_3, \mathbf{x}_3) & k(\mathbf{x}_3, \mathbf{x}_3) & k(\mathbf{x}_4, \mathbf{x}_3) \\ k(\mathbf{x}_4, \mathbf{x}_1) & k(\mathbf{x}_4, \mathbf{x}_4) & k(\mathbf{x}_4, \mathbf{x}_3) & k(\mathbf{x}_4, \mathbf{x}_4) \end{pmatrix} = \begin{pmatrix} 9 & 1 & 1 & 1 \\ 1 & 9 & 1 & 1 \\ 1 & 1 & 9 & 1 \\ 1 & 1 & 1 & 9 \end{pmatrix}$$

The objective function for the dual form of optimization is

$$Q(\alpha) = \sum_{i=1}^{4} \alpha_i - \frac{1}{2} \cdot \sum_{i=1}^{4} \sum_{j=1}^{4} \alpha_i \cdot \alpha_j \cdot t_i \cdot t_j \cdot k(\mathbf{x}_i, \mathbf{x}_j)$$

$$Q(\alpha) = \alpha_1 + \alpha_2 + \alpha_3 + \alpha_4 - \frac{1}{2} \cdot (9\alpha_1^2 - 2\alpha_1\alpha_2 - 2\alpha_1\alpha_3 + 2\alpha_1\alpha_4$$

$$9\alpha_2^2 + 2\alpha_2\alpha_3 - 2\alpha_2\alpha_4 + 9\alpha_3^2 - 2\alpha_3\alpha_4 + 9\alpha_4^2)$$

We maximize the objective function $Q(\alpha)$ by determining the partial derivatives

$$\frac{\partial Q(\alpha)}{\partial \alpha_1} = 1 - 9 \cdot \alpha 1 + \alpha 2 + \alpha 3 - \alpha 4 = 0$$

$$\frac{\partial Q(\alpha)}{\partial \alpha_2} = 1 - +\alpha 1 - 9 \cdot \alpha 2 - \alpha 3 + \alpha 4 = 0$$

$$\frac{\partial Q(\alpha)}{\partial \alpha_3} = 1 + \alpha 1 - \alpha 2 - 9 \cdot \alpha 3 + \alpha 4 = 0$$

$$\frac{\partial Q(\alpha)}{\partial \alpha_4} = 1 - \alpha 1 + \alpha 2 + \alpha 3 - 9 \cdot \alpha 4 = 0$$

that lead to four equations that can be solved by

$$\begin{pmatrix} 9 & -1 & -1 & 1 \\ -1 & 9 & 1 & -1 \\ -1 & 1 & 9 & -1 \\ 1 & -1 & -1 & 9 \end{pmatrix} \cdot \begin{pmatrix} \alpha_1 \\ \alpha_2 \\ \alpha_3 \\ \alpha_4 \end{pmatrix} = \begin{pmatrix} 1 \\ 1 \\ 1 \\ 1 \end{pmatrix}$$

with the optimum values of the Lagrange multipliers

$$\alpha_{opt,1} = \alpha_{opt,2} = \alpha_{opt,3} = \alpha_{opt,4} = \frac{1}{8}$$

with all input vectors being support vectors.

To compute the output

(1) we compute the bias

$$b = \frac{1}{4} \sum_{i=1}^{4} \left(t_i - \sum_{j=1}^{4} \alpha_j \cdot t_j \cdot k(\mathbf{x}_i, \mathbf{x}_j) \right), \qquad (11.40)$$

$$b = \frac{1}{4} \left(\cdot \left(-1 - \frac{1}{8} \cdot (-9 + 1 + 1 - 1) \right) + \left(1 - \frac{1}{8} \cdot (-1 + 9 + 1 - 1) \right) + \right.$$

$$\left. \left(1 - \frac{1}{8} \cdot (-1 + 1 + 9 - 1) \right) + \left(-1 - \frac{1}{8} \cdot (-1 + 1 + 1 - 9) \right) \right) = 0.$$

In this case we had an optimum Lagrange multipliers $\alpha_{opt,i}$, se we could as well use the form

$$b_{opt} = 1 - \sum_{i=1}^{N} \alpha_{opt,i} \cdot t_i \cdot \cdot k(\mathbf{x}_i, \mathbf{x}^{(s)}), \quad for \ \ t^{(s)} = 1.$$

(2) then the output

$$o = sgn\left(\sum_{i=1}^{4} \alpha_i \cdot t_i \cdot k(\mathbf{x}, \mathbf{x}_i) + b \right). \qquad (11.41)$$

For the query vector

$$\mathbf{x}_q = \begin{pmatrix} -1 \\ -1 \end{pmatrix}$$

we get

$$o = sgn\left(\frac{1}{8} \cdot (-9 + 1 + 1 - 1) \right) = sgn(-1) = -1$$

Since the feature vector $\Phi(\mathbf{x}_i)$ has a finite dimension, we can determine the hyperplane (line) by

$$\mathbf{w} = \sum_{i=1}^{4} \alpha_i \cdot t_i \cdot \Phi(\mathbf{x}_i)$$

$$\mathbf{w}_{opt} = \frac{1}{8}\left(-\phi(\mathbf{x}_1) + \phi(\mathbf{x}_2) + \phi(\mathbf{x}_3) - \phi(\mathbf{x}_4)\right)$$

and

$$\mathbf{w}_{opt} = \begin{pmatrix} 0 \\ 0 \\ -\frac{1}{\sqrt{2}} \\ 0 \\ 0 \\ 0 \end{pmatrix}.$$

With bias zero

$$\mathbf{w}_{opt}^T \cdot \Phi(\mathbf{x}) + 0 = 0$$

we get the hyperplane (line)

$$(0, 0, -\frac{1}{\sqrt{2}}, 0, 0, 0) \cdot \begin{pmatrix} 1 \\ x_1^2 \\ \sqrt{2} \cdot x_1 \cdot x_2 \\ x_2^2 \\ \sqrt{2} \cdot x_1 \\ \sqrt{2} \cdot x_2 \end{pmatrix} = -x_1 \cdot x_2 = 0.$$

11.7   Constructing Kernels

We have seen that a way to characterize Mercer kernels is that they give rise to positive kernel matrices K [Saitoh (1988)]. However this condition tells us only whether a candidate kernel is actually an inner-product kernel in some space and therefore if it is admissible for use in a support vector machine. Therefore, it says nothing about how to construct the functions.

The choice of the kernel defines if the problem is solve or not. One possible approach is to build a specific kernel for a specific task. For example, consider we would like to apply the feature transformation given by

$$\phi(\mathbf{x}) = (x_1^2, \sqrt{2} \cdot x_1 \cdot x_2, x_2^2)^T.$$

An inner-product between two such vectors would be given by
$$\phi(\mathbf{x})^T \cdot \phi(\mathbf{z}) = (x_1^2, \sqrt{2} \cdot x_1 \cdot x_2, x_2^2) \cdot (z_1^2, \sqrt{2} \cdot z_1 \cdot z_2, z_2^2)^T.$$
Which is the same as writing
$$\phi(\mathbf{x})^T \cdot \phi(\mathbf{z}) = x_1^2 \cdot z_1^2 + 2 \cdot x_1 \cdot x_2 \cdot z_1 \cdot z_2 + x_2^2 \cdot z_2^2 = (x_1 \cdot z_1 + x_2 \cdot z_2)^2.$$
Compactly, we can write
$$\phi(\mathbf{x})^T \cdot \phi(\mathbf{z}) = (x_1 \cdot z_1 + x_2 \cdot z_2)^2 = (\mathbf{x}^T \cdot \mathbf{z})^2.$$
Which can be seen as our kernel
$$k(\mathbf{x}, \mathbf{z}) = \phi(\mathbf{x})^T \cdot \phi(\mathbf{z}) = (\mathbf{x}^T \cdot \mathbf{z})^2.$$

Despite some simple examples, constructing a kernel function is not easy. One powerful technique that allows us to do it is to build them out of simpler kernels as building blocks. Being $f()$ any function, $q()$ is a polynomial with nonnegative coefficients, A is a symmetric positive semidefinite matrix, x_a and x_b are variables (not necessarily disjoint) with $x = (x_a, x_b)$, and k_a and k_b are valid kernel functions over their respective spaces.

Even if there are some techniques to construct new kernels, many existing, well-known kernels solve large amounts of problems. Let us go through some of the most noticeable ones.

11.7.1 *Gaussian Kernel*

The Gaussian kernel corresponds to a feature vector with infinite dimensionality. It can be written as
$$k(\mathbf{x}, \mathbf{x}') = \exp\left(-\frac{\|\mathbf{x} - \mathbf{x}'\|^2}{2 \cdot \sigma^2}\right).$$
Or, alternatively, using
$$\|\mathbf{x} - \mathbf{x}'\|^2 = \mathbf{x}^T \cdot \mathbf{x} + (\mathbf{x}')^T \cdot \mathbf{x}' - 2 \cdot \mathbf{x}^T \cdot \mathbf{x}'$$
we get
$$k(\mathbf{x}, \mathbf{x}') = \exp\left(\frac{\mathbf{x}^T \cdot \mathbf{x}}{2 \cdot \sigma^2}\right) \cdot \exp\left(\frac{\mathbf{x}^T \cdot \mathbf{x}'}{\sigma^2}\right) \cdot \exp\left(\frac{\mathbf{x}'^T \cdot \mathbf{x}'}{2 \cdot \sigma^2}\right).$$

11.7.2 *Sigmoidal Kernel*

Another kernel function is the sigmoidal kernel given by
$$k(\mathbf{x}, \mathbf{x}') = \tanh(a \cdot \mathbf{x}^T \cdot \mathbf{x}' + b) \tag{11.42}$$
whose kernel matrix in general is not positive semidefinite. This form of kernel has, however, been used in practice (Vapnik, 1995) because it gives kernel expansions such as the support vector machine and it is similar to the one used in neural network models.

11.7.3 *Generative mode Kernels*

Given a generative model $p(\mathbf{x})$ we can define a kernel by

$$k(\mathbf{x}, \mathbf{x'}) = p(\mathbf{x}) \cdot p(\mathbf{x'}). \tag{11.43}$$

Two inputs $\mathbf{x}$ and $\mathbf{x'}$ are similar if they both have high probabilities.

11.8 Conclusion

A support vector machine (SVM) is basically a two-class classifier. Yet, one can change the quadratic problem formulation to allow for multi-class classification. Alternatively, the data set can be divided into two parts in different ways and a separate SVM is trained for each way of division. Multiclass classification is then done by combining the output of all the SVM classifiers, like for example by the majority rule.

An SVM can be a linear machine using a linear kernel. In such case, it simply constructs a hyperplane as the decision surface in such a way that the margin of separation between positive and negative examples is maximized with a good generalization performance.

Furthermore, the support vector learning algorithm may construct many different learning machines by applying multiple kernels. Three common ones are:

(1) Polynomial learning machine with the kernel

$$k(\mathbf{x}, \mathbf{x'}) = (\mathbf{x}^T \mathbf{x}_i + 1)^p = (\langle \mathbf{x} | \mathbf{x'} \rangle + 1)^p$$

(2) Radial-basis-function network support vector machine with the kernel

$$k(\mathbf{x}, \mathbf{x'}) = \exp\left(-\frac{\|\mathbf{x} - \mathbf{x'}\|^2}{2 \cdot \sigma^2}\right)$$

In the radial-basis function type of a support vector machine, the number of radial-basis functions and their centers are determined by their number of support-vectors and their values.

(3) A perceptron with one hidden layer using the kernel

$$k(\mathbf{x}, \mathbf{x'}) = \tanh(a \cdot \mathbf{x}^T \cdot \mathbf{x'} + b)$$

A perceptron with one hidden layer type of support vector machine is somewhat restricted, this is due to the fact that the determination of whether a given kernel satisfies Mercer's theorem can indeed be a difficult matter. The number of hidden units corresponds to the number of support-vectors.

For all three machine types, the dimensionality of the feature space is determined by the number of support vectors extracted from the training data by the solution to the constrained-optimization problem.

11.8.1 SVMs, MLPs and RBFNs

Feed-forward networks with hidden nonlinear units are universal approximators. This is because the hidden layer applies a nonlinear transformation from the input space to a hidden space. The idea is to transform the input vector to a higher dimensional space in which linear classification in the output layer using a simple perceptron can be done. For an output neuron with M hidden neurons

$$o = \sigma \left(\sum_{i=1}^{M} w_i \cdot \sigma \left(\sum_{j=0}^{D} W_{ij} \cdot x_j \right) + b \right) \qquad (11.44)$$

such networks correspond to a sigmoidal kernel.

However, attempting to build a network with only one layer to approximate complex functions often requires a very large number of nodes. These nodes' many outputs represent a high dimensional vector M that is classified by the output neuron corresponding to a perceptron.

For a RBF network the number of hidden units (the number of radial-basis functions) corresponds to the the size N of the training test

$$o = \sigma \left(\sum_{i=1}^{N} w_i \cdot \phi(\|\mathbf{x} - \mathbf{x}_i\|) + b \right). \qquad (11.45)$$

Yet, we have seen that the number can be reduced by representing the training set by K cluster centers.

$$o = \sigma \left(\sum_{i=1}^{K} w_i \cdot \phi(\|\mathbf{x} - \mathbf{c}_i\|) + b \right). \qquad (11.46)$$

The use of kernel functions can turn any algorithm that only depends on dot products into a nonlinear algorithm, like an SVM machine into a Kernel Machine.

$$o = sgn \left(\sum_{i=1}^{N_s} \alpha_i \cdot t_i \cdot k(\mathbf{x}, \mathbf{x}_i) + b \right). \qquad (11.47)$$

In an SVM the number of hidden units corresponds to the number of N_s support-vectors and their values. The support-vectors do not cover the training set like the cluster centers in the RBF network. Because of that, the SVM is more prone to outliers that may become support-vectors. Their number is related to the size of the training set.

All in all, we have the following relations

$$M \ll N, \quad K \ll N. \quad N_s \ll N. \tag{11.48}$$

Usually the numbers M and K have to be determined by empirical experiments, however we may assume

$$M \approx K \approx N_s. \tag{11.49}$$

With big training sets the number of hidden units in all three approaches becomes very large leading to a very high dimensional vector to be classified by the output neuron. The high dimensionality of the vector influences negatively the classification of the output neurons during learning and generalization. This is the problem of the curse of dimensionality. Deep neural networks can avoid the curse of dimensionality problem by constraining the number of hidden neurons per layer. So, these deep networks present a solution to avoid the curse of dimensionality whenever the training data set is big. However if the size of the training set is moderate, one can and most likely should use regular MLPs, SVMs or RBF networks.

11.9   Exercises and Answers

The original support vector machine (SVM) is a binary classifier that finds an hyperplane that separates two classes. However, unlike perceptrons and logistic regressions it does not find any hyperplane that separates the two classes. SVMs look for the best possible hyperplane. But what does this mean?

To explain the process we will use the following figure with a two-dimensional example:

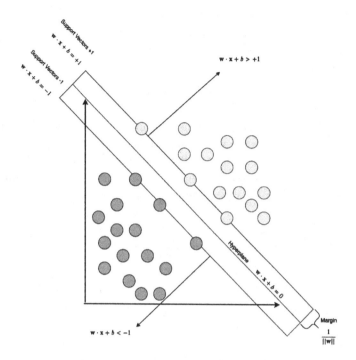

Between two sets of points from two classes, only a few will be on close to the frontier. These points are called the support vectors. The separation hyperplane defined by the weight vector $\mathbf{w}$ and bias term b will have to be placed somewhere between these.

The key idea is to maximize the distance between the boundary and both classes. To measure this distance, we have a quantity called the margin m which is defined as the distance between the support vectors and the boundary and can be computed through $m = \frac{1}{\|\mathbf{w}\|_2}$.

So, the learning procedure would be to find the weight vector that maximizes m. However, we need to restrict the optimization procedure such that the boundary hyperplane correctly classifies the points. To that end, we define the constraint:

$$\begin{cases} \mathbf{w}^T \mathbf{x}^{(i)} + b = +1 & t^{(i)} = +1 \\ \mathbf{w}^T \mathbf{x}^{(i)} + b = -1 & t^{(i)} = -1 \end{cases} \iff t^{(i)} \left(\mathbf{w}^T \mathbf{x}^{(i)} + b \right) \geq 1$$

where $\mathbf{x}^{(i)}$ is a support vector and $t^{(i)}$ is its target.

There are two ways to solve the optimization problem. The primal way finds $\mathbf{w}$ and b directly. Using it, we get the parameters directly and, so, after learning, the SVM classifies points with:

$$SVM\left(\mathbf{x};\mathbf{w},b\right) = sgn\left(\mathbf{w}^T\mathbf{x} + b\right)$$

The dual way is sometimes easier to optimize and uses the support vectors directly. Each point $\mathbf{x}^{(i)}$ gets a coefficient α_i which determines its contribution to the boundary. So, all non support vectors will have a zero coefficient. With this formulation, the optimizer tries to find the coefficients and, in the end, the SVM uses them to classify points as follows:

$$SVM\left(\mathbf{x};\mathbf{w},b\right) = sgn\left(\sum_{i=1}^{N} t^{(i)}\alpha_i\mathbf{x}^T\mathbf{x}^{(i)} + b\right)$$

As we can see, this dual version writes the decision function for a point based on its inner product with the training vectors. It is in this formulation that we can see where the kernel trick enters. If we replace the dot product $\mathbf{x}^T\mathbf{x}^{(i)}$ by a kernel function $K\left(\mathbf{x},\mathbf{x}^{(i)}\right)$ we can interpret the kernel as an inner product in a high dimensional space where the problem is separable.

1)

Consider the training set:

$$\mathbf{x}^{(1)} = \begin{pmatrix} 0 \\ 0 \\ 2 \end{pmatrix}, \mathbf{x}^{(2)} = \begin{pmatrix} 0 \\ 1 \\ 8 \end{pmatrix}, \mathbf{x}^{(3)} = \begin{pmatrix} 1 \\ 0 \\ 6 \end{pmatrix}, \mathbf{x}^{(4)} = \begin{pmatrix} 1 \\ 1 \\ 7 \end{pmatrix}, \mathbf{x}^{(5)} = \begin{pmatrix} 1 \\ 1 \\ 3 \end{pmatrix}$$

With targets:

$$t^{(1)} = +1, t^{(2)} = +1, t^{(3)} = -1, t^{(4)} = -1, t^{(5)} = +1$$

After training an SVM, we get the following coefficients:

$$\alpha^{(1)} = 0, \alpha^{(2)} = 1, \alpha^{(3)} = 0.5, \alpha^{(4)} = 1, \alpha^{(5)} = 0.5$$

a) How many support vectors are required?

Solution:

Four. All that have $\alpha_i > 0$.

---

b) Using a linear kernel and $b = -3$, how does this SVM classify $\mathbf{x} = \begin{pmatrix} 1\ 1\ 8 \end{pmatrix}^T$.

Solution:

$$o(\mathbf{x}) = sgn\left(\sum_{i=1}^{4} t^{(i)}\alpha_i \mathbf{x}^T \mathbf{x}^{(i)} + b\right)$$

$$= sgn((+1)(1)\begin{pmatrix} 1 & 1 & 8 \end{pmatrix}\begin{pmatrix} 0 \\ 1 \\ 8 \end{pmatrix} + (-1)\left(\frac{1}{2}\right)\begin{pmatrix} 1 & 1 & 8 \end{pmatrix}\begin{pmatrix} 1 \\ 0 \\ 6 \end{pmatrix}$$

$$+ (-1)(1)\begin{pmatrix} 1 & 1 & 8 \end{pmatrix}\begin{pmatrix} 1 \\ 1 \\ 7 \end{pmatrix} + (+1)\left(\frac{1}{2}\right)\begin{pmatrix} 1 & 1 & 8 \end{pmatrix}\begin{pmatrix} 1 \\ 1 \\ 3 \end{pmatrix} - 3)$$

$$= sgn\left(65 - 24.5 - 58 + 13 - 3\right)$$

$$= sgn\left(-7.5\right)$$

$$= -1$$

---

2)

Consider the training set put on a design matrix with the examples on the columns:

$$\mathbf{X} = \begin{pmatrix} 3.29\ 2.29\ 2.07\ 1.84\ 3.06\ 1.41\ 0.70\ 0.22\ 1.18\ 0.83 \\ 1.60\ 1.81\ 0.91\ 1.37\ 1.66\ 0.51\ 1.25\ 0.35\ 0.25\ 0.62 \end{pmatrix}$$

With targets placed on a row vector:

$$\mathbf{t} = \begin{pmatrix} +1\ +1\ +1\ +1\ +1\ -1\ -1\ -1\ -1\ -1 \end{pmatrix}$$

After training an SVM, we get the following coefficients:

$$\alpha = \begin{pmatrix} 0\ 0\ 3.36\ 0\ 0\ 3.36\ 0\ 0\ 0\ 0 \end{pmatrix}$$

a) How many support vectors are required?

Solution:

Two. All that have $\alpha_i > 0$.

b) What is the weight vector?

Solution:

Looking at the classification function:

$$o\left(\mathbf{x}\right) = sgn\left(\sum_{i=1}^{2} t^{(i)}\alpha_i \mathbf{x}^T \mathbf{x}^{(i)} + b\right)$$

We can rewrite is as:

$$o\left(\mathbf{x}\right) = sgn\left(\sum_{i=1}^{2} t^{(i)}\alpha_i \left(\mathbf{x}^{(i)}\right)^T \mathbf{x} + b\right)$$

Which can be written in terms of the weight vector as:

$$o\left(\mathbf{x}\right) = sgn\left(\mathbf{w}^T \mathbf{x} + b\right)$$

With:

$$\mathbf{w} = \sum_{i=1}^{2} t^{(i)}\alpha_i \mathbf{x}^{(i)}$$

So, we can get the weight vector:

$$\mathbf{w} = (+1)(3.36)\begin{pmatrix} 2.07 \\ 0.91 \end{pmatrix} + (-1)(3.36)\begin{pmatrix} 1.41 \\ 0.51 \end{pmatrix} = \begin{pmatrix} 2.2176 \\ 1.344 \end{pmatrix}$$

c) What is the boundary equation?

To get the boundary equation, we need the weight vector $\mathbf{w}$ and the bias b. We have the weight vector from the previous question. All we need is the bias.

We know that, for any support vector $\mathbf{x}^{(i)}$ with target $t^{(i)}$, we have that:

$$\mathbf{w}^T\mathbf{x}^{(i)} + b = t^{(i)}$$

So, we can take a support vector like $\mathbf{x}^{(3)} = \begin{pmatrix} 2.07 \\ 0.91 \end{pmatrix}$ and use it to get the bias:

$$\mathbf{w}^T\mathbf{x}^{(i)} + b = t^{(i)}$$

$$\begin{pmatrix} 2.2176 \\ 1.344 \end{pmatrix}^T \begin{pmatrix} 2.07 \\ 0.91 \end{pmatrix} + b = +1$$

$$b = 1 - 5.81$$

$$b = -4.81$$

Now we have all we need:

$$\mathbf{w}^T\mathbf{x} + b = 0 \iff 2.2176x_1 + 1.344x_2 - 4.81 = 0$$

---

d) What is the value of the margin?

Solution:

For the boundary line we have:

$$\mathbf{w}^T\mathbf{x} + b = 0 \iff 2.2176x_1 + 1.344x_2 - 4.81 = 0$$

The margin is the distance between any support vector and the boundary line. As was shown above, this distance can be computed as follows:

$$margin = \frac{1}{\|\mathbf{w}\|_2} = \frac{1}{\sqrt{2.2176^2 + 1.344^2}} = 0.386$$

e) Using the coefficient formulation, how does this SVM classify $\mathbf{x} = \left(1\ 3\right)^T$.

Solution:

$$o\left(\mathbf{x}\right) = sgn\left(\sum_{i=1}^{2} t^{(i)}\alpha_i \mathbf{x}^T \mathbf{x}^{(i)} + b\right)$$

$$= sgn\left((+1)(3.36)\left(1\ 3\right)\binom{2.07}{0.91} + (-1)(3.36)\left(1\ 3\right)\binom{1.41}{0.51} - 4.81\right)$$

$$= sgn\left(1.44\right)$$

$$= +1$$

f) What about with the weight vector?.

Solution:

$$o\left(\mathbf{x}\right) = sgn\left(\mathbf{w}^T\mathbf{x} + b\right)$$

$$= sgn\left(\binom{2.2176}{1.344}^T\binom{1}{3} - 4.81\right)$$

$$= sgn\left(1.44\right)$$

$$= +1$$

3)

Consider the training set:

$$\mathbf{X} = \begin{pmatrix} 0.68 & -0.25 & 0.83 & 1.44 & 1.14 & -2.19 & -2.47 & -1.19 & -2.3 & -0.94 \\ 1.26 & -0.51 & -0.32 & 1.04 & 3.21 & 5.1 & 3.76 & 6.39 & 3.48 & 5.04 \end{pmatrix}$$

With targets:

$$\mathbf{t} = \left(+1\ +1\ +1\ +1\ +1\ -1\ -1\ -1\ -1\ -1\right)$$

After running an SVM we get the weight vector $w = \left(0.544\ -0.474\right)^T$ and bias $b = 1.902$.

a) What are the support vectors?

Solution:

We know that, for any support vector $\mathbf{x}^{(i)}$ with target $t^{(i)}$, we have that:

$$\mathbf{w}^T \mathbf{x}^{(i)} + b = t^{(i)}$$

So, all we need to do is check this condition for every point:

- For $\mathbf{x}^{(1)}$: $\begin{pmatrix} 0.544 & -0.474 \end{pmatrix} \begin{pmatrix} 0.68 \\ 1.26 \end{pmatrix} + 1.902 = 1.67 \neq +1$, so it is not a support vector.

- For $\mathbf{x}^{(2)}$: $\begin{pmatrix} 0.544 & -0.474 \end{pmatrix} \begin{pmatrix} -0.25 \\ -0.51 \end{pmatrix} + 1.902 = 2.01 \neq +1$, so it is not a support vector.

- For $\mathbf{x}^{(3)}$: $\begin{pmatrix} 0.544 & -0.474 \end{pmatrix} \begin{pmatrix} 0.83 \\ -0.32 \end{pmatrix} + 1.902 = 2.51 \neq +1$, so it is not a support vector.

- For $\mathbf{x}^{(4)}$: $\begin{pmatrix} 0.544 & -0.474 \end{pmatrix} \begin{pmatrix} 1.44 \\ 1.04 \end{pmatrix} + 1.902 = 2.19 \neq +1$, so it is not a support vector.

- For $\mathbf{x}^{(5)}$: $\begin{pmatrix} 0.544 & -0.474 \end{pmatrix} \begin{pmatrix} 1.14 \\ 3.21 \end{pmatrix} + 1.902 = 1 = +1$, so it is a support vector.

- For $\mathbf{x}^{(6)}$: $\begin{pmatrix} 0.544 & -0.474 \end{pmatrix} \begin{pmatrix} -2.19 \\ 5.1 \end{pmatrix} + 1.902 = -1.71 \neq -1$, so it is not a support vector.

- For $\mathbf{x}^{(7)}$: $\begin{pmatrix} 0.544 & -0.474 \end{pmatrix} \begin{pmatrix} -2.47 \\ 3.76 \end{pmatrix} + 1.902 = -1.22 \neq -1$, so it is not a support vector.

- For $\mathbf{x}^{(8)}$: $\begin{pmatrix} 0.544 & -0.474 \end{pmatrix} \begin{pmatrix} -1.19 \\ 6.39 \end{pmatrix} + 1.902 = -1.78 \neq -1$, so it is not a support vector.

- For $\mathbf{x}^{(9)}$: $\begin{pmatrix} 0.544 & -0.474 \end{pmatrix} \begin{pmatrix} -2.3 \\ 3.48 \end{pmatrix} + 1.902 = -1 = -1$, so it is a support vector.

- For $\mathbf{x}^{(10)}$: $\begin{pmatrix} 0.544 & -0.474 \end{pmatrix} \begin{pmatrix} -0.94 \\ 5.04 \end{pmatrix} + 1.902 = -1 = -1$, so it is a support vector.

So, we have three support vectors: $\mathbf{x}^{(5)}$, $\mathbf{x}^{(9)}$ and $\mathbf{x}^{(10)}$.

b) What are the dual coefficients α_i?

Solution:

Looking at the classification function:

$$o\left(\mathbf{x}\right) = sgn\left(\mathbf{w}^T\mathbf{x} + b\right)$$

Which can be written in terms of the coefficients as follows:

$$o\left(\mathbf{x}\right) = sgn\left(\sum_{i=1}^{10} t^{(i)}\alpha_i\mathbf{x}^T\mathbf{x}^{(i)} + b\right)$$

So, for a support vector $\mathbf{x}$ with target t, we must have:

$$\sum_{i=1}^{10} t^{(i)}\alpha_i\mathbf{x}^T\mathbf{x}^{(i)} + b = t$$

For the first support vector:

$$\sum_{i=1}^{10} t^{(i)}\alpha_i\mathbf{x}^T\mathbf{x}^{(i)} + b =$$

$$t^{(5)}\alpha_5\mathbf{x}^T\mathbf{x}^{(5)} + t^{(9)}\alpha_9\mathbf{x}^T\mathbf{x}^{(9)} + t^{(10)}\alpha_{10}\mathbf{x}^T\mathbf{x}^{(10)} + 1.902 = +1$$

$$\alpha_5\left(1.14\ 3.21\right)\begin{pmatrix}1.14\\3.21\end{pmatrix} - \alpha_9\left(1.14\ 3.21\right)\begin{pmatrix}-2.3\\3.48\end{pmatrix} - \alpha_{10}\left(1.14\ 3.21\right)\begin{pmatrix}-0.94\\5.04\end{pmatrix} + 1.902 = +1$$

$$11.6037\alpha_5 - 8.5488\alpha_9 - 15.1068\alpha_{10} + 1.902 = +1$$

$$11.6037\alpha_5 - 8.5488\alpha_9 - 15.1068\alpha_{10} = -0.902$$

For the second support vector:

$$\sum_{i=1}^{10} t^{(i)}\alpha_i\mathbf{x}^T\mathbf{x}^{(i)} + b =$$

$$t^{(5)}\alpha_5\mathbf{x}^T\mathbf{x}^{(5)} + t^{(9)}\alpha_9\mathbf{x}^T\mathbf{x}^{(9)} + t^{(10)}\alpha_{10}\mathbf{x}^T\mathbf{x}^{(10)} + 1.902 = -1$$

$$\alpha_5\left(-2.3\ 3.48\right)\begin{pmatrix}1.14\\3.21\end{pmatrix} - \alpha_9\left(-2.3\ 3.48\right)\begin{pmatrix}-2.3\\3.48\end{pmatrix} - \alpha_{10}\left(-2.3\ 3.48\right)\begin{pmatrix}-0.94\\5.04\end{pmatrix} + 1.902 = -1$$

$$8.5488\alpha_5 - 17.4004\alpha_9 - 19.7012\alpha_{10} + 1.902 = -1$$

$$8.5488\alpha_5 - 17.4004\alpha_9 - 19.7012\alpha_{10} = -2.902$$

For the third support vector:

$$\sum_{i=1}^{10} t^{(i)}\alpha_i \mathbf{x}^T \mathbf{x}^{(i)} + b = t$$

$$t^{(5)}\alpha_5 \mathbf{x}^T \mathbf{x}^{(5)} + t^{(9)}\alpha_9 \mathbf{x}^T \mathbf{x}^{(9)} + t^{(10)}\alpha_{10} \mathbf{x}^T \mathbf{x}^{(10)} + 1.902 = -1$$

$$\alpha_5 \left(-0.94\ 5.04\right)\begin{pmatrix} 1.14 \\ 3.21 \end{pmatrix} - \alpha_9 \left(-0.94\ 5.04\right)\begin{pmatrix} -2.3 \\ 3.48 \end{pmatrix} - \alpha_{10}\left(-0.94\ 5.04\right)\begin{pmatrix} -0.94 \\ 5.04 \end{pmatrix} + 1.902 = -1$$

$$15.1068\alpha_5 - 19.7012\alpha_9 - 26.2852\alpha_{10} + 1.902 = -1$$

$$15.1068\alpha_5 - 19.7012\alpha_9 - 26.2852\alpha_{10} = -2.902$$

Combining the three equations in a system and solving it we get:

$$\alpha_5 = 0.2606$$

$$\alpha_9 = 0.0016$$

$$\alpha_{10} = 0.2600$$

c) What is the value of the margin?

Solution:

The margin is the distance between any support vector and the boundary line. As was shown above, this distance can be computed as follows:

$$margin = \frac{1}{\|\mathbf{w}\|_2} = \frac{1}{\sqrt{0.544^2 + -0.474^2}} = 1.385$$

Thinking Questions

a) Think about the VC dimension of an SVM. Will it be closer to the dimension of the weight vector? Will it be related to the number of support vectors?

b) Think about how the choice for SVM kernel related to the feature transformations we applied with linear regression.

c) How do you think the kernel related to the use of hidden layers in MLPs?

d) Is an MLP with linear hidden layers able to separate nonlinear problems?

e) What about an SVM with a linear kernel?

Chapter 12

Deep Learning

Fig. 12.1 In deep learning many hidden layers of artificial neural networks are used to learn complex mappings from input to output from large sets of training examples.

12.1   Introduction

The term "Deep Learning" was introduced to the machine learning community by Rina Dechter in 1986 [Dechter (1986)] (see Figure 12.2 (a)) and to artificial neural networks by Igor Aizenberg and colleagues in 2000 [Aizenberg *et al.* (2000)]. However, it only became really popular after an overview article by Juergen Schmidhuber [Schmidhuber (2014)], see Figure 12.2 (b).

(a)   (b)

Fig. 12.2   (a) Rina Dechter and (b) Juergen Schmidhuber.

A deep artificial network uses many hidden layers to increase the model's power, see Figure 12.3. These layers are trained by backpropagation like we have seen for the regular MLP. With many hidden layers it is typical to use vector notation to write a more compact version of the algorithm. In the exercises section, we will go into the details on how to apply, implement and think about backpropagation with many layers. In fact, deep learning as a field proposes a compendium of heuristics and techniques that can be applied to MLPs with the aim of improving results on specific tasks.

12.1.1   *Loss Function*

The first step of the general approach in deep learning is to write down a loss function that depends on the data and the network weighs [Goodfellow *et al.* (2016)]. As we have seen before, a typical example of such a function is the cross entropy error.

Assume we refer to the whole set of parameters in a network as θ. Now, concretely, the loss function depends on a comparison between the model outputs o and the targets t. Since the outputs depend on the inputs and

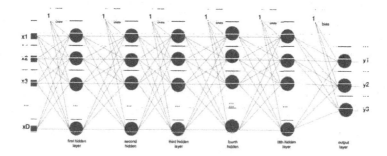

Fig. 12.3 A feed forward network with many hidden layers is called a deep network, in our example the network has five hidden layers. Depending on the training set more hidden layers can be used. Deep learning is not a new algorithm. In fact, it is really a large MLP trained by backpropagation. Furthermore, different heuristics and methods, made possible by the increase in computing power, are used with the aim of improving the results. These models achieved tremendous results and represent one of the most successful tools in engineering.

the parameters, we can write $o = f(\mathbf{x}, \theta)$. But given that the inputs are fixed, we can introduce a short notation for the outputs

$$o_\theta = f(\mathbf{x}, \theta).$$

With that, the loss function can be written as

$$L(f(\mathbf{x}, \theta), \mathbf{y}) = L(\mathbf{y}, o_\theta). \tag{12.1}$$

Following the same reasoning, the inputs are also fixed. For that reason, it is common to write the loss function as depending on the parameters

$$L(f(\mathbf{x}, \theta), \mathbf{y}) = L(\mathbf{y}, o_\theta) = L(\theta). \tag{12.2}$$

12.1.2 *Mini-Batch*

Having a loss function, training is performed through backpropagation of gradients. In the typical MLP, the gradients were determined using the whole training data set. This is called the batch gradient descent. The model updates parameters after processing the whole training data (one epoch). Deep learning usually works with extremely large training sets. For that reason, using the full data to compute one gradient iteration can be too time consuming and even unnecessary. A subset of the data can be enough to have a reasonable estimate of the gradient at a given iteration. For MLPs we have also covered the stochastic gradient descent procedure where one updates model parameters after processing every instance, however, gradients based on only one example can be very noisy and may delay convergence [Goodfellow *et al.* (2016)]. Therefore, a solution is to use mini batch gradient descent . This is basically a trade-off between the two approaches where learning is preformed in small groups. For example, if the training set is composed by 50000 instances, and the size of a mini-batch is set to 50, then there will be 1000 mini batches.

12.2   Why Deep Networks?

According to the universality theorem, a neural network with a single large enough hidden layer is capable of approximating any continuous function. So, the big question is why should we use (see Figure 12.4) a "deep" neural network instead of a "fat" neural network?

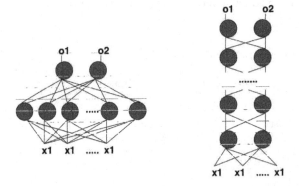

Fig. 12.4   Why should we use a "deep" neural network (right side) instead of a "fat" neural network (left side)?

Attempting to build a network with only one layer to approximate complex functions often requires a very large number of hidden nodes. Empirical experiments indicate that "deep" neural networks give better results than "fat" neural networks. As we will see, there are several hints on why this happens.

12.2.1 *Hierarchical Organization*

The principles of hierarchical organization appear in nature, for example, the structure of matter itself is hierarchically organized including elementary particles, atomic nuclei, atoms, and molecules [Resnikoff (1989)]. The idea of hierarchical structures is based on the decomposition of a hierarchy into simpler parts. Hierarchy offers a more efficient way of representing information. Deep learning enables high-level abstractions in data by architectures composed of multiple nonlinear transformations. It offers a natural progression from low-level structures to high-level structure, as demonstrated by natural complexity [LeCun and Bengio (1998a); Riesenhuber *et al.* (1999); Riesenhuber and Poggio (2000, 2002)].

12.2.2 *Boolean Functions*

A good example of the power of hierarchy appears in the case of boolean functions. Any such function can be represented by a truth table. For D variables there are 2^D rows in the table. Alternatively, the same function can be described by a disjunctive normal form (DNF) which is an expression of made by an lot of *OR*s between *AND*s. Each of the *AND*s can be implemented by one perceptron. We can construct an hidden layer with these perceptrons. Then, all of their outputs (the logical results of the *AND*s) is fed into an output perceptron that computes the *OR* between all. For large and complex DNF, the size of the hidden layer can explode. Alternatively, one can represent the formula by a logical circuit of bigger depth but of much lesser complexity, which is the idea behind using a deep network.

12.2.3 *Curse of dimensionality*

In a "fat" neural network there are many hidden neurons, their outputs represent a high dimensional vector that is classified by the output neurons. The high dimensionality of this vector influences negatively the classification of the output neurons during learning and generalization. This corresponds to the phenomenon of the curse of dimensionality. Deep neural networks can avoid this curse of dimensionality problem by constraining the number of hidden neurons in each layer by distributing them across several layers.

12.2.4 *Local Minima*

It is assumed that an artificial neural network with several hidden layers is less likely to be stuck in a local minima as demonstrated by empirical experiments. It was commonly thought that simple gradient descent would get trapped in poor local minima. However, in practice, although poor local minima present a big problem with small networks [Swirszcz *et al.* (2016)], they rarely are a problem with deep networks. In these, most local minima are equivalent and close to the global minimum [Choromanska *et al.* (2015)]. For large networks, the loss function may have a large number of saddle points where the gradient is zero [Dauphin *et al.* (2014)]. Saddle points need to be traded differently than local minima with advanced momentum techniques. Also with saddle points Newton's method cannot be used.

12.2.5 *Can represent big training sets*

By increasing the number of layers we can increase the number of parameters faster. By doing so, we can add enough degrees of freedom to model large training sets. This is extremely helpful since nowadays, for specific tasks, a really large amount is collected.

12.2.6 *Efficient Model Selection*

Ideally, to overcome overfitting one has to use a model that has the right capacity. However, this task is difficult and costly since it involves the search through many different architectures. Many experiments with different number of neurons and hidden layers have to be done. Using an over-parameterized deep learning network, one can constraint it to the right complexity through regularization. This way, the search for the model of the right capacity is done by a search for the correct regularization parameters. This kind of search is easier to implement since for example for l_2

$$\Delta w_j = -\eta \left(\frac{\partial E}{\partial w_j} \right) - \alpha \cdot w_j$$

or l_1 regularization

$$\Delta w_j = -\eta \left(\frac{\partial E}{\partial w_j} \right) - \alpha \cdot sign(w_j)$$

all we have to do is find the right value for one parameter α. So, the search for the correct model complexity can be done efficiently through empirical experiments.

12.2.7 *Criticism of Deep Neural Networks*

It seems as well that the deep learning revolution results mainly from brute force, it is not based on new mathematical models and appears to be biologically unlikely [Serre (2019)]. Deep neural networks require a very large labeled training set. This requirement can become a bottleneck, since in many special applications it is difficult to generate labels for enough examples. Often these huge sets have to be manually labeled by some experts which results in high costs. For example medical classification of tumors would require a relatively expensive big labeled data set.

12.3 Vanishing Gradients Problem

There are two main technical problems in the learning process with a deep neural network: overfitting and vanishing gradients. Overfitting can be overcome by regularization. We already introduced the l_2, l_1 and l_p regularization methods. Furthermore, in a later section we describe an additional stochastic regularization method called dropout. So, in this section we focus on the vanishing gradients problem.

As more layers using the sigmoid activation functions are added to neural networks, the gradients of the error function approaches zero during the backpropagation algorithm [Goodfellow *et al.* (2016)]. This happens because the sigmoid function squashes the input into an output between 0 and 1. With that, large change in the input to the sigmoid function will cause small changes in the output and the derivative becomes small, see Figure 12.5. The same applies to the tanh function which squashes the input into an output between -1 and 1. This is a problem because during backpropagation, in each iteration, weights receive an update proportional to the partial derivative with respect to that weight. If that derivative is too small, the weights will practically not change and the network does not learn.

For shallow network with only a few layers this is not a problem. However, when more layers are used, backpropagation computes gradients through the chain rule and thus multiplies several small values to compute

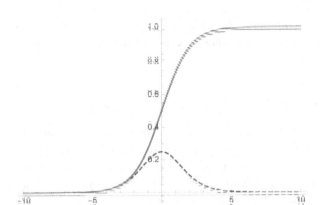

Fig. 12.5   The sigmoid function and the derivative indicated by dashed line.

the gradient of the layers closer to the input. By doing so, as the gradients get closer to the input layer, their value decreases exponentially leading to a vanishingly small value preventing the weight from changing its value. Hochreiter's diploma thesis of 1991 formally identified the reason for this failure in the vanishing gradients problem [Hochreiter (1991)].

The simplest solution to this problem is to use an activation function that does not cause a small derivative. An example of such an activation function is the rectified activation function. Besides changing the activation function we will go through two more solutions: residual connections and batch normalization.

12.3.1   *Rectified Linear Unit (ReLU)*

Rectifier also known as a ramp function

$$f(x) = \max(0, x). \tag{12.3}$$

is defined as the positive part of its argument [Jarrett *et al.* (2009)], [Nair and Hinton (2009)], [Goodfellow *et al.* (2016)]. The function is non-differentiable at zero; however, it is differentiable anywhere else and we can use the subderivative with sgn_0 function

$$f'(x) = sgn_0(x) = \begin{cases} 1 \text{ if } x \geq 0 \\ 0 \text{ if } x < 0 \end{cases}. \tag{12.4}$$

The rectifier has fewer vanishing gradient problems when compared to a sigmoidal activation function since it does not cause a small derivative, see Figure 12.6.

(a)
(b)

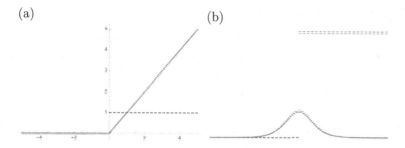

Fig. 12.6 (a) Rectifier activation function (ReLU), the derivative is indicated by the doted line. (b) Comparing the derivatives of the sigmoid activation function and the rectifier activation function indicated by a doted line.

The rectifier is a biological plausible activation function [Hahnloser *et al.* (2000)]. A unit (neuron) employing it is also called a rectified linear unit (ReLU). The function is very computationally efficient since it is only based on comparison, addition and multiplication. The use of rectified linear units leads to a sparse activation, in a randomly initialized network, only about 50% of hidden units are activated (having a non-zero output).

Despite all their advantages, rectified linear units can become inactive for essentially all inputs and so become stuck in an inactive state. In some cases, large numbers of units in a network can become stuck in dead states. This problem typically arises when the learning rate is set too high. Depending on the task, this can be a problem since dead states cannot recover during mini-batch learning or during stochastic gradient descent. However for batch learning (whole training sample) this can be a positive property since the model capacity decreases, it is a form of regularization.

12.3.1.1 *Leaky ReLU*

The dead states can be mitigated by using leaky ReLUs [Maas *et al.* (2013)] instead

$$f(x) = \max(0.01 \cdot x, x). \tag{12.5}$$

Leaky ReLUs do not "die" since they replace the inactive state by a small negative linear value, see Figure 12.7 (a). The derivative is given by

$$f'(x) = \begin{cases} 1 & \text{if } x \geq 0 \\ 0.01 & \text{if } x < 0 \end{cases}. \tag{12.6}$$

12.3.1.2   *Parametric ReLU*

Parametric ReLUs (PReLU) [He *et al.* (2015b)] make the coefficient of leakage α into a parameter that is learned along with the other neural network parameters

$$f(x) = \max(\alpha \cdot x, x). \tag{12.7}$$

12.3.1.3   *Exponential Linear Units (ELU)*

Exponential Linear Units [Clevert *et al.* (2015)]

$$f(x) = \max(\alpha \cdot x, x) \tag{12.8}$$

compared with Leaky ReLU adds some robustness to noise since they are closer to zero mean outputs, see Figure 12.7 (b). However the function is computationally inefficient since it requires the $exp()$ operation.

(a)   (b)

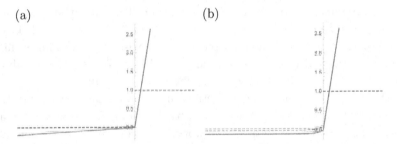

Fig. 12.7   (a) Leaky ReLU, the derivative is indicated by the doted line. (b) Exponential Linear Units (ELU), the derivative is indicated by the doted line.

12.3.1.4   *Maxout Unit*

The unit (neuron) does not have the basic form of dot product, instead each unit has two sets of weights $\mathbf{w}_1, \mathbf{w}_2$ and biases b_1, b_2, and the activation function is the max of the inputs [Goodfellow *et al.* (2013)]

$$\max(\mathbf{w}_1 \cdot \mathbf{x} + b_1, \mathbf{w}_2 \cdot \mathbf{x} + b_2). \tag{12.9}$$

Both ReLU and Leaky ReLU are a special case of this form, for ReLU $\mathbf{w}_1 = (0, 0, \cdots, 0)^T, b_1 = 0$. The Maxout neuron therefore enjoys all the benefits of a ReLU unit (linear regime of operation, no saturation) and does not die. However, unlike the ReLU neurons it doubles the number of parameters for every single unit, leading to a high total number of parameters. The number of sets can also be more than two.

12.3.1.5 *Which activation to Use?*

As we have seen there are many possible activation functions. As a general rule of thumb, in deep learning one should avoid sigmoidal activation functions and try rectified linear units (ReLU). During the experiments one should be careful with the learning rates since too high learning rates result in inactive units during mini-batch learning. Further experiments can be done with Leaky ReLU, then Maxout and finally ELU verifying if the empirical results [Goodfellow *et al.* (2016)] payoff the increase in complexity.

12.3.2 *Residual Learning*

The residual neural network (ResNet) is an artificial neural network that is motivated by the pyramidal cells in the cerebral cortex. In a cortical layer, pyramidal cells (neurons) get the input from the following layers skipping intermediary layers [Thomson (2010)]. An implementation of this principle avoids the vanishing gradients problem through skip connections, or shortcuts to jump over some layers [He *et al.* (2015a)], [Srivastava *et al.* (2015)].

Consider a neural network with input $\mathbf{x}$ and target $\mathbf{y}$. The goal of training is that the output $\mathbf{o}$ of the neural network becomes similar to the desired target $\mathbf{y}$ by minimizing a loss function

$$L(\mathbf{y}, o_\theta).$$

Assuming that the dimension of both vectors $\mathbf{x}$ and $\mathbf{y}$ are the same, we define the difference (or the residual) between both vectors as

$$R(\mathbf{x}) = \mathbf{y} - \mathbf{x} \tag{12.10}$$

and define the target of the network as $R(\mathbf{x})$. The corresponding network tries to learn the residual $R(\mathbf{x})$ instead of $\mathbf{y}$

$$L(R(\mathbf{x}), o_\theta).$$

This operation corresponds to adding the input $\mathbf{x}$ to the output of a network o_θ by skipped connections. This form of learning is called residual learning, see Figure 12.8.

If the dimension of both vectors $\mathbf{x}$ and $\mathbf{y}$ are not same we can perform a linear projection W_p by the shortcut connections to match the dimensions:

$$dim(\mathbf{y}) = dim(W_p \cdot \mathbf{x}).$$

A building block is defined with the residual units

$$o_\theta = f(\mathbf{x}, \theta)$$

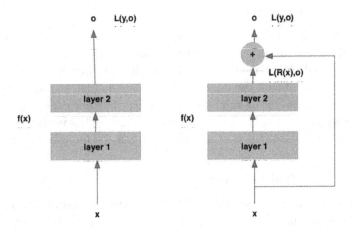

Fig. 12.8   Residual learning.

as

$$o = f(\mathbf{x}, \theta_i) + \mathbf{x}. \tag{12.11}$$

A network can be composed of many hidden units, the connections usually skip two layers which represents a residual building block, see Figure 12.9.

With many skip connections over layers the network reuses activations from a previous layer until the adjacent layer learns its weights. During training, the weights adapt to mute the upstream layer, and amplify the previously-skipped layer. With many skip connections, the network can start making progress even if several layers have not started learning yet.

12.3.3   *Batch Normalization*

Another approach to fight the vanishing gradients problem is to do batch normalization. This can be done to a point where even sigmoidal units work [Ioffe and Szegedy (2015)]. Furthermore, this technique can also make the resulting network much less sensitive to the weight initialization.

In the intermediate layers of an artificial deep neural network the distribution of the activations is constantly changing during training. This slows down the training process because each layer must learn to adapt themselves to a new distribution in every training step. Batch normalization is a method that we can use to normalize the inputs of each layer, in order to fight the internal covariate shift problem. The basic idea is to normalize

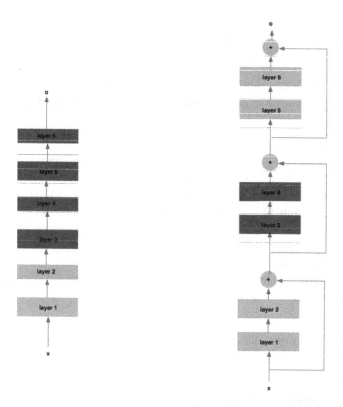

Fig. 12.9 A network can be composed of many hidden units, the connections usually skip two layers which represents a residual building block. With many skip connections over layers the network reuses activations from a previous layer until the adjacent layer learns its weights. During training, the weights adapt to mute the upstream layer, and amplify the previously-skipped layer. With many skip connections, the network can start making progress even if several layers have not started learning yet.

the training data so that it resembles a normal distribution (zero mean and a unitary variance). In order to zero-center and normalize the inputs, the algorithm needs to estimate the inputs mean and standard deviation. It does it by evaluating the mean and standard deviation of the inputs over the current mini batch. Concretely, at training time, a batch normalization layer does the following:

- Calculate the mean μ_B and variance σ_B^2 of the layers input over the min batch

$$\mu_B = \frac{1}{m_B} \sum_{k=1}^{m_B} \mathbf{x}_k, \quad \sigma_B^2 = \frac{1}{m_B} \sum_{k=1}^{m_B} (\mathbf{x}_k - \mu_B)^2$$

where m_B is the number of instances in the mini-batch.

- Normalize the layer inputs using the previously calculated batch statistics

$$\hat{\mathbf{x}}_k = \frac{\mathbf{x}_k - \mu_B}{\sqrt{\sigma_B^2 + \epsilon}}$$

where $\hat{\mathbf{x}}_k$ is the zero-centered and normalized input and ϵ is a smoothing term, that is, a tiny number to avoid division by zero (like 0.001).

- Scale and shift in order to obtain the output of the layer

$$\mathbf{z}_k = BN_{\gamma, \beta}(\mathbf{x}_k) = \gamma \cdot \hat{\mathbf{x}}_k + \beta$$

where $\mathbf{z}_k$ is the output of the BN operation. This operation's parameters γ and β are learned during training (trough gradient descent) along with the original network weights and biases.

At test time, the mean and the variance are fixed. They are estimated using the previously calculated means and variances of each training batch by computing the whole training set's mean and standard deviation.

12.4   Regularization by Dropout

Having covered the main solutions to the vanishing gradient's problem, we can focus on another solution for the other main problem, overfitting. Besides the regularization techniques based on weight penalties, in deep learning it is very common to use dropout (Dilution) [Hertz et al. (1991)] which is a stochastic regularization method. In each forward pass, a randomly selected set of neurons is ignored (dropped) for one pass [Hinton et al. (2012)] , [Goodfellow et al. (2016)]. The probability of dropping the set out is described by a hyper-parameter; usually 0.5 is commonly used. For input nodes, this should be low, because information is directly lost when input nodes are ignored. Then only the reduced network is trained on the data in that training step, see Figure 12.10.

In the next training step the removed nodes are then reinserted into the network with their original weights. By avoiding training all nodes on all training data, dropout decreases overfitting and it also significantly improves training speed. Furthermore, it reduces the possibility for many

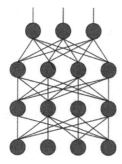 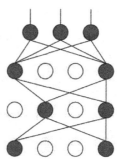

Fig. 12.10   In each forward pass, a randomly selected set of neurons is ignored.

node interactions, leading each individual unit to learn more robust features. It is a stochastic process, since at each training step a different (randomly chosen) set of neurons is dropped out and not allowed to learn.

12.5   Weight Initialization

Besides the two main technical problems we have covered, in deep networks, initialization can also play an important role. In a typical shallow MLP the weights are initialized with small random numbers (Gaussian with zero mean and 0.01 standard deviation). This works for small networks, but creates problems with deeper networks since all activations can become zero and the gradients will be all zero.

To circumvent this issue many techniques have been proposed like the Xavier initialization. In this approach weights are chosen from a Gaussian distribution with zero mean and a variance of $1/D$, where D specifies the number of input neurons. However when using ReLU all activations can become zero. This problem can be solved by setting the variance to $2/D$ [Glorot and Bengio (2010)].

12.6   Faster Optimizers

Training a very large deep neural network can be a slow process. The gradient descent can be very slow if η is too small, and can oscillate widely if η is too large. For that reason, some techniques were proposed to learn more effectively. These techniques are also particularly suited for the saddle points problem that is present in deep networks.

12.6.1   *Momentum*

In some cases one can speed up training by including momentum term with weight α in the update rule

$$\Delta w_{ti}(\tau + 1) = -\eta \frac{\partial E}{\partial w_{ti}} + \alpha \cdot \Delta w_{ti}(\tau) \tag{12.12}$$

where τ indicates the time step of the algorithm. With that, the update rule becomes

$$w_{ti}^{new} = w_{ti}^{old} + \Delta w_{ti}(\tau + 1).$$

Including momentum prohibits fast changes of the direction of the gradient [Hertz *et al.* (1991)] by taking into account the previous gradient. The momentum parameter α is chosen between 0 and 1, usually 0.9 is a good value. Building on the idea of momentum there are other alternative methods that we will cover.

12.6.2   *Nestrov Momentum*

The idea of Nesterov momentum optimization is to measure the gradient of the cost function not at the local position but slightly ahead in the direction of the momentum [Nesterov (1983)], [Nesterov (2004)], [Sutskever *et al.* (2013)] $w_{ti} + \Delta w_{ti}(\tau)$

$$\Delta w_{ti}(\tau + 1) = -\eta \frac{\partial E(w_{ti} + \Delta w_{ti}(\tau))}{\partial w_{ti}} + \alpha \cdot \Delta w_{ti}(\tau), \tag{12.13}$$

and

$$w_{ti}^{new} = w_{ti}^{old} + \Delta w_{ti}(\tau + 1).$$

12.6.3   *AdaGrad*

The AdaGrad algorithm scales down the gradient vector along the steepest dimensions and uses a different learning rate for every parameter w_i at every time step [Duchi *et al.* (2011)]. It scales them inversely proportional to the square root of the sum of all squared values of the gradient representing the scale variable $s_{ti}(\tau)$. At the beginning of learning with $\tau = 0$ the scale variable is initialized to zero $s_{ti}(0) = 0$. In the first iteration we determine the scale variable by accumulating the squared gradient

$$s_{ti}(\tau + 1) = s_{ti}(\tau) + \frac{\partial E}{\partial w_{ti}} \cdot \frac{\partial E}{\partial w_{ti}} \tag{12.14}$$

and we preform the scaled gradient descent with

$$w_{ti}^{new} = w_{ti}^{old} - \eta \cdot \frac{\frac{\partial E}{\partial w_{ti}}}{\sqrt{s_{ti}(\tau + 1) + \epsilon}} \tag{12.15}$$

where ϵ is a smoothing term, a very tiny number to avoid division by zero (like $0.00000001 = 10^{-8}$).

12.6.4 *RMSProp*

The AdaGrad algorithm can slow down a bit too much and may end up never converging to a minimum. RMSProp changes the gradient into an exponential weighted moving average [Goodfellow *et al.* (2016)]. It discard history from extreme past so that it can converge rapidly, accumulating only the gradients from the most recent iterations. At the beginning of learning with $\tau = 0$ the scale variable is initialized to zero $s_{ti}(0) = 0$. In the first iteration we determine the scale variable

$$s_{ti}(\tau + 1) = \alpha \cdot s_{ti}(\tau) + (1 - \alpha) \cdot \frac{\partial E}{\partial w_{ti}} \cdot \frac{\partial E}{\partial w_{ti}} \tag{12.16}$$

with α being the decay rate with a typical value of 0.9. Then we preform the scaled gradient descent

$$w_{ti}^{new} = w_{ti}^{old} - \eta \cdot \frac{\frac{\partial E}{\partial w_{ti}}}{\sqrt{s_{ti}(\tau + 1) + \epsilon}} \tag{12.17}$$

where, again, ϵ is a smoothing term.

12.6.5 *Adam*

Adam which stands for adaptive moment estimation [Kingma and Ba (2014)], combines the ideas of momentum

$$\Delta w_{ti}(\tau + 1) = -(1 - \alpha_1)\frac{\partial E}{\partial w_{ti}} + \alpha_1 \cdot \Delta w_{ti}(\tau) \tag{12.18}$$

and RMSProp

$$s_{ti}(\tau + 1) = \alpha_2 \cdot s_{ti}(\tau) + (1 - \alpha_2) \cdot \frac{\partial E}{\partial w_{ti}} \cdot \frac{\partial E}{\partial w_{ti}}. \tag{12.19}$$

At the beginning of learning with $\tau = 0$ the scale variable is initialized to zero $s_{ti}(0) = 0$. The procedure then corrects the values in relation to time τ (taking the power of the value τ)

$$\Delta w_{ti}(\tau + 1) = \frac{\Delta w_{ti}(\tau + 1)}{1 - \alpha_1^{\tau+1}} \tag{12.20}$$

and

$$s_{ti}(\tau + 1) = \frac{s_{ti}(\tau + 1))}{1 - \alpha_2^{\tau+1}}. \tag{12.21}$$

Then we apply the update

$$w_{ti}^{new} = w_{ti}^{old} + \eta \cdot \frac{\Delta w_{ti}(\tau + 1)}{\sqrt{s_{ti}(\tau + 1) + \epsilon}} \tag{12.22}$$

where ϵ is a smoothing term (10^{-8}). Usually this approach requires less tuning than gradient descent with the default values $\alpha_1 = 0.9$, $\alpha_2 = 0.999$, $\eta = 0.001$. Adam is regarded as robust, however there are some cases when other methods like momentum or Nestrov momentum give better results.

12.6.6   *Notation*

In the deep learning community one often uses vector notation and indicates the free parameter as θ since beside the network weights there are as well other parameters like γ and β in the batch normalization [Goodfellow *et al.* (2016)]. For example, in Adam, the vector notation for momentum would be

$$\mathbf{m} = \alpha_1 \cdot \mathbf{m} - (1 - \alpha_1)\nabla_\theta L(\theta) \tag{12.23}$$

and for RMSProp would be

$$\mathbf{s} = \alpha_2 \cdot \mathbf{s} + (1 - \alpha_2)\nabla_\theta L(\theta) \odot \nabla_\theta L(\theta) \tag{12.24}$$

where $\odot$ represents the element-wise multiplication. The correction of values in relation to time τ (taking the power of the value τ) would be

$$\mathbf{m} = \frac{\mathbf{m}}{1 - \alpha_1^\tau} \tag{12.25}$$

and

$$\mathbf{s} = \frac{\mathbf{s}}{1 - \alpha_2^\tau}. \tag{12.26}$$

Finally, the update would be

$$\theta = \theta + \eta \cdot \mathbf{m} \oslash \sqrt{\mathbf{s} + \epsilon} \tag{12.27}$$

where $\oslash$ represents the element-wise division.

12.7 Transfer Learning

With many parameters, one of the main requirements that deep learning imposes is a large labeled training set. As we have discussed before, this may be expensive and even impossible to match. However, the general structure of a deep network lends itself to a technique that can help overcome this issue in some tasks. Transfer learning exploits the situation where what has been learned in one setting can be used in another setting. It is assumed that the distribution in the first learning task is to some extent similar to the distribution in the second learning task and can be reused to speed up the training [Goodfellow *et al.* (2016)], see Figure 12.11. To achieve this reuse, we basically build a new network where some of the hidden layers are fixed with the weights that were learned in the network we applied to the first task. Then, when we apply learning to the new network we only update weights in non-reused layers. The general idea is that we depart from some knowledge about the old task and fine tune the extra layers to the new task.

12.8 Conclusion

To train a deep neural network we have to preform several empirical experiments in which we determine model parameters, complexity and which techniques to include. In that sense, deep learning is an art since there are many different methods and many parameters and one needs to know what they do to change them intelligently. A good approach is to build a first prototype for the task at hand. This prototype can be motivated by existing models that one can access in public repositories. Having the starting point, a highly iterative process starts in which a lot of experimental results are accumulated. It is important to have a logbook of different experiments that guides the search for the best one. Also, the logbook should make it possible to reproduce previous experiments. Having a general grasp of the basic deep learning techniques, in the next chapter we will dive into the deep learning approach to a more specific problem, namely visual pattern recognition or image classification.

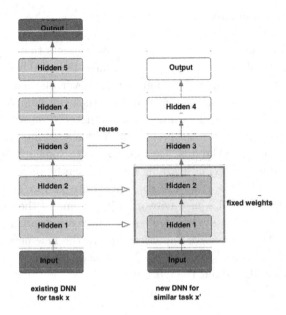

Fig. 12.11   If we assume that the distribution in a first learning task x is to some extent similar to the distribution in a second learning task x'. One can apply transfer learning and reuse part of what was learned in the first task to help solve the second. The hidden layers 1 and 2 are fixed, the hidden layer 3 is initialized with the weights for the task x and can adapt during the learning process.

12.9   Exercises and Answers

Throughout these notes we will use a superscript $[l]$ to refer to a quantity from layer l and a superscript (n) to refer to the n-th training example.

In general, the backpropagation algorithm can be described in three different phases.

Phase 1: Forward propagation

We can look at a multi-layer a perceptron as a set of functions that are applied in composition to an input. Following the figure below, for a general layer $l \in \{1, \ldots, L\}$, where L is the total number of layers, we denote the following quantities:

- $\mathbf{x}^{[l]}$ is the vector that contains the activations of the layer's units
- $\mathbf{z}^{[l]}$ is the vector that contains the net inputs to layer l units

- $\mathbf{W}^{[l]}$ is the weight matrix that makes the connections between layer $l-1$ and l. Specifically, w_{ij} is the weight that connects unit j of layer $l-1$ to unit i of layer l
- $\mathbf{b}^{[l]}$ is the bias vector that contains the bias of each unit in layer l
- $f^{[l]}$ is the activation function of the units in layer l

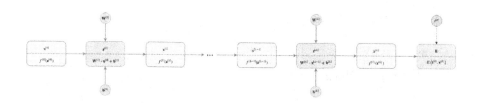

The figure also shows how to move forward from input $\mathbf{x}^{[0]}$ to the output $\mathbf{x}^{[L]}$ and the error computation between that output and the intended target $t^{(n)}$. The moving forward is what defines the forward propagation step. Each step follows the same logic behind the linear models we've seen before: a dot product between weights and input plus a bias. However, the multiple units in a layer serve as inputs to multiple perceptrons (units) in the next layer. So, instead of a weight vector, we have a weight matrix and instead of a bias scalar we have a bias vector.

Looking carefully at the figure we see the same pattern repeated when going from one layer to the next:

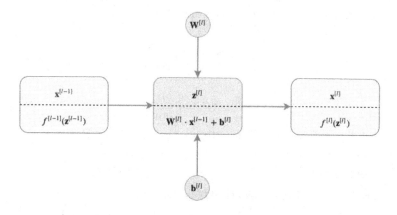

Concretely, we can write the forward propagation equations:

$$\mathbf{x}^{[0]} = Input$$
$$\mathbf{z}^{[1]} = \mathbf{W}^{[1]}\mathbf{x}^{[0]} + \mathbf{b}^{[1]}$$
$$\mathbf{x}^{[1]} = f^{[1]}\left(\mathbf{z}^{[1]}\right)$$
$$\mathbf{z}^{[2]} = \mathbf{W}^{[2]}\mathbf{x}^{[1]} + \mathbf{b}^{[2]}$$
$$\mathbf{x}^{[2]} = f^{[2]}\left(\mathbf{z}^{[2]}\right)$$
$$\vdots$$
$$\mathbf{z}^{[L-1]} = \mathbf{W}^{[L-1]}\mathbf{x}^{[L-2]} + \mathbf{b}^{[L-1]}$$
$$\mathbf{x}^{[L-1]} = f^{[L-1]}\left(\mathbf{z}^{[L-1]}\right)$$
$$\mathbf{z}^{[L]} = \mathbf{W}^{[L]}\mathbf{x}^{[L-1]} + \mathbf{b}^{[L]}$$
$$\mathbf{x}^{[L]} = f^{[L]}\left(\mathbf{z}^{[L]}\right)$$
And verify the same pattern:
$$\mathbf{z}^{[l]} = \mathbf{W}^{[l]}\mathbf{x}^{[l-1]} + \mathbf{b}^{[l]}$$
$$\mathbf{x}^{[l]} = f^{[l]}\left(\mathbf{z}^{[l]}\right)$$

So, to start the algorithm, for each example, we start at layer 1 and go all the way to layer L applying the forward recursion to get the final output.

Phase 2: Backward propagation

Just like in the linear models, the interesting question is how to choose the model's parameters. Like before, we apply gradient descent:

$$\mathbf{W}^{[l]} = \mathbf{W}^{[l]} - \eta\frac{\partial E}{\partial \mathbf{W}^{[l]}}$$

$$\mathbf{b}^{[l]} = \mathbf{b}^{[l]} - \eta\frac{\partial E}{\partial \mathbf{b}^{[l]}}$$

Much like before, we will need to use the chain rule. However, since we will be working with derivatives of vectors and matrices we will need a few simple rules to avoid mismatches in matrix dimensions.

(1) Deriving matrix multiplication (symbol ·):

    (a) Derivative of a quantity on the right: transpose and multiply on the left

(b) Derivative of a quantity on the left: transpose and multiply on the right

(2) Chain rule product corresponds to Hadamard (i.e. element-wise) product (symbol $\circ$)

Applying the chain rule corresponds to travelling back in our network and multiplying the derivatives as we go. So, let us try to find the gradient for the last layer's parameters:

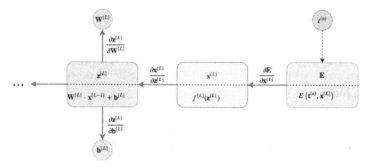

We see that it works just like the linear models. So, why stop there? We can keep going towards the layer before the last:

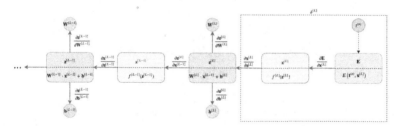

By doing so, we immediately notice that we can reuse part of the math we did for the last layer. We call this quantity the delta of the last layer (i.e. $\delta^{[L]}$). We can interpret it as the "error" that layer $L-1$ sees. Doing it for the next layer, we see the same pattern:

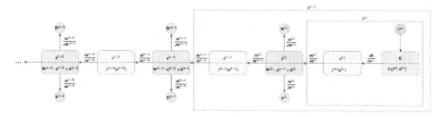

So, again, we have a delta which is the error that the current layer sees and we use it to get our gradient. The pattern keeps appearing until the first layer. So, we also have a recursion to go back... the backward recursion:

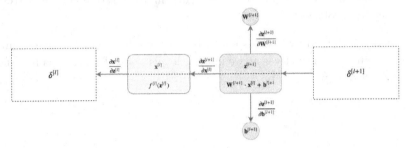

Now that we've seen it in pictures, let us write it all down. For the first layer, we have:

$$\frac{\partial E}{\partial \mathbf{W}^{[L]}} = \frac{\partial E}{\partial \mathbf{x}^{[L]}} \circ \frac{\partial \mathbf{x}^{[L]}}{\partial \mathbf{z}^{[L]}} \cdot \frac{\partial \mathbf{z}^{[L]}}{\partial \mathbf{W}^{[L]}}^{T}$$

$$\frac{\partial E}{\partial \mathbf{b}^{[L]}} = \frac{\partial E}{\partial \mathbf{x}^{[L]}} \circ \frac{\partial \mathbf{x}^{[L]}}{\partial \mathbf{z}^{[L]}} \cdot \frac{\partial \mathbf{z}^{[L]}}{\partial \mathbf{b}^{[L]}}^{T}$$

$$\delta^{[L]} = \frac{\partial E}{\partial \mathbf{x}^{[L]}} \circ \frac{\partial \mathbf{x}^{[L]}}{\partial \mathbf{z}^{[L]}}$$

For the second to last layer we have:

$$\frac{\partial E}{\partial \mathbf{W}^{[L-1]}} = \frac{\partial \mathbf{z}^{[L]}}{\partial \mathbf{x}^{[L-1]}}^{T} \cdot \left(\frac{\partial E}{\partial \mathbf{x}^{[L]}} \circ \frac{\partial \mathbf{x}^{[L]}}{\partial \mathbf{z}^{[L]}} \right) \circ \frac{\partial \mathbf{x}^{[L-1]}}{\partial \mathbf{z}^{[L-1]}} \cdot \frac{\partial \mathbf{z}^{[L-1]}}{\partial \mathbf{W}^{[L-1]}}^{T}$$

$$\frac{\partial E}{\partial \mathbf{b}^{[L-1]}} = \frac{\partial \mathbf{z}^{[L]}}{\partial \mathbf{x}^{[L-1]}}^{T} \cdot \left(\frac{\partial E}{\partial \mathbf{x}^{[L]}} \circ \frac{\partial \mathbf{x}^{[L]}}{\partial \mathbf{z}^{[L]}} \right) \circ \frac{\partial \mathbf{x}^{[L-1]}}{\partial \mathbf{z}^{[L-1]}} \cdot \frac{\partial \mathbf{z}^{[L-1]}}{\partial \mathbf{b}^{[L-1]}}^{T}$$

$$\delta^{[L-1]} = \frac{\partial \mathbf{z}^{[L]}}{\partial \mathbf{x}^{[L-1]}}^{T} \cdot \delta^{[L]} \circ \frac{\partial \mathbf{x}^{[L-1]}}{\partial \mathbf{z}^{[L-1]}}$$

For layer $L - 2$ we have:

$$\frac{\partial E}{\partial \mathbf{W}^{[L-2]}} =$$

$$\frac{\partial \mathbf{z}^{[L-1]}}{\partial \mathbf{x}^{[L-2]}}^T \cdot \left(\frac{\partial \mathbf{z}^{[L]}}{\partial \mathbf{x}^{[L-1]}}^T \cdot \left(\frac{\partial E}{\partial \mathbf{x}^{[L]}} \circ \frac{\partial \mathbf{x}^{[L]}}{\partial \mathbf{z}^{[L]}} \right) \circ \frac{\partial \mathbf{x}^{[L-1]}}{\partial \mathbf{z}^{[L-1]}} \right) \circ \frac{\partial \mathbf{x}^{[L-2]}}{\partial \mathbf{z}^{[L-2]}} \cdot \frac{\partial \mathbf{z}^{[L-2]}}{\partial \mathbf{W}^{[L-2]}}^T$$

$$\frac{\partial E}{\partial \mathbf{b}^{[L-2]}} =$$

$$\frac{\partial \mathbf{z}^{[L-1]}}{\partial \mathbf{x}^{[L-2]}}^T \cdot \left(\frac{\partial \mathbf{z}^{[L]}}{\partial \mathbf{x}^{[L-1]}}^T \cdot \left(\frac{\partial E}{\partial \mathbf{x}^{[L]}} \circ \frac{\partial \mathbf{x}^{[L]}}{\partial \mathbf{z}^{[L]}} \right) \circ \frac{\partial \mathbf{x}^{[L-1]}}{\partial \mathbf{z}^{[L-1]}} \right) \circ \frac{\partial \mathbf{x}^{[L-2]}}{\partial \mathbf{z}^{[L-2]}} \cdot \frac{\partial \mathbf{z}^{[L-2]}}{\partial \mathbf{b}^{[L-2]}}^T$$

$$\delta^{[L-2]} = \frac{\partial \mathbf{z}^{[L-1]}}{\partial \mathbf{x}^{[L-2]}}^T \cdot \delta^{[L-1]} \circ \frac{\partial \mathbf{x}^{[L-2]}}{\partial \mathbf{z}^{[L-2]}}$$

In general, we can write down the backward recursion as follows:

$$\delta^{[L]} = \frac{\partial E}{\partial \mathbf{x}^{[L]}} \circ \frac{\partial \mathbf{x}^{[L]}}{\partial \mathbf{z}^{[L]}}$$

$$\delta^{[l]} = \frac{\partial \mathbf{z}^{[l+1]}}{\partial \mathbf{x}^{[l]}}^T \cdot \delta^{[l+1]} \circ \frac{\partial \mathbf{x}^{[l]}}{\partial \mathbf{z}^{[l]}}$$

To complete the backward step all we need to do is to go from layer L to layer 1 and compute all deltas. Having the deltas, we can go to the last step.

Phase 3: Update the parameters

As we have seen in the last section, having the delta for a given layer, all we have to do to compute the gradients for its parameters is:

$$\frac{\partial E}{\partial \mathbf{W}^{[l]}} = \delta^{[l]} \cdot \frac{\partial \mathbf{z}^{[l]}}{\partial \mathbf{W}^{[l]}}^T$$

$$\frac{\partial E}{\partial \mathbf{b}^{[l]}} = \delta^{[l]} \cdot \frac{\partial \mathbf{z}^{[l]}}{\partial \mathbf{b}^{[l]}}^T$$

So, the last phase is to go from layer 1to layer L computing the gradients and performing the updates:

$$\mathbf{W}^{[l]} = \mathbf{W}^{[l]} - \eta \frac{\partial E}{\partial \mathbf{W}^{[l]}}$$

$$\mathbf{b}^{[l]} = \mathbf{b}^{[l]} - \eta \frac{\partial E}{\partial \mathbf{b}^{[l]}}$$

1)

Consider a network with three layers: 5 inputs, 3 hidden units and 2 outputs where all units use a sigmoid activation function.

    a) Initialize all connection weights to 0.1 and all biases to 0. Using the squared error loss do a **stochastic gradient descent** update (with learning rate $\eta = 1$) for the training example

$$\left\{ \mathbf{x} = \left(\,1\;1\;0\;0\;0\,\right)^{T}, \mathbf{t} = \begin{pmatrix} 1 \\ 0 \end{pmatrix} \right\}$$

Solution:

    We start by writing the connection weights and the biases:

$$\mathbf{W}^{[1]} = \begin{pmatrix} 0.1\;0.1\;0.1\;0.1\;0.1 \\ 0.1\;0.1\;0.1\;0.1\;0.1 \\ 0.1\;0.1\;0.1\;0.1\;0.1 \end{pmatrix}$$

$$\mathbf{b}^{[1]} = \begin{pmatrix} 0 \\ 0 \\ 0 \end{pmatrix}$$

$$\mathbf{W}^{[2]} = \begin{pmatrix} 0.1\;0.1\;0.1 \\ 0.1\;0.1\;0.1 \end{pmatrix}$$

$$\mathbf{b}^{[2]} = \begin{pmatrix} 0 \\ 0 \end{pmatrix}$$

We are now ready to do forward propagation:

$$\mathbf{x}^{[0]} = \begin{pmatrix} 1 \\ 1 \\ 0 \\ 0 \\ 0 \end{pmatrix}$$

$$\mathbf{z}^{[1]} = \begin{pmatrix} 0.1\;0.1\;0.1\;0.1\;0.1 \\ 0.1\;0.1\;0.1\;0.1\;0.1 \\ 0.1\;0.1\;0.1\;0.1\;0.1 \end{pmatrix} \begin{pmatrix} 1 \\ 1 \\ 0 \\ 0 \\ 0 \end{pmatrix} + \begin{pmatrix} 0 \\ 0 \\ 0 \end{pmatrix} = \begin{pmatrix} 0.2 \\ 0.2 \\ 0.2 \end{pmatrix}$$

$$\mathbf{x}^{[1]} = \sigma\left(\begin{pmatrix} 0.2 \\ 0.2 \\ 0.2 \end{pmatrix}\right) = \begin{pmatrix} \sigma\left(0.2\right) \\ \sigma\left(0.2\right) \\ \sigma\left(0.2\right) \end{pmatrix}$$

$$\mathbf{z}^{[2]} = \begin{pmatrix} 0.1\ 0.1\ 0.1 \\ 0.1\ 0.1\ 0.1 \end{pmatrix} \begin{pmatrix} \sigma\left(0.2\right) \\ \sigma\left(0.2\right) \\ \sigma\left(0.2\right) \end{pmatrix} + \begin{pmatrix} 0 \\ 0 \end{pmatrix} = \begin{pmatrix} 0.16495 \\ 0.16495 \end{pmatrix}$$

$$\mathbf{x}^{[2]} = \sigma\left(\begin{pmatrix} 0.16495 \\ 0.16495 \end{pmatrix}\right) = \begin{pmatrix} \sigma\left(0.16495\right) \\ \sigma\left(0.16495\right) \end{pmatrix} = \begin{pmatrix} 0.5411 \\ 0.5411 \end{pmatrix}$$

Now we want to do the backward phase. Recall the squared error measure:

$$E\left(\mathbf{t}, \mathbf{x}^{[2]}\right) = \frac{1}{2}\sum_{i=1}^{1}\left(\mathbf{x}^{[2]} - \mathbf{t}\right)^2 = \frac{1}{2}\left(\mathbf{x}^{[2]} - \mathbf{t}\right)^2$$

In general, we will need to know how to derive all functions in our network. Let us compute them beforehand:

$$\frac{\partial E}{\partial \mathbf{x}^{[2]}}\left(\mathbf{t}, \mathbf{x}^{[2]}\right) = \frac{\partial E}{\partial\left(\mathbf{x}^{[2]} - \mathbf{t}\right)^2}\frac{\partial\left(\mathbf{x}^{[2]} - \mathbf{t}\right)^2}{\partial\left(\mathbf{x}^{[2]} - \mathbf{t}\right)}\frac{\partial\left(\mathbf{x}^{[2]} - \mathbf{t}\right)}{\partial \mathbf{x}^{[2]}} = \frac{1}{2}\left[2\left(\mathbf{x}^{[2]} - \mathbf{t}\right)\right] = \mathbf{x}^{[2]} - \mathbf{t}$$

$$\frac{\partial \mathbf{x}^{[l]}}{\partial \mathbf{z}^{[l]}}\left(\mathbf{z}^{[l]}\right) = \sigma\left(\mathbf{z}^{[l]}\right)\left(1 - \sigma\left(\mathbf{z}^{[l]}\right)\right)$$

$$\frac{\partial \mathbf{z}^{[l]}}{\partial \mathbf{W}^{[l]}}\left(\mathbf{W}^{[l]}, \mathbf{b}^{[l]}, \mathbf{x}^{[l-1]}\right) = \mathbf{x}^{[l-1]}$$

$$\frac{\partial \mathbf{z}^{[l]}}{\partial \mathbf{b}^{[l]}}\left(\mathbf{W}^{[l]}, \mathbf{b}^{[l]}, \mathbf{x}^{[l-1]}\right) = 1$$

$$\frac{\partial \mathbf{z}^{[l]}}{\partial \mathbf{x}^{[l-1]}}\left(\mathbf{W}^{[l]}, \mathbf{b}^{[l]}, \mathbf{x}^{[l-1]}\right) = \mathbf{W}^{[l]}$$

To start the recursion, we need the delta from the last layer:

$$\delta^{[2]} = \frac{\partial E}{\partial \mathbf{x}^{[2]}} \circ \frac{\partial \mathbf{x}^{[2]}}{\partial \mathbf{z}^{[2]}}$$

$$= \left(\mathbf{x}^{[2]} - \mathbf{t} \right) \circ \sigma \left(\mathbf{z}^{[2]} \right) \left(1 - \sigma \left(\mathbf{z}^{[2]} \right) \right)$$

$$= \left(\begin{pmatrix} 0.5411 \\ 0.5411 \end{pmatrix} - \begin{pmatrix} 1 \\ 0 \end{pmatrix} \right) \circ \begin{pmatrix} 0.16495 \\ 0.16495 \end{pmatrix} \circ \left(1 - \begin{pmatrix} 0.16495 \\ 0.16495 \end{pmatrix} \right)$$

$$= \begin{pmatrix} -0.11394 \\ 0.13437 \end{pmatrix}$$

Now, we can use the recursion to compute the delta from the hidden layer:

$$\delta^{[1]} = \frac{\partial \mathbf{z}^{[2]}}{\partial \mathbf{x}^{[1]}}^{T} \cdot \delta^{[2]} \circ \frac{\partial \mathbf{x}^{[l]}}{\partial \mathbf{z}^{[l]}}$$

$$= \left(\mathbf{W}^{[2]} \right)^{T} \cdot \delta^{[2]} \circ \sigma \left(\mathbf{z}^{[1]} \right) \circ \left(1 - \sigma \left(\mathbf{z}^{[1]} \right) \right)$$

$$= \left(\mathbf{W}^{[2]} \right)^{T} \cdot \delta^{[2]} \circ \sigma \left(\mathbf{z}^{[1]} \right) \circ \left(1 - \sigma \left(\mathbf{z}^{[1]} \right) \right)$$

$$= \begin{pmatrix} 0.1 & 0.1 \\ 0.1 & 0.1 \\ 0.1 & 0.1 \end{pmatrix} \cdot \begin{pmatrix} -0.11394 \\ 0.13437 \end{pmatrix} \circ \sigma \left(\begin{pmatrix} 0.2 \\ 0.2 \\ 0.2 \end{pmatrix} \right) \circ \left(1 - \sigma \left(\begin{pmatrix} 0.2 \\ 0.2 \\ 0.2 \end{pmatrix} \right) \right)$$

$$= \begin{pmatrix} 0.00050575 \\ 0.00050575 \\ 0.00050575 \end{pmatrix}$$

Finally, we can go to the last phase and perform the updates. We start with the first layer:

$$\frac{\partial E}{\partial \mathbf{W}^{[1]}} = \delta^{[1]} \cdot \frac{\partial \mathbf{z}^{[1]}}{\partial \mathbf{W}^{[1]}}^{T}$$

$$= \delta^{[1]} \cdot \left(\mathbf{x}^{[0]} \right)^{T}$$

$$= \begin{pmatrix} 0.00050575 \\ 0.00050575 \\ 0.00050575 \end{pmatrix} \cdot \begin{pmatrix} 1 & 1 & 0 & 0 & 0 \end{pmatrix}$$

$$= \begin{pmatrix} 0.00050575 & 0.00050575 & 0 & 0 & 0 \\ 0.00050575 & 0.00050575 & 0 & 0 & 0 \\ 0.00050575 & 0.00050575 & 0 & 0 & 0 \end{pmatrix}$$

$$\mathbf{W}^{[1]} = \mathbf{W}^{[1]} - \eta \frac{\partial E}{\partial \mathbf{W}^{[1]}}$$

$$= \begin{pmatrix} 0.1\ 0.1\ 0.1\ 0.1\ 0.1 \\ 0.1\ 0.1\ 0.1\ 0.1\ 0.1 \\ 0.1\ 0.1\ 0.1\ 0.1\ 0.1 \end{pmatrix} - 1 \begin{pmatrix} 0.00050575\ 0.00050575\ 0\ 0\ 0 \\ 0.00050575\ 0.00050575\ 0\ 0\ 0 \\ 0.00050575\ 0.00050575\ 0\ 0\ 0 \end{pmatrix}$$

$$= \begin{pmatrix} 0.09949\ 0.09949\ 0.1\ 0.1\ 0.1 \\ 0.09949\ 0.09949\ 0.1\ 0.1\ 0.1 \\ 0.09949\ 0.09949\ 0.1\ 0.1\ 0.1 \end{pmatrix}$$

$$\frac{\partial E}{\partial \mathbf{b}^{[1]}} = \delta^{[1]} \cdot \frac{\partial \mathbf{z}^{[1]}}{\partial \mathbf{b}^{[1]}}^T$$

$$= \delta^{[1]}$$

$$= \begin{pmatrix} 0.00050575 \\ 0.00050575 \\ 0.00050575 \end{pmatrix}$$

$$\mathbf{b}^{[1]} = \mathbf{b}^{[1]} - \eta \frac{\partial E}{\partial \mathbf{b}^{[1]}}$$

$$= \begin{pmatrix} 0 \\ 0 \\ 0 \end{pmatrix} - 1 \begin{pmatrix} 0.00050575 \\ 0.00050575 \\ 0.00050575 \end{pmatrix}$$

$$= \begin{pmatrix} -0.00050575 \\ -0.00050575 \\ -0.00050575 \end{pmatrix}$$

All that is left is to update the weights for the output layer.

$$\frac{\partial E}{\partial \mathbf{W}^{[2]}} = \delta^{[2]} \cdot \frac{\partial \mathbf{z}^{[2]}}{\partial \mathbf{W}^{[2]}}^T$$

$$= \delta^{[2]} \cdot \left(\mathbf{x}^{[1]} \right)^T$$

$$= \begin{pmatrix} -0.11394 \\ 0.13437 \end{pmatrix} \cdot \left(\sigma(0.2)\ \sigma(0.2)\ \sigma(0.2) \right)$$

$$= \begin{pmatrix} -0.062647\ -0.062647\ -0.062647 \\ 0.073881\quad 0.073881\quad 0.073881 \end{pmatrix}$$

$$\mathbf{W}^{[2]} = \mathbf{W}^{[2]} - \eta \frac{\partial E}{\partial \mathbf{W}^{[2]}}$$

$$= \begin{pmatrix} 0.1\ 0.1\ 0.1 \\ 0.1\ 0.1\ 0.1 \end{pmatrix} - 1 \begin{pmatrix} -0.062647\ -0.062647\ -0.062647 \\ 0.073881\quad 0.073881\quad 0.073881 \end{pmatrix}$$

$$= \begin{pmatrix} 0.162647\ 0.162647\ 0.162647 \\ 0.026119\ 0.026119\ 0.026119 \end{pmatrix}$$

$$\frac{\partial E}{\partial \mathbf{b}^{[2]}} = \delta^{[2]} \cdot \frac{\partial \mathbf{z}^{[2]}}{\partial \mathbf{b}^{[2]}}^T$$

$$= \delta^{[2]}$$

$$= \begin{pmatrix} -0.11394 \\ 0.13437 \end{pmatrix}$$

$$\mathbf{b}^{[2]} = \mathbf{b}^{[2]} - \eta \frac{\partial E}{\partial \mathbf{b}^{[2]}}$$

$$= \begin{pmatrix} 0 \\ 0 \end{pmatrix} - 1 \begin{pmatrix} -0.11394 \\ 0.13437 \end{pmatrix}$$

$$= \begin{pmatrix} 0.11394 \\ -0.13437 \end{pmatrix}$$

$$\frac{\partial E}{\partial \mathbf{b}^{[1]}} = \delta^{[1]} \cdot \frac{\partial \mathbf{z}^{[1]}}{\partial \mathbf{b}^{[1]}}^T$$

b) Compute the MLP class for the query point $\mathbf{x} = \begin{pmatrix} 1 & 0 & 0 & 0 & 1 \end{pmatrix}^T$.

Solution:

We use the weights and biases from the previous exercise:

$$\mathbf{W}^{[1]} = \begin{pmatrix} 0.09949 & 0.09949 & 0.1 & 0.1 & 0.1 \\ 0.09949 & 0.09949 & 0.1 & 0.1 & 0.1 \\ 0.09949 & 0.09949 & 0.1 & 0.1 & 0.1 \end{pmatrix}$$

$$\mathbf{b}^{[1]} = \begin{pmatrix} 0.00050575 \\ 0.00050575 \\ 0.00050575 \end{pmatrix}$$

$$\mathbf{W}^{[2]} = \begin{pmatrix} -0.062647 & -0.062647 & -0.062647 \\ 0.073881 & 0.073881 & 0.073881 \end{pmatrix}$$

$$\mathbf{b}^{[2]} = \begin{pmatrix} 0.11394 \\ -0.13437 \end{pmatrix}$$

To get the class label we need to get the MLP output for the point. To get that, we just need to do forward propagation:

$$\mathbf{x}^{[0]} = \begin{pmatrix} 1 \\ 0 \\ 0 \\ 0 \\ 1 \end{pmatrix}$$

$$\mathbf{z}^{[1]} = \begin{pmatrix} 0.09949 \ 0.09949 \ 0.1 \ 0.1 \ 0.1 \\ 0.09949 \ 0.09949 \ 0.1 \ 0.1 \ 0.1 \\ 0.09949 \ 0.09949 \ 0.1 \ 0.1 \ 0.1 \end{pmatrix} \begin{pmatrix} 1 \\ 0 \\ 0 \\ 0 \\ 1 \end{pmatrix} + \begin{pmatrix} 0.00050575 \\ 0.00050575 \\ 0.00050575 \end{pmatrix} = \begin{pmatrix} 0.19949 \\ 0.19949 \\ 0.19949 \end{pmatrix}$$

$$\mathbf{x}^{[1]} = \sigma \left(\begin{pmatrix} 0.19949 \\ 0.19949 \\ 0.19949 \end{pmatrix} \right) = \begin{pmatrix} 0.54971 \\ 0.54971 \\ 0.54971 \end{pmatrix}$$

$$\mathbf{z}^{[2]} = \begin{pmatrix} -0.062647 \ -0.062647 \ -0.062647 \\ 0.073881 \ \ 0.073881 \ \ 0.073881 \end{pmatrix} \begin{pmatrix} 0.54971 \\ 0.54971 \\ 0.54971 \end{pmatrix} + \begin{pmatrix} 0.11394 \\ -0.13437 \end{pmatrix}$$

$$= \begin{pmatrix} 0.382162 \\ -0.091297 \end{pmatrix}$$

$$\mathbf{x}^{[2]} = \sigma \left(\begin{pmatrix} 0.382162 \\ -0.091297 \end{pmatrix} \right) = \begin{pmatrix} 0.59439 \\ 0.47719 \end{pmatrix}$$

Now, we just need to choose the label with highest output:

$$label = \arg\max_i \mathbf{x}^{[2]} = \arg\max_i \begin{pmatrix} \mathbf{x}_1^{[2]} \\ \mathbf{x}_2^{[2]} \end{pmatrix} = \arg\max_i \begin{pmatrix} 0.59439 \\ 0.47719 \end{pmatrix} = 1$$

2)

Consider a network with four layers with the following numbers of units: $4, 4, 3, 3$. Assume all units use the hyperbolic tangent activation function.

a) Initialize all connection weights and biases to 0.1. Using the squared error loss do a **stochastic gradient descent** update (with learning rate $\eta = 0.1$) for the training example:

$$\left\{ \mathbf{x} = \begin{pmatrix} 1 \ 0 \ 1 \ 0 \end{pmatrix}^T, \mathbf{t} = \begin{pmatrix} 0 \\ 1 \\ 0 \end{pmatrix} \right\}$$

Solution:

Before moving forward, we recall and derive the tanh activation function.

$$\tanh (x) = \frac{2}{1 + \exp (-2x)} - 1$$

$$\frac{\partial}{\partial x} \tanh (x) = \frac{\partial}{\partial x} \left(\frac{2}{1 + \exp (-2x)} - 1 \right)$$

$$= \frac{\partial}{\partial x} \left(\frac{2}{1 + \exp (-2x)} \right)$$

$$= 2 \frac{\partial}{\partial x} \left(\frac{1}{1 + \exp (-2x)} \right)$$

$$= 2 \left(\frac{\partial \left(\frac{1}{1+\exp(-2x)} \right)}{\partial (1+\exp(-2x))} \frac{\partial (1+\exp(-2x))}{\partial (\exp(-2x))} \frac{\partial (\exp(-2x))}{\partial (-2x)} \frac{\partial (-2x)}{\partial x} \right)$$

$$= 2 \left(-\frac{1}{(1 + \exp (-2x))^2} (1) \exp (-2x) (-2) \right)$$

$$= 4 \left(\frac{\exp (-2x)}{(1 + \exp (-2x))^2} \right)$$

$$= 4 \left(\frac{1 + \exp (-2x) - 1}{(1 + \exp (-2x))^2} \right)$$

$$= 4 \left(\frac{1 + \exp (-2x)}{(1 + \exp (-2x))^2} - \frac{1}{(1 + \exp (-2x))^2} \right)$$

$$= 4 \left(\frac{1}{1 + \exp (-2x)} - \frac{1}{(1 + \exp (-2x))^2} \right)$$

$$= \frac{4}{1 + \exp (-2x)} \left(1 - \frac{1}{1 + \exp (-2x)} \right)$$

$$= 2 \frac{2}{1 + \exp (-2x)} \left(1 - \frac{1}{1 + \exp (-2x)} \right)$$

$$= \frac{2}{1 + \exp (-2x)} \left(2 - \frac{2}{1 + \exp (-2x)} \right)$$

$$= (\tanh (x) + 1) (2 - (\tanh (x) + 1))$$

$$= (\tanh (x) + 1) (2 - \tanh (x) - 1)$$

$$= (\tanh (x) + 1) (1 - \tanh (x))$$

$$= \tanh (x) - \tanh (x)^2 + 1 - \tanh (x)$$

$$1 - \tanh (x)^2$$

We start by writing the connection weights and the biases:

$$\mathbf{W}^{[1]} = \begin{pmatrix} 0.1\ 0.1\ 0.1\ 0.1 \\ 0.1\ 0.1\ 0.1\ 0.1 \\ 0.1\ 0.1\ 0.1\ 0.1 \\ 0.1\ 0.1\ 0.1\ 0.1 \end{pmatrix}$$

$$\mathbf{b}^{[1]} = \begin{pmatrix} 0.1 \\ 0.1 \\ 0.1 \\ 0.1 \end{pmatrix}$$

$$\mathbf{W}^{[2]} = \begin{pmatrix} 0.1\ 0.1\ 0.1\ 0.1 \\ 0.1\ 0.1\ 0.1\ 0.1 \\ 0.1\ 0.1\ 0.1\ 0.1 \end{pmatrix}$$

$$\mathbf{b}^{[2]} = \begin{pmatrix} 0.1 \\ 0.1 \\ 0.1 \end{pmatrix}$$

$$\mathbf{W}^{[3]} = \begin{pmatrix} 0.1\ 0.1\ 0.1 \\ 0.1\ 0.1\ 0.1 \\ 0.1\ 0.1\ 0.1 \end{pmatrix}$$

$$\mathbf{b}^{[3]} = \begin{pmatrix} 0.1 \\ 0.1 \\ 0.1 \end{pmatrix}$$

We are now ready to do forward propagation:

$$\mathbf{x}^{[0]} = \begin{pmatrix} 1 \\ 0 \\ 1 \\ 0 \end{pmatrix}$$

$$\mathbf{z}^{[1]} = \begin{pmatrix} 0.1\ 0.1\ 0.1\ 0.1 \\ 0.1\ 0.1\ 0.1\ 0.1 \\ 0.1\ 0.1\ 0.1\ 0.1 \\ 0.1\ 0.1\ 0.1\ 0.1 \end{pmatrix} \begin{pmatrix} 1 \\ 0 \\ 1 \\ 0 \end{pmatrix} + \begin{pmatrix} 0.1 \\ 0.1 \\ 0.1 \\ 0.1 \end{pmatrix} = \begin{pmatrix} 0.3 \\ 0.3 \\ 0.3 \\ 0.3 \end{pmatrix}$$

$$\mathbf{x}^{[1]} = tanh\left(\begin{pmatrix} 0.3 \\ 0.3 \\ 0.3 \\ 0.3 \end{pmatrix}\right) = \begin{pmatrix} 0.2913 \\ 0.2913 \\ 0.2913 \\ 0.2913 \end{pmatrix}$$

$$\mathbf{z}^{[2]} = \begin{pmatrix} 0.1\ 0.1\ 0.1\ 0.1 \\ 0.1\ 0.1\ 0.1\ 0.1 \\ 0.1\ 0.1\ 0.1\ 0.1 \end{pmatrix} \begin{pmatrix} 0.2913 \\ 0.2913 \\ 0.2913 \\ 0.2913 \end{pmatrix} + \begin{pmatrix} 0.1 \\ 0.1 \\ 0.1 \end{pmatrix} = \begin{pmatrix} 0.2165 \\ 0.2165 \\ 0.2165 \end{pmatrix}$$

$$\mathbf{x}^{[2]} = tanh\left(\begin{pmatrix} 0.2165 \\ 0.2165 \\ 0.2165 \end{pmatrix}\right) = \begin{pmatrix} 0.2132 \\ 0.2132 \\ 0.2132 \end{pmatrix}$$

$$\mathbf{z}^{[3]} = \begin{pmatrix} 0.1\ 0.1\ 0.1 \\ 0.1\ 0.1\ 0.1 \\ 0.1\ 0.1\ 0.1 \end{pmatrix} \begin{pmatrix} 0.2132 \\ 0.2132 \\ 0.2132 \end{pmatrix} + \begin{pmatrix} 0.1 \\ 0.1 \\ 0.1 \end{pmatrix} = \begin{pmatrix} 0.16396 \\ 0.16396 \\ 0.16396 \end{pmatrix}$$

$$\mathbf{x}^{[3]} = tanh\left(\begin{pmatrix} 0.16396 \\ 0.16396 \\ 0.16396 \end{pmatrix}\right) = \begin{pmatrix} 0.16251 \\ 0.16251 \\ 0.16251 \end{pmatrix}$$

Now we want to do the backward phase. Recall the squared error measure:

$$E\left(\mathbf{t}, \mathbf{x}^{[L]}\right) = \frac{1}{2} \sum_{i=1}^{1} \left(\mathbf{x}^{[L]} - \mathbf{t}\right)^2 = \frac{1}{2}\left(\mathbf{x}^{[L]} - \mathbf{t}\right)^2$$

In general, we will need to know how to derive all functions in our network. Let us compute them beforehand:

$$\frac{\partial E}{\partial \mathbf{x}^{[L]}}\left(\mathbf{t}, \mathbf{x}^{[L]}\right)$$

$$= \frac{\partial E}{\partial \left(\mathbf{x}^{[L]} - \mathbf{t}\right)^2} \frac{\partial \left(\mathbf{x}^{[L]} - \mathbf{t}\right)^2}{\partial \left(\mathbf{x}^{[L]} - \mathbf{t}\right)} \frac{\partial \left(\mathbf{x}^{[L]} - \mathbf{t}\right)}{\partial \mathbf{x}^{[L]}} = \frac{1}{2}\left[2\left(\mathbf{x}^{[L]} - \mathbf{t}\right)\right] = \mathbf{x}^{[L]} - \mathbf{t}$$

$$\frac{\partial \mathbf{x}^{[l]}}{\partial \mathbf{z}^{[l]}}\left(\mathbf{z}^{[l]}\right) = 1 - tanh\left(\mathbf{z}^{[l]}\right)^2$$

$$\frac{\partial \mathbf{z}^{[l]}}{\partial \mathbf{W}^{[l]}} \left(\mathbf{W}^{[l]}, \mathbf{b}^{[l]}, \mathbf{x}^{[l-1]} \right) = \mathbf{x}^{[l-1]}$$

$$\frac{\partial \mathbf{z}^{[l]}}{\partial \mathbf{b}^{[l]}} \left(\mathbf{W}^{[l]}, \mathbf{b}^{[l]}, \mathbf{x}^{[l-1]} \right) = 1$$

$$\frac{\partial \mathbf{z}^{[l]}}{\partial \mathbf{x}^{[l-1]}} \left(\mathbf{W}^{[l]}, \mathbf{b}^{[l]}, \mathbf{x}^{[l-1]} \right) = \mathbf{W}^{[l]}$$

To start the recursion, we need the delta from the last layer:

$$\delta^{[3]} = \frac{\partial E}{\partial \mathbf{x}^{[3]}} \circ \frac{\partial \mathbf{x}^{[3]}}{\partial \mathbf{z}^{[3]}}$$

$$= \left(\mathbf{x}^{[3]} - \mathbf{t} \right) \circ \left(1 - tanh \left(\mathbf{z}^{[3]} \right)^2 \right)$$

$$= \left(\begin{pmatrix} 0.16251 \\ 0.16251 \\ 0.16251 \end{pmatrix} - \begin{pmatrix} 0 \\ 1 \\ 0 \end{pmatrix} \right) \circ \left(\begin{pmatrix} 1 \\ 1 \\ 1 \end{pmatrix} - \begin{pmatrix} tanh \left(0.16396 \right)^2 \\ tanh \left(0.16396 \right)^2 \\ tanh \left(0.16396 \right)^2 \end{pmatrix} \right)$$

$$= \begin{pmatrix} 0.15822 \\ -0.81538 \\ 0.15822 \end{pmatrix}$$

Now, we can use the recursion to compute the delta from the hidden layers:

$$\delta^{[2]} = \frac{\partial \mathbf{z}^{[3]}}{\partial \mathbf{x}^{[2]}}^{T} \cdot \delta^{[3]} \circ \frac{\partial \mathbf{x}^{[2]}}{\partial \mathbf{z}^{[2]}}$$

$$= \left(\mathbf{W}^{[3]} \right)^{T} \cdot \delta^{[3]} \circ \left(1 - tanh \left(\mathbf{z}^{[2]} \right)^2 \right)$$

$$= \begin{pmatrix} 0.1\ 0.1\ 0.1 \\ 0.1\ 0.1\ 0.1 \\ 0.1\ 0.1\ 0.1 \end{pmatrix} \cdot \begin{pmatrix} 0.15822 \\ -0.81538 \\ 0.15822 \end{pmatrix} \circ \left(\begin{pmatrix} 1 \\ 1 \\ 1 \end{pmatrix} - \begin{pmatrix} tanh \left(0.2165 \right)^2 \\ tanh \left(0.2165 \right)^2 \\ tanh \left(0.2165 \right)^2 \end{pmatrix} \right)$$

$$= \begin{pmatrix} -0.0476 \\ -0.0476 \\ -0.0476 \end{pmatrix}$$

$$\delta^{[1]} = \frac{\partial \mathbf{z}^{[2]}}{\partial \mathbf{x}^{[1]}}^T \cdot \delta^{[2]} \circ \frac{\partial \mathbf{x}^{[1]}}{\partial \mathbf{z}^{[1]}}$$

$$= \left(\mathbf{W}^{[2]}\right)^T \cdot \delta^{[2]} \circ \left(1 - tanh\left(\mathbf{z}^{[1]}\right)^2\right)$$

$$= \begin{pmatrix} 0.1\ 0.1\ 0.1 \\ 0.1\ 0.1\ 0.1 \\ 0.1\ 0.1\ 0.1 \\ 0.1\ 0.1\ 0.1 \end{pmatrix} \cdot \begin{pmatrix} -0.0476 \\ -0.0476 \\ -0.0476 \end{pmatrix} \circ \left(\begin{pmatrix} 1 \\ 1 \\ 1 \\ 1 \end{pmatrix} - \begin{pmatrix} tanh\,(0.3)^2 \\ tanh\,(0.3)^2 \\ tanh\,(0.3)^2 \\ tanh\,(0.3)^2 \end{pmatrix} \right)$$

$$= \begin{pmatrix} -0.0131 \\ -0.0131 \\ -0.0131 \\ -0.0131 \end{pmatrix}$$

Finally, we can go to the last phase and perform the updates. We start with the first layer:

$$\frac{\partial E}{\partial \mathbf{W}^{[1]}} = \delta^{[1]} \cdot \frac{\partial \mathbf{z}^{[1]}}{\partial \mathbf{W}^{[1]}}^T$$

$$= \delta^{[1]} \cdot \left(\mathbf{x}^{[0]}\right)^T$$

$$= \begin{pmatrix} -0.0131 \\ -0.0131 \\ -0.0131 \\ -0.0131 \end{pmatrix} \cdot \begin{pmatrix} 1\ 0\ 1\ 0 \end{pmatrix}$$

$$= \begin{pmatrix} -0.0131\ 0\ -0.0131\ 0\ 0 \\ -0.0131\ 0\ -0.0131\ 0\ 0 \\ -0.0131\ 0\ -0.0131\ 0\ 0 \\ -0.0131\ 0\ -0.0131\ 0\ 0 \end{pmatrix}$$

$$\mathbf{W}^{[1]} = \mathbf{W}^{[1]} - \eta \frac{\partial E}{\partial \mathbf{W}^{[1]}}$$

$$= \begin{pmatrix} 0.1\ 0.1\ 0.1\ 0.1 \\ 0.1\ 0.1\ 0.1\ 0.1 \\ 0.1\ 0.1\ 0.1\ 0.1 \\ 0.1\ 0.1\ 0.1\ 0.1 \end{pmatrix} - 0.1 \begin{pmatrix} -0.0131\ 0\ -0.0131\ 0\ 0 \\ -0.0131\ 0\ -0.0131\ 0\ 0 \\ -0.0131\ 0\ -0.0131\ 0\ 0 \\ -0.0131\ 0\ -0.0131\ 0\ 0 \end{pmatrix}$$

$$= \begin{pmatrix} 0.10131\ 0.1\ 0.10131\ 0.1 \\ 0.10131\ 0.1\ 0.10131\ 0.1 \\ 0.10131\ 0.1\ 0.10131\ 0.1 \\ 0.10131\ 0.1\ 0.10131\ 0.1 \end{pmatrix}$$

$$\frac{\partial E}{\partial \mathbf{b}^{[1]}} = \delta^{[1]} \cdot \frac{\partial \mathbf{z}^{[1]}}{\partial \mathbf{b}^{[1]}}^T$$

$$= \delta^{[1]}$$

$$= \begin{pmatrix} -0.0131 \\ -0.0131 \\ -0.0131 \\ -0.0131 \end{pmatrix}$$

$$\mathbf{b}^{[1]} = \mathbf{b}^{[1]} - \eta \frac{\partial E}{\partial \mathbf{b}^{[1]}}$$

$$= \begin{pmatrix} 0.1 \\ 0.1 \\ 0.1 \\ 0.1 \end{pmatrix} - 0.1 \begin{pmatrix} -0.0131 \\ -0.0131 \\ -0.0131 \\ -0.0131 \end{pmatrix}$$

$$= \begin{pmatrix} 0.10131 \\ 0.10131 \\ 0.10131 \\ 0.10131 \end{pmatrix}$$

Now the second:

$$\frac{\partial E}{\partial \mathbf{W}^{[2]}} = \delta^{[2]} \cdot \frac{\partial \mathbf{z}^{[2]}}{\partial \mathbf{W}^{[2]}}^T$$

$$= \delta^{[2]} \cdot \left(\mathbf{x}^{[1]} \right)^T$$

$$= \begin{pmatrix} -0.0476 \\ -0.0476 \\ -0.0476 \end{pmatrix} \cdot \begin{pmatrix} 0.2913 & 0.2913 & 0.2913 & 0.2913 \end{pmatrix}$$

$$= \begin{pmatrix} -0.01387 & -0.01387 & -0.01387 & -0.01387 \\ -0.01387 & -0.01387 & -0.01387 & -0.01387 \\ -0.01387 & -0.01387 & -0.01387 & -0.01387 \end{pmatrix}$$

$$\mathbf{W}^{[2]} = \mathbf{W}^{[2]} - \eta \frac{\partial E}{\partial \mathbf{W}^{[2]}}$$

$$= \begin{pmatrix} 0.1 & 0.1 & 0.1 & 0.1 \\ 0.1 & 0.1 & 0.1 & 0.1 \\ 0.1 & 0.1 & 0.1 & 0.1 \end{pmatrix} - 0.1 \begin{pmatrix} -0.01387 & -0.01387 & -0.01387 & -0.01387 \\ -0.01387 & -0.01387 & -0.01387 & -0.01387 \\ -0.01387 & -0.01387 & -0.01387 & -0.01387 \end{pmatrix}$$

$$= \begin{pmatrix} 0.101387 & 0.101387 & 0.101387 & 0.101387 \\ 0.101387 & 0.101387 & 0.101387 & 0.101387 \\ 0.101387 & 0.101387 & 0.101387 & 0.101387 \end{pmatrix}$$

$$\frac{\partial E}{\partial \mathbf{b}^{[2]}} = \delta^{[2]} \cdot \frac{\partial \mathbf{z}^{[2]}}{\partial \mathbf{b}^{[2]}}^T$$

$$= \delta^{[2]}$$

$$= \begin{pmatrix} -0.0476 \\ -0.0476 \\ -0.0476 \end{pmatrix}$$

$$\mathbf{b}^{[2]} = \mathbf{b}^{[2]} - \eta \frac{\partial E}{\partial \mathbf{b}^{[2]}}$$

$$= \begin{pmatrix} 0.1 \\ 0.1 \\ 0.1 \end{pmatrix} - 0.1 \begin{pmatrix} -0.0476 \\ -0.0476 \\ -0.0476 \end{pmatrix}$$

$$= \begin{pmatrix} 0.10476 \\ 0.10476 \\ 0.10476 \end{pmatrix}$$

All that is left is to update the parameters for the output layer.

$$\frac{\partial E}{\partial \mathbf{W}^{[3]}} = \delta^{[3]} \cdot \frac{\partial \mathbf{z}^{[3]}}{\partial \mathbf{W}^{[3]}}^T$$

$$= \delta^{[3]} \cdot \left(\mathbf{x}^{[2]} \right)^T$$

$$= \begin{pmatrix} 0.15822 \\ -0.81538 \\ 0.15822 \end{pmatrix} \cdot \begin{pmatrix} 0.2132 & 0.2132 & 0.2132 \end{pmatrix}$$

$$= \begin{pmatrix} 0.03373 & 0.03373 & 0.03373 \\ -0.17384 & -0.17384 & -0.17384 \\ 0.03373 & 0.03373 & 0.03373 \end{pmatrix}$$

$$\mathbf{W}^{[3]} = \mathbf{W}^{[3]} - \eta \frac{\partial E}{\partial \mathbf{W}^{[3]}}$$

$$= \begin{pmatrix} 0.1 & 0.1 & 0.1 \\ 0.1 & 0.1 & 0.1 \\ 0.1 & 0.1 & 0.1 \end{pmatrix} - 0.1 \begin{pmatrix} 0.03373 & 0.03373 & 0.03373 \\ -0.17384 & -0.17384 & -0.17384 \\ 0.03373 & 0.03373 & 0.03373 \end{pmatrix}$$

$$= \begin{pmatrix} 0.096627 & 0.096627 & 0.096627 \\ 0.117384 & 0.117384 & 0.117384 \\ 0.096627 & 0.096627 & 0.096627 \end{pmatrix}$$

$$\frac{\partial E}{\partial \mathbf{b}^{[3]}} = \delta^{[3]} \cdot \frac{\partial \mathbf{z}^{[3]}}{\partial \mathbf{b}^{[3]}}^T$$

$$= \delta^{[3]}$$

$$= \begin{pmatrix} 0.15822 \\ -0.81538 \\ 0.15822 \end{pmatrix}$$

$$\mathbf{b}^{[3]} = \mathbf{b}^{[3]} - \eta \frac{\partial E}{\partial \mathbf{b}^{[3]}}$$

$$= \begin{pmatrix} 0.1 \\ 0.1 \\ 0.1 \end{pmatrix} - 0.1 \begin{pmatrix} 0.15822 \\ -0.81538 \\ 0.15822 \end{pmatrix}$$

$$= \begin{pmatrix} 0.084178 \\ 0.181538 \\ 0.084178 \end{pmatrix}$$

b) Reusing the computations from the previous exercise do a **gradient descent** update (with learning rate $\eta = 0.1$) for the batch with the training example from the a) and the following:

$$\left\{ \mathbf{x} = \begin{pmatrix} 0 & 0 & 10 & 0 \end{pmatrix}^T, \mathbf{t} = \begin{pmatrix} 0 \\ 0 \\ 1 \end{pmatrix} \right\}$$

Solution:

Recall the squared error measure:

$$E\left(\mathbf{t}, \mathbf{x}^{[L]}\right) = \frac{1}{2} \sum_{i=1}^{2} \left(\mathbf{x}^{[L]} - \mathbf{t}\right)^2$$

Notice that the derivative of the sum is equal to the sum of the derivatives. For this reason, all we have to do is to compute the derivative for the new example and the final gradient will be the sum of both individual derivatives: the one for the new example and the one from the previous exercise.

We start by writting the connection weights and the biases:

$$\mathbf{W}^{[1]} = \begin{pmatrix} 0.1 & 0.1 & 0.1 & 0.1 \\ 0.1 & 0.1 & 0.1 & 0.1 \\ 0.1 & 0.1 & 0.1 & 0.1 \\ 0.1 & 0.1 & 0.1 & 0.1 \end{pmatrix}$$

$$\mathbf{b}^{[1]} = \begin{pmatrix} 0.1 \\ 0.1 \\ 0.1 \\ 0.1 \end{pmatrix}$$

$$\mathbf{W}^{[2]} = \begin{pmatrix} 0.1\ 0.1\ 0.1\ 0.1 \\ 0.1\ 0.1\ 0.1\ 0.1 \\ 0.1\ 0.1\ 0.1\ 0.1 \end{pmatrix}$$

$$\mathbf{b}^{[2]} = \begin{pmatrix} 0.1 \\ 0.1 \\ 0.1 \end{pmatrix}$$

$$\mathbf{W}^{[3]} = \begin{pmatrix} 0.1\ 0.1\ 0.1 \\ 0.1\ 0.1\ 0.1 \\ 0.1\ 0.1\ 0.1 \end{pmatrix}$$

$$\mathbf{b}^{[3]} = \begin{pmatrix} 0.1 \\ 0.1 \\ 0.1 \end{pmatrix}$$

We are now ready to do forward propagation:

$$\mathbf{x}^{[0]} = \begin{pmatrix} 0 \\ 0 \\ 10 \\ 0 \end{pmatrix}$$

$$\mathbf{z}^{[1]} = \begin{pmatrix} 0.1\ 0.1\ 0.1\ 0.1 \\ 0.1\ 0.1\ 0.1\ 0.1 \\ 0.1\ 0.1\ 0.1\ 0.1 \\ 0.1\ 0.1\ 0.1\ 0.1 \end{pmatrix} \begin{pmatrix} 0 \\ 0 \\ 10 \\ 0 \end{pmatrix} + \begin{pmatrix} 0.1 \\ 0.1 \\ 0.1 \\ 0.1 \end{pmatrix} = \begin{pmatrix} 1.1 \\ 1.1 \\ 1.1 \\ 1.1 \end{pmatrix}$$

$$\mathbf{x}^{[1]} = tanh \left(\begin{pmatrix} 1.1 \\ 1.1 \\ 1.1 \\ 1.1 \end{pmatrix} \right) = \begin{pmatrix} 0.8005 \\ 0.8005 \\ 0.8005 \\ 0.8005 \end{pmatrix}$$

$$\mathbf{z}^{[2]} = \begin{pmatrix} 0.1\ 0.1\ 0.1\ 0.1 \\ 0.1\ 0.1\ 0.1\ 0.1 \\ 0.1\ 0.1\ 0.1\ 0.1 \end{pmatrix} \begin{pmatrix} 0.8005 \\ 0.8005 \\ 0.8005 \\ 0.8005 \end{pmatrix} + \begin{pmatrix} 0.1 \\ 0.1 \\ 0.1 \end{pmatrix} = \begin{pmatrix} 0.4202 \\ 0.4202 \\ 0.4202 \end{pmatrix}$$

$$\mathbf{x}^{[2]} = tanh\left(\begin{pmatrix} 0.4202 \\ 0.4202 \\ 0.4202 \end{pmatrix}\right) = \begin{pmatrix} 0.3971 \\ 0.3971 \\ 0.3971 \end{pmatrix}$$

$$\mathbf{z}^{[3]} = \begin{pmatrix} 0.1\ 0.1\ 0.1 \\ 0.1\ 0.1\ 0.1 \\ 0.1\ 0.1\ 0.1 \end{pmatrix} \begin{pmatrix} 0.3971 \\ 0.3971 \\ 0.3971 \end{pmatrix} + \begin{pmatrix} 0.1 \\ 0.1 \\ 0.1 \end{pmatrix} = \begin{pmatrix} 0.2191 \\ 0.2191 \\ 0.2191 \end{pmatrix}$$

$$\mathbf{x}^{[3]} = tanh\left(\begin{pmatrix} 0.2191 \\ 0.2191 \\ 0.2191 \end{pmatrix}\right) = \begin{pmatrix} 0.2157 \\ 0.2157 \\ 0.2157 \end{pmatrix}$$

To start the recursion, we need the delta from the last layer:

$$\delta^{[3]} = \frac{\partial E}{\partial \mathbf{x}^{[3]}} \circ \frac{\partial \mathbf{x}^{[3]}}{\partial \mathbf{z}^{[3]}}$$

$$= \left(\mathbf{x}^{[3]} - \mathbf{t}\right) \circ \left(1 - tanh\left(\mathbf{z}^{[3]}\right)^2\right)$$

$$= \left(\begin{pmatrix} 0.2157 \\ 0.2157 \\ 0.2157 \end{pmatrix} - \begin{pmatrix} 0 \\ 0 \\ 1 \end{pmatrix}\right) \circ \left(\begin{pmatrix} 1 \\ 1 \\ 1 \end{pmatrix} - \begin{pmatrix} tanh\,(0.2191)^2 \\ tanh\,(0.2191)^2 \\ tanh\,(0.2191)^2 \end{pmatrix}\right)$$

$$= \begin{pmatrix} 0.2057 \\ 0.2057 \\ -0.7478 \end{pmatrix}$$

Now, we can use the recursion to compute the delta from the hidden layers:

$$\delta^{[2]} = \frac{\partial \mathbf{z}^{[3]}}{\partial \mathbf{x}^{[2]}}^T \cdot \delta^{[3]} \circ \frac{\partial \mathbf{x}^{[2]}}{\partial \mathbf{z}^{[2]}}$$

$$= \left(\mathbf{W}^{[3]}\right)^T \cdot \delta^{[3]} \circ \left(1 - tanh\left(\mathbf{z}^{[2]}\right)^2\right)$$

$$= \begin{pmatrix} 0.1\ 0.1\ 0.1 \\ 0.1\ 0.1\ 0.1 \\ 0.1\ 0.1\ 0.1 \end{pmatrix} \cdot \begin{pmatrix} 0.2057 \\ 0.2057 \\ -0.7478 \end{pmatrix} \circ \left(\begin{pmatrix} 1 \\ 1 \\ 1 \end{pmatrix} - \begin{pmatrix} tanh\,(0.4202)^2 \\ tanh\,(0.4202)^2 \\ tanh\,(0.4202)^2 \end{pmatrix}\right)$$

$$= \begin{pmatrix} -0.0283 \\ -0.0283 \\ -0.0283 \end{pmatrix}$$

$$\delta^{[1]} = \frac{\partial \mathbf{z}^{[2]}}{\partial \mathbf{x}^{[1]}}^T \cdot \delta^{[2]} \circ \frac{\partial \mathbf{x}^{[1]}}{\partial \mathbf{z}^{[1]}}$$

$$= \left(\mathbf{W}^{[2]} \right)^T \cdot \delta^{[2]} \circ \left(1 - tanh\left(\mathbf{z}^{[1]} \right)^2 \right)$$

$$= \begin{pmatrix} 0.1 \ 0.1 \ 0.1 \\ 0.1 \ 0.1 \ 0.1 \\ 0.1 \ 0.1 \ 0.1 \\ 0.1 \ 0.1 \ 0.1 \end{pmatrix} \cdot \begin{pmatrix} -0.0283 \\ -0.0283 \\ -0.0283 \end{pmatrix} \circ \left(\begin{pmatrix} 1 \\ 1 \\ 1 \\ 1 \end{pmatrix} - \begin{pmatrix} tanh\left(1.1\right)^2 \\ tanh\left(1.1\right)^2 \\ tanh\left(1.1\right)^2 \\ tanh\left(1.1\right)^2 \end{pmatrix} \right)$$

$$= \begin{pmatrix} -0.00305 \\ -0.00305 \\ -0.00305 \\ -0.00305 \end{pmatrix}$$

Finally, we can go to the last phase and perform the updates. Recall that the gradient will be the sum of the individual gradients.

Let us start with the first layer:

$$\frac{\partial E}{\partial \mathbf{W}^{[1]}} = \delta^{[1](1)} \cdot \frac{\partial \mathbf{z}^{[1](1)}}{\partial \mathbf{W}^{[1]}}^T + \delta^{[1](2)} \cdot \frac{\partial \mathbf{z}^{[1](2)}}{\partial \mathbf{W}^{[1]}}^T$$

$$= \delta^{[1](1)} \cdot \left(\mathbf{x}^{[0](1)} \right)^T + \delta^{[1](2)} \cdot \left(\mathbf{x}^{[0](2)} \right)^T$$

$$= \begin{pmatrix} -0.0131 \\ -0.0131 \\ -0.0131 \\ -0.0131 \end{pmatrix} \cdot \left(1\ 0\ 1\ 0 \right) + \begin{pmatrix} -0.00305 \\ -0.00305 \\ -0.00305 \\ -0.00305 \end{pmatrix} \cdot \left(0\ 0\ 10\ 0 \right)$$

$$= \begin{pmatrix} -0.0131 \ 0 \ -0.0436 \ 0 \ 0 \\ -0.0131 \ 0 \ -0.0436 \ 0 \ 0 \\ -0.0131 \ 0 \ -0.0436 \ 0 \ 0 \\ -0.0131 \ 0 \ -0.0436 \ 0 \ 0 \end{pmatrix}$$

$$\mathbf{W}^{[1]} = \mathbf{W}^{[1]} - \eta \frac{\partial E}{\partial \mathbf{W}^{[1]}}$$

$$= \begin{pmatrix} 0.1 \ 0.1 \ 0.1 \ 0.1 \\ 0.1 \ 0.1 \ 0.1 \ 0.1 \\ 0.1 \ 0.1 \ 0.1 \ 0.1 \\ 0.1 \ 0.1 \ 0.1 \ 0.1 \end{pmatrix} - 0.1 \begin{pmatrix} -0.0131 \ 0 \ -0.0436 \ 0 \ 0 \\ -0.0131 \ 0 \ -0.0436 \ 0 \ 0 \\ -0.0131 \ 0 \ -0.0436 \ 0 \ 0 \\ -0.0131 \ 0 \ -0.0436 \ 0 \ 0 \end{pmatrix}$$

$$= \begin{pmatrix} 0.10131 \ 0.1 \ 0.10436 \ 0.1 \\ 0.10131 \ 0.1 \ 0.10436 \ 0.1 \\ 0.10131 \ 0.1 \ 0.10436 \ 0.1 \\ 0.10131 \ 0.1 \ 0.10436 \ 0.1 \end{pmatrix}$$

$$\frac{\partial E}{\partial \mathbf{b}^{[1]}} = \delta^{[1](1)} \cdot \frac{\partial \mathbf{z}^{[1](1)}}{\partial \mathbf{b}^{[1]}}^T + \delta^{[1](2)} \cdot \frac{\partial \mathbf{z}^{[1](2)}}{\partial \mathbf{b}^{[1]}}^T$$

$$= \delta^{[1](1)} + \delta^{[1](2)}$$

$$= \begin{pmatrix} -0.0131 \\ -0.0131 \\ -0.0131 \\ -0.0131 \end{pmatrix} + \begin{pmatrix} -0.00305 \\ -0.00305 \\ -0.00305 \\ -0.00305 \end{pmatrix}$$

$$= \begin{pmatrix} -0.0161 \\ -0.0161 \\ -0.0161 \\ -0.0161 \end{pmatrix}$$

$$\mathbf{b}^{[1]} = \mathbf{b}^{[1]} - \eta \frac{\partial E}{\partial \mathbf{b}^{[1]}}$$

$$= \begin{pmatrix} 0.1 \\ 0.1 \\ 0.1 \\ 0.1 \end{pmatrix} - 0.1 \begin{pmatrix} -0.0161 \\ -0.0161 \\ -0.0161 \\ -0.0161 \end{pmatrix}$$

$$= \begin{pmatrix} 0.10161 \\ 0.10161 \\ 0.10161 \\ 0.10161 \end{pmatrix}$$

Now the second:

$$\frac{\partial E}{\partial \mathbf{W}^{[2]}} = \delta^{[2](1)} \cdot \frac{\partial \mathbf{z}^{[2](1)}}{\partial \mathbf{W}^{[2]}}^T + \delta^{[2](2)} \cdot \frac{\partial \mathbf{z}^{[2](2)}}{\partial \mathbf{W}^{[2]}}^T$$

$$= \delta^{[2](1)} \cdot \left(\mathbf{x}^{[1](1)} \right)^T + \delta^{[2](2)} \cdot \left(\mathbf{x}^{[1](2)} \right)^T$$

$$= \begin{pmatrix} -0.0476 \\ -0.0476 \\ -0.0476 \end{pmatrix} \cdot \begin{pmatrix} 0.2913 & 0.2913 & 0.2913 & 0.2913 \end{pmatrix}$$

$$+ \begin{pmatrix} -0.0283 \\ -0.0283 \\ -0.0283 \end{pmatrix} \cdot \begin{pmatrix} 0.8005 & 0.8005 & 0.8005 & 0.8005 \end{pmatrix}$$

$$= \begin{pmatrix} -0.03656 & -0.03656 & -0.03656 & -0.03656 \\ -0.03656 & -0.03656 & -0.03656 & -0.03656 \\ -0.03656 & -0.03656 & -0.03656 & -0.03656 \end{pmatrix}$$

$$\mathbf{W}^{[2]} = \mathbf{W}^{[2]} - \eta \frac{\partial E}{\partial \mathbf{W}^{[2]}}$$

$$= \begin{pmatrix} 0.1\ 0.1\ 0.1\ 0.1 \\ 0.1\ 0.1\ 0.1\ 0.1 \\ 0.1\ 0.1\ 0.1\ 0.1 \end{pmatrix}$$

$$- 0.1 \begin{pmatrix} -0.03656\ -0.03656\ -0.03656\ -0.03656 \\ -0.03656\ -0.03656\ -0.03656\ -0.03656 \\ -0.03656\ -0.03656\ -0.03656\ -0.03656 \end{pmatrix}$$

$$= \begin{pmatrix} 0.103656\ 0.103656\ 0.103656\ 0.103656 \\ 0.103656\ 0.103656\ 0.103656\ 0.103656 \\ 0.103656\ 0.103656\ 0.103656\ 0.103656 \end{pmatrix}$$

$$\frac{\partial E}{\partial \mathbf{b}^{[2]}} = \delta^{[2](1)} \cdot \frac{\partial \mathbf{z}^{[2](1)}}{\partial \mathbf{b}^{[2]}}^T + \delta^{[2](2)} \cdot \frac{\partial \mathbf{z}^{[2](2)}}{\partial \mathbf{b}^{[2]}}^T$$

$$= \delta^{[2](1)} + \delta^{[2](2)}$$

$$= \begin{pmatrix} -0.0476 \\ -0.0476 \\ -0.0476 \end{pmatrix} + \begin{pmatrix} -0.02835 \\ -0.02835 \\ -0.02835 \end{pmatrix}$$

$$= \begin{pmatrix} -0.07597 \\ -0.07597 \\ -0.07597 \end{pmatrix}$$

$$\mathbf{b}^{[2]} = \mathbf{b}^{[2]} - \eta \frac{\partial E}{\partial \mathbf{b}^{[2]}}$$

$$= \begin{pmatrix} 0.1 \\ 0.1 \\ 0.1 \end{pmatrix} - 0.1 \begin{pmatrix} -0.07597 \\ -0.07597 \\ -0.07597 \end{pmatrix}$$

$$= \begin{pmatrix} 0.107597 \\ 0.107597 \\ 0.107597 \end{pmatrix}$$

All that is left is to update the parameters for the output layer.

$$\frac{\partial E}{\partial \mathbf{W}^{[3]}} = \delta^{[3](1)} \cdot \frac{\partial \mathbf{z}^{[3](1)}}{\partial \mathbf{W}^{[3]}}^T + \delta^{[3](2)} \cdot \frac{\partial \mathbf{z}^{[3](2)}}{\partial \mathbf{W}^{[3]}}^T$$

$$= \delta^{[3](1)} \cdot \left(\mathbf{x}^{[2](1)} \right)^T + \delta^{[3](2)} \cdot \left(\mathbf{x}^{[2](2)} \right)^T$$

$$= \begin{pmatrix} 0.15822 \\ -0.81538 \\ 0.15822 \end{pmatrix} \cdot \begin{pmatrix} 0.2132 & 0.2132 & 0.2132 \end{pmatrix}$$

$$+ \begin{pmatrix} 0.2057 \\ 0.2057 \\ -0.7478 \end{pmatrix} \cdot \begin{pmatrix} 0.3971 & 0.3971 & 0.3971 \end{pmatrix}$$

$$= \begin{pmatrix} 0.11539 & 0.11534 & 0.11534 \\ -0.09218 & -0.09218 & -0.09218 \\ -0.26323 & -0.26323 & -0.26323 \end{pmatrix}$$

$$\mathbf{W}^{[3]} = \mathbf{W}^{[3]} - \eta \frac{\partial E}{\partial \mathbf{W}^{[3]}}$$

$$= \begin{pmatrix} 0.1 & 0.1 & 0.1 \\ 0.1 & 0.1 & 0.1 \\ 0.1 & 0.1 & 0.1 \end{pmatrix} - 0.1 \begin{pmatrix} 0.11539 & 0.11534 & 0.11534 \\ -0.09218 & -0.09218 & -0.09218 \\ -0.26323 & -0.26323 & -0.26323 \end{pmatrix}$$

$$= \begin{pmatrix} 0.08846 & 0.08846 & 0.08846 \\ 0.10922 & 0.10922 & 0.10922 \\ 0.12632 & 0.12632 & 0.12632 \end{pmatrix}$$

$$\frac{\partial E}{\partial \mathbf{b}^{[3]}} = \delta^{[3](1)} \cdot \frac{\partial \mathbf{z}^{[3](1)}}{\partial \mathbf{b}^{[3]}}^T + \delta^{[3](2)} \cdot \frac{\partial \mathbf{z}^{[3](2)}}{\partial \mathbf{b}^{[3]}}^T$$

$$= \delta^{[3](1)} + \delta^{[3](2)}$$

$$= \begin{pmatrix} 0.3639 \\ -0.6097 \\ -0.5896 \end{pmatrix}$$

$$\mathbf{b}^{[3]} = \mathbf{b}^{[3]} - \eta \frac{\partial E}{\partial \mathbf{b}^{[3]}}$$

$$= \begin{pmatrix} 0.1 \\ 0.1 \\ 0.1 \end{pmatrix} - 0.1 \begin{pmatrix} 0.3639 \\ -0.6097 \\ -0.5896 \end{pmatrix}$$

$$= \begin{pmatrix} 0.0636 \\ 0.1609 \\ 0.1589 \end{pmatrix}$$

c) Compute the MLP class for the query point

$$\left\{ \mathbf{x} = \left(1\ 1\ 1\ 0\right)^T, \mathbf{t} = \begin{pmatrix} 0 \\ 0 \\ 1 \end{pmatrix} \right\}$$

using both models from a) and b). Which has smallest squared error? Which model has better classification accuracy?

Solution:

Let us start with model a):

$$\mathbf{x}^{[0]} = \begin{pmatrix} 1 \\ 1 \\ 1 \\ 0 \end{pmatrix}$$

$$\mathbf{z}^{[1]} = \begin{pmatrix} 0.10131\ 0.1\ 0.10131\ 0.1 \\ 0.10131\ 0.1\ 0.10131\ 0.1 \\ 0.10131\ 0.1\ 0.10131\ 0.1 \\ 0.10131\ 0.1\ 0.10131\ 0.1 \end{pmatrix} \begin{pmatrix} 1 \\ 1 \\ 1 \\ 0 \end{pmatrix} + \begin{pmatrix} 0.10131 \\ 0.10131 \\ 0.10131 \\ 0.10131 \end{pmatrix}$$

$$= \begin{pmatrix} 0.4039 \\ 0.4039 \\ 0.4039 \\ 0.4039 \end{pmatrix}$$

$$\mathbf{x}^{[1]} = tanh\left(\begin{pmatrix} 0.4039 \\ 0.4039 \\ 0.4039 \\ 0.4039 \end{pmatrix} \right) = \begin{pmatrix} 0.3833 \\ 0.3833 \\ 0.3833 \\ 0.3833 \end{pmatrix}$$

$$\mathbf{z}^{[2]} = \begin{pmatrix} 0.101387\ 0.101387\ 0.101387\ 0.101387 \\ 0.101387\ 0.101387\ 0.101387\ 0.101387 \\ 0.101387\ 0.101387\ 0.101387\ 0.101387 \end{pmatrix} \begin{pmatrix} 0.3833 \\ 0.3833 \\ 0.3833 \\ 0.3833 \end{pmatrix} + \begin{pmatrix} 0.10476 \\ 0.10476 \\ 0.10476 \end{pmatrix}$$

$$= \begin{pmatrix} 0.2602 \\ 0.2602 \\ 0.2602 \end{pmatrix}$$

$$\mathbf{x}^{[2]} = tanh\left(\begin{pmatrix} 0.2602 \\ 0.2602 \\ 0.2602 \end{pmatrix}\right) = \begin{pmatrix} 0.2545 \\ 0.2545 \\ 0.2545 \end{pmatrix}$$

$$\mathbf{z}^{[3]} = \begin{pmatrix} 0.096627 \; 0.096627 \; 0.096627 \\ 0.117384 \; 0.117384 \; 0.117384 \\ 0.096627 \; 0.096627 \; 0.096627 \end{pmatrix} \begin{pmatrix} 0.2545 \\ 0.2545 \\ 0.2545 \end{pmatrix} + \begin{pmatrix} 0.084178 \\ 0.181538 \\ 0.084178 \end{pmatrix} = \begin{pmatrix} 0.1579 \\ 0.2712 \\ 0.1579 \end{pmatrix}$$

$$\mathbf{x}^{[3]} = tanh\left(\begin{pmatrix} 0.1579 \\ 0.2712 \\ 0.1579 \end{pmatrix}\right) = \begin{pmatrix} 0.1567 \\ 0.2647 \\ 0.1567 \end{pmatrix}$$

$$E\left(\mathbf{t}, \mathbf{x}^{[3]}\right) = \frac{1}{2}\sum_{i=1}^{2}\left(\mathbf{x}^{[3]} - \mathbf{t}\right)^2 = 0.8058$$

Now model b):

$$\mathbf{x}^{[0]} = \begin{pmatrix} 1 \\ 1 \\ 1 \\ 0 \end{pmatrix}$$

$$\mathbf{z}^{[1]} = \begin{pmatrix} 0.10131 \; 0.1 \; 0.10436 \; 0.1 \\ 0.10131 \; 0.1 \; 0.10436 \; 0.1 \\ 0.10131 \; 0.1 \; 0.10436 \; 0.1 \\ 0.10131 \; 0.1 \; 0.10436 \; 0.1 \end{pmatrix} \begin{pmatrix} 1 \\ 1 \\ 1 \\ 0 \end{pmatrix} + \begin{pmatrix} 0.10161 \\ 0.10161 \\ 0.10161 \\ 0.10161 \end{pmatrix} = \begin{pmatrix} 0.4073 \\ 0.4073 \\ 0.4073 \\ 0.4073 \end{pmatrix}$$

$$\mathbf{x}^{[1]} = tanh\left(\begin{pmatrix} 0.4073 \\ 0.4073 \\ 0.4073 \\ 0.4073 \end{pmatrix}\right) = \begin{pmatrix} 0.3862 \\ 0.3862 \\ 0.3862 \\ 0.3862 \end{pmatrix}$$

$$\mathbf{z}^{[2]} = \begin{pmatrix} 0.103656 \; 0.103656 \; 0.103656 \; 0.103656 \\ 0.103656 \; 0.103656 \; 0.103656 \; 0.103656 \\ 0.103656 \; 0.103656 \; 0.103656 \; 0.103656 \end{pmatrix} \begin{pmatrix} 0.3862 \\ 0.3862 \\ 0.3862 \\ 0.3862 \end{pmatrix} + \begin{pmatrix} 0.107597 \\ 0.107597 \\ 0.107597 \end{pmatrix}$$

$$= \begin{pmatrix} 0.2677 \\ 0.2677 \\ 0.2677 \end{pmatrix}$$

$$\mathbf{x}^{[2]} = tanh\left(\begin{pmatrix} 0.2677 \\ 0.2677 \\ 0.2677 \end{pmatrix}\right) = \begin{pmatrix} 0.2615 \\ 0.2615 \\ 0.2615 \end{pmatrix}$$

$$\mathbf{z}^{[3]} = \begin{pmatrix} 0.08846\ 0.08846\ 0.08846 \\ 0.10922\ 0.10922\ 0.10922 \\ 0.12632\ 0.12632\ 0.12632 \end{pmatrix} \begin{pmatrix} 0.2615 \\ 0.2615 \\ 0.2615 \end{pmatrix} + \begin{pmatrix} 0.0636 \\ 0.1609 \\ 0.1589 \end{pmatrix} = \begin{pmatrix} 0.1330 \\ 0.2467 \\ 0.2581 \end{pmatrix}$$

$$\mathbf{x}^{[3]} = tanh\left(\begin{pmatrix} 0.1330 \\ 0.2467 \\ 0.2581 \end{pmatrix}\right) = \begin{pmatrix} 0.1322 \\ 0.2418 \\ 0.2525 \end{pmatrix}$$

$$E\left(\mathbf{t}, \mathbf{x}^{[3]}\right) = \frac{1}{2} \sum_{i=1}^{2} \left(\mathbf{x}^{[3]} - \mathbf{t}\right)^2 = 0.6347$$

Model b) has a lower error and is the only one that classifies the point correctly. However, the difference between a correct classification and an incorrect classification seems to be small in terms of squared error. Perhaps we need a better error function...

---

3)

Let us repeat the exact same exercise as in 2) but this time we will change:

- The output units have a softmax activation function
- The error function is cross-entropy

a) Initialize all connection weights and biases to 0.1. Using the squared error loss do a **stochastic gradient descent** update (with learning rate $\eta = 0.1$) for the training example:

$$\left\{\mathbf{x} = \begin{pmatrix} 1\ 0\ 1\ 0 \end{pmatrix}^T, \mathbf{t} = \begin{pmatrix} 0 \\ 1 \\ 0 \end{pmatrix}\right\}$$

Solution:

Before moving forward, we recall and derive the *softmax* activation function. This activation function will work differently from what we have seen so far. This happens because each unit's output depends not only on its input but on the inputs of the other units. Let us make this more concrete. This function receives a vector $\mathbf{z} \in \mathbb{R}^d$ and outputs a vector $\mathbf{x} \in \mathbb{R}^d$.

$$softmax\left(\begin{bmatrix} z_1 & z_2 & \cdots & z_d \end{bmatrix}^T\right) = \begin{bmatrix} x_1 & x_2 & \cdots & x_d \end{bmatrix}^T$$

In general, we have that $x_i = \frac{\exp(z_i)}{\sum_{k=1}^{d}\exp(z_k)}$. Notice how each x_i depends not only on z_i like before. So, let us try to find the derivative of a given x_i with respect to a general z_i.

$$\frac{\partial x_i}{\partial z_j} = \frac{\partial}{\partial z_j} \frac{\exp(z_i)}{\sum_{k=1}^{d}\exp(z_k)}$$

If we have $i = j$ we have to use the rule to derive a quotient:

$$\frac{\partial x_i}{\partial z_j} = \frac{\partial}{\partial z_j} \frac{\exp(z_i)}{\sum_{k=1}^{d}\exp(z_k)}$$

$$= \frac{\left(\frac{\partial}{\partial z_j}\exp(z_i)\right)\left(\sum_{k=1}^{d}\exp(z_k)\right) - (\exp(z_i))\left(\frac{\partial}{\partial z_j}\sum_{k=1}^{d}\exp(z_k)\right)}{\left(\sum_{k=1}^{d}\exp(z_k)\right)^2}$$

$$= \frac{\exp(z_i)\sum_{k=1}^{d}\exp(z_k) - \exp(z_i)\exp(z_j)}{\left(\sum_{k=1}^{d}\exp(z_k)\right)^2}$$

$$= \frac{\exp(z_i)\left(\sum_{k=1}^{d}\exp(z_k) - \exp(z_j)\right)}{\left(\sum_{k=1}^{d}\exp(z_k)\right)^2}$$

$$= \frac{\exp(z_i)}{\sum_{k=1}^{d}\exp(z_k)} \frac{\sum_{k=1}^{d}\exp(z_k) - \exp(z_j)}{\sum_{k=1}^{d}\exp(z_k)}$$

$$= \frac{\exp(z_i)}{\sum_{k=1}^{d}\exp(z_k)}\left(\frac{\sum_{k=1}^{d}\exp(z_k)}{\sum_{k=1}^{d}\exp(z_k)} - \frac{\exp(z_j)}{\sum_{k=1}^{d}\exp(z_k)}\right)$$

$$= \frac{\exp(z_i)}{\sum_{k=1}^{d}\exp(z_k)}\left(1 - \frac{\exp(z_j)}{\sum_{k=1}^{d}\exp(z_k)}\right)$$

$$= x_i(1 - x_j)$$

$$= x_i(1 - x_i)$$

If we have $i \neq j$ we can factor out the numerator:

$$
\begin{aligned}
\frac{\partial x_i}{\partial z_j} &= \frac{\partial}{\partial z_j} \frac{\exp(z_i)}{\sum_{k=1}^{d} \exp(z_k)} \\
&= \exp(z_i) \frac{\partial}{\partial z_j} \frac{1}{\sum_{k=1}^{d} \exp(z_k)} \\
&= \exp(z_i) \frac{\partial \left(\frac{1}{\sum_{k=1}^{d} \exp(z_k)} \right)}{\partial \left(\sum_{k=1}^{d} \exp(z_k) \right)} \frac{\partial \left(\sum_{k=1}^{d} \exp(z_k) \right)}{\partial z_j} \\
&= \exp(z_i) \left(-\frac{1}{\left(\sum_{k=1}^{d} \exp(z_k) \right)^2} \right) \exp(z_j) \\
&= -\frac{\exp(z_i)}{\sum_{k=1}^{d} \exp(z_k)} \frac{\exp(z_j)}{\sum_{k=1}^{d} \exp(z_k)} \\
&= -x_i x_j
\end{aligned}
$$

We start by writting the connection weights and the biases:

$$
\mathbf{W}^{[1]} = \begin{pmatrix} 0.1 \ 0.1 \ 0.1 \ 0.1 \\ 0.1 \ 0.1 \ 0.1 \ 0.1 \\ 0.1 \ 0.1 \ 0.1 \ 0.1 \\ 0.1 \ 0.1 \ 0.1 \ 0.1 \end{pmatrix}
$$

$$
\mathbf{b}^{[1]} = \begin{pmatrix} 0.1 \\ 0.1 \\ 0.1 \\ 0.1 \end{pmatrix}
$$

$$
\mathbf{W}^{[2]} = \begin{pmatrix} 0.1 \ 0.1 \ 0.1 \ 0.1 \\ 0.1 \ 0.1 \ 0.1 \ 0.1 \\ 0.1 \ 0.1 \ 0.1 \ 0.1 \end{pmatrix}
$$

$$
\mathbf{b}^{[2]} = \begin{pmatrix} 0.1 \\ 0.1 \\ 0.1 \end{pmatrix}
$$

$$
\mathbf{W}^{[3]} = \begin{pmatrix} 0.1 \ 0.1 \ 0.1 \\ 0.1 \ 0.1 \ 0.1 \\ 0.1 \ 0.1 \ 0.1 \end{pmatrix}
$$

$$\mathbf{b}^{[3]} = \begin{pmatrix} 0.1 \\ 0.1 \\ 0.1 \end{pmatrix}$$

We are now ready to do forward propagation:

$$\mathbf{x}^{[0]} = \begin{pmatrix} 1 \\ 0 \\ 1 \\ 0 \end{pmatrix}$$

$$\mathbf{z}^{[1]} = \begin{pmatrix} 0.1\ 0.1\ 0.1\ 0.1 \\ 0.1\ 0.1\ 0.1\ 0.1 \\ 0.1\ 0.1\ 0.1\ 0.1 \\ 0.1\ 0.1\ 0.1\ 0.1 \end{pmatrix} \begin{pmatrix} 1 \\ 0 \\ 1 \\ 0 \end{pmatrix} + \begin{pmatrix} 0.1 \\ 0.1 \\ 0.1 \\ 0.1 \end{pmatrix} = \begin{pmatrix} 0.3 \\ 0.3 \\ 0.3 \\ 0.3 \end{pmatrix}$$

$$\mathbf{x}^{[1]} = tanh\left(\begin{pmatrix} 0.3 \\ 0.3 \\ 0.3 \\ 0.3 \end{pmatrix}\right) = \begin{pmatrix} 0.2913 \\ 0.2913 \\ 0.2913 \\ 0.2913 \end{pmatrix}$$

$$\mathbf{z}^{[2]} = \begin{pmatrix} 0.1\ 0.1\ 0.1\ 0.1 \\ 0.1\ 0.1\ 0.1\ 0.1 \\ 0.1\ 0.1\ 0.1\ 0.1 \end{pmatrix} \begin{pmatrix} 0.2913 \\ 0.2913 \\ 0.2913 \\ 0.2913 \end{pmatrix} + \begin{pmatrix} 0.1 \\ 0.1 \\ 0.1 \end{pmatrix} = \begin{pmatrix} 0.2165 \\ 0.2165 \\ 0.2165 \end{pmatrix}$$

$$\mathbf{x}^{[2]} = tanh\left(\begin{pmatrix} 0.2165 \\ 0.2165 \\ 0.2165 \end{pmatrix}\right) = \begin{pmatrix} 0.2132 \\ 0.2132 \\ 0.2132 \end{pmatrix}$$

$$\mathbf{z}^{[3]} = \begin{pmatrix} 0.1\ 0.1\ 0.1 \\ 0.1\ 0.1\ 0.1 \\ 0.1\ 0.1\ 0.1 \end{pmatrix} \begin{pmatrix} 0.2132 \\ 0.2132 \\ 0.2132 \end{pmatrix} + \begin{pmatrix} 0.1 \\ 0.1 \\ 0.1 \end{pmatrix} = \begin{pmatrix} 0.16396 \\ 0.16396 \\ 0.16396 \end{pmatrix}$$

$$\mathbf{x}^{[3]} = softmax\left(\begin{pmatrix} 0.16396 \\ 0.16396 \\ 0.16396 \end{pmatrix}\right) = \begin{pmatrix} 0.3333 \\ 0.3333 \\ 0.3333 \end{pmatrix}$$

Recall the cross-entropy loss:

$$E\left(\mathbf{t}, \mathbf{x}^{[3]}\right) = -\sum_{i=1}^{d} t_i \log x_i^{[3]}$$

What will differ is the delta of the last layer. For the remaining layers we can use the same approach as before. So, for a given $z_i^{[3]}$ the derivative of the error function will be as follows.

$$\delta_i^{[3]} = \frac{\partial E\left(\mathbf{t}, \mathbf{x}^{[3]}\right)}{\partial z_i}$$

$$= \frac{\partial}{\partial z_i}\left(-\sum_{k=1}^{d} t_k \log x_k^{[3]}\right)$$

$$= -\sum_{k=1}^{d} t_k \frac{\partial}{\partial z_i} \log x_k^{[3]}$$

$$= -\sum_{k=1}^{d} t_k \frac{1}{x_k^{[3]}} \frac{\partial x_k^{[3]}}{\partial z_i}$$

$$= -\sum_{k=i} t_k \frac{1}{x_k^{[3]}} \frac{\partial x_k^{[3]}}{\partial z_i} - \sum_{k \neq i} t_k \frac{1}{x_k^{[3]}} \frac{\partial x_k^{[3]}}{\partial z_i}$$

$$= -\sum_{k=i} t_k \frac{1}{x_k^{[3]}} \left(x_i^{[3]}\left(1 - x_i^{[3]}\right)\right) - \sum_{k \neq i} t_k \frac{1}{x_k^{[3]}} \left(-x_k^{[3]} x_i^{[3]}\right)$$

$$= -t_i \frac{1}{x_i^{[3]}} \left(x_i^{[3]}\left(1 - x_i^{[3]}\right)\right) - \sum_{k \neq i} t_k \frac{1}{x_k^{[3]}} \left(-x_k^{[3]} x_i^{[3]}\right)$$

$$= -t_i \left(1 - x_i^{[3]}\right) + \sum_{k \neq i} t_k x_i^{[3]}$$

$$= -t_i + t_i x_i^{[3]} + \sum_{k \neq i} t_k x_i^{[3]}$$

$$= -t_i + x_i^{[3]}\left(t_i + \sum_{k \neq i} t_k\right)$$

$$= -t_i + x_i^{[3]}\left(\sum_{k=1}^{d} t_k\right)$$

$$= -t_i + x_i^{[3]}$$

$$= x_i^{[3]} - t_i$$

The remaining derivatives can be computed as before:

$$\frac{\partial \mathbf{x}^{[l]}}{\partial \mathbf{z}^{[l]}}\left(\mathbf{z}^{[l]}\right) = 1 - tanh\left(\mathbf{z}^{[l]}\right)^2$$

$$\frac{\partial \mathbf{z}^{[l]}}{\partial \mathbf{W}^{[l]}}\left(\mathbf{W}^{[l]}, \mathbf{b}^{[l]}, \mathbf{x}^{[l-1]}\right) = \mathbf{x}^{[l-1]}$$

$$\frac{\partial \mathbf{z}^{[l]}}{\partial \mathbf{b}^{[l]}}\left(\mathbf{W}^{[l]}, \mathbf{b}^{[l]}, \mathbf{x}^{[l-1]}\right) = 1$$

$$\frac{\partial \mathbf{z}^{[l]}}{\partial \mathbf{x}^{[l-1]}}\left(\mathbf{W}^{[l]}, \mathbf{b}^{[l]}, \mathbf{x}^{[l-1]}\right) = \mathbf{W}^{[l]}$$

To start the recursion, we need the delta from the last layer:

$$
\delta^{[3]} = \begin{pmatrix} \delta_1^{[3]} \\ \delta_2^{[3]} \\ \delta_3^{[3]} \end{pmatrix} = \begin{pmatrix} \frac{\partial E\left(\mathbf{t},\mathbf{x}^{[3]}\right)}{\partial z_1} \\ \frac{\partial E\left(\mathbf{t},\mathbf{x}^{[3]}\right)}{\partial z_2} \\ \frac{\partial E\left(\mathbf{t},\mathbf{x}^{[3]}\right)}{\partial z_3} \end{pmatrix}
$$

$$
= \begin{pmatrix} x_1^{[3]} - t_1 \\ x_2^{[3]} - t_2 \\ x_3^{[3]} - t_3 \end{pmatrix}
$$

$$
= \left(\mathbf{x}^{[3]} - \mathbf{t}\right)
$$

$$
= \begin{pmatrix} 0.3333 \\ 0.3333 \\ 0.3333 \end{pmatrix} - \begin{pmatrix} 0 \\ 1 \\ 0 \end{pmatrix}
$$

$$
= \begin{pmatrix} 0.3333 \\ -0.6666 \\ 0.3333 \end{pmatrix}
$$

Now, we can use the recursion to compute the delta from the hidden layers:

$$
\delta^{[2]} = \frac{\partial \mathbf{z}^{[3]}}{\partial \mathbf{x}^{[2]}}^T \cdot \delta^{[3]} \circ \frac{\partial \mathbf{x}^{[2]}}{\partial \mathbf{z}^{[2]}}
$$

$$
= \left(\mathbf{W}^{[3]}\right)^T \cdot \delta^{[3]} \circ \left(1 - tanh\left(\mathbf{z}^{[2]}\right)^2\right)
$$

$$
= \begin{pmatrix} 0.1 & 0.1 & 0.1 \\ 0.1 & 0.1 & 0.1 \\ 0.1 & 0.1 & 0.1 \end{pmatrix} \cdot \begin{pmatrix} 0.3333 \\ -0.6667 \\ 0.3333 \end{pmatrix} \circ \left(\begin{pmatrix} 1 \\ 1 \\ 1 \end{pmatrix} - \begin{pmatrix} tanh\left(0.2165\right)^2 \\ tanh\left(0.2165\right)^2 \\ tanh\left(0.2165\right)^2 \end{pmatrix} \right)
$$

$$
= \begin{pmatrix} 0 \\ 0 \\ 0 \end{pmatrix}
$$

$$\delta^{[1]} = \frac{\partial \mathbf{z}^{[2]}}{\partial \mathbf{x}^{[1]}}^T \cdot \delta^{[2]} \circ \frac{\partial \mathbf{x}^{[1]}}{\partial \mathbf{z}^{[1]}}$$

$$= \left(\mathbf{W}^{[2]}\right)^T \cdot \delta^{[2]} \circ \left(1 - tanh\left(\mathbf{z}^{[1]}\right)^2\right)$$

$$= \begin{pmatrix} 0.1 \ 0.1 \ 0.1 \\ 0.1 \ 0.1 \ 0.1 \\ 0.1 \ 0.1 \ 0.1 \\ 0.1 \ 0.1 \ 0.1 \end{pmatrix} \cdot \begin{pmatrix} 0 \\ 0 \\ 0 \end{pmatrix} \circ \left(\begin{pmatrix} 1 \\ 1 \\ 1 \\ 1 \end{pmatrix} - \begin{pmatrix} tanh\,(0.3)^2 \\ tanh\,(0.3)^2 \\ tanh\,(0.3)^2 \\ tanh\,(0.3)^2 \end{pmatrix} \right)$$

$$= \begin{pmatrix} 0 \\ 0 \\ 0 \\ 0 \end{pmatrix}$$

Finally, we can go to the last phase and perform the updates. We start with the first layer:

$$\frac{\partial E}{\partial \mathbf{W}^{[1]}} = \delta^{[1]} \cdot \frac{\partial \mathbf{z}^{[1]}}{\partial \mathbf{W}^{[1]}}^T$$

$$= \delta^{[1]} \cdot \left(\mathbf{x}^{[0]}\right)^T$$

$$= \begin{pmatrix} 0 \\ 0 \\ 0 \\ 0 \end{pmatrix} \cdot \begin{pmatrix} 1 \ 0 \ 1 \ 0 \end{pmatrix}$$

$$= \begin{pmatrix} 0\ 0\ 0\ 0\ 0 \\ 0\ 0\ 0\ 0\ 0 \\ 0\ 0\ 0\ 0\ 0 \\ 0\ 0\ 0\ 0\ 0 \end{pmatrix}$$

$$\mathbf{W}^{[1]} = \mathbf{W}^{[1]} - \eta\frac{\partial E}{\partial \mathbf{W}^{[1]}}$$

$$= \begin{pmatrix} 0.1\ 0.1\ 0.1\ 0.1 \\ 0.1\ 0.1\ 0.1\ 0.1 \\ 0.1\ 0.1\ 0.1\ 0.1 \\ 0.1\ 0.1\ 0.1\ 0.1 \end{pmatrix} - 0.1 \begin{pmatrix} 0\ 0\ 0\ 0\ 0 \\ 0\ 0\ 0\ 0\ 0 \\ 0\ 0\ 0\ 0\ 0 \\ 0\ 0\ 0\ 0\ 0 \end{pmatrix}$$

$$= \begin{pmatrix} 0.1\ 0.1\ 0.1\ 0.1 \\ 0.1\ 0.1\ 0.1\ 0.1 \\ 0.1\ 0.1\ 0.1\ 0.1 \\ 0.1\ 0.1\ 0.1\ 0.1 \end{pmatrix}$$

$$\frac{\partial E}{\partial \mathbf{b}^{[1]}} = \delta^{[1]} \cdot \frac{\partial \mathbf{z}^{[1]}}{\partial \mathbf{b}^{[1]}}^T$$

$$= \delta^{[1]}$$

$$= \begin{pmatrix} 0 \\ 0 \\ 0 \\ 0 \end{pmatrix}$$

$$\mathbf{b}^{[1]} = \mathbf{b}^{[1]} - \eta \frac{\partial E}{\partial \mathbf{b}^{[1]}}$$

$$= \begin{pmatrix} 0.1 \\ 0.1 \\ 0.1 \\ 0.1 \end{pmatrix} - 0.1 \begin{pmatrix} 0 \\ 0 \\ 0 \\ 0 \end{pmatrix}$$

$$= \begin{pmatrix} 0.1 \\ 0.1 \\ 0.1 \\ 0.1 \end{pmatrix}$$

Now the second:

$$\frac{\partial E}{\partial \mathbf{W}^{[2]}} = \delta^{[2]} \cdot \frac{\partial \mathbf{z}^{[2]}}{\partial \mathbf{W}^{[2]}}^T$$

$$= \delta^{[2]} \cdot \left(\mathbf{x}^{[1]} \right)^T$$

$$= \begin{pmatrix} 0 \\ 0 \\ 0 \end{pmatrix} \cdot \begin{pmatrix} 0.2913 \, 0.2913 \, 0.2913 \, 0.2913 \end{pmatrix}$$

$$= \begin{pmatrix} 0\,0\,0\,0 \\ 0\,0\,0\,0 \\ 0\,0\,0\,0 \end{pmatrix}$$

$$\mathbf{W}^{[2]} = \mathbf{W}^{[2]} - \eta \frac{\partial E}{\partial \mathbf{W}^{[2]}}$$

$$= \begin{pmatrix} 0.1 \, 0.1 \, 0.1 \, 0.1 \\ 0.1 \, 0.1 \, 0.1 \, 0.1 \\ 0.1 \, 0.1 \, 0.1 \, 0.1 \end{pmatrix} - 0.1 \begin{pmatrix} 0\,0\,0\,0 \\ 0\,0\,0\,0 \\ 0\,0\,0\,0 \end{pmatrix}$$

$$= \begin{pmatrix} 0.1 \, 0.1 \, 0.1 \, 0.1 \\ 0.1 \, 0.1 \, 0.1 \, 0.1 \\ 0.1 \, 0.1 \, 0.1 \, 0.1 \end{pmatrix}$$

$$\frac{\partial E}{\partial \mathbf{b}^{[2]}} = \delta^{[2]} \cdot \frac{\partial \mathbf{z}^{[2]}}{\partial \mathbf{b}^{[2]}}^T$$

$$= \delta^{[2]}$$

$$= \begin{pmatrix} 0 \\ 0 \\ 0 \end{pmatrix}$$

$$\mathbf{b}^{[2]} = \mathbf{b}^{[2]} - \eta \frac{\partial E}{\partial \mathbf{b}^{[2]}}$$

$$= \begin{pmatrix} 0.1 \\ 0.1 \\ 0.1 \end{pmatrix} - 0.1 \begin{pmatrix} 0 \\ 0 \\ 0 \end{pmatrix}$$

$$= \begin{pmatrix} 0.1 \\ 0.1 \\ 0.1 \end{pmatrix}$$

All that is left is to update the parameters for the output layer.

$$\frac{\partial E}{\partial \mathbf{W}^{[3]}} = \delta^{[3]} \cdot \frac{\partial \mathbf{z}^{[3]}}{\partial \mathbf{W}^{[3]}}^T$$

$$= \delta^{[3]} \cdot \left(\mathbf{x}^{[2]} \right)^T$$

$$= \begin{pmatrix} 0.3333 \\ -0.6666 \\ 0.3333 \end{pmatrix} \cdot \begin{pmatrix} 0.2132 & 0.2132 & 0.2132 \end{pmatrix}$$

$$= \begin{pmatrix} 0.0711 & 0.0711 & 0.0711 \\ -0.1421 & -0.1421 & -0.1421 \\ 0.0711 & 0.0711 & 0.0711 \end{pmatrix}$$

$$\mathbf{W}^{[3]} = \mathbf{W}^{[3]} - \eta \frac{\partial E}{\partial \mathbf{W}^{[3]}}$$

$$= \begin{pmatrix} 0.1 & 0.1 & 0.1 \\ 0.1 & 0.1 & 0.1 \\ 0.1 & 0.1 & 0.1 \end{pmatrix} - 0.1 \begin{pmatrix} 0.0711 & 0.0711 & 0.0711 \\ -0.1421 & -0.1421 & -0.1421 \\ 0.0711 & 0.0711 & 0.0711 \end{pmatrix}$$

$$= \begin{pmatrix} 0.0929 & 0.0929 & 0.0929 \\ 0.1142 & 0.1142 & 0.1142 \\ 0.0929 & 0.0929 & 0.0929 \end{pmatrix}$$

$$\frac{\partial E}{\partial \mathbf{b}^{[3]}} = \delta^{[3]} \cdot \frac{\partial \mathbf{z}^{[3]}}{\partial \mathbf{b}^{[3]}}^T$$

$$= \delta^{[3]}$$

$$= \begin{pmatrix} 0.3333 \\ -0.6666 \\ 0.3333 \end{pmatrix}$$

$$\mathbf{b}^{[3]} = \mathbf{b}^{[3]} - \eta \frac{\partial E}{\partial \mathbf{b}^{[3]}}$$

$$= \begin{pmatrix} 0.1 \\ 0.1 \\ 0.1 \end{pmatrix} - 0.1 \begin{pmatrix} 0.3333 \\ -0.6666 \\ 0.3333 \end{pmatrix}$$

$$= \begin{pmatrix} 0.0667 \\ 0.1667 \\ 0.0667 \end{pmatrix}$$

b) Reusing the computations from the previous exercise do a **gradient descent** update (with learning rate $\eta = 0.1$) for the batch with the training example from the a) and the following:

$$\left\{ \mathbf{x} = \begin{pmatrix} 0 & 0 & 10 & 0 \end{pmatrix}^T, \mathbf{t} = \begin{pmatrix} 0 \\ 0 \\ 1 \end{pmatrix} \right\}$$

Solution:

Since the derivative of the sum is equal to the sum of the derivatives. For this reason, all we have to do is to compute the derivative for the new example and the final gradient will be the sum of both individual derivatives: the one for the new example and the one from the previous exercise.

We start by writting the connection weights and the biases:

$$\mathbf{W}^{[1]} = \begin{pmatrix} 0.1 & 0.1 & 0.1 & 0.1 \\ 0.1 & 0.1 & 0.1 & 0.1 \\ 0.1 & 0.1 & 0.1 & 0.1 \\ 0.1 & 0.1 & 0.1 & 0.1 \end{pmatrix}$$

$$\mathbf{b}^{[1]} = \begin{pmatrix} 0.1 \\ 0.1 \\ 0.1 \\ 0.1 \end{pmatrix}$$

$$\mathbf{W}^{[2]} = \begin{pmatrix} 0.1\ 0.1\ 0.1\ 0.1 \\ 0.1\ 0.1\ 0.1\ 0.1 \\ 0.1\ 0.1\ 0.1\ 0.1 \end{pmatrix}$$

$$\mathbf{b}^{[2]} = \begin{pmatrix} 0.1 \\ 0.1 \\ 0.1 \end{pmatrix}$$

$$\mathbf{W}^{[3]} = \begin{pmatrix} 0.1\ 0.1\ 0.1 \\ 0.1\ 0.1\ 0.1 \\ 0.1\ 0.1\ 0.1 \end{pmatrix}$$

$$\mathbf{b}^{[3]} = \begin{pmatrix} 0.1 \\ 0.1 \\ 0.1 \end{pmatrix}$$

We are now ready to do forward propagation:

$$\mathbf{x}^{[0]} = \begin{pmatrix} 0 \\ 0 \\ 10 \\ 0 \end{pmatrix}$$

$$\mathbf{z}^{[1]} = \begin{pmatrix} 0.1\ 0.1\ 0.1\ 0.1 \\ 0.1\ 0.1\ 0.1\ 0.1 \\ 0.1\ 0.1\ 0.1\ 0.1 \\ 0.1\ 0.1\ 0.1\ 0.1 \end{pmatrix} \begin{pmatrix} 0 \\ 0 \\ 10 \\ 0 \end{pmatrix} + \begin{pmatrix} 0.1 \\ 0.1 \\ 0.1 \\ 0.1 \end{pmatrix} = \begin{pmatrix} 1.1 \\ 1.1 \\ 1.1 \\ 1.1 \end{pmatrix}$$

$$\mathbf{x}^{[1]} = tanh \left(\begin{pmatrix} 1.1 \\ 1.1 \\ 1.1 \\ 1.1 \end{pmatrix} \right) = \begin{pmatrix} 0.8005 \\ 0.8005 \\ 0.8005 \\ 0.8005 \end{pmatrix}$$

$$\mathbf{z}^{[2]} = \begin{pmatrix} 0.1\ 0.1\ 0.1\ 0.1 \\ 0.1\ 0.1\ 0.1\ 0.1 \\ 0.1\ 0.1\ 0.1\ 0.1 \end{pmatrix} \begin{pmatrix} 0.8005 \\ 0.8005 \\ 0.8005 \\ 0.8005 \end{pmatrix} + \begin{pmatrix} 0.1 \\ 0.1 \\ 0.1 \end{pmatrix} = \begin{pmatrix} 0.4202 \\ 0.4202 \\ 0.4202 \end{pmatrix}$$

$$\mathbf{x}^{[2]} = tanh \left(\begin{pmatrix} 0.4202 \\ 0.4202 \\ 0.4202 \end{pmatrix} \right) = \begin{pmatrix} 0.3971 \\ 0.3971 \\ 0.3971 \end{pmatrix}$$

$$\mathbf{z}^{[3]} = \begin{pmatrix} 0.1\ 0.1\ 0.1 \\ 0.1\ 0.1\ 0.1 \\ 0.1\ 0.1\ 0.1 \end{pmatrix} \begin{pmatrix} 0.3971 \\ 0.3971 \\ 0.3971 \end{pmatrix} + \begin{pmatrix} 0.1 \\ 0.1 \\ 0.1 \end{pmatrix} = \begin{pmatrix} 0.2191 \\ 0.2191 \\ 0.2191 \end{pmatrix}$$

$$\mathbf{x}^{[3]} = tanh \left(\begin{pmatrix} 0.2191 \\ 0.2191 \\ 0.2191 \end{pmatrix} \right) = \begin{pmatrix} 0.3333 \\ 0.3333 \\ 0.3333 \end{pmatrix}$$

To start the recursion, we need the delta from the last layer:

$$
\delta^{[3]} = \begin{pmatrix} \delta_1^{[3]} \\ \delta_2^{[3]} \\ \delta_3^{[3]} \end{pmatrix} = \begin{pmatrix} \frac{\partial E\left(\mathbf{t}, \mathbf{x}^{[3]}\right)}{\partial z_1} \\ \frac{\partial E\left(\mathbf{t}, \mathbf{x}^{[3]}\right)}{\partial z_2} \\ \frac{\partial E\left(\mathbf{t}, \mathbf{x}^{[3]}\right)}{\partial z_3} \end{pmatrix}
$$

$$
= \begin{pmatrix} x_1^{[3]} - t_1 \\ x_2^{[3]} - t_2 \\ x_3^{[3]} - t_3 \end{pmatrix}
$$

$$
= \left(\mathbf{x}^{[3]} - \mathbf{t} \right)
$$

$$
= \begin{pmatrix} 0.3333 \\ 0.3333 \\ 0.3333 \end{pmatrix} - \begin{pmatrix} 0 \\ 0 \\ 1 \end{pmatrix}
$$

$$
= \begin{pmatrix} 0.3333 \\ 0.3333 \\ -0.6666 \end{pmatrix}
$$

Now, we can use the recursion to compute the delta from the hidden layers:

$$
\delta^{[2]} = \frac{\partial \mathbf{z}^{[3]}}{\partial \mathbf{x}^{[2]}}^T \cdot \delta^{[3]} \circ \frac{\partial \mathbf{x}^{[2]}}{\partial \mathbf{z}^{[2]}}
$$

$$
= \left(\mathbf{W}^{[3]} \right)^T \cdot \delta^{[3]} \circ \left(1 - tanh\left(\mathbf{z}^{[2]}\right)^2 \right)
$$

$$
= \begin{pmatrix} 0.1\ 0.1\ 0.1 \\ 0.1\ 0.1\ 0.1 \\ 0.1\ 0.1\ 0.1 \end{pmatrix} \cdot \begin{pmatrix} 0.3333 \\ 0.3333 \\ -0.6666 \end{pmatrix} \circ \left(\begin{pmatrix} 1 \\ 1 \\ 1 \end{pmatrix} - \begin{pmatrix} tanh\left(0.4202\right)^2 \\ tanh\left(0.4202\right)^2 \\ tanh\left(0.4202\right)^2 \end{pmatrix} \right)
$$

$$
= \begin{pmatrix} 0 \\ 0 \\ 0 \end{pmatrix}
$$

$$\delta^{[1]} = \frac{\partial \mathbf{z}^{[2]}}{\partial \mathbf{x}^{[1]}}^T \cdot \delta^{[2]} \circ \frac{\partial \mathbf{x}^{[1]}}{\partial \mathbf{z}^{[1]}}$$

$$= \left(\mathbf{W}^{[2]}\right)^T \cdot \delta^{[2]} \circ \left(1 - tanh\left(\mathbf{z}^{[1]}\right)^2\right)$$

$$= \begin{pmatrix} 0.1\ 0.1\ 0.1 \\ 0.1\ 0.1\ 0.1 \\ 0.1\ 0.1\ 0.1 \\ 0.1\ 0.1\ 0.1 \end{pmatrix} \cdot \begin{pmatrix} 0 \\ 0 \\ 0 \end{pmatrix} \circ \left(\begin{pmatrix} 1 \\ 1 \\ 1 \\ 1 \end{pmatrix} - \begin{pmatrix} tanh\,(1.1)^2 \\ tanh\,(1.1)^2 \\ tanh\,(1.1)^2 \\ tanh\,(1.1)^2 \end{pmatrix} \right)$$

$$= \begin{pmatrix} 0 \\ 0 \\ 0 \\ 0 \end{pmatrix}$$

Finally, we can go to the last phase and perform the updates. Recall that the gradient will be the sum of the individual gradiens!

Let us start with the first layer:

$$\frac{\partial E}{\partial \mathbf{W}^{[1]}} = \delta^{[1](1)} \cdot \frac{\partial \mathbf{z}^{[1](1)}}{\partial \mathbf{W}^{[1]}}^T + \delta^{[1](2)} \cdot \frac{\partial \mathbf{z}^{[1](2)}}{\partial \mathbf{W}^{[1]}}^T$$

$$= \delta^{[1](1)} \cdot \left(\mathbf{x}^{[0](1)}\right)^T + \delta^{[1](2)} \cdot \left(\mathbf{x}^{[0](2)}\right)^T$$

$$= \begin{pmatrix} 0 \\ 0 \\ 0 \\ 0 \end{pmatrix} \cdot (1\ 0\ 1\ 0) + \begin{pmatrix} 0 \\ 0 \\ 0 \\ 0 \end{pmatrix} \cdot (0\ 0\ 10\ 0)$$

$$= \begin{pmatrix} 0\ 0\ 0\ 0\ 0 \\ 0\ 0\ 0\ 0\ 0 \\ 0\ 0\ 0\ 0\ 0 \\ 0\ 0\ 0\ 0\ 0 \end{pmatrix}$$

$$\mathbf{W}^{[1]} = \mathbf{W}^{[1]} - \eta \frac{\partial E}{\partial \mathbf{W}^{[1]}}$$

$$= \begin{pmatrix} 0.1\ 0.1\ 0.1\ 0.1 \\ 0.1\ 0.1\ 0.1\ 0.1 \\ 0.1\ 0.1\ 0.1\ 0.1 \\ 0.1\ 0.1\ 0.1\ 0.1 \end{pmatrix} - 0.1 \begin{pmatrix} 0\ 0\ 0\ 0\ 0 \\ 0\ 0\ 0\ 0\ 0 \\ 0\ 0\ 0\ 0\ 0 \\ 0\ 0\ 0\ 0\ 0 \end{pmatrix}$$

$$= \begin{pmatrix} 0.1\ 0.1\ 0.1\ 0.1 \\ 0.1\ 0.1\ 0.1\ 0.1 \\ 0.1\ 0.1\ 0.1\ 0.1 \\ 0.1\ 0.1\ 0.1\ 0.1 \end{pmatrix}$$

$$\frac{\partial E}{\partial \mathbf{b}^{[1]}} = \delta^{[1](1)} \cdot \frac{\partial \mathbf{z}^{[1](1)}}{\partial \mathbf{b}^{[1]}}^T + \delta^{[1](2)} \cdot \frac{\partial \mathbf{z}^{[1](2)}}{\partial \mathbf{b}^{[1]}}^T$$

$$= \delta^{[1](1)} + \delta^{[1](2)}$$

$$= \begin{pmatrix} 0 \\ 0 \\ 0 \\ 0 \end{pmatrix} + \begin{pmatrix} 0 \\ 0 \\ 0 \\ 0 \end{pmatrix}$$

$$= \begin{pmatrix} 0 \\ 0 \\ 0 \\ 0 \end{pmatrix}$$

$$\mathbf{b}^{[1]} = \mathbf{b}^{[1]} - \eta \frac{\partial E}{\partial \mathbf{b}^{[1]}}$$

$$= \begin{pmatrix} 0.1 \\ 0.1 \\ 0.1 \\ 0.1 \end{pmatrix} - 0.1 \begin{pmatrix} 0 \\ 0 \\ 0 \\ 0 \end{pmatrix}$$

$$= \begin{pmatrix} 0.1 \\ 0.1 \\ 0.1 \\ 0.1 \end{pmatrix}$$

Now the second:

$$\frac{\partial E}{\partial \mathbf{W}^{[2]}} = \delta^{[2](1)} \cdot \frac{\partial \mathbf{z}^{[2](1)}}{\partial \mathbf{W}^{[2]}}^T + \delta^{[2](2)} \cdot \frac{\partial \mathbf{z}^{[2](2)}}{\partial \mathbf{W}^{[2]}}^T$$

$$= \delta^{[2](1)} \cdot \left(\mathbf{x}^{[1](1)} \right)^T + \delta^{[2](2)} \cdot \left(\mathbf{x}^{[1](2)} \right)^T$$

$$= \begin{pmatrix} 0 \\ 0 \\ 0 \end{pmatrix} \cdot \begin{pmatrix} 0.2913 & 0.2913 & 0.2913 & 0.2913 \end{pmatrix}$$

$$+ \begin{pmatrix} 0 \\ 0 \\ 0 \end{pmatrix} \cdot \begin{pmatrix} 0.8005 & 0.8005 & 0.8005 & 0.8005 \end{pmatrix}$$

$$= \begin{pmatrix} 0 & 0 & 0 & 0 \\ 0 & 0 & 0 & 0 \\ 0 & 0 & 0 & 0 \end{pmatrix}$$

$$\mathbf{W}^{[2]} = \mathbf{W}^{[2]} - \eta \frac{\partial E}{\partial \mathbf{W}^{[2]}}$$

$$= \begin{pmatrix} 0.1\ 0.1\ 0.1\ 0.1 \\ 0.1\ 0.1\ 0.1\ 0.1 \\ 0.1\ 0.1\ 0.1\ 0.1 \end{pmatrix} - 0.1 \begin{pmatrix} 0\ 0\ 0\ 0 \\ 0\ 0\ 0\ 0 \\ 0\ 0\ 0\ 0 \end{pmatrix}$$

$$= \begin{pmatrix} 0.1\ 0.1\ 0.1\ 0.1 \\ 0.1\ 0.1\ 0.1\ 0.1 \\ 0.1\ 0.1\ 0.1\ 0.1 \end{pmatrix}$$

$$\frac{\partial E}{\partial \mathbf{b}^{[2]}} = \delta^{[2](1)} \cdot \frac{\partial \mathbf{z}^{[2](1)}}{\partial \mathbf{b}^{[2]}}^T + \delta^{[2](2)} \cdot \frac{\partial \mathbf{z}^{[2](2)}}{\partial \mathbf{b}^{[2]}}^T$$

$$= \delta^{[2](1)} + \delta^{[2](2)}$$

$$= \begin{pmatrix} 0 \\ 0 \\ 0 \end{pmatrix} + \begin{pmatrix} 0 \\ 0 \\ 0 \end{pmatrix}$$

$$= \begin{pmatrix} 0 \\ 0 \\ 0 \end{pmatrix}$$

$$\mathbf{b}^{[2]} = \mathbf{b}^{[2]} - \eta \frac{\partial E}{\partial \mathbf{b}^{[2]}}$$

$$= \begin{pmatrix} 0.1 \\ 0.1 \\ 0.1 \end{pmatrix} - 0.1 \begin{pmatrix} 0 \\ 0 \\ 0 \end{pmatrix}$$

$$= \begin{pmatrix} 0.1 \\ 0.1 \\ 0.1 \end{pmatrix}$$

All that is left is to update the parameters for the output layer.

$$\frac{\partial E}{\partial \mathbf{W}^{[3]}} = \delta^{[3](1)} \cdot \frac{\partial \mathbf{z}^{[3](1)}}{\partial \mathbf{W}^{[3]}}^T + \delta^{[3](2)} \cdot \frac{\partial \mathbf{z}^{[3](2)}}{\partial \mathbf{W}^{[3]}}^T$$

$$= \delta^{[3](1)} \cdot \left(\mathbf{x}^{[2](1)} \right)^T + \delta^{[3](2)} \cdot \left(\mathbf{x}^{[2](2)} \right)^T$$

$$= \begin{pmatrix} 0.3333 \\ -0.6666 \\ 0.3333 \end{pmatrix} \cdot \begin{pmatrix} 0.2132 \ 0.2132 \ 0.2132 \end{pmatrix}$$

$$+ \begin{pmatrix} 0.3333 \\ 0.3333 \\ -0.6666 \end{pmatrix} \cdot \begin{pmatrix} 0.3971 \ 0.3971 \ 0.3971 \end{pmatrix}$$

$$= \begin{pmatrix} 0.2034 & 0.2034 & 0.2034 \\ -0.0098 & -0.0098 & -0.0098 \\ -0.1937 & -0.1937 & -0.1937 \end{pmatrix}$$

$$\mathbf{W}^{[3]} = \mathbf{W}^{[3]} - \eta \frac{\partial E}{\partial \mathbf{W}^{[3]}}$$

$$= \begin{pmatrix} 0.1 \ 0.1 \ 0.1 \\ 0.1 \ 0.1 \ 0.1 \\ 0.1 \ 0.1 \ 0.1 \end{pmatrix} - 0.1 \begin{pmatrix} 0.2034 & 0.2034 & 0.2034 \\ -0.0098 & -0.0098 & -0.0098 \\ -0.1937 & -0.1937 & -0.1937 \end{pmatrix}$$

$$= \begin{pmatrix} 0.0797 \ 0.0797 \ 0.0797 \\ 0.1009 \ 0.1009 \ 0.1009 \\ 0.1194 \ 0.1194 \ 0.1194 \end{pmatrix}$$

$$\frac{\partial E}{\partial \mathbf{b}^{[3]}} = \delta^{[3](1)} \cdot \frac{\partial \mathbf{z}^{[3](1)}}{\partial \mathbf{b}^{[3]}}^T + \delta^{[3](2)} \cdot \frac{\partial \mathbf{z}^{[3](2)}}{\partial \mathbf{b}^{[3]}}^T$$

$$= \delta^{[3](1)} + \delta^{[3](2)}$$

$$= \begin{pmatrix} 0.3333 \\ -0.6666 \\ 0.3333 \end{pmatrix} + \begin{pmatrix} 0.3333 \\ 0.3333 \\ -0.6666 \end{pmatrix}$$

$$= \begin{pmatrix} 0.6666 \\ -0.3333 \\ -0.3333 \end{pmatrix}$$

$$\mathbf{b}^{[3]} = \mathbf{b}^{[3]} - \eta \frac{\partial E}{\partial \mathbf{b}^{[3]}}$$

$$= \begin{pmatrix} 0.1 \\ 0.1 \\ 0.1 \end{pmatrix} - 0.1 \begin{pmatrix} 0.6666 \\ -0.3333 \\ -0.3333 \end{pmatrix}$$

$$= \begin{pmatrix} 0.3333 \\ 1.3333 \\ 1.3333 \end{pmatrix}$$

c) Compute the MLP class for the query point

$$\left\{ \mathbf{x} = \begin{pmatrix} 1 \ 1 \ 1 \ 0 \end{pmatrix}^{T}, \mathbf{t} = \begin{pmatrix} 0 \\ 0 \\ 1 \end{pmatrix} \right\}$$

using both models from a) and b). Which has smallest cross-entropy loss? Which model has better classification accuracy?

Solution: Let us start with model a):

$$\mathbf{x}^{[0]} = \begin{pmatrix} 1 \\ 1 \\ 1 \\ 0 \end{pmatrix}$$

$$\mathbf{z}^{[1]} = \begin{pmatrix} 0.1 \ 0.1 \ 0.1 \ 0.1 \\ 0.1 \ 0.1 \ 0.1 \ 0.1 \\ 0.1 \ 0.1 \ 0.1 \ 0.1 \\ 0.1 \ 0.1 \ 0.1 \ 0.1 \end{pmatrix} \begin{pmatrix} 1 \\ 1 \\ 1 \\ 0 \end{pmatrix} + \begin{pmatrix} 0.1 \\ 0.1 \\ 0.1 \\ 0.1 \end{pmatrix} = \begin{pmatrix} 0.4 \\ 0.4 \\ 0.4 \\ 0.4 \end{pmatrix}$$

$$\mathbf{x}^{[1]} = \tanh\left(\begin{pmatrix} 0.4 \\ 0.4 \\ 0.4 \\ 0.4 \end{pmatrix} \right) = \begin{pmatrix} 0.3799 \\ 0.3799 \\ 0.3799 \\ 0.3799 \end{pmatrix}$$

$$\mathbf{z}^{[2]} = \begin{pmatrix} 0.1 \ 0.1 \ 0.1 \ 0.1 \\ 0.1 \ 0.1 \ 0.1 \ 0.1 \\ 0.1 \ 0.1 \ 0.1 \ 0.1 \end{pmatrix} \begin{pmatrix} 0.3799 \\ 0.3799 \\ 0.3799 \\ 0.3799 \end{pmatrix} + \begin{pmatrix} 0.1 \\ 0.1 \\ 0.1 \end{pmatrix} = \begin{pmatrix} 0.2519 \\ 0.2519 \\ 0.2519 \end{pmatrix}$$

$$\mathbf{x}^{[2]} = tanh \left(\begin{pmatrix} 0.2519 \\ 0.2519 \\ 0.2519 \end{pmatrix} \right) = \begin{pmatrix} 0.2468 \\ 0.2468 \\ 0.2468 \end{pmatrix}$$

$$\mathbf{z}^{[3]} = \begin{pmatrix} 0.0929 \ 0.0929 \ 0.0929 \\ 0.1142 \ 0.1142 \ 0.1142 \\ 0.0929 \ 0.0929 \ 0.0929 \end{pmatrix} \begin{pmatrix} 0.2468 \\ 0.2468 \\ 0.2468 \end{pmatrix} + \begin{pmatrix} 0.0667 \\ 0.1667 \\ 0.0667 \end{pmatrix} = \begin{pmatrix} 0.1354 \\ 0.2512 \\ 0.1354 \end{pmatrix}$$

$$\mathbf{x}^{[3]} = tanh \left(\begin{pmatrix} 0.1354 \\ 0.2512 \\ 0.1354 \end{pmatrix} \right) = \begin{pmatrix} 0.3202 \\ 0.3595 \\ 0.3202 \end{pmatrix}$$

$$E\left(\mathbf{t}, \mathbf{x}^{[3]}\right) = \frac{1}{2} \sum_{i=1}^{2} \left(\mathbf{x}^{[3]} - \mathbf{t}\right)^2 = 1.1387$$

Now model b):

$$\mathbf{x}^{[0]} = \begin{pmatrix} 1 \\ 1 \\ 1 \\ 0 \end{pmatrix}$$

$$\mathbf{z}^{[1]} = \begin{pmatrix} 0.1 \ 0.1 \ 0.1 \ 0.1 \\ 0.1 \ 0.1 \ 0.1 \ 0.1 \\ 0.1 \ 0.1 \ 0.1 \ 0.1 \\ 0.1 \ 0.1 \ 0.1 \ 0.1 \end{pmatrix} \begin{pmatrix} 1 \\ 1 \\ 1 \\ 0 \end{pmatrix} + \begin{pmatrix} 0.1 \\ 0.1 \\ 0.1 \\ 0.1 \end{pmatrix} = \begin{pmatrix} 0.4 \\ 0.4 \\ 0.4 \\ 0.4 \end{pmatrix}$$

$$\mathbf{x}^{[1]} = tanh \left(\begin{pmatrix} 0.4 \\ 0.4 \\ 0.4 \\ 0.4 \end{pmatrix} \right) = \begin{pmatrix} 0.3799 \\ 0.3799 \\ 0.3799 \\ 0.3799 \end{pmatrix}$$

$$\mathbf{z}^{[2]} = \begin{pmatrix} 0.1 \ 0.1 \ 0.1 \ 0.1 \\ 0.1 \ 0.1 \ 0.1 \ 0.1 \\ 0.1 \ 0.1 \ 0.1 \ 0.1 \end{pmatrix} \begin{pmatrix} 0.3799 \\ 0.3799 \\ 0.3799 \\ 0.3799 \end{pmatrix} + \begin{pmatrix} 0.1 \\ 0.1 \\ 0.1 \end{pmatrix} = \begin{pmatrix} 0.2519 \\ 0.2519 \\ 0.2519 \end{pmatrix}$$

$$\mathbf{x}^{[2]} = tanh \left(\begin{pmatrix} 0.2519 \\ 0.2519 \\ 0.2519 \end{pmatrix} \right) = \begin{pmatrix} 0.2468 \\ 0.2468 \\ 0.2468 \end{pmatrix}$$

$$\mathbf{z}^{[3]} = \begin{pmatrix} 0.0797 \ 0.0797 \ 0.0797 \\ 0.1009 \ 0.1009 \ 0.1009 \\ 0.1194 \ 0.1194 \ 0.1194 \end{pmatrix} \begin{pmatrix} 0.2468 \\ 0.2468 \\ 0.2468 \end{pmatrix} + \begin{pmatrix} 0.3333 \\ 1.3333 \\ 1.3333 \end{pmatrix} = \begin{pmatrix} 0.0923 \\ 0.2081 \\ 0.2217 \end{pmatrix}$$

$$\mathbf{x}^{[3]} = softmax \left(\begin{pmatrix} 0.0923 \\ 0.2081 \\ 0.2217 \end{pmatrix} \right) = \begin{pmatrix} 0.3067 \\ 0.3443 \\ 0.3490 \end{pmatrix}$$

$$E\left(\mathbf{t}, \mathbf{x}^{[3]}\right) = 1.0526$$

Model b) has a lower error and is the only one that classifies the point correctly.

Thinking Questions

a) Try to repeat the problems in the lecture with invented (differentiable) activation functions.

b) Think about how the number of parameters to estimate grows with the number of layers. Do we need more or less data to estimate them properly?

Chapter 13

Convolutional Networks

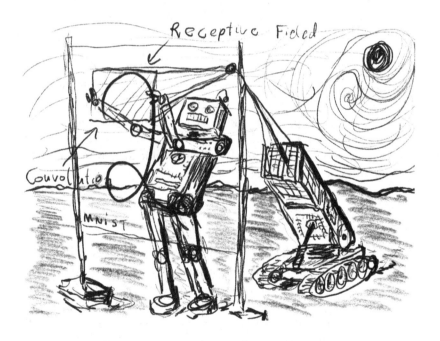

Fig. 13.1 A convolutional network represents a marriage between hierarchical neural networks and digital image processing.

13.1 Hierarchical Networks

13.1.1 *Biological Vision*

In biological vision, outside light is captured in photoreceptors in the retina. One can think about the firings of these cells as the representation of an input image. In a simplified manner, we can say that the primary visual cortex is composed by cells that receive connections from the retina. Each V1 cell is connected to a subset of the retina, so it is usually said that neurons at this stage have a local view of the input. The experimental work of Hubel and Wiesel [Hubel and Wiesel (1962)], [Hubel and Wiesel (1968)] that was performed first in the cat and later in the macaque monkey [Hubel and Wiesel (1968)] indicated that the V1 is composed by two main types of cells [Hubel (1988)], the simple cells and the complex cells. Simple cells react to stimuli with specific orientations and positions. Whereas complex cells react to stimuli with specific orientations but allow for positional shifts. For this work it has further been proposed that there in the V1 and in later stages there is a kind of hierarchy where the complexity of the preferred stimuli of neurons increases as we move away from the eye [Hubel (1988)] and at the end of the ventral stream, the cells are tuned to highly complex stimuli such as faces [Gross and Mishkin (1977)]. These findings led to vision models that implement a kind of hierarchical template matching. Specifically, a pattern is passed through layers of units with progressively more complex features at progressively less specific locations. Hierarchical in that features at a later stage are built from features at earlier stages.

13.1.2 *Neocognitron*

The Neocognitron [Fukushima (1980)], [Fukushima (1988)], [Fukushima (2001)], [Fukushima (2003)] was one of the first models of pattern recognition inspired by the biological hypotheses we described earlier (see Figure 13.2).

This model is an evolution of a previously proposed Cognitron [Fukushima (1975)] which only included the idea of simple cells. The fact that it exploits the aforementioned working principles and the fact that it is tailored for image data makes it very good at learning and generalizing from few typical examples [Shouno *et al.* (1999)], [Fukushima (2004)], [Fukushima (2005)]. Although it is mostly based on unsupervised learning [Fukushima (1980)], [Fukushima (1988)] we will later see that it provided

Fig. 13.2 Kunihiko Fukushima, the father of convolutional networks and the inventor of one of the first hierarchical artificial neural networks, the cognitron and the neocognitron.

the starting point for the supervised, deep learning approach of convolution networks.

In the neocognitron, all units have a local view, unlike the common fully connected networks we have seen throughout the book. This local view corresponds to the idea of receptive fields in biological neurons (see Figure 13.3).

The neocognitron gradually reduces information from the input layer through the output layer where it provides a classification for the input. This is done by integrating local features into more global features in sequential transformations. Each of these transformations is composed by two different steps. The first step reduces the information by representing it with previously learned templates represented by S-cells (resembling simple cells). The second step blurs the information with C-cells (resembling complex cells) to allow positional shifts, giving the model some invariance under shifts and distortions.

A stage is a sequence of two layers of different types in which the first is an S-cell layer and the second is a C-cell layer. A network can be composed of several stages. The cells in a stage are arranged in cell-planes, and each of these planes reacts to a specific stimulus in different positions. Cells in

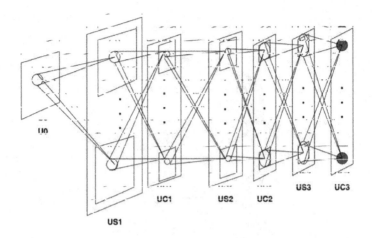

Fig. 13.3   Hierarchical network structure of the neocognitron.

higher stages (closer to the output) tend to have larger receptive fields and tend to be less sensitive to the position of the stimulus. The first layer of the first stage has the same size as the patterns to be recognized, and the last layer of the last stage has only a set of cells in which each cell represents one of the classes to be recognized. This organization implies that the dimensions of the layers are progressively reduced from the input layer to the output layer. This thinning-out takes place through the integration of local features into more global features.

13.1.3   *Map transformation cascade*

A less complex description of the neocognitron is the hierarchical neural network called map transformation cascade [Wichert], [Kemke and Wichert (1993)], [Cardoso and Wichert (2010)].

In this model, the information is processed sequentially, each layer only processes information after the previous layer is finished. The input image is tiled with a squared mask, to give rise to a collection of image parts (or sub-patterns). Each of these are matched to previously learned templates in a process that mimics the simple cells. At this step, the image is basically represented as a template map where each sub-pattern is replaced by the label of the template to which it was matched. In the following step, this map representation of the pattern is transformed by losing the exact positional information in a process that resembles complex cells. Specifically, the map is tiled with a squared mask, and for each only the presence or absence of the templates is stored, thus eliminating the positional information of each inside the mask.

The layers of a Map Transformation Cascade can be seen as filters, since they have a clear and interpretable output, which is a modification of the input information. Several filters transform and map the input pattern into a space where patterns of the same class are close. The output of the filters is then passed to a simple classifier which produces a final classification.

To get a more detailed sense of the model, let us go through each type of layer using the classical MNIST database (Modified National Institute of Standards and Technology database) of 0 to 9 handwritten digits, see Figure 13.4.

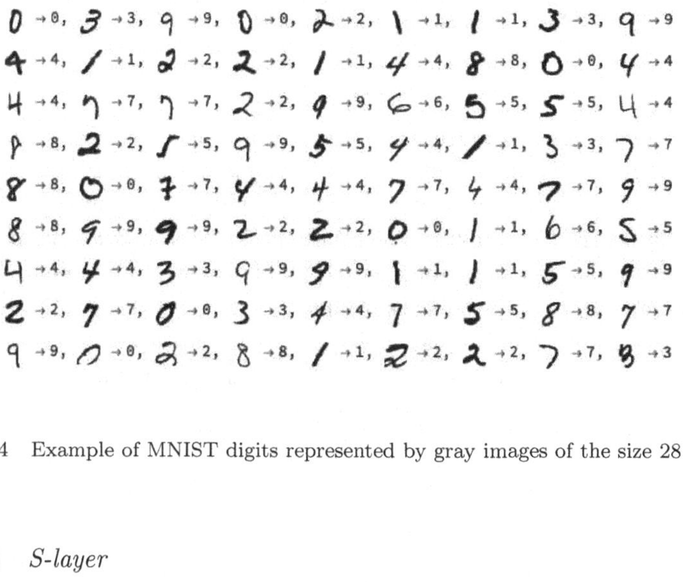

$0 \to 0, \ 3 \to 3, \ 9 \to 9, \ 0 \to 0, \ 2 \to 2, \ 1 \to 1, \ 1 \to 1, \ 3 \to 3, \ 9 \to 9$

$4 \to 4, \ 1 \to 1, \ 2 \to 2, \ 2 \to 2, \ 1 \to 1, \ 4 \to 4, \ 8 \to 8, \ 0 \to 0, \ 4 \to 4$

$4 \to 4, \ 7 \to 7, \ 7 \to 7, \ 2 \to 2, \ 9 \to 9, \ 6 \to 6, \ 5 \to 5, \ 5 \to 5, \ 4 \to 4$

$8 \to 8, \ 2 \to 2, \ 5 \to 5, \ 9 \to 9, \ 5 \to 5, \ 4 \to 4, \ 1 \to 1, \ 3 \to 3, \ 7 \to 7$

$8 \to 8, \ 0 \to 0, \ 7 \to 7, \ 4 \to 4, \ 4 \to 4, \ 7 \to 7, \ 4 \to 4, \ 7 \to 7, \ 9 \to 9$

$8 \to 8, \ 9 \to 9, \ 9 \to 9, \ 2 \to 2, \ 2 \to 2, \ 0 \to 0, \ 1 \to 1, \ 6 \to 6, \ 5 \to 5$

$4 \to 4, \ 4 \to 4, \ 3 \to 3, \ 9 \to 9, \ 9 \to 9, \ 1 \to 1, \ 1 \to 1, \ 5 \to 5, \ 9 \to 9$

$2 \to 2, \ 7 \to 7, \ 0 \to 0, \ 3 \to 3, \ 4 \to 4, \ 7 \to 7, \ 5 \to 5, \ 8 \to 8, \ 7 \to 7$

$9 \to 9, \ 0 \to 0, \ 2 \to 2, \ 8 \to 8, \ 1 \to 1, \ 2 \to 2, \ 2 \to 2, \ 7 \to 7, \ 8 \to 3$

Fig. 13.4   Example of MNIST digits represented by gray images of the size 28 × 28.

13.1.3.1   S-layer

The S-layer tries to mimic the idea of simple cells in the visual cortex by mapping the input into a template space [Cardoso and Wichert (2010)]. The input is tiled with squared overlapping masks, where each sub-pattern is replaced by a number indicating the corresponding template. These templates are previously learned using a clustering algorithm like K-means, see Figure 13.5 and Figure 13.6.

During mapping, the corresponding sub-patterns of an input pattern are mapped into the corresponding templates. The binary input pattern

Fig. 13.5   Example of a binary input pattern .

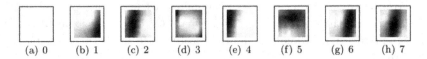

Fig. 13.6   (a) Represents the background information by the template 0. (b) to (h) represent the seven learned templates $1, 2, 3, 4, 5, 6, 7$.

is tiled with a squared mask M of size $j \times j$. The tiling can be generated dynamically by scanning a mask over the input pattern. In each position, a mask is applied to the input, and the sub-pattern is compared with the previously learned templates. For each position, the input is mapped into the most similar template represented by the index i (between 0 and k). The index 0 represents the background, by convention, and the indices 1 to k represent learned templates. For each sub-pattern $\mathbf{x}$ the most similar template i is determined according to the Euclidean distance:

$$\{i|\min_i d(\mathbf{x}, \mathbf{c}_i), i \in \{0, 1, ..., k\}\}. \tag{13.1}$$

In Figure 13.7 we see the representation of Figure 13.5 in the template space.

13.1.3.2   *C-layer*

The C-layer, which tries to mimic the idea of complex cells transforms the input it receives from the S-layer. The transformation performed by the C-layer is fixed and cannot be modified. Its purpose is to allow positional shifts, thus giving the model some invariance. The template representation of a pattern is tiled m times with a squared mask M of size $l \times l$. In each position, a vector $\mathbf{c}_h$, with $h \in \{1, 2, ..., m\}$, of dimensions $l \times l$, is determined. The vector $\mathbf{c}_h$ describes the presence of each template inside

0	0	0	0	0	0	0	0	0	0	0	0	0	0	0	0	0	0	0
0	0	0	0	0	0	0	3	3	1	1	3	3	3	0	0	0	0	0
0	0	0	0	0	3	1	1	1	1	1	1	1	3	3	3	0	0	0
0	0	0	0	3	1	1	1	1	1	5	5	1	7	2	3	3	0	0
0	0	0	3	1	1	7	3	5	5	5	5	5	5	2	4	3	0	0
0	0	3	1	1	7	5	5	5	5	5	5	5	7	2	4	0	0	0
0	0	3	1	6	7	2	4	3	3	3	3	1	6	7	2	4	3	0
0	0	1	6	7	2	4	3	0	0	0	3	6	7	2	4	3	0	0
0	3	1	6	7	2	4	3	0	0	0	3	6	7	2	4	3	0	0
0	3	1	7	2	4	3	0	0	0	0	3	6	7	2	4	3	0	0
0	1	6	7	2	4	3	0	0	0	0	1	6	7	2	4	3	0	0
0	1	6	7	2	4	0	0	0	0	0	1	6	7	2	4	3	0	0
0	1	6	7	2	4	0	0	0	0	3	1	6	7	4	4	0	0	0
0	1	6	7	2	3	0	0	0	3	1	6	7	2	4	3	0	0	0
0	1	6	7	2	4	3	3	3	1	1	7	7	2	4	3	0	0	0
0	1	6	7	2	4	1	1	1	1	7	7	2	4	3	0	0	0	0
0	3	6	5	5	1	1	1	7	7	5	5	3	3	3	0	0	0	0
0	3	3	5	5	5	5	5	5	5	5	3	3	3	0	0	0	0	0
0	0	3	3	5	5	5	5	5	4	3	3	0	0	0	0	0	0	0
0	0	0	3	3	3	3	3	3	3	3	0	0	0	0	0	0	0	0
0	0	0	0	0	0	0	0	0	0	0	0	0	0	0	0	0	0	0

Fig. 13.7 The representation of the pattern of Figure 13.5 in the template space. Only the information in the center, where the pattern is represented, is shown here. The background information is represented by 0.

the mask M. By keeping only the information about wether or not a template is present, this step loses the specific positional information inside the mask. Figure 13.8 shows the input into a C-layer mask. The output of the C-layer mask for this position will be the set of all present classes. The background and the frequency information is discarded by the C-layer [Cardoso and Wichert (2010)].

The output of a mask of a C-layer s represented by a binary vector. A 'one' represents a class at the corresponding position of a binary vector; its absence is denoted by a 'zero'. The class set $\{1, 2, 3, 4, 5, 6, 7\}$ is represented by a binary vector of seven dimensions. The presence of the classes $\{1, 6, 3\}$ is represented by the binary vector $\mathbf{u} = [1\ 0\ 1\ 0\ 0\ 1\ 0]$, with ones in the corresponding positions 1, 3, and 6. We call this vector the unsharp vector.

0	0	0	1	6
0	0	0	3	6
0	0	0	3	3
0	0	0	0	3
0	0	0	0	0

Fig. 13.8 C-layer mask input in a given position when scanning Figure 13.7, its output is $\{1, 6, 3\}$. It indicates the presence of these classes.

The template representation of a pattern is transformed into an unsharp template representation. For p classes, we get an unsharp vector $\mathbf{u}$ of dimension p. The more ones are present in the unsharp vector $\mathbf{u}$, the more information is lost. The result of a transformation of m squared masks M covering a class pattern is a $(m \times p)$-dimensional binary unsharp template vector $\mathbf{U}$. This binary vector is composed by m unsharp vectors

$$\mathbf{U} = (\mathbf{u}_1, \mathbf{u}_2, ..., \mathbf{u}_m).$$

13.1.3.3 *Cascade*

Multiple combinations of the previous two steps can be applied in cascade until a final representation is reached. That representation can then be used to feed an output classifier layer that makes the final decision.

13.1.3.4 *Experiments*

The map transformation cascade (MTC) shows good generalization for a small number of training examples and achieved performance similar to that of the neocognitron in combination with a simple nearest neighbor in the output layer. The combination of MTC and a linear SVM achieves competitive results, [Cardoso and Wichert (2013)]. The proposed MTC network achieved as well a higher noise tolerance than some related models [Cardoso and Wicher (2014)].

13.2 Convolutional Neural Networks

The basic idea behind convolutional networks [LeCun and Bengio (1998a)],[LeCun and Bengio (1998b)], [LeCun *et al.* (1990)], [LeCun *et al.* (1995)] is to take a neocognitron architecture and train it by error backpropagation. In the exercises section, we will go into the details of the CNN architecture and its specific terminology. However, for now it is helpful to draw a parallelism between it and the neocognitron. The original CNN was also composed of multiple stages of S- and C-cell layers where, in each layer, cells are organized in cell planes that share the same stimulus or, in this case, the same weights. Also, cells in higher stages (closer to the output) tend to have larger receptive fields and tend to be less sensitive to the position of the stimulus.

In CNNs, the S-layers are called convolution layers. This is because of the image processing operation of a convolution. This operation takes a small matrix called a kernel and slides through an image and at each position (see Figure 13.9), computes the sum of the neighborhood values weighted by the values in the kernel as is shown in Figure 13.10.

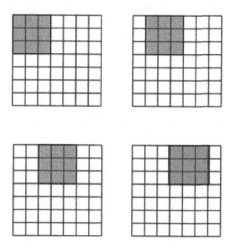

Fig. 13.9   An example of a convolution of the size 3 × 3 moving with a stride value two over an input of the size 7 × 7.

Sometimes, it can be helpful to pad the input such that the convolution analyzes all positions as in Figure 13.11. Now, if we assume the kernel stores a given stimulus (or local feature) this is exactly what each cell plane in the old S-layer did: at each position, react highly if the stimulus is present. From this, it follows that the receptive field is the same size as the kernel, because this is the neighborhood that is actually analyzed around each position. Each position of the convolution output corresponds to the output of one unit. So, if we assume that the units have nonlinear

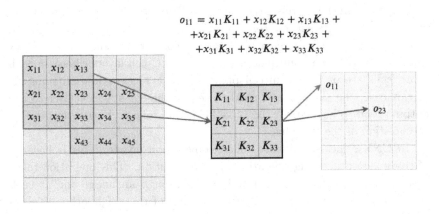

$$o_{11} = x_{11}K_{11} + x_{12}K_{12} + x_{13}K_{13} +$$
$$+x_{21}K_{21} + x_{22}K_{22} + x_{23}K_{23} +$$
$$+x_{31}K_{31} + x_{32}K_{32} + x_{33}K_{33}$$

Fig. 13.10   An example of the convolution operation.

Fig. 13.11   Zero padding pads the input volume with zeros around the border. An inout window of the size 5×5 becomes a window of the size 7×7 so that a convolution of the size 4×4 can move with a stride value one.

activation functions, we would have to pass the convolution output values through one. Notice that, the whole cell plane performs the convolution for a single kernel. So, all units share the same kernel. Which, in neural network terms, means that they all share the same weights. This is a good way to avoid overfitting. With many units sharing weights, the number of free parameters in the model is considerably reduced.

The C-layers are called max-pooling (or mean-pooling) layers or sub-sampling layers. The name comes from the idea of a pooling operation using a given aggregating function. Units in these layers are also arranged in cell planes and each plane performs the pooling of the corresponding plane in the previous layer. Figure 13.12 provides an illustration of that operation. Basically, the size of the plane is reduced by combining neighborhood positions through their maximum (or mean) value. Pooling makes

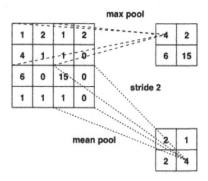

Fig. 13.12   A C-cell layer does not learn, however its task is to preform a downsampling and is called a sub-sampling layer. Alternatively a max operation over an input window is preformed, instead of the mean value a maximal value is determined.

the representations smaller and more manageable and operates over each activation map independently.

Figure 13.13 shows an overview representation of the two described operations. Besides these two newly introduced layers, a CNN can be finished with a set of fully-connected layers (basically an MLP) that performs the classification. No matter how many or of what kind, all layers are trained through the backpropagation algorithm. As an example, see Figure 13.14. With all of that, deep convolutional networks are deep networks that, besides including many of the techniques we have seen in the previous chapter, can also include convolution or pooling layers. They exhibit a key advantage when working with images because weight sharing and sparseness connectivity (see Figure 13.15) exploit the repetitive two-dimensional structure of images to reduce tremendously the number of parameters without loosing the capability to learn them.

13.2.1   *CNNs and Kernels in Image Processing*

Recall that convolution is the process of adding each element of the image to its local neighbors, weighted by a kernel. For example, if the input plane

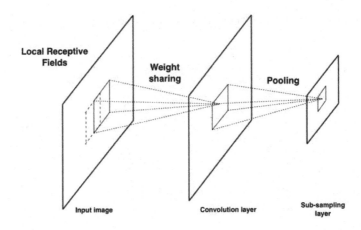

Fig. 13.13 A convolutional network, the receptive fields define a convolution. The S-layers are called convolution layers and the C-layers are called sub-sampling layers.

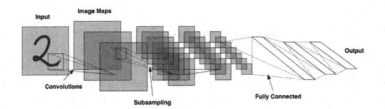

Fig. 13.14 The LeNet-5 architecture is one of the first CNN architectures by Yann LeCun in 1998 that was successfully applied to handwritten digit recognition (MNIST) [LeCun and Bengio (1998a)],[LeCun and Bengio (1998b)], [LeCun *et al.* (1990)]. In LeNet-5 the newly introduced convolution network layers are followed by fully-connected layers.

is represented by some values (like for example pixels of a gray image)

$$
\begin{pmatrix}
f(x-1,y-1) & f(x-1,y) & f(x-1,y+1) \\
f(x,y-1) & f(x,y) & f(x,y+1) \\
f(x+11,y-1) & f(x+11,y) & f(x+1,y+1)
\end{pmatrix} \tag{13.2}
$$

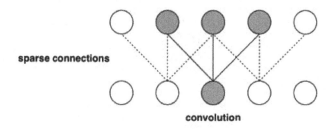

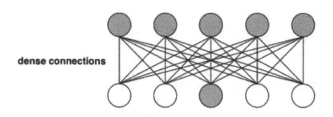

Fig. 13.15   Parameter sharing, convolution share the same parameters across all spatial locations. This is the same principle as in Neococgnitron or MTC network. This is not the case with a fully connected (dense) network.

and the convolution kernel is represented by the weights

$$
\begin{pmatrix}
w(-1,-1) & w(-1,0) & w(-1,-1) \\
w(0,-1) & w(0,0) & w(0,-1) \\
w(1,-1) & w(1,0) & w(1,-1)
\end{pmatrix}
\tag{13.3}
$$

then the value of the convolution output at the position (x, y) is

$$
g(x, y) = \sum_{s=-1}^{1} \sum_{t=-1}^{1} w(s, t) \cdot f(x + s, y + t)
\tag{13.4}
$$

Images in the red, green, and blue (RGB) color space consist of colored pixels that are defined by three numbers: one for red, one for green and one for blue (RGB image). The range of different colors that can be produced is dependent on the pixel depth. For instance, for a 12 bit pixel depth, four bits per primary color yields

$$
2^4 \cdot 2^4 \cdot 2^4 = 4096
$$

different colors. An extreme case is an image with only black and white pixels which requires only a single bit for each pixel. Alternatively, a black and white picture with 256 different grey values requires 8 bits per pixel.

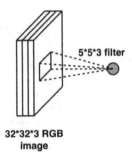

**32*32*3 RGB
image**

Fig. 13.16   An input RGB image of the size 32×32 and its input to a convolution of the size 5×5.

An input RGB image of the size 32×32 and its input to a convolution of the size 5×5 is shown in the Figure 13.16. The mean value of the three RGB numbers represents approximately the gray value.

The idea of using convolution in image processing existed before CNNs. In fact, one may think of this operation as a kind of feature extraction where the feature to be extracted is represented in the kernel. Traditionally the hard part was to choose the right kernels [Wichert (2015)]. In fact, many well-known kernels existed beforehand and were proposed to extract certain types of features.

13.2.1.1   *Edge detection*

An image may be converted into a set of curves or edges. The basic idea behind edge detection is to localize the discontinuities in the intensity function of the image. Many approaches to edge detection are based on the rapid changes and discontinuities in the gray level. If we represent the gray levels as two-dimensional functions, the discontinuities can be detected using maxima in the first derivative or zero-crossings in the second derivative. In one dimension, the largest change corresponds to the derivative that has the maximum magnitude (second derivative is zero). In two dimensions, the derivative is represented by the gradient [Paulus and Hornegger (2003)]. The gradient of a continuous function $f(x, y)$ that represents an image is given by

$$\bigtriangledown f(x, y) = \left(\frac{\partial f}{\partial x}, \frac{\partial f}{\partial y} \right). \tag{13.5}$$

It points in the direction of the most rapid change in intensity. The gradient defines the edge direction and the edge strength. The edge direction is usually defined to be orthogonal to the gradient. The gradient direction is given by

$$\nabla f(x,y) = \left(\frac{\partial f}{\partial x}, \frac{\partial f}{\partial y}\right) \tag{13.6}$$

and the edge strength is given by the gradient magnitude

$$\|\nabla f(x,y)\| = \sqrt{\left(\frac{\partial f}{\partial x}\right)^2 + \left(\frac{\partial f}{\partial y}\right)^2}. \tag{13.7}$$

A digital image can be differentiated either by reconstructing a continuous image $f(x,y)$ and then computing the gradient or via a discrete derivative, computing a finite difference

$$\frac{\partial f}{\partial x}(x,y) \approx f(x+1,y) - f(x,y) \tag{13.8}$$

and

$$\frac{\partial f}{\partial y}(x,y) \approx f(x,y+1) - f(x,y). \tag{13.9}$$

In this latter approach, the equations can be interpreted as functions

$$h_x(x,y) = \begin{cases} -1 & \text{if} & x = 0 \\ 0 & \text{if} & x = 1 \\ 1 & \text{if} & x = 2 \\ 0 & \text{if } (x < 0) \vee (x > 2) \end{cases} \tag{13.10}$$

and

$$h_y(x,y) = \begin{cases} -1 & \text{if} & y = 0 \\ 0 & \text{if} & y = 1 \\ 1 & \text{if} & y = 2 \\ 0 & \text{if } (y < 0) \vee (y > 2) \end{cases} \tag{13.11}$$

or as symmetric kernels

$$h_x = \begin{pmatrix} -1 & 0 & 1 \end{pmatrix} \tag{13.12}$$

and

$$h_y = \begin{pmatrix} -1 \\ 0 \\ -1 \end{pmatrix} \tag{13.13}$$

which can then be used in a convolution operation. For an image f of the size $n \times m$ and the masks h_x and h_y the derivative is simply computed by convolutions (denoted by the symbol $*$)

$$\frac{\partial f}{\partial x}(x, y) \approx f * h_x = \sum_{i=0}^{n-1} f(i, y) \cdot h_x(x - i, y) \tag{13.14}$$

and

$$\frac{\partial f}{\partial y}(x, y) \approx f * h_y \sum_{j=0}^{m-1} f(x, j) \cdot h_x(x, y - j). \tag{13.15}$$

Since the distance from the central point where the derivative is estimated is one pixel to the right, the computation yields only half of the derivative. Better approximations of the derivatives can be given through different kernels. For instance, the Sobel operators (kernels)

$$s_x = \begin{pmatrix} -1 & 0 & 1 \\ -2 & 0 & 2 \\ -1 & 0 & 1 \end{pmatrix} \tag{13.16}$$

and

$$s_y = \begin{pmatrix} 1 & 2 & 1 \\ 0 & 0 & 0 \\ -1 & -2 & -1 \end{pmatrix} = s_x^T \tag{13.17}$$

with

$$\frac{\partial f}{\partial x}(x, y) \approx f * \left(\frac{1}{8} \cdot s_x \right) \tag{13.18}$$

and

$$\frac{\partial f}{\partial y}(x, y) \approx f * \left(\frac{1}{8} \cdot s_y \right). \tag{13.19}$$

where we multiply the Sobel operator with a term $1/8$ to approximate the right gradient value. For edge detection this normalization factor is not required (see Figure 13.17).

13.2.1.2 *Other types of kernels*

In digital image processing many applications for kernels exist. We have covered, as an example, the edge extraction vertical Sobel

$$\text{vertical sobel kernel} = \begin{pmatrix} -1 & 0 & 1 \\ -2 & 0 & 2 \\ -1 & 0 & 1 \end{pmatrix} \tag{13.20}$$

 (a)   (b)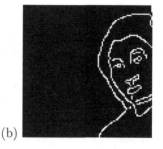

Fig. 13.17   (a) Example of an RGB image, represented as a gray image. (b) Gradient image computed with Sobel operator [Wichert (2015)].

with

$$g(x,y) = -f(x-1,y-1) + f(x-1,y+1) - 2 \cdot f(x,y-1) + $$
$$2 \cdot f(x,y+1) - f(x+1,y-1) + f(x+1,y+1).$$

Yet, there are many more. For instance, for edge detection we have the laplacian operator that is sensitive to noise

$$edge\ detection\ kernel = \begin{pmatrix} -1 & -1 & -1 \\ -1 & 8 & -1 \\ -1 & -1 & -1 \end{pmatrix}, \qquad (13.21)$$

for image sharpening we have the sharpen kernel

$$sharpen\ kernel = \begin{pmatrix} 0 & -1 & 0 \\ -1 & 5 & -1 \\ 0 & -1 & 0 \end{pmatrix}, \qquad (13.22)$$

and for blurring we can use a Gaussian kernel

$$Gaussian\ blur\ kernel = \begin{pmatrix} \frac{1}{16} & \frac{2}{16} & \frac{1}{16} \\ \frac{2}{16} & \frac{4}{16} & \frac{2}{16} \\ \frac{1}{16} & \frac{2}{16} & \frac{1}{16} \end{pmatrix}. \qquad (13.23)$$

13.2.1.3 *Features*

In convolutional networks kernels are used and since the network is trained by backpropagation, the algorithm learns which kernels are most suitable to the task at hand. Instead of inventing features that may be meaningful for classification (like edges) one learns these features by building a generic model using a large labeled data set. These features may be generic for any image task or may be task specific, it is hard for us humans to interpret the weights of the CNN and see which features are being used. However, they achieve great results and early layers are at least generic enough to be often useful for transfer learning.

13.2.2   *Data Augmentation*

Convolutional neural networks require big training sets that describe the classes due to differences in position, contrast and color since their invariant properties can be rather limited when compared to the neocognitron. Furthermore, there are lots of parameters to estimate. So, one can increase the training set by data augmentation. Typically, it is possible to flip original images, crop and rescale some parts of them, change their color distribution or even add some random pixels to them, thus generating a new labeled data set with more examples.

13.2.3   *Case Studies*

13.2.3.1   *LeNet-5*

The LeNet-5 architecture was one of the first CNN architectures. It was proposed by Yann LeCun in 1998 and it was successfully applied to handwritten digit recognition (MNIST) [LeCun and Bengio (1998a)],[LeCun and Bengio (1998b)], [LeCun *et al.* (1990)], see Figure 13.14.

13.2.3.2   *AlexNet*

The AlexNet CNN architecture won the 2012 ImageNet ILSVRC challenge with 17% error rate [Krizhevsky *et al.* (2017)]. It is quite similar to LeNet-5, only much larger. It contained eight layers; the first five were convolutional layers, some of them followed by max-pooling layers, and the last three were fully connected layers. It used for the first time ReLU to deal with the vanishing gradients problem. Furthermore, it used mini-batches of size 128 in a gradient descent with a momentum value of 0.9. As regularization it used dropout with the value 0.5 as well as l_2 regularization with the value $\lambda/2 = 0.0005$ also called weight decay.

13.2.3.3   *GoogLeNet*

The GoogLeNet architecture [Szegedy *et al.* (2015)] won the ILSVRC 2014 challenge with an error rate below 7%. The network was much deeper than previous CNNs. It was composed of 22 layers and an efficient intercept module. It is build out of stack interception modules with dimension reduction on top of each other. GoogLeNet led to the revolution of depth where huge networks with up to hundred layers are used. This network required big training sets and relayed on heavy computing resources. Of course such network architectures have nothing to do with brain or the visual cortex.

13.3   Exercises and Answers

Convolution Networks are a way to structure a network's architecture such that it uses knowledge from how images are built to reduce the number of free parameters and thus increase generalization. The cornerstone of these networks is the convolution operation. Let us recall the convolution operation.

Convolution Operation:

The convolution which is represented by the symbol $*$. Given a $k_h \times k_w$ kernel matrix $\mathbf{K}_{ij}$. For a given input matrix $\mathbf{x} \in \mathbb{R}^{H \times W}$, the convolution of $\mathbf{x}$ by $\mathbf{K}$ is as a matrix $\mathbf{o} = \mathbf{x} * \mathbf{K}$ where the coordinates are defined as:

$$o_{ij} = (\mathbf{x} * \mathbf{K})_{ij} = \sum_{h=1}^{k_h} \sum_{w=1}^{k_w} x_{(i+h-1)(j+w-1)} K_{hw}$$

The following figure presents an example where we show the computation performed by convolution to get two output positions.

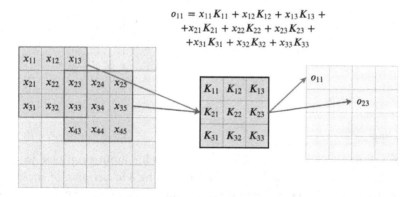

We can think of each step as a dot product between the kernel and the image's window. So, the result will be high if the window is similar to the kernel. This tells us that convolving an image with a kernel corresponds to searching for occurrences of the feature represented by that kernel in the image.

Looking at the way convolution is defined, we can see that it corresponds to sliding a window with the same size as the kernel through the image. Concretely, the window start at the top left corner and its contents are multiplied by the kernel and summed. This process achieves the top left corner of the output. Afterwards, the window shifts one position to right and the same process is applied. Eventually, we can no longer slide the window to the right without crossing the input boundary. Then, the window goes back to the left side but shited down by one position. If we define the amount that the window is shifted accross the image's width from step to step s_w, we say that the regular convolution has a horizontal stride of one $s_w = 1$. The same reasoning tell us that the vertical (or height) stride $s_h = 1$ as well.

Variable Stride:

With the previous definition in mind, we can change the stride value and move the window more from step to step. This may cause convolution to skip input positions. The following figure provides an example where $s_w = 2$ and $s_h = 1$.

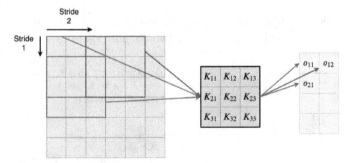

Padding:

If we want convolution to look around all possible input positions, we can use a technique called padding. The trick is to add a frame of invented pixels around the image. Several values can be placed on these pixels. A typical choice is to put all zeros which is called zero padding. The following figure shows convolution applied to a padded image where $p_h = 1$ because we added a row of imaginary pixels above and below. Also, we have that

$p_w = 1$ because we added a column on the left and on the right.

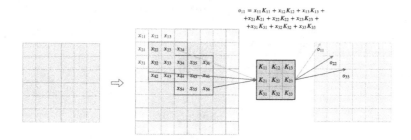

Convolution with Channels:

Usually, convolution is not applied to a single two-dimensional matrix but to a collection of matrices where each is called a channel. Think about an image in RGB where each color has its matrix of pixels. In this case, each color is a channel.

In this formulation, the kernel has the same number of channels as the input. Now, convolution between an input with channels and a kernel with channels corresponds to applying the old convolution between the corresponding channels independently and summing the results. The figure below provides an example.

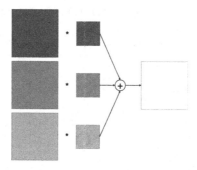

Convolution Layer:

A convolution layer computes the convolution operation between an input and a set of different kernels. Since each convolution results in a two-dimensional matrix (one for each kernel), we say that the output of a layer with k kernels is an new representation of an image with k channels.

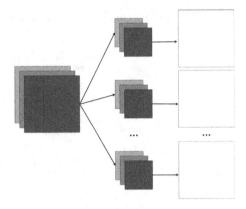

Thinking about what the layer is doing, we see that each channels correspond to a map that pinpoints where the feature represented by that kernel seems to appear.

Pooling Operation:

The pooling operation is very similar to the convolution operation. However, there is no kernel. For each window in the input, a fixed operation is applied. Usually, two kinds of pooling are used: max pooling and average pooling. For the figure below, the first one would correspond to $o_{11} = \max{(x_{11}, x_{12}, x_{13}, x_{21}, x_{22}, x_{23}, x_{31}, x_{32}, x_{33})}$. Where as the second one would be $o_{11} = mean{(x_{11}, x_{12}, x_{13}, x_{21}, x_{22}, x_{23}, x_{31}, x_{32}, x_{33})}$.

$$o_{11} = operation{(x_{11}, x_{12}, x_{13}, x_{21}, x_{22}, x_{23}, x_{31}, x_{32}, x_{33})}$$

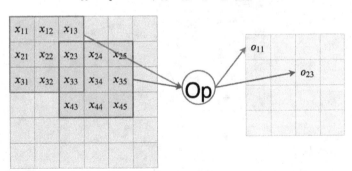

This process is usually done to change the resolution. This not only allows for noise to fade but also yields a smaller image, which will result in less parameters and thus more generalization. However, if the pooling operation is over done, the resolution is too small and we may lose not only noise but also very important features.

Pooling Layer:

A pooling layer applies the pooling operation to every channel independently. The figure below provides an illustration.

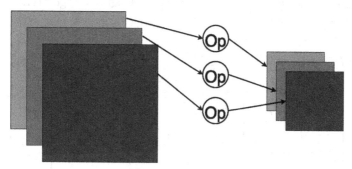

1)

a) For a kernel of shape $(k_h, k_w) = (5, 3)$ with one channel, a stride of $(s_h, s_w) = (1, 1)$ and an input of shape $(H, W, C) = (6, 5)$ with one channel, what padding (p_h, p_w) is required such that the output has the same shape as the input (also called same padding)?

Solution:

The input will be something like the following:

$$\begin{pmatrix} I_{110} & I_{120} & I_{130} & I_{140} & I_{150} \\ I_{210} & I_{220} & I_{230} & I_{240} & I_{250} \\ I_{310} & I_{320} & I_{330} & I_{340} & I_{350} \\ I_{410} & I_{420} & I_{430} & I_{440} & I_{450} \\ I_{510} & I_{520} & I_{530} & I_{540} & I_{550} \\ I_{610} & I_{620} & I_{630} & I_{640} & I_{650} \end{pmatrix}$$

where I_{hwc} corresponds to the input value at height h, width w and channel c.

Let us focus on one dimension at a time.

For the height, a general slice at width w and channel c will have the following values:

$$\begin{pmatrix} I_{1wc} \\ I_{2wc} \\ I_{3wc} \\ I_{4wc} \\ I_{5wc} \\ I_{6wc} \end{pmatrix}$$

If we center the kernel at all possible heights we get the following possibilities:

$$\begin{pmatrix} ? \\ ? \\ I_{1wc} \\ I_{2wc} \\ I_{3wc} \\ I_{4wc} \\ I_{5wc} \\ I_{6wc} \end{pmatrix}, \begin{pmatrix} ? \\ I_{1wc} \\ I_{2wc} \\ I_{3wc} \\ I_{4wc} \\ I_{5wc} \\ I_{6wc} \end{pmatrix}, \begin{pmatrix} I_{1wc} \\ I_{2wc} \\ I_{3wc} \\ I_{4wc} \\ I_{5wc} \\ I_{6wc} \end{pmatrix}, \begin{pmatrix} I_{1wc} \\ I_{2wc} \\ I_{3wc} \\ I_{4wc} \\ I_{5wc} \\ I_{6wc} \end{pmatrix}, \begin{pmatrix} I_{1wc} \\ I_{2wc} \\ I_{3wc} \\ I_{4wc} \\ I_{5wc} \\ I_{6wc} \\ ? \end{pmatrix}, \begin{pmatrix} I_{1wc} \\ I_{2wc} \\ I_{3wc} \\ I_{4wc} \\ I_{5wc} \\ I_{6wc} \\ ? \\ ? \end{pmatrix}$$

So, we will need two extra dimensions on both sides to cover the top and bottom cases. For that reason, $p_h = 2$.

Repeating the same reasoning for the width and the channels, we get $p_w = 1$ and $p_c = 0$.

---

b) For a general kernel shape (k_h, k_w), a general input shape (H, W) and a fixed stride of $(s_h, s_w) = (1, 1)$. Can you derive a general formula for (p_h, p_w) such that the output has shape (H, W)?

Solution:

For an input of height H, if we want the output to have also height H we will have:

$$H = H - f_h + 2p_h + 1 \iff p_h = \frac{f_h - 1}{2}$$

For the width we will have:

$$W = W - f_w + 2p_w + 1 \iff p_w = \frac{f_w - 1}{2}.$$

---

2)

Connsider the following network:

- Input:
  - $(H, W, C) = (28, 28, 3)$
- Convolution:
  - Number of kernels: 8
  - For all kernels the shapes are: $(k_h, k_w, k_c) = (5, 5, 3)$
  - The strides are: $(s_h, s_w) = (1, 1)$
  - Same padding
- Pooling:
  - $(k_h, k_w) = (4, 4)$
  - $(s_h, s_w) = (2, 2)$

a) List and count all parameters in this network.

Solution:

Each kernel channels is a matrix of shape 5×5. Each kernel has three channels. So, each kernel will require $3 \times 5 \times 5 = 75$ parameters.

The convolution layer has 8 kernels, so the total amount of parameters for all kernels is $8 \times 75 = 600$.

Besides the kernel weights, there will also be biases. More specifically, 8biases, one per kernel. So, $600 + 8 = 608$ parameters.

The pooling layer has a fixed operation, so there are no parameters.

In total, the network has 608 parameters.

---

b) What is the output's shape?

Solution:

Since the convolution layer has same padding, the output of that layer will have the same height and width of the input 28×28. The number of kernels in the layer is 8 so the output of the layer will be 8 channels of shape 28×28.

The pooling layer applies a pooling operation to each channel independently. So, the number of channels will not change. However, the height and width do change.

Horizontally, we can move a 4×4 window with a two pixel stride for 13 positions before we cross the input boundary. Namely, we will have windows starting at widths $1, 3, 5, 7, 9, 11, 13, 15, 17, 19, 21, 23, 25$.

Vertically we get the same thing. So, the final output of the whole network corresponds to 8 channels of shape 13×13.

---

3)

Connsider the following network:

- Input:
  - $(H, W, C) = (10, 10, 1)$
- Convolution:
  - Number of kernels: 8
  - $(k_h, k_w, k_c) = (5, 5, 1)$
  - $(s_h, s_w) = (1, 1)$
  - Same padding
- Convolution:
  - Number of kernels: 12
  - $(k_h, k_w, k_c) = (3, 3, 8)$
  - $(s_h, s_w) = (1, 1)$
  - Same padding

a) List and count all parameters in this network.

Solution:

The first convolution layer has 8 kernels with one channel with shape $(5, 5)$. So, there will be eight matrices of shape 5×5. So, a total of $8 \times 5 \times 5 = 200$ parameters.

Besides the weights, there will also be biases. More specifically, 8biases, one per kernel. So, a total of $200 + 8 = 208$ parameters.

The second convolution layer has 12 kernels where each has 8 channels with shape $(3, 3)$ and 12 biases. So, the second layer will have $12 \times 8 \times 3 \times 3 + 12 = 876$ parameters.

Finally, the whole network will have a total of $208 + 876 = 1084$ parameters.

---

b) What is the output's shape?

Solution:

Since the first convolution layer has same padding the height and width do not change. So, with 8 kernels, the output will have 8 channels where each has a shape of 10×10.

The second convolution layer is similar. The same padding will keep the height and width constant. With 12 kernels, the final output will have 12 channels of 10×10 values.

4)

Given an input image of shape $(10, 10, 1)$ connected to a layer of $(10, 10, 5)$ units.

a) How many parameters does the network have if it is fully connected?

Solution:

Every input unit will be connected to all units in the next layer. So, there will be $(10 \times 10 \times 1) \times (10 \times 10 \times 5)$ weight connections. Also, each unit in the layer has its bias term, so there will be $10 \times 10 \times 5$ bias parameters.

b) What about if it is a convolution layer with 5 kernels of shape $(3, 3, 1)$ with same padding and unitary stride.

Solution:

The convolution layer has 5 kernels where each has shape $(3, 3, 1)$ and 3 biases. So, the total number of parameters is $5 \times 1 \times 3 \times 3 + 3 = 48$.

5)

For the following input image:

$$I = \begin{pmatrix} 10 & 10 & 10 & 10 & 10 & 10 \\ 5 & 5 & 5 & 5 & 5 & 5 \\ 2 & 2 & 2 & 0 & 0 & 2 \\ 2 & 2 & 2 & 0 & 0 & 2 \\ 50 & 10 & 50 & 50 & 50 & 10 \\ 50 & 10 & 50 & 50 & 50 & 10 \end{pmatrix}$$

a) What is the output provided by a convolution layer with the following properties:

- Zero Padding: $(1,1)$
- Stride: $(1,1)$
- Kernel Shape: $(3,3)$
- Number of kernels: 2
- Kernels:

$$\begin{pmatrix} 1 & 1 & 1 \\ 1 & 0 & 1 \\ 1 & 1 & 1 \end{pmatrix}, \begin{pmatrix} 0 & 0 & 0 \\ 0 & 1 & 0 \\ 0 & 0 & 0 \end{pmatrix}$$

Solution:

First, let us compute the output dimensions:

$$Output_h = \left\lfloor \frac{6 - 3 + 2 \times 1}{1} \right\rfloor + 1 = 6$$

$$Output_w = \left\lfloor \frac{6 - 3 + 2 \times 1}{1} \right\rfloor + 1 = 6$$

The first channel of the output will be:

$$pad\,(I,(1,1)) * \begin{pmatrix} 1 & 1 & 1 \\ 1 & 0 & 1 \\ 1 & 1 & 1 \end{pmatrix} = \begin{pmatrix} 0 & 0 & 0 & 0 & 0 & 0 & 0 & 0 \\ 0 & 10 & 10 & 10 & 10 & 10 & 10 & 0 \\ 0 & 5 & 5 & 5 & 5 & 5 & 5 & 0 \\ 0 & 2 & 2 & 2 & 0 & 0 & 2 & 0 \\ 0 & 2 & 2 & 2 & 0 & 0 & 2 & 0 \\ 0 & 50 & 10 & 50 & 50 & 50 & 10 & 0 \\ 0 & 50 & 10 & 50 & 50 & 50 & 10 & 0 \\ 0 & 0 & 0 & 0 & 0 & 0 & 0 & 0 \end{pmatrix} * \begin{pmatrix} 1 & 1 & 1 \\ 1 & 0 & 1 \\ 1 & 1 & 1 \end{pmatrix}$$

$$= \begin{pmatrix} 20 & 35 & 35 & 35 & 35 & 20 \\ 29 & 46 & 44 & 42 & 42 & 27 \\ 16 & 25 & 21 & 19 & 19 & 12 \\ 66 & 120 & 116 & 154 & 114 & 62 \\ 74 & 216 & 174 & 252 & 172 & 112 \\ 70 & 210 & 170 & 250 & 170 & 110 \end{pmatrix}$$

The second channel of the output will be:

$$pad\,(I,(1,1)) * \begin{pmatrix} 0\,0\,0 \\ 0\,1\,0 \\ 0\,0\,0 \end{pmatrix} = \begin{pmatrix} 0 & 0 & 0 & 0 & 0 & 0 & 0 & 0 \\ 0 & 10 & 10 & 10 & 10 & 10 & 10 & 0 \\ 0 & 5 & 5 & 5 & 5 & 5 & 5 & 0 \\ 0 & 2 & 2 & 2 & 0 & 0 & 2 & 0 \\ 0 & 2 & 2 & 2 & 0 & 0 & 2 & 0 \\ 0 & 50 & 10 & 50 & 50 & 50 & 10 & 0 \\ 0 & 50 & 10 & 50 & 50 & 50 & 10 & 0 \\ 0 & 0 & 0 & 0 & 0 & 0 & 0 & 0 \end{pmatrix} * \begin{pmatrix} 0\,0\,0 \\ 0\,1\,0 \\ 0\,0\,0 \end{pmatrix}$$

$$= \begin{pmatrix} 10 & 10 & 10 & 10 & 10 & 10 \\ 5 & 5 & 5 & 5 & 5 & 5 \\ 2 & 2 & 2 & 0 & 0 & 2 \\ 2 & 2 & 2 & 0 & 0 & 2 \\ 50 & 10 & 50 & 50 & 50 & 10 \\ 50 & 10 & 50 & 50 & 50 & 10 \end{pmatrix}$$

b) Take the output from **a)** and apply a max pooling layer with the following properties:

- Zero Padding: $(0,0)$
- Stride: $(2,2)$
- Kernel Shape: $(2,2)$

Solution:
First, let us compute the output dimensions:

$$Output_h = \left\lfloor \frac{6 - 2 + 2 \times 0}{2} \right\rfloor + 1 = 3$$

$$Output_w = \left\lfloor \frac{6 - 2 + 2 \times 0}{2} \right\rfloor + 1 = 3$$

The first channel of the output will be:

$$maxpool \begin{pmatrix} 20 & 35 & 35 & 35 & 35 & 20 \\ 29 & 46 & 44 & 42 & 42 & 27 \\ 16 & 25 & 21 & 19 & 19 & 12 \\ 66 & 120 & 116 & 154 & 114 & 62 \\ 74 & 216 & 174 & 252 & 172 & 112 \\ 70 & 210 & 170 & 250 & 170 & 110 \end{pmatrix} = \begin{pmatrix} 46 & 44 & 42 \\ 120 & 154 & 114 \\ 216 & 252 & 172 \end{pmatrix}$$

The second channel of the output will be:

$$maxpool \begin{pmatrix} 10 & 10 & 10 & 10 & 10 & 10 \\ 5 & 5 & 5 & 5 & 5 & 5 \\ 2 & 2 & 2 & 0 & 0 & 2 \\ 2 & 2 & 2 & 0 & 0 & 2 \\ 50 & 10 & 50 & 50 & 50 & 10 \\ 50 & 10 & 50 & 50 & 50 & 10 \end{pmatrix} = \begin{pmatrix} 10 & 10 & 10 \\ 2 & 2 & 2 \\ 50 & 50 & 50 \end{pmatrix}$$

---

6)

For the following kernels, describe what kind of feature they extract from the image:

$$F_1 = \begin{pmatrix} -10 & -10 & -10 \\ 5 & 5 & 5 \\ -50 & -10 & -10 \end{pmatrix}, F_2 = \begin{pmatrix} 2 & 2 & 2 \\ 2 & -12 & 2 \\ 2 & 2 & 2 \end{pmatrix}, F_3 = \begin{pmatrix} -20 & -10 & 0 & 5 & 10 \\ -10 & 0 & 5 & 10 & 5 \\ 0 & 5 & 10 & 5 & 0 \\ 5 & 10 & 5 & 0 & -10 \\ 10 & 5 & 0 & -10 & -20 \end{pmatrix}$$

Solution:

F_1: Thin horizontal line

F_2: Frame with no center

F_3: Diagonal line

---

7)

Get some information about Tensorflow/Keras at

$$https: //www.tensorflow.org/tutorials$$

and about Colab

$$https: //colab.research.google.com/github/tensorflow/$$

$$docs/blob/master/site/en/tutorials/quickstart/beginner.ipynb$$

or Google it..

Using Tensorflow/Keras explore the use of different neural network architectures to achieve the highest performance on the test set of the famous MNIST data set

$$http: //yann.lecun.com/exdb/mnist/$$

More specifically:

- Explore the use of Feed-Forward and Convolutional Neural Networks
- Explore networks with a different number of hidden layers
- Assess the impact of different regularization methods

Thinking Questions

Can you see why is it said that a CNN is a smart way to regularize an MLP through a different architecture? Think about some key factors like free parameters, bias and generalization.

Chapter 14

Recurrent Networks

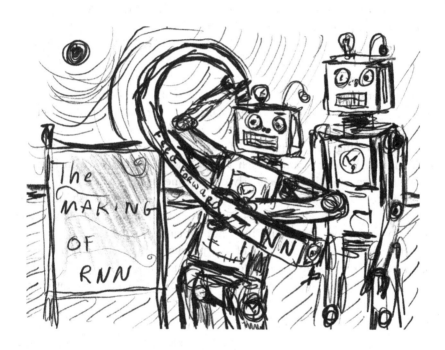

Fig. 14.1 When applying machine learning to sequences, we often want to turn an input sequence into an output sequence in a different domain. Recurrent neural networks or RNNs are a family of neural networks for processing sequential data, like a sequence of values.

14.1   Sequence Modelling

There are many machine learning scenarios where the inputs are sequences. For example, we often want to turn an input sequence into an output sequence in a different domain like mapping a sequence of sounds into a sequence of word identities. Another possible setting is one where we want to classify a given sequence like qualifying a restaurant review based on the text. Finally, we may even want to predict the next word in an input sequence.

Let us consider that each input is a sequence of vectors

$$\mathbf{x}^{(1)}, \cdots, \mathbf{x}^{(T)} \tag{14.1}$$

where the superscript denotes the position of the vector in the sequence (typically called the timestep). A training set of many examples can contain many of such sequences, with variable lengths.

A traditional fully connected feedforward network can only deal with input vectors and not sequences. So, if we wanted to apply one to this type of data, we could do one of two things. On the one hand, we could train a single network that receives sequence elements. By doing so, we would lose completely the sense of order. On the other hand, we could create one network for each possible timestep. In that case we will not only have problems dealing with sequences of variable lengths, but we will also be extremely inefficient because each network will have to learn insights by itself that are shared independently of the timestep.

A system that can process sequences of variable length should share the same weights at all timesteps and should be able to model transitions between timesteps. With that in mind, we can describe the state of such a system in time as a function of the previous timestep and the shared parameters. For instance, consider a dynamical system with inputs from $t = 1$ to $t = 3$ where parameters $\mathbf{w}$ are shared in that they do not change across timesteps t. Then, the state of the system at time t can be written as

$$\mathbf{s}^{(t)} = f(\mathbf{s}^{(t-1)}; \mathbf{w}). \tag{14.2}$$

The system equation can be unfolded to yield

$$\mathbf{s}^{(3)} = f(\mathbf{s}^{(2)}; \mathbf{w}) = f(f(\mathbf{s}^{(1)}; \mathbf{w}); \mathbf{w}). \tag{14.3}$$

This sort of equation can be described by a graph called the unrolled graph, see Figure 14.2. We will see later that this unfolding can be very helpful when we describe how to learn the system's parameters.

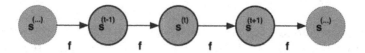

Fig. 14.2 We can describe the state of a system in time by a graph, called the unrolled graph. For a dynamical system parameters **w** do not change over time steps t.

Recurrent neural networks or RNNs are a family of neural networks that follows the ideas described in the aforementioned system to process sequential data. In a network of this sort, we represent all the information the network has received up until timestep t with a variable $\mathbf{h}^{(t-1)}$. With that, at time t the network receives the t-th element $\mathbf{x}^{(t)}$ in the sequence and combines both pieces of information to get its new state

$$\mathbf{h}^{(t)} = f(\mathbf{h}^{(t-1)}, \mathbf{x}^{(t)}; \mathbf{w}). \tag{14.4}$$

Note that by following this logic, the network ends up in a state, which is a fixed length vector $\mathbf{h}^{(T)}$, that encodes the whole sequence. In the next section we will see that this happens in most RNNs. What differs is the way the specific model uses the information in the hidden state depending on the use case. As we have discussed before, a recurrent net can be used with many different types of targets.

Much like before, this kind of system can be unfolded and represented as a graph like the one in Figure 14.3. By doing so, the network is shaped exactly like a simple, known to us feedforward net. Later we will see that this the key reason why we can apply the typical backpropagation idea to train these models.

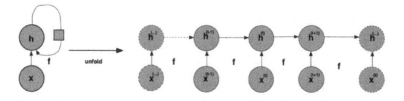

Fig. 14.3 Unfolding computational graphs. The model maps an arbitrary length sequence to a fixed length vector $\mathbf{h}^{(t)}$.

14.2   Recurrent Neural Networks

Having gone through the general idea behind recurrent networks it is now time to get concrete. To do so, it will be helpful to describe the details of an RNN departing from the well known MLP. To make things easier let us recast a single hidden layer MLP in the typical RNN notation. In a feedforward network with one hidden layer there are two sets of parameters connecting layers. First, we have the connection weights from input $\mathbf{x}$ to the hidden units, these can be represented by a matrix U, and the hidden units' biases that can be represented by a bias vector $\mathbf{b}$. Second, we have the weights from the hidden units $\mathbf{h}$ to the output $\mathbf{o}$ represented by the matrix V, and the output bias vector $\mathbf{c}$ [Goodfellow *et al.* (2016)].

Now imagine we want to apply the feedforward network to the input sequence elements $\mathbf{x}^{(t)}$ independently where each results in an output $\mathbf{o}^{(t)}$ over time. So, for each input in

$$\mathbf{x}^{(1)}, \mathbf{x}^{(2)}, \cdots, \mathbf{x}^{(t-2)}, \mathbf{x}^{(t-1)}, \mathbf{x}^{(t)}, \cdots, \mathbf{x}^{(T)} \tag{14.5}$$

the hidden layer states would be given by

$$h_i^{(t)} = \phi \left(\sum_{j=1}^{D} U_{ij} \cdot x_j^{(t)} + b_i \right), \tag{14.6}$$

$$\mathbf{h}^{(t)} = \phi \left(U \cdot \mathbf{x}^{(t)} + \mathbf{b} \right) \tag{14.7}$$

where ϕ is the activation function. Resulting in

$$\mathbf{h}^{(\tau)}, \cdots \mathbf{h}^{(t)}, \mathbf{h}^{(t-1)}, \mathbf{h}^{(t-2)}, \cdots, \mathbf{h}^{(2)}, \mathbf{h}^{(1)} \tag{14.8}$$

and the output states would be given by

$$\mathbf{o}^{(t)} = \varphi \left(V \cdot \mathbf{h}^{(t)} + \mathbf{c} \right) \tag{14.9}$$

resulting in the sequence of outputs

$$\mathbf{o}^{(\tau)}, \cdots \mathbf{o}^{(t)}, \mathbf{o}^{(t-1)}, \mathbf{o}^{(t-2)}, \cdots, \mathbf{o}^{(2)}, \mathbf{o}^{(1)}. \tag{14.10}$$

14.2.1   *Elman recurrent neural networks*

Let us take the setting we just described and add recurrent connections such that we model the sequence instead of looking at its elements independently. By doing so, we will get a specific type of recurrent neural networks that produces an output at each timestep using recurrent connections between hidden units called Elman or Vanilla RNN. To put a connection between hidden layers at sequential timsteps means we need connection weights. These weights are also shared across all connections between pairs of hidden states and can be represented by a squared matrix W [Elman (1990)],[Hertz *et al.* (1991)].

The hidden activations at time t depend on the input at that time $\mathbf{x}^{(t)}$ like in the previously described MLP. Additionally, they also depend on the previous hidden state $\mathbf{h}^{(t-1)}$. Using the respective connections weights and the biases to combine the two pieces of information, we get the network's new state

$$\mathbf{h}^{(t)} = \phi\left(U \cdot \mathbf{x}^{(t)} + \mathbf{b} + W \cdot \mathbf{h}^{(t-1)}\right). \tag{14.11}$$

For the first timestep, we will need to specify an initial state (typically, it can be an all zeros vector)

$$\mathbf{h}^{(0)} = initial\ state. \tag{14.12}$$

Any activation can be used, but the classical description uses $\phi() = \tanh()$, so we get

$$\mathbf{h}^{(t)} = \tanh\left(U \cdot \mathbf{x}^{(t)} + \mathbf{b} + W \cdot \mathbf{h}^{(t-1)}\right). \tag{14.13}$$

The output values are computed just like in the MLP setting

$$\mathbf{o}^{(t)} = \varphi\left(V \cdot \mathbf{h}^{(t)} + \mathbf{c}\right). \tag{14.14}$$

If we are classifying each sequence element we can use the *softmax* activation to get a distribution over possible output values

$$\mathbf{o}^{(t)} = softmax\left(V \cdot \mathbf{h}^{(t)} + \mathbf{c}\right). \tag{14.15}$$

A good example would be in part of speech tagging in an English sentence.

So, by running the network with the aforementioned equations, we will get again a sequence of outputs

$$\mathbf{o}^{(\tau)}, \cdots \mathbf{o}^{(t)}, \mathbf{o}^{(t-1)}, \mathbf{o}^{(t-2)}, \cdots, \mathbf{o}^{(2)}, \mathbf{o}^{(1)}. \tag{14.16}$$

Assuming that the hidden layer's activation function maps into the interval $[0, 1]$ like for example a sigmoid activation function $\sigma()$ does, then we can interpret the recurrent connections as a conditional probability

$$p(h_i^{(t)}|h_i^{(t-1)}) \tag{14.17}$$

in which the probability of a state $h_i^{(t)}$ is conditionally dependent on the preceding state $h_i^{(t-1)}$.

The recurrent neural network is universal in the sense that any function computable by a Turing machine can be computed by such a recurrent network of a finite size. A theorem was formulated by Siegelmann and Sontag [Siegelmann and Sontag (1991)], [Siegelmann and Sontag (1995)] (see Figure 14.4) stating that all Turing machines may be simulated by fully connected recurrent networks built on neurons with sigmoidal activation functions.

Fig. 14.4   Hava Siegelmann is a professor of computer science, and a world leader in the fields of Lifelong Learning, Artificial Intelligence, Machine Learning, Neural Networks, and Computational Neuroscience.

Throughout all of this description we assumed we had all the parameters. So far, we have said next to nothing about learning. We will postpone this issue a little bit further. Yet, as we have said before, a key element is the ability to unfold the network as a graph. For a network of the sort we just described, we would get an unrolled graph like the one in Figure 14.5.

14.2.2   *Jordan recurrent neural networks*

If instead of connecting the hidden layers across timesteps we connect the output of the previous step to the hidden layer of the next step we get a Jordan RNN [Jordan (1986)], [Hertz *et al.* (1991)]. These are less powerful because they lack hidden-to-hidden connections and require that the output units capture all of the information about the past that the network will use

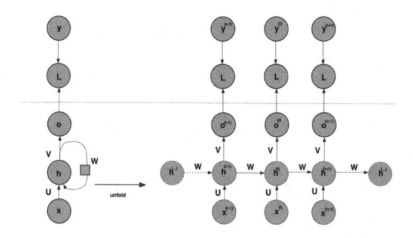

Fig. 14.5 Recurrent networks that produce an output at each timestep and have recurrent connections between hidden units (represented by the matrix W) are called vanilla recurrent neural networks or Elman recurrent neural networks. The outputs are indicated by $\mathbf{o}^{(t)}$ and the target values by $\mathbf{y}^{(t)}$, the costs are represented by a loss function L.

to predict the future (see Figure 14.6). For example they cannot simulate a universal Turing machine.

The activation of the hidden units is defined as a function of the input at that time $\mathbf{x}^{(t)}$ weighted by the matrix U, the bias $\mathbf{b}$ and information from the previous timestep output $\mathbf{o}^{(t-1)}$ weighted by the matrix W

$$\mathbf{h}^{(t)} = \phi\left(U \cdot \mathbf{x}^{(t)} + \mathbf{b} + W \cdot \mathbf{o}^{(t-1)}\right). \tag{14.18}$$

Just like before, we would need to specify an initial state

$$\mathbf{o}^{(0)} = initial\ state. \tag{14.19}$$

Then the output values are computed as before

$$\mathbf{o}^{(t)} = \varphi\left(V \cdot \mathbf{h}^{(t)} + \mathbf{c}\right) \tag{14.20}$$

resulting in the sequence of outputs

$$\mathbf{o}^{(\tau)}, \cdots \mathbf{o}^{(t)}, \mathbf{o}^{(t-1)}, \mathbf{o}^{(t-2)}, \cdots, \mathbf{o}^{(2)}, \mathbf{o}^{(1)}. \tag{14.21}$$

14.2.3 *Single Output*

At this point the reader may be getting that there can be a lot flexibility assembling the structure of the network. In fact, in the exercises section we

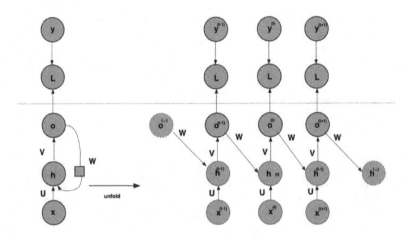

Fig. 14.6   Recurrent networks that produce an output at each time step and have recurrent connections only from the output at one time step to the hidden units at the next time step are less powerful because they lack hidden-to-hidden recurrent connection. The output is indicated by $\mathbf{o}^{(t)}$ and the target value by $\mathbf{y}^{(t)}$, the costs are represented by a loss function L.

will go into this fact. For now, let us describe another classical example. In Figure 14.7 we see a network, with recurrent connections between hidden units, that reads an entire sequence and then produces a single output. The single output is indicated by $\mathbf{o}^{(T)}$ and the single target value by $\mathbf{y}^{(T)}$.

Just like in Vanilla networks, the hidden activations are a function of the current input $\mathbf{x}^{(t)}$ weighted by the matrix U, the bias $\mathbf{b}$ and the previous state $\mathbf{h}^{(t-1)}$ weighted by the matrix W

$$\mathbf{h}^{(t)} = \phi\left(U \cdot \mathbf{x}^{(t)} + \mathbf{b} + W \cdot \mathbf{h}^{(t-1)}\right) \tag{14.22}$$

where, again, we need to specify an initial state

$$\mathbf{h}^{(0)} = initial\ state. \tag{14.23}$$

After we run the recurrence across all steps, the output value is computed only for the last timestep T

$$\mathbf{o}^{(\tau)} = \varphi\left(V \cdot \mathbf{h}^{(\tau)} + \mathbf{c}\right) \tag{14.24}$$

resulting in one output value.

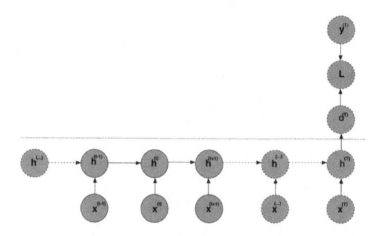

Fig. 14.7 Recurrent networks, with connections between hidden units, that read an entire sequence and then produce a single output. The single output is indicated by $\mathbf{o}^{(T)}$ and the single target value by $\mathbf{y}^{(T)}$, the cost is represented by a loss function L.

14.2.4 *Backpropagation Trough Time*

To learn the parameters of a recurrent network we use what is called backpropagation through time (BPTT) [Werbos (1988)], [Mozer (1995)], [Goodfellow *et al.* (2016)]. Looking at the unrolled graph, we see that propagating gradients from future timesteps to previous ones follows the exact same logic we used in an MLP to propagate gradients from closer to the output layers to closer to the input layers. The main difference is that for different layers we had always different weights, whereas in this case, for different timesteps the weights are the same.

Thinking about the unrolled graphs, we can imagine that doing backpropagation in a recurrent network with T steps would be somewhat similar to doing T backpropagations in parallel for T MLPs. However, in an RNN there is a key difference that hampers parallelization, both in forward and in backward propagation a given timestep depends on the values that come from other timesteps to move on.

In the exercises section, we will go into the details on how to use and implement this procedure. However, the idea is always the same. We have a loss function we want to minimize and to do so we need gradients with respect to all the parameters. So, for N examples, if we have sequence inputs to sequence outputs a cross-entropy loss would be something like

$$E(\mathbf{w}) = -\sum_{n=1}^{N}\sum_{t=1}^{T}\sum_{k=1}^{K} y_{nk}^{(t)} \log o_{nk}^{(t)} \tag{14.25}$$

and a squared loss would be something like

$$E(\mathbf{w}) = \frac{1}{2}\cdot\sum_{n=1}^{N}\sum_{t=1}^{T}\|\mathbf{y}_{n}^{(t)} - \mathbf{o}_{n}^{(t)}\|^{2}, \tag{14.26}$$

see Figure 14.8.

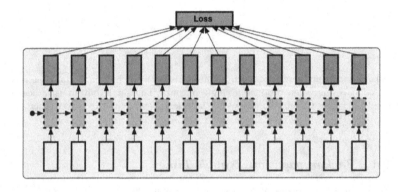

Fig. 14.8 Backpropagation through time (BPTT). The forward step is preformed through the entire sequence to compute the loss function (error/cost function). The gradient is defined by the entire sequence.

Alternatively, for a sequence input and a single output at time step T cross-entropy would be

$$E(\mathbf{w}) = -\sum_{n=1}^{N}\sum_{k=1}^{K} y_{nk}^{(T)} \log o_{nk}^{(T)} \tag{14.27}$$

and squared error would be

$$E(\mathbf{w}) = \frac{1}{2}\cdot\sum_{n=1}^{N}\|\mathbf{y}_{n}^{(T)} - \mathbf{o}_{n}^{(T)}\|^{2}. \tag{14.28}$$

Having the loss function, the gradients are derived in the same way as before as we will se in the exercises section. Despite the similarities with typical backpropagation there are some specific issues. Namely, BPTT has difficulty with local minima. The recurrent feedback in RNNs tends to create chaotic responses in the error surface which cause local minima to occur frequently and in poor locations. The basic problem is that gradients propagated over many stages tend to either vanish (most of the time) or explode. Because of that the activation function $\phi() = \tanh()$ is used to keep the gradient in the linear region which means that the gradient of $\tanh()$ is close to linear (close to one) on both sides of 0. With a *ReLU* activation function the RNN would enter an unstable regime (with the subderivative around zero). Even if we assume that the parameters are such that the recurrent network is stable without exploding gradients, the difficulty with long-term dependencies arises from the exponentially smaller weights given to long-term interactions. A solution is to clip the norm $\|\mathbf{g}\|$ of the gradient $\mathbf{g}$ where v is the norm threshold. The gradient is normalzsed and multiplied with the scalar v.

$$\mathbf{g} = \begin{cases} \frac{\mathbf{g} \cdot v}{\|g\|} & if \ \|g\| > v \\ g & else \end{cases}. \tag{14.29}$$

14.2.5 *Deep Recurrent Networks*

Empirical experiments suggest that we need enough depth in order to perform the required mappings. There are three possible ways of recurrent connections in a deep recurrent neural network that can be combined

- Deeper computation can be introduced from the input to the hidden state.
- From the previous hidden state to the next hidden state. The hidden recurrent state can be broken down into groups organized hierarchically.
- Deeper computation can be introduced from the hidden state to the output.

The hidden recurrent state can be organized by groups hierarchically [Schmidhuber (1992)], [Goodfellow *et al.* (2016)], deeper computation can be introduced by units leading to increased capacity and the path length, the resulting path length can be shorten by skip connections, see Figure 14.9.

14.3 Long Short Term Memory

As noted before the gradients propagated over many stages tend to either vanish (most of the time) or explode because of the rounding errors involved

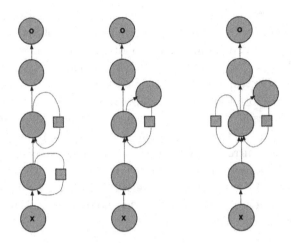

Fig. 14.9   From left to right: The hidden recurrent state can be organized by groups hierarchically, deeper computation can be introduced by units leading to increased capacity and the path length, the resulting path length can be shorten by skip connections.

in the computational process. If we preform many time steps the long term dependencies between distant time steps cannot be learned since the computation uses finite precision-numbers. To some extent the problem can be solved by the Long Short Term Memory (LSTM) [Hochreiter and Schmidhuber (1997)]. The name should not be confused with the psychological long and short term memory models of human problem solving [Anderson (1995)].

LSTMs are composed of several gates that allow the gradients to flow unchanged. They solve partially the vanishing gradient problem, however they can still suffer from the exploding gradient problem. There are three types of gates, forget gate, input gate and the output gate. Each gate has its own weight matrices and bias vector parameters which needs to be learned during training. A gate is described by a sigmoid activation function and a Hadamard product (point wise multiplication operation), see Figure 14.10. The output of a sigmoid activation function is a number between zero and one, describing how much of each component should be let through. A value of zero means no information is let through, while a value of one indicates that all information is let through.

In an Elman RNN the hidden activations at time t depend on the input

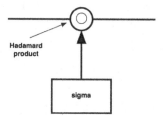

Fig. 14.10 A gate is described by a sigmoid activation function and a Hadamard product. The output of a sigmoid activation function is a number between zero and one, describing how much of each component should be let through. A value of zero means no information is let through, whereas a value of one indicates that all information is let through.

at that time $\mathbf{x}^{(t)}$ and on the previous hidden state $\mathbf{h}^{(t-1)}$ with

$$\mathbf{h}^{(t)} = \tanh\left(U \cdot \mathbf{x}^{(t)} + \mathbf{b} + W \cdot \mathbf{h}^{(t-1)}\right).$$

In an LSTM there are four activation vectors corresponding to the three gates and a cell input activation:

- the forget gate activation vector

$$\mathbf{f}^{(t)} = \sigma\left(U_f \cdot \mathbf{x}^{(t)} + \mathbf{b}_f + W_f \cdot \mathbf{h}^{(t-1)}\right), \qquad (14.30)$$

- the input gate activation vector

$$\mathbf{i}^{(t)} = \sigma\left(U_i \cdot \mathbf{x}^{(t)} + \mathbf{b}_i + W_i \cdot \mathbf{h}^{(t-1)}\right), \qquad (14.31)$$

- the output gate activation vector

$$\mathbf{og}^{(t)} = \sigma\left(U_{og} \cdot \mathbf{x}^{(t)} + \mathbf{b}_{og} + W_{og} \cdot \mathbf{h}^{(t-1)}\right), \qquad (14.32)$$

- the cell input activation with tanh

$$\mathbf{ci}^{(t)} = \tanh\left(U_{ci} \cdot \mathbf{x}^{(t)} + \mathbf{b}_{ci} + W_{ci} \cdot \mathbf{h}^{(t-1)}\right). \qquad (14.33)$$

In an LSTM eight weight matrices and four bias vectors need to be learned during training, four times more than in an Elman RNN.

The cell activation vector $\mathbf{c}^{(t)}$ is determined using the forget gate operation with the old cell activation vector $\mathbf{c}^{(t-1)}$ and the input gate operation with the cell input activation vector $\mathbf{ci}^{(t)}$ by

$$\mathbf{c}^{(t)} = \mathbf{f}^{(t)} \circ \mathbf{c}^{(t-1)} + \mathbf{i}^{(t)} \circ \mathbf{ci}^{(t)}. \qquad (14.34)$$

With the cell activation vector $\mathbf{c}^{(t)}$, the new hidden state $\mathbf{h}^{(t)}$ is determined using the output gate operation

$$\mathbf{h}^{(t)} = \mathbf{og}^{(t)} \circ \tanh(\mathbf{c}^{(t)}). \tag{14.35}$$

The key to LSTMs is the cell activation $\mathbf{c}^{(t-1)}$, with only some minor linear interactions representing the dependencies between the elements in the input sequence. The forget gate controls if the cell activation remains, the input gate adds new values and the output gate controls the extent to which the previous cell activation is used to compute the output activation of the LSTM unit representing the hidden layer values, see Figure 14.11.

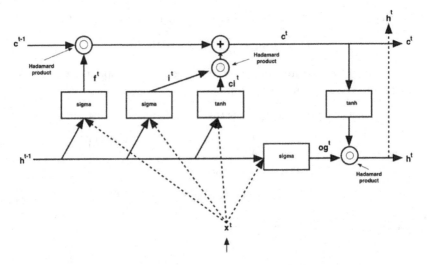

Fig. 14.11 Architecture of the Long Short-Term Memory (LSTM) and its gate that processes the data sequentially and keep its hidden state through time.

Variations of LSTMs can be built including or omitting the forget, input and output gates or introducing new alternative gates. For example, gated recurrent units (GRUs) [Cho *et al.* (2014)] have fewer parameters than LSTMs, as they lack an output gate. Transformer models are a different approach to the same issues [Polosukhin *et al.* (2017)] that facilitate more parallelization during training allowing larger data set, yet they go way beyond the scope of this book.

14.4 Process Sequences

We can represent different categories of neural networks for sequence processing by unrolled graphs [Goodfellow *et al.* (2016)] in Figure 14.12 the most common types are depicted. Specifically, we can process sequences by conventional feed-forward networks without any feedback connections, this the MLP case we have seen at the beginning of the chapter. Alternatively, we can have a one to many architecture where given a single input, a network generates a sequence; a typical case would be generating captions from images. Another structure is the many to one RNN used for classification of whole sequence, this the architecture we analyzed in the "Single Output" section. In the rightmost sketch, we see a many to many architecture that maps a sequence into another sequence which is the exact same architecture we have seen for example for the Vanilla RNN. This can be used for frame classification, like video annotation or speech recognition or speech translation. The other version of many to many is the encoder-decoder strategy. These networks start with an encoder RNN that reads the input sequence and represents it in its final hidden state vector. Being then followed by a decoder RNN that generates the output sequence from the previous one's final state, see Figure 14.13. For that reason, we can say that the final hidden state of the encoder RNN is used to compute a fixed-size context variable C which represents a compressed representation of the input sequence and is given as input to the decoder RNN. Such

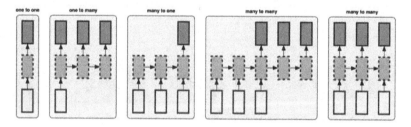

Fig. 14.12 Conventional feed-forward network without any feedback connections is called a one to one network. In the following we see a one to many RNN, many to one RNN and many to many RNN.

an architecture is widely used for machine translation, it concatenates the source and target sequence and makes only prediction on the target sequence. It uses a special symbol $< EOS >$ to indicate the beginning of

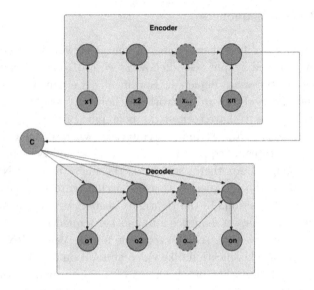

Fig. 14.13   A sequence to sequence architecture is composed of an encoder RNN that reads the input sequence decoder RNN that generates the output sequence. The final hidden state of the encoder RNN is used to compute a fixed-size context variable C which represents a compressed representation of the input sequence and is given as input to the decoder RNN.

the sequence, see Figure 14.14. When the model was first proposed, no one would have believed that it can solve the translation problem, but it turns out to work quite well. Its main limitations are that it is based on a fixed

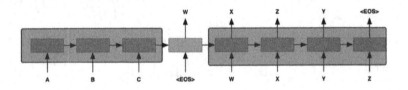

Fig. 14.14   Schematic representation on the basis of neural machine translation.

size vocabulary and does not work well with morphologically rich languages like Polish [Wolk and Marasek (2019)].

14.5 Exercises and Answers

Below we present a simple recurrent network that maps a sequence of inputs to a sequence of targets. In this example we use only one hidden layer that has a feedback connection.

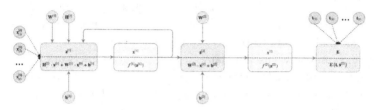

When one thinks about how to apply backpropagation to learn the parameters on such a network it may not seem obvious at first. However, if we unfold the network's function graph, the recurrent network becomes a much like a regular one.

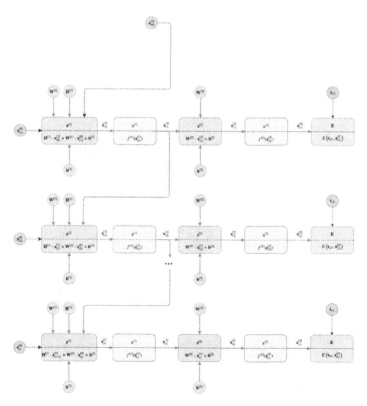

Unfolding corresponds to making copies of the network structure to match the total number of sequence elements. This implies that between copies of the network the weights are shared! This means that $\mathbf{W}^{[1]}$ at the bottom of the unfolded graph is the same as the $\mathbf{W}^{[1]}$ at the top. This weight sharing will influence the way we apply the backward pass. Namely, to update a parameter, we need to sum accross all paths that lead to all copies of that parameter. A requirment of this approach is that we need to initialize $\mathbf{x}^{[1]}_{(0)}$ to feed as hidden state to the first copy of the network.

As an example, we used a many-to-many recurrent network and showed unfolding corresponds to making copies of its structure for every time step. However, many other architecture templates exist. For example, we could have a many-to-one network. In this case, we will see that sometimes what we have to replicate is just the recursion part. For example, for the network:

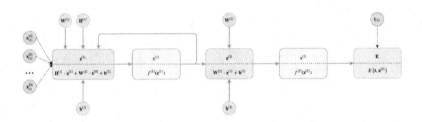

the unfolding would be done as follows:

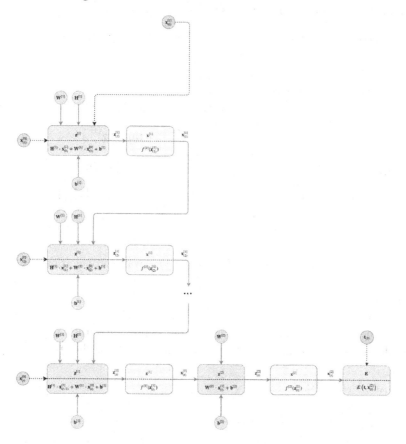

Note that the recursion is copied throughout all time steps but since there is only one output, we only place an output layer after the last time step.

On the exercises below we will go through the details of both of these architectures.

1)

Consider a recurrent network with one hidden layer to solve a **many-to-many** task. Take into account that:

- The recurrent connections happen between the hidden layers
- The hidden activation function is the hyperbolic tangent

- The output activation function is softmax
- The error function is the cross-entropy between output and target

a) Write down the model equations for forward propagation.

Solution:

For all $t \in \{1, \ldots, T\}$:

$$\mathbf{z}_{(t)}^{[1]} = z^{[1]}\left(\mathbf{H}^{[1]}, \mathbf{x}_{(t-1)}^{[1]}, \mathbf{W}^{[1]}, \mathbf{x}_{(t)}^{[0]}, \mathbf{b}^{[1]}\right) \qquad = \mathbf{H}^{[1]}\mathbf{x}_{(t-1)}^{[1]} + \mathbf{W}^{[1]}\mathbf{x}_{(t)}^{[0]} + \mathbf{b}^{[1]}$$

$$\mathbf{x}_{(t)}^{[1]} = f^{[1]}\left(\mathbf{z}_{(t)}^{[1]}\right) \qquad = \tanh\left(\mathbf{z}_{(t)}^{[1]}\right)$$

$$\mathbf{z}_{(t)}^{[2]} = z^{[2]}\left(\mathbf{W}^{[2]}, \mathbf{x}_{(t)}^{[1]}, \mathbf{b}^{[2]}\right) \qquad = \mathbf{W}^{[2]}\mathbf{x}_{(t)}^{[1]} + \mathbf{b}^{[2]}$$

$$\mathbf{x}_{(t)}^{[2]} = f^{[2]}\left(\mathbf{z}_{(t)}^{[2]}\right) \qquad = softmax\left(\mathbf{z}_{(t)}^{[2]}\right)$$

$$e_{(t)} = E\left(\mathbf{x}_{(t)}^{[2]}, \mathbf{t}_{(t)}\right) \qquad = -\mathbf{t}_{(t)} \cdot \log \mathbf{x}_{(t)}^{[2]}$$

b) Write down the model equations for backward propagation.

Solution:

Since we are working with a many to many network each time step yields an error that will be propagated backwards. For the output layer, the deltas are independent of other time steps. Applying the chain–rule we get:

$$\delta_{(t)}^{[2]} = \frac{\partial E}{\partial \mathbf{x}_{(t)}^{[2]}} \frac{\partial \mathbf{x}_{(t)}^{[2]}}{\mathbf{z}_{(t)}^{[2]}}$$

$$= \mathbf{x}_{(t)}^{[2]} - \mathbf{t}_{(t)}$$

For the last time step T, the delta for the hidden layer is independent of all other time steps. Using the chain-rule we get:

$$\delta_{(T)}^{[1]} = \delta_{(T)}^{[2]} \frac{\partial \mathbf{z}_{(T)}^{[2]}}{\partial \mathbf{x}_{(T)}^{[1]}} \frac{\partial \mathbf{x}_{(T)}^{[1]}}{\partial \mathbf{z}_{(T)}^{[1]}}$$

$$= \left(\frac{\partial \mathbf{z}_{(T)}^{[2]}}{\partial \mathbf{x}_{(T)}^{[1]}}\right)^{T} \bullet \delta_{(T)}^{[2]} \circ \frac{\partial \mathbf{x}_{(T)}^{[1]}}{\partial \mathbf{z}_{(T)}^{[1]}}$$

$$= \left(\mathbf{W}^{[2]}\right)^{T} \bullet \delta_{(T)}^{[2]} \circ \left(1 - \tanh^2 \mathbf{z}_{(T)}^{[1]}\right)$$

For all other time steps $t \in \{1, \ldots, T-1\}$, the delta for the hidden layer depends on the nexttime step's hidden layer. Using the chain-rule we get:

$$\delta_{(t)}^{[1]} = \left(\delta_{(t)}^{[2]} \frac{\partial \mathbf{z}_{(t)}^{[2]}}{\partial \mathbf{x}_{(t)}^{[1]}} + \delta_{(t+1)}^{[1]} \frac{\partial \mathbf{z}_{(t+1)}^{[1]}}{\partial \mathbf{x}_{(t)}^{[1]}} \right) \frac{\partial \mathbf{x}_{(t)}^{[1]}}{\partial \mathbf{z}_{(t)}^{[1]}}$$

$$= \left(\left(\frac{\partial \mathbf{z}_{(t)}^{[2]}}{\partial \mathbf{x}_{(t)}^{[1]}} \right)^T \bullet \delta_{(t)}^{[2]} + \left(\frac{\partial \mathbf{z}_{(t+1)}^{[1]}}{\partial \mathbf{x}_{(t)}^{[1]}} \right)^T \bullet \delta_{(t+1)}^{[1]} \right) \circ \frac{\partial \mathbf{x}_{(t)}^{[1]}}{\partial \mathbf{z}_{(t)}^{[1]}}$$

$$= \left(\left(\mathbf{W}^{[2]} \right)^T \bullet \delta_{(t)}^{[2]} + \mathbf{H}^T \bullet \delta_{(t+1)}^{[1]} \right) \circ \left(1 - \tanh^2 \mathbf{z}_{(t)}^{[1]} \right)$$

c) Perform a stochastic gradient descent update for:

$$\mathbf{x}^{(1)} = \left[\begin{pmatrix} 4 \\ 0 \\ 0 \\ 0 \end{pmatrix}, \begin{pmatrix} 0 \\ 8 \\ 2 \\ 0 \end{pmatrix} \right]$$

With targets:

$$t^{(1)} = \left[\begin{pmatrix} 1 \\ 0 \end{pmatrix}, \begin{pmatrix} 0 \\ 1 \end{pmatrix} \right]$$

Initialize all weights and biases to 0.1, using 3 units per hidden layer, initializing the hidden state to all zeros and using $\eta = 1.0$.

Solution:

Initializing the parameters, we have:

$$\mathbf{W}^{[1]} = \begin{pmatrix} 0.1 & 0.1 & 0.1 & 0.1 \\ 0.1 & 0.1 & 0.1 & 0.1 \\ 0.1 & 0.1 & 0.1 & 0.1 \end{pmatrix}$$

$$\mathbf{b}^{[1]} = \begin{pmatrix} 0.1 \\ 0.1 \\ 0.1 \end{pmatrix}$$

$$\mathbf{H}^{[1]} = \begin{pmatrix} 0.1 & 0.1 & 0.1 \\ 0.1 & 0.1 & 0.1 \\ 0.1 & 0.1 & 0.1 \end{pmatrix}$$

$$\mathbf{W}^{[2]} = \begin{pmatrix} 0.1\ 0.1\ 0.1 \\ 0.1\ 0.1\ 0.1 \end{pmatrix}$$

$$\mathbf{b}^{[2]} = \begin{pmatrix} 0.1 \\ 0.1 \end{pmatrix}$$

$$\mathbf{x}_{(0)}^{[1]} = \begin{pmatrix} 0 \\ 0 \\ 0 \end{pmatrix}$$

Now, we can use **a)** to apply forward propagation. Let us start with time step $t = 1$:

$$\mathbf{z}_{(1)}^{[1]} = \begin{pmatrix} 0.1\ 0.1\ 0.1 \\ 0.1\ 0.1\ 0.1 \\ 0.1\ 0.1\ 0.1 \end{pmatrix} \begin{pmatrix} 0 \\ 0 \\ 0 \end{pmatrix} + \begin{pmatrix} 0.1\ 0.1\ 0.1\ 0.1 \\ 0.1\ 0.1\ 0.1\ 0.1 \\ 0.1\ 0.1\ 0.1\ 0.1 \end{pmatrix} \begin{pmatrix} 4 \\ 0 \\ 0 \\ 0 \end{pmatrix} + \begin{pmatrix} 0.1 \\ 0.1 \\ 0.1 \end{pmatrix}$$

$$= \begin{pmatrix} 0.5 \\ 0.5 \\ 0.5 \end{pmatrix}$$

$$\mathbf{x}_{(1)}^{[1]} = \tanh \begin{pmatrix} 0.5 \\ 0.5 \\ 0.5 \end{pmatrix}$$

$$\mathbf{z}_{(1)}^{[2]} = \begin{pmatrix} 0.1\ 0.1\ 0.1 \\ 0.1\ 0.1\ 0.1 \end{pmatrix} \tanh \begin{pmatrix} 0.5 \\ 0.5 \\ 0.5 \end{pmatrix} + \begin{pmatrix} 0.1 \\ 0.1 \end{pmatrix}$$

$$= \begin{pmatrix} 0.3 \tanh 0.5 + 0.1 \\ 0.3 \tanh 0.5 + 0.1 \end{pmatrix}$$

$$\mathbf{x}_{(1)}^{[2]} = softmax \begin{pmatrix} 0.3 \tanh 0.5 + 0.1 \\ 0.3 \tanh 0.5 + 0.1 \end{pmatrix}$$

$$= \begin{pmatrix} 0.5 \\ 0.5 \end{pmatrix}$$

Now we can apply the same logic to the second time step.

$$\mathbf{z}_{(2)}^{[1]} = \begin{pmatrix} 0.1\,0.1\,0.1 \\ 0.1\,0.1\,0.1 \\ 0.1\,0.1\,0.1 \end{pmatrix} \tanh \begin{pmatrix} 0.5 \\ 0.5 \\ 0.5 \end{pmatrix} + \begin{pmatrix} 0.1\,0.1\,0.1\,0.1 \\ 0.1\,0.1\,0.1\,0.1 \\ 0.1\,0.1\,0.1\,0.1 \end{pmatrix} \begin{pmatrix} 0 \\ 8 \\ 2 \\ 0 \end{pmatrix} + \begin{pmatrix} 0.1 \\ 0.1 \\ 0.1 \end{pmatrix}$$

$$= \begin{pmatrix} 1.1 + 0.3 \tanh 0.5 \\ 1.1 + 0.3 \tanh 0.5 \\ 1.1 + 0.3 \tanh 0.5 \end{pmatrix}$$

$$\mathbf{x}_{(2)}^{[1]} = \tanh \begin{pmatrix} 1.1 + 0.3 \tanh 0.5 \\ 1.1 + 0.3 \tanh 0.5 \\ 1.1 + 0.3 \tanh 0.5 \end{pmatrix}$$

$$\mathbf{z}_{(2)}^{[2]} = \begin{pmatrix} 0.1\,0.1\,0.1 \\ 0.1\,0.1\,0.1 \end{pmatrix} \tanh \begin{pmatrix} 1.1 + 0.3 \tanh 0.5 \\ 1.1 + 0.3 \tanh 0.5 \\ 1.1 + 0.3 \tanh 0.5 \end{pmatrix} + \begin{pmatrix} 0.1 \\ 0.1 \end{pmatrix}$$

$$= \begin{pmatrix} 0.3 \tanh (1.1 + 0.3 \tanh 0.5) + 0.1 \\ 0.3 \tanh (1.1 + 0.3 \tanh 0.5) + 0.1 \end{pmatrix}$$

$$\mathbf{x}_{(2)}^{[2]} = softmax \begin{pmatrix} 0.3 \tanh (1.1 + 0.3 \tanh 0.5) + 0.1 \\ 0.3 \tanh (1.1 + 0.3 \tanh 0.5) + 0.1 \end{pmatrix}$$

$$= \begin{pmatrix} 0.5 \\ 0.5 \end{pmatrix}$$

After finishing forward propagation, we can use **b)** to perform backward propagation. For the output layers we have:

$$\delta_{(2)}^{[2]} = \mathbf{x}_{(2)}^{[2]} - \mathbf{t}_{(2)} = \begin{pmatrix} 0.5 \\ 0.5 \end{pmatrix} - \begin{pmatrix} 0 \\ 1 \end{pmatrix} = \begin{pmatrix} 0.5 \\ -0.5 \end{pmatrix}$$

$$\delta_{(1)}^{[2]} = \mathbf{x}_{(1)}^{[2]} - \mathbf{t}_{(1)} = \begin{pmatrix} 0.5 \\ 0.5 \end{pmatrix} - \begin{pmatrix} 1 \\ 0 \end{pmatrix} = \begin{pmatrix} -0.5 \\ 0.5 \end{pmatrix}$$

For the hidden layer of the last time step we have:

$$\delta_{(2)}^{[1]} = \left(\mathbf{W}^{[2]}\right)^T \bullet \delta_{(2)}^{[2]} \circ \left(1 - \tanh^2 \mathbf{z}_{(2)}^{[1]}\right)$$

$$= \begin{pmatrix} 0.1 & 0.1 \\ 0.1 & 0.1 \\ 0.1 & 0.1 \end{pmatrix} \bullet \begin{pmatrix} 0.5 \\ -0.5 \end{pmatrix} \circ \begin{pmatrix} 1 - \tanh^2\left(1.1 + 0.3\tanh 0.5\right) \\ 1 - \tanh^2\left(1.1 + 0.3\tanh 0.5\right) \\ 1 - \tanh^2\left(1.1 + 0.3\tanh 0.5\right) \end{pmatrix}$$

$$= \begin{pmatrix} 0 \\ 0 \\ 0 \end{pmatrix} \circ \begin{pmatrix} 1 - \tanh^2\left(1.1 + 0.3\tanh 0.5\right) \\ 1 - \tanh^2\left(1.1 + 0.3\tanh 0.5\right) \\ 1 - \tanh^2\left(1.1 + 0.3\tanh 0.5\right) \end{pmatrix}$$

$$= \begin{pmatrix} 0 \\ 0 \\ 0 \end{pmatrix}$$

For the hidden layer of the first time step we have:

$$\delta_{(1)}^{[1]} = \left(\left(\mathbf{W}^{[2]}\right)^T \bullet \delta_{(1)}^{[2]} + \left(\mathbf{H}^{[1]}\right)^T \bullet \delta_{(2)}^{[1]}\right) \circ \left(1 - \tanh^2 \mathbf{z}_{(1)}^{[1]}\right)$$

$$= \left(\begin{pmatrix} 0.1 & 0.1 \\ 0.1 & 0.1 \\ 0.1 & 0.1 \end{pmatrix} \bullet \begin{pmatrix} -0.5 \\ 0.5 \end{pmatrix} + \begin{pmatrix} 0.1 & 0.1 & 0.1 \\ 0.1 & 0.1 & 0.1 \\ 0.1 & 0.1 & 0.1 \end{pmatrix} \bullet \begin{pmatrix} 0 \\ 0 \\ 0 \end{pmatrix}\right)$$

$$\circ \begin{pmatrix} 1 - \tanh^2 0.5 \\ 1 - \tanh^2 0.5 \\ 1 - \tanh^2 0.5 \end{pmatrix}$$

$$= \left(\begin{pmatrix} 0 \\ 0 \\ 0 \end{pmatrix} + \begin{pmatrix} 0 \\ 0 \\ 0 \end{pmatrix}\right) \circ \begin{pmatrix} 1 - \tanh^2 0.5 \\ 1 - \tanh^2 0.5 \\ 1 - \tanh^2 0.5 \end{pmatrix}$$

$$= \begin{pmatrix} 0 \\ 0 \\ 0 \end{pmatrix}$$

Having the deltas, we can compute the specific gradients for all parameters. Each gradient corresponds to the sum across all backward paths that lead to that parameter.

$$\frac{\partial E}{\partial \mathbf{H}^{[1]}} = \sum_{t=1}^{T} \delta_{(t)}^{[1]} \frac{\partial \mathbf{z}_{(t)}^{[1]}}{\partial \mathbf{H}^{[1]}}$$

$$= \delta_{(1)}^{[1]} \bullet \left(\frac{\partial \mathbf{z}_{(1)}^{[1]}}{\partial \mathbf{H}^{[1]}} \right)^{T} + \delta_{(2)}^{[1]} \bullet \left(\frac{\partial \mathbf{z}_{(2)}^{[1]}}{\partial \mathbf{H}^{[1]}} \right)^{T}$$

$$= \delta_{(1)}^{[1]} \bullet \left(\mathbf{x}_{(0)}^{[0]} \right)^{T} + \delta_{(2)}^{[1]} \bullet \left(\mathbf{x}_{(1)}^{[1]} \right)^{T}$$

$$= \begin{pmatrix} 0 \\ 0 \\ 0 \end{pmatrix} (0\ 0\ 0) + \begin{pmatrix} 0 \\ 0 \\ 0 \end{pmatrix} (\tanh 0.5\ \tanh 0.5\ \tanh 0.5)$$

$$= \begin{pmatrix} 0\ 0\ 0 \\ 0\ 0\ 0 \\ 0\ 0\ 0 \end{pmatrix}$$

$$\frac{\partial E}{\partial \mathbf{W}^{[1]}} = \sum_{t=1}^{T} \delta_{(t)}^{[1]} \frac{\partial \mathbf{z}_{(t)}^{[1]}}{\partial \mathbf{W}^{[1]}}$$

$$= \delta_{(1)}^{[1]} \bullet \left(\frac{\partial \mathbf{z}_{(1)}^{[1]}}{\partial \mathbf{W}^{[1]}} \right)^{T} + \delta_{(2)}^{[1]} \bullet \left(\frac{\partial \mathbf{z}_{(2)}^{[1]}}{\partial \mathbf{W}^{[1]}} \right)^{T}$$

$$= \delta_{(1)}^{[1]} \bullet \left(\mathbf{x}_{(1)}^{[0]} \right)^{T} + \delta_{(2)}^{[1]} \bullet \left(\mathbf{x}_{(2)}^{[0]} \right)^{T}$$

$$= \begin{pmatrix} 0 \\ 0 \\ 0 \end{pmatrix} (4\ 0\ 0\ 0) + \begin{pmatrix} 0 \\ 0 \\ 0 \end{pmatrix} (0\ 8\ 2\ 0)$$

$$= \begin{pmatrix} 0\ 0\ 0\ 0 \\ 0\ 0\ 0\ 0 \\ 0\ 0\ 0\ 0 \end{pmatrix}$$

$$\frac{\partial E}{\partial \mathbf{b}^{[1]}} = \sum_{t=1}^{T} \delta_{(t)}^{[1]} \frac{\partial \mathbf{z}_{(t)}^{[1]}}{\partial \mathbf{b}^{[1]}}$$

$$= \delta_{(1)}^{[1]} \circ \frac{\partial \mathbf{z}_{(1)}^{[1]}}{\partial \mathbf{b}^{[1]}} + \delta_{(2)}^{[1]} \circ \frac{\partial \mathbf{z}_{(2)}^{[1]}}{\partial \mathbf{b}^{[1]}}$$

$$= \delta_{(1)}^{[1]} \circ \mathbf{1} + \delta_{(2)}^{[1]} \circ \mathbf{1}$$

$$= \begin{pmatrix} 0 \\ 0 \\ 0 \end{pmatrix} + \begin{pmatrix} 0 \\ 0 \\ 0 \end{pmatrix}$$

$$= \begin{pmatrix} 0 \\ 0 \\ 0 \end{pmatrix}$$

$$\frac{\partial E}{\partial \mathbf{W}^{[2]}} = \sum_{t=1}^{T} \delta_{(t)}^{[2]} \frac{\partial \mathbf{z}_{(t)}^{[2]}}{\partial \mathbf{W}^{[2]}}$$

$$= \delta_{(1)}^{[2]} \bullet \left(\frac{\partial \mathbf{z}_{(1)}^{[2]}}{\partial \mathbf{W}^{[2]}} \right)^T + \delta_{(2)}^{[2]} \bullet \left(\frac{\partial \mathbf{z}_{(2)}^{[2]}}{\partial \mathbf{W}^{[2]}} \right)^T$$

$$= \begin{pmatrix} -0.5 \\ 0.5 \end{pmatrix} \bullet \left(\tanh \begin{pmatrix} 0.5 \\ 0.5 \\ 0.5 \end{pmatrix} \right)^T + \begin{pmatrix} 0.5 \\ -0.5 \end{pmatrix}$$

$$\bullet \left(\tanh \begin{pmatrix} 1.1 + 0.3 \tanh 0.5 \\ 1.1 + 0.3 \tanh 0.5 \\ 1.1 + 0.3 \tanh 0.5 \end{pmatrix} \right)^T$$

$$\frac{\partial E}{\partial \mathbf{b}^{[2]}} = \sum_{t=1}^{T} \delta_{(t)}^{[2]} \frac{\partial \mathbf{z}_{(t)}^{[2]}}{\partial \mathbf{b}^{[2]}}$$

$$= \delta_{(1)}^{[2]} \circ \frac{\partial \mathbf{z}_{(1)}^{[2]}}{\partial \mathbf{b}^{[2]}} + \delta_{(2)}^{[2]} \circ \frac{\partial \mathbf{z}_{(2)}^{[2]}}{\partial \mathbf{b}^{[2]}}$$

$$= \delta_{(1)}^{[2]} \circ \mathbf{1} + \delta_{(2)}^{[2]} \circ \mathbf{1}$$

$$= \begin{pmatrix} -0.5 \\ 0.5 \end{pmatrix} + \begin{pmatrix} 0.5 \\ -0.5 \end{pmatrix}$$

$$= \begin{pmatrix} 0 \\ 0 \end{pmatrix}$$

Having the gradients, we can perform the stochastic gradient descent updates for all parameters:

$$\mathbf{H}^{[1]} = \mathbf{H}^{[1]} - \eta \frac{\partial E}{\partial \mathbf{H}^{[1]}}$$

$$= \begin{pmatrix} 0.1\ 0.1\ 0.1 \\ 0.1\ 0.1\ 0.1 \\ 0.1\ 0.1\ 0.1 \end{pmatrix} - 1 \begin{pmatrix} 0\ 0\ 0 \\ 0\ 0\ 0 \\ 0\ 0\ 0 \end{pmatrix}$$

$$= \begin{pmatrix} 0.1\ 0.1\ 0.1 \\ 0.1\ 0.1\ 0.1 \\ 0.1\ 0.1\ 0.1 \end{pmatrix}$$

$$\mathbf{W}^{[1]} = \mathbf{W}^{[1]} - \eta \frac{\partial E}{\partial \mathbf{W}^{[1]}}$$

$$= \begin{pmatrix} 0.1\ 0.1\ 0.1\ 0.1 \\ 0.1\ 0.1\ 0.1\ 0.1 \\ 0.1\ 0.1\ 0.1\ 0.1 \end{pmatrix} - 1 \begin{pmatrix} 0\ 0\ 0\ 0 \\ 0\ 0\ 0\ 0 \\ 0\ 0\ 0\ 0 \end{pmatrix}$$

$$= \begin{pmatrix} 0.1\ 0.1\ 0.1\ 0.1 \\ 0.1\ 0.1\ 0.1\ 0.1 \\ 0.1\ 0.1\ 0.1\ 0.1 \end{pmatrix}$$

$$\mathbf{b}^{[1]} = \mathbf{b}^{[1]} - \eta \frac{\partial E}{\partial \mathbf{b}^{[1]}}$$

$$= \begin{pmatrix} 0.1 \\ 0.1 \\ 0.1 \end{pmatrix} - 1 \begin{pmatrix} 0 \\ 0 \\ 0 \end{pmatrix}$$

$$= \begin{pmatrix} 0.1 \\ 0.1 \\ 0.1 \end{pmatrix}$$

$$\mathbf{W}^{[2]} = \mathbf{W}^{[2]} - \eta \frac{\partial E}{\partial \mathbf{W}^{[2]}}$$

$$= \begin{pmatrix} -0.0915\ -0.0915\ -0.0915 \\ 0.2915\ \ \ 0.2915\ \ \ 0.2915 \end{pmatrix}$$

$$\mathbf{b}^{[2]} = \mathbf{b}^{[2]} - \eta \frac{\partial E}{\partial \mathbf{b}^{[2]}}$$

$$= \begin{pmatrix} 0.1 \\ 0.1 \end{pmatrix} - 1 \begin{pmatrix} 0 \\ 0 \end{pmatrix}$$

$$= \begin{pmatrix} 0.1 \\ 0.1 \end{pmatrix}$$

2)

Consider a recurrent network with one hidden layer to solve a **many-to-many** task. Take into account that:

- The recurrent connections happen between the hidden layers
- The hidden activation function is the hyperbolic tangent
- The output activation function is the identity
- The error function is the half squared error between output and target

a) Write down the model equations for forward propagation.

Solution:

For all $t \in \{1, \ldots, T\}$:

$$z_{(t)}^{[1]} = z^{[1]}\left(\mathbf{H}^{[1]}, \mathbf{x}_{(t-1)}^{[1]}, \mathbf{W}^{[1]}, \mathbf{x}_{(t)}^{[0]}, \mathbf{b}^{[1]}\right) \qquad = \mathbf{H}^{[1]}\mathbf{x}_{(t-1)}^{[1]} + \mathbf{W}^{[1]}\mathbf{x}_{(t)}^{[0]} + \mathbf{b}^{[1]}$$

$$\mathbf{x}_{(t)}^{[1]} = f^{[1]}\left(\mathbf{z}_{(t)}^{[1]}\right) \qquad = \tanh\left(\mathbf{z}_{(t)}^{[1]}\right)$$

$$z_{(t)}^{[2]} = z^{[2]}\left(\mathbf{W}^{[2]}, \mathbf{x}_{(t)}^{[1]}, \mathbf{b}^{[2]}\right) \qquad = \mathbf{W}^{[2]}\mathbf{x}_{(t)}^{[1]} + \mathbf{b}^{[2]}$$

$$\mathbf{x}_{(t)}^{[2]} = f^{[2]}\left(\mathbf{z}_{(t)}^{[2]}\right) \qquad = \mathbf{z}_{(t)}^{[2]}$$

$$e_{(t)} = E\left(\mathbf{x}_{(t)}^{[2]}, \mathbf{t}_{(t)}\right) \qquad = \frac{1}{2}\left\|\mathbf{t}_{(t)} - \mathbf{x}_{(t)}^{[2]}\right\|_2^2$$

---

b) Write down the model equations for backward propagation.

Solution:

Since we are working with a many to many network eachtime step yields an error that will be propagated backwards. For the output layer, the deltas are independent of othertime steps. Applying the chain–rule we get:

$$\delta_{(t)}^{[2]} = \frac{\partial E}{\partial \mathbf{x}_{(t)}^{[2]}} \frac{\partial \mathbf{x}_{(t)}^{[2]}}{\mathbf{z}_{(t)}^{[2]}}$$

$$= \left(\mathbf{x}_{(t)}^{[2]} - \mathbf{t}_{(t)}\right) \circ \mathbf{1}$$

$$= \mathbf{x}_{(t)}^{[2]} - \mathbf{t}_{(t)}$$

For the lasttime step T, the delta for the hidden layer is independent of all othertime steps. Using the chain-rule we get:

$$\delta_{(T)}^{[1]} = \delta_{(T)}^{[2]} \frac{\partial \mathbf{z}_{(T)}^{[2]}}{\partial \mathbf{x}_{(T)}^{[1]}} \frac{\partial \mathbf{x}_{(T)}^{[1]}}{\partial \mathbf{z}_{(T)}^{[1]}}$$

$$= \left(\frac{\partial \mathbf{z}_{(T)}^{[2]}}{\partial \mathbf{x}_{(T)}^{[1]}} \right)^T \bullet \delta_{(T)}^{[2]} \circ \frac{\partial \mathbf{x}_{(T)}^{[1]}}{\partial \mathbf{z}_{(T)}^{[1]}}$$

$$= \left(\mathbf{W}^{[2]} \right)^T \bullet \delta_{(T)}^{[2]} \circ \left(1 - \tanh^2 \mathbf{z}_{(T)}^{[1]} \right)$$

For all othertime steps $t \in \{1, \ldots, T-1\}$, the delta for the hidden layer depends on the nexttime step's hidden layer. Using the chain-rule we get:

$$\delta_{(t)}^{[1]} = \left(\delta_{(t)}^{[2]} \frac{\partial \mathbf{z}_{(t)}^{[2]}}{\partial \mathbf{x}_{(t)}^{[1]}} + \delta_{(t+1)}^{[1]} \frac{\partial \mathbf{z}_{(t+1)}^{[1]}}{\partial \mathbf{x}_{(t)}^{[1]}} \right) \frac{\partial \mathbf{x}_{(t)}^{[1]}}{\partial \mathbf{z}_{(t)}^{[1]}}$$

$$= \left(\left(\frac{\partial \mathbf{z}_{(t)}^{[2]}}{\partial \mathbf{x}_{(t)}^{[1]}} \right)^T \bullet \delta_{(t)}^{[2]} + \left(\frac{\partial \mathbf{z}_{(t+1)}^{[1]}}{\partial \mathbf{x}_{(t)}^{[1]}} \right)^T \bullet \delta_{(t+1)}^{[1]} \right) \circ \frac{\partial \mathbf{x}_{(t)}^{[1]}}{\partial \mathbf{z}_{(t)}^{[1]}}$$

$$= \left(\left(\mathbf{W}^{[2]} \right)^T \bullet \delta_{(t)}^{[2]} + \mathbf{H}^T \bullet \delta_{(t+1)}^{[1]} \right) \circ \left(1 - \tanh^2 \mathbf{z}_{(t)}^{[1]} \right)$$

c) Perform a stochastic gradient descent update for:

$$x^{(1)} = \left[\begin{pmatrix} 4 \\ 0 \\ 0 \\ 0 \end{pmatrix}, \begin{pmatrix} 0 \\ 8 \\ 2 \\ 0 \end{pmatrix} \right]$$

With targets:

$$t^{(1)} = \left[\begin{pmatrix} 1 \\ 0 \end{pmatrix}, \begin{pmatrix} 0 \\ 1 \end{pmatrix} \right]$$

Initialize all weights and biases to 0.1, using 3 units per hidden layer, initializing the hidden state to all zeros and using $\eta = 1.0$.

Solution:

Initializing the parameters, we have:

$$\mathbf{W}^{[1]} = \begin{pmatrix} 0.1 \ 0.1 \ 0.1 \ 0.1 \\ 0.1 \ 0.1 \ 0.1 \ 0.1 \\ 0.1 \ 0.1 \ 0.1 \ 0.1 \end{pmatrix}$$

$$\mathbf{b}^{[1]} = \begin{pmatrix} 0.1 \\ 0.1 \\ 0.1 \end{pmatrix}$$

$$\mathbf{H}^{[1]} = \begin{pmatrix} 0.1\ 0.1\ 0.1 \\ 0.1\ 0.1\ 0.1 \\ 0.1\ 0.1\ 0.1 \end{pmatrix}$$

$$\mathbf{W}^{[2]} = \begin{pmatrix} 0.1\ 0.1\ 0.1 \\ 0.1\ 0.1\ 0.1 \end{pmatrix}$$

$$\mathbf{b}^{[2]} = \begin{pmatrix} 0.1 \\ 0.1 \end{pmatrix}$$

$$\mathbf{x}_{(0)}^{[1]} = \begin{pmatrix} 0 \\ 0 \\ 0 \end{pmatrix}$$

Now, we can use **a)** to apply forward propagation. Let us start with time step $t = 1$:

$$\mathbf{z}_{(1)}^{[1]} = \begin{pmatrix} 0.1\ 0.1\ 0.1 \\ 0.1\ 0.1\ 0.1 \\ 0.1\ 0.1\ 0.1 \end{pmatrix} \begin{pmatrix} 0 \\ 0 \\ 0 \end{pmatrix} + \begin{pmatrix} 0.1\ 0.1\ 0.1\ 0.1 \\ 0.1\ 0.1\ 0.1\ 0.1 \\ 0.1\ 0.1\ 0.1\ 0.1 \end{pmatrix} \begin{pmatrix} 4 \\ 0 \\ 0 \\ 0 \end{pmatrix} + \begin{pmatrix} 0.1 \\ 0.1 \\ 0.1 \end{pmatrix}$$

$$= \begin{pmatrix} 0.5 \\ 0.5 \\ 0.5 \end{pmatrix}$$

$$\mathbf{x}_{(1)}^{[1]} = \tanh \begin{pmatrix} 0.5 \\ 0.5 \\ 0.5 \end{pmatrix}$$

$$\mathbf{z}_{(1)}^{[2]} = \begin{pmatrix} 0.1\ 0.1\ 0.1 \\ 0.1\ 0.1\ 0.1 \end{pmatrix} \tanh \begin{pmatrix} 0.5 \\ 0.5 \\ 0.5 \end{pmatrix} + \begin{pmatrix} 0.1 \\ 0.1 \end{pmatrix}$$

$$= \begin{pmatrix} 0.3\tanh 0.5 + 0.1 \\ 0.3\tanh 0.5 + 0.1 \end{pmatrix}$$

$$\mathbf{x}_{(1)}^{[2]} = \begin{pmatrix} 0.3\tanh 0.5 + 0.1 \\ 0.3\tanh 0.5 + 0.1 \end{pmatrix}$$

Now we can apply the same logic to the second time step.

$$\mathbf{z}_{(2)}^{[1]} = \begin{pmatrix} 0.1\ 0.1\ 0.1 \\ 0.1\ 0.1\ 0.1 \\ 0.1\ 0.1\ 0.1 \end{pmatrix} \tanh \begin{pmatrix} 0.5 \\ 0.5 \\ 0.5 \end{pmatrix} + \begin{pmatrix} 0.1\ 0.1\ 0.1\ 0.1 \\ 0.1\ 0.1\ 0.1\ 0.1 \\ 0.1\ 0.1\ 0.1\ 0.1 \end{pmatrix} \begin{pmatrix} 0 \\ 8 \\ 2 \\ 0 \end{pmatrix} + \begin{pmatrix} 0.1 \\ 0.1 \\ 0.1 \end{pmatrix}$$

$$= \begin{pmatrix} 1.1 + 0.3 \tanh 0.5 \\ 1.1 + 0.3 \tanh 0.5 \\ 1.1 + 0.3 \tanh 0.5 \end{pmatrix}$$

$$\mathbf{x}_{(2)}^{[1]} = \tanh \begin{pmatrix} 1.1 + 0.3 \tanh 0.5 \\ 1.1 + 0.3 \tanh 0.5 \\ 1.1 + 0.3 \tanh 0.5 \end{pmatrix}$$

$$\mathbf{z}_{(2)}^{[2]} = \begin{pmatrix} 0.1\ 0.1\ 0.1 \\ 0.1\ 0.1\ 0.1 \end{pmatrix} \tanh \begin{pmatrix} 1.1 + 0.3 \tanh 0.5 \\ 1.1 + 0.3 \tanh 0.5 \\ 1.1 + 0.3 \tanh 0.5 \end{pmatrix} + \begin{pmatrix} 0.1 \\ 0.1 \end{pmatrix}$$

$$= \begin{pmatrix} 0.3 \tanh (1.1 + 0.3 \tanh 0.5) + 0.1 \\ 0.3 \tanh (1.1 + 0.3 \tanh 0.5) + 0.1 \end{pmatrix}$$

$$\mathbf{x}_{(2)}^{[2]} = \begin{pmatrix} 0.3 \tanh (1.1 + 0.3 \tanh 0.5) + 0.1 \\ 0.3 \tanh (1.1 + 0.3 \tanh 0.5) + 0.1 \end{pmatrix}$$

After finishing forward propagation, we can use **b)** to perform backward propagation. For the output layers we have:

$$\delta_{(2)}^{[2]} = \mathbf{x}_{(2)}^{[2]} - \mathbf{t}_{(2)} = \begin{pmatrix} 0.3 \tanh (1.1 + 0.3 \tanh 0.5) + 0.1 \\ 0.3 \tanh (1.1 + 0.3 \tanh 0.5) + 0.1 \end{pmatrix} - \begin{pmatrix} 0 \\ 1 \end{pmatrix}$$

$$= \begin{pmatrix} 0.3 \tanh (1.1 + 0.3 \tanh 0.5) + 0.1 \\ 0.3 \tanh (1.1 + 0.3 \tanh 0.5) - 0.9 \end{pmatrix}$$

$$= \begin{pmatrix} o_{21} \\ o_{22} \end{pmatrix}$$

$$\delta_{(1)}^{[2]} = \mathbf{x}_{(1)}^{[2]} - \mathbf{t}_{(1)} = \begin{pmatrix} 0.3 \tanh 0.5 + 0.1 \\ 0.3 \tanh 0.5 + 0.1 \end{pmatrix} - \begin{pmatrix} 1 \\ 0 \end{pmatrix}$$

$$= \begin{pmatrix} 0.3 \tanh 0.5 - 0.9 \\ 0.3 \tanh 0.5 + 0.1 \end{pmatrix}$$

$$= \begin{pmatrix} o_{11} \\ o_{12} \end{pmatrix}$$

For the hidden layer of the last time step we have:

$$\delta_{(2)}^{[1]} = \left(\mathbf{W}^{[2]}\right)^T \bullet \delta_{(2)}^{[2]} \circ \left(1 - \tanh^2 \mathbf{z}_{(2)}^{[1]}\right)$$

$$= \begin{pmatrix} 0.1 \; 0.1 \\ 0.1 \; 0.1 \\ 0.1 \; 0.1 \end{pmatrix} \bullet \begin{pmatrix} 0.3 \tanh\left(1.1 + 0.3 \tanh 0.5\right) + 0.1 \\ 0.3 \tanh\left(1.1 + 0.3 \tanh 0.5\right) - 0.9 \end{pmatrix}$$

$$\circ \begin{pmatrix} 1 - \tanh^2\left(1.1 + 0.3 \tanh 0.5\right) \\ 1 - \tanh^2\left(1.1 + 0.3 \tanh 0.5\right) \\ 1 - \tanh^2\left(1.1 + 0.3 \tanh 0.5\right) \end{pmatrix}$$

$$= \begin{pmatrix} 0.06 \tanh\left(1.1 + 0.3 \tanh 0.5\right) - 0.08 \\ 0.06 \tanh\left(1.1 + 0.3 \tanh 0.5\right) - 0.08 \\ 0.06 \tanh\left(1.1 + 0.3 \tanh 0.5\right) - 0.08 \end{pmatrix}$$

$$\circ \begin{pmatrix} 1 - \tanh^2\left(1.1 + 0.3 \tanh 0.5\right) \\ 1 - \tanh^2\left(1.1 + 0.3 \tanh 0.5\right) \\ 1 - \tanh^2\left(1.1 + 0.3 \tanh 0.5\right) \end{pmatrix}$$

$$= \begin{pmatrix} h_2 \\ h_2 \\ h_2 \end{pmatrix}$$

Where:

$$h_2 = \left(0.06 \tanh\left(1.1 + 0.3 \tanh 0.5\right) - 0.08\right)\left(1 - \tanh^2\left(1.1 + 0.3 \tanh 0.5\right)\right)$$

For the hidden layer of the first time step we have:

$$\delta_{(1)}^{[1]} = \left(\left(\mathbf{W}^{[2]} \right)^T \bullet \delta_{(1)}^{[2]} + \left(\mathbf{H}^{[1]} \right)^T \bullet \delta_{(2)}^{[1]} \right) \circ \left(1 - \tanh^2 \mathbf{z}_{(1)}^{[1]} \right)$$

$$\left(\mathbf{W}^{[2]} \right)^T \bullet \delta_{(1)}^{[2]} \circ \left(1 - \tanh^2 \mathbf{z}_{(1)}^{[1]} \right) + \left(\mathbf{H}^{[1]} \right)^T \bullet \delta_{(2)}^{[1]} \circ \left(1 - \tanh^2 \mathbf{z}_{(1)}^{[1]} \right)$$

$$= \begin{pmatrix} 0.1 & 0.1 \\ 0.1 & 0.1 \\ 0.1 & 0.1 \end{pmatrix} \bullet \begin{pmatrix} 0.3\tanh 0.5 - 0.9 \\ 0.3\tanh 0.5 + 0.1 \end{pmatrix} \circ \begin{pmatrix} 1 - \tanh^2 0.5 \\ 1 - \tanh^2 0.5 \\ 1 - \tanh^2 0.5 \end{pmatrix}$$

$$+ \begin{pmatrix} 0.1 & 0.1 & 0.1 \\ 0.1 & 0.1 & 0.1 \\ 0.1 & 0.1 & 0.1 \end{pmatrix}$$

$$\bullet \begin{pmatrix} (0.06\tanh(1.1 + 0.3\tanh 0.5) - 0.08)\left(1 - \tanh^2(1.1 + 0.3\tanh 0.5) \right) \\ (0.06\tanh(1.1 + 0.3\tanh 0.5) - 0.08)\left(1 - \tanh^2(1.1 + 0.3\tanh 0.5) \right) \\ (0.06\tanh(1.1 + 0.3\tanh 0.5) - 0.08)\left(1 - \tanh^2(1.1 + 0.3\tanh 0.5) \right) \end{pmatrix}$$

$$\circ \begin{pmatrix} 1 - \tanh^2 0.5 \\ 1 - \tanh^2 0.5 \\ 1 - \tanh^2 0.5 \end{pmatrix}$$

$$= \begin{pmatrix} 0.06\tanh 0.5 - 0.08 \\ 0.06\tanh 0.5 - 0.08 \\ 0.06\tanh 0.5 - 0.08 \end{pmatrix} \circ \begin{pmatrix} 1 - \tanh^2 0.5 \\ 1 - \tanh^2 0.5 \\ 1 - \tanh^2 0.5 \end{pmatrix}$$

$$+ \begin{pmatrix} 0.3\left(0.06\tanh(1.1 + 0.3\tanh 0.5) - 0.08 \right)\left(1 - \tanh^2(1.1 + 0.3\tanh 0.5) \right) \\ 0.3\left(0.06\tanh(1.1 + 0.3\tanh 0.5) - 0.08 \right)\left(1 - \tanh^2(1.1 + 0.3\tanh 0.5) \right) \\ 0.3\left(0.06\tanh(1.1 + 0.3\tanh 0.5) - 0.08 \right)\left(1 - \tanh^2(1.1 + 0.3\tanh 0.5) \right) \end{pmatrix}$$

$$\circ \begin{pmatrix} 1 - \tanh^2 0.5 \\ 1 - \tanh^2 0.5 \\ 1 - \tanh^2 0.5 \end{pmatrix}$$

$$= \begin{pmatrix} h_1 \\ h_1 \\ h_1 \end{pmatrix}$$

Where:

$$h_1 = (0.06\tanh 0.5 - 0.08)\left(1 - \tanh^2 0.5 \right)$$
$$+ \left(0.3\left(0.06\tanh(1.1 + 0.3\tanh 0.5) - 0.08 \right) \cdot \left(1 - \tanh^2(1.1 + 0.3\tanh 0.5) \right) \right)$$
$$\cdot \left(1 - \tanh^2 0.5 \right)$$

Having the deltas, we can compute the specific gradients for all parameters. Each gradient corresponds to the sum across all backward paths that lead to that parameter.

$$\frac{\partial E}{\partial \mathbf{H}^{[1]}} = \sum_{t=1}^{T} \delta_{(t)}^{[1]} \frac{\partial \mathbf{z}_{(t)}^{[1]}}{\partial \mathbf{H}^{[1]}}$$

$$= \delta_{(1)}^{[1]} \bullet \left(\frac{\partial \mathbf{z}_{(1)}^{[1]}}{\partial \mathbf{H}^{[1]}} \right)^{T} + \delta_{(2)}^{[1]} \bullet \left(\frac{\partial \mathbf{z}_{(2)}^{[1]}}{\partial \mathbf{H}^{[1]}} \right)^{T}$$

$$= \delta_{(1)}^{[1]} \bullet \left(\mathbf{x}_{(0)}^{[0]} \right)^{T} + \delta_{(2)}^{[1]} \bullet \left(\mathbf{x}_{(1)}^{[1]} \right)^{T}$$

$$= \begin{pmatrix} h_1 \\ h_1 \\ h_1 \end{pmatrix} (0\,0\,0) + \begin{pmatrix} h_2 \\ h_2 \\ h_2 \end{pmatrix} (\tanh 0.5 \ \tanh 0.5 \ \tanh 0.5)$$

$$= \begin{pmatrix} h_2 \tanh 0.5 \ h_2 \tanh 0.5 \ h_2 \tanh 0.5 \\ h_2 \tanh 0.5 \ h_2 \tanh 0.5 \ h_2 \tanh 0.5 \\ h_2 \tanh 0.5 \ h_2 \tanh 0.5 \ h_2 \tanh 0.5 \end{pmatrix}$$

$$\frac{\partial E}{\partial \mathbf{W}^{[1]}} = \sum_{t=1}^{T} \delta_{(t)}^{[1]} \frac{\partial \mathbf{z}_{(t)}^{[1]}}{\partial \mathbf{W}^{[1]}}$$

$$= \delta_{(1)}^{[1]} \bullet \left(\frac{\partial \mathbf{z}_{(1)}^{[1]}}{\partial \mathbf{W}^{[1]}} \right)^{T} + \delta_{(2)}^{[1]} \bullet \left(\frac{\partial \mathbf{z}_{(2)}^{[1]}}{\partial \mathbf{W}^{[1]}} \right)^{T}$$

$$= \delta_{(1)}^{[1]} \bullet \left(\mathbf{x}_{(1)}^{[0]} \right)^{T} + \delta_{(2)}^{[1]} \bullet \left(\mathbf{x}_{(2)}^{[0]} \right)^{T}$$

$$= \begin{pmatrix} h_1 \\ h_1 \\ h_1 \end{pmatrix} (4\,0\,0\,0) + \begin{pmatrix} h_2 \\ h_2 \\ h_2 \end{pmatrix} (0\,8\,2\,0)$$

$$= \begin{pmatrix} 4h_1\,0\,0\,0 \\ 4h_1\,0\,0\,0 \\ 4h_1\,0\,0\,0 \end{pmatrix} + \begin{pmatrix} 0\,8h_2\,2h_2\,0 \\ 0\,8h_2\,2h_2\,0 \\ 0\,8h_2\,2h_2\,0 \end{pmatrix}$$

$$= \begin{pmatrix} 4h_1\,8h_2\,2h_2\,0 \\ 4h_1\,8h_2\,2h_2\,0 \\ 4h_1\,8h_2\,2h_2\,0 \end{pmatrix}$$

$$\frac{\partial E}{\partial \mathbf{b}^{[1]}} = \sum_{t=1}^{T} \delta_{(t)}^{[1]} \frac{\partial \mathbf{z}_{(t)}^{[1]}}{\partial \mathbf{b}^{[1]}}$$

$$= \delta_{(1)}^{[1]} \circ \frac{\partial \mathbf{z}_{(1)}^{[1]}}{\partial \mathbf{b}^{[1]}} + \delta_{(2)}^{[1]} \circ \frac{\partial \mathbf{z}_{(2)}^{[1]}}{\partial \mathbf{b}^{[1]}}$$

$$= \delta_{(1)}^{[1]} \circ \mathbf{1} + \delta_{(2)}^{[1]} \circ \mathbf{1}$$

$$= \begin{pmatrix} h_1 \\ h_1 \\ h_1 \end{pmatrix} + \begin{pmatrix} h_2 \\ h_2 \\ h_2 \end{pmatrix}$$

$$= \begin{pmatrix} h_1 + h_2 \\ h_1 + h_2 \\ h_1 + h_2 \end{pmatrix}$$

HHH

$$\frac{\partial E}{\partial \mathbf{W}^{[2]}} = \sum_{t=1}^{T} \delta_{(t)}^{[2]} \frac{\partial \mathbf{z}_{(t)}^{[2]}}{\partial \mathbf{W}^{[2]}}$$

$$= \delta_{(1)}^{[2]} \bullet \left(\frac{\partial \mathbf{z}_{(1)}^{[2]}}{\partial \mathbf{W}^{[2]}} \right)^T + \delta_{(2)}^{[2]} \bullet \left(\frac{\partial \mathbf{z}_{(2)}^{[2]}}{\partial \mathbf{W}^{[2]}} \right)^T$$

$$= \begin{pmatrix} o_{11} \\ o_{12} \end{pmatrix} \bullet \left(\tanh \begin{pmatrix} 0.5 \\ 0.5 \\ 0.5 \end{pmatrix} \right)^T + \begin{pmatrix} o_{21} \\ o_{22} \end{pmatrix} \bullet \left(\tanh \begin{pmatrix} 1.1 + 0.3 \tanh 0.5 \\ 1.1 + 0.3 \tanh 0.5 \\ 1.1 + 0.3 \tanh 0.5 \end{pmatrix} \right)^T$$

$$= \begin{pmatrix} w_{21} \ w_{21} \ w_{21} \\ w_{22} \ w_{22} \ w_{22} \end{pmatrix}$$

Where:

$$w_{21} = o_{11} \tanh 0.5 + o_{21} \tanh (1.1 + 0.3 \tanh 0.5)$$

$$w_{22} = o_{12} \tanh 0.5 + o_{22} \tanh (1.1 + 0.3 \tanh 0.5)$$

$$\frac{\partial E}{\partial \mathbf{b}^{[2]}} = \sum_{t=1}^{T} \delta_{(t)}^{[2]} \frac{\partial \mathbf{z}_{(t)}^{[2]}}{\partial \mathbf{b}^{[2]}}$$

$$= \delta_{(1)}^{[2]} \circ \frac{\partial \mathbf{z}_{(1)}^{[2]}}{\partial \mathbf{b}^{[2]}} + \delta_{(2)}^{[1]} \circ \frac{\partial \mathbf{z}_{(2)}^{[2]}}{\partial \mathbf{b}^{[2]}}$$

$$= \delta_{(1)}^{[2]} \circ \mathbf{1} + \delta_{(2)}^{[2]} \circ \mathbf{1}$$

$$= \begin{pmatrix} o_{11} \\ o_{12} \end{pmatrix} + \begin{pmatrix} o_{21} \\ o_{22} \end{pmatrix}$$

$$= \begin{pmatrix} o_{11} + o_{21} \\ o_{12} + o_{22} \end{pmatrix}$$

Having the gradients, we can perform the stochastic gradient descent updates for all parameters:

$$\mathbf{H}^{[1]} = \mathbf{H}^{[1]} - \eta \frac{\partial E}{\partial \mathbf{H}^{[1]}}$$

$$= \begin{pmatrix} 0.1 \ 0.1 \ 0.1 \\ 0.1 \ 0.1 \ 0.1 \\ 0.1 \ 0.1 \ 0.1 \end{pmatrix} - 1 \begin{pmatrix} h_2 \tanh 0.5 \ h_2 \tanh 0.5 \ h_2 \tanh 0.5 \\ h_2 \tanh 0.5 \ h_2 \tanh 0.5 \ h_2 \tanh 0.5 \\ h_2 \tanh 0.5 \ h_2 \tanh 0.5 \ h_2 \tanh 0.5 \end{pmatrix}$$

$$= \begin{pmatrix} 0.1039 \ 0.1039 \ 0.1039 \\ 0.1039 \ 0.1039 \ 0.1039 \\ 0.1039 \ 0.1039 \ 0.1039 \end{pmatrix}$$

$$\mathbf{W}^{[1]} = \mathbf{W}^{[1]} - \eta \frac{\partial E}{\partial \mathbf{W}^{[1]}}$$

$$= \begin{pmatrix} 0.1 \ 0.1 \ 0.1 \ 0.1 \\ 0.1 \ 0.1 \ 0.1 \ 0.1 \\ 0.1 \ 0.1 \ 0.1 \ 0.1 \end{pmatrix} - 1 \begin{pmatrix} 4h_1 \ 8h_2 \ 2h_2 \ 0 \\ 4h_1 \ 8h_2 \ 2h_2 \ 0 \\ 4h_1 \ 8h_2 \ 2h_2 \ 0 \end{pmatrix}$$

$$= \begin{pmatrix} 0.2723 \ 0.1669 \ 0.1167 \ 0.1 \\ 0.2723 \ 0.1669 \ 0.1167 \ 0.1 \\ 0.2723 \ 0.1669 \ 0.1167 \ 0.1 \end{pmatrix}$$

$$\mathbf{b}^{[1]} = \mathbf{b}^{[1]} - \eta \frac{\partial E}{\partial \mathbf{b}^{[1]}}$$

$$= \begin{pmatrix} 0.1 \\ 0.1 \\ 0.1 \end{pmatrix} - 1 \begin{pmatrix} h_1 + h_2 \\ h_1 + h_2 \\ h_1 + h_2 \end{pmatrix}$$

$$= \begin{pmatrix} 0.1515 \\ 0.1515 \\ 0.1515 \end{pmatrix}$$

$$\mathbf{W}^{[2]} = \mathbf{W}^{[2]} - \eta \frac{\partial E}{\partial \mathbf{W}^{[2]}}$$

$$= \begin{pmatrix} 0.1\ 0.1\ 0.1 \\ 0.1\ 0.1\ 0.1 \end{pmatrix} - 1 \begin{pmatrix} w_{21}\ w_{21}\ w_{21} \\ w_{22}\ w_{22}\ w_{22} \end{pmatrix}$$

$$= \begin{pmatrix} 0.1531\ 0.1531\ 0.1531 \\ 0.5360\ 0.5360\ 0.5360 \end{pmatrix}$$

$$\mathbf{b}^{[2]} = \mathbf{b}^{[2]} - \eta \frac{\partial E}{\partial \mathbf{b}^{[2]}}$$

$$= \begin{pmatrix} 0.1 \\ 0.1 \end{pmatrix} - 1 \begin{pmatrix} o_{11} + o_{21} \\ o_{12} + o_{22} \end{pmatrix}$$

$$= \begin{pmatrix} 0.5078 \\ 0.5078 \end{pmatrix}$$

---

3)

Consider a recurrent network with one hidden layer to solve a **many-to-one** task. Take into account that:

- The recurrent connections happen between the hidden layers
- The hidden activation function is the hyperbolic tangent
- The output activation function is the softmax
- The error function is the cross-entropy between output and target

a) Write down the model equations for forward propagation.

Solution:

Timesteps before the last $t \in \{1, \ldots, T-1\}$ are only processed until the hidden layer:

$$\mathbf{z}_{(t)}^{[1]} = \mathbf{H}^{[1]}\mathbf{x}_{(t-1)}^{[1]} + \mathbf{W}^{[1]}\mathbf{x}_{(t)}^{[0]} + \mathbf{b}^{[1]}$$

$$\mathbf{x}_{(t)}^{[1]} = \tanh\left(\mathbf{z}_{(t)}^{[1]}\right)$$

The lasttime step receives the hidden state from the previoustime step and performs the full network operation until the output:

$$\mathbf{z}^{[1]}_{(T)} = \mathbf{H}^{[1]}\mathbf{x}^{[1]}_{(T-1)} + \mathbf{W}^{[1]}\mathbf{x}^{[0]}_{(T)} + \mathbf{b}^{[1]}$$

$$\mathbf{x}^{[1]}_{(T)} = \tanh\left(\mathbf{z}^{[1]}_{(T)}\right)$$

$$\mathbf{z}^{[2]}_{(T)} = \mathbf{W}^{[2]}\mathbf{x}^{[1]}_{(T)} + \mathbf{b}^{[2]}$$

$$\mathbf{x}^{[2]}_{(T)} = softmax\left(\mathbf{z}^{[2]}_{(T)}\right)$$

$$e = -\mathbf{t} \bullet \log\mathbf{x}^{[2]}_{(T)}$$

b) Write down the model equations for backward propagation.

Solution:

Since we are working with a many to one network only the lasttime step will have a delta for the output layer. So, applying the chain–rule we get:

$$\delta^{[2]}_{(T)} = \frac{\partial E}{\partial\mathbf{x}^{[2]}_{(T)}}\frac{\partial\mathbf{x}^{[2]}_{(T)}}{\mathbf{z}^{[2]}_{(T)}}$$

$$= \mathbf{x}^{[2]}_{(T)} - \mathbf{t}_{(T)}$$

For the lasttime step T, the delta for the hidden layer is independent of all othertime steps. Using the chain-rule we get:

$$\delta^{[1]}_{(T)} = \delta^{[2]}_{(T)}\frac{\partial\mathbf{z}^{[2]}_{(T)}}{\partial\mathbf{x}^{[1]}_{(T)}}\frac{\partial\mathbf{x}^{[1]}_{(T)}}{\partial\mathbf{z}^{[1]}_{(T)}}$$

$$= \left(\frac{\partial\mathbf{z}^{[2]}_{(T)}}{\partial\mathbf{x}^{[1]}_{(T)}}\right)^T \bullet \delta^{[2]}_{(T)} \circ \frac{\partial\mathbf{x}^{[1]}_{(T)}}{\partial\mathbf{z}^{[1]}_{(T)}}$$

$$= \left(\mathbf{W}^{[2]}\right)^T \bullet \delta^{[2]}_{(T)} \circ \left(1 - \tanh^2 \mathbf{z}^{[1]}_{(T)}\right)$$

For all othertime steps $t \in \{1,\ldots,T-1\}$, the delta for the hidden layer depends only on the nexttime step's hidden layer. Using the chain-rule we get:

$$\delta^{[1]}_{(t)} = \delta^{[1]}_{(t+1)}\frac{\partial\mathbf{z}^{[1]}_{(t+1)}}{\partial\mathbf{x}^{[1]}_{(t)}}\frac{\partial\mathbf{x}^{[1]}_{(t)}}{\partial\mathbf{z}^{[1]}_{(t)}}$$

$$= \left(\frac{\partial\mathbf{z}^{[1]}_{(t+1)}}{\partial\mathbf{x}^{[1]}_{(t)}}\right)^T \bullet \delta^{[1]}_{(t+1)} \circ \frac{\partial\mathbf{x}^{[1]}_{(t)}}{\partial\mathbf{z}^{[1]}_{(t)}}$$

$$= \left(\mathbf{H}^{[1]}\right)^T \bullet \delta^{[1]}_{(t+1)} \circ \left(1 - \tanh^2 \mathbf{z}^{[1]}_{(t)}\right)$$

c) Perform a stochastic gradient descent update for:

$$x^{(1)} = \left[\begin{pmatrix} 4 \\ 0 \\ 0 \\ 0 \end{pmatrix}, \begin{pmatrix} 0 \\ 8 \\ 2 \\ 0 \end{pmatrix} \right]$$

With targets:

$$\mathbf{t} = \begin{pmatrix} 0 \\ 1 \end{pmatrix}$$

Initialize all weights and biases to 0.1, using 3 units per hidden layer, initializing the hidden state to all zeros and using $\eta = 1.0$.

Solution:

Initializing the parameters, we have:

$$\mathbf{W}^{[1]} = \begin{pmatrix} 0.1 & 0.1 & 0.1 & 0.1 \\ 0.1 & 0.1 & 0.1 & 0.1 \\ 0.1 & 0.1 & 0.1 & 0.1 \end{pmatrix}$$

$$\mathbf{b}^{[1]} = \begin{pmatrix} 0.1 \\ 0.1 \\ 0.1 \end{pmatrix}$$

$$\mathbf{H}^{[1]} = \begin{pmatrix} 0.1 & 0.1 & 0.1 \\ 0.1 & 0.1 & 0.1 \\ 0.1 & 0.1 & 0.1 \end{pmatrix}$$

$$\mathbf{W}^{[2]} = \begin{pmatrix} 0.1 & 0.1 & 0.1 \\ 0.1 & 0.1 & 0.1 \end{pmatrix}$$

$$\mathbf{b}^{[2]} = \begin{pmatrix} 0.1 \\ 0.1 \end{pmatrix}$$

$$\mathbf{x}^{[1]}_{(0)} = \begin{pmatrix} 0 \\ 0 \\ 0 \end{pmatrix}$$

Now, we can use **a)** to apply forward propagation. Let us start with time step $t = 1$:

$$\mathbf{z}^{[1]}_{(1)} = \begin{pmatrix} 0.1 \; 0.1 \; 0.1 \\ 0.1 \; 0.1 \; 0.1 \\ 0.1 \; 0.1 \; 0.1 \end{pmatrix} \begin{pmatrix} 0 \\ 0 \\ 0 \end{pmatrix} + \begin{pmatrix} 0.1 \; 0.1 \; 0.1 \; 0.1 \\ 0.1 \; 0.1 \; 0.1 \; 0.1 \\ 0.1 \; 0.1 \; 0.1 \; 0.1 \end{pmatrix} \begin{pmatrix} 4 \\ 0 \\ 0 \\ 0 \end{pmatrix} + \begin{pmatrix} 0.1 \\ 0.1 \\ 0.1 \end{pmatrix}$$

$$= \begin{pmatrix} 0.5 \\ 0.5 \\ 0.5 \end{pmatrix}$$

$$\mathbf{x}^{[1]}_{(1)} = \tanh \begin{pmatrix} 0.5 \\ 0.5 \\ 0.5 \end{pmatrix}$$

Now we can apply the same logic to the second time step.

$$\mathbf{z}^{[1]}_{(2)} = \begin{pmatrix} 0.1 \; 0.1 \; 0.1 \\ 0.1 \; 0.1 \; 0.1 \\ 0.1 \; 0.1 \; 0.1 \end{pmatrix} \tanh \begin{pmatrix} 0.5 \\ 0.5 \\ 0.5 \end{pmatrix} + \begin{pmatrix} 0.1 \; 0.1 \; 0.1 \; 0.1 \\ 0.1 \; 0.1 \; 0.1 \; 0.1 \\ 0.1 \; 0.1 \; 0.1 \; 0.1 \end{pmatrix} \begin{pmatrix} 0 \\ 8 \\ 2 \\ 0 \end{pmatrix} + \begin{pmatrix} 0.1 \\ 0.1 \\ 0.1 \end{pmatrix}$$

$$= \begin{pmatrix} 1.1 + 0.3 \tanh 0.5 \\ 1.1 + 0.3 \tanh 0.5 \\ 1.1 + 0.3 \tanh 0.5 \end{pmatrix}$$

$$\mathbf{x}^{[1]}_{(2)} = \tanh \begin{pmatrix} 1.1 + 0.3 \tanh 0.5 \\ 1.1 + 0.3 \tanh 0.5 \\ 1.1 + 0.3 \tanh 0.5 \end{pmatrix}$$

$$\mathbf{z}^{[2]}_{(2)} = \begin{pmatrix} 0.1 \; 0.1 \; 0.1 \\ 0.1 \; 0.1 \; 0.1 \end{pmatrix} \tanh \begin{pmatrix} 1.1 + 0.3 \tanh 0.5 \\ 1.1 + 0.3 \tanh 0.5 \\ 1.1 + 0.3 \tanh 0.5 \end{pmatrix} + \begin{pmatrix} 0.1 \\ 0.1 \end{pmatrix}$$

$$= \begin{pmatrix} 0.3 \tanh \left(1.1 + 0.3 \tanh 0.5 \right) + 0.1 \\ 0.3 \tanh \left(1.1 + 0.3 \tanh 0.5 \right) + 0.1 \end{pmatrix}$$

$$\mathbf{x}^{[2]}_{(2)} = softmax \begin{pmatrix} 0.3 \tanh \left(1.1 + 0.3 \tanh 0.5 \right) + 0.1 \\ 0.3 \tanh \left(1.1 + 0.3 \tanh 0.5 \right) + 0.1 \end{pmatrix}$$

$$= \begin{pmatrix} 0.5 \\ 0.5 \end{pmatrix}$$

After finishing forward propagation, we can use **b)** to perform backward propagation. For the output layer in the lasttime step we have:

$$\delta_{(2)}^{[2]} = \mathbf{x}_{(2)}^{[2]} - \mathbf{t}_{(2)} \;\; = \begin{pmatrix} 0.5 \\ 0.5 \end{pmatrix} - \begin{pmatrix} 0 \\ 1 \end{pmatrix} = \begin{pmatrix} 0.5 \\ -0.5 \end{pmatrix}$$

For the hidden layer of the lasttime step we have:

$$
\begin{aligned}
\delta_{(2)}^{[1]} &= \left(\mathbf{W}^{[2]} \right)^T \bullet \delta_{(2)}^{[2]} \circ \left(1 - \tanh^2 \mathbf{z}_{(2)}^{[1]} \right) \\
&= \begin{pmatrix} 0.1 \; 0.1 \\ 0.1 \; 0.1 \\ 0.1 \; 0.1 \end{pmatrix} \bullet \begin{pmatrix} 0.5 \\ -0.5 \end{pmatrix} \circ \begin{pmatrix} 1 - \tanh^2 (1.1 + 0.3 \tanh 0.5) \\ 1 - \tanh^2 (1.1 + 0.3 \tanh 0.5) \\ 1 - \tanh^2 (1.1 + 0.3 \tanh 0.5) \end{pmatrix} \\
&= \begin{pmatrix} 0 \\ 0 \\ 0 \end{pmatrix} \circ \begin{pmatrix} 1 - \tanh^2 (1.1 + 0.3 \tanh 0.5) \\ 1 - \tanh^2 (1.1 + 0.3 \tanh 0.5) \\ 1 - \tanh^2 (1.1 + 0.3 \tanh 0.5) \end{pmatrix} \\
&= \begin{pmatrix} 0 \\ 0 \\ 0 \end{pmatrix}
\end{aligned}
$$

For the hidden layer of the firs time step we have:

$$
\begin{aligned}
\delta_{(1)}^{[1]} &= \left(\mathbf{H}^{[1]} \right)^T \bullet \delta_{(2)}^{[1]} \circ \left(1 - \tanh^2 \mathbf{z}_{(1)}^{[1]} \right) \\
&= \begin{pmatrix} 0.1 \; 0.1 \; 0.1 \\ 0.1 \; 0.1 \; 0.1 \\ 0.1 \; 0.1 \; 0.1 \end{pmatrix} \bullet \begin{pmatrix} 0 \\ 0 \\ 0 \end{pmatrix} \circ \begin{pmatrix} 1 - \tanh^2 0.5 \\ 1 - \tanh^2 0.5 \\ 1 - \tanh^2 0.5 \end{pmatrix} \\
&= \begin{pmatrix} 0 \\ 0 \\ 0 \end{pmatrix} \circ \begin{pmatrix} 1 - \tanh^2 0.5 \\ 1 - \tanh^2 0.5 \\ 1 - \tanh^2 0.5 \end{pmatrix} \\
&= \begin{pmatrix} 0 \\ 0 \\ 0 \end{pmatrix}
\end{aligned}
$$

Having the deltas, we can compute the specific gradients for all parameters. Each gradient corresponds to the sum across all backward paths that lead to that parameter.

$$\frac{\partial E}{\partial \mathbf{H}^{[1]}} = \sum_{t=1}^{T} \delta_{(t)}^{[1]} \frac{\partial \mathbf{z}_{(t)}^{[1]}}{\partial \mathbf{H}^{[1]}}$$

$$= \delta_{(1)}^{[1]} \bullet \left(\frac{\partial \mathbf{z}_{(1)}^{[1]}}{\partial \mathbf{H}^{[1]}} \right)^{T} + \delta_{(2)}^{[1]} \bullet \left(\frac{\partial \mathbf{z}_{(2)}^{[1]}}{\partial \mathbf{H}^{[1]}} \right)^{T}$$

$$= \delta_{(1)}^{[1]} \bullet \left(\mathbf{x}_{(0)}^{[0]} \right)^{T} + \delta_{(2)}^{[1]} \bullet \left(\mathbf{x}_{(1)}^{[1]} \right)^{T}$$

$$= \begin{pmatrix} 0 \\ 0 \\ 0 \end{pmatrix} (0\ 0\ 0) + \begin{pmatrix} 0 \\ 0 \\ 0 \end{pmatrix} \left(\tanh 0.5 \ \tanh 0.5 \ \tanh 0.5 \right)$$

$$= \begin{pmatrix} 0\ 0\ 0 \\ 0\ 0\ 0 \\ 0\ 0\ 0 \end{pmatrix}$$

$$\frac{\partial E}{\partial \mathbf{W}^{[1]}} = \sum_{t=1}^{T} \delta_{(t)}^{[1]} \frac{\partial \mathbf{z}_{(t)}^{[1]}}{\partial \mathbf{W}^{[1]}}$$

$$= \delta_{(1)}^{[1]} \bullet \left(\frac{\partial \mathbf{z}_{(1)}^{[1]}}{\partial \mathbf{W}^{[1]}} \right)^{T} + \delta_{(2)}^{[1]} \bullet \left(\frac{\partial \mathbf{z}_{(2)}^{[1]}}{\partial \mathbf{W}^{[1]}} \right)^{T}$$

$$= \delta_{(1)}^{[1]} \bullet \left(\mathbf{x}_{(1)}^{[0]} \right)^{T} + \delta_{(2)}^{[1]} \bullet \left(\mathbf{x}_{(2)}^{[0]} \right)^{T}$$

$$= \begin{pmatrix} 0 \\ 0 \\ 0 \end{pmatrix} (4\ 0\ 0\ 0) + \begin{pmatrix} 0 \\ 0 \\ 0 \end{pmatrix} (0\ 8\ 2\ 0)$$

$$= \begin{pmatrix} 0\ 0\ 0\ 0 \\ 0\ 0\ 0\ 0 \\ 0\ 0\ 0\ 0 \end{pmatrix}$$

$$\frac{\partial E}{\partial \mathbf{b}^{[1]}} = \sum_{t=1}^{T} \delta_{(t)}^{[1]} \frac{\partial \mathbf{z}_{(t)}^{[1]}}{\partial \mathbf{b}^{[1]}}$$

$$= \delta_{(1)}^{[1]} \circ \frac{\partial \mathbf{z}_{(1)}^{[1]}}{\partial \mathbf{b}^{[1]}} + \delta_{(2)}^{[1]} \circ \frac{\partial \mathbf{z}_{(2)}^{[1]}}{\partial \mathbf{b}^{[1]}}$$

$$= \delta_{(1)}^{[1]} \circ \mathbf{1} + \delta_{(2)}^{[1]} \circ \mathbf{1}$$

$$= \begin{pmatrix} 0 \\ 0 \\ 0 \end{pmatrix} + \begin{pmatrix} 0 \\ 0 \\ 0 \end{pmatrix}$$

$$= \begin{pmatrix} 0 \\ 0 \\ 0 \end{pmatrix}$$

For the output layer parameters there is no sum because, unlike the many-to-many network, this network only has an output layer for the last-time step:

$$\frac{\partial E}{\partial \mathbf{W}^{[2]}} = \delta_{(T)}^{[2]} \frac{\partial \mathbf{z}_{(T)}^{[2]}}{\partial \mathbf{W}^{[2]}}$$

$$= \delta_{(2)}^{[2]} \bullet \left(\frac{\partial \mathbf{z}_{(2)}^{[2]}}{\partial \mathbf{W}^{[2]}} \right)^{T}$$

$$= \begin{pmatrix} 0.5 \\ -0.5 \end{pmatrix} \bullet \left(\tanh \begin{pmatrix} 1.1 + 0.3 \tanh 0.5 \\ 1.1 + 0.3 \tanh 0.5 \\ 1.1 + 0.3 \tanh 0.5 \end{pmatrix} \right)^{T}$$

$$= \begin{pmatrix} 0.5 \\ -0.5 \end{pmatrix} \bullet \begin{pmatrix} d & d & d \end{pmatrix}$$

$$= \begin{pmatrix} 0.5d & 0.5d & 0.5d \\ -0.5d & -0.5d & -0.5d \end{pmatrix}$$

Where $d = \tanh(1.1 + 0.3 \tanh 0.5)$.

$$\frac{\partial E}{\partial \mathbf{b}^{[2]}} = \delta_{(T)}^{[2]} \frac{\partial \mathbf{z}_{(T)}^{[2]}}{\partial \mathbf{b}^{[2]}}$$

$$= \delta_{(2)}^{[2]} \circ \frac{\partial \mathbf{z}_{(2)}^{[2]}}{\partial \mathbf{b}^{[2]}}$$

$$= \delta_{(2)}^{[2]} \circ \mathbf{1}$$

$$= \begin{pmatrix} 0.5 \\ -0.5 \end{pmatrix}$$

Having the gradients, we can perform the stochastic gradient descent updates for all parameters:

$$\mathbf{H}^{[1]} = \mathbf{H}^{[1]} - \eta \frac{\partial E}{\partial \mathbf{H}^{[1]}}$$

$$= \begin{pmatrix} 0.1\ 0.1\ 0.1 \\ 0.1\ 0.1\ 0.1 \\ 0.1\ 0.1\ 0.1 \end{pmatrix} - 1 \begin{pmatrix} 0\ 0\ 0 \\ 0\ 0\ 0 \\ 0\ 0\ 0 \end{pmatrix}$$

$$= \begin{pmatrix} 0.1\ 0.1\ 0.1 \\ 0.1\ 0.1\ 0.1 \\ 0.1\ 0.1\ 0.1 \end{pmatrix}$$

$$\mathbf{W}^{[1]} = \mathbf{W}^{[1]} - \eta \frac{\partial E}{\partial \mathbf{W}^{[1]}}$$

$$= \begin{pmatrix} 0.1\ 0.1\ 0.1\ 0.1 \\ 0.1\ 0.1\ 0.1\ 0.1 \\ 0.1\ 0.1\ 0.1\ 0.1 \end{pmatrix} - 1 \begin{pmatrix} 0\ 0\ 0\ 0 \\ 0\ 0\ 0\ 0 \\ 0\ 0\ 0\ 0 \end{pmatrix}$$

$$= \begin{pmatrix} 0.1\ 0.1\ 0.1\ 0.1 \\ 0.1\ 0.1\ 0.1\ 0.1 \\ 0.1\ 0.1\ 0.1\ 0.1 \end{pmatrix}$$

$$\mathbf{b}^{[1]} = \mathbf{b}^{[1]} - \eta \frac{\partial E}{\partial \mathbf{b}^{[1]}}$$

$$= \begin{pmatrix} 0.1 \\ 0.1 \\ 0.1 \end{pmatrix} - 1 \begin{pmatrix} 0 \\ 0 \\ 0 \end{pmatrix}$$

$$= \begin{pmatrix} 0.1 \\ 0.1 \\ 0.1 \end{pmatrix}$$

$$\mathbf{W}^{[2]} = \mathbf{W}^{[2]} - \eta \frac{\partial E}{\partial \mathbf{W}^{[2]}}$$

$$= \begin{pmatrix} 0.1\ 0.1\ 0.1 \\ 0.1\ 0.1\ 0.1 \end{pmatrix} - 1 \begin{pmatrix} 0.5d & 0.5d & 0.5d \\ -0.5d & -0.5d & -0.5d \end{pmatrix}$$

$$= \begin{pmatrix} 0.1 - 0.5d\ 0.1 - 0.5d\ 0.1 - 0.5d \\ 0.1 + 0.5d\ 0.1 + 0.5d\ 0.1 + 0.5d \end{pmatrix}$$

$$= \begin{pmatrix} -0.3225 & -0.3225 & -0.3225 \\ 0.5225 & 0.5225 & 0.5225 \end{pmatrix}$$

$$\mathbf{b}^{[2]} = \mathbf{b}^{[2]} - \eta \frac{\partial E}{\partial \mathbf{b}^{[2]}}$$

$$= \begin{pmatrix} 0.1 \\ 0.1 \end{pmatrix} - 1 \begin{pmatrix} 0.5 \\ -0.5 \end{pmatrix}$$

$$= \begin{pmatrix} -0.4 \\ 0.6 \end{pmatrix}$$

---

4)

Consider a recurrent network with one hidden layer to solve a **many-to-one** task. Take into account that:

- The recurrent connections happen between the hidden layers
- The hidden activation function is the hyperbolic tangent
- The output activation function is the identity
- The error function is the half squared error between output and target

a) Write down the model equations for forward propagation.

Solution:

Time steps before the last $t \in \{1, \dots, T-1\}$ are only processed until the hidden layer:

$$\mathbf{z}_{(t)}^{[1]} = \mathbf{H}^{[1]} \mathbf{x}_{(t-1)}^{[1]} + \mathbf{W}^{[1]} \mathbf{x}_{(t)}^{[0]} + \mathbf{b}^{[1]}$$

$$\mathbf{x}_{(t)}^{[1]} = \tanh\left(\mathbf{z}_{(t)}^{[1]}\right)$$

The lasttime step receives the hidden state from the previoustime step and performs the full network operation until the output:

$$\mathbf{z}_{(T)}^{[1]} = \mathbf{H}^{[1]} \mathbf{x}_{(T-1)}^{[1]} + \mathbf{W}^{[1]} \mathbf{x}_{(T)}^{[0]} + \mathbf{b}^{[1]}$$

$$\mathbf{x}_{(T)}^{[1]} = \tanh\left(\mathbf{z}_{(T)}^{[1]}\right)$$

$$\mathbf{z}_{(T)}^{[2]} = \mathbf{W}^{[2]} \mathbf{x}_{(T)}^{[1]} + \mathbf{b}^{[2]}$$

$$\mathbf{x}_{(T)}^{[2]} = \mathbf{z}_{(T)}^{[2]}$$

$$e = -\mathbf{t} \bullet \log \mathbf{x}_{(T)}^{[2]}$$

b) Write down the model equations for backward propagation.

Solution:

Since we are working with a many to one network only the lasttime step will have a delta for the output layer. So, applying the chain–rule we get:

$$\delta_{(T)}^{[2]} = \frac{\partial E}{\partial \mathbf{x}_{(T)}^{[2]}} \frac{\partial \mathbf{x}_{(T)}^{[2]}}{\mathbf{z}_{(T)}^{[2]}}$$

$$= \left(\mathbf{x}_{(T)}^{[2]} - \mathbf{t}_{(T)} \right) \circ 1$$

$$= \mathbf{x}_{(T)}^{[2]} - \mathbf{t}_{(T)}$$

For the last time step T, the delta for the hidden layer is independent of all other time steps. Using the chain-rule we get:

$$\delta_{(T)}^{[1]} = \delta_{(T)}^{[2]} \frac{\partial \mathbf{z}_{(T)}^{[2]}}{\partial \mathbf{x}_{(T)}^{[1]}} \frac{\partial \mathbf{x}_{(T)}^{[1]}}{\partial \mathbf{z}_{(T)}^{[1]}}$$

$$= \left(\frac{\partial \mathbf{z}_{(T)}^{[2]}}{\partial \mathbf{x}_{(T)}^{[1]}} \right)^T \bullet \delta_{(T)}^{[2]} \circ \frac{\partial \mathbf{x}_{(T)}^{[1]}}{\partial \mathbf{z}_{(T)}^{[1]}}$$

$$= \left(\mathbf{W}^{[2]} \right)^T \bullet \delta_{(T)}^{[2]} \circ \left(1 - \tanh^2 \mathbf{z}_{(T)}^{[1]} \right)$$

For all other time steps $t \in \{1, \ldots, T-1\}$, the delta for the hidden layer depends only on the nexttime step's hidden layer. Using the chain-rule we get:

$$\delta_{(t)}^{[1]} = \delta_{(t+1)}^{[1]} \frac{\partial \mathbf{z}_{(t+1)}^{[1]}}{\partial \mathbf{x}_{(t)}^{[1]}} \frac{\partial \mathbf{x}_{(t)}^{[1]}}{\partial \mathbf{z}_{(t)}^{[1]}}$$

$$= \left(\frac{\partial \mathbf{z}_{(t+1)}^{[1]}}{\partial \mathbf{x}_{(t)}^{[1]}} \right)^T \bullet \delta_{(t+1)}^{[1]} \circ \frac{\partial \mathbf{x}_{(t)}^{[1]}}{\partial \mathbf{z}_{(t)}^{[1]}}$$

$$= \left(\mathbf{H}^{[1]} \right)^T \bullet \delta_{(t+1)}^{[1]} \circ \left(1 - \tanh^2 \mathbf{z}_{(t)}^{[1]} \right)$$

c) Perform a stochastic gradient descent update for:

$$x^{(1)} = \left[\begin{pmatrix} 4 \\ 0 \\ 0 \\ 0 \end{pmatrix}, \begin{pmatrix} 0 \\ 8 \\ 2 \\ 0 \end{pmatrix} \right]$$

With targets:

$$\mathbf{t} = \begin{pmatrix} 0 \\ 1 \end{pmatrix}$$

Initialize all weights and biases to 0.1, using 3 units per hidden layer, initializing the hidden state to all zeros and using $\eta = 1.0$.

Solution:

Initializing the parameters, we have:

$$\mathbf{W}^{[1]} = \begin{pmatrix} 0.1\ 0.1\ 0.1\ 0.1 \\ 0.1\ 0.1\ 0.1\ 0.1 \\ 0.1\ 0.1\ 0.1\ 0.1 \end{pmatrix}$$

$$\mathbf{b}^{[1]} = \begin{pmatrix} 0.1 \\ 0.1 \\ 0.1 \end{pmatrix}$$

$$\mathbf{H}^{[1]} = \begin{pmatrix} 0.1\ 0.1\ 0.1 \\ 0.1\ 0.1\ 0.1 \\ 0.1\ 0.1\ 0.1 \end{pmatrix}$$

$$\mathbf{W}^{[2]} = \begin{pmatrix} 0.1\ 0.1\ 0.1 \\ 0.1\ 0.1\ 0.1 \end{pmatrix}$$

$$\mathbf{b}^{[2]} = \begin{pmatrix} 0.1 \\ 0.1 \end{pmatrix}$$

$$\mathbf{x}^{[1]}_{(0)} = \begin{pmatrix} 0 \\ 0 \\ 0 \end{pmatrix}$$

Now, we can use **a)** to apply forward propagation. Let us start with time step $t = 1$:

$$\mathbf{z}^{[1]}_{(1)} = \begin{pmatrix} 0.1\ 0.1\ 0.1 \\ 0.1\ 0.1\ 0.1 \\ 0.1\ 0.1\ 0.1 \end{pmatrix} \begin{pmatrix} 0 \\ 0 \\ 0 \end{pmatrix} + \begin{pmatrix} 0.1\ 0.1\ 0.1\ 0.1 \\ 0.1\ 0.1\ 0.1\ 0.1 \\ 0.1\ 0.1\ 0.1\ 0.1 \end{pmatrix} \begin{pmatrix} 4 \\ 0 \\ 0 \\ 0 \end{pmatrix} + \begin{pmatrix} 0.1 \\ 0.1 \\ 0.1 \end{pmatrix}$$

$$= \begin{pmatrix} 0.5 \\ 0.5 \\ 0.5 \end{pmatrix}$$

$$\mathbf{x}^{[1]}_{(1)} = \tanh \begin{pmatrix} 0.5 \\ 0.5 \\ 0.5 \end{pmatrix}$$

Now we can apply the same logic to the second time step.

$$z_{(2)}^{[1]} = \begin{pmatrix} 0.1\ 0.1\ 0.1 \\ 0.1\ 0.1\ 0.1 \\ 0.1\ 0.1\ 0.1 \end{pmatrix} \tanh \begin{pmatrix} 0.5 \\ 0.5 \\ 0.5 \end{pmatrix} + \begin{pmatrix} 0.1\ 0.1\ 0.1\ 0.1 \\ 0.1\ 0.1\ 0.1\ 0.1 \\ 0.1\ 0.1\ 0.1\ 0.1 \end{pmatrix} \begin{pmatrix} 0 \\ 8 \\ 2 \\ 0 \end{pmatrix} + \begin{pmatrix} 0.1 \\ 0.1 \\ 0.1 \end{pmatrix}$$

$$= \begin{pmatrix} 1.1 + 0.3 \tanh 0.5 \\ 1.1 + 0.3 \tanh 0.5 \\ 1.1 + 0.3 \tanh 0.5 \end{pmatrix}$$

$$x_{(2)}^{[1]} = \tanh \begin{pmatrix} 1.1 + 0.3 \tanh 0.5 \\ 1.1 + 0.3 \tanh 0.5 \\ 1.1 + 0.3 \tanh 0.5 \end{pmatrix}$$

$$z_{(2)}^{[2]} = \begin{pmatrix} 0.1\ 0.1\ 0.1 \\ 0.1\ 0.1\ 0.1 \end{pmatrix} \tanh \begin{pmatrix} 1.1 + 0.3 \tanh 0.5 \\ 1.1 + 0.3 \tanh 0.5 \\ 1.1 + 0.3 \tanh 0.5 \end{pmatrix} + \begin{pmatrix} 0.1 \\ 0.1 \end{pmatrix}$$

$$= \begin{pmatrix} 0.3 \tanh (1.1 + 0.3 \tanh 0.5) + 0.1 \\ 0.3 \tanh (1.1 + 0.3 \tanh 0.5) + 0.1 \end{pmatrix}$$

$$x_{(2)}^{[2]} = \begin{pmatrix} 0.3 \tanh (1.1 + 0.3 \tanh 0.5) + 0.1 \\ 0.3 \tanh (1.1 + 0.3 \tanh 0.5) + 0.1 \end{pmatrix}$$

After finishing forward propagation, we can use **b)** to perform backward propagation. For the output layer in the lasttime step we have:

$$\delta_{(2)}^{[2]} = x_{(2)}^{[2]} - t_{(2)}$$

$$= \begin{pmatrix} 0.3 \tanh (1.1 + 0.3 \tanh 0.5) + 0.1 \\ 0.3 \tanh (1.1 + 0.3 \tanh 0.5) + 0.1 \end{pmatrix} - \begin{pmatrix} 0 \\ 1 \end{pmatrix}$$

$$= \begin{pmatrix} o \\ o - 1 \end{pmatrix}$$

Where $o = 0.3 \tanh (1.1 + 0.3 \tanh 0.5) + 0.1$.

For the hidden layer of the lasttime step we have:

$$\delta^{[1]}_{(2)} = \left(\mathbf{W}^{[2]}\right)^T \bullet \delta^{[2]}_{(2)} \circ \left(1 - \tanh^2 \mathbf{z}^{[1]}_{(2)}\right)$$

$$= \begin{pmatrix} 0.1\ 0.1 \\ 0.1\ 0.1 \\ 0.1\ 0.1 \end{pmatrix} \bullet \begin{pmatrix} o \\ o-1 \end{pmatrix} \circ \begin{pmatrix} 1 - \tanh^2\left(1.1 + 0.3\tanh 0.5\right) \\ 1 - \tanh^2\left(1.1 + 0.3\tanh 0.5\right) \\ 1 - \tanh^2\left(1.1 + 0.3\tanh 0.5\right) \end{pmatrix}$$

$$= \begin{pmatrix} 0.2o - 0.1 \\ 0.2o - 0.1 \\ 0.2o - 0.1 \end{pmatrix} \circ \begin{pmatrix} 1 - \tanh^2\left(1.1 + 0.3\tanh 0.5\right) \\ 1 - \tanh^2\left(1.1 + 0.3\tanh 0.5\right) \\ 1 - \tanh^2\left(1.1 + 0.3\tanh 0.5\right) \end{pmatrix}$$

$$= \begin{pmatrix} h_2 \\ h_2 \\ h_2 \end{pmatrix}$$

Where $h_2 = (0.2o - 0.1)\left(1 - \tanh^2\left(1.1 + 0.3\tanh 0.5\right)\right)$.
For the hidden layer of the firsttime step we have:

$$\delta^{[1]}_{(1)} = \left(\mathbf{H}^{[1]}\right)^T \bullet \begin{pmatrix} h_2 \\ h_2 \\ h_2 \end{pmatrix} \circ \left(1 - \tanh^2 \mathbf{z}^{[1]}_{(1)}\right)$$

$$= \begin{pmatrix} 0.1\ 0.1\ 0.1 \\ 0.1\ 0.1\ 0.1 \\ 0.1\ 0.1\ 0.1 \end{pmatrix} \bullet \begin{pmatrix} h_2 \\ h_2 \\ h_2 \end{pmatrix} \circ \begin{pmatrix} 1 - \tanh^2 0.5 \\ 1 - \tanh^2 0.5 \\ 1 - \tanh^2 0.5 \end{pmatrix}$$

$$= \begin{pmatrix} 0.3h_2 \\ 0.3h_2 \\ 0.3h_2 \end{pmatrix} \circ \begin{pmatrix} 1 - \tanh^2 0.5 \\ 1 - \tanh^2 0.5 \\ 1 - \tanh^2 0.5 \end{pmatrix}$$

$$= \begin{pmatrix} h_1 \\ h_1 \\ h_1 \end{pmatrix}$$

Where $h_1 = 0.3h_2\left(1 - \tanh^2 0.5\right)$.

Having the deltas, we can compute the specific gradients for all parameters. Each gradient corresponds to the sum across all backward paths that lead to that parameter.

$$\frac{\partial E}{\partial \mathbf{H}^{[1]}} = \sum_{t=1}^{T} \delta_{(t)}^{[1]} \frac{\partial \mathbf{z}_{(t)}^{[1]}}{\partial \mathbf{H}^{[1]}}$$

$$= \delta_{(1)}^{[1]} \bullet \left(\frac{\partial \mathbf{z}_{(1)}^{[1]}}{\partial \mathbf{H}^{[1]}} \right)^{T} + \delta_{(2)}^{[1]} \bullet \left(\frac{\partial \mathbf{z}_{(2)}^{[1]}}{\partial \mathbf{H}^{[1]}} \right)^{T}$$

$$= \delta_{(1)}^{[1]} \bullet \left(\mathbf{x}_{(0)}^{[0]} \right)^{T} + \delta_{(2)}^{[1]} \bullet \left(\mathbf{x}_{(1)}^{[1]} \right)^{T}$$

$$= \begin{pmatrix} h_1 \\ h_1 \\ h_1 \end{pmatrix} (0\ 0\ 0) + \begin{pmatrix} h_2 \\ h_2 \\ h_2 \end{pmatrix} (\tanh 0.5 \ \tanh 0.5 \ \tanh 0.5)$$

$$= \begin{pmatrix} h_2 \tanh 0.5 \ h_2 \tanh 0.5 \ h_2 \tanh 0.5 \\ h_2 \tanh 0.5 \ h_2 \tanh 0.5 \ h_2 \tanh 0.5 \\ h_2 \tanh 0.5 \ h_2 \tanh 0.5 \ h_2 \tanh 0.5 \end{pmatrix}$$

$$\frac{\partial E}{\partial \mathbf{W}^{[1]}} = \sum_{t=1}^{T} \delta_{(t)}^{[1]} \frac{\partial \mathbf{z}_{(t)}^{[1]}}{\partial \mathbf{W}^{[1]}}$$

$$= \delta_{(1)}^{[1]} \bullet \left(\frac{\partial \mathbf{z}_{(1)}^{[1]}}{\partial \mathbf{W}^{[1]}} \right)^{T} + \delta_{(2)}^{[1]} \bullet \left(\frac{\partial \mathbf{z}_{(2)}^{[1]}}{\partial \mathbf{W}^{[1]}} \right)^{T}$$

$$= \delta_{(1)}^{[1]} \bullet \left(\mathbf{x}_{(1)}^{[0]} \right)^{T} + \delta_{(2)}^{[1]} \bullet \left(\mathbf{x}_{(2)}^{[0]} \right)^{T}$$

$$= \begin{pmatrix} h_1 \\ h_1 \\ h_1 \end{pmatrix} (4\ 0\ 0\ 0) + \begin{pmatrix} h_2 \\ h_2 \\ h_2 \end{pmatrix} (0\ 8\ 2\ 0)$$

$$= \begin{pmatrix} 4h_1\ 0\ 0\ 0 \\ 4h_1\ 0\ 0\ 0 \\ 4h_1\ 0\ 0\ 0 \end{pmatrix} + \begin{pmatrix} 0\ 8h_2\ 2h_2\ 0 \\ 0\ 8h_2\ 2h_2\ 0 \\ 0\ 8h_2\ 2h_2\ 0 \end{pmatrix}$$

$$= \begin{pmatrix} 4h_1\ 8h_2\ 2h_2\ 0 \\ 4h_1\ 8h_2\ 2h_2\ 0 \\ 4h_1\ 8h_2\ 2h_2\ 0 \end{pmatrix}$$

$$\frac{\partial E}{\partial \mathbf{b}^{[1]}} = \sum_{t=1}^{T} \delta_{(t)}^{[1]} \frac{\partial \mathbf{z}_{(t)}^{[1]}}{\partial \mathbf{b}^{[1]}}$$

$$= \delta_{(1)}^{[1]} \circ \frac{\partial \mathbf{z}_{(1)}^{[1]}}{\partial \mathbf{b}^{[1]}} + \delta_{(2)}^{[1]} \circ \frac{\partial \mathbf{z}_{(2)}^{[1]}}{\partial \mathbf{b}^{[1]}}$$

$$= \delta_{(1)}^{[1]} \circ \mathbf{1} + \delta_{(2)}^{[1]} \circ \mathbf{1}$$

$$= \begin{pmatrix} h_1 \\ h_1 \\ h_1 \end{pmatrix} + \begin{pmatrix} h_2 \\ h_2 \\ h_2 \end{pmatrix}$$

$$= \begin{pmatrix} h_1 + h_2 \\ h_1 + h_2 \\ h_1 + h_2 \end{pmatrix}$$

For the output layer parameters there is no sum because, unlike the many-to-many network, this network only has an output layer for the last-time step:

$$\frac{\partial E}{\partial \mathbf{W}^{[2]}} = \delta_{(T)}^{[2]} \frac{\partial \mathbf{z}_{(T)}^{[2]}}{\partial \mathbf{W}^{[2]}}$$

$$= \delta_{(2)}^{[2]} \bullet \left(\frac{\partial \mathbf{z}_{(2)}^{[2]}}{\partial \mathbf{W}^{[2]}} \right)^T$$

$$= \begin{pmatrix} o \\ o-1 \end{pmatrix} \bullet \left(\tanh \begin{pmatrix} 1.1 + 0.3 \tanh 0.5 \\ 1.1 + 0.3 \tanh 0.5 \\ 1.1 + 0.3 \tanh 0.5 \end{pmatrix} \right)^T$$

$$= \begin{pmatrix} o \\ o-1 \end{pmatrix} \bullet \begin{pmatrix} w & w & w \end{pmatrix}$$

$$= \begin{pmatrix} ow & ow & ow \\ (o-1)w & (o-1)w & (o-1)w \end{pmatrix}$$

Where $w = \tanh(1.1 + 0.3 \tanh 0.5)$.

$$\frac{\partial E}{\partial \mathbf{b}^{[2]}} = \delta_{(T)}^{[2]} \frac{\partial \mathbf{z}_{(T)}^{[2]}}{\partial \mathbf{b}^{[2]}}$$

$$= \delta_{(2)}^{[2]} \circ \frac{\partial \mathbf{z}_{(2)}^{[2]}}{\partial \mathbf{b}^{[2]}}$$

$$= \delta_{(2)}^{[2]} \circ \mathbf{1}$$

$$= \begin{pmatrix} o \\ o - 1 \end{pmatrix}$$

Having the gradients, we can perform the stochastic gradient descent updates for all parameters:

$$\mathbf{H}^{[1]} = \mathbf{H}^{[1]} - \eta \frac{\partial E}{\partial \mathbf{H}^{[1]}}$$

$$= \begin{pmatrix} 0.1\ 0.1\ 0.1 \\ 0.1\ 0.1\ 0.1 \\ 0.1\ 0.1\ 0.1 \end{pmatrix} - 1 \begin{pmatrix} h_2 \tanh 0.5\ h_2 \tanh 0.5\ h_2 \tanh 0.5 \\ h_2 \tanh 0.5\ h_2 \tanh 0.5\ h_2 \tanh 0.5 \\ h_2 \tanh 0.5\ h_2 \tanh 0.5\ h_2 \tanh 0.5 \end{pmatrix}$$

$$= \begin{pmatrix} 0.1039\ 0.1039\ 0.1039 \\ 0.1039\ 0.1039\ 0.1039 \\ 0.1039\ 0.1039\ 0.1039 \end{pmatrix}$$

$$\mathbf{W}^{[1]} = \mathbf{W}^{[1]} - \eta \frac{\partial E}{\partial \mathbf{W}^{[1]}}$$

$$= \begin{pmatrix} 0.1\ 0.1\ 0.1\ 0.1 \\ 0.1\ 0.1\ 0.1\ 0.1 \\ 0.1\ 0.1\ 0.1\ 0.1 \end{pmatrix} - 1 \begin{pmatrix} 4h_1\ 8h_2\ 2h_2\ 0 \\ 4h_1\ 8h_2\ 2h_2\ 0 \\ 4h_1\ 8h_2\ 2h_2\ 0 \end{pmatrix}$$

$$= \begin{pmatrix} 0.1079\ 0.1669\ 0.1167\ 0.1 \\ 0.1079\ 0.1669\ 0.1167\ 0.1 \\ 0.1079\ 0.1669\ 0.1167\ 0.1 \end{pmatrix}$$

$$\mathbf{b}^{[1]} = \mathbf{b}^{[1]} - \eta \frac{\partial E}{\partial \mathbf{b}^{[1]}}$$

$$= \begin{pmatrix} 0.1 \\ 0.1 \\ 0.1 \end{pmatrix} - 1 \begin{pmatrix} h_1 + h_2 \\ h_1 + h_2 \\ h_1 + h_2 \end{pmatrix}$$

$$= \begin{pmatrix} 0.1104 \\ 0.1104 \\ 0.1104 \end{pmatrix}$$

$$\mathbf{W}^{[2]} = \mathbf{W}^{[2]} - \eta \frac{\partial E}{\partial \mathbf{W}^{[2]}}$$

$$= \begin{pmatrix} 0.1 \; 0.1 \; 0.1 \\ 0.1 \; 0.1 \; 0.1 \end{pmatrix} - 1 \begin{pmatrix} ow & ow & ow \\ (o-1)\,w & (o-1)\,w & (o-1)\,w \end{pmatrix}$$

$$= \begin{pmatrix} -0.1987 & -0.1987 & -0.1987 \\ 0.6463 & 0.6463 & 0.6463 \end{pmatrix}$$

$$\mathbf{b}^{[2]} = \mathbf{b}^{[2]} - \eta \frac{\partial E}{\partial \mathbf{b}^{[2]}}$$

$$= \begin{pmatrix} 0.1 \\ 0.1 \end{pmatrix} - 1 \begin{pmatrix} o \\ o-1 \end{pmatrix}$$

$$= \begin{pmatrix} -0.2535 \\ 0.7465 \end{pmatrix}$$

Thinking Questions

Why is it said that backpropagation through time is very hard to implement in parallel?

Chapter 15

Autoencoders

Fig. 15.1 An autoencoder is a neural network that is trained to attempt to copy its input to its output. By copying the input through a restricted channel, useful properties of the data are learned.

15.1   Eigenvectors and Eigenvalues

Consider a matrix C of dimensions $m \times m$. All vectors $\mathbf{u}$ that do not change direction when multiplied by C make up the set of C's eigenvectors. Although these special vectors do not change direction, they may well change orientation or even magnitude. So, we may write

$$C \cdot \mathbf{u} = \lambda \cdot \mathbf{u} \tag{15.1}$$

and we call λ the eigenvalue that corresponds to $\mathbf{u}$.

For an $m \times m$ matrix there are m orthogonal directions along which all vectors are eigenvectors. So, it is common to restrict the concept of eigenvectors to normalized vectors only. That is, vectors with norm equal to one. So, we can rewrite our condition for a given eigenvector $\mathbf{u}_i$, which is a unitary norm vector along the i-th direction, with $i = 1, \cdots, m$ as

$$C \cdot \mathbf{u}_i = \lambda_i \cdot \mathbf{u}_i,$$

which can be rearranged to yield

$$(\lambda_i \cdot I - C) \cdot \mathbf{u}_i = 0.$$

So, we have m conditions, one for each eigenvalue eigenvector pair. Note that for each of the m directions we can have two unitary norm eigenvectors: a "positive" one $\mathbf{u}_i$ and a "negative" one $-\mathbf{u}_i$. So we could also write

$$C \cdot (-\mathbf{u}_i) = \lambda_i \cdot (-\mathbf{u}_i). \tag{15.2}$$

It is common to write an $m \times m$ orthonormal matrix U where the normalized eigenvectors are placed in the columns. One may think of this matrix U as defining a coordinate system. For example, in two-dimensions, the identity matrix

$$\begin{pmatrix} 1 & 0 \\ 0 & 1 \end{pmatrix},$$

contains the directions of the typical coordinate system in the columns. Following the same reasoning, U contains the directions of a coordinate system where the two axis are the two directions for which there are eigenvectors.

15.2   The Karhunen-Loève transform

A real matrix C is positive definite if $\mathbf{z}^\top \cdot C \cdot \mathbf{z} > 0$ for any non-zero column vector $\mathbf{z}$ of real numbers. A symmetric and positive-definite matrix can be diagonalized using its eigendecomposition as

$$U^{-1} \cdot C \cdot U = \Lambda = diag(\lambda_1, \lambda_2, \cdots . \lambda_m) \tag{15.3}$$

where U is the orthonormal $m \times m$ matrix of eigenvectors. An orthonormal matrix is one where

$$U^\top \cdot U = I, \tag{15.4}$$

which means that its inverse equals its transpose $U^{-1} = U^\top$. Using this, we can rewrite the diagonalization as

$$U^\top \cdot C \cdot U = \Lambda = diag(\lambda_1, \lambda_2, \cdots .\lambda_m). \tag{15.5}$$

Multiplying both sides by U, we get

$$U \cdot \Lambda = C \cdot U. \tag{15.6}$$

Using the fact that both Λ and C are symmetric, we get

$$U^\top \cdot \Lambda = U^\top \cdot C. \tag{15.7}$$

Given a data set, consider its covariance matrix Σ or C as we had above. Applying the diagonalization idea, we know that the covariance becomes diagonal when multiplied by $U^\top$. A diagonal covariance means that all the variance is along the axis of the coordinate system and, in this case, the variances will be determined by the eigenvalues. So, we can see that multiplying on the left by $U^\top$ is the same as rotating the coordinate system for the data set from the original one into the eigenvector coordinate system.

This is exactly the idea behind the Karhunen-Loève (KL) transform. That is, to rotate the coordinate system under which the data is described using the eigenvector matrix U with

$$\mathbf{y} = U^\top \cdot \mathbf{x}. \tag{15.8}$$

After this rotation, if we recompute the covariance matrix, it will be diagonal.

Let us look at the example from the probability chapter. Our data was

$$Data = \{(2.1, 2), (2.3, 2), (2.9, 3), (4.1, 4), (5, 4.8), (2, 2.5), (2.2, 1.5),$$

$$(4, 5), (4, 2), (2.8, 4), (3, 3.4), (3.5, 3.8), (4.5, 4.7), (3.5, 3)\}.$$

Let us plot it again to get a feel for it, check Figure 15.2. We saw that the covariance matrix Σ was given by

$$\Sigma = \begin{pmatrix} 0.912582 & 0.82456 \\ 0.82456 & 1.34247 \end{pmatrix}. \tag{15.9}$$

The eigenvalues corresponding to the covariance matrix of the data set Σ are

$$\lambda_1 = 1.97964, \quad \lambda_2 = 0.275412$$

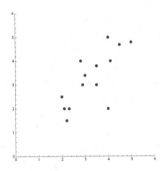

Fig. 15.2   The points in the data set *Data*.

and the corresponding normalized eigenvectors are

$$\mathbf{u}_1 = \begin{pmatrix} 0.611454 \\ 0.79128 \end{pmatrix}, \quad \mathbf{u}_2 = \begin{pmatrix} -0.79128 \\ 0.611454 \end{pmatrix}.$$

The transform matrix U is thus given by

$$U = \begin{pmatrix} 0.611454 & -0.79128 \\ 0.79128 & 0.611454 \end{pmatrix}. \tag{15.10}$$

With that, the Karhunen-Loève transform for the data set Σ is given by

$$\mathbf{y} = U^\top \cdot \mathbf{x} = \begin{pmatrix} 0.611454 & 0.79128 \\ -0.79128 & 0.611454 \end{pmatrix} \cdot \mathbf{x}. \tag{15.11}$$

Applying the transform to all points in Figure 15.2, we get Figure 15.3 and confirm the idea of coordinate system rotation.

15.2.1   *Principal component analysis*

Principal component analysis (PCA) is a technique that is useful for the compression of data. The purpose is to apply a transformation to the points that reduces the dimensionality of a data set by finding a new set of variables, smaller than the original set of variables, that nonetheless retains most of the sample's information.

Departing from the premise that uncorrelated features with higher variance contain more information. We can achieve a PCA departing from a KL transformation matrix U and removing columns that correspond to smaller λ_i, that is, dimensions with small variance. Following this reasoning, the first principal component corresponds to the normalized eigenvector with the highest variance and so on. According to the Kaiser criterion, the

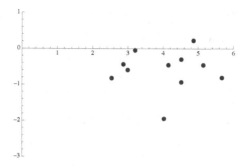

Fig. 15.3 The Karhunen-Loève transform for the the data set. We can see that It rotates the coordinate system (the points) in such a way that the new covariance matrix is diagonal.

eigenvectors whose eigenvalues are below 1 can be discarded [de Sá (2001)], [Wichert (2015)].

Applying the aforementioned logic and removing columns from U, we will end up with s non-discarded eigenvectors as the columns of a new matrix W of dimension $m \times s$. This PCA matrix W corresponds to a linear mapping from $\mathbb{R}^m \to \mathbb{R}^s$,

$$\mathbf{z} = W^\top \cdot \mathbf{x} \tag{15.12}$$

with $dim(s) \leq dim(m)$.

Using the Kaiser criterion, the PCA for our example data set would be given by

$$\mathbf{z} = W^\top \cdot \mathbf{x} = \begin{pmatrix} 0.611454 \, 0.79128 \end{pmatrix} \cdot \mathbf{x} \tag{15.13}$$

(see Figure 15.4). Since PCA depends on the covariance matrix, it must be

Fig. 15.4 Our two dimensional data set is projected onto one dimension.

recomputed every time we get new data.

15.2.1.1   *Examples*

Suppose we have a covariance matrix

$$C = \begin{pmatrix} 3 & 1 \\ 1 & 21 \end{pmatrix}. \tag{15.14}$$

What is the corresponding KL transformation matrix? First, we have to compute the eigenvalues. Recall that for every eigenvector we had

$$(\lambda_i \cdot I - C) \cdot \mathbf{u}_i = 0.$$

For any eigenvalue, the system has to become linear dependable (singular). So, the determinant has to become zero. Hence, we may write

$$|\lambda \cdot I - C| = 0. \tag{15.15}$$

Solving the equation we get

$$\lambda^2 - 24 \cdot \lambda + 62 = 0 \tag{15.16}$$

yielding the two eigenvalues

$$\lambda_1 = 2.94461, \quad \lambda_2 = 21.05538.$$

To compute the eigenvectors we have to solve two singular, dependent systems

$$(\lambda_1 \cdot I - C) \cdot \mathbf{u}_1 = 0$$

and

$$(\lambda_2 \cdot I - C) \cdot \mathbf{u}_i 2 = 0.$$

For $\lambda_1 = 2.94461$ we get

$$\left(\begin{pmatrix} 2.94461 & 0 \\ 0 & 2.94461 \end{pmatrix} - \begin{pmatrix} 3 & 1 \\ 1 & 21 \end{pmatrix} \right) \cdot \begin{pmatrix} u_1 \\ u_2 \end{pmatrix} = 0 \tag{15.17}$$

and we have to find a nontrivial solution for

$$\begin{pmatrix} -0.05538 & -1 \\ -1 & -18.055 \end{pmatrix} \cdot \begin{pmatrix} u_1 \\ u_2 \end{pmatrix} = 0. \tag{15.18}$$

Because the system is linear dependable, the left column is a multiple value of the right column, and there are infinitely many solutions. We only have to determine the direction of the eigenvectors; if we simply suppose that $u_1 = 1$,

$$\begin{pmatrix} -0.05538 & -1 \\ -1 & -18.055 \end{pmatrix} \cdot \begin{pmatrix} 1 \\ u_2 \end{pmatrix} = 0$$

and

$$\begin{pmatrix} -0.05538 \\ -1 \end{pmatrix} = \begin{pmatrix} 1 \\ 18.055 \end{pmatrix} \cdot u_2$$

we get

$$\mathbf{u}_1 = \begin{pmatrix} u_1 \\ u_2 \end{pmatrix} = \begin{pmatrix} 1 \\ -0.05539 \end{pmatrix}.$$

For $\lambda_2 = 21.05538$ we get

$$\begin{pmatrix} 18.055 & -1 \\ -1 & 0.05538 \end{pmatrix} \cdot \begin{pmatrix} u_1 \\ u_2 \end{pmatrix} = 0 \qquad (15.19)$$

and using the same reasoning, we end up with

$$\mathbf{u}_2 = \begin{pmatrix} u_1 \\ u_2 \end{pmatrix} = \begin{pmatrix} 1 \\ 18.055 \end{pmatrix}.$$

The two normalized vectors $\mathbf{u}_1$, $\mathbf{u}_2$ define the columns of U

$$U = \begin{pmatrix} 0.998469 & 0.0553016 \\ -0.0553052 & 0.99847 \end{pmatrix}.$$

Because $\lambda_1 = 2.94461 < \lambda_2 = 21.05538$ the second eigenvector is more significant, however we cannot apply the Kaiser criterion.

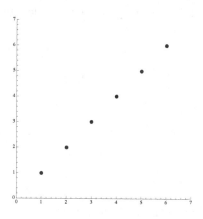

Fig. 15.5 The data points of the data set Ψ.

Now consider a second example with the data set in Figure 15.5 given by

$$\Psi = \{(1,1), (2,2), (3,3), (4,4), (5,5), (6,6)\}$$

the covariance matrix is

$$C = \begin{pmatrix} 3.5 & 3.5 \\ 3.5 & 3.5 \end{pmatrix}. \tag{15.20}$$

The two two eigenvalues are

$$\lambda_1 = 7, \quad \lambda_2 = 0$$

and the two normalized eigenvectors are

$$\mathbf{u}_1 = \begin{pmatrix} \frac{1}{\sqrt{2}} \\ \frac{1}{\sqrt{2}} \end{pmatrix}, \quad \mathbf{u}_2 = \begin{pmatrix} -\frac{1}{\sqrt{2}} \\ \frac{1}{\sqrt{2}} \end{pmatrix}.$$

The matrix that describes the KL transformation is given by

$$U = \begin{pmatrix} \frac{1}{\sqrt{2}} & \frac{1}{\sqrt{2}} \\ \frac{1}{\sqrt{2}} & -\frac{1}{\sqrt{2}} \end{pmatrix} = \frac{1}{\sqrt{2}} \cdot \begin{pmatrix} 1 & 1 \\ 1 & -1 \end{pmatrix} = \sqrt{2} \cdot \begin{pmatrix} \frac{1}{2} & \frac{1}{2} \\ \frac{1}{2} & -\frac{1}{2} \end{pmatrix}. \tag{15.21}$$

Applying PCA we map the two dimensional data set Ψ into one dimension because λ_2 is zero (see Figure 15.6). For example, the data point $(1, 1)$ is mapped on the x-axis

$$\begin{pmatrix} \sqrt{2} \\ 0 \end{pmatrix} = \begin{pmatrix} \sqrt{2} \cdot \frac{1+1}{2} \\ \sqrt{2} \cdot \frac{1-1}{2} \end{pmatrix} = \sqrt{2} \cdot \begin{pmatrix} \frac{1}{2} & \frac{1}{2} \\ \frac{1}{2} & -\frac{1}{2} \end{pmatrix} \cdot \begin{pmatrix} 1 \\ 1 \end{pmatrix} \tag{15.22}$$

with the value $\sqrt{2} \approx 1.4142$ corresponding to the length of the vector $(1, 1)$.

Fig. 15.6   The data set Ψ projected onto one dimension.

15.3   Singular Value Decomposition

In singular value decomposition any matrix A can be factorized as

$$A = U \cdot S \cdot V^T, \tag{15.23}$$

where U is an orthogonal matrix with orthonormal eigenvectors from $A \cdot A^T$ and V an orthogonal matrix with orthonormal eigenvectors from $A^T \cdot A$. S is a diagonal matrix with m elements equal to the root of the positive eigenvalues of $A \cdot A^T$ or $A^T \cdot A$.

15.3.1 *Example*

For matrix

$$A = \begin{pmatrix} 3 & 2 & 2 \\ 2 & 3 & -2 \end{pmatrix} \tag{15.24}$$

we get

$$A \cdot A^T = \begin{pmatrix} 17 & 8 \\ 8 & 17 \end{pmatrix} \tag{15.25}$$

with eigenvalues $\lambda_1 = 25$, $\lambda_2 = 9$ and orthonormal eigenvectors

$$u_1 = \begin{pmatrix} \frac{1}{\sqrt{2}} \\ \frac{1}{\sqrt{2}} \end{pmatrix}, \quad u_2 = \begin{pmatrix} \frac{1}{\sqrt{2}} \\ -\frac{1}{\sqrt{2}} \end{pmatrix}. \tag{15.26}$$

Furthermore, for

$$A^T \cdot A = \begin{pmatrix} 13 & 12 & 2 \\ 12 & 13 & -2 \\ 2 & -2 & 8 \end{pmatrix} \tag{15.27}$$

we get the eigenvalues $\lambda_1 = 25$, $\lambda_2 = 9$, $\lambda_3 = 0$ and the orthonormal eigenvectors

$$u_1 = \begin{pmatrix} \frac{1}{\sqrt{2}} \\ \frac{1}{\sqrt{2}} \\ 0 \end{pmatrix}, \quad u_2 = \begin{pmatrix} \frac{1}{\sqrt{18}} \\ -\frac{1}{\sqrt{18}} \\ \frac{4}{\sqrt{18}} \end{pmatrix}, \quad u_3 = \begin{pmatrix} \frac{2}{3} \\ -\frac{2}{3} \\ -\frac{1}{3} \end{pmatrix}. \tag{15.28}$$

The singular value decomposition for A is

$$A = U \cdot S \cdot V^T = \begin{pmatrix} \frac{1}{\sqrt{2}} & \frac{1}{\sqrt{2}} \\ \frac{1}{\sqrt{2}} & -\frac{1}{\sqrt{2}} \end{pmatrix} \cdot \begin{pmatrix} 5 & 0 & 0 \\ 0 & 3 & 0 \end{pmatrix} \cdot \begin{pmatrix} \frac{1}{\sqrt{2}} & \frac{1}{\sqrt{2}} & 0 \\ \frac{1}{\sqrt{18}} & -\frac{1}{\sqrt{18}} & \frac{4}{\sqrt{18}} \\ \frac{2}{3} & -\frac{2}{3} & -\frac{1}{3} \end{pmatrix}. \tag{15.29}$$

15.3.2 *Pseudoinverse*

The Pseudoinverse of A, denoted by $A^\dagger$ is defined as

$$A^\dagger = V \cdot S^\dagger U^T \tag{15.30}$$

where $S^\dagger$ is formed from S by taking the reciprocal of all the non-zero elements, leaving all the zeros alone and making the matrix the right shape: if S is an $m \times n$ matrix, then $S^\dagger$ must be an $n \times m$ matrix [Bishop (2006)].

15.3.3   *SVD and PCA*

We can use SVD to perform PCA instead of performing the typical eigen-decomposition, because SVD is more numerically stable if the columns are close to collinear. With a symmetric positive definite covariance matrix C, we have that

$$U = V = C \cdot C^T = C^T \cdot C = C \cdot C = C^2 \tag{15.31}$$

where $U = V$ is an orthogonal matrix with m orthonormal eigenvectors from C^2 and $S = \Lambda$ is a diagonal matrix with m elements equal to the root of the eigenvalues. So, we get

$$U \cdot \Lambda \cdot U^T = C. \tag{15.32}$$

The only difference to the Karhunen-Loève transform is that we determine the eigenvectors of C^2 instead of C and that resulting eigenvalues are the root of the eigenvalues of C.

15.4   **Autoencoders**

An autoencoder is a neural network that tries to solve the same problem of dimensionality reduction that PCA attempted to solve. To achieve that, the network is trained to attempt to copy its input to the output. In the mean time, internally, it has a hidden layer **h** that describes a code used to represent the input [Goodfellow *et al.* (2016)], see Figure 15.7. This code can be used as a reduced version of the input data.

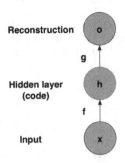

Fig. 15.7   An autoencoder is a neural network that is trained to attempt to copy its input to its output. Internally, it has a hidden layer **h** that describes a code used to represent the input.

An autoencoder may be viewed as consisting of two parts: an encoder function $\mathbf{h} = f(\mathbf{x})$ that maps the input to the hidden representation and a decoder function that produces a reconstruction $\mathbf{r} =: \mathbf{o} = g(\mathbf{h})$ departing from the hidden representation.

As the target output of a network is the same as its input, we do not need additional labels as targets. For that reason, this instance of back-propagation is seen as an instance of unsupervised learning.

At this point one may think that this is quite a strange formulation. After all, why would a network need to learn to copy its input? Was it not the goal to learn the structure of the data in lower dimensions? Autoencoders are designed to be unable to learn to copy perfectly, they are restricted in ways that allow them to copy only approximately. Namely, in some cases, they need to copy through a restricted channel. So, if the decoder needs to reproduce the original input using only the hidden state, then, the encoder must produce a constraint hidden state that contains all the relevant information compressed. Traditionally, the hidden state can then be seen as compressed representation of the input using better features.

On a final note before moving on, it is sometimes useful to represent the encoder and the decoder by stochastic mappings $p_{encoder}(\mathbf{h}|\mathbf{x})$ and $p_{decoder}(\mathbf{x}|\mathbf{h})$ [Alain *et al.* (2015)], see Figure 15.8.

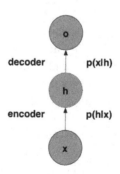

Fig. 15.8   An autoencoder can be represented as an encoder and a decoder that are seen as stochastic mappings $p_{encoder}(\mathbf{h}|\mathbf{x})$ and $p_{decoder}(\mathbf{x}|\mathbf{h})$.

15.5   Undercomplete Autoencoders

One way to obtain useful features from the autoencoder is to constrain **h** to have a smaller dimension than **x**. An autoencoder whose code dimension is less than the input dimension is called undercomplete, see Figure 15.9. Learning an undercomplete representation forces the autoencoder to

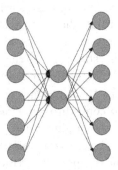

Fig. 15.9   An autoencoder whose code dimension is less than the input dimension is called undercomplete,

capture the most important features of the training data by minimizing the loss/error function

$$L(\mathbf{x}, f(g(\mathbf{x}))) = E(\mathbf{w}) = \frac{1}{2} \cdot \sum_{k=1}^{N} (\mathbf{x}_k - f(g(\mathbf{x}_k)))^2. \qquad (15.33)$$

When the decoder is linear and L is the mean squared error, an undercomplete autoencoder learns to span the same subspace as PCA. Autoencoders with nonlinear encoder functions f and nonlinear decoder functions g can learn a more powerful nonlinear generalization of PCA, the structure of the manifold [Hinton and Salakhutdinov (2006)], [Goodfellow *et al.* (2016)], see Figure 15.10. A manifold is a topological space (which may also be a separated space) which locally resembles real n-dimensional space, for example the real coordinate space R^n is the prototypical n-manifold, a circle is a compact 1-manifold. The mapped data concentrates around a low-dimensional manifold or a small set of such manifolds. An important characterization of a manifold is the set of its tangent planes. At a point **x** on a d-dimensional manifold, the tangent plane is given by basis vectors that span the local directions of variation allowed on the manifold, see Figure 15.11.

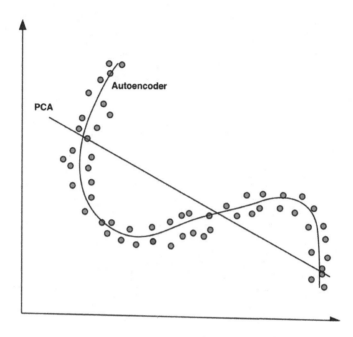

Fig. 15.10 When the decoder is linear and L is the mean squared error, an under-complete autoencoder learns to span the same subspace as PCA. Autoencoders with nonlinear encoder functions f and nonlinear decoder functions g can learn a more powerful nonlinear generalization of PCA, the structure of the manifold.

15.6 Overcomplete Autoencoders

Another way to obtain useful features from the autoencoder is to allow $\mathbf{h}$ to have bigger dimension than $\mathbf{x}$ but constraining the usage of the hidden layer through regularization. An autoencoder whose code dimension is bigger than the input dimension is called overcomplete [Bengio (2009)], [Goodfellow *et al.* (2016)], see Figure 15.12. In overcomplete autoencoders a linear encoder and a linear decoder without regularization can learn to copy the input to the output without learning anything useful about the data distribution. So, we need to adapt the loss function to encourages the model to have other properties besides the ability to copy its input to its output

$$L(\mathbf{x}, f(g(\mathbf{x})) + \Omega(\mathbf{h})) \tag{15.34}$$

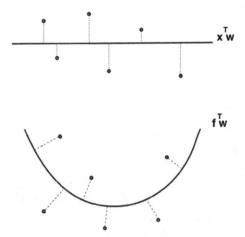

Fig. 15.11   At a point **x** on a d-dimensional manifold, the tangent plane is given by basis vectors that span the local directions of variation allowed on the manifold.

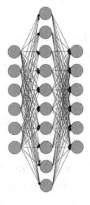

Fig. 15.12   An autoencoder whose code dimension is bigger than the input dimension is called overcomplete.

where $\Omega(\mathbf{h})$ can be a non-sparsity penalty, for example

$$L(\mathbf{x}, f(g(\mathbf{x})) + \Omega(\mathbf{h})) = \frac{1}{2} \cdot \sum_{k=1}^{N} (\mathbf{x}_k - f(g(\mathbf{x}_k)))^2 + \lambda \cdot \|\mathbf{h}\|_1. \qquad (15.35)$$

An autoencoder that has been regularized to be sparse must respond to unique statistical features of the data set it has been trained on, rather than simply acting as an identity function. In this way, training to perform the copying task with a sparsity penalty can yield a model that learns useful features.

With a prior that actually pushes the representations to zero like $\lambda \cdot \|\mathbf{h}\|_1$, one can indirectly control the average number of zeros in the representation resulting in a sparse code with a very small number of non-zero units. This type of code is known to be very biologically plausible and may allow for a very efficient storage in a fault tolerant answering mechanism known as an associative memory [Willshaw *et al.* (1969)], [Palm (1982)], [Bentz *et al.* (1989)], [Hecht-Nielsen (1989)], [Palm *et al.* (1997)].

15.6.1 *Denoising Autoencoders*

A denoising autoencoder or DAE minimizes

$$L(\mathbf{x}, f(g(\tilde{\mathbf{x}})) + \Omega(\mathbf{h}))\qquad(15.36)$$

where $\tilde{\mathbf{x}}$ is a copy of $\mathbf{x}$ that has been corrupted by some form of noise [Vincent *et al.* (2008)]. Denoising autoencoders must therefore undo this corruption rather than simply copying their input. A corruption process $C(\tilde{\mathbf{x}}, \mathbf{x})$ represents a conditional distribution over corrupted samples $\tilde{\mathbf{x}}$ given a data sample $\mathbf{x}$. The autoencoder then learns a reconstruction distribution $p_{reconstruct}(\mathbf{x}|\tilde{\mathbf{x}})$ from samples $(\tilde{\mathbf{x}}, \mathbf{x})$, see Figure 15.13. Sample a corrupted

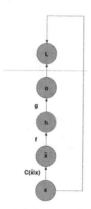

Fig. 15.13   A denoising autoencoder or DAE minimizes $L(\mathbf{x}, f(g(\tilde{\mathbf{x}})))$ where $\tilde{\mathbf{x}}$ is a copy of $\mathbf{x}$ that has been corrupted by some form of noise.

version $\tilde{\mathbf{x}}$ from $C(\tilde{\mathbf{x}}, \mathbf{x})$ and use $(\tilde{\mathbf{x}}, \mathbf{x})$ as a training example for estimating the autoencoder reconstruction distribution

$$p_{reconstruct}(\mathbf{x}|\tilde{\mathbf{x}}) = p_{decoder}(\mathbf{x}|\mathbf{h}) \qquad (15.37)$$

with $\mathbf{h}$ being the output of the encoder $\mathbf{h} = f(\tilde{\mathbf{x}})$.

15.7   Exercises and Answers

A Principal Component Analysis (PCA)

Lower dimensional problems are generally easier to deal with than higher dimensional ones. Furthermore, it is often the case when data is represented with a needlessly large amount of features. For instance, think about images. A large number of pixels will correspond to a data collection with a large amount of features. However, images really live in a lower dimensional space since they capture a three-dimensional world. PCA is a technique that tries to discover the lower dimensional space where high dimensional points really live.

To exemplify the reasoning behind it, let us look at a group of two-dimensional points.

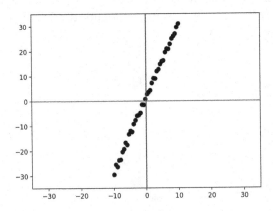

By looking at the data, we can see that although there are two features, the data seems to really vary accross a one dimensional diagonal line. The idea is to find that line and use it as our coordinates system.

The covariance matrix describes the variations of the data accross all dimensions. Through linear algebra, we can find the coordinate system that fits the data variation by computing the eigenvectors of the covariance matrix.

Eigenvalues and Eigenvectors

An eigenvector of a matrix is a vector for which the transformation of that vector by that matrix yields the same vector multiplied by a scalar called the eigenvalue. In practice, this means the following:

$$\mathbf{Cu} = \lambda \mathbf{u} \Longleftrightarrow (\mathbf{C} - \lambda \mathbf{I})\,\mathbf{u} = \mathbf{0}$$

Many eigenvectors exist with different scales. So, for the condition to met we must have an indetermined system with nontrivial solutions. This means that the determinant of the coefficients must equal zero. In fact, the determinant of the coefficients is called the characteristic polynomial:

$$|\mathbf{C} - \lambda \mathbf{I}|$$

The eigenvalues λ are such that:

$$|\mathbf{C} - \lambda \mathbf{I}| = 0$$

Finding the list of eigenvalues we can find each corresponding eigenvector by choosing any vector that verifies $(\mathbf{C} - \lambda \mathbf{I})\,\mathbf{u} = \mathbf{0}$. However, it is usual to work with orthonormal eigenvectors, so, typically, one normalizes the chosen vector.

For our example, the eigenvectors define the two directions denoted by blue and red.

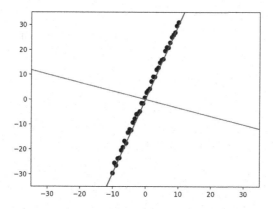

The K-L transform

If we consider a coordinate system defined by the eigenvectors, we see in the figure below that mostly one feature varies while the other remains more or less constant.

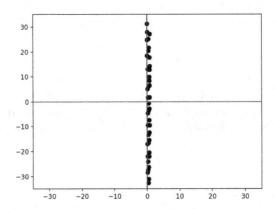

The matrix that rotates the coordinate system from the original one to the eigenvector defined one is called the K-L transform and is defined by placing the eigenvector on the columns:

$$\mathbf{U}_{KL} = \begin{pmatrix} | & | & & | \\ \mathbf{u}_1 & \mathbf{u}_2 & \cdots & \mathbf{u}_d \\ | & | & & | \end{pmatrix}$$

So, to map a point $\mathbf{x}$ on the original coordinate system to the new one we do:

$$\mathbf{x}_{eig} = \mathbf{U}_{KL}^T \mathbf{x}$$

Mapping to a lower dimensional space

Some dimensions are more relevant than others. The idea behind PCA is to discard the low importance dimensions. In our case, that would mean discard the red one and keep only the blue one:

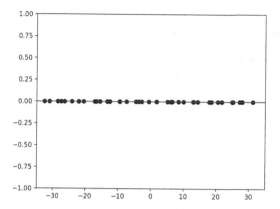

As we can see, most variations is kept and few information was lost.

If we discard the most significant dimesion, we see that we lose all information since all points collapse:

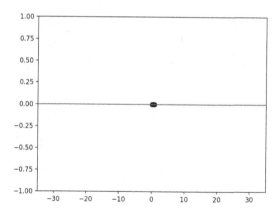

With that said, the key idea here is to define importance. How to we know which eigendimensions to discard? The eigenvalues store this information. Larger eigenvalues mean more variation. So, one well known criterion, the Kaiser criterion, is to discard all dimensions with eigenvalue $\lambda_i < 1$.

So, to build the PCA transformation matrix, all we need to do is take the K-L matrix and remove the columns that correspond to eigenvectors we want to discard.

Exercise:

Given the following training data:

$$\mathbf{x}^{(1)} = \begin{pmatrix} 0 \\ 0 \end{pmatrix}, \mathbf{x}^{(2)} = \begin{pmatrix} 4 \\ 0 \end{pmatrix}, \mathbf{x}^{(3)} = \begin{pmatrix} 2 \\ 1 \end{pmatrix}, \mathbf{x}^{(4)} = \begin{pmatrix} 6 \\ 3 \end{pmatrix}$$

a) Compute the K-L transformation.

Solution:

First, we compute the mean vector:

$$\mu = \frac{1}{4}\left(\begin{pmatrix} 0 \\ 0 \end{pmatrix} + \begin{pmatrix} 4 \\ 0 \end{pmatrix} + \begin{pmatrix} 2 \\ 1 \end{pmatrix} + \begin{pmatrix} 6 \\ 3 \end{pmatrix} \right) = \begin{pmatrix} 3 \\ 1 \end{pmatrix}$$

Now, we can compute the covariance matrix. First, we compute the individual contributions from each point:

$$\mathbf{x}^{(1)} \rightarrow \left(\begin{pmatrix} 0 \\ 0 \end{pmatrix} - \begin{pmatrix} 3 \\ 1 \end{pmatrix} \right) \left(\begin{pmatrix} 0 \\ 0 \end{pmatrix} - \begin{pmatrix} 3 \\ 1 \end{pmatrix} \right)^T = \begin{pmatrix} -3 \\ -1 \end{pmatrix} (-3 \ {-1}) = \begin{pmatrix} 9 & 3 \\ 3 & 1 \end{pmatrix}$$

$$\mathbf{x}^{(2)} \rightarrow \left(\begin{pmatrix} 4 \\ 0 \end{pmatrix} - \begin{pmatrix} 3 \\ 1 \end{pmatrix} \right) \left(\begin{pmatrix} 4 \\ 0 \end{pmatrix} - \begin{pmatrix} 3 \\ 1 \end{pmatrix} \right)^T = \begin{pmatrix} 1 \\ -1 \end{pmatrix} (1 \ {-1}) = \begin{pmatrix} 1 & -1 \\ -1 & 1 \end{pmatrix}$$

$$\mathbf{x}^{(3)} \rightarrow \left(\begin{pmatrix} 2 \\ 1 \end{pmatrix} - \begin{pmatrix} 3 \\ 1 \end{pmatrix} \right) \left(\begin{pmatrix} 2 \\ 1 \end{pmatrix} - \begin{pmatrix} 3 \\ 1 \end{pmatrix} \right)^T = \begin{pmatrix} -1 \\ 0 \end{pmatrix} (-1 \ 0) = \begin{pmatrix} 1 & 0 \\ 0 & 0 \end{pmatrix}$$

$$\mathbf{x}^{(4)} \rightarrow \left(\begin{pmatrix} 6 \\ 3 \end{pmatrix} - \begin{pmatrix} 3 \\ 1 \end{pmatrix} \right) \left(\begin{pmatrix} 6 \\ 3 \end{pmatrix} - \begin{pmatrix} 3 \\ 1 \end{pmatrix} \right)^T = \begin{pmatrix} 3 \\ 2 \end{pmatrix} (3 \ 2) = \begin{pmatrix} 9 & 6 \\ 6 & 4 \end{pmatrix}$$

Now, we can get the covariance matrix:

$$C = \frac{1}{4-1}\left(\begin{pmatrix} 9 & 3 \\ 3 & 1 \end{pmatrix} + \begin{pmatrix} 1 & -1 \\ -1 & 1 \end{pmatrix} + \begin{pmatrix} 1 & 0 \\ 0 & 0 \end{pmatrix} + \begin{pmatrix} 9 & 6 \\ 6 & 4 \end{pmatrix} \right)$$

$$= \frac{1}{3} \begin{pmatrix} 20 & 8 \\ 8 & 6 \end{pmatrix} = \begin{pmatrix} \frac{20}{3} & \frac{8}{3} \\ \frac{8}{3} & 2 \end{pmatrix}$$

To get the intended transformation we need to compute C's eigenvectors. We know that the eigenvalues λ of a matrix are the roots of the characteristic polynomial:

$$|\mathbf{C} - \lambda \mathbf{I}| = 0$$

Since we are working with two-dimensional data we know that there will be two eigenvalues. So, our equation becomes:

$$|\mathbf{C} - \lambda\mathbf{I}| = \left|\begin{pmatrix} \frac{20}{3} & \frac{8}{3} \\ \frac{8}{3} & 2 \end{pmatrix} - \begin{pmatrix} \lambda & 0 \\ 0 & \lambda \end{pmatrix}\right|$$

$$= \left|\begin{pmatrix} \frac{20}{3} - \lambda & \frac{8}{3} - 0 \\ \frac{8}{3} - 0 & 2 - \lambda \end{pmatrix}\right|$$

$$= \left(\frac{20}{3} - \lambda\right)(2 - \lambda) - \left(\frac{8}{3} - 0\right)\left(\frac{8}{3} - 0\right)$$

$$= \frac{40}{3} - \frac{20}{3}\lambda - 2\lambda + \lambda^2 - \frac{64}{9}$$

$$= \lambda^2 - \frac{26}{3}\lambda + \frac{56}{9}$$

$$= 0$$

Solving the second degree equation, we get:

$$\lambda_1 = 0.79 \vee \lambda_2 = 7.88$$

Having the eigenvalues, we can get the eigenvectors. If we have that $\lambda_1 = 0.79$, then the corresponding eigenvector $u_1 = \begin{pmatrix} u_{11} \\ u_{12} \end{pmatrix}$ will verify the following:

$$\mathbf{C}\mathbf{u}_1 = \lambda_1\mathbf{u}_1 \iff (\mathbf{C} - \lambda_1\mathbf{I})\mathbf{u}_1 = 0$$

Which yields:

$$(\mathbf{C} - \lambda_1\mathbf{I})\mathbf{u}_1 = \mathbf{0}$$

$$\left[\begin{pmatrix} \frac{20}{3} & \frac{8}{3} \\ \frac{8}{3} & 2 \end{pmatrix} - \begin{pmatrix} \lambda_1 & 0 \\ 0 & \lambda_1 \end{pmatrix}\right]\begin{pmatrix} u_{11} \\ u_{12} \end{pmatrix} = \begin{pmatrix} 0 \\ 0 \end{pmatrix}$$

$$\begin{pmatrix} \frac{20}{3} - \lambda_1 & \frac{8}{3} \\ \frac{8}{3} & 2 - \lambda_1 \end{pmatrix}\begin{pmatrix} u_{11} \\ u_{12} \end{pmatrix} = \begin{pmatrix} 0 \\ 0 \end{pmatrix}$$

$$\begin{pmatrix} \left(\frac{20}{3} - \lambda_1\right)u_{11} + \frac{8}{3}u_{12} \\ \frac{8}{3}u_{11} + (2 - \lambda_1)u_{12} \end{pmatrix} = \begin{pmatrix} 0 \\ 0 \end{pmatrix}$$

So, the following condition must be met:

$$u_{12} = -\frac{3}{8}\left(\frac{20}{3} - \lambda_1\right)u_{11}$$

With that, a solution for the system will be:

$$\mathbf{u}_1 = \begin{pmatrix} u_{11} \\ -\frac{3}{8}\left(\frac{20}{3} - \lambda_1\right)u_{11} \end{pmatrix}$$

We can choose for instance $u_{11} = 1$ and get:

$$\mathbf{u}_1 = \begin{pmatrix} 1 \\ -\frac{3}{8}\left(\frac{20}{3} - 0.79\right) \end{pmatrix} = \begin{pmatrix} 1 \\ -2.2 \end{pmatrix}$$

However, it is usual to work with normalized eigenvectors:

$$\mathbf{u}_1 = \frac{\mathbf{u}_1}{\|\mathbf{u}_1\|_2} = \begin{pmatrix} 0.4138 \\ -0.9104 \end{pmatrix}$$

For $\lambda_2 = 7.88$, the corresponding eigenvector $\mathbf{u}_2 = \begin{pmatrix} u_{21} \\ u_{22} \end{pmatrix}$ will verify the following:

$$\mathbf{C}\mathbf{u}_2 = \lambda_2\mathbf{u}_2 \Longleftrightarrow (\mathbf{C} - \lambda_2\mathbf{I})\,\mathbf{u}_2 = 0$$

Which yields:

$$(\mathbf{C} - \lambda_2\mathbf{I})\,\mathbf{u}_2 = 0$$

$$\left[\begin{pmatrix} \frac{20}{3} & \frac{8}{3} \\ \frac{8}{3} & 2 \end{pmatrix} - \begin{pmatrix} \lambda_2 & 0 \\ 0 & \lambda_2 \end{pmatrix} \right] \begin{pmatrix} u_{21} \\ u_{22} \end{pmatrix} = \begin{pmatrix} 0 \\ 0 \end{pmatrix}$$

$$\begin{pmatrix} \frac{20}{3} - \lambda_2 & \frac{8}{3} \\ \frac{8}{3} & 2 - \lambda_2 \end{pmatrix} \begin{pmatrix} u_{21} \\ u_{22} \end{pmatrix} = \begin{pmatrix} 0 \\ 0 \end{pmatrix}$$

$$\begin{pmatrix} \left(\frac{20}{3} - \lambda_2\right) u_{21} + \frac{8}{3}u_{22} \\ \frac{8}{3}u_{21} + (2 - \lambda_2)\,u_{22} \end{pmatrix} = \begin{pmatrix} 0 \\ 0 \end{pmatrix}$$

Again, the following condition must be met:

$$u_{22} = -\frac{3}{8}\left(\frac{20}{3} - \lambda_2\right) u_{21}$$

So, a solution for the system will be:

$$\mathbf{u}_2 = \begin{pmatrix} u_{21} \\ -\frac{3}{8}\left(\frac{20}{3} - \lambda_1\right) u_{21} \end{pmatrix}$$

We can choose for instance $u_{21} = 1$ and get:

$$\mathbf{u}_2 = \begin{pmatrix} 1 \\ -\frac{3}{8}\left(\frac{20}{3} - 7.88\right) \end{pmatrix} = \begin{pmatrix} 1 \\ 0.45 \end{pmatrix}$$

However, it is usual to work with normalized eigenvectors:

$$\mathbf{u}_2 = \frac{\mathbf{u}_2}{\|\mathbf{u}_2\|_2} = \begin{pmatrix} 0.9119 \\ 0.4104 \end{pmatrix}$$

Having the eigenvectors, we can place them on the columns of a matrix to build the K-L transformation:

$$U_{K-L} = \begin{pmatrix} 0.4138 & 0.9119 \\ -0.9104 & 0.4104 \end{pmatrix}$$

b) What is the rotation applied to go from the original coordinate system to the eigenvector coordinate system?

Solution:

$$\mathbf{U}\mathbf{e}_1 = \begin{pmatrix} 0.4138 & 0.9119 \\ -0.9104 & 0.4104 \end{pmatrix} \begin{pmatrix} 1 \\ 0 \end{pmatrix} = \mathbf{u}_1$$

$$\mathbf{u}_1\mathbf{e}_1 = \left\| \begin{pmatrix} 0.4138 \\ -0.9104 \end{pmatrix} \right\|_2 \left\| \begin{pmatrix} 1 \\ 0 \end{pmatrix} \right\|_2 \cos \alpha = 0.4138$$

$$\alpha = \arccos(0.4138) = 1.1442 rad \simeq 65 deg$$

Let us graphically analyze what happened. The original points in the original coordinate system:

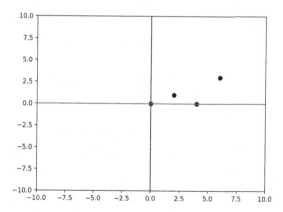

The eigenvectors are as follows:

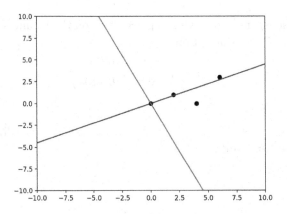

Mapping the points to this new eigenspace through $\mathbf{x}_{eig} = \mathbf{U}^T\mathbf{x}$, we get:

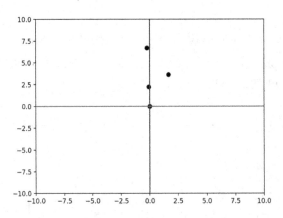

Through this we can see that the 65 degree rotation was negative (i.e. counter-clockwise).

c) Which eigenvector is most significant?

Solution:

The most significant eigenvector is the largest one. In this case λ_2.

d) Can we apply the Kaiser criterion?

Solution:

Yes, since $\lambda_1 < 1$ we can apply the criterion and discard it.

e) Map the points onto the most significant dimension.

Solution:

We can map the points to the eigenspace through $\mathbf{x}_{eig} = \mathbf{U}^T \mathbf{x}$:

$$\mathbf{x}_{eig}^{(1)} = \begin{pmatrix} 0.4138 & 0.9119 \\ -0.9104 & 0.4104 \end{pmatrix}^T \begin{pmatrix} 0 \\ 0 \end{pmatrix} = \begin{pmatrix} 0 \\ 0 \end{pmatrix}$$

$$\mathbf{x}_{eig}^{(2)} = \begin{pmatrix} 0.4138 & 0.9119 \\ -0.9104 & 0.4104 \end{pmatrix}^T \begin{pmatrix} 4 \\ 0 \end{pmatrix} = \begin{pmatrix} 1.66 \\ 3.65 \end{pmatrix}$$

$$\mathbf{x}_{eig}^{(3)} = \begin{pmatrix} 0.4138 & 0.9119 \\ -0.9104 & 0.4104 \end{pmatrix}^T \begin{pmatrix} 2 \\ 1 \end{pmatrix} = \begin{pmatrix} -0.08 \\ 2.23 \end{pmatrix}$$

$$\mathbf{x}_{eig}^{(4)} = \begin{pmatrix} 0.4138 & 0.9119 \\ -0.9104 & 0.4104 \end{pmatrix}^T \begin{pmatrix} 6 \\ 3 \end{pmatrix} = \begin{pmatrix} -0.25 \\ 6.70 \end{pmatrix}$$

PCA corresponds to keeping only the most significant dimensions. In this case, we discard the first dimension and get:

$$\mathbf{x}_{PCA}^{(1)} = \begin{pmatrix} 0 \end{pmatrix}$$

$$\mathbf{x}_{PCA}^{(2)} = \begin{pmatrix} 3.65 \end{pmatrix}$$

$$\mathbf{x}_{PCA}^{(3)} = \begin{pmatrix} 2.23 \end{pmatrix}$$

$$\mathbf{x}_{PCA}^{(4)} = \begin{pmatrix} 6.70 \end{pmatrix}$$

Which yields:

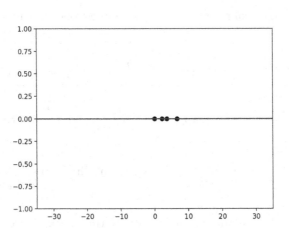

B Autoencoders

Another way to embed high dimensional data into a lower dimensional space is to use a neural network. To that end, we build a regular neural network that maps an input to an output with the dimension of the lower dimensional target space. Such network is called the encoder.

However, we do not know what the target should be. Unlike classification, there is no correct output for each point. Several different good embeddings may be possible.

The way to solve this network is to append a second neural network to the encoder. This new network takes the embedding as input and outputs a vector of the same dimensionality of the original input point.

If we look at the two networks together as one full system called an autoencoder, we know that for an input vector $\mathbf{x}$ the output should, ideally, be the same vector $\mathbf{x}$. This architecture is presented in the figure below.

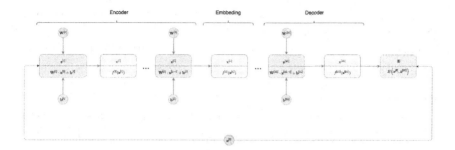

Using an autoencoder, we have a way to unsupervisedly learn the weights for both the encoder and the decoder. After doing so, we can separate the two modules and use the encoder as dimensionality reduction machinel. As the image below suggests, all we have to do to map an input to a lower dimensional embbeding is to do forward propagation on the encoder network.

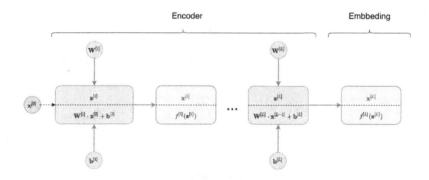

Exercise:

Consider the following point from a training collection of unsupervised data:

$$\mathbf{x} = \begin{pmatrix} 8 \\ 0 \\ 4 \end{pmatrix}$$

a) Build a one hidden layer autoencoder to map this data to two dimensions. Initialize all weights to 1 and all biases to zero. Use linear activation functions. Specify all forward operations, all backward operations and the loss function.

Solution:

The autoencoder has an input layer with 3 units, an hidden layer with 2 units and an output layer with 3 outputs. So, the initialized parameters are as follows:

$$\mathbf{W}^{[1]} = \begin{pmatrix} 1 & 1 & 1 \\ 1 & 1 & 1 \end{pmatrix}$$

$$\mathbf{b}^{[1]} = \begin{pmatrix} 0 \\ 0 \end{pmatrix}$$

$$\mathbf{W}^{[2]} = \begin{pmatrix} 1 & 1 \\ 1 & 1 \\ 1 & 1 \end{pmatrix}$$

$$\mathbf{b}^{[2]} = \begin{pmatrix} 0 \\ 0 \\ 0 \end{pmatrix}$$

The forward operations are as follows:

$$\mathbf{z}^{[1]} = \mathbf{W}^{[1]}\mathbf{x}^{[0]} + \mathbf{b}^{[1]}$$

$$\mathbf{x}^{[1]} = \mathbf{z}^{[1]}$$

$$\mathbf{z}^{[2]} = \mathbf{W}^{[2]}\mathbf{x}^{[1]} + \mathbf{b}^{[2]}$$

$$\mathbf{x}^{[2]} = \mathbf{z}^{[2]}$$

$$E\left(\mathbf{x}^{[2]}, \mathbf{t}\right) = \frac{1}{2}\left\|\mathbf{x}^{[2]} - \mathbf{t}\right\|_2^2$$

The backward operations are as follows:

$$\frac{\partial E}{\partial \mathbf{x}^{[2]}}\left(\mathbf{t}, \mathbf{x}^{[2]}\right) = \frac{\partial E}{\partial \left(\mathbf{x}^{[2]} - \mathbf{t}\right)^2} \frac{\partial \left(\mathbf{x}^{[2]} - \mathbf{t}\right)^2}{\partial \left(\mathbf{x}^{[2]} - \mathbf{t}\right)} \frac{\partial \left(\mathbf{x}^{[2]} - \mathbf{t}\right)}{\partial \mathbf{x}^{[2]}} = \frac{1}{2}\left[2\left(\mathbf{x}^{[2]} - \mathbf{t}\right)\right] = \mathbf{x}^{[2]} - \mathbf{t}$$

$$\frac{\partial \mathbf{x}^{[2]}}{\partial \mathbf{z}^{[2]}}\left(\mathbf{z}^{[2]}\right) = 1$$

$$\frac{\partial \mathbf{z}^{[2]}}{\partial \mathbf{W}^{[2]}}\left(\mathbf{W}^{[2]}, \mathbf{b}^{[2]}, \mathbf{x}^{[1]}\right) = \mathbf{x}^{[1]}$$

$$\frac{\partial \mathbf{z}^{[2]}}{\partial \mathbf{b}^{[2]}}\left(\mathbf{W}^{[2]}, \mathbf{b}^{[2]}, \mathbf{x}^{[1]}\right) = 1$$

$$\frac{\partial \mathbf{z}^{[2]}}{\partial \mathbf{x}^{[1]}}\left(\mathbf{W}^{[2]}, \mathbf{b}^{[2]}, \mathbf{x}^{[1]}\right) = \mathbf{W}^{[2]}$$

$$\frac{\partial \mathbf{x}^{[1]}}{\partial \mathbf{z}^{[1]}}\left(\mathbf{z}^{[1]}\right) = 1$$

$$\frac{\partial \mathbf{z}^{[1]}}{\partial \mathbf{W}^{[1]}}\left(\mathbf{W}^{[1]}, \mathbf{b}^{[1]}, \mathbf{x}^{[0]}\right) = \mathbf{x}^{[0]}$$

$$\frac{\partial \mathbf{z}^{[1]}}{\partial \mathbf{b}^{[1]}}\left(\mathbf{W}^{[1]}, \mathbf{b}^{[1]}, \mathbf{x}^{[0]}\right) = 1$$

$$\frac{\partial \mathbf{z}^{[1]}}{\partial \mathbf{x}^{[0]}}\left(\mathbf{W}^{[1]}, \mathbf{b}^{[1]}, \mathbf{x}^{[0]}\right) = \mathbf{W}^{[1]}$$

b) Use a learning rate of 0.001 for an iteration of stochastic gradient descent backpropagation using the half-squared error.

Solution:

In an autoencoder the target equals the input. So, we have to do the iteration with $\mathbf{x} = \begin{pmatrix} 8 \\ 0 \\ 4 \end{pmatrix}$ and $\mathbf{t} = \begin{pmatrix} 8 \\ 0 \\ 4 \end{pmatrix}$:

$$\mathbf{z}^{[1]} = \begin{pmatrix} 1 & 1 & 1 \\ 1 & 1 & 1 \end{pmatrix} \begin{pmatrix} 8 \\ 0 \\ 4 \end{pmatrix} = \begin{pmatrix} 12 \\ 12 \end{pmatrix}$$

$$\mathbf{x}^{[1]} = \begin{pmatrix} 12 \\ 12 \end{pmatrix} = \begin{pmatrix} 12 \\ 12 \end{pmatrix}$$

$$\mathbf{z}^{[2]} = \begin{pmatrix} 1 & 1 \\ 1 & 1 \\ 1 & 1 \end{pmatrix} \begin{pmatrix} 12 \\ 12 \end{pmatrix} = \begin{pmatrix} 24 \\ 24 \\ 24 \end{pmatrix}$$

$$\mathbf{x}^{[2]} = \begin{pmatrix} 24 \\ 24 \\ 24 \end{pmatrix} = \begin{pmatrix} 24 \\ 24 \\ 24 \end{pmatrix}$$

Now, we can compute the deltas:

$$\delta^{[2]} = \frac{\partial E}{\partial \mathbf{x}^{[2]}} \circ \frac{\partial \mathbf{x}^{[2]}}{\partial \mathbf{z}^{[2]}}$$

$$= \left(\mathbf{x}^{[2]} - \mathbf{t} \right) \circ \mathbf{1}$$

$$= \left(\begin{pmatrix} 24 \\ 24 \\ 24 \end{pmatrix} - \begin{pmatrix} 8 \\ 0 \\ 4 \end{pmatrix} \right) \circ \begin{pmatrix} 1 \\ 1 \\ 1 \end{pmatrix}$$

$$= \begin{pmatrix} 16 \\ 24 \\ 20 \end{pmatrix}$$

$$\delta^{[1]} = \frac{\partial \mathbf{z}^{[2]}}{\partial \mathbf{x}^{[1]}}^{T} \cdot \delta^{[2]} \circ \frac{\partial \mathbf{x}^{[l]}}{\partial \mathbf{z}^{[l]}}$$

$$= \left(\mathbf{W}^{[2]} \right)^{T} \cdot \delta^{[2]} \circ \mathbf{1}$$

$$= \begin{pmatrix} 1 & 1 & 1 \\ 1 & 1 & 1 \end{pmatrix} \cdot \begin{pmatrix} 16 \\ 24 \\ 20 \end{pmatrix} \circ \begin{pmatrix} 1 \\ 1 \end{pmatrix}$$

$$= \begin{pmatrix} 60 \\ 60 \end{pmatrix}$$

The gradients become:

$$\frac{\partial E}{\partial \mathbf{W}^{[1]}} = \delta^{[1]} \cdot \frac{\partial \mathbf{z}^{[1]}}{\partial \mathbf{W}^{[1]}}^{T}$$

$$= \delta^{[1]} \cdot \left(\mathbf{x}^{[0]} \right)^{T}$$

$$= \begin{pmatrix} 60 \\ 60 \end{pmatrix} \cdot \begin{pmatrix} 8 & 0 & 4 \end{pmatrix}$$

$$= \begin{pmatrix} 480 & 0 & 204 \\ 480 & 0 & 240 \end{pmatrix}$$

$$\frac{\partial E}{\partial \mathbf{b}^{[1]}} = \delta^{[1]} \circ \frac{\partial \mathbf{z}^{[1]}}{\partial \mathbf{b}^{[1]}}$$

$$= \delta^{[1]} \circ \mathbf{1}$$

$$= \begin{pmatrix} 60 \\ 60 \end{pmatrix} \cdot \begin{pmatrix} 1 \\ 1 \end{pmatrix}$$

$$= \begin{pmatrix} 60 \\ 60 \end{pmatrix}$$

$$\frac{\partial E}{\partial \mathbf{W}^{[2]}} = \delta^{[2]} \cdot \frac{\partial \mathbf{z}^{[2]}}{\partial \mathbf{W}^{[2]}}^{T}$$

$$= \delta^{[2]} \cdot \left(\mathbf{x}^{[1]}\right)^{T}$$

$$= \begin{pmatrix} 16 \\ 24 \\ 20 \end{pmatrix} \cdot \begin{pmatrix} 12 & 12 \end{pmatrix}$$

$$= \begin{pmatrix} 192 & 192 \\ 288 & 288 \\ 240 & 240 \end{pmatrix}$$

$$\frac{\partial E}{\partial \mathbf{b}^{[2]}} = \delta^{[2]} \circ \frac{\partial \mathbf{z}^{[2]}}{\partial \mathbf{b}^{[2]}}$$

$$= \delta^{[2]} \circ \mathbf{1}$$

$$= \begin{pmatrix} 16 \\ 24 \\ 20 \end{pmatrix} \cdot \begin{pmatrix} 1 \\ 1 \\ 1 \end{pmatrix}$$

$$= \begin{pmatrix} 16 \\ 24 \\ 20 \end{pmatrix}$$

So, we get the updates:

$$\mathbf{W}^{[1]} = \mathbf{W}^{[1]} - \eta \frac{\partial E}{\partial \mathbf{W}^{[1]}}$$

$$= \begin{pmatrix} 1 & 1 & 1 \\ 1 & 1 & 1 \end{pmatrix} - 0.001 \begin{pmatrix} 480 & 0 & 240 \\ 480 & 0 & 240 \end{pmatrix}$$

$$= \begin{pmatrix} 1 & 1 & 1 \\ 1 & 1 & 1 \end{pmatrix} - \begin{pmatrix} 0.480 & 0 & 0.240 \\ 0.480 & 0 & 0.240 \end{pmatrix}$$

$$= \begin{pmatrix} 0.52 & 1 & 0.76 \\ 0.52 & 1 & 0.76 \end{pmatrix}$$

$$\mathbf{b}^{[1]} = \mathbf{b}^{[1]} - \eta \frac{\partial E}{\partial \mathbf{b}^{[1]}}$$

$$= \begin{pmatrix} 0 \\ 0 \end{pmatrix} - 0.001 \begin{pmatrix} 60 \\ 60 \end{pmatrix}$$

$$= \begin{pmatrix} -0.06 \\ -0.06 \end{pmatrix}$$

$$\mathbf{W}^{[2]} = \mathbf{W}^{[2]} - \eta \frac{\partial E}{\partial \mathbf{W}^{[2]}}$$

$$= \begin{pmatrix} 1 & 1 \\ 1 & 1 \\ 1 & 1 \end{pmatrix} - 0.001 \begin{pmatrix} 192 & 192 \\ 288 & 288 \\ 240 & 240 \end{pmatrix}$$

$$= \begin{pmatrix} 0.808 & 0.808 \\ 0.712 & 0.712 \\ 0.760 & 0.760 \end{pmatrix}$$

$$\mathbf{b}^{[2]} = \mathbf{b}^{[2]} - \eta \frac{\partial E}{\partial \mathbf{b}^{[2]}}$$

$$= \begin{pmatrix} 0 \\ 0 \\ 0 \end{pmatrix} - 0.001 \begin{pmatrix} 16 \\ 24 \\ 20 \end{pmatrix}$$

$$= \begin{pmatrix} -0.016 \\ -0.024 \\ -0.020 \end{pmatrix}$$

c) Encode the point with the resulting autoencoder. That is, use it to map $\mathbf{x}$ to the two-dimensional manifold discovered in **b)**.

Solution:
All we need to do is to perform forward propagation until the hidden layer:

$$\mathbf{z}^{[1]} = \begin{pmatrix} 0.52 & 1 & 0.76 \\ 0.52 & 1 & 0.76 \end{pmatrix} \begin{pmatrix} 8 \\ 0 \\ 4 \end{pmatrix} + \begin{pmatrix} -0.06 \\ -0.06 \end{pmatrix} = \begin{pmatrix} 7.14 \\ 7.14 \end{pmatrix}$$

$$\mathbf{x}^{[1]} = \begin{pmatrix} 7.14 \\ 7.14 \end{pmatrix} \qquad\qquad = \begin{pmatrix} 7.14 \\ 7.14 \end{pmatrix}$$

d) Decode the encoding from **c)** and measure the squared error.

Solution:
To decode, all we need to do is to perform forward propagation from the hidden layer until the output layer:

$$\mathbf{z}^{[2]} = \begin{pmatrix} 0.808\ 0.808 \\ 0.712\ 0.712 \\ 0.760\ 0.760 \end{pmatrix} \begin{pmatrix} 7.14 \\ 7.14 \end{pmatrix} + \begin{pmatrix} -0.016 \\ -0.024 \\ -0.020 \end{pmatrix} = \begin{pmatrix} 11.52224 \\ 10.14336 \\ 10.83280 \end{pmatrix}$$

$$\mathbf{x}^{[2]} = \begin{pmatrix} 11.52224 \\ 10.14336 \\ 10.83280 \end{pmatrix}$$

The error is simply the loss function applied to the original point and the decoded version:

$$E\left(\mathbf{x}^{[2]}, \mathbf{t}\right) = \frac{1}{2} \left\| \begin{pmatrix} 11.52224 \\ 10.14336 \\ 10.83280 \end{pmatrix} - \begin{pmatrix} 8 \\ 0 \\ 4 \end{pmatrix} \right\|_2^2 = 80.99$$

As we can see, one iteration was not nearly enough. In practice, we would run SGD on several points for many epochs.

Thinking Questions

a) Name possible applications of an autoencoder.

Solution:

- Dimensionality reduction:
- Generating Sparse Codes
- Pretraining: An autoencoder can be used to pretrain another neural network, e.g. a classifier. For instance, we could take the trained encoder, add a few dense layers for prediction and re-train the resulting model end-to-end with a prediction loss such as the binary cross entropy.
- Outlier detection: The reconstruction error is often large for inputs which are very different from the usual patterns observed in the training data. This can be used for outlier/anomaly detection by simply using the reconstruction error as an outlier score.
- Generative model: The learned decoder can be used as a generative model. Similarly as a GAN, it can be used for generating additional synthetic training samples, which is particularly useful in a setting where only few labeled samples are available. The Variational Autoencoder (VAE) is especially suited for this, since the latent dimensions are independently Gaussian distributed with unit variance, so we can just sample from these distributions and decode the resulting latent vector.

b) Consider a linear autoencoder without regularization or denoising. What happens if the number of dimensions of the latent space is set larger than the dimensionality of the data space.

Solution:

In this case, the autoencoder will simply learn the identity function and achieve zero reconstruction error. Since the latent space has a sufficient number of dimensions, the autoencoder can just copy the input into the latent space and back. This is a general problem if the autoencoder is given too much capacity. By introducing a bottleneck, the autoencoder is forced to learn compact and expressive representations. One can as well introduce l2 or l1 regularization to constraint the capacity of the Autoencoder.

c) When is an autoencoder equivalent to a PCA? What are the main differences?

Solution:

Linear units where the number of the hidden units corresponds to the number of the principal components (the eigenvectors with large eigenvalues) In PCA the eigenvalues indicate which dimensions are important. In a linear autoencoder the number of hidden units has to be determined by experiments.

Chapter 16

Epilogue

Fig. 16.1 New methods in machine learning are required that do not rely on backpropagation.

Throughout the book we have seen that biology provided some inspiration for current state-of-the-art deep learning models. However, we have also seen that invariably a departure from it is done and backpropagation based optimization is used for learning. Think about, for instance, in the departure from neocognitron [Fukushima (1988)] to convolution networks [LeCun *et al.* (1990)], [LeCun *et al.* (1995)], [LeCun and Bengio (1998a)].

This change created tremendous engineering tools for tasks where large sets of labeled data exist. The results were so good that it is now common to identify artificial intelligence with deep learning, leaving aside a lot of other trends like symbol manipulating systems. This results from the paradox of artificial intelligence, a discipline whose principal purpose is its own definition since the terms "intelligence" and "intelligent human behavior" are not very well defined and understood.

However, we see that human brains can learn from much less examples, in notoriously difficult tasks, while providing deeper understanding a generalization capability. This led the machine learning pioneer Geoffrey Hinton to suggest that entirely new methods will probably have to be invented (see Figure 16.2). He stated[1]: "I don't think it's how the brain works.... We clearly don't need all the labeled data."

Fig. 16.2   Machine learning and artificial intelligence pioneer Geoffrey Hinton.

Perhaps some of these new methods may come from a deeper under-

---

[1]Interview with Steve LeVine, Sep 15, 2017, AXIOS, https://www.axios.com.

standing of biological networks. However, we believe that cognitive science may be the key. New methods should be related to the important question posed by the cognitive science researcher Douglas Hoffstadter (see Figure 16.3), [Hofstadter (1995)]: "What is a concept?". From this key question, many others follow. How do fluid boundaries come about? How do they give rise to generalization? What makes something similar to something else? For example, what makes an uppercase letter 'A' recognizable as such. What is the essence of 'A'-ness? Current, supervised machine learning tries to find regularities from a labeled data set but cannot answer these questions. For example, even in a very functional deep learning model applied to a simple task, we cannot access this information since the network is a kind of black box that is determined by the statistical properties of the training sample.

Fig. 16.3   Writer and cognitive science researcher Douglas Hoffstader.

Bibliography

Abu-Mostafa, Y. S., Magdon-Ismail, M. and Lin, H.-T. (2012). *Learning from Data - A Short Course* (AMLbook.com).

Aizenberg, I., Aizenberg, N. N. and Vandewalle, J. P. (2000). *Multi-Valued and Universal Binary Neurons* (Springer).

Alain, G., Bengio, Y., Yao, L., Thibodeau-Laufer, E., Yosinski, J. and Vincent, P. (2015). Generative stochastic networks, *ArXiv Quantum Physics e-prints* **abs/1503.05571**.

Anderson, J. R. (1995). *Cognitive Psychology and its Implications*, 4th edn. (W. H. Freeman and Company).

Bebis, G. and Georgiopoulos, M. (1994). Feed-forward neural networks, *IEEE Potentials* **13**, 4, pp. 27–31.

Bengio, Y. (2009). Learning deep architectures for ai, *Foundations and Trends in Machine Learning* **2**, 8, pp. 1795–1797.

Bentz, H. J., Hagstroem, M. and Palm, G. (1989). Information storage and effective data retrieval in sparse matrices, *Neural Networks* **2**, 4, pp. 289–293.

Bishop, C. (2006). *Pattern Recognition and Machine Learning* (Springer).

Blumer, A., Ehrenfeucht, A., Haussler, D. and Warmuth, M. (1989). Learnability and the vapnik-chervonenkis dimension, *Journal of the ACM* **36**, 4, pp. 929–965.

Böhm, C., Berchtold, S. and Kei, A. K., D. (2001). Searching in high-dimensional spaces—index structures for improving the performance of multimedia databases, *ACM Computing Surveys* **33**, 3, pp. 322–373.

Broomhead, D. and Lowe, D. (1988). Multivariable functional interpolation and adaptive networks, *Complex Systems* **2**, pp. 321–355.

Bryson, A. E. and Ho, Y.-C. (1969). *Applied optimal control : optimization, estimation, and control* (Blaisdell Pub. Co.).

Cardoso, A. and Wicher, A. (2014). Noise tolerance in a neocognitron like network, *Neural Networks* **49**, 32-38, p. 2014.

Cardoso, A. and Wichert, A. (2010). Neocognitron and the map transformation cascade, *Neural Networks* **23**, 1, pp. 74–88.

Cardoso, A. and Wichert, A. (2013). Handwritten digit recognition using biologically inspired features, *Neurocomputing* **99**, pp. 575–589.

Cho, K., van Merrienboer, B., Gulcehre, C., Bahdanau, D., Bougares, F., Schwenk, H. and Bengio, Y. (2014). Learning phrase representations using rnn encoder-decoder for statistical machine translation, *ArXiv Quantum Physics e-prints* **abs/1406.1078**.

Choromanska, A., Henaff, M., Mathieu, M., Arous, G. B. and LeCun, Y. (2015). The loss surfaces of multilayer networks, in *Proceedings of the 18th International Conference on Artificial Intelligence and Statistics*, Vol. 38, pp. 192–204.

Churchland, P. S. and Sejnowski, T. J. (1994). *The Computational Brain* (The MIT Press).

Clevert, D. A., Unterthiner, T. and Hochreiter, S. (2015). Fast and accurate deep network learning by exponential linear units (elus, *ArXiv Quantum Physics e-prints* **abs/1511.07289**.

Cortes, C. and Vapnik, V. (1995). Support-vector networks, *Machine Learning* **20**, pp. 273–297.

Cover, T. M. (1965). Geometrical and statistical properties of systems of linear inequalities with applications in pattern recognition, *IEEE Transactions on Electronic Computers* **3**, 326-334.

Cybenko, G. (1989). Approximations by superpositions of sigmoidal functions, *Mathematics of Control, Signals, and Systems* **2**, 4, pp. 303–314.

Dauphin, Y., Pascanu, R., Gulcehre, C., Cho, K., Ganguli, S. and Bengio, Y. (2014). Identifying and attacking the saddle point problem in high-dimensional non-convex optimization, *ArXiv Quantum Physics e-prints* **abs/1406.2572**.

Davis, C. (1962). The norm of the schur product operation, *Numerische Mathematik* **4**, 1, pp. 343–344.

de Sá, J. P. M. (2001). *Pattern Recognition: Concepts, Methods and Applications* (Springer-Verlag).

Dechter, R. (1986). Learning while searching in constraint-satisfaction problems, in *AAAI-86 Proceedings*, pp. 178–183.

Duchi, J., Hazan, E. and Singer, Y. (2011). Adaptive subgradient methods for online learning and stochastic optimization, *Journal of Machine Learning Research* **12**, pp. 2121–2159.

Duda, R. O., Hart, P. E. and Stork, D. G. (2000). *Pattern Classification (2nd Edition)* (Wiley-Interscience), ISBN 0471056693.

Elman, J. (1990). Finding structure in time, *Cognitive Science* **14**, pp. 179–211.

Fukushima, K. (1975). Cognitron: A self-organizing multilayered neural network, *Biological Cybernetics* **20**, pp. 121–136.

Fukushima, K. (1980). Neocognitron: a self organizing neural network model for a mechanism of pattern recognition unaffected by shift in position. *Biol Cybern* **36**, 4, pp. 193–202.

Fukushima, K. (1988). Neocognitron: A hierarchical neural network capable of visual pattern recognition, *Neural Networks* **1**, pp. 119–130.

Fukushima, K. (2001). Recognition of partly occluded patterns: a neural network model. *Biol Cybern* **84**, 4, pp. 251–259.

Fukushima, K. (2003). Neocognitron for handwritten digit recognition. *Neuro-computing* **51**, pp. 161–180.

Fukushima, K. (2004). Neocognitron capable of incremental learning. *Neural Netw* **17**, 1, pp. 37–46.

Fukushima, K. (2005). Restoring partly occluded patterns: a neural network model, *Neural Netw.* **18**, 1, pp. 33–43, doi:http://dx.doi.org/10.1016/j.neunet.2004.05.001.

Glorot, X. and Bengio, Y. (2010). Understanding the difficulty of training deep feedforward neural networks, in *Proceedings of the 13th International Conference on Artificial Intelligence and Statistics*, Vol. 9.

Goodfellow, I., Bengio, Y. and Courville, A. (2016). *Deep Learning* (MIT Press).

Goodfellow, I. J., Warde-Farley, D., Mirza, M., Courville, A. and Bengio, Y. (2013). Maxout networks, in S. Dasgupta and D. McAllester (eds.), *ICML'13*, pp. 1319–1327.

Gross, C. and Mishkin (1977). The neural basis of stimulus equivalence across retinal translation, in S. Harnad, R. Dorty, J. Jaynes, L. Goldstein and Krauthamer (eds.), *Lateralization in the nervous system* (Academic Press, New York), pp. 109–122.

Hahnloser, R. H. R., Sarpeshkar, R., Mahowald, M. A., Douglas, R. J. and Seung, H. S. (2000). Digital selection and analogue amplification coexist in a cortex-inspired silicon circuit, *Nature* **405**, pp. 947–951.

Haykin, S. O. (2008). *Neural Networks and Learning Machines (3rd Edition)* (Prentice Hall).

He, K., Zhang, X., Ren, S. and Sun, J. (2015a). Deep residual learning for image recognition, *ArXiv Quantum Physics e-prints* **abs/1512.03385**.

He, K., Zhang, X., Ren, S. and Sun, J. (2015b). Delving deep into rectifiers: Surpassing human-level performance on imagenet classification, *ArXiv Quantum Physics e-prints* **abs/1511.07289**.

Hecht-Nielsen, R. (1989). *Neurocomputing* (Addison-Wesley).

Hertz, J., Krogh, A. and Palmer, R. G. (1991). *Introduction to the Theory of Neural Computation* (Addison-Wesley).

Hinton, G. E. and Salakhutdinov, R. (2006). Reducing the dimensionality of data with neural networks, *Science* **313**, 5786, pp. 504–507.

Hinton, G. E., Srivastava, N., Krizhevsky, I., Alexs Sutskever and Salakhutdinov, R. R. (2012). Improving neural networks by preventing co-adaptation of feature detectors, *ArXiv Quantum Physics e-prints* **abs/1207.0580**.

Hochreiter, S. (1991). *Untersuchungen zu dynamischen neuronalen Netzen*, Master's thesis, T.U. Munchen.

Hochreiter, S. and Schmidhuber, J. (1997). Long short-term memory, *Neural Computation* **9**, 8, pp. 1735–1780.

Hoeffding, W. (1963). Probability inequalities for sums of bounded random variables, *Journal of the American Statistical Association* **58**, 301, p. 30.

Hofstadter, D. (1995). *Fluid Concepts and Creative Analogies: Computer Models of the Fundamental Mechanisms of Thought* (Basic Books).

Hornik, K. (1991). Approximation capabilities of multilayer feedforward networks, *Neural Networks* **4**, 2, pp. 251–257.

Hornik, K., Stinchcombe, M. and White, H. (1989). Multilayer feedforward networks are universal approximators, *Neural Networks* **2**, 5, pp. 359–366.

Hubel, D. H. (1988). *Eye, Brain, and Vision* (Scientific Ammerican Library, Oxford, England).

Hubel, D. H. and Wiesel, T. N. (1962). Receptive fields, binocular interaction and functional architecture in the cat's visual cortex. *J Physiol* **160**, pp. 106–154.

Hubel, D. H. and Wiesel, T. N. (1968). Receptive fields and functional architecture of monkey striate cortex. *J Physiol* **195**, 1, pp. 215–243.

Ioffe, S. and Szegedy, C. (2015). Batch normalization: Accelerating deep network training by reducing internal covariate shift, in *Proceedings of the 32nd International Conference on Machine Learning*, Vol. 37.

Jarrett, K., Kavukcuoglu, K., Ranzato, M. and LeCun, Y. (2009). What is the best multi-stage architecture for object recognition? in *ICCV'09*.

Jordan, M. (1986). Attractor dynamics and parallelism in a connectionist sequential machine, in *Proceedings of the Eigth Annual Conference on the Cognitive Science Society* (Erlbaum, Hillsdale), pp. 531–546.

Kemke, C. and Wichert, A. (1993). Hierarchical self-organizing feature maps for speech recognition, in *Proceedings World Congres on Neural Networks* (Lawrence Erlbaum), pp. 45–47.

Kingma, D. and Ba, J. (2014). dam: A method for stochastic optimization, *ArXiv Quantum Physics e-prints* **abs/1412.6980**.

Kolmogorov, A. (1933). *Grundbegriffe der Wahrscheinlichkeitsrechnung* (Springer-Verlag).

Kolmogorov, A. (1998). On tables of random numbers, *Theoretical Computer Science* **207**, 2, pp. 387–395.

Krizhevsky, A., Sutskever, I. and Hinton, G. E. (2017). Imagenet classification with deep convolutional neural networks, *Communications of the ACM* **60**, 6, pp. 84–90.

LeCun, Y. and Bengio, Y. (1998a). *Convolutional networks for images, speech, and time series* (MIT Press, Cambridge, MA, USA), ISBN 0-262-51102-9, pp. 255–258.

LeCun, Y. and Bengio, Y. (1998b). *Pattern recognition* (MIT Press, Cambridge, MA, USA), ISBN 0-262-51102-9, pp. 864–868.

LeCun, Y., Boser, B., Denker, J. S., Henderson, D., Howard, R. E., Hubbard, W. and Jackel, L. D. (1990). Handwritten digit recognition with a back-propagation network, in D. Touretzky (ed.), *Advances in Neural Information Processing Systems 2 (NIPS*89)* (Morgan Kaufman, Denver, CO).

LeCun, Y., Jackel, L., Bottou, L., Brunot, A., Cortes, C., Denker, J., Drucker, H., Guyon, I., Muller, U., Sackinger, E., Simard, P. and Vapnik, V. (1995). Comparison of learning algorithms for handwritten digit recognition, URL citeseer.ist.psu.edu/article/lecun95comparison.html.

Lloyd, S. P. (1982). Least squares quantization in pcm, *IEEE Transactions on Information Theory* **28**, 2, pp. 129–137.

Luger, G. F. and Stubblefield, W. A. (1998). *Artificial Intelligence, Structures and Strategies for Complex Problem Solving*, 3rd edn. (Addison-Wesley).

Maas, A. L., Hannun, A. Y. and Ng, A. Y. (2013). Rectifier nonlinearities improve neural network acoustic models, in *CML Workshop on Deep Learning for Audio, Speech, and Language Processing*, Vol. 28.

McClelland, J. and Rumelhart, D. (1986a). *Explorations in Parallel Distributed Processing - IBM version* (The MIT Press).

McClelland, J. and Rumelhart, D. (1986b). *Explorations in the Microstructure of Cognition. Volume 1: Foundations* (The MIT Press).

McClelland, J. and Rumelhart, D. (1986c). *Explorations in the Microstructure of Cognition. Volume 2: Psychological and Biological Models* (The MIT Press).

McCulloch, W. and Pitts, W. (1943). A logical calculus of the ideas immanent in nervous activity, *Bulletin of Mathematical Biophysics* **5**, pp. 115–133.

Mercer, J. (1909). Functions of positive and negative type, and their connection with the theory of integral equations, *Transactions of the London Philosophical Society (A)* **209**, 415-446.

Minsky, M. and Papert, S. (1972). *Perceptrons: An Introduction to Computational Geometry* (MIT Press).

Mitchell, T. (1997). *Machine Learning* (McGraw-Hill).

Mozer, M. C. (1995). A focused backpropagation algorithm for temporal pattern recognition, *Complex Systems* **3**, 4, pp. 349–381.

Nair, V. and Hinton, G. E. (2009). 3d object recognition with deep belief nets, in Y. Bengio, D. Schuurmans, J. D. Lafferty, C. K. I. Williams and A. Culotta (eds.), *Advances in Neural Information Processing Systems 22,* (Curran Associates, Inc.), pp. 1339–1347.

Nesterov, Y. (1983). A method of solving a convex programming problem with convergence rate o(1/(k*k)), *Soviet Mathematics Doklady* **27**, pp. 372–376.

Nesterov, Y. (2004). *ntroductory lectures on convex optimization : a basic course. Applied optimization.* (Kluwer Academic).

Newell, A. (1990). *Unified Theories of Cognition* (Harvard University Press).

Newell, A. and Simon, H. (1976). Computer science as empirical inquiry: symbols and search. *Communication of the ACM* **19**, 3, pp. 113–126.

Palm, G. (1982). *Neural Assemblies, an Alternative Approach to Artificial Intelligence* (Springer-Verlag).

Palm, G., Schwenker, F., Sommer, F. and Strey, A. (1997). Neural associative memories, in A. Krikelis and C. Weems (eds.), *Associative Processing and Processors* (IEEE Press), pp. 307–325.

Parker, D. B. (1985). Learning-logic: Casting the cortex of the human brain in silicon, Technical Report Tr-47, Center for Computational Research in Economics and Management Science. MIT Cambridge, MA.

Paulus, D. and Hornegger, J. (2003). *Applied Pattern Recognition, Fourth Edition: Algorithms and Implementation in C++* (GWV-Vieweg;).

Polosukhin, I., Kaiser, A. N., Lukasz; Gomez, Jones, L., Uszkoreit, J., Parmar, N., Shazeer, N. and Vaswani, A. (2017). Attention is all you need, *ArXiv Quantum Physics e-prints* **abs/1706.03762**.

Powell, M. (1988). Radial basis function approximations to polynomials, in *Numerical Analysis 1987 Proceedings,*, pp. 223–241.

Rao, C. R. (1973). *Linear Statistical Inference and its Applications: Second Editon* (John Wiley and Sons).

Reid, C. (1996). *Hilbert* (Spriner Verlag).

Resnikoff, H. L. (1989). *The Illusion of Reality* (Springer-Verlag).

Riesenhuber, M. and Poggio, T. (2000). Models of object recognition, *Nat Neuroscience* **3**, pp. 1199–1204.

Riesenhuber, M. and Poggio, T. (2002). Neural mechanisms of object recognition, *Current Opinion in Neurobiology* **12**, pp. 162–168.

Riesenhuber, M., Poggio, T. and models of object recognition in cortex, H. (1999). Hierarchical models of object recognition in cortex, *Nature Neuroscience* **2**, pp. 1019–1025.

Rissanen, J. (1978). Modeling by shortest data description, *Automatica* **14**, 5, pp. 465–471.

Rissanen, J. (1998). *Stochastic Complexity in Statistical Inquiry* (World Scientific).

Robert, C. P. (2007). *The Bayesian Choice: From Decision-Theoretic Foundations to Computational Implementation (Springer Texts in Statistics) 2nd Edition* (Springer).

Rosenblatt, F. (1962). *Principles of neurodynamics: Perceptrons and the theory of brain mechanisms* (Spartan Books).

Saitoh, S. (1988). *Theory of Reproducing Kernels and Its Applications* (Longman Scientific and Technical).

Schmidhuber, J. (1992). Learning complex, extended sequences using the principle of history compression, *Neural Computation* **4**, 2, pp. 234–242.

Schmidhuber, J. (2014). Deep learning in neural networks: An overview, *Neural Networks* **61**, pp. 85–117.

Seber, G. A. F. and Wild, C. J. (1989). *Nonlinear Regression* (John Wiley qnd Sons).

Serre, T. (2019). Deep learning: The good, the bad, and the ugly, *Annual Review of Vision Science* **5**, pp. 399–426.

Shannon, C. E. (1948). A mathematical theory of communication, *Bell System Technical Journal* , pp. 1–54.

Shawe-Taylor, J. and Cristianini, N. (2004). *Kernel Methods for Pattern Analysis* (Cambridge University Press).

Shouno, H., Fukushima, F. and Okada, M. (1999). Recognition of handwritten digits in the real world by neocognitron, in *Knowledge-based Intelligent Techniques in Character Recognition* (CRC Press).

Siegelmann, H. and Sontag, E. (1991). Turing computability with neural nets, *pplied Mathematics Letters* **4**, 6, pp. 77–80.

Siegelmann, H. and Sontag, E. (1995). On the computational power of neural nets, *Journal of Computer and System Sciences* **50**, pp. 132–150.

Simon, H. A. (1991). *Models of my Life* (Basic Books, New York).

Srivastava, R. K., Greff, K. and Schmidhuber, J. (2015). Highway networks, *ArXiv Quantum Physics e-prints* **abs/1505.00387**.

Sutskever, I., Martens, J., Dahl, G. and Hinton, G. (2013). On the importance of initialization and momentum in deep learning, in *Proceedings of the 30th International Conference on Machine Learning*, Vol. 28, pp. 1139–1147.

Swirszcz, G., Czarnecki, W. M. and Pascanu, R. (2016). Local minima in training of neural networks, *ArXiv Quantum Physics e-prints* **abs/1611.06310**.

Szegedy, C., Liu, W., Jia, Y., Sermanet, P., Reed, S., Anguelov, D., Erhan, D., Vanhoucke, V. and Rabinovich, A. (2015). Going deeper with convolutions, in *Proceedings of the IEEE Conference on Computer Vision and Pattern Recognition*, pp. 1–9.

Tarski, A. (1956). *Logic, Semantics,Metamathematics* (Oxford University Press, London).

Thomson, A. (2010). Neocortical layer 6, a review, *Frontiers in Neuroanatomy* **4**, 13.

Tibshirani, R. (1996). Regression shrinkage and selection via the lasso, *Journal of the Royal Statistical Society. Series B* **58**, 1, pp. 267–288.

Tikhonov, A. N. and Arsenin, V. Y. (1977). *Solutions of Ill-Posed Problems* (V. H. Winston and Sons).

Topsoe, F. (1974). *Informationstheorie* (Teubner Sudienbucher).

Vapnik, V. N. and Chervonenkis, A. Y. (1971). On the uniform convergence of relative frequencies of events to their probabilities, *Theory of Probability and Its Applications* **16**, 2, p. 264.

Vincent, P., Larochelle, H., Y., Bengio and Manzagol, P. A. (2008). Extracting and composing robust features with denoising autoencoders, in *ICML'08: Proceedings of the 25th international conference on Machine learning*, pp. 1096–1103.

Wasserman, P. D. (1993). *Advanced Methods in Neurl Computing* (Van Nostrand Reinhold).

Werbos, P. (1974). *Beyond regression : new tools for prediction and analysis in the behavioral sciences*, Ph.D. thesis, Harvard University.

Werbos, P. J. (1988). Generalization of backpropagation with application to a recurrent gas market model, *Neural Networks* **1**, 4, pp. 339–356.

White, H. (1992). *Artificial Neural Networks - Approximation and Learning Theorz* (Blackwell).

Wichert, A. (1993). MTCn-nets, in *Proceedings World Congres on Neural Networks* (Lawrence Erlbaum), pp. 59–62.

Wichert, A. (2009). Sub-symbols and icons, *Cognitive Computation* **1**, 4, pp. 342–347.

Wichert, A. (2013). *Principles of Quantum Artificial Intelligence* (World Scientific).

Wichert, A. (2015). *Intelligent Big Multimedia Databases* (World Scientific).

Wichert, A., Abler, B., Grothe, J., Walter, H. and Sommer, F. T. (2002). Exploratory analysis of event-related fmri demonstrated in a working memory study, in F. Sommer and A. Wichert (eds.), *Exploratory analysis and data modeling in functional neuroimaging*, chap. 5 (MIT Press, Boston, MA), pp. 77–108.

Widrow, B. and Hoff, M. (1960). Adaptive switching circuits, *IRE WESCON Convention Record* **4**, pp. 96–104.

Widrow, B. and Hoff, M. (1962). Associative storage and retrieval of digital information in networks of adaptive 'neurons', *Biological Prototypes and Synthetic Systems* **1**, p. 160.

Willshaw, D., Buneman, O. and Longuet-Higgins, H. (1969). Nonholgraphic associative memory, *Nature* **222**, pp. 960–962.

Winston, P. H. (1992). *Artificial Intelligence*, 3rd edn. (Addison-Wesley).

Wolk, K. and Marasek, K. (2019). Survey on neural machine translation into polish, in K. Choros, M. Kopel, E. Kukla and A. Sieminski (eds.), *Multimedia and Network Information System, Proceedings of the 11th International Conference MISSI 2018*, pp. 260–272.

Index

Printed in the United States
by Baker & Taylor Publisher Services